CATCH
THE
GLEAM

CATCH
THE
GLEAM

MOUNT ROYAL,
FROM COLLEGE TO UNIVERSITY,
1910–2009

DONALD NOEL BAKER

UNIVERSITY OF
CALGARY
PRESS

University of Calgary Press
2500 University Drive NW
Calgary, Alberta
Canada T2N 1N4
www.uofcpress.com

LIBRARY AND ARCHIVES CANADA CATALOGUING IN PUBLICATION

Baker, Donald N. (Donald Noel), 1936-
        Catch the gleam : Mount Royal, from college to university, 1910-2009 / Donald N. Baker.

(The west, 1922-6519 ; 2)
Includes bibliographical references and index.
ISBN 978-1-55238-532-6

        1. Mount Royal University–History. I. Title. II. Series: West series (Calgary, Alta.) ; 2

LE3.M97B34 2011   378.7123'38   C2011-901725-3

The University of Calgary Press acknowledges the support of the Alberta Foundation for the Arts for our publications. We acknowledge the financial support of the Government of Canada through the Canada Book Fund for our publishing activities. We acknowledge the financial support of the Canada Council for the Arts for our publishing program.

This book has been published with the support of Mount Royal University.

Printed and bound in Canada by Houghton Boston
∞ This book is printed on FSC Certified Starbrite Dull Text paper

Cover design, page design, and typesetting by Melina Cusano

*It makes little difference
whether that college is state or
private endowed, if it only opens up
some celestial vision or enables the
young mind to catch the gleam.*

– George W. Kerby, Principal's Report to
Board of Governors, 3 July 1912

Table of Contents

Foreword

This is the history of Mount Royal College from its founding in December 1910 through several major stages of development to its transformation into Mount Royal University in September 2009. At the end of the first year of operation, in July 1912, Principal George W. Kerby told the board of governors that "it makes little difference whether that college is state or private endowed, if it only opens up some celestial vision or enables the young mind to catch the gleam." Though his language was freighted with religious implication, as befitted a Methodist minister, his words aptly describe the overarching goal of the college in all of its later phases – that of enabling students to catch the gleam of understanding, to perceive the underlying realities, to experience the joy of intellectual discovery.

The college's story falls into two parts. The first is about the development of the original Methodist-inspired and religiously affiliated college from its legal establishment in December 1910 until it exhausted its mission and resources as a private institution in August 1966; the second is about its transformation into a public college with a community college mandate in 1966 through to its conversion into Mount Royal University in September 2009. Within each part, there were distinct phases and transformational moments which involved a mix of significant changes: in mandate, governance, scale of operation, student clientele, faculty qualifications, and public image. Yet, the college's story is not only of change and transformation but also of continuity in underlying purpose and stress on the quality of student experience and student academic success.

The story told here is mainly that of the people who comprised the college over time – the students, without whom it would not have existed and whose life stories cast its shadow widely, the faculty members who developed and delivered its programs and facilitated student learning, the support staff who kept the wheels turning, the administrators and board members who set or kept the strategic directions, volunteers who participated in program advisory committees and fundraising, and donors who have supported students, faculty, and facilities. But those participants did not make the college as they pleased, for it developed in symbiotic relationship with the community in which it was and is embedded and in ongoing interactions with government ministers, ministry officials, and other post-secondary institutions at home and abroad. Thus, in addition to being about institutional transformation, the story of the college casts a century-long light on Calgary's dynamic economy and society, the development of Alberta policy for higher education, and the changing character of higher education in Alberta and Canada.

While the transformation of formerly religiously affiliated colleges into public universities is familiar in Canada, there is one difference in the case of Mount Royal. It was the only such institution that passed through four decades as a public college with a university-transfer and community college vocation. That period confirmed and prolonged key traits of the private college that preceded it. These included its insistence on the importance of a liberal arts core curriculum, its ongoing response to needs not met or inadequately met by other institutions, its community focus, its commitment to good teaching and effective learning, and its strong student orientation. The public college added work-study co-operative programs, external program quality assurance, sophisticated institutional research and analysis, fundraising, and international partnerships, among other things.

Though much of this book discusses the college's internal life, I have placed Mount Royal's story in a broader context – its fit with the dynamic evolving community it served, its place in Alberta government policy on higher education, its role vis-à-vis other post-secondary institutions, its struggle for differentiation within the college system and then, as a new university, its effort to achieve recognition for its degree programs in the framework of academic credibility in Canada. The college's ambitions had broader repercussions. Among other things, they contributed to the formation of an arms-length agency in Alberta with powers to review all programs offered by public and private universities and colleges and to review proposed changes in mandates or internal governance systems. Mount Royal can also be seen as the cause of Grant MacEwan College's conversion into a university. It also fueled the national debate over how new degree programs and new universities can be fitted into a national framework of academic recognition.

I must declare my *parti pris*. I am at once an historian by profession and a participant in some of the events described in this book – as a former president of Mount Royal College, and as the director of the Secretariat for the Postsecondary Education Quality Assessment Board of Ontario, which played a critical role in the recognition of college degree programs and promoting the idea of a degree-level qualifications framework for Canada. I have tried throughout to wear my hat as an historian, but there may be moments when others may see some bias. Related to my role is the question of authorial voice. In order to keep an even-handed approach, I have referred to myself in the third person. I confess to an abiding affection and respect for Mount Royal, which elicits a striking loyalty in most people who were at one time part of its family.

Acknowledgments

This book began at the initiation of Hunter Wight, vice-president, University Advancement, who wanted a history prepared for Mount Royal's centennial celebrations in 2011. I think Hunter wanted a coffee table book for alumni, but as I got deeper into the project the book took on its own life and a more scholarly character. Throughout, he has been a valuable source of assistance and support. Anticipating the centennial anniversary, he arranged for the appointment of Patricia Roome, a member of the Department of History, to serve as the first director of the Mount Royal University Archives. This was an inspired choice, as Pat has brought order to chaotic holdings and has expanded the collection. In addition to bringing things to my attention, she has been an insightful critic of the text and contributed to the selection of images for the book. I am grateful as well to Janice Nermo, the archivist technician in the Archives, and Mary Chau, records administrator of the Executive Records Centre, for their assistance in accessing and verifying documentation. Jennifer Dunne, the photo designer in the Archives, was invaluable in preparing all the images for publication. I also want to convey my profound appreciation to Janis Frantz, secretary to the president since the 1980s, to Bridget Damps who for about the same length of time has prepared minutes and agendas for the Academic Council and board of governors, and Brigitte Wenn of Hunter Wight's office for greatly facilitating my work in many ways. Cathy Nickel, formerly coordinator of college communications, corrected a number of errors, brought her usual good cheer and insight to the project, and, with photo designer Jennifer Dunne, selected the photographs.

There is no published history of the college. There are two drafts--one, begun by John Howse in the early 1970s, was left incomplete; the other, by Dr. Robert MacDonald, supplemented by interviews that he and Reverend Stephen Wilks had with former students, staff and governors, focuses largely on the college's internal community. Among those who have provided me with information and comments on parts of the manuscript are former presidents Douglas Lauchlan and Thomas Wood and the current president, David Marshall, who has been very forthcoming and generous with his support. I have also benefited from comments by former academic vice-president Judith Eifert and current academic vice-president, Robin Fisher; Kenneth Robson, former Dean of Arts and vice-president, Student Services and Campus Life; Bruce Mahon, former Director of Human Resources; Donna Spaulding, Dean of Continuing Education and Extension; Lorna Smith, Director of Mount Royal International Education; Manuel Mertin, current Dean of Arts; Michael Fellows, former chair of the Department of Political Science; and Jerre Paquette, former chair of the Department of English and former president of the Mount Royal Faculty Association. I am grateful as well for a discussion with David Hyttenrauch, president of the Mount Royal Faculty Association, concerning the final stages in the conversion process. Carole Simpson, Director, and Melanie Rogers, Manager of Communications and Stewardship, both of the Mount Royal University Foundation, were helpful with fundraising information. Peter Seto, Director of the Office of Institutional Analysis and Planning, Keri Rank, and other members of the staff provided data.

I also benefited from the insightful comments made by the anonymous readers for the University of Calgary Press and discussions with Terry Miosi (formerly of the Postsecondary Education Quality

Assessment Board in Ontario), Michael Skolnik (University of Toronto), Marc Shell (Harvard University), and John (Jamil) Brownson (United Arab Emirates University). I also want to convey my gratitude for the editorial work of Curtis Fahey and Ellen Dahl and the final copy editing of Peter Enman of the University of Calgary Press. Melina Cusano of the press was responsible for the magnificent book design and Karen Buttner was responsible for technical matters.

The staffs of the archives and libraries I consulted were unfailingly congenial and helpful. These included Mount Royal's library, Alberta's public archives, the Glenbow Museum, the libraries of the University of Alberta, University of Calgary, and the University of Toronto, notably Victoria University, the John Robarts Library, and the Ontario Institute for Studies in Education. Finally, my wife, Heather D. Baker, helped in amassing materials, reorganizing mounds of documents I managed to keep scrambled, catching errors, preparing the draft of the index, and otherwise assisting at every stage. I also owe her a profound debt for putting up with lost weekends and vacations.

Of course, I accept the responsibility for any remaining errors or distortions.

Mount Royal University
wishes to thank our generous supporters

Edco Financial Holdings Ltd.
N. Murray Edwards

Libin Family: Alvin, Bobby, Eda, Nora and Louis
In Memory of Mona Libin,
Mount Royal Alumnus

To all those who made Mount Royal
what it was, what it is, and what it will be.

SEPTEMBER 1905	*Province of Alberta established*
SEPTEMBER 1908	*University of Alberta begins operation*
AUGUST 1910	*Initial meeting of Mount Royal College board of governors*
	William H. Cushing named chairman of board
NOVEMBER 1910	*Board appoints Rev. George W. Kerby as Principal*
DECEMBER 1910	*Mount Royal College Act*
7 SEPTEMBER 1911	*Mount Royal College opens for first classes*

CHAPTER 1

FOUNDING THE COLLEGE

A real college . . . grows up in the soil and from the manhood and womanhood which serve it. The college should give to its young people great impulses. It should impart not only knowledge, but it should form taste. It should be a place where the spirit is more important than the letter, where teacher and student co-operate in a common endeavor to learn, and where contact with inspiring personality holds a chief place; and furthermore, it must be borne in mind that an institution that leaves God out of its curriculum, leaves out the greatest factor that builds up the college.

– Board of Governors, Mount Royal College, 1914[1]

Before the establishment of public schools and universities, churches assumed most of the responsibility for providing education in Canada. In the Maritime provinces, Quebec and Ontario, there were Roman Catholic, Methodist, Presbyterian, Baptist, and Anglican schools and colleges, and many of these later evolved into public institutions. Catholic tributaries fed into Concordia University, the University of Windsor, and the University of Ottawa; a Baptist college became McMaster University; and Methodist colleges grew into Mount Allison University, the University of Winnipeg, the University of Regina – and Mount Royal College in Calgary.

By comparison with eastern Canada, where many universities began as private, religiously affiliated institutions, Alberta and Saskatchewan moved swiftly after their creation in 1905 to establish public universities and tight government control over higher education. They did not want to repeat the denominational struggles experienced elsewhere. Even so, churches spawned private colleges. There were seven in Alberta by 1914: Alberta College (Edmonton, Methodist, 1903), Alberta Industrial Academy (Leduc, Seventh-Day Adventist, 1907), Mount Royal College (Calgary, Methodist, 1910), Camrose Lutheran College (1910), Alberta College South (Strathcona, Methodist, 1911), Collège Saint-Jean (Pincher Creek, then Edmonton, Roman Catholic, 1911), and Robertson College (Strathcona, Presbyterian, 1911).[2]

Having begun educational activity before public schools existed, the Methodists had a broad conception of what was required. In the Canadian west, they were particularly concerned about students in rural districts where one-room elementary schools were the norm. A residential college in the city offering more advanced academic programs in a Christian environment would meet a substantial need for parents wanting their children to go beyond the elementary level. In addition, as only a small minority of adults completed high school, Methodist colleges were also aimed at enabling adults to complete high school, start degree-level education, secure an education to become a minister, or be trained for the world of work. In frontier conditions, moreover, there was need for cultural literacy and stimulation – for music and speech lessons, concerts and plays, recreation and sports, debates and discussions, public speakers. Thus, Methodist colleges were

broad-gauged in purpose. Their aim was not merely to impart literacy but to provide a practical education, to shape individual and social character, to nurture the best in individuals and society, and to serve as sources of illumination in the community. Mount Royal College conformed to the pattern.

Though part of a broad educational expansion by the Methodist Church in the period, the college owed its particular origins in 1910–11 to the dreams, energies, and resources of Methodists in Calgary and southern Alberta. As their hopes were translated into reality, the founders discovered that the circumstances that provided opportunities also set constraints on their ambitions. The college was to be shaped by a blend of Methodist ideas, educational needs in Calgary and southern Alberta, the vision of its founders, and the interplay between its ambitions and limits imposed by resources and government policy.

The Early Calgary Community

High in the Rockies, along the Icefields Parkway that skirts the Columbia Glacier and runs between Lake Louise and Jasper, are the glacial sources of two major rivers – the North Saskatchewan, which flows east along a northerly route, and the Bow, which flows east along a southerly route that passes through Montana. In mid-prairies they merge to form the Saskatchewan River, which feeds into the Hudson Bay and Missouri River watersheds. The rivers were the original pathways of trade and settlement; their canyons became the routes into the Rockies for the railways and road systems. The major urban centres were built on their banks – notably, Edmonton on the North Saskatchewan, gateway to the Yellowhead Pass, and Calgary on the Bow, gateway to the Rogers Pass.

In 1870 the province of Manitoba had joined the Canadian confederation and was followed in 1871 by British Columbia. Between them lay the vast North-West Territories, which was administered until 1872 by the Hudson's Bay Company. The Canadian government then opened the Territories to settlement, and waves of settlers moved in. Native communities were undermined by the decimation of the buffalo stocks and the erosive effects of alcohol. Dislocated, tribes signed over their land and moved onto reserves where the government provided food and shelter. Treaty No. 7 (1877) established the reserves nearest Calgary.[3]

Development of the Canadian Pacific Railroad (CPR) spurred population growth in the West. In 1888 the North-West Territories were granted a legislature with limited powers. In 1905 Ottawa carved out the provinces of Alberta and Saskatchewan, leaving the Territories label to describe the lands north of the 60th parallel.[4] Calgary's settlement began with the establishment in 1875 of the North-West Mounted Police Fort (Fort Calgary) and the opening of the Hudson's Bay Company and I. G. Baker trading posts nearby. The name "Calgary," borrowed from a Scottish town, supposedly meant "clear running water" in Gaelic, a claim later muddied by scholars.[5] "During June 1883, about 65 miles of track was put down, an average of better than 2.5 miles per working day . . . On July 7, 6.02 miles of iron was put down . . . On August 15, Calgary was reached."[6] By the end of that year there were sixty tent and wooden structures. On 7 November 1884 Calgary was incorporated as a town. Almost a decade later, on 1 January 1894, when it had barely 3,800 residents, it was incorporated as a city. A fire that destroyed many of its original wooden structures led to a regulation that all large buildings must be made of sandstone from the banks of the Bow River, lending the downtown a distinctive buff coloration.[7] Though Calgary was the main entrepôt in southern Alberta, it grew slowly until the early 1900s, when the federal government changed its policy from leasing large tracts of land to ranchers to one of granting homesteads to newcomers. A headline in the *Lethbridge Herald* on 20 September 1909 described the resulting land rush – "BIG MASS OF MEN FIGHT IN A STRUGGLE FOR LAND."[8] In 1901, there were 73,000 people in Alberta; by 1911, 374,000; and by 1921, 588,454. The newly opened frontier led to an economic boom, with men and capital pouring into the region.

From 1901 to 1911, Calgary's population rose from 4,091 to 43,704. The city's growth derived from the railroads, which began with the east-west lines of the CPR but expanded in the 1890s to include a north-south line from Edmonton to Fort Macleod. By 1914, the city rivalled Winnipeg as a wholesale centre.[9] In 1908 streetcars appeared and the city opened a public library. The number of homes grew from 1,689 in 1901 to over 11,000 in 1911. In the latter year, more than 20 per cent of the workforce was employed in construction. However, the boom was followed by a bust. In 1913–14 real estate values crashed, costing thousands of jobs and hundreds of fortunes. By 1921, construction workers formed only 7.6 per cent of the workforce. The 1911 census revealed a frontier demography: 155 men for every 100 women.[10] A year later the Calgary Stampede, the public stage for fearless cowboys, was inaugurated. Large-scale construction attracted single men from the East, and on the weekends, when ranch hands came to town, the male ratio was even higher. Not surprisingly, Calgary's downtown catered to the young men through bars, bawdy houses, and gaming places.[11] Tensions grew between the denizens of the inner city and those who favoured a community ruled by Victorian and Christian values.[12]

THE METHODISTS IN CALGARY

Prominent among the advocates of moral order were the Methodists. Beginning as a dissenting religion in Great Britain in the eighteenth century, Methodism had grown rapidly among those whose lives were most affected by industrialization and urbanization. Crossing the Atlantic to the American colonies, it had moved into British North America and finally to the West.[13] An "inward religion, the religion of the heart,"[14] Methodism was spread by ministers who travelled through their "circuits" on horseback and delivered an emotional style of religion including mass rallies, crusading hymns, emotional prayer meetings, exuberant testimonials, and public conversions. It "was adapted perfectly to a place where there was everything to do, where most people were poor, their greatest assets strength of will and strength of body, where life was hard and good fortune chancy, but where everything was to be gained if only the effort made were great enough"; in uncertain frontier conditions, it provided personal moral certainty and belief in the power of free will "to act rather than to be acted upon" in both temporal and spiritual matters.[15] Methodists wanted to "find the meaning of their lives in seeking the realization of the kingdom of God in the very fabric of society."[16] Methodists promoted literacy and organized schools, both to help people find salvation by reading the Bible and to enable them to shape their own society: "our own tradition . . . is to think of the state as the potential instrument of God and to think of the function of the church as being to make it actually so."[17] Like American Methodists, Canadian Methodists were comfortable with the individualistic values of the capitalist order; they were spiritual and material strivers, self-improvers and political activists, "not the defeated and hopeless."[18]

Central Methodist Church, 1911.
Glenbow Archives NA-920-8.

From 1901 to 1911, the number of Methodists in Alberta rose from 10,000 to 61,000 and proportionately from 13.7 to 16.3 per cent of the population. While the countryside drew immigrants from central and eastern Europe, Calgary attracted people with British or eastern Canadian roots. From 1901 to 1941, people of British origin constituted 71–82 per cent of the city's population, with all other ethnic groups remaining small. Religious orientation reflected the ethnic roots: Anglican, 23–25 per cent; Methodist, 19–20 per cent; Presbyterian, 26–27 per cent; Catholic, 9–12 per cent; Lutheran, 6–8 per cent.[19] Calgary's Methodists steadily outgrew their churches. The Reverend John McDougall had first offered religious services in the fort and the I. G. Baker trading post, and in 1877 his chapel was built of logs. It was followed in 1883 by a wood and canvas structure, in 1884 by a wood-frame building, and in 1889 by a brick church.[20]

The members of this church, known first as Calgary Methodist and later as Central Methodist, included many business and civic leaders. Its first board of trustees included A. M. Armour and T. B. Braden, founders of the *Calgary Herald*; James A. Lougheed, a Conservative lawyer who became the first senator from Alberta (1889); William H. Cushing, who created a sash-and-door company in 1885, helped build the first wood and tent church, became city councillor and mayor (1900–1901) and a Liberal provincial cabinet minister from 1905 to 1910; and Richard Bedford Bennett, a young lawyer brought to Calgary by Lougheed and later a Conservative member of the provincial and federal legislatures and prime minister of Canada. The meeting to incorporate the City of Calgary was held in the church, and such influential groups as the United Farmers of Alberta and the United Farm Women of Alberta also used it for meetings. Piety, politics, and business went hand in hand. Lougheed and Cushing were typical of the "booster businessmen" who reconciled promotion of their private interests with community service, within and without the church.[21]

Inspired by the "Social Gospel," which proposed applying Christian ethics to social issues, the Calgary congregation sought to strengthen "the institution of marriage and a man's support of his wife and family" through such campaigns as those for prohibition and against prostitution.[22] The 1898 national plebiscite on prohibition revealed that "wherever the Methodist Church was strong, the prohibition vote was strong" – in Calgary, 57.6 per cent.[23] Implicit in such campaigns was the perception that "women were morally superior to men."[24] "Women were viewed as the backbone of the society which the Social Gospel attempted to improve. Women were the bearers of children, the keepers of the family, and the upholders of morality."[25] As a result, Methodists were early champions of women's right to vote. But there were limits on such inclusiveness. Some Methodists were "infected with the social Darwinism of the period, and exhibited a degree of ambivalence toward 'lesser breeds'" such as Aboriginals and many European immigrants. Many were enthusiastic supporters of the British Empire and saw Victorian Anglo-Saxon culture as civilization itself.[26]

Whereas Methodism in eastern and central Canada had spread as a form of religious dissent against the hierarchical worldview of the Anglican establishment, Methodism in the west began as a missionary activity aimed at indigenous peoples, trappers, and ranch hands. It then evolved into an expression of the emerging middle class attempting to establish their moral order in frontier conditions. For some this meant dealing directly with the fallen in their midst; for others, it meant shunning them.[27]

METHODISTS AND EDUCATION

By 1909–10, Calgary's Methodists were sufficiently numerous, confident, and concerned about the lack of educational opportunities to consider establishing a college. In this, in the words of the historian of Calgary Methodist Church, "it may be reasonably assumed that these laymen had derived some of their thinking on education from long exposure to the sermons and conversation of a succession of Ryersonian ministers."[28] Indeed, informing all Canadian Methodist thinking about education were the views of Egerton Ryerson (1803–82). Originally an itinerant preacher offering "his first sermons in a log schoolhouse . . . in the light of a tallow candle pinned to the wall by a hunting knife,"[29] Ryerson was the most influential Methodist in the nineteenth century. He was founder and editor of the *Christian Guardian* (1829), creator of the Methodist Book Concern (precursor of Ryerson Press), and first principal of Victoria College (1842–44), the major training ground for Methodist ministers.[30] His greatest influence, however, was as superintendent of education for Upper Canada (and Ontario) for thirty-one years (1845–76), when he laid the foundations of Ontario's public-education system. He established the first normal school and model schools for in-class instruction of new teachers, created a press to publish textbooks, and established the *Journal of Education* to inform teachers of new pedagogical ideas.

"My leading idea," Ryerson wrote, "has been . . . not only to impart to the public mind the greatest amount of useful knowledge, based upon, and interwoven throughout with sound Christian principles, but to render the Educational System, in its various ramifications and applications, the indirect but powerful, instrument of British Constitutional Government."[31] "By education, I mean not the mere acquisition of certain arts, or of certain branches of knowledge, but that instruction and discipline which qualify and dispose the subjects of it for their appropriate duties and employment of life, as Christians, as persons of business, and also as members of the civil community in which they live."[32] He thought an educated populace was the best guarantee of good government, freedom, and the law.[33] Ryerson's wide-ranging ideas permeated school systems throughout Canada.[34] In Calgary, the first superintendent of public schools, Dr. A. Melville Scott, was "a staunch Victorian Methodist" of Ryersonian vision who "gave his full support to the civilizing and moralizing mission of the public school on the prairie frontier."[35] Scott was to play a critical role in shaping the new public-school system and the new Methodist college during his tenure, which lasted from 1905 to 1935.

Methodist educational institutions in Canada began in 1829 with establishment of an academy in Cobourg, Ontario, that Ryerson later converted into Victoria College. In the 1830s Methodists in Upper Canada established Albert College in Belleville and Alma College in Saint Thomas. Loyalist Methodists in Lower Canada founded Stanstead Academy.[36] In 1842 Methodists in Nova Scotia opened Sackville Wesleyan Academy.[37] In 1871 a Methodist school was established in Winnipeg.[38] In Alberta the first Methodist initiative was Alberta College, founded in 1903 in Edmonton. Open to residential and day students, it offered elementary, junior, and senior high-school programs, academic upgrading courses, vocational courses in business, lessons in elocution, art, and music, and first-year university courses in affiliation with McGill University. In Saskatchewan, Regina College opened its doors in 1912 as a "preparatory residential school for both sexes offering courses in collegiate first-year university, . . . music and business, and an elementary course for older students" who "have not been able to obtain a good public school education."[39]

The Methodists focused on niches not served or not served well by public systems. Their colleges were dynamic institutions, abandoning elementary education as public schools developed, focusing on students with academic deficiencies or social problems as secondary schools emerged, adding career programs to prepare people for the workforce, and forging partnerships with public institutions where appropriate.

Loosely coordinating the colleges was the Methodists' Education Society, which named a Board of Education to oversee educational activities. For nearly three decades, both prior to and after the Methodists' integration into the United Church in 1926, the board's secretary was the Reverend John W. Graham in Toronto. The board's role was to recommend approval of new institutions for "connexion" to the church, appoint their board members, coordinate theological education, make loans to probationers

studying to be ministers, and disseminate grants to "connexional" institutions, mainly to those offering theological programs for probationers. The board held that the colleges were alternatives to public institutions, not competitors with them. Its 1905–6 annual report noted: "The trend towards the educational institutions of the church seems entirely due to the fact that a Christian people desire that the education of their children should be under the direction of Christian men and the influence of Christian principles. . . . We should regard it as the greatest of all mistakes that the church and state should enter into antagonistic competition in this important work, or that to enjoy the advantage of the one, they must be deprived of the other." In 1905–6 there were eleven colleges with 3,130 students, 157 faculty, property worth $1,623,434, and endowments of $1,069,432. By 1910, there were 3,929 students;[40] and by 1919, there were seventeen institutions with 4,674 students (of whom 204 were in theology), 270 instructors, property worth $4 million, furniture and equipment worth $374,800, endowments of $6,267,357, and debts of $740,069.[41]

The colleges differed markedly. As Graham explained to an American questioner, "our Methodist colleges are not of one type – they largely represent the evolution of history."[42] The growing number and diversity soon raised questions. How did they all relate to the church's mission and priorities? How much financial support should be given? Should they compete with public or private institutions? Should there be a common core curriculum? Should new colleges receive funding when existing ones were suffering financially? The Methodist college in Calgary was to take root in the ebullient phase of the church's approach to providing education. It was to spend most of its life as a private church-related institution in a more questioning environment.

THE REVEREND GEORGE W. KERBY

The minister of Calgary Methodist Church from 1903 to 1910, the Reverend George William Kerby (1860–1944), was a key member of the group that founded the Methodist college in Calgary. He subsequently served as principal from its founding in 1910 to his retirement at the end of June 1942. His long tenure as

Founder and Principal Rev. Dr. George W. Kerby, ca. 1912.
Photographer A.L. Hess; Glenbow Archives NA-2345-3.

Paris (Ontario) and daughter of the Reverend James Spencer, editor of the *Christian Guardian*. Before accepting the call to Calgary, Kerby served in pastorates in Woodstock, Hamilton, St. Catharines, Brantford, Montreal, and Toronto and spent two years (1902–3) as an evangelist for the Ontario Methodist Conference, speaking to mass rallies in Canada and United States. Timothy C. Eaton, then expanding his business through mail-order catalogues, encouraged Kerby to accept the offer in Calgary and gave the Kerbys a new mattress to help them cope in the Wild West.[46]

What Calgary gained when Kerby arrived was an energetic, visionary, and charismatic minister, a master builder and promoter. He had many contacts across the country, in the church, in fraternal clubs, and in social-reform organizations. An inveterate joiner, he belonged to, and often served as president of, such organizations as the Rotary Club, the Independent Order of Oddfellows, the Red Cross Society, the Calgary Board of Trade, the Canadian Club, the Calgary Branch of the Canadian Authors Society, the Alberta and Canadian Home and School Federations, and the Calgary Public School Board. He had joined the Masonic Lodge in 1899 and was a lifelong member, serving as grand chaplain of the Grand Lodge of Alberta, 1915–18, and as grand master of the Grand Lodge of Alberta in 1931.[47] A tireless traveller and speaker, he was never without some fraternal connection, group to address, or local contact in Canada, the United States, Great Britain, or Europe. In a city full of "booster businessmen," Kerby found a propitious climate – a fast-growing congregation, a frontier society with "moral mud holes,"[48] and men with new fortunes to spend on worthy causes. In 1905, the province of Alberta came into existence and elections were held, with some of Kerby's new friends emerging as key political figures.

Though plans for a new church had been drafted, Kerby, who was used to large churches and evangelical rallies, found the size much too small and ordered it enlarged. Learning that Hull Opera House held the largest audiences in Calgary, "the top-hatted Kerby was [soon] seated in the somber varnished offices of Calgary's leading law firm—Lougheed and Bennett. Kerby, arguing that he could preach in an opera house as well as in a cathedral, simply told lawyer R. B. Bennett [a pillar of the church] he needed some place

principal enabled him to leave a deep impression on the college's environment and direction.[43]

Born on a farm in Lambton County, Ontario, in an Anglican family of United Empire Loyalist origins, Kerby became a Methodist in the 1870s by conversion and decided to enter the ministry. Completing his secondary education as a ministerial "probationer" at Cobourg Collegiate, he then attended Victoria University, graduating in 1888 with an honours BA in theology and philosophy. As a student, he became "social editor" of *Acta Victoriana*, a monthly publication, and one of the more "prominent" students.[44] (After being awarded an honorary degree of Doctor of Divinity on 29 April 1912,[45] he was known as Dr. Kerby.) In October 1888 he married Emily Spencer (1859–1938), principal of an elementary school in bigger if he was to reach the citizens of Calgary."[49] This marked the beginning of a lifelong friendship between Kerby and a man whose political career passed through Alberta's legislature to Ottawa, where he became prime minister. James Lougheed, the other legal partner, and another pillar of the church and good friend of Kerby, also became a politician and eventually a Senator.

With the help of such friends, Kerby mobilized the funds and got the job done. Dedicated in February 1905, the new church held thirteen hundred people. It was the largest building in Calgary. Though overflow crowds attended services to hear the vivacious Kerby, the audience was even bigger, for he had arranged for the Calgary exchange of the Bell Telephone Company to broadcast services over party lines. "This may be termed an unqualified success from the listening point of view," the *Calgary Herald* wrote. "Every word the preacher uttered and every one of the anthems, solos and hymns, were as distinct as if the listener were in church."[50] Kerby urged Methodists "to swarm" in suburbs to establish new churches. By 1911, there were ten new churches and Calgary Methodist had become Calgary Central Methodist, the mother church for the suburban brood. In 1906–7 Kerby served as president of the Alberta Methodist Conference.

In 1906 the Methodist Church adopted the report of a "committee on sociological questions" that recommended paying attention to the social factors inhibiting the practice of Christian values.[51] An apostle of the "social gospel," Kerby held that many people were diverted from attending to their salvation by family and social conditions and that the church needed to demonstrate its continuing relevance by addressing those conditions. With great verve, he addressed the social gospel to local conditions and demonstrated personal commitment by enlisting in social-reform movements. One of them was directed to "the young man problem." "The weakest point in the church's campaign for bringing the world to Christ," he wrote, "is the relation of the church to the young."[52] Seeking to create a dynamic environment for young people, he was "an originator of the Forward Movement in Bible study and evangelistic work" for young Methodists across Canada.[53] In Montreal, he had created a youth choir. In Calgary, he initiated the Young Men's Club (Men's Own), which met on Sunday afternoons to listen to speakers, and an AOTS (As One That Serves) young men's club, and, for the purposes of these clubs, he turned the church basement into a gymnasium and games room.[54]

Kerby's concern for young men was matched by that of his wife, Emily Spencer Kerby, for the plight of women. A "daughter of the parsonage,"[55] she was a strong advocate of women's rights[56] and chafed at the segregation of men and women in church affairs. "Why in the discussion of the place of women in the church, should sex enter at all?" she asked.[57] Under a pseudonym, she published pieces on women's issues and rights, including sterilization and birth control, both of which she supported: birth control because it enabled women to take control of their own bodies, sterilization because the alternative was blemished children that became unwanted.[58] In July 1907 she initiated a fundraising campaign to house young women who found little accommodation in Calgary, and by November the group had raised enough money to rent a house for a month, commencing the local chapter of the Young Women's Christian Association (YWCA).[59] She was a charter member and later president of the Calgary Local Council of Women (CLCW) and, as convener of its Franchise Committee, helped organize a large delegation to present a petition to Premier Arthur Sifton urging passage of the suffrage bill in 1916.[60] Later she joined Nellie McClung in pressing for the same rights at the federal level.[61] She argued that the church should treat women equally with men, including ordination as ministers, but it was sixteen years after her death before the church conceded the ordination of women in 1954.[62]

Kerby's readiness to move beyond the ministry was foreshadowed in his book *The Broken Trail: Pages from a Pastor's Experience in Western Canada* (1909), which recounted "some of the more outstanding experiences of my pastorate in the West" and underlined his social concerns.[63] "The deadest man in God's world is the one who shuts his eyes so that he cannot see the tattered garments of the poor; who stops his ears so that he cannot hear the cry of the hungry; and who shuts his hand so that he cannot help a deserving fellow. God save you and me from being mean and small in our charities." The themes of this work included the centrality of the family in society and of the mother in the family, the degenerating temptations of alcohol, tobacco, drugs, and popular entertainments, the importance of loving other human beings and extending a helping hand to them, and the need for constructive activities for young people. Kerby criticized the church's neglect of "the forbidden city" around his downtown church: "the trend of modern church life is to get away from the centre of vice and crime to some popular and fashionable suburb where salvation is easy and service claims but little sacrifice." One now had to look outside the church to address social issues. There was also the assimilation of immigrants, "one of the most serious of our national problems." He proposed a "League of Social Service which shall recognize no distinction in church or creed or caste, nothing but a divine and universal sisterhood." Recognizing that this work required many hands, he wrote that "denominationalism has had its day."[64]

Kerby may not have been thinking of anything more than the need for the Methodists to create a college, but he was nearing fifty and may have been thinking of his own future too.[65] Because of the church's itinerancy rule, the earlier renewal of his appointment in Calgary had required the approval of the Alberta and national conferences.[66] As he neared the end of his second term, he would have had to break precedent to be reappointed for a third term. He also may have sensed that the heroic age of building Methodism in Calgary was past and that only more routine tasks lay ahead. His keen interest in social issues hinted at a desire to become more directly involved in them. Thus, creation of the new college came at a propitious moment for Kerby, enabling him to remain in Calgary and in a church project, one with a wider audience than the pulpit.[67] "It seems clear," the historian of Central Methodist Church has written, "that if Kerby did not suggest the idea he was one of the first to take it up, and that he was in on the discussions of it which took place during 1909 and 1910."[68]

Emily Spencer Kerby (R) with Harriett E. Crandell, wife of E.H. Crandell, a member of the Mount Royal College Board of Governors, ca. 1910. Mount Royal University Archives HA49.

LAUNCHING MOUNT ROYAL COLLEGE

In early 1910 the dream took practical form when a committee of Calgary and southern Alberta Methodists was formed to seek approval from the Alberta Conference to establish a "Methodist preparatory college" in Calgary.[69] Committee members "recognized the need for emphasizing moral and spiritual values in education" and thought that public education "lacks the opportunity of touching the life of future citizens that is afforded in a well-conducted residential college with Christian ideals."[70] They were also concerned about weaknesses in the public schools, such as the lack of aesthetic and practical education and the early school-leaving age, and planned to counteract them. Many of the same men were also to be involved in the effort to launch a University of Calgary. The Methodists were not alone in creating new schools in this period. However, two things distinguished their efforts from the others – co-education, and survival. Except for St. Hilda's Ladies College (Anglican), which lasted until the 1930s, all of the rest disappeared.[71]

In July 1910 a committee of the Alberta Conference endorsed establishment of the college and the naming of a provisional governing board.[72] In August the General Conference of the national church approved "the principle of a preparatory college at Calgary and request[ed] the proposed board of governors to submit full financial and academic plans to the Board of the Educational Society, and recommend that the Board shall have full authority to approve the same. . . ."[73] Kerby and William G. Hunt convened a meeting on 2 August 1910 to name the governors and appoint officers: the Honourable William H. Cushing, chairman; Dr. A. Melville Scott, vice-chairman; Charles F. Adams, secretary; and A. Judson Sayre, treasurer. With the principal and other board members resident in Calgary, the officers constituted the Executive Committee, which was granted the authority "to deal with all matters and transact all business of the board and of the college between meetings of the board. . . ."[74]

The board members were what Bob Edwards of *The Eye Opener* called "the Moguls of Methodism."[75] Of them, Cushing stood out. Owner of a major lumber company which by 1910 employed 200 workers,[76]

First Chairman of the Mount Royal College Board of Governors, The Honourable William Cushing, Alberta Minister of Public Works. Glenbow Archives NA-1201-1.

Cushing was "a sort of super-elder" who held a church office in every year from 1883 to 1925.[77] He was also a politician – city alderman and briefly mayor of Calgary in the 1890s, member of the Territorial legislature, Liberal member of the Alberta legislature beginning in 1905, and minister of public works. When he stood for re-election in 1910, he defeated the Conservative candidate, R. B. Bennett. (Bennett's political fortunes improved in October 1911 when he was elected to the federal House of Commons in a by-election.[78]) When Cushing resigned from the cabinet in opposition to the railroad financing policy of Premier Alexander C. Rutherford, the government fell.[79] After that, he focused on business and volunteer activities, including the college, the hospital, and social services. A man who practised his values, he once sheltered Chinese immigrants in his home when they were threatened with violence.[80] Cushing served as chairman of the Mount Royal board until 1926 and as a member until his death in January 1934.

Dr. A. Melville Scott, the vice-chairman, Calgary's first superintendent of education, brought considerable prestige to the new venture (he was also to serve on the Senate of the stillborn University of Calgary).[81] As Max Foran observed in his history of Calgary, citing Scott as an example, "the institutional voice of authority commanded more respect in Calgary than in centres where the population was larger, more mobile and certainly more diverse in occupation or origin."[82] Scott remained superintendent until 1935 and on the Mount Royal board through the 1930s.

A. Judson Sayre, the treasurer, was an American Methodist who arrived in Calgary in 1905 and created the Calgary Colonization Company to invest in land and real estate projects. With the closing of the American frontier by the end of the nineteenth century, a number of Americans like Sayre moved into Alberta to seize remaining frontier opportunities; in 1911, there were 3,500 Americans in Calgary, nearly one in ten of the inhabitants. Sayre was prominent in developing the poshest residential district in the city, Mount Royal, sometimes called "American Hill."[83] Sayre had earlier shown his commitment to Methodism by donating funds for a residence at Wesley College in North Dakota.[84] A great booster of the new college, he continued on its board until the 1920s when he retired to California and remained a donor until he died in the late 1930s.

Charles F. Adams, a lawyer, served as the board's secretary and put his legal expertise to use for the college. The Executive Committee, for its part, soon came to include the four officers and six others: Dr. T. H. Crawford (a medical doctor), Albert B. Cushing (owner of a lumber firm, youngest brother of William H. Cushing),[85] O. S. Chapin (a businessman), William L. Hunt (a businessman, chairman of the committee to replace Kerby as minister), George W. Morfitt (a businessman), and Kerby. All were from Calgary. The Executive Committee met monthly, while the full board met annually, usually in November or December. There were thirty-three board members – twenty-one from Calgary, ten from other Alberta communities, one from England, and one from Saskatchewan.

Twenty-five were laymen, and eight clergymen; four were doctors; all were men.[86]

On 7 September the board discussed potential leaders for the new college. George Kerby was not among the latter, perhaps because a resolution had been passed asking him to serve as "acting principal," subject to the approval of his church.[87] Kerby was also named chairman of the committee to select staff and a principal. Not surprisingly, the committee recommended Kerby and, on 4 November 1910, the board confirmed the appointment. The minutes indicate that Kerby, who left the room for the discussion, "replied very feelingly and accepted same, subject to the approval of the Quarterly Official Board of the Central Methodist Church." His salary was $3,000 plus a $600 housing allowance.[88] With this appointment, Kerby's career as a pastor ended, his eight years in Calgary constituting "the longest term of a continuous pastorate in Canadian Methodism."[89] To this point, Kerby had been just one member of the group creating the college. However, in the words of the historian of Methodist Central, "once the decision was taken to establish the school, he took over the primary leadership role, and this was a great accomplishment. But he did not do it alone, and there were certainly more laymen than clergy involved during the stages which led up to his appointment."[90]

Chaired by Charles Adams, the committee on legal issues secured incorporation in October and prepared a petition to the provincial government for a charter. In a meeting on 4 November, the board of governors decided on the name "Calgary College." However, the charter came up just after the legislature stripped degree granting from the proposed charter for the University of Calgary and changed its name to Calgary College.[91] Kerby asked for the clause in the Methodists' charter to be left blank during the first reading so he could "consult his colleagues."[92] The Executive Committee reviewed alternatives – Bow Valley, King, Central, North Western, and McDougall – and settled on Mount Royal College.[93] On 16 December 1910 the Act to Incorporate Mount Royal College was passed. Its mandate was "to establish, equip, maintain and conduct in or near the City of Calgary an institution of learning for the education and instruction of youths of both sexes, or of either sex, in the elementary and secondary branches of knowledge and to do all such acts, matters and things as are incidental or conducive to the attainment of the said objects."[94]

Kerby's committee for recruiting staff moved quickly.[95] The college reported to the Alberta Conference that the staff and students were "composed of different denominations. No religious tests are allowed to be put to either students or professors. At the same time the relation of the college to the Church insures the Christian character of the institution."[96] As always, Kerby was in a hurry. When he wanted to begin making commitments to faculty members in November 1910, the board decided that it was premature, given the need to fund, design, and build facilities. As a result, the board deferred appointments until 24 March 1911.[97] The initial faculty included: John H. Beasley, MA (Mount Allison), dean of the boys' residence, science and mathematics instructor, at an annual salary of $1,200;[98] W. G. Bennett (Leeds, Queen's, Ontario Normal School), head of the Commercial Department, salary of $1,200; Miss Margaret A. Graham, MA (Toronto, post-graduate studies in Germany and France), modern languages, salary of $800; Nora M. Powers, MA (Dalhousie), classics, from Halifax Lady's College (Presbyterian), salary of $800; and F. Arthur Oliver, ACTM (Toronto Conservatory, post-graduate studies in Germany), director of the Conservatory of Music.[99] "There will be nothing sectarian about our college," Kerby said. "The teachers are of different religious denominations, and in their selection I did not take that into consideration at all, so long as I was satisfied that their qualifications were all right, and that they were men of Christian character."[100] Among the other early teachers was Emily Kerby, who taught in the elementary school program.[101] Initially, though not subsequently, instructors were described as "professors" in college publications.[102] As the college was to be residential, the initial staff also included Miss S. Rae, who, for $20 a month, "would clean the girls' residence corridors and stairs, spend the afternoons darning and mending for students, and help with the dishes each evening."[103]

The committee to select a site for the new college, chaired by Dr. Crawford, first considered locating the college near the proposed university (whose site was still uncertain but was generally thought to be on the north side of the Bow River). For start-up operations,

Dr. Blow offered space in his downtown building, at no cost.[104] Several real estate developers offered land on the condition that the college must build on it – for example, S. O. Tregillus and Thomas Jackson offered thirty acres adjacent to the land they had donated to the university on the same condition. Because of the continuing campaign by supporters of the university, the committee recommended building on a temporary site in October 1910. Ten lots near the intersection of 7th Avenue and 11th Street West were purchased "in the name of individual board members and hence the board was not bound to take them over." The plan was to build on the seven most westerly lots (whose address became 1128 7th Avenue West). Central Calgary was still residential, and the campus was within walking or streetcar distance for many residents.

The building committee, chaired by Chapin and consisting as well of Hunt and James Garden, a building contractor, steward of Central Methodist, and alderman, moved quickly to launch construction. Garden designed a three-storey, L-shaped building and supervised the construction. The original plan was for 140 residential students and a residence for the principal, but in the end there were rooms for only 100 residents and no residence for the principal. The building ran 130 feet along 11th Street and 176 feet along 7th Street.[105] The board approved the project on 8 November 1910. A building loan of $75,000 was provided by the Merchants Bank of Canada. As this would not cover all costs, the board arranged for a $25,000 loan from Sir John Langham, a British supporter. The letter for the loan declared that "the board of governors is easily worth from three to five million dollars, so that our guarantee will remain ample."[106] The college's annual report to the Alberta Conference said that the building was "admirably adapted for doing first class work."[107] The Executive Committee furnished "the college with good, substantial furnishings in every way, rather than the cheaper line of furnishings, having in view the fact that the furnishings, if of a high grade, could nearly all be used in the permanent college buildings later on, and it was thought that as a matter of economy this would be the wiser course." The total cost of the project was $59,000, which Kerby said was "not an unreasonable amount for so good or commodious a building."[108]

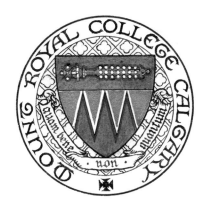

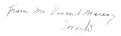

An early proposed design of the Mount Royal College badge, believed to have been designed by Alexander Scott Carter, one of Canada's pre-eminent heraldic artists, and subsequent evolution of the graphics used for promotional and ceremonial purposes. Mount Royal University Archives 1912-1.

Mount Royal College badge used approximately 1912–1950. Mount Royal University Archives *Calendar 1912–13.*

Mount Royal College badge used approximately 1970–2009. Mount Royal University Archives *Calendar 1970–71.*

"At the request of the Executive of the board of governors,"[109] Kerby left on a tour of educational institutions in eastern Canada and the United States. From 9 January to 9 March 1911, he visited "some sixty-five institutions" in seven U.S. states and five provinces. The institutions included "independent, state and denominational schools, colleges and universities, agricultural colleges, technical institutes, household science and art schools, technical and commercial high schools, conservatories of music, business colleges, institutes of research, schools of law, medicine, mine and forestry, teachers' colleges, schools of applied science. . . ." Along the way he attended "eight educational meetings" and "also delivered some eleven special addresses and sermons, gave several interviews to the leading press of eastern Canada and the United States, on the objects of my tour and the development of our Canadian West, and in addition wrote a series

of letters, some eleven in number, to the press of East and Western Canada."[110]

Somewhere along his trip Kerby saw a motto that he liked and used for Mount Royal – *Quam bene non quantum* ("how well, not how much"). Kerby's acquaintance, the young Vincent Massey, who visited Calgary in August 2011[111] and whose family, through the Massey Foundation, was the largest benefactor of the Methodist Church, apparently arranged for a badge or crest with an "escutcheon emblazoned with the Royal Sceptre and the Snow-Capped Mountains suggestive of the college name." All later Mount Royal badges were to be based on that original design, though notably different in expression from time to time. After what appears to have been a colour selection conflicting with that of the University of Alberta, the "college colours" became the royal blue and white that endured throughout the life of the college.[112]

The tour gave Kerby insights that he hoped "will help us to understand better the present and future possibilities of Mount Royal College and the relation of education generally to the development of the national life and the best interests of our civilization." These included the importance of co-education, of a practical and useful education, of physical education ("fair play helps to make fair men"), and of a residential campus because a home-like environment was important for developing character. "These are some of the things that mark the new era in educational work," said Kerby, "and schools and colleges are coming to realize as never before that to fail at the point of character is to fail at every point."[113]

Meanwhile, student recruitment began. The calendar was printed and circulated. Notices went to Methodist churches. Advertisements described the college as "a high-class residential college," "non-sectarian in the best sense," with an "ideal location," and having "staff of highest scholarship and experience."[114] The fees were $340 for students receiving "room, board, light, heat, laundry (12 pieces) and tuition in any of the yearly courses," and $90 (or $9 a month) for day students.[115] Through the next thirty years, the fees were not to change much. In 1942–43, junior-college students paid $320 in board and tuition and high-school students $400 in board and tuition,[116] testimony to the college's concern for the cost of education and to the economic hardship of the intervening decades.

The College Opens

When the college opened its doors on Monday, 5 September 1911, Calgarians were invited to an open house and hundreds came. The *Morning Albertan* said the building was "unpretentious but substantial."[117] The *Calgary Daily Herald*, declaring it "one of the best and most up-to-date colleges to be found anywhere on the continent, "described the "throngs" who "wandered up and down flights of stairs and conversed enthusiastically about the color harmony, bright airy classrooms, sitting rooms, etc."[118] The dining room was "a bright, spacious room, where all dine together, as one big family." The basement held the kitchen, pantries, dining room the laundry and furnace rooms, and the Household Science and Manual Training

rooms. The main floor contained the general office and the principal's office, the board room, library, and classrooms. "The second and third floors are dormitories and teachers' residence, with a reception room in each dormitory. The west building is the Ladies' Residence, with separate entrance. The east building is the Boys' Residence, with separate entrance also."[119] The visits ended in the dining room, "where Mrs. Kerby and the board of governors' wives and faculty served delicious tea and viands." "The crowds continued to pour in after 8 o'clock and the music discoursed by the orchestra was a unique feature of the evening."[120] The high society flavour of the event was suggested by reports on the ladies' gowns: "a becoming gown of taupe gray satin toque designed of palest yellow roses"; "a pretty gray gown of rajah silk and becoming white chapeau"; "an attractive little gown of delft blue and white foulard with small hat of Milan straw adorned with a black yellow plume and bandings of black velvet ribbon."[121] The student newspaper, the *Chinook*, reported that some things had not gone as planned: "… the electrical lights took a rest for a while, but even those who, on account of this did not see the whole college thoroughly, saw enough to make them decide that it would be a thoroughly healthful and comfortable home for any student residing within its walls."[122]

The *Morning Albertan* said that as of 5 September there were "about 75" students registered. By the end of the first year the total was 179.[123] The Principal's Reports to the board recorded the number of people living in the residence. In 1911–12, there were 50 males and 43 females, including 7 teachers and 8 students from the Normal School; the other 7 rooms were occupied by residential staff.[124] The 1913 *Annual Report of the Department of Education* listed the college's enrolment as 48 students under age 14 (20 boys, 28 girls) and 240 over 14 (96 boys, 144 girls), all aimed at "preparation for Provincial Department Examinations."[125]

The founders had much to celebrate. In less than a year they had secured a charter, selected a site, built a campus, recruited a staff and the first cohort of students, and developed a curriculum. Yet there was a price for such speed. "I have learned with deep regret and pain that some of the members of our board feel that I have not taken them into my confidence in this

The original Mount Royal College building, ca. 1912,
located at 7th Avenue and 11th Street S.W. Photographer H.
Pollard; Mount Royal University Archives HB172-1.

DINING HALL

MAIN ENTRANCE AND CORRIDOR

An interior corridor in the original Mount
Royal College building, ca. 1912. Photographer
Novelty Manufacturing & Art Co. Ltd.; Mount
Royal University Archives *Calendar 1912–13.*

The dining hall in the original Mount Royal College
building, ca. 1912. Photographer Novelty Manufacturing &
Art Co. Ltd., Montreal; Mount Royal University Archives
Calendar 1916–17.

work," Kerby wrote in January 1912. "Nothing, I assure you, could have been farther from my mind or intention." If he had neglected to keep anyone adequately informed, he said, "I must humbly ask your pardon." In response to rumours about Mrs. Kerby, whom he had described in December as "Lady Principal or Superintendent," he said that without her knowledge the Executive Committee had set a monthly payment of $60 in recognition of her contribution. "While she thoroughly appreciated the kindness of the board," he declared, "she was entirely opposed to receiving any remuneration whatever, and she desires me to say that she must decline to receive any salary for the future, and furthermore I desire on her part, as well as my own, to have the privilege of paying back to the board . . . the entire amount that has been paid to her during that past three or four months."[126] This decision meant that his wife's major contributions to the college were not to be formally recognized.

THE GATHERING GLOOM

Inspired by his exposure to prestigious institutions during his trip, Kerby conjured up the broad, sunlit uplands ahead. The goal must be to create "something of a national institution. . . . There is no reason . . . why Mount Royal College should not become one of the famous colleges of Canada. We have here the location, and the climate, and the other conditions that make this possible, Mount Royal College will be largely what we make it; if we hold our ideals high, if we lay the foundation for a great institution, we can have it."[127] It would need a campus of twenty to twenty-five acres, with buildings for arts and science, preparatory studies, manual training and household science, as well as a gymnasium, "possibly a library," and "a residence for the president." It also required an endowment fund: "If we are to have a college that is worthwhile, we must not only have buildings properly equipped, but we must have sufficient endowment to carry on the work along the highest lines of efficiency." A million dollars would suffice; Kerby proposed raising half a million in the near future.[128]

In the ebullient atmosphere of the time, in which fortunes were being made in property while men slept, such dreams seemed more realistic than they proved to be in practice. Kerby's calculations included the value of land donated to the college. In November 1911 James Shouldice and A. S. McKay, developers, donated fifty acres on the north side of the Bow River for a campus, on the condition that the college build facilities on it.[129] In December 1911 the board's Executive Committee accepted the donation, together with eleven lots donated by Scott and Hartfront Ltd., twenty-four lots from Dr. William Egbert (a member of the Methodist elite, Freemason, Liberal politician, and subsequently Alberta's Lieutenant Governor, 1925–31),[130] and other land donated by John Hextall (an Englishman who had bought the Bowness district in the hope of making it a high-class residential area and who had swapped land with the city in 1911 in exchange for a streetcar line that was never built).[131] In a submission to the Methodist Board of Education in April 1912, the college listed its property assets as worth $222,000 (fifty acres valued at $100,000, forty-five acres elsewhere valued at $30,000, sixty-eight lots valued at $10,000, ten lots – site of the college building – valued at $25,000, and the building itself, valued at $57,000). In addition, the college had "money subscriptions" amounting to $203,000 ($198,000 from nine contributors, "other promises valued at say $5,000"), along with $75,000 in liabilities.[132] In July 1912 Kerby estimated that the college had "a total in land and money promises of nearly $300,000, as well as $2,000 in cash from Sir John Langham, a member of our board of governors."[133] However, the property boom was about to end in a bust, undermining not only the value of properties the college hoped to sell and the fortunes of some donors, but also hopes for the college's future beyond its temporary facility and limited mandate. "Would-be millionaires found themselves struggling to survive. As the autumn winds blew cold, men searched for work amid the 400 boarded up real estate offices lining the city streets. Scores of half-finished buildings made the once-booming city look like a ghost town."[134] Thus, far from having the resources to contemplate more commitments, the college soon found that it did not have enough cash to pay for its temporary campus. Its mortgage with the Merchant Bank of Canada remained $65,000,[135] its debt to Langham at $25,000,[136] and its revenues were about to collapse when the First World War disrupted civil life.

TENSIONS IN THE CHURCH

In the beginning, Mount Royal College, unlike some of its sister institutions, received little notice from the church's Board of Education. The board's minutes recorded every stage in the development of Regina College until its early approval as a "connexional" college.[137] J. H. Riddell, principal of Alberta College, regularly reported on plans to divide the college into two parts, a theological college (Alberta College South) and a non-degree college (Alberta College North).[138] By contrast, there were no reports from Kerby and no mention of Mount Royal prior to its launching in September 1911. The absence probably reflected Kerby's style: he would deliver a college in short order while giving no hostages to church maneuvring.

One result was a longer period prior to "connexional" status than Kerby had anticipated. In 1910, as we have seen, the General Conference had asked the college "to submit full financial and academic plans to the Board of the Educational Society."[139] Preparing for the Board of Education's annual meeting in October 1911, general secretary Graham wrote Kerby to remind him to submit the documents. Caught up in start-up activities, Kerby sent a quick note in response. The college's calendar "speaks for itself concerning the scope of our work – which is up to the end of 2nd year University." "The general scheme, as accepted by the board of governors, involves an investment of at least 1 mill[ion] dollars in buildings, etc. and endowment. . . . We have promises of several valuable sites for the permanent buildings, the last one 50 acres in one solid block, one of the finest anywhere here. I have this legally signed up . . . Our present building will cost about $75,000. It is growing in value every day. We have furnished it with the best of furniture, so that it is one of the best equipped colleges in Canada." On academic directions, he wrote: "The ultimate form of our work may be different from the present. It seemed necessary in starting to have the many lines and departments we have . . . I do not want the Board of Education to tie our hands so far as the future is concerned on any line. The future will care for itself."[140] Unfortunately, Kerby's letter arrived in Toronto on 6 October, two days after the meeting. Thus, the first mention of Mount Royal in the minutes was as follows: ". . . the secretary stated that he had written to

the board of the college for information regarding their proposed plans, academic and financial, but so far had received no reply, and, there being nothing before the board, no action was taken."[141]

There was, of course, more to the story. When the proposal to create Mount Royal had been considered by the Alberta Methodist Conference, the college's founders had agreed not to duplicate Alberta College's theological programs for "probationers." At the new college's initial board meeting on 2 August 1910, W. G. Hunt had "pointed out the development and growth of Alberta College and the fact that very few in attendance at Alberta College came from South of the Red Deer River and hence the manifest opportunity for another college along the lines of Alberta College to be located at Calgary."[142] The phrase "along the lines" inspired suspicion that Mount Royal would not keep the agreement. When word spread that the assistant pastor of Central Methodist, "appointed to Victoria College" as a probationary ministerial student, had "applied to be allowed to attend Mount Royal College Calgary," Reverend Arthur Barner, president of the Alberta Conference, wrote confidentially to Graham in August 1911 warning that "such a movement ought to be jealously guarded for fear of friction between the North and the South here and for the sake of building up one strong Theological College in this province. Now it would seem that we have reached the place where we have to do something for I hear of several other young men who wish to pursue the same course." That Barner and Graham saw Kerby as trouble was plain: "I think from what you said to me in Calgary last June that we are of one mind in regard to this principal."[143]

In September 1911, Principal Riddell of Alberta College also conveyed his concerns to Graham: "It is reported that Victoria College is transferring some of the students sent to her by Alberta Conference to Mount Royal College. . . . We have no objection to Mount Royal doing the work it set out to do and assured us it was going to do. We have gone to great expense to put a large building on the university grounds and have made preparation to do this preparatory work for our ministers. If another college is going to come into the field and divides this work it will be suicidal to all our work." He asked why Mount Royal had "not come out openly before the Conference and got the mind of this Conference on the matter and not seek to get students by this round-about way after declaring most emphatically that they had no intention of interfering with Alberta College."[144]

This was the environment prior to the board's meeting in October 1911. When he learned that the board had not approved connexional status, Kerby responded angrily. Referring to the publicity about the college "in the *Guardian* and other papers," reports to Graham about fundraising and the acquisition of land, the fact the board had a copy of the calendar, and Graham's own urging for the board to take action, he went on: "I had a feeling at the General Conference that the board seemed to be suspicious that there was something dark about the starting of Mount Royal College. It was and is our desire to be related to the Methodist Church, but if the Methodist Church does not want this relation I presume we can get along or give some other church that relation."[145] On probationers, Kerby distinguished between preparatory academic and theological study. "I have a number of young probationers here taking their Literary and Matriculation work, only I understand that this action of the board leads you to hesitate to advance their fees. I remember that when I was recommended to Victoria College as a probationer, instead of going to Victoria College, I went to the [Cobourg] Collegiate Institute and I had my fees paid just the same. We are not trying to steal a march or build up Mount Royal College at the expense of any other college or any other department of our work." Indeed, probationers in other colleges might suffer financially, if the same rule were applied to them: "A move of that kind would hurt our other colleges here in Alberta more than it would hurt us."[146]

In December 1911 W. G. Hunt advised Graham that "a Special Committee has been appointed to draft an application and forward same to you." Yet, as of 9 March 1912, when Graham replied to Kerby, the application had not been submitted. "Your letter of last October, which arrived too late for the Annual Meeting of the Board of Education," Graham wrote, "really proffered no request from your board of governors to have the Institution connexionalized. You should send me a definite request in the form of a resolution of your board . . . asking [to] . . . be connexionalized," together with anything further on financial and academic plans.[147] Kerby explained that "when your letter came [in September 1911] there was very little time to get our board together. . . . It does seem to me that we have carried out our end of this contract, [though] it might have been better for the information to have been sent over the signature of the Secretary of our Board, but as you know, the time was short." The college would report soon but "it will be difficult for some members of our board to believe that the Methodist Church really desires to connexionalize Mount Royal College."[148]

In April 1912 Charles Adams, the board's secretary, forwarded a copy of "the report of the Special Committee on Church Connection as submitted to the March meeting of the Executive Committee of the board," a certified copy of the resolution passed by the Executive Committee requesting connexional status, the charter, and information on the college's property holdings. With respect to "educational scope and work," the report said "we refer the Board [of Education] to the college Calendar. . . ." There was no reference to probationers or to constraints on the college's mandate.[149]

One can only guess at the ensuing dialogue. When the board considered Mount Royal's application in October 1912, the motion was moved by Graham and seconded by Riddell. It approved "the establishment of Mount Royal College in Calgary . . . and hereby endorse[s] it as a connexional institution of the Methodist Church. . . ." The resolution also expressed "deep appreciation for the splendid enterprise and loyal devotion of the citizens of Calgary in establishing such a creditable institution and we hope that abundant success may crown the efforts of the Rev. Principal Kerby and his associates to make Mount Royal College worthy of the best traditions of Methodism."[150] In January 1913, the Special Committee of the General Conference approved connexional status for Mount Royal "under the assumption that the Theological work shall be done at Edmonton."[151]

Though Kerby later served on the church's Board of Education, he never belonged to the inner circle.[152] Indeed, some tensions continued. In 1921, Riddell, then principal of Wesley College and a member of Mount Royal's board, queried a financial statement, sending a copy to Graham. This infuriated Kerby: "Dr. Riddell might have at least done us the courtesy of waiting to hear from us in reply to his letter before notifying you."[153]

Though becoming a connexional college might have opened the way for a small annual grant from the Board of Education, neither Regina College nor Mount Royal received grants until 1923–24. Such grants were taken from the "connexional" funds that each congregation forwarded to Toronto to pay for administration and publications, ministers' pensions, salaries for ministers in new churches, and loans to probationers.[154] One of the reasons was limited funds, and the financial claims of new colleges inspired concerns in older ones: "With all due respect to the policy adopted by this Board of Education," the treasurer of Alma College in St. Thomas, Ontario, wrote, "it does seem to me of at least equal value to foster work already on its feet as to launch new schemes to the possible peril of those already established."[155]

Indeed, the growing number of Methodist colleges inspired more than financial concerns. There were also questions about mandate and why the church should sustain colleges as public education developed. In 1911 the Board of Education learned that Vincent Massey, vice-chair of the Massey Foundation, the largest donor to the church, had recommended "the appointment of a Commission to enquire and report a policy in respect of secondary education in our colleges."[156] It took until 1918 before the commission was established and 1921 before its report was available. In the meantime, the seventeen colleges continued on their separate paths, with little coordination except for those offering theological programs.

THE EDUCATIONAL CONTEXT

In 1911 the college's founders were only dimly aware that denial of degree-conferring powers to Calgary College reflected an enduring policy rather than a short-term response to a political demand. The men who ran the North-West Territories and the successor provinces of Alberta and Saskatchewan wanted to avoid the denominational struggles that had been waged in Ontario and Manitoba, and that implied government control of degree granting.[157] The pattern was set in 1903 by Frederick W. G. Haultain, head of the government of the Territories, who, in response

to a proposed private university, passed an ordinance which declared that "the first principle . . . is to make the university free from all influence of government, sect, or politics, in fact the institution is to be governed by its graduates."[158] When Premier Rutherford, a former minister of education in the Territorial assembly, drafted the charter for the University of Alberta (which began operating in 1908), it reflected that "principle." He also personally recruited the president, Dr. Henry Wallace Tory, a fellow graduate of McGill University and a member of the Methodists' Board of Education.[159] Tory also regarded denominationalism as "the greatest danger to good educational work. Church colleges were small, inefficient, financially wasteful, and unable to offer the scientific education needed in the 20th century."[160]

It was in this context that Tory persuaded Alberta College, which was further encouraged by the Board of Education, to separate its degree and non-degree activities, and to incorporate the religious degree-granting activities with the university as an affiliated Alberta Theological College. Thus, its independent degree-granting capacity was made subject to the university's approval.[161] The revision of the University of Alberta Act (1910) drafted by Tory reinforced the university's role in degree granting. Religious and "junior colleges" were required to affiliate with the university to offer degree-level courses, while the university also became responsible for certifying professional education.[162] In June 1914 the *Edmonton Journal* wrote that "no such highly unified system of higher education exists anywhere on the American continent as has been achieved in the province of Alberta in the past six years."[163]

Though the university's curriculum expanded beyond its arts and science base, with the addition of law (1912), applied science (engineering, 1913), medicine (1913), pharmacy (1914), agriculture (1915), and accounting (1916), its enrolment remained around 300–400 until 1919–20, when it rose to about 1,000. In 1912 the university added also a Department of Extension, whose purpose was to "take the university to the people" through agricultural extension activities and travelling lecture programs.[164]

However sensible it was for a province with a small population to support only one university, the fact that Rutherford had it located in his Strathcona constituency ensured controversy. Calgarians had expected to be awarded the university because Edmonton had been designated as the capital. The ensuing fracas was one of the first rounds in an enduring north-south rivalry. In 1909 *The Eye Opener* epitomized the gap in public benefits: "Well, Strathcona has another plum, the Agricultural College, to be run as an adjunct of the University. . . . There are five, and five only, big important institutes in Alberta—the capital and parliament buildings; the Univeristy of Alberta; the Agricultural College; the Penitentiary; and the Asylum for the Insane. Ponoka has the Bug House. But where are the rest? On the banks of the Sakatchewan [river], of course."[165] Though, in December 1910, the government, then led by Clifford Sifton, had stripped degree-granting authority from the bill proposed by R. B. Bennett, leader of the Conservative opposition,[166] the campaign for the university continued. It was led by Dr. T. H. Blow, chairman of the board of governors of the proposed University of Calgary, and W. J. Tregillus, president of the United Farmers of Alberta (UFA).[167] The UFA provided land, the city council passed a bylaw granting $150,000 for the construction of the first building, and Lord Strathcona donated $25,000. Many donors were also supporters of Mount Royal, including Blow, Tregillus, Sayre, Hextall, Hunt, Crandell, Shouldice, Sinnott, A. B. Cushing, Bennett, and W. G. Hunt.[168] Despite the lack of a statutory foundation, the "university" began operations on 4 October 1912 with 125 students registered in a "Faculty of Arts" and a "Faculty of Law." The *Chinook* declared it "an accomplished fact."[169] Though the proponents suggested that the university might specialize in science and technology, bills proposing degree-granting powers for Calgary College were defeated again in 1912 and 1913.[170]

To lay the issue to rest, the government appointed a royal commission to recommend future directions for post-secondary education. Consisting of the presidents of the universities of Toronto, Saskatchewan, and Dalhousie, the commission concluded that, with limited funds and a small pool of qualified students, the province should fund only one university: "We see no reason for advising a departure from the historic policy of Western Canada, which was inaugurated by the Province of Manitoba, adopted by the North West Territories, and re-affirmed by the Province of

Alberta, to establish one University and one only to be supported and controlled by the Province for the purpose of giving instruction, granting degrees and controlling the requirements for admission to the professions."[171] Calgary College was bankrupt. The commission recommended establishing a new kind of institution to offer technical and practical subjects.[172]

When the report became public on 7 March 1915, two hundred people met in Calgary's city council chamber. Kerby moved, and Dr. A. O. Macrae, principal of Western Canada College, seconded a motion that the report be accepted and a committee struck to meet with the government to discuss alternatives. However, the majority rejected the report, leaving only the determination to send a delegation. The delegation proposed establishing two institutions – Calgary College, a junior college, to be funded by the city; and the technical institute, to be funded by the province. However, the minister of education, J. R. Boyle, rejected the junior college and incorporated an art program in the Institute and located the Normal School on its proposed campus.[173] As a result, Mount Royal was to develop for decades without a public competitor for the programs it offered.

"The only publicly supported technical institute on the continent," the Alberta Institute of Technology and Art opened its doors in October 1916 with the mandate to provide technical training to returning soldiers, industrial arts teachers, and the "maturing youth of the province." Students did not need to be high-school graduates to enter. It began with five students and seven instructors. The royal commission had anticipated credit transfer and governance issues that would arise decades later, but nothing was done to ensure that courses were transferable to the university, while the idea of a governing board made up of representatives of the city and province was set aside in favour of direct administration by the province.[174] In 1922 the Institute moved into a new facility on the northern slopes of the Bow River overlooking downtown Calgary. It shared the building with the Calgary Normal School, which in 1925 added first-year arts courses for its students, leading to an affiliation with the University of Alberta and to a seat for the Institute on the university Senate.[175] An Art Department was added in 1926 – precursor of the Alberta College of Art and Design.[176]

During the debate in 1912–13, when a government official suggested that colleges might offer degree programs if the university approved, Kerby hailed this as a sign that the Department of Education was rising above its "brand of narrow-mindedness." "Though this scarcely affects Mount Royal now," he wrote, "it may quite possibly in the future, as the intention is to broaden out by taking the work of the second year in a short time, and in some future date Mount Royal may possibly avail itself of the privileges conferred upon all colleges by this amendment."[177] In the meantime, there was much work for the college to do to make up for deficiencies in public schooling – in access for rural students, values, practical preparation, aesthetic awareness and sensibilities, and encouraging students to remain in school beyond fourteen, the legal minimum age for dropping out. The low minimal age deeply concerned Kerby and other Methodists. "Out of 380,000 between the ages of 13 and 14" in Canada, Kerby remarked, "only 36,000 continue their education between the ages of 14 and 15. This is less than 10 percent. This means that comparatively few of our boys and girls are receiving even a high school education. Indeed, many of them never complete the public school course [grade 8] . . . The low age limit of school accounts for much of the general shallowness of our time. Boys and girls leave school when they reach 14 years of age, having received just enough education to make them shallow."[178] For Methodists, there appeared to be fertile terrain for what the college had to offer.

Such was the context in which Mount Royal took shape. The college was another expression of the Methodist Church's educational mission fusing gospel, social development, and civic enlightenment. Its major opportunities consisted of niches not served, or not served adequately, by public-education systems. Its chief constraints arose partly from the limits of its resources in the dismal financial circumstances from 1913 to the Second World War, and partly from the emergence of educational systems that diminished the need for some of the things it did. And yet hard times were a challenge that the college was able to meet. The early decades were the period in which the college's essential character was forged. It learned to live parsimoniously. It offered a stimulating and supportive learning and living environment for students. Its programs were attuned to what students needed and wanted. It was flexible in permitting students to combine studies from different academic streams. It began developing post–high-school career programs. It was academically entrepreneurial, constantly searching for new needs to meet, and promoting itself vigorously and imaginatively.

1914–1918	*Canada joins Great Britain in First World War*
OCTOBER 1914	*Literary Society established*
1921	*Massey Foundation report on Methodist colleges issues harsh criticism of Mount Royal*
1921–22	*College bailed out financially by Methodist Church*
JUNE 1924	*Business manager hired to assist with financial operations*
JUNE 1925	*United Church established and Mount Royal becomes a secondary school affiliated with the new church*
FALL 1929	*Commencement of the Great Depression*
1930–1931	*Lowest enrolment point*

CHAPTER 2

TAKING ROOT, 1911–1931

*All-round manly Christian character;
education as an aid to the service of society; a
stimulation of true patriotism and citizenship;
high ideals of scholarship; to assist students
in "finding themselves".*

– Methodist Yearbook, 1915[1]

Born as an expression of hope and idealism in the ebullient phase of "the open frontier" before 1914, Mount Royal College found itself during the next three decades in a struggle to survive. The open frontier had required a westward flow of people and capital, but, with the First World War, people and capital began moving elsewhere. As Max Foran has written, "removal of the crucial variables of immigration and capital investment meant an end to externally motivated growth, or in short, to the vibrancy of the open frontier."[2] Calgary and its hinterland endured thirty years of consolidation, of "the closed frontier," as they adjusted to narrower possibilities and learned to rely on their own resources. Neither Kerby nor the governors had anticipated an era of hardship. They had expected their college to grow steadily, move onto a handsome new campus, and eventually add degree granting to its credentials. Instead, they had to pursue their dream in a context in which the college's survival from one year to the next was a major preoccupation.

George Kerby remained principal from 1910 to 1942, when he reached eighty-two years of age. Broadly speaking, his principalship fell in two parts: the period from 1911 to 1931, during which the college worked out its initial mandate, and the period after 1931, when it formed an affiliation agreement with the University of Alberta and established an identity for itself as a "junior college."

It would be hard to exaggerate the financial and enrolment challenges Mount Royal College faced during its first twenty years. It was only three years old when the war began in August 1914, an event that led to a sharp decline in enrolment and growing deficits. During the war, agricultural production in Canada, Australia, the United States, and elsewhere expanded to make up for the disruption of agriculture in Europe. Following the war, when European agriculture revived, market gluts led to the world agricultural depression that lasted until the Second World War. As the college relied heavily on its boarding school function for revenue and as most residential students came from rural areas, rural penury implied scarcity for the college. In 1923 a CPR official estimated that 80 per cent of Alberta farmers were bankrupt; from 1921 to 1926, thirteen of Alberta's twenty towns shrank in population.[3] Though there was a brief economic recovery in the late 1920s, the onset of the Great Depression in 1929–30 brought yet more hardship. From 1930 to 1935, "the net income per farmer was less than $400 annually"[4] – barely enough to pay the college's residential and tuition fees. With ranchers similarly hard-hit, flight from the land continued, with pools of unemployed growing in urban centres.[5] Given the circumstances, it was remarkable that the college survived while all of the other private colleges initiated in Calgary before 1914 disappeared.

DEVELOPING A "CHARACTER FACTORY"

During its first two decades, the college most completely realized the Methodist vision of what it should be – apart from imparting knowledge and practical skills, that meant building personal character. In 1915, the *Methodist Yearbook* explained the purpose of the colleges: "All-round manly Christian character; education as an aid to the service of society; a stimulation of true patriotism and citizenship; high ideals of scholarship; to assist students in "finding themselves."[6] That emphasis on character development had accounted for the draconian disciplinary conditions in earlier generations of Methodist schools. However, for Kerby, a progressive educator, more was to be gained by love and engagement than by harsh discipline: "the

Science of Religious Education . . . can eliminate dishonesty, lying, cruelty and other vices . . . and establish the moral health of society."[7] Moreover, in his view, building character was complex. It required the interlocking relationships and responsibilities of the home, school, and church in shaping the minds and values of young people. Though the chief responsibility lay with the home, not all homes had a positive environment or coped well with young people oriented toward peers and popular diversions. The question was how the school and the church could reinforce the home or, where necessary, provide an alternative environment. The college was part of that broader set of relationships, though a singular one, because it combined church and school for some students while for others it combined home, church, and school.

Thus, in addition to serving as principal of the college, Kerby attempted to link home, school, and church in other venues. From 1912 to 1916 he served as a trustee on the Calgary school board (the last two years as chairman). In the 1920s and 1930s, he became a leader of the emerging home and school movement, with the aim of nudging public education to reflect the Methodists' vision of education. When parent-teacher groups in Calgary combined in November 1926 to form the Local Federation of Home and School Association, he became its first president. When the Canadian National Federation of Home and School (1927) and the Alberta Home and School Federation (1929) were formed, Kerby became the first president of each. By the mid-1930s, he was vice-president of the International Federation of Home and School Associations.[8]

Shaping character was his lifelong preoccupation. The church needed to offer "something better and brighter than the bar, the brothel or the gambling room.""We must make our churches character factories, not cold-storage plants. . . . We should have services or meetings that will appeal to the physical, social, intellectual, as well as the spiritual." "I believe . . . that it is possible to be ten minutes ahead of the devil."[9] In its operations, the college combined the functions of home, school, and church. "A college is a character factory, a place for the making of men and women."[10] The residence program added the home to the mix. "Here," Kerby said, "the most important of our educational work is done: the work of character

The Curriculum

In the Victorian era, the badges of learning were Latin for boys, piano and fine arts for girls, and elocution ("expression") for everyone. As a co-educational institution, Mount Royal offered those badges. The key languages were available – and even Latin lingered on well after the college became public. There were to be music courses for regular students and music lessons for members of the community through the Conservatory of Music: "It is the purpose of the college to establish a first-class Conservatory of Music. Students will be prepared for the various local examinations in music, of the Toronto Conservatory and Royal Academy of Music and other similar musical institutions."[12] The college would mount a "Fine Art School" to provide "china painting, painting in oils and water-colours," a "School of Expression, Physical Culture and Dramatic Art" to offer elocution and public-speaking lessons, and "a full Ladies' College Course and Special Courses for Boys."[13]

The academic year consisted of two twenty-week semesters. The curriculum was divided into two divisions, "the Preparatory and Collegiate, or Junior and Senior," and remained largely unchanged from 1911 to 1931. The preparatory division was for students of ten years of age (grades 4–8) and older. "Pupils entering the college will be placed in the work of the year for which they are fitted, and all students will be pushed on as fast as they can profitably go." The courses included arithmetic, art, reading, literature, writing, composition, spelling, grammar, British history, Canadian history, Canadian civics, nature study, agriculture (grades 7–8), manual training for boys, and "household science and art" for girls.[14] The collegiate division offered "the work of the High School course, Teachers' Certificate, and Matriculation." High school ended with grade 11. (Grade 12 was considered equivalent to first-year university.) The division also offered a General Course "designed for those who seek a thorough and liberal training without reference to university entrance" – a terminal high-school program. Collegiate-division courses built on those in the Preparatory program but were more intensive. High-school students were required to take two languages (French, Latin, German, or Greek). English included elocution, which began with "scientific breathing,

Reverend George Kerby shares his philosophy on education for young men in *Keep a Grip on Harry*, published ca. 1904. Mount Royal University Archives A-2007-27.

education, education for life, education by contact and by contagion, social education, as well as the development of personality."[11] As a devotee of progressive education, Kerby wanted to deliver a child-centred education. This was a lofty notion, easier to declare than to implement, but it indicated the ideal he was promulgating.

. . . the basis of all voice culture." The curriculum included three years of art courses.[15]

There were three academic streams. "The Matriculation and Teachers' Courses" led to "University and Normal [School] work respectively." Within this stream, "the Undergraduate Course" was "designed for those who wish one year of undergraduate work before taking up their professional studies." Another stream, "the General Course," was "designed for those who seek a thorough and liberal training without reference to university entrance." The third stream consisted of "Special Courses" for students not aiming at completing matriculation or a high-school diploma.[16] In addition, the Department of Commerce offered short courses to "train students as Bookkeepers, Commercial Teachers, Stenographers, Typists, [and] Operators" of business machines ("dictaphone, adding machine, comptometer, posting machine, "various duplicating devices").[17]

With typical verve, Kerby immediately asked universities to recognize "the matriculation examinations set and examined by themselves," as George Chown, the registrar of Queen's University, put it in a letter to President Tory of the University of Alberta. "So far as we can understand it," Chown wrote, "it is an attempt to get from under the provincial matriculation. Queen's has always stood for uniformity of matriculation examinations and will not now if it understands the situation, countenance any attempt to establish different matriculation standards within a province."[18] Tory responded that "I have already written telling them [the college] that they must conform to the usual examination set by ourselves or by the Department of Education. These are the terms we give to Alberta College and Western Canada College."[19] After some tergiversation, the college conducted its examinations "in accordance with the Regulations of the Department of Education of Alberta." Grades were based on

The cooking class, 1916. Mount Royal University Archives G1246-7.

"daily recitations and written tests" (40 per cent) and final examinations (60 per cent).[20]

The first calendar anticipated offering "two years of university." "Mount Royal College will be in affiliation with McGill, Toronto and Alberta Universities. Students may take the first two years of any of these universities at Mount Royal College."[21] This claim drew the university's attention: "I notice from the Calendar . . . that they claim they will be affiliated with McGill, Toronto and the University of Alberta," Dr. Tory wrote to Queen's. "Our regulation for affiliated schools is this – any school sending up students to our examinations is considered affiliated at hoc, provided they succeed in passing the examination."[22] He wrote Kerby on 7 December 1911 stating that "the only thing necessary for you to secure affiliation with the university, as a preparatory college, is to send students to the matriculation examinations . . . [or] if you have a reasonable number of students, . . . at your own building."[23] In June 1912 Tory advised Kerby of wording the university would find acceptable for the college calendar: "Under the regulations of the Senate of the University of Alberta, preparatory schools which send students to the university matriculation examinations are affiliated with the university." Thus, in 1912–13, "Mount Royal College will be in the advantageous position of affiliation with the University of Alberta." However, Tory added, "with respect to affiliation beyond the matriculation examination that is of course another matter and will be dealt with by the Senate when the time arrives to discuss it. Up to the present time we have not granted affiliation beyond [course] articulation."[24]

A year later the college's calendar diluted its claim: "For the present Mount Royal College takes up only the first year undergraduate work. This is covered by the work of Grade 12 of the Alberta Education Department."[25] Later, the wording became: "The Undergraduate Course includes the first year of university work, and is designed for those who wish one year of undergraduate work before taking up their professional studies."[26] Following a change in course classification by the department in 1926, the college modified its advertising to reflect the fact that it offered "first-year university courses (formerly designated second-year courses)."[27]

THE CAMPUS EXPERIENCE

From the outset, Kerby sought to create a campus environment that would be enriching, stimulating, and uplifting. "An air of culture and luxury is felt everywhere," the *Chinook*, the new student publication, said. "It is not often statues and classical pictures adorn the walls and corridors . . . Moreover, the soft strains of music are heard on every hand."[28] Within weeks of the start of classes in 1911, there were student clubs, publications, athletic teams, intramural and external leagues, concerts, lecture series, debates, a college song, and a college "yell."[29] This was a period when people were expected to manufacture their own entertainments, and the students responded avidly. Kerby believed in the importance of fun, as suggested by the initial reception he and Mrs. Kerby held for faculty and more than one hundred students in September 1911. The evening included musical entertainment by students, a reading, card games such as Pit and "tic-tac-toe," and ended with a rendition of "Auld Lang Syne."[30] In 1913 the occasion included "Spin the Pan," "Grunt," "college songs and yells," and a "peanut stabbing contest. . . ."[31] There were annual Halloween masquerade dances, with students competing in costumes.[32] In 1912, "all were masked with the exception of the University of Alberta Rugby Team, which, as it was in the city at the time, had been invited to this event of the season." The students played charades, showed moving pictures, while "gypsy queens . . . were relating the present, past and future to many eager students."[33]

The core of campus intellectual life was the Literary Society. Its first meeting on 11 October 1911 reflected Kerby's approach. There was a piano solo by a student, games, "a candy feed," and a lecture by Margaret M. Graham, a faculty member, offering "a very educative, as well as pleasing, description of the city of Venice and its peculiar citizens." On another occasion, the guest speaker was a "Major Shoff" who had "served in the English, German, American, Mexican and other armies, and, as you would expect, has had many rare and exciting adventures."[34] Stanley M. Sweetman, a student from Calgary, was elected the first president. Meeting weekly on Friday evenings, the Literary Society was the principal venue

Dramatic Club, ca. 1915. Mount Royal University Archives *Calendar 1916–17.*

Literary Society, 1920. Mount Royal University Archives HC6-4-1.

for readings of student work, lectures, debates, music recitals, and games.[35]

"The most important business that has come before the club" was the decision in its first meetings to create the *Chinook*, a student publication that was to appear two or three times a year, and a "bi-weekly paper, containing principally the news of the college, read at the meetings of the Literary Club."[36] The first editor-in-chief of the *Chinook* was Varian Green, a student from Calgary, followed later by W. Burn, E. B. J. Fallis, Lucile Trego, Claire Gemmill, and G. T. Walters. The *Chinook* published student and faculty essays, poems, jokes, descriptions of college clubs and activities, lists of prize winners, sketches of teachers, and items on former students.

The Literary Society also spawned a Debating Club that was a major part of college life for decades. It was a useful means for engaging students in discussion of "the big questions," fostering self-confidence, and improving oratorical skills. The first debate, between teams from grades 8 and 9, was held on 22 November 1912 on the topic: "Resolved that city life is more beneficial to human welfare than life in the country."[37] In December 1912 the topic was: "Resolved that women's suffrage should be granted to Canada by amendment to the BNA Act."[38] Public speaking and debating became part of the "expression" program.[39] In 1919 a mock parliament was added.[40] The 1921–22 calendar indicated that "Leader of Government" and "Leader of Opposition" had become offices in the Literary Society.[41]

As the spiritual environment was always a concern, the college insisted on chapel attendance, compulsory religion classes, Scripture readings, grace at meals, and prayers at ceremonies. Kerby held services every weekday morning, wearing his academic gown, leading a parade of teachers and students into the chapel.[42] The college also housed chapters of the YWCA (formed in 1913),[43] while Mrs. Kerby acted as the "Bible and Mission Study Class Teacher"[44] (she gave up her Sunday School class in Central Methodist Church to do this) and J. E. Lovering of the faculty led the Boys Bible Class.[45] After the war, Arnold Rosborough assumed the latter role.[46] In 1922, Kerby noted that there were still "Sunday afternoon Bible and Mission study classes, Mrs. Kerby taking charge of the girls in this work and Mr. Miller, the boys."[47]

To recognize student achievements, Kerby ensured that there were many prizes. The annual academic awards included gold and silver medals "for General Proficiency in the Academic and Commercial Departments" and prizes "for conduct and for highest proficiency in various subjects (Scripture, History, English, Science, Mathematics, Latin, Greek, Moderns, and Writing)," penmanship, "highest standing in private expression," "highest standard in reading," and winners of the oration contest.[48] Among the initial prize winners was John H. Garden (later Kerby's successor), second in general proficiency in the academic program and winner of the good-conduct prize for senior boy students. The prizes came to include the "interclass debating cup," prizes for students with the neatest room, fewest demerit points, and neatest notebooks, and prizes for field-day sport winners (including track events, tennis, the thread-and-needle race, the cup-and-bowl race, and the necktie race).[49] Kerby advised the board of student successes. In 1914, he reported that "some of the highest marks taken in the province were taken by Mount Royal College students" in recent Department examinations, and that "the student taking the highest marks in Classics in the Freshman Class this year at Toronto University [sic] was prepared at Mount Royal College."[50]

For all the fun of campus life, there also needed to be discipline. "The conduct of all students," the calendar said, "should be that observed by Christian ladies and gentlemen, who try their best to do unto others as they would be done unto, and also to do all they possibly can to assist their fellow students to do what is right and fitting."[51] Chapel services were intended to offer moral instruction and acquaint students with "the subject of character and conduct and religious and moral ideals, in relation to their lives. The interest the students evince in these services and the other evidence we have lead us to believe that no work being done by the college is more vital than this."[52] Whereas earlier generations of Methodists had enforced strict rules to constrain flawed human nature,[53] Kerby saw young people, in the words of historian Michael Owen, as "innocents who, without the proper guidance and training, love and affection, would be corrupted by a noxious social environment."[54] This optimism was conveyed in the calendar: "Refinement and love is the basis of our government. The development of

unselfishness and self-control makes restrictive rules less necessary. Prohibitions are always in the interests of the health, happiness and progress of the student family, and the highest welfare of the individual. We take it for granted that the girls and boys entering Mount Royal College intend to do right." Still, there was need for guidance, and on occasion students were sent home.[55]

The Student Council was invited to establish minor rules. As the names of the early presidents indicated, the council was dominated by boys – Percy Morecombe (1912–13), Percy W. Smith (1914–15), H. P. Young (1915–16), and Mansfield G. Newton (1918–19). To stimulate more female participation, Kerby split the council in 1919–20 – one for the boys, another for the girls.[56] However, the councils soon disappeared, replaced by a "General Executive" made up of representatives of the Literary Society, Social Committee, Editorial Committee, and numerous athletic committees, all with faculty participation. The first student organization listed in the annual calendar was the Literary Society, followed by the editors of the *Chinook*. Though photographs of sports teams, *Chinook* editors, and the Literary Society leaders appeared in publications, there were no pictures of Student Council members in the first three decades.[57]

The rules written by Kerby originally included a requirement to attend daily chapel service during the week, Sunday evening service, and Bible study. The chapel or church service requirement continued until 1931–32, when Mount Royal became a junior college.[58] The Bible study requirement was to remain in force to the end of the private college. Some rules were protective of young students: "For many reasons, but especially for the serious mental deterioration which results from their use, tobacco, narcotics and alcoholic beverages are strictly prohibited . . . Smoking is especially injurious to the memory and general brain power of young students." "Lady students will be chaperoned to and from trains, to church, and on long walks. Strangers calling on students must present letters of introduction from parents." "Request for the absence of any student from college must be sent direct to the principal. Students are not free to be out with friends, except by special permission. These permissions should rarely be given." Some rules betrayed the sexism of the time: "Students in the Ladies' Residence make their own beds, and are required to maintain an orderly room" – not an obligation for the boys, though all rooms were regularly inspected for neatness.[59] There was a dress code: "The college costume for class-room wear for the ladies is navy blue skirt and blue or white middy blouse . . . The college costume for boys is dark blue suits and college caps."[60]

When discipline was required, Kerby said, its purpose was to assist students to develop their capacity for moral judgment. The daily schedule was intended to keep students busy from morning to night. Students "below passing grade in any study or those found out of their rooms between bells are required to study in the study hall. Throughout evening study hours students are required to be in their rooms and at study, except when arrangements are made for study hall." Faculty members spent at least two evenings a week in the residence during the study hours. Even the home was not to interfere: "Students will not be allowed to use the telephone. Parents or friends wishing to communicate by 'phone may do so at any time, giving their message over the 'phone to the Dean or teacher in charge."[61]

THE FIRST WORLD WAR

The outbreak of war in August 1914 was greeted "with an enthusiasm which in retrospect seems almost as barbaric as the actual war itself. The city, already tense with suspense from the slow deterioration of events in Europe, exploded into patriotic fever." "Not even at the height of the real estate or oil excitement was there such an outburst of pent-up feelings," said the *Calgary Herald*.[62] For, Kerby, an ardent advocate of the British Empire, serving king and country went with serving God and man. At a November 1914 meeting of the Methodist Church's Board of Education, he moved a motion conveying its "hearty appreciation" for receipt of an address entitled "Canada's Duty."[63] In 1916 he became the chief recruiting officer for District 13 and district representative under the Military Service Act, with the honorary rank of major and title as chaplain. Gordon Bennett, head of the business program and dean of boys, was granted a leave to enlist and later became a major and second-in-command of the 191st Regiment based in Red Deer. Two board members,

G. W. Morfitt and the Reverend Robert Pearson, enlisted.[64]

Even before the outbreak of war, a mobilization of male spirits had begun. In 1913 the Lord Strathcona Trust had sponsored Cadet Corps No. 135, a military simulacrum of the Boy Scout movement emerging around the world. The college participated because training and discipline were "a most valuable experience to the boys."[65] With the start of the war, the activity took on a more serious dimension. Training began in the use of weapons, semaphore, Morse code, and the telegraph. The Christmas 1914 edition of the *Chinook* included a photograph of about forty non-uniformed boys, all wearing fedoras, lined up behind Lieutenant Gordon Bennett, head of Cadet Corps No. 135;[66] pictures of cadets appeared in college calendars during the war and into the peace.[67] "After all," the *Chinook* proclaimed, "why should England tremble, when there are so many cadets from the different organizations who will soon be ready to enlist to do their duty for the British Empire."[68] In 1915 the *Chinook* carried reports on the twice-weekly drills, the "grumbling around the halls," and the value of military discipline, notably "the absolute obedience to the commands and laws laid down by the officers."[69] In 1915 Kerby reported on the "splendid year" experienced by the boys and said that there were plans for a corps for the girls, but the latter never materialized. The following year, he indicated that calls for volunteers had reduced the number of boys registered, particularly in the matriculation and commercial programs aimed at older students. Over forty students had enlisted.[70]

Student publications were filled with patriotic effusions, though reports also gave a sense of the grim realities in the field. "May each one of us remember them [the soldiers in the trenches] and hope for a speedy cessation of the awful carnage that has overclouded Europe," the *Chinook* declared.[71] In the fall of 1918, Literary Society meetings provided a venue for papers on the history and character of the belligerent countries. Among the topics were "The Causes of the War," "The Colonies and the War," "Austria-Hungary, France, and the Kaiser."[72] A prize was offered for the best essay on "Why the Allies Must Win." Conservatory instructor Wilfred Oaten sang the national anthems of the Allies.

In 1918 the honour roll of those who had enlisted "to fight for the right in the great world-wide conflict" included 120 names, of whom 9 had died.[73] At war's end, Kerby greeted students somberly. "The war is over. The daily casualty list has ceased. On every ship and train are the returning boys. Soon all, save those who sleep 'In Flanders Field where Poppies Blow,' will be home." Students must remember that "the spirit of courage and sacrifice and determination is still needed to make secure for all time the fruits of victory." Education was more valuable than ever, as it gave "a resolute, unshakeable persistence in the realization of a life purpose that is worthwhile."[74] This echoed a theme struck by the Methodist Church: "The present world strife emphasizes the fact that knowledge is power, that training spells efficiency, that schools and teachers exert a most potent influence upon the plastic life of youth, and at the same time sounds a deeper note of warning in showing that wrong ideas and false ideals are a positive menace to a nation's life. The horrors of the Hun in Belgium have burned upon the consciousness of the race as with indelible letters of fire the truth that the production of character is infinitely above mere culture or the development of a keen, merciless intellect."[75]

The war has "taught us many lessons," the *Chinook* declared: "courage in facing tremendous dangers; determination before the seemingly impossible, sacrifice, self-restraint and generosity for the good of others." It had also "shattered the prestige of many established customs" and led to a "demand for improved conditions of life." "Impatient souls are already speaking of revolution." "We need to keep cool, to keep our ideals high, and put forth the best that is in us for the betterment of Alberta and of Canada."[76] Over time, this "war culture" was to give way to second thoughts about mingling the secular and the spiritual, eroding certainty and encouraging anti-war sentiments.[77]

In all Methodist colleges, the disruptions of economic and social life triggered by the war caused enrolment and revenues to drop, inflated costs, and reduced charitable donations. Mount Royal's enrolment fell from 278 in 1914 to 192 in 1915, 162 in 1916, and 208 in 1917.[78] "The financial problem of our colleges has been most acute," a Methodist publication explained, "chiefly due to the withdrawal of large numbers of men students who have enlisted for overseas service

and a resultant large decrease in the amount received as fees."[79] The number of Mount Royal's boarders fell in half, a crucial matter since the boarders paid for the utilities and food services. By the end of the war, the college was deep in debt.

THE CHURCH EXAMINES ITS COLLEGES

The college's connection to the Methodist Church was mainly a result of its roots in the Methodist community rather of its connexional status. Most, though not all, of the church's grants went to institutions with theological programs, notably Victoria College, Mount Allison University, and, in the west, Wesley College in Winnipeg and Alberta College in Edmonton. In September 1915 the board debated whether to launch an external commission to review "the necessity for the continuance of each school or college." This led to the establishment of the Commission of Seven which, in 1919, with the addition of two corresponding members, became known as the Commission of Nine.[80] The effort to clarify the church's educational role was paralleled by efforts to develop more effective Sunday schools and youth activities.[81] In January 1919 the church accepted a proposal from the Massey Foundation for a joint "enquiry into Methodist educational institutions and to issue a report for the information of all who might be interested."[82] Its members were Vincent Massey (vice-president of the foundation), the Reverend James Smyth (principal of Wesleyan Theological College in Montreal), George H. Locke (chief librarian of Toronto), and Professor J. C. Robertson (dean of the Faculty of Arts, Victoria College).[83]

The commission's report in January 1921 addressed basic questions. Why was the church "undertaking what would seem to be the duty and concern of the State – the provision of education needed to fit young people for the duties of citizenship?" The connection to colleges about which it knew little could not continue: "where the Church will not assume responsibility and exercise supervision, it should not lend the prestige or its name." The report also challenged institutional rationales, such as compensating for the lack of public educational opportunities (a transitional need), providing a Christian environment (an argument for hostels rather than for colleges), meeting the needs of students whose education had been hindered (trying to be all things to all people, offering "pot-boiler" courses to generate revenue), and fostering experimentation (there was none to be found). Rather than "dissipating" energies on unnecessary functions, the "agents of the church should be devoting [themselves] to their proper calling. . . . " The institutions placed too much emphasis on facilities and too little on personnel: "Education is chiefly a matter of brains and personality. . . . Let them find men of the highest qualifications and pay them adequately and the other material problems will offer no lasting difficulty." Many principals lacked qualifications: "In any other than a church institution, it would as a rule be regarded as axiomatic that the head of an educational institution should be an educationist of recognized standing." There were problems with academic standards. While "auxiliary subjects" such as music, fine arts, and bookkeeping might be offered, they should not be offered as specializations but rather as supplements to provide a balanced education "that would take due account of all the capacities that call for development if the pupil is to be prepared adequately to fill his place in the community."[84]

The commissioners' reviews of individual institutions were frank. Mount Royal College lacked adequate facilities, was heavily indebted, registered most students in music and arts courses rather than in academic subjects, was in unnecessary competition with the private sector in business topics, lacked sufficient academic staff, and had no credible long-term rationale: "As the province develops and abnormal conditions pass away, what sphere of work, uncultivated by others, will remain to Mount Royal College? That is the question the answer to which must determine its future policy. [We] would suggest that no extensive plans for the future should be framed in simple reliance on the virtues of the sort of institution which attempts to meet educational demands of every description that may be made by any class in the community." The commissioners "strongly recommend[ed] that serious consideration be given to . . . changing Mount Royal College into a hostel for the accommodation primarily of Methodist students in attendance at the high schools, normal schools, and other educational institutions."[85]

Stunned, Kerby hastened to limit the damage. When the report came before the Board of Education on 30 March 1921, he supported its referral to the Commission of Nine to formulate recommendations for the General Conference of 1922.[86] He prompted his own board to respond, which it did in a message dated 21 April 1921, signed by Charles Adam, board secretary, declaring that the report had inflicted a "grave injustice, doubtless without intention," through its "incorrect statements and recommendations." The college rejected the hostel idea and warned of damage to donations and student and staff recruitment if it became public. While there were facilities limitations, the college's long-term plans included more residences and classrooms, a gymnasium, an assembly hall – and transformation into a junior college.[87]

The battle to rehabilitate the college's reputation shifted to the Commission of Nine.[88] Dr. George J. Trueman, one of the nine, president of Mount Allison University beginning in 1923, visited in February 1921.[89] The report of the Commission of Nine was submitted to the General Conference in 1922,[90] after which Trueman sent Kerby his confidential report. Of all the colleges he had visited, the disparity between the views of the principal and the rest of the staff was greatest at Mount Royal, the principal describing "an end toward which he was constantly striving," the teachers "not so fully conscious of this," seeing "things more as they actually were." Noting the amount of time Kerby spent away from the college, Trueman described Kerby as neither a scholar nor a manager but as a motivational speaker. "Dr. Kerby does not make the mistake of so many school principals, who give themselves to the study of books, but he studies people as individuals and as they group themselves in society. He is not spending his time in teaching, nor experimenting with different methods of teaching, reading, arithmetic, etc. . . . On the other hand he is using his great energy, tact, public spirit and knowledge of people to encourage and inspire his students, and to animate his teachers with his own fine purpose. Thus becoming the motive power behind the whole organization, he succeeds in passing on his fine faith and courage to the student and teaching bodies." He recommended designating a coordinator for academic activities.[91]

When the Board of Education considered the recommendations of the Commission of Nine on 18 April 1922, Kerby moved that the board, "in forwarding these approved principles and their suggested recommendations to the several colleges . . . does not desire to convey the impression that it is endeavoring to superimpose a set of regulations to which the college must at once rigidly conform as a condition to receive recognition from the Methodist Church, but rather it is presenting a group of educational ideals which the board of any Methodist college should make every endeavour to realize as soon as possible in the life and work of the institution for the direction of whose policy it is responsible."[92] The motion was approved, along with another from Kerby to set aside the recommendations relating to Mount Royal. Thus, the report's chief effect was an internal administrative realignment a few years later.[93]

In 1924–25 the Methodists negotiated a merger with the Congregationalists and most Presbyterians to form the United Church of Canada. The merger appealed to Kerby's non-sectarian outlook, but his flexibility was not tested, for there was no similar Congregationalist or Presbyterian college with which Mount Royal was required to merge. The United Church quickly confirmed its commitment to the colleges. In a communication in October 1926, J. W. Graham, now Secretary of the United Church's Board of Secondary Schools and Colleges, underlined the importance of the colleges as supplements to the Christian home and alternatives to secular public institutions.[94] For the college, one benefit of the union was the inclusion of Presbyterian and Congregationalist ministers on Mount Royal's board, opening new links into the communities of southern Alberta. Indeed, it was "the only" United Church college "serving the central and southern parts of the province. As such, its constituency will be greatly extended, and we naturally look forward to a widening interest in the college's life and work."[95] On one Sunday in 1927, the board members and local ministers presented information to seventeen congregations and urged parents to send students and others to provide support.[96] The church's broader base helped strengthen non-denominationalism in the college. In 1929–30, a "Purpose of the College Statement" declared that Mount Royal, "although under the auspices of the United Church of Canada, yet its doors are open to all."[97]

"GRACE, GRIT AND GREENBACKS"

Following the war, the college revived. In 1918, it introduced a fee discount of 5 per cent "when two or more students attend from the same family" and for the sons and daughters of ministers.[98] Aggressive recruiting paid dividends, as enrolment climbed to 277 in 1918, 291 in 1919, and 371 in 1920. Boarders once again filled the residence. However, things then turned down. In January 1921, when the first reunion of the Old Boys and Girls club was held, Kerby said that 2,500 students had already passed through the college and predicted 600 students for the fall.[99] In fact, only 205 students registered and by February 1922, the total was only 167.[100] The world agricultural depression, together with over-expansion into dryland areas of southern Alberta, was driving thousands of farmers into bankruptcy, undercutting the college's rural constituency.[101]

The college launched a vigorous campaign to recruit students, including newspaper ads, letters to clergymen, and Kerby's tours of small towns. In December 1923 Kerby told the board that he had "been out somewhere every week all Fall and have brought the college to the attention of the community."[102] This aggressive recruiting raised enrolment to 330 in 1923–24. "It has not been an easy task," he told the board in 1924. "It takes grace, grit and greenbacks to finance colleges in these days. Grace is always available from Him who giveth liberally, and upbraideth not. . . . Grit is a matter of sheer willpower, dogged determination, and unswerving loyalty to an ideal. Greenbacks are largely a question of economic conditions. Twenty more resident students may mean all the difference between balancing your budget or showing a deficit."[103]

Recognizing that Kerby's grit and determination were not likely enough to sustain the college, the Executive Committee in June 1924 hired a young business manager and student recruiter, George Walters. Walters travelled around the province in a college automobile, contacting teachers and visiting the homes of prospective students.[104] His efforts, combined with Kerby's, kept enrolment over 300 for the next two years; in 1927, rising prosperity helped raise it to 363 students, a level sustained in 1928–29 and 1929–30, mainly because of increased numbers of day and music students.[105]

Walters' appointment posed the question of how his responsibilities dovetailed with those of Kerby. Trueman had called for better academic management, but the Executive Committee's main concern was finances – hence the appointment of a business manager rather than of an academic dean. In early 1925, Kerby volunteered to step down or take a cut in salary. In April the Executive Committee met without Kerby to discuss management issues. The upshot was a vote to ask Kerby to stay on, to accept his offer of a reduced salary, and to "outline the principal's duties more clearly." More specifically, it decided "that amongst other duties the principal continue to devote his attention to what might be termed the inspiration including the publicity work of the college, as well as continue to be responsible for the branch of religious teaching or religious education on the college curriculum, that he be expected to give intensive direction towards the obtaining of new pupils, also in canvassing for donations," and "that the Accountant, Mr. Walters, have charge of the general administration of the business affairs of the college, including the purchasing of supplies and the dealing with the employees other than staff." In June 1925, a special board meeting became more directive: "It was suggested that the principal hold a regularly monthly meeting with his staff."[106]

The college experienced significant staff and student turnover in the late 1920s. Of greater concern, its academic performance was also suffering. Walters reported to board chairman Stanley in November 1929 that student results on provincial examinations had been poor. "Of the [examination] units written by grade 12 students, 82.3 per cent passed in the public schools as compared with 44.2 per cent in MRC. Of grade 11 students writing, 85.8 per cent passed in the public schools as against 30 per cent in MRC." Of 81 resident students in 1928–29, 24 had left before the end of April 1929; of 146 students who might have returned in September 1929, only 19 had. "We have not fallen down on obtaining 'new business,'" Walters wrote. "If this were a manufacturing plant one would say the trouble was not with the selling department, but with the factory." There was no management of academic affairs. As a result, Walters had taken up the slack, negotiating appointments with new faculty members, assigning teaching loads, and overhauling a timetable that had led to 157 course conflicts among

32 students, making sure students took the courses they required to graduate. He recommended hiring a dean to manage academic affairs, leaving the principal free to focus on external matters.[107] Instead, the board named him assistant to the principal, in addition to being recruiter, registrar, business manager, and accountant – a chief operations officer.

STUDENT LIFE

As a marketing device, the college's early calendars included the hometowns of students. Of the 180 on the list in 1912–13, 122 came from Calgary, 50 from small towns in Alberta, and 8 from elsewhere (the United States, Ireland, Ontario). The names were mainly English, Scottish, and Irish. Later calendars mentioned only the hometowns of prize winners: of the fifteen medals awarded for "general proficiency" (high academic performance) in 1921, seven went to students from Calgary, one to a student from Edmonton, six to students from small Alberta centres (Delacour, Irvine, Rose Lynn, Spirit River), and one to a student from Poland (Stanley Chambers). The other prize winners included students from Aldersyde, Blackie, Blairmore, Carbon, Cheadle, Commerce, Drumheller, Edmonton, Foleet, Gleichen, Glenview, Keoma, Fort Macleod, Morley, Nordegg, Rosebud, Rumsey, Wetaskiwin, Delisle (Saskatchewan), and Hudson's Hope and Vancouver in British Columbia.[108] The pattern was continued in later years.[109] Kerby frequently toured high schools in the small towns, speaking on topics such as "Power and Aim," "with graphic language and apt illustrations, showing how one without the other was valueless but when combined, possibilities were limitless."[110]

Despite the college's roots in rural areas where European immigrants settled, the ethnic composition of the students was heavily Anglo-Saxon. In May 1933 Kerby described that year's 387 students: "The racial groups represented in the student body are Scotch, Irish, English, American, Scandinavian, Italian, German and Canadian; of whom the larger portion are Canadian-born. The registration according to religious denominations are: United Church, 50 per cent of the total, with the balance made up in the following the order named – Anglican, Roman

A typical girls' dorm room, 1917. Mount Royal University Archives G1246-11.

The women's hockey team, 1928. Mount Royal University Archives G427.

Lacrosse team, 1912. Photographer W.J. Oliver; Mount Royal University Archives HC4.

Catholic, Presbyterian, Baptist, Jewish, Christian Science, Lutheran and some undenominational."[111]

In the 1920s, prior to the addition of the junior-college division, student life continued along familiar tracks. There were the annual start-of-the-year teas hosted by the Kerbys, an annual college dinner, and parties at Halloween, Christmas, and Valentine's. The responsibility for organizing some social events was vouchsafed to students. Such occasions were accompanied by costumes, games, grand marches, and eating competitions (e.g., eating pumpkin pie without hands).[112] Faculty and administrative staff attended.[113] Students also organized an annual athletic dinner and invited board members, staff, and members of the community.[114]

The college negotiated use of the Mewata Armouries for two afternoons a week for indoor recreational or athletic activities. With the opening of the college's new gymnasium in early 1928, the potential for in-house activities, both social and recreational, multiplied. Basketball was popular with both boys and girls. The girls played against high-school teams and at one point entered the City League "with an undaunted spirit" and "put up a four-square contest."[115] The boys played against local high schools and in the Tuxis church league.[116]

Proceeds from the tuck shop, the Bon Marché, which was organized by the girls to sell sundries to students, provided funds for student activities, such as renting Crystal Rink for Saturday morning hockey practice or resurfacing the tennis courts.[117] The hockey team played against high-school teams, the Normal School, the Institute of Technology, and others.[118] There continued to be an annual track and field day. In addition to winter sports, there was recreational skating for girls and on occasion a "girls' tramp" led by Margaret Carrick, with wieners and marshmallows toasted with "much smoke and little flame" on one occasion and with "grub and ukuleles" on another.[119]

During the 1920s the Literary Society and the *Chinook* continued. Among other short-term student publications was the *Bug House Bugle*, which consisted solely of cartoons drawn by students. Another in the 1928–31 period was a mimeographed circular for which students submitted jokes, cartoons ("gorilla of my dreams"), wrote stories, and poems in English and French; it included advertisements from the Union Milk Company, the Strand film house, the Bow Marsh Confectionery, and other firms.[120]

With a view to launching an alumni group, Kerby had organized the Old Boys and Girls Association at the end of the 1911–12 year. Its first officers included Wilson Gouge as president, Harold Timmons as vice-president, and Flossie Wilson as secretary-treasurer.[121] They were followed during the latter part of the war by Lester McKinnon as president and Harold A. Young as vice-president, with Flossie Wilson continuing as secretary-treasurer.[122] In 1921–22, the body was reconstituted as the Alumni Association of Mount Royal College, with "Rev. Capt. John Garden, B. A.," as president, Myram Tisdale as vice-president, and Arthur Clarke as assistant secretary.[123] Flossie Wilson was the chief continuing member through the first two decades. However, the association waxed and waned, only occasionally surfacing in anniversary celebrations and needing to be re-established from time to time. In 1922, Kerby said that "the newly formed Alumni

Student staff of *The Chinook*, 1928. Mount Royal University Archives G421.

Association is getting in touch with ex-students and holding each year, during the Christmas vacation, a reunion with a view of keeping alive the interest in the college on the part of all ex-students."[124] The college began naming class "representatives," all whom, in 1929–30, were located in Alberta, BC, Manitoba, and Saskatchewan.[125]

Though it is impossible to track most former students from this early period, notes on some appeared periodically in the *Chinook*. The 1927 report recorded the range of outcomes one would expect for a young institution – former students getting married, taking jobs, pursuing further studies. Charles Broad, president of the Alumni Association, was working for the United Grain Growers in Calgary. "Ronnie Martin has become a famous hockey player" (he played for the Detroit Olympics in 1927 and for other professional teams until 1940). Helen Bellamy was a nurse working at the General Hospital in Calgary. Marion Chapin was pursuing further studies at the Agriculture College in Pullman, Washington, "and has been selected for one of the leading sororities." Henry Langford, who spent four years at the college (1916–20), was now "a legal light in the office of his uncle in Toronto," while Ted Walters, who spent the same years at the college, was enrolled in "post-graduate work in Geology" at the University of Toronto. Harold Palmer was working for Imperial Oil and expecting to attend the University

FIGURE 2.1 MALE AND FEMALE STUDENTS, 1920S

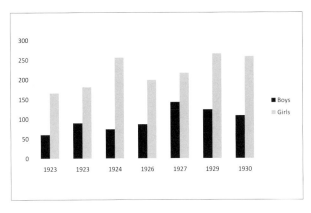

SOURCE: Data from Principal's Reports to the Executive Committee of the Board of Governors.

THE CONSERVATORY

During the college's first few decades, the bulk of the college's registrations consisted of students taking music, speech, and art lessons. As most of them took music lessons, the Conservatory not only played a larger role in the college's life in those years than it did later, but also a major role in defining the college's identity in the community. As we have seen, Kerby ensured that both the Conservatory and what became known as the School of Expression were woven into the fabric of the college's internal life.

Under the direction of William V. Oaten, the music director for Central Methodist, the Conservatory had begun operations in 1911, with seventy-five students registered in music lessons – "a most phenomenal record for the first year, and . . . an indication of the future that is in store for this, one of the first Conservatories of Western Canada." By 1913–14, the Conservatory had five teachers and ninety-six students. Lessons were provided in piano, voice, organ, violin, and theory. In 1915 the college made the Toronto Conservatory's exams its standard and became a "Local Centre" for their administration.[128] The examinations promoted "a growing interest and a natural aspiration to greater aims, leading to and eventually culminating in the highest proficiency." In addition to diplomas offered by the Toronto Conservatory of Music, the Conservatory offered its own diploma for pianoforte teachers, "the only diploma awarded by the Conservatory." Theory lessons were taught by correspondence. In the 1920s the Conservatory taught primarily piano, violin, and voice, with some training in the saxophone and other wind instruments.[129]

The Conservatory's faculty members and students provided music in local Methodist churches and gave concerts to the college community which in many cases became public events. Music was pervasive in college life. In February 1913, for example, the students of Wilfred Oaten and Lillian G. Wilson, a voice teacher, performed. Literary Society meetings were enlivened by recitals, such as piano solos by Mary Blanchard, Etta Wilson, Elizabeth Sayre, and Arthur Clark, a vocal solo by Aileen Sibbald,[130] and a cornet solo by J. Randall.[131] Students also performed for the Debating Club.[132] All students were encouraged to attend cultural events and concerts in the city, and the

of Alberta in the fall. Janet O'Donnell, while boarding in the college, was attending the Calgary Normal School. Zoe Trotter was a journalist working for the *Albertan*. Bella Siskin, "one of our students from Russia last year, is studying dentistry at a dental college in New York City." Derwent Thomas was a law student at Harvard University.[126]

Statistics gathered by the Methodist Church for 1918 indicated that Mount Royal's 19 faculty members ranked sixth in size and its 280 students placed seventh. Alberta College, with 1,275 students and 35 faculty members, was the largest.[127] More troubling, as indicated in the Massey report, the college's academic enrolment fell from 44 per cent before 1914 to 25–33 per cent in the 1920s, while registrations in commerce stabilized at 8–10 per cent of the total. Registrations in music courses rose to 45 per cent in the late 1920s, while those in fine arts settled at 6–8 per cent and elocution at 8–10 per cent. Girls outnumbered boys, three to one. Not by design but by circumstance, the college had become a finishing school for girls. In that context, both the Conservatory and the School of Expression were important activities.

DR. ROGERS AT WORK IN HIS STUDIO

Dr. Rogers teaching a Conservatory student, ca. 1920.
Photographer Novelty Manufacturing & Art Co. Ltd.;
Mount Royal University Archives *Calendar 1920–21.*

Chinook's critics often reviewed such performances.[133] Radio and phonographs were not yet widely available and school performances, concerts, debates, and lectures were occasions for the entire community, not just for parents or colleagues.

Through its music lessons, performances, and examinations, the Conservatory "exerted a marked influence in the musical culture of the city," the *Albertan* noted in 1913.[134] Its students often earned prizes in music festivals. In 1923, for example, they won two gold and five silver medals at the Alberta Music Festival.[135] The annual June recital by advanced students was a popular success: "the newspapers next day were united in their praise of the high standards of performance and in stating that Calgary could claim a musical academy equal to any in the West so far as standards and thoroughness of teaching were concerned."[136]

The Conservatory was intended to be self-funding. Music lessons were offered in four terms of nine weeks, each course consisting of one or two thirty-minute lessons a week. The initial fees were $27 for two lessons a week, per nine-week term, or a total of $108 per year, more than the $90 for a full-time day student. The college extracted 20 per cent of fee revenues to cover facilities and administrative costs. Because of the noise of lessons, the Conservatory soon relocated much of its teaching to the Mason and Risch building at the southwest corner of 8th Avenue and 4th Street. Some teachers also taught in their homes.[137]

From 1917, when Oaten resigned, to 1925, there were three directors of the Conservatory, all organists and all involved in local Methodist churches: Dr. J. E. Hodgson (1917–20), a graduate in music from Durham and McGill universities, the organist at Wesleyan Methodist, former organist for the Glasgow Choral Union and Scottish Orchestra, and director of the Conservatory of Music for Regina College in 1911;[138] Dr. Frederic Rogers (1920–22), organist and choirmaster for Central Methodist;[139] and Clifford Higgins, organist at Knox Presbyterian.[140]

In 1925, with the appointment of Percy Newcombe, the choir director of Central Methodist, director of the Apollo Choir (1910–18), and founder of the first Calgary Symphony Orchestra in 1910, the Conservatory found its leader for the next sixteen years.[141] Newcombe continued the Conservatory's close interaction with churches throughout southern Alberta. The annual recitals were held in Central Methodist Church, and Conservatory students belonged to the church's choir, which entered into the annual music festivals.[142] Programs offered instruction "from primary to advanced grades" in "Pianoforte; Singing; Violin and other stringed instruments; the Organ, Cornet and other orchestral instruments; Theory of Music, Composition, Harmony, Counterpoint, Form, Fugue, Orchestration, Choral and Orchestral Conducting and Musical History."[143]

The School of Expression

Like the music courses of the Conservatory, the School of Expression served both the college's regular students and a wider group of all ages wanting lessons in public speaking, acting, and art. "We believe that all students should take some instruction in the art of Expression and Public Speaking, and more and more this work will be emphasized. . .," Kerby reported to the Methodist Church in 1914.[144] The public speaking and related dramatic readings were in due course to feed into a vigorous theatre program that became a feature of the college's life from the 1930s forward.

The Expression program included both speech and fine arts. Initially, the speech program was described as "elocution" and its purpose was "to train mind, body and voice to express thought in a manner that will be pleasing and convincing, whether in conversation, reading or public address. . . . The course includes studies in pantomime and training and harmonic gymnastics. Studies for interpretation are selected from standard authors, thus increasing the student's knowledge of the best literature."[145] The Expression program produced short plays performed by students sometimes with musical accompaniment, as in *The College Ball* in June 1914 when the college's Male Quartet performed.[146]

In 1915–16 the speech and drama classes were offered by the School of Expression, which now offered a two-year diploma program in expression. The program's goal was "to develop in the student the greatest possible power of expression, to cultivate beauty of speech, to train the intellect, to broaden the sympathies and give keener insight into the deeper understanding of life." The program was intended to foster creativity, not imitation, to enable the student to form his or her "own mental images and have a definite idea of the author's meaning." It included the study of "English literature (16th, 18th and 19th century), a history of English Literature, Composition, Philosophy of Expression, Physical Training, Voice Culture, Dramatic Arts, Story Telling, Public Speaking."[147] That there were insufficient students for the two-year diploma was suggested by the fact that by the end of the 1920s the School of Expression, Oratory and Dramatic Art offered a three-year program that could be taken "in connection with other courses in the college."[148]

As in music, so in drama the school became the organizing centre for both community and college productions. The casts included students, faculty, and community members. In 1913 the plays included *The Rector* and Madame *De Portment School*, in 1914, *The College Hall*, and in 1918–19, *Their Nearest Male Relations*, *The Makers of Dreams*, and *Why Girls Leave Home*.[149] The school also organized public recitals for the dramatic reading of pieces by such authors as Robert Service, Lucy Maud Montgomery, and Rudyard Kipling.[150]

The Fine Arts program also began with classes for members of the community. The early classes were offered in leather tooling, china painting, drawing, painting, metal work, and wood carving.[151] Students also designed covers for internal publications — for example, Elaine Strong for the Christmas 1913 edition of the *Chinook*.[152] A Fine Art department appeared in 1918 headed by Edna Carder. In addition to the original subjects, others were added in "sketching from nature," painting in oils, art lectures, design ("the study of the principles of design and their application to objects"), and watercolour painting. Diplomas were offered to students who completed "two years, ten hours a week, freehand drawing," "one year, two hours a week, design," and "two years, one hour a week, history of art."[153]

By the end of the 1920s, the Fine Art department also reflected the lack of internal clientele by separating its academic program from the classes in sketching, watercolour, weaving, and textiles stamping. Rather than offering "unrelated subjects," the calendar said, the department "was "a center of sound artistic training, where every student, regardless of what particular branch they may be pursuing, will be allowed to proceed only along the lines of accepted artistic principles; so that when they leave the school they will have a foundation which will enable them to express their own particular talent in the creation of works of merit." Exhibitions of student and faculty work, the calendar boasted, "have become an outstanding event, and are conceded to be among the best of their kind in Western Canada."[154] Melville Scott wrote in 1927 that the college's "aim has been to make it a centre of literary, musical and artistic culture – a place for the development of ideals and the scattering of light."[155]

Dr. George and Mrs. Emily Kerby outside the original Mount Royal College Building, ca. 1928. Glenbow Archives NA-4855-9.

READY FOR TRANSFORMATION

As the 1920s came to a close, Mount Royal had survived the first stage of the "closed frontier," when capital and people stopped flowing into Alberta and the world agricultural depression crushed the countryside. Its leaders could not have anticipated that still worse conditions were on the way. But it was already clear that the spread of public schools in rural districts and the expansion of high-school opportunities in the cities were confining the college's enrolment base. In order to do more than survive, it needed to expand its mandate, to find a new clientele, and to improve its academic operations. The opportunity to do so came even before the Great Depression hit in 1929–30. It was an opportunity that enabled the private college to carry on for the next three decades. By then, the college was surviving but not thriving. Its academic quality was in doubt. Its mission of serving needs not met or inadequately met by other public institutions was losing force as public schools spread. With the start of the Depression, moreover, families could no longer afford to send students to board. What was to save the college was the adoption of a new mission.

1929	First college gymnasium opens
1931	Affiliation agreement signed with University of Alberta, making Mount Royal a "junior college" and eliminating primary and junior high-school education
	Junior College Community Players formed
1934	Proposed Education Project for Urban and Rural Leadership and Culture
1937	Mount Royal College Symphony established by Jascha Galperin
June 1942	Dr. George W. Kerby retires as Principal

CHAPTER 3

BECOMING A JUNIOR COLLEGE, 1931–1942

To students who are looking forward to securing a university degree, the Junior college affords an opportunity to complete their first year without the necessity of leaving their own homes or going far from their own communities. To those who are preparing to enter more directly into modern life, the Junior College serves a useful purpose as a finishing school, where they may receive one or two more years of higher education.

– Mount Royal College, *Calendar*, 1940–41, 19

The first of the major transformations that Mount Royal underwent as it worked its way through a century to becoming a university occurred in 1931, when it became a "junior college" in affiliation with the University of Alberta. This status derived entirely from the affiliation agreement and was limited to offering the university's courses. For the next twenty years, the college was proxy for the public junior college that Calgarians had demanded in the 1920s. The success of the new vocation rested in part on hard economic times because the chance to pursue first-year university studies while living at home was attractive to some Calgary students.

In January 1931, a local newspaper described the Depression as a "character test": "Nothing is to be gained by continual bemoaning [of] the fact that boom conditions have departed for a while. . . . The temptation to get rich quickly without working was too strong for many of us. We were in danger of losing that which no material wealth can give – our virility and courage which met and vanquished worse troubles than we are facing today."[1] Little did the editorial writers know how much more testing lay ahead.

Fiscal orthodoxy required governments to balance budgets, and as their revenues fell they slashed expenditures, even as the numbers of unemployed and indigents soared. The burden of caring for the unemployed fell on the cities, which mounted relief programs – soup kitchens, "pogeys" (temporary accommodations), work projects, and recreation. New Year's celebrations in Calgary in 1931 suggested the temper of the times: "Fires, break-ins and street brawls made the advent of 1931 a memorable event in down-town Calgary. With hundreds of unemployed men roaming the streets, and wild hoodlums on the spree, the spirit of the New Year was dangerous, and Calgary's police force was prepared to handle any situation that might arise."[2] In Calgary in 1934, more than 8,000 people, about 12 per cent of the population, were on relief.

The parlous state of the economy had political repercussions. The federal Conservative government formed in 1930 by R. B. Bennett, Kerby's friend, had the double misfortune of being in office when the Depression hit and being devoted to fiscal orthodoxy, handcuffing its ability to respond to growing misery. Though it initiated major institutional changes,[3] the Bennett government's principal social reform – the Relief Act of 1932 – boomeranged. Camps created under the act to provide unemployed single men with a subsistence living (twenty cents a day for six-and-a-half days of work) quickly became cauldrons of discontent. In June 1935 residents of camps in British Columbia launched "a march on Ottawa," "riding the rods" atop CPR freight trains that passed through Calgary and ended in Regina in a bloody confrontation with police. Bennett, who had ordered the police to stop the march, was defeated at the polls in October, replaced by a Liberal government led by Mackenzie King. In the same year, Alberta's United Farmers government was replaced by the first Social Credit government, led by William ("Bible Bill") Aberhart, who promised to distribute money directly to citizens. Since he could not print currency, this was a promise

Aberhart could not keep, but it indicated an empathy appreciated by voters.[4]

Calgary's economy continued to evolve. Workers in the service sector became the most numerous, rising from 19.2 per cent of the total workforce in 1911 to 29.8 per cent in 1921 and remaining at that level for several decades before growing further. The sector included companies serving the fledgling oil and gas industries in the Turner Valley, a base that made Calgary the energy centre when the far larger fields in Leduc near Edmonton opened in 1947. Oil output rose from 168,000 barrels in 1925 to 1.4 million in 1930 but, as the *Calgary Daily Herald* remarked, "the quest for oil in Alberta has hardly started."[5] The relocation of railroad repair shops from Calgary to northern yards caused employment in transportation in the city to fall from 14.5 per cent of total employment in 1921 to 7.2 per cent three decades later. Construction accounted for 9–10 per cent of the workforce, half the pre-war figure. Though the proportion of manufacturing employees remained at 15–17 per cent, the number of manufacturing firms rose from 149 in 1921 to 207 in 1941 and employees in the sector doubled (from 2,516 to 5,239).[6]

Economic hardship slowed population growth in the 1920s and nearly stopped it in the 1930s. However, one major change came rapidly: in 1921 there was an even balance of males and females, an indication of how quickly the closed frontier had reduced the high proportion of males.[7] The change from the open to the closed frontier was also reflected in Calgary's planning. As there were many unfinished housing projects and the city could collect barely half of the taxes due, it retrenched, limiting services to outlying districts, encouraging downtown housing, and cutting back on transportation and road development. In 1930 it adopted a plan to develop only a small city in the future.[8]

The Depression also stifled the expansion of university education to Calgary. While the university's enrolment remained about 1,600 students annually from 1929 to 1935, enrolment at the Provincial Institute of Technology plummeted from 2,000 in 1929 to 690 in 1936 (it did not return to the 1929 level until 1950).[9] The only fresh public educational initiative in the 1930s was establishment of the Banff School of Fine Arts.[10]

Becoming Mount Royal Junior College

The story of how Mount Royal College became a junior college in affiliation with the university is intertwined with the history of Calgary College. In the mid-1920s there was renewed agitation for the revival of Calgary College as a junior college or branch campus of the University of Alberta. This idea was promoted by a General Citizens Committee that included Kerby. When the minister of education, Perren Baker, held "out little hope to a representative gathering of Calgary citizens for the establishment of a two-year university course in this city in the fall of 1925,"[11] the committee called a large public meeting on 10 January 1925 at which presentations were made on the development of junior colleges in the United States and in BC. As the new college could use facilities at the Provincial Institute, the Normal School, and high schools, the attendees thought the capital cost would be minimal. It was unfair for Calgarians to pay the cost of room and board for higher education while Edmontonians did not. Calgary, it was claimed, was the only city of its size in Canada lacking degree-level education. Besides, the cost would be small, around $20,000 annually.[12]

Privately, the minister of education wrote to president Tory of the university to solicit his views. Tory drafted a nine-page response in which he argued that Alberta could not afford yet another new institution. The university's grant had been cut; it was running a deficit; its salaries were too low to fill all faculty positions; and some operations still existed only on paper. Taking money from the university's allocation "would be a crime against higher education in this province." Thus: "I am for the moment both on educational and economic grounds unalterably opposed." If there were to be a junior college in Calgary "it should be the outgrowth of a municipal effort and not a charge upon the treasury of the province."[13]

Recognizing that the failure of the public initiative might open the way for a private one, Kerby wrote Tory to propose a policy like that in Saskatchewan, where "the Senate has empowered the University Council to recognize the work of what may be called 'Junior Colleges' in the province…. Similar action on the part of the Senate of Alberta University would

enable institutions such as Mount Royal College to make their contribution towards this movement if they so desired."[14] Tory replied that he was aware of developments in Saskatchewan but concerned about the plight of his university: "I have been very anxious that the university should get squarely on its feet before any competition with its classes is established. I would gladly welcome in the future the development of the junior college idea just as soon as the population and a real demand for it warrant the step." However, he added, "I should be glad to discuss with you some time when I see you the position in which your college finds itself with regard to the possibility of such additions to the staff as would make another year's work possible. Please treat this as a private letter and see me about the matter sometime."[15]

On 19 March 1925 minister Baker told the legislature that, while he could not recommend increased funding for higher education until elementary and secondary education were firmly established, the government was prepared to amend the School Act to permit school boards to establish colleges funded by themselves and in affiliation with the university.[16] However, no school board stepped forward.[17] Thus, in 1927 Baker went a step further. Referring to Mount Royal, he expressed support for alternatives to public institutions: "we need variety … but under the state system we cannot very well get it.'"[18]

Responding to the opportunity, Mount Royal's board of governors struck a committee to explore the potential for affiliation with the University of Alberta on the model of the agreement between the University of Saskatchewan and Regina College.[19] Dr. George Stanley, the chairman, declared that "we have adopted the idea and propose to undertake it as soon as the demand seems to warrant it." The experience in Saskatchewan showed that "pupils up from Regina College take their place alongside of the others and are holding their own quite satisfactorily."[20] In the summer of 1928, the Executive Committee of the Alberta Conference of the United Church met with Premier John E. Brownlee to promote the junior-college role for Mount Royal.[21] Kerby reported that the minister of education was "in hearty agreement," though wishing to leave the decision to the university.[22] In response to a query from Kerby about the intentions of the Calgary school board, Dr. Melville Scott, the

George D. Stanley, Chairman, 1926-54. Photographer William Kensit Studio; Mount Royal University Executive Records GO010-05S.

superintendent, replied: "I do not quite see what relation it has to any extension of work which may be contemplated by Mount Royal College."[23] The way was clear.

Following preliminary discussions with the new president of the university, Dr. Robert C. Wallace, the college's board of governors approved the report of its "Committee on Junior College" on 21 December 1928, recommending that the college should request affiliation. In January 1929, Kerby told the board that "we believe that the time has come when we should try to determine a policy for the future of the college, … and we must look not only to the new few years,

but fifty years ahead."[24] He advised Wallace and Brownlee of the intention to apply for affiliation and told the premier that "we are very anxious to secure from the Government a site for new buildings on the land on which the Technical Institute is located."[25] To discuss next steps, Kerby, Stanley, and Scott travelled to Edmonton to meet with university officials.[26] That meeting was followed by a letter from Kerby requesting an opportunity to address the Senate and to present the college's "request for the taking on of junior college work, which means an additional year to what we are now doing."[27] The reasons he adduced for approving the affiliation included these: accessibility for students in Calgary who could not afford to relocate to Edmonton; a new educational opportunity for students "who wish to go beyond the high school course but who do not desire and possibly cannot afford to pursue the full university course"; and satisfaction of the college's desire for "a closer relationship with the provincial university," inasmuch as "junior college status would in a larger and more real sense make us a part of the University itself." The proposed junior college curriculum would "stress the social and humanities part of the Arts curriculum."[28]

Meanwhile, the university developed a policy to govern its relations with junior colleges. Among other things, the policy required: "a minimum staff of six teachers giving the major part of their time to junior college work," consisting of "university graduates with special training in their particular fields and [with] at least one year of post-graduate study"; separation "both in organization and in buildings from the work of the primary grades"; and "regular university examinations or as an alternative the grade 12 departmental examinations and the regular university examinations for the second year."[29] Following review by the university's Committee on Junior Colleges, the Senate approved affiliation in December 1930.[30] The agreement, signed in February 1931, was for five years, and renewable.[31] It empowered Mount Royal to offer "the first year of the course [program] leading to the BA and BSc in Arts degrees."[32] While the college's leaders had hoped to offer second-year courses as well, this was a substantial first step for a college that needed to build new facilities, acquire laboratory equipment, develop a library, recruit qualified faculty, terminate its primary programs, and find a clientele for its new post-secondary courses.

The university named a team to help the college meet the requirements,[33] and Mount Royal's board undertook to "take the necessary steps to inaugurate the Junior College work by the fall of 1931, complying with the conditions stipulated by the Senate of the University of Alberta."[34] The details included how to handle Christmas examinations, the timing of faculty travel to Edmonton to mark examinations jointly with university staff, and procedures for university approval of faculty appointments.[35] One other step was required of the college – the formal approval of the United Church, which granted it by a resolution dated 16 April 1931," subject to the proviso that "it is understood that this action . . . does not commit this board to any financial obligations."[36] Kerby formally advised United Church ministers and others of the affiliation in May 1931.[37] The college promptly added the phrase "in affiliation with the University of Alberta as a Junior College" to its publications. Its calendar thenceforth included a section entitled Mount Royal Junior College to describe university courses.

Kerby was quick to predict a great success. "The staff will be made up of specialists with one or more years of post-graduate work. The library will compare favorably with that of any Canadian university and will be fully adequate for the courses taught. Laboratory equipment for science classes will be similar to that employed at the University of Alberta. Examinations will be similar to those of the university and in addition, students may take the Grade 12 examinations instead of first-year university if desired."[38] For the public he explained that a junior college was a bridge between the high school and university, just as the junior high-school was a bridge between elementary and secondary education.[39]

The university's Committee on Junior Colleges found the proposed faculty members "well qualified." Nearly all had at least an MA and two were Ph.D. candidates. The list included people who, beyond undergraduate work, had studied at the Sorbonne, Oxford, the University of Chicago, and Columbia University.

It was a list of which the college was rightly proud.[40] The first classes in the junior college began on 23 September 1931. On 22 October, there was a large "inaugural ceremony" chaired by Dr. Stanley, now a Conservative Member of Parliament, that featured an address by Premier Brownlee, remarks by the mayor of Calgary, the minister of education, the dean of arts at the university (Walter A. R. Kerr), and presentation of the "Historic Roll" bearing the names of students registered in university courses to President Wallace. Jascha Galperin of the Conservatory entertained with a rendition of "Gypsy Airs" by Sarasate.[41]

As part of the preparations for its new role, the college sought funds for two major developments – additional facilities suitable for the laboratories and classrooms of a junior college, and enhanced library holdings.

"A new building was an immediate and absolute necessity in order to carry on the work" of the junior college, the board's Staff Committee decided.[42] The college's existing facilities were cramped and aging. There was classroom space for only two hundred students at a time. The "Barn" was in constant need of maintenance – painting, oiling, varnishing, calcimining, tiling, and, until 1926, when natural-gas heating was installed, operating and maintaining the coal-fired heating system.[43] To add space, the college had bought nearby houses, including one, in 1928, that had a 31 x 52–foot barn at the rear that was converted into the college's first gymnasium, which opened with a basketball game on 23 January 1929.[44] Though the college still owned the fifty acres donated by Shouldice and McKay in 1911, lots donated by Dr. T. H. Blow, and lots offered by Judson Sayre when he moved to Los Angeles in the early 1920s,[45] it could not afford to pay the taxes on them. In 1926–27 it had accepted an offer from Dr. Blow to find a purchaser for the lots he had donated to provide the college with cash and relieve the tax burden.[46] In 1928 Kerby reviewed the potential for building on the fifty-acre site and concluded it was not feasible, given the lack of services, public transportation, and cash.[47] Ultimately, the fifty acres were returned to the donor families.[48] Kerby and the board dreamed of an inexpensive alternative – building on vacant space on the government-owned site occupied by the Institute of Technology.[49] It was serviced, there was vacant space, and the college would need only to raise money for construction.[50] Kerby presented the idea to Premier Brownlee in January and June 1929.[51] The three institutions could share facilities; a common site would enhance the visibility of all three and rationalize the cost of public transit to them; and the province could enable, at no cash cost, a private alternative to the public college sought by Calgarians.[52] In the end, the college was offered a long-range lease at a nominal rate and the board had architectural renderings prepared. However, the college still needed to raise funding for construction and was unable to do so. The idea receded, though it was to be revived briefly after the Second World War when the next expansion was to occur.[53]

For want of an alternative, the college added to its existing facilities. In 1931, it added a 32 x 55–foot extension to the Barn to provide laboratory space on the lower floor for about forty students and a large space on the upper floor for the junior college and music recitals. It renovated the houses it had acquired. Once again, James Garden oversaw construction.[54] Even with the addition, college facilities remained cramped. There were no adequate study, recreation, dining, and lounge facilities. Being short of space and of funding to build became permanent features of college life.

Though it had been unable to raise funds for a new campus, the college was more successful in raising funds for its library. Learning that the Carnegie Educational Foundation would make grants to Canadian universities for innovative projects, the board argued that the college's junior-college role was an innovation. As a result, the foundation provided a grant of $500 for each of three years for the acquisition of library books.[55] Among other donors were the T. Eaton Company, which donated $1,500, the publisher J. W. McConnell, and E. W. Beatty, each of whom donated $1,000.[56]

"There can be no doubt," Kerby said, "that the junior college will greatly increase our prestige and widen our scope of usefulness; and that numbers of people are looking forward to the junior college is evidenced from the inquiries that are constantly coming . . . It would seem . . . that we are at a turning point in our history."[57] Indeed, as a result the college was to undergo a major transformation in governance (university control over faculty appointments, the content of the courses, the setting of examinations, and the

grading of examinations passed to the university), faculty qualifications, its program base, its student clientele, and in public image. The disappearance of elementary students and the addition of adults altered the tone of campus life. At almost every level of its being the college experienced fundamental change as a result of the affiliation agreement.

THE JUNIOR COLLEGE IN OPERATION

The change of mandate came just in time. In 1930–31 the number of students declined by more than sixty from the previous year.[58] The number of students able to pay boarding fees dropped sharply; in November 1934, there were only twenty-one resident students; in 1937–38, forty-four.[59] The new post-secondary students, however, made up the difference. Though enrolment declined slightly from 1935 to 1937, at the nadir of the Depression, it grew rapidly in the late 1930s. By 1938–39 there were 499 students, twice the level reached in the 1920s.[60] The growth occurred chiefly in day and older students who either lived or boarded in Calgary.[61]

In May 1932, Kerby, reporting that that there were seventy-four university students from Calgary in Mount Royal's "second-year classes alone," assessed the implications. "This means a saving to the citizens of Calgary . . . of many thousands of dollars. Not only so, but it has made possible the keeping of these students in their own home and community, which is a decided advantage to them and their parents." Without Mount Royal, he said, "the majority" of the students "would not have been able to begin the course at all. The present economic situation would have prevented them from going elsewhere, or securing employment, which would have meant for them an idle year."[62] Moreover, as the students were attending for financial reasons, not because they were academically weak, they were performing very well. The "percentage of junior college students passing in all subjects in the University of Alberta final examinations was practically on a par with the university classes and in addition the college had two of its students lead the entire university in the marks obtained in History 2 and Physics 7 courses."[63] In 1934, in a private memo to President Wallace, J. W.

Inaugural second-year University Transfer class, 1931–32.
Photographer W. J. Oliver; Mount Royal University
Archives G425-1.

Shipley of Chemistry commented on "the excellent record which the students of Mount Royal made in Chemistry 1 this year." A statistical report comparing the college's transfer students with the regular student body for 1933–34 indicated that in first-year Arts, 41 per cent of 44 regular university students passed all courses while only 19 per cent (of 26 students) of Mount Royal's transfer students did but that in second-year Arts the numbers were respectively 44 per cent (of 211) and 35 per cent (of 75) – an indication that students needed to adjust before performing well. In five courses, the highest mark was awarded to a former Mount Royal student.[64] In 1936 eight Mount Royal students led the university in course examinations and one tied for the highest marks; in 1937 thirteen former college students received first-class standing; in 1939 five won medals or scholarships, including the student who led the university. The latter accomplishment inspired President Walter Kerr to comment publicly on the quality of the college's work.[65]

By 1937, six years of schooling (grades 4 through 9) had disappeared from the college's curriculum and another year of university-level courses had been added (that is, first-year university courses as distinct from grade 12 courses). The university courses were organized in two basic streams, one "leading to the degrees of B.A. or B.Sc. in Arts or LL.B," the other to the "B.Com." Students in the first stream were required to choose from courses in English, French, German, Latin and Greek, history, political economy, philosophy, mathematics, physics, and chemistry. Those in the business stream were required to take English, accounting, mathematics, political economy, and "a modern language."[66] In 1938, the college added first-year studies leading to the Bachelor of Commerce.[67] Thus, by the end of the decade, the college's advertisements proclaimed that it offered first-year university courses leading to these degrees: BA, B.Sc. in Arts, LL.B, and B.Com. and B.Sc. in Engineering. Some ads declared that "you who seek careers in medicine or dentistry can now take your first-year pre-medical course at Mount Royal College." In addition, the ads proclaimed that the college offered high-school courses in grades 10, 11, and 12 courses leading to senior matriculation, that the School of Commerce offered "business" and "secretarial" courses and a "placement service" for students, and that the Conservatory offered "private and class instruction in public speaking, dramatic art, voice training," preparing students "in all branches of music" to meet the standards of the Toronto Conservatory of Music and the Royal Schools of Music.[68]

PROPOSING AN ADULT EDUCATION PROGRAM

Mount Royal's role as a junior college placed it among a small group of Canadian institutions at the time. There were only eight other schools that also offered the first two years of a four-year BA or B.Sc. degree program: Memorial University College (Newfoundland), Prince of Wales College (Prince Edward Island), Alma College (Ontario), Victoria College (BC), and four affiliates of the University of Saskatchewan (including Regina College).[69]

In 1932, the board of governors carefully defined the new mandate to put the role of the junior college in a broader perspective than its university-level courses and affiliation with the university. "The junior college has two distinct, but yet complementary, functions," it declared:

- One of these is to duplicate the curricula of the first two years of the university, and thus meet the needs of those who intend to go on to complete their university course.

- The other, and more important function, is to be of service to that great group of high school graduates who feel that they have not the time, money or academic desire to spend four or more years in a university. The junior college offers terminal facilities, in the shape of finishing courses for such students.

- The function, then, of the junior college, is specific and semi-professional. It is an institution distinct from both from the university and the high school.[70]

Such institutions would later be known as "community" rather than as "junior colleges." From at least 1930 Kerby had promoted this broader idea of the junior college's role. Students who "want a sound, thorough but more limited training . . . look to occupations of the semi-professional type. The individuals of this group make up the bulk of our population. They are the men and women who carry on business and the affairs of common life."[71]

In 1933, Kerby suggested approaching the Carnegie Foundation with a project to address the plight of young people left derelict by the Depression.[72] The resulting proposal, "The Mount Royal College Education Project for Urban and Rural Leadership and Culture," submitted to the foundation in February 1934, envisaged a "cultural course preparatory to occupational life." It was for rural and urban youth, aged seventeen to twenty-eight, who had not completed high school, did not intend to go to university, and planned either to stay at work or to find a job if they did not have one. It was essentially a job readiness program. The core curriculum included English and citizenship. It was to be student-centred and aimed at moving each individual to a further point in his or her personal learning curve. There were no textbooks or requirements. Success would depend on the availability of inspiring teachers and on student motivation.

The curriculum was designed "to give encouragement to independent and self-directed study, and furnish opportunity for creative self-expression, through social studies, in literature interpretation, and through writing, dramatics, fine art, music and school and community activities."[73] The program was said to be similar to those offered by "the famous folk schools in Denmark."[74] In words that would be echoed by the college over many decades to come, the board's committee on new courses explained that a "school which merely meets the demands of yesterday, or even today, is not enough in a rapidly changing civilization such as ours. Education should be adjusted to meet the needs of all of all the peoples of the world, from children to adults. A changing social and economic and political condition makes this imperative."[75]

At the best of times such a proposal would have inspired skepticism, but then it stirred concerns in government and university circles. When Kerby and Stanley arrived at the Carnegie Foundation's headquarters in New York to discuss the proposal, they met President Wallace of the university on his way out.[76] Not surprisingly, the message they received was that they must avoid duplicating university or Technical Institute programs. Already, in 1931, Kerby had proposed joining the university in its rural extension work but the university had let the idea die.[77] Perhaps this proposal appeared to be an effort to outflank the university in that regard. As for the Technical Institute, the proposal amounted to a job readiness plan. To allay concerns that this somehow competed with the Technical Institute, the college revised the proposal to focus more on job satisfaction than on job readiness training, making the whole idea weaker. Perhaps because of such resistance from government-funded operations, the college vaunted its role as a private institution. It declared that it was "a logical institution to undertake this experiment for Southern Alberta, and this because of its location, its long years of successful work as a residential, co-educational college, and from the fact that it is an independent institution and therefore is not compelled to follow the details or the methods of a proscribed state system of education in this new adventure."[78] The fact that the proposal included a request for an annual grant of $45,000 plus $200,000 for facilities and equipment to add fifty students in "business, speech and drama" did not help

the college's cause. After more than a year of discussions with the Technical Institute and the foundation, the foundation rejected the application in November 1934; following further discussions, it repeated its rejection in April 1935.[79]

The college decided to proceed on its own by offering "special cultural and occupational courses ... to provide cultural combined with practical training for both rural and urban students."[80] While the program soon disappeared, it reflected the college's commitment to facilitate the learning of people, whatever their initial level of education. The project applied progressive education theory to adult education: its aim was less to achieve objective standards than to maximize personal development; objective standards were less important than the extent of the movement along one's own learning curve. The project can be seen as a pioneering effort to expand the notion of what Canadian colleges could and should do. The spirit behind it was to be expressed in new forms over time, notably in "continuing education" after 1945 and in the "community college philosophy" of the 1960s.

THE CHANGING CAMPUS CULTURE

In the interwar years, campus life continued to be filled with the activities of clubs and societies, though the nature of the activities changed as older students replaced younger ones. In 1933, for example, the principal noted that about a quarter of the students in academic programs (46 of 197) were taking evening courses, a factor that by itself altered the tone of campus life.[81] The roster of clubs and their activities also began to change, and for the same reason. In 1931–32, the first year of the junior college, the clubs included the Athletic, Literary, and Debating Clubs, the Political Economy Club, the French Club, the Chess Club, the Students' Christian Movement, class organizations, and a general students' executive.[82] As the junior-college function took deeper root, the Chemistry Club was added, and the conservative Intervarsity Christian Fellowship emerged beside the Students' Christian Movement (SCM).[83] In 1921, the student body included "twelve religious denominations and thirteen nationalities."[84]

1931

margaret, Betsy, mildred, Jean, marion.

Students relaxing on the lawn outside the College building, 1931. Mount Royal University Archives G473.

The traditional Valentine, Halloween, and Christmas parties continued but were enhanced by the creative participation of older students.[85] New social diversions appeared. In 1935, there was a "cabaret" and "the sophomore class . . . invited Mr. X and Cavewoman to the 'Caveman's Council,' at 'Gug's Grotto," accompanied by sketches of an ape-like cave man and gorgeous cave woman.[86] There were themed dances, such as the Rugby Ball in October 1936 (the hall was decorated as a rugby field and the orchestra was dressed in rugby uniforms), and the "Barnyard Frolic," sponsored by the Student Council in November 1936.[87]

The older students did not want to live in the residences or under the rules set for the residences, and by the mid-1930s, the residence was half-empty. The rules were eased. "Senior students" were exempted from mandatory study time in the evenings. As recently as November 1931 the Executive Committee had reaffirmed its ban on smoking in college buildings; in 1936, it reversed the policy, permitting smoking in the common room.[88] The annual calendars stopped printing the names and hometowns of prize winners in favour of listing the "undergraduate" medals and prizes available to students. By 1938–39, the regulation on "dress and outfits" no longer contained a dress code and indicated only the need for residential students to have a "napkin ring, teaspoon, glass, fruit knife for use when eating fruit in room, clothes and shoe brushes, toilet soap and necessary toilet articles."[89]

The Literary Society continued, though "unfortunately the greater part of the work fell on a talented few."[90] By contrast, there appeared to be a campus-wide enthusiasm for theatre arts. The Department of Speech and Drama, as it was called in 1935–36, offered four streams of courses – speech, drama, interpretive reading, and creative English. A "certificate of proficiency" was awarded to a student who "satisfactorily completes the required courses in that division." A "diploma of proficiency" was awarded "to any student who has passed the Normal Entrance of Junior

Matriculation departmental examinations and completed the required courses in the three of the four divisions of the work in this department." The college had an agreement with Emerson College of Oratory in Boston "to give this diploma credit as equivalent to at least their first year's work" toward a bachelor's degree in speech and drama.[91] The college's own offerings included "audience speaking," "interpretive reading," "stage techniques" ("Play Acting I and II, Play Direction I and II, Public Performances I and II, Scenery and Costume Design, Completion of an original project, Make-up") and "Creative English" ("short story writing," "story writing," "private lessons in creative writing," "conferences with criticism," an "author's club," "discussion groups," "contests").[92]

With the older student body, the college committed itself more thoroughly to theatre than it had ever done in the past. Its calendar declared that "progressive educationalists acknowledge that the experience of being in a publicly-presented play has many worthy and varied educative outcomes."[93] Beginning in 1931 with about thirty charter members, the Junior College Community Players had organized monthly plays, lectures, contests, children's theatre, and puppet theatre, a festival of plays by Calgary writers, a repertoire theatre group, and competition in the annual Alberta Dramatic Festival.[94] By November 1931, the Players had presented three one-act plays which, according to the reviewer for the *Albertan*, were modest successes: "Amateur dramatics are much more enjoyable for the audience and of more value to the actors when they are not overly ambitious . . . The plays . . . were clean and refreshing but were not too subtle, and did not draw on stronger emotions than amateurs can command. They attained their object, which is better than missing a higher aim."[95] In 1932–33, the Players produced thirty-five plays and dramatic sketches, including *Pillars of Society*, which ran for three nights and an additional night in Cochrane. In addition to plays by established playwrights, the productions included some written by the theatre writing class, for example, a one-act play by Lucille Walters and six short plays by other students in 1933.[96] The Players continued the vigorous schedule in later years, including presenting productions in provincial competitions.[97] The enthusiasm was shared by junior high-school students, who

put on skits during graduation ceremonies and social occasions.[98]

Debating and public speaking also remained lively activities. The interclass debate competitions continued, with the debating cup awarded to the best team each year at convocation. The college fielded a debate team to compete with the University of Alberta, the Young Liberal Club, and other teams.[99] On one occasion, a team consisting of Doris Hunt, the French instructor (1931–38), and Gordon Fairbanks, a student, debated in French; in 1934 the team debated in Montreal in both English and French.[100] In the spring of 1936, a college team "successfully destroyed" the Normal School team on a resolution on whether Canada should pursue an isolationist North American policy vis-à-vis the United States; representing the negative position, the team won with its argument that an isolationist policy severing the connection to the Empire and ignoring the League of Nations would lead to annexation of the smaller country by the larger.[101]

Sports continued to build a sense of community and school morale. Rugby, which had been played as early as 1913 but languished later, was re-introduced in 1933, with the team competing against local high schools, such as Central, and more distant ones, like Red Deer.[102] Hockey and basketball teams competed against high schools, the Normal School, the Institute of Technology, and church and community teams. Other sports included bowling, gymnastics, skiing, and swimming.[103] Kerby's monthly reports were filled with the trials and tribulations of sporting teams, and the press covered many events.[104] In 1934 the college hired Sheila Jean Ritchie, a graduate of McGill, to develop its first physical-education program.[105]

For some reason student publications languished in the 1930s. The *Chinook* disappeared in the early 1930s. However, the tradition of student publication revived at the end of the decade. In 1939, the students produced a special commemorative edition of the *Chinook* entitled *Arpi-Huba* after a Sarcee legend in memory of Emily Spencer Kerby.[106] It consisted mainly of photos of students, with a witty saying for each, for example, Don Swanson, president of the Students' Council in 1938–39: "He fills our life with gay sweet song, the trouble is, the notes are wrong." The publication warmly anticipated the pending visit of the King and Queen: "This special mark of favor to

Canada has created immense satisfaction among Canadian people."[107] In the same year, a new yearbook, *Varshicom* (a name made from "the three fields of learning in the college, namely, university, high school and commercial"), had appeared. In 1942, a new student publication entitled the *Scratch Pad* appeared ("published bi-weekly by the students of Mount Royal College"), becoming the first regularly appearing student publication (albeit in mimeographed format) since the demise of the *Chinook*, which had been printed.[108] It featured reports on campus events, cartoons, commentaries, editorials, and social news and gossip. It appeared four times a year. In an introductory editorial, Garden saluted its emergence. The *Scratch Pad* "will do much to weld us into a happy college family with a high spirit de corps in all our work. . . . No doubt this paper will also see the humorous side of life which is so important, especially in time of war. . . . Baby Scratchpad, Mount Royal College has indeed waited thirty-one years for your appearance, and hails you with a blare of trumpets and college yells."[109] Sections had titles such as "The Ed. Sez," "Wormwood Natterings," "Dissa and Datta about Stuffa and Matta." There were funny stories made up by students.

The periodic exhibition of artwork by students and staff continued. In 1931 the wives of the members of the board introduced an annual tea that included musical entertainment by students. Within three years it included exhibitions of student and faculty art work. The first such exhibit boasted eighty paintings, including works by Margaret Carrick, landscapes by Annora Brown (later famous for her paintings of wild flowers),[110] and animal studies and a crayon drawing of a mountain cabin by Betty McNaught.[111] Carrick contributed often to the exhibits, as did Doris Hunt.[112] In 1935, she completed a Mount Royal College tapestry that remains part of the institution's permanent collection.

With the conversion to the junior college role in 1931, the morning chapel session became optional. Kerby tried to keep it interesting by inviting distinguished guests, such as Max Eastman from the League of Nations, various ministers, and J. W. Graham of the United Church's Board of Secondary Schools.[113] Religious Knowledge classes continued to be held on Sundays, their subjects ranging from interpretation of the New Testament to moral problem solving

Margaret Carrick, Dean of Girls and House Directress, ca. 1930. Mount Royal University Archives HA94.

and "creative living." That there was sometimes lively dialogue among young Christians on campus was suggested in 1937 by Kerby's remark that the Students' Christian Movement (SCM) was having "one of the most interesting years since the Junior College was formed."[114] He continued to insist on the non-denominational nature of the college: "We do not countenance sectarian propaganda in any form, but we do assume and expect that every member of our faculty will both by precept and example uphold the ideals which make for Christian character and good citizenship. We like to think of our teachers as a group of liberal-minded men and women, highly cultured, and employing the best standards and ideals of a great profession."[115]

FIGURE 3.1 ENROLMENT TRENDS (REGISTRANTS), 1911-42

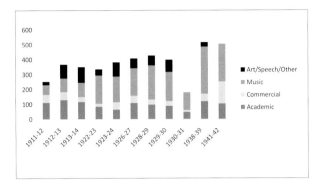

SOURCE: Data from Principal's Reports to the Executive Committee of the Board of Governors

FIGURE 3.2 PERCENTAGE OF ENROLMENT BY PROGRAM TYPE, 1911-42

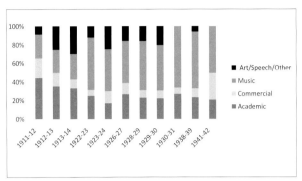

SOURCE: Data from the Principal's Reports to the Executive Committee of the Board of Governors.

The older students began to display more interest in the role of the Student Council than had been the case earlier. Its role was "the transaction of business in which students are particularly interested. This relates to social events, Literary Society, clubs, etc., and athletic activities. The work of preparing and publishing the yearbook and the college paper, the *Scratch Pad*, is done under the supervision of the council."[116] However, it was only after the Second World War, when the number of older students soared, that students organized to promote their own interests in matters such as food services and lounge and study space.

As Figures 3.1 and 3.2 illustrate, the college had a total of 9,606 day and resident students from 1911 to 1940. Of them, 1,502 (15.6 per cent) had lived in the residences. In addition, the college had enrolled 7,006 students in music, art and physical education courses.[117] Almost all of the music students were very young; the art students tended to be mature women. The place of the college among United Church colleges was indicated in a 1938–39 survey. Of the 716 resident students and 3,262 day students in Methodist colleges, Mount Royal had respectively 46 (6.4 per cent) and 458 (14 per cent), less than half the size of Alberta College. The survey showed that 121 Mount Royal students were registered in academic programs, 305 in music courses, 48 in "commercial" programs, and 30 in "other" activities.[118] In an internal report, the college noted that its total registration of 504 was "one of the largest in the history of the college." The report indicated that "the students registered in the

university courses at the college during the past eight years total some 800. In last year's graduating class at the University of Alberta, twenty-five were former students of Mount Royal College, many of them gaining first class honours in their graduation and five of them winning scholarships totaling $3,000 to the University of Alberta, the University of Wisconsin, Berkeley University, California [sic], and Northwestern University." The student body was "made up of all denominations, about 50 per cent United Church and the balance divided among other churches. Each year we have two or three young men among our students who are looking forward to the ministry in the United Church or some other denomination."[119]

In 1940–41, *Varshicom* included notices on former students, sixty-three males, seventy-eight females. Of the males, twenty-three were serving in the air force, seven in the army, one in the navy, and one in the Royal Canadian Mounted Police; five were teaching, three were farming, five were clerks or stenographers, and nineteen were attending university. Of the females, two were in the Women's Auxiliary, four were teaching, two were attending Normal School, two were in nursing, ten were married or at "home," thirty-five were serving as clerks or stenographers, one was a journalist, and the rest were attending school or doing something else.[120] The distribution was not surprising, given wartime conditions; however, the proportion of young women planning to attend university was notably high, given the typical female participation rates of the time.

The Conservatory

In the 1930s the Conservatory expanded its role in the cultural life of Calgary,[121] despite – and in some cases because of – the Depression. Money was a recurrent problem. The minutes of a Conservatory meeting in 1937 recorded a discussion of the challenges. It was resolved "that more of the percentages from student fees be spent on improving the Conservatory—or, as Mr. Newcombe said, 'the gas tax be spent on the road.'"[122] Jascha Galperin, a vigorous and entrepreneurial young man who had moved to Calgary from Europe, had immediately breathed new life into the Conservatory after joining it in 1933. Where Newcombe had linked Conservatory performance to churches, Galperin linked it to the broader musical community. He immediately became a member of the "executive" of the Conservatory, which in that period consisted of Newcombe, Leonard Leacock, Jean Cotton, Mrs. A. Newcombe, and occasionally Kerby. A few weeks after Galperin arrived, Kerby asked the Conservatory to designate a representative "to attend the weekly meeting of the academic faculty and Mr. Galperin was appointed to do so,"[123] bringing him into the centre of the college's activities.

The "Baby Symphony" with Jascha Galperin, conductor, ca. 1938. Photographer W. J. Oliver; Glenbow Archives NA-5215-1.

Galperin exposed students to demanding classical works. This brought some student protests, for in March 1934 Mrs. Newcombe suggested that "student recitals be made more interesting and shorter." Galperin responded "that these recitals were especially beneficial to the students and would give them occasion to perform extended compositions." A compromise was reached: "it was decided that the programs be limited to twelve members of the orchestra and the time limit to be one and one half hours." The recitals were held monthly, with an annual recital required of all advanced students "towards the close of the college year;" the college boasted that they "became a marked event in musical circles in Calgary."[124]

To highlight both the teachers and students of the Conservatory in classical and popular music, Galperin organized concert series to promote Conservatory performers, for example, the Aeolian Chamber Music series, which played works by composers such as Fauré, Schubert, Beethoven, and Haydn.[125] He later established a chamber group consisting of himself, students (initially, Albert McCalla, Louise Augade, Muriel Herries-Clark, and Earl Ruttan), and "outside artists."[126] A born promoter, Galperin wanted Conservatory groups to perform at college events, such as convocations and meetings of Mrs. Kerby's Mount Royal College Educational Club. The tussle over limited space was a continuing concern, notably the competing demands of the drama and music groups for use of the auditorium.[127] On 9 September 1935, the Conservatory, on a motion from Kerby, committed to establishing an orchestra.[128] In 1937 Galperin had enough players to establish the Mount Royal College Orchestra. Its first annual concert was held on 15 June 1938 in the Grand Theatre; in the same month it won the highest commendation in the annual Kiwanis Music Festival in Edmonton. In 1944, in recognition of the addition of brass, clarinets, and flute, it became known as the Mount Royal College Symphony Orchestra. From the outset it had been supplemented by the "Baby Symphony," which consisted of children from the ages of four to twelve.[129] Its first concert was for the Women's Musical Club of Calgary in the Palliser Hotel in March 1938.[130] To promote broader interest in music, Galperin suggested that "explanatory remarks be given before each number to add to the interest and educational value of the program."[131] And in 1938 he established the Sonata Club from "among our own student body" to meet monthly to discuss music; it shortly became known as the Junior Chamber Music Club.[132]

Following Newcombe's retirement in September 1939, Galperin became the director of the Conservatory.[133] The collapse of the Calgary Symphony Orchestra in that year opened the door for him to make the Baby Symphony and the Junior Symphony into the major sources of live music in Calgary. In 1941, the growing numbers of older students enabled the minimum age for the Junior Symphony to be raised from twelve to fourteen years. "Woodwinds, brasses and drums" were then added to the original strings. It was popular. In 1942, "hundreds could not obtain tickets" because tickets were "sold out early" for its concert in the Grand Theatre.[134] The quality of the Junior Symphony was underlined by a British adjudicator who remarked that "this is quite the most extraordinary orchestra of its kind in Canada or on the other side of the Atlantic for that matter."[135] The *Albertan* described it as "an organization unique of its kind, not only in Canada, but in the entire British Empire. The purpose of the orchestra is to encourage appreciation and rendition of orchestral music by young people, to give the public symphonic concerns, and to discover a talent among the children of Calgary."[136] Not satisfied with a local audience, Galperin arranged for performances on CBC radio (sometimes with remarks by Kerby).[137] The broadcasts continued until the fall of 1943.[138]

In 1941, the executive of the Conservatory included many veteran instructors, including Galperin, Jean Cotton, Mrs. Newcombe, Mr. McCalla, and Leonard Leacock.[139] By late 1942, however, much of the faculty had changed. Two noteworthy additions were Norma Piper, the diva soprano who had made an international career,[140] and Gladys Egbert (1896–1968), a long-time piano teacher in the community (Leacock had been one of her pupils).[141] The new team discussed how to recruit students, including "a lengthy and animated discussion on the advantages and disadvantages . . . of house-to-house canvassers or agents as a means of getting students. . . . It was decided that it was really the only means that achieved results in creating a reservoir of talent for the continuation of the Mount Royal College Junior Symphony Orchestra. . . ." Instructors were to be used for the purpose.[142]

To enhance the Conservatory's credibility, Galperin negotiated an affiliation agreement with the Toronto Conservatory of Music to make the Conservatory a testing centre in 1942.[143] He sought to broaden the Conservatory's appeal by adding new instruments to its teaching roster. With Earl Ruttan, for example, he attracted some two hundred students for classes in violin, banjo, and Spanish and Hawaiian guitar.[144] In these and other ways, Galperin helped considerably in raising the Conservatory's – and the college's – profile in the community.

Finances

For members of the board of governors and administrators, finances were a constant preoccupation. The college could not survive without maximizing its revenues and minimizing its expenditures. From 1911 to 1940, the college's total revenues were just under $1.4 million and its expenditures were $1.5 million, for a net loss of $115,000. In only five years did the college have a surplus, three of them in the late 1920s. To offset the shortfalls and generate funds for capital purposes, Kerby and the board had raised $211,408 in donations, leaving the college with a small net operating surplus for the period.[145] But cash flow did not tell the whole story, for the college remained indebted. Still, given the harsh financial circumstances, the wonder was that the college had survived, not that it still owed payments on its mortgage.

Figure 3.3 summarizes the annual budget balances from 1912 to 1940. It shows that, though the overall balance at the end of the period was positive, the college experienced a deficit in most years. The heaviest deficits occurred during the First World War and the 1920s, with smaller ones in the 1930s. The peak years for donations were in the 1920s, with the total declining sharply in the 1930s.

The plunge in enrolment during the First World War caused revenue to fall from nearly $50,000 in 1914 to just over $30,000 in 1916–17 (nearly 40 per cent) while tuition revenues fell from $16,000 to less than $10,000, and donations from $15,546 in 1913 and $19,271 in 1914 to $3,838 in 1915.[146] In response, Kerby reduced his salary.[147] By 1918, the college's debt had reached $83,500 (with "unpaid subscriptions" of $50,000 from nineteen pledges) and mounted to $97,000 a few months later.[148] In addition to its other debts, the college owed property-secured mortgages and loans totalled $68,999 in June 1920.[149] In 1919–20, interest payments alone amounted to nearly $9,000.[150]

Mount Royal was not alone in experiencing financial problems. College petitions to the Methodist church for funding assistance led the church to include their needs in 1919 in its "Forward Movement" fundraising campaign. From the proceeds the Board of Education was awarded $750,000 to allocate to the colleges.[151] Mount Royal submitted a claim for $97,367, "most of which is immediately payable and pressing,"

FIGURE 3.3 REVENUES AND EXPENSES, 1912–40

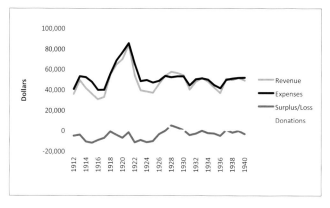

SOURCE: Data from the Principal's Reports to the Executive Committee of the Board of Governors.

and the church allocated it $70,000.[152] Though Kerby said that "every dollar" from the Forward Movement campaign "has gone to the reduction of our indebtedness" and "that Mount Royal College has been as economically and efficiently managed as any institution in connection with the Methodist Church," the college still had a $40,000 debt in 1921, just before enrolments collapsed again.[153] Indeed, thanks to deferred mortgage payments in the 1920s and 1930s, it was to remain in debt until 1950.

In addition to the special funds, the college also applied to the church for "connexional" funding. The formula for distributing grants had evolved over time but was based on a constant principle – the major portion of funds raised within a regional conference would be directed to the theological school in that conference, that the funds raised across the country would pay for the Department of Education and special grants to institutions, and that any balance would be split among the theological schools. The charges against the fund included "the salary of a special teacher to teach religion to all of the students and, in co-operation with other members of the staff, to direct the religious life of the college." As it was not approved to offer theology, Mount Royal had not benefited from the fund. In 1923–24, 80 per cent of the connexional funds contributed by the Alberta Conference, as well as 12 per cent of the national surplus, went to Alberta College South, where teaching "probationers" occurred.

Like other institutions without probationers, Mount Royal's connexional grant was to be $500.[154]

The enrolment downturn in 1922–23 soon led to a financial crisis. In 1923, O. S. Chapin reported to the board that the "auditor forecasts a 'jam' or crisis before the end of the year and that, giving most favorable aspect to the college's position, we are running behind approximately $7,000 and $9,000 per annum; . . . the gross annual income of the college has dropped during the past year from $80,000 to $39,000."[155] In order to keep the college afloat, members of the board signed personal financial guarantees, an action that came back to haunt their estates in the 1930s when the families of some board members discovered there were lingering obligations.[156] On other occasions board members made outright donations – in 1926, for example, seven members contributed $200 each; on other occasions, the levy was $25. Some board members made regular annual donations, including Sayre, who had retired to California and contributed annually until his death in the late 1930s.[157] Supporters were encouraged to remember the college in their wills.[158] In the early 1920s Kerby and Carrick took voluntary deferred compensation to help the college meet ends.[159] Mrs. Kerby and Mrs. George Walters donated free instructional services.[160] Maintenance was deferred. Students who had not paid their fees were tracked down by credit collectors and assets such as automobiles were seized.[161] The college sought and received in-kind donations such as coal and paint.[162]

In the 1920s the financial contribution of the boarding operation was critical to the college's financial health. In 1919–20, for example, boarding fees provided 53 per cent of the revenues, compared to the 37 per cent provided by tuition fees, while the boarding function accounted for only 33 per cent of expenditures (faculty salaries accounted for 27 per cent, administrative costs 14 per cent, and maintenance and utilities 11 per cent, the remainder going to books and sundries).[163] In 1924–25 boarding fees provided 51 per cent of the revenue while boarding consumed only 38 per cent of expenditures; the profit paid the operating costs of college facilities.[164] To fill the residences, single staff members were obliged to live in them and students were accepted from the Technical Institute and Normal School.[165] When Leonard Leacock was hired to teach piano in 1924, he initially shared a room with a student. During the summer, the residences hosted the Methodist School of Religion and Stampede visitors; in 1925, the college earned nearly $400 in rent from Stampede visitors, and in 1928, $900.[166]

Though there were rough financial periods in the 1930s – in 1931, when enrolment fell sharply again, and in 1935–36, when the Depression hit bottom – the effects were not as dramatic as they had been earlier, thanks to the tough-minded attitude of the Executive Committee, which slashed salaries in the early 1930s, terminated positions, and raised the administrative charge for Conservatory teachers.[167] Once again employees took voluntary salary cuts and deferred payments – to a combined total of $9,000 for Kerby, Walters, and Carrick. Faculty salaries were reduced. The Executive Committee negotiated a reduction from 7 to 6 per cent in the interest rate on the remaining mortgage. In 1934, Frank Langford, who had replaced Graham has Secretary of the Board of Christian Education of the United Church, commended the college for "the sound condition of its finances."[168]

When the Second World War started in September 1939, Kerby and Stanley, fearing another financial disaster like that during the First World War, hastened to visit President Kerr of the university to ask for permission to admit university students with one academic deficiency (the university would permit none).[169] They noted that because of uncertainty "we have only twenty-eight students whom we have been able to register for university courses. This will seriously affect our income. . . . "[170] The request implied that the college and university would have different admission standards, and Kerr denied the request.[171]

Among Kerby's other concerns was the decline in the number of boarders. By November 1938, there were only forty-four, a year later, thirty-three. These numbers included thirteen instructors and "other boarders."[172] Thus, from being a source of revenue, the residence had become a fiscal drain. When asked whether the college could accommodate military officers from Military District No. 13, Kerby the board agreed "to accept as many officers as could be accommodated in rooms not occupied by students in the west end of the college building." A year later the board agreed to advertise rooms for soldiers and their wives.[173] In May 1942 boarding rates were raised by 10 per cent along with the commission paid to "field representatives" recruiting students.[174]

While facing straitened financial circumstances, the executive committee in 1940 addressed the mortgage owed to Mrs. Langford. The college had paid $56,000 in interest and only $5,000 on the principal of $30,000. After several months of negotiations with Henry Langford, her son, the board signed an agreement to provide either a payment of $1,500 annually "for the remainder of her life or for a period of ten years, at expiry of which the mortgage would be discharged without any further payments if all payments had been made to such date." As a result, the obligation was to end in 1951.[175]

FACULTY

During Kerby's tenure, the college annually employed ten to sixteen full-time academic staff members, including administrators.[176] Low salaries, new opportunities in public schools, and a requirement to live in or spend time in the student residence resulted in a steady turnover.[177] There was also a lingering differentiation by gender in the teaching staff. In 1914 Marion Wilkie was added to teach French and German, Muriel Crow to teach drama, and Katherine MacEachern to teach stenography. At the same time, Kirk Johnson was hired to teach in the junior academic stream and Arthur Rosborough to teach physics and mathematics.[178] The pattern was to continue – the languages, cultural, secretarial, and home-economics courses were taught by women, the arts, science, and commercial programs by men. In 1941–42 there were twelve academic faculty members, nine of them women (six unmarried, three married).[179] The requirement for single faculty members to live in the residence was not always a welcome obligation. Walter Hepburn of the Commerce Department noted in his letter of resignation in 1929 that residential life had added to his "burdensome" workload.[180] A small faculty also meant that some programs were hostage to personnel changes.

Faculty members were expected to engage in social activities with students and to participate in committees, such as those responsible for the residences, the library, admissions, and athletics. Students who fell below satisfactory levels on examinations were referred to the Standing Committee to determine how deficiencies could be addressed.[181] For lack of

Faculty in 1938–39. Mount Royal University Archives *Calendar 1938–39.*

resources, the college rejected requests for leaves so faculty could further their academic credentials, and several were turned down.[182]

The board's Staff Committee was responsible for recruiting new faculty, but it usually delegated authority to Kerby to make appointments during his trips.[183] In 1926–27 a half-dozen new faculty members were graduates of Maritime universities (notably Dalhousie); their references included letters of support from inspectors of schools, university presidents, and teachers. In 1926 the faculty included eight holders of bachelor's degrees (one also held an M.Sc.), two holders of credentials in fine arts, two holders of diplomas (home economics, commerce), three normal school graduates, and one member trained in "Literary Interpretation."[184] This situation contrasted with the composition of the faculty after the affiliation agreement with the University of Alberta. Thereafter all faculty members teaching university-level courses held an MA or M.Sc., while some others had credentials more appropriate to music or art.

OTHER LINKS TO THE COMMUNITY

With an annual budget that ranged from $40,000 to $60,000, the college was a small but important economic presence in the community. It employed ten to eighteen faculty members, a small administrative staff (business manager, secretary), a nutritionist, cooks, and cleaning and maintenance staff, and processed fees for dozens of Conservatory teachers. It did business with many companies in Calgary. In return, the community supported the college in various ways – in-kind donations, as we have seen, and notably in the provision of scholarships, medals, and prizes for students. The Scholarship Committee annually canvassed people to provide awards. Donations came from board members (Macdonald, Stanley, Henry Jenkins, Sher Willows, James Garden, W. J. Snodden, F. Stappels), employees of the college (Kerby, Walters, Carrick), and businesses (e.g., F. E. Osborne, a stationer, D. E. Black, a jeweller), and such prominent businessmen or local notables as Nat Christie, John Burns, William Heron, A. E. Cross, and R. B. Bennett. In 1936 Imperial Oil, Eaton's, Union Milk, and the *Calgary Herald*, whose managing editor, Leigh Spence, was a board member, were among the benefactors. The Kiwanis Club offered $100 to students entering with the highest standing in grade 12 departmental examinations. B'nai Brith and the Calgary Council of Jewish Women provided bursaries. Some donations were for students from particular regions, such as the Canadian Western Natural Gas bursary for a student from Foremost.[185] In 1935 and 1936, $125 scholarships were awarded to students from small towns around the province, while students from Calgary high schools received $50 scholarships for grade 11.[186]

Kerby incarnated a lively link to the community. Even in his seventies he remained active in a dozen organizations and was a tireless professional speaker. In February 1936, for example, he spoke in one week to the Probus Club, Father's and Mother's Evening at Elbow Park and Bow View Schools, Leisure Time League at the YMCA, the Provincial Home and School Association, and the Masonic Order.[187] Renowned for funerary orations, he bade farewell to many dignitaries. When King George V died in 1935, Kerby, as a past Grand Master, led the Masons' memorial service at Knox United Church.[188] He also spoke at receptions held when R. B. Bennett resigned as Conservative leader and announced his departure from Canada, as well as events held at Central United Church and others hosted by officers of the militia, of which he was a chaplain.[189]

Except for Conservatory teachers, faculty members were not as prominent in the community as some were to become later. As a kind of exception, C. F. Burchill, a business instructor, spoke to the Elks Club in 1934 on the applicability of Major C. H. Douglas's social credit theory to Alberta.[190] The college also organized speaker's series. The speakers included Dr. E. K. Broadus of the University of Alberta, who spoke on "English Poetry since 1802" and "The Uncelestial City,"[191] and others who discussed folk songs and folklore in Quebec and the merits of the Roman statesman Cato compared to those of Sir Robert Walpole.[192]

The Mount Royal College Education Club organized an ambitious monthly schedule of speakers. Established by Mrs. Kerby in 1923,[193] the club was intended to bring women together for various purposes. The club's mandate evolved. The first version envisioned a "current events and ceramic club"; in 1924–25 the mandate became studying "world events, and the geography and history of the world."[194] In addition, the club organized music concerts, poetry readings, travelogues, and photographic displays. The lecture topics were wide-ranging, including topics on Russian society, the role of the East India Company (Mrs. Kerby), the impact of the Roman Empire on law, education, and literature, the Renaissance, George Bernard Shaw, hydro-electric power on the Shannon River, Spanish drama from medieval mystery plays to the present, the evolution of Scottish literature, France and French culture, and the nationalization of the Mexican petroleum industry.[195] In 1935 the club had seventy-five members and a waiting list.

On 3 October 1938, Mrs. Kerby died unexpectedly at the age of seventy-eight.[196] The Education Club was to continue, though in attenuated form, becoming an annual luncheon in the postwar period.[197]

Passing the Torch

In 1936, celebrating the college's twenty-fifth anniversary, Kerby had declared that "the college was at first a dream, a vision, and an ideal, before it began to be a concrete reality. The dream is not yet completely fulfilled and the ideal is not yet fully realized. . . . It is, however, a going concern, . . . a centre of cultural influence for southern Alberta and the millions of people who will yet find their home in this potentially great province."[198] In 1941, Kerby was over eighty and the Executive Committee began anticipating a change in leadership. Thinking about a successor was well advanced when Kerby convened the Executive Committee on 3 December 1941 to announce his retirement "in the spring of 1942, in order that a younger man might be secured to assume the responsibilities of the principalship." Dr. Stanley then "voiced the fact that all the citizens of Calgary and the province owed a debt of gratitude to Dr. Kerby for the life's work he had put into the inauguration, building, and successful operation of Mount Royal College during the past thirty years." Two subcommittees were formed, "one to arrange for Dr. Kerby's future financial position with regard to the college, and another to look into the matter of possible candidates."[199] (Kerby had reduced his salary on several occasions, at a cost to his retirement situation.) The subcommittee to recommend a successor met on 11 December 1941. Kerby himself had a successor in mind – the Reverend John Henderson Garden, then minister of Ryerson United Church in Hamilton, Ontario. Three other candidates, all United Church ministers, were identified. While no other non-ministers were considered, the subcommittee "agreed that recommendations need not necessarily be confined to ministers, as there was nothing in the college charter to prevent a layman from being principal. It was also agreed, however, that other things being equal, preference should be given to a minister of the United Church."[200] There was no public search. In a meeting on 23 January 1942, the subcommittee recommended Garden and the

John H. Garden, Mount Royal College Principal 1942–58. Mount Royal University Executive Records GO010-05G.

Executive Committee offered him the post effective 1 July 1942.[201] Kerby became "principal emeritus" and continued to live in his house by the college until his death in February 1944.[202]

Each head of the college has faced some particular challenges. Those faced by Kerby included translating the original mandate into operational practice, establishing the role and reputation of the college in the minds of parents and students in southern Alberta, building its credibility with other post-secondary institutions and the government, finding the means for financial survival and facility expansion, adapting the college's mandate to meet changing educational opportunities, and making the college a cultural resource for the Calgary community. By the time of his retirement, he – and the college – had met those challenges. To be sure, the college remained small, with just under five hundred students, most of them still in the high-school stream. But the concepts that were to lead to a broader mandate and larger operation were in place.

KERBY MEMORIAL BUILDING

 1 9 4 8

July 1942	*Rev. John H. Garden appointed Principal*
1944	*Revised Act makes college a "junior college" by legislation*
	Petroleum Engineering program added
1948–49	*Evening College commences*
	Kerby Memorial Building and Stanley Gymnasium open
1951	*University of Alberta Centre opens in Calgary*
1957	*Mount Royal re-negotiates affiliation agreement while retaining freedom to offer courses transferring to other jurisdictions*
1957–58	*Wing added to Kerby Memorial Building*
1958	*Principal Garden departs*

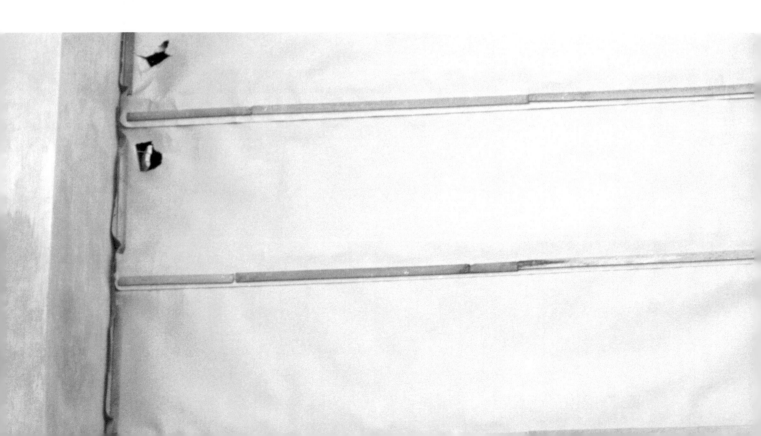

CHAPTER 4

BROADENING THE MANDATE, 1942–1958

The college with a university atmosphere.

– Advertising slogan, *Calgary Herald*[1]

John H. Garden's term as principal from July 1942 to December 1958 fell into two parts. The dividing point was the University of Alberta's decision in 1951 to open its own centre in Calgary to deliver its programs, depriving Mount Royal of its unique role in delivering university courses in Calgary. Already the college had escaped the university's control over its offering of courses transferable to universities outside Alberta. After the university's arrival, the college had no alternative but to accelerate the broadening of its mandate. Once again it was to undergo a transformation affecting its program mix, delivery methods, credentials, student clientele faculty qualifications, and public image.

Garden assumed office nearly two years into the Second World War, which precipitated an unprecedented mobilization of Canadian society and boosted the economy out of the Depression. In Alberta, the move from rural to urban districts intensified; at war's end 44 per cent of the population lived in towns and cities. The discovery of petroleum deposits in the Leduc-Woodbend area south of Edmonton in 1947 greatly accelerated economic growth. The frontier that had closed in 1914 reopened. Once again people and capital flooded in. While Edmonton became the centre for construction industries, Calgary became the head-office city for the energy and related service industries. In two decades the share of provincial wealth generated by agriculture fell from over one half to less than one quarter.[2] The changing source of wealth was symbolized by the founding of the Calgary Petroleum Club in 1948 by oilmen who felt awkward in the Ranchmen's Club. And yet, almost paradoxically, Calgary became increasingly identified as a frontier town, thanks to such branding activities as the white cowboy hat and books on the West by authors like Grant MacEwan, a member of Mount Royal's board and later Lieutenant Governor of Alberta.[3]

Calgary grew steadily, rising from 97,241 residents in 1944 to 323,389 in 1965, and then nearly trebling again by the end of the twentieth century. Though the rate of growth was uneven, the city grew by about 100,000 people per decade. Its boundaries sprawled outward. The small-city strategy adopted in 1931 gave way to a sprawling city pattern. The population became diverse and better educated, as energy-related head-office and service industries grew. From 1935 to 1971, the Social Credit party formed the provincial governments. Born in the Depression, it was led initially by evangelical ministers – William Aberhart 1935 to 1943, Ernest Manning from then to 1968 – who blended religion and populism.[4]

Until the 1960s Alberta's higher educational system was geared to the needs of a slow-moving economy. Its main purpose was to prepare teachers, engineers, accountants, lawyers, nurses, doctors, and agronomists. The university's admission requirements were stringent, focused solely on high-school graduates. Its principal adaptation to another kind of clientele came when it absorbed war veterans who nearly doubled the university's student body in one year.[5] That wave also swept over Mount Royal.

The New Broom

Principal Garden's major challenges included reorganizing to provide better academic management, maintaining a sound financial situation, expanding facilities to match enrolment growth and more a more varied curriculum, coping with the University of Alberta before and after it opened its centre in Calgary, revising the college's legal mandate, and finding ways to reorient the college in the wake of the affiliation agreement with the university.[6]

The younger brother of James Garden, the builder and board member, John H. Garden, born in Aberdeen, had migrated with his family in 1908 to Calgary, where he became a member of Calgary Methodist Church and of Kerby's Young Men's Club. One of the first students in the new college, he spent two years there before enrolling in Victoria University. During the war he joined the military and rose to the rank of captain. After completing an honours BA (Toronto), he was ordained as a minister by the

Faculty, ca. 1942. Mount Royal University Archives *Commemorative Yearbook 1971–72.*

Alberta Methodist Conference and served in churches in Calgary, Brandon, and Hamilton, where he was at the time of his appointment to the college. In 1927, he was awarded a BD by Stephen's College. In 1921, he had become head of Mount Royal's alumni association and in 1923 had joined the board as the alumni representative. His inauguration occurred on 29 October 1942, with Jascha Galperin and the Junior Symphony providing the music. In October 1945 he was awarded an honorary DD by Victoria University, after which he was commonly referred to as Dr. Garden.[7]

Months before Kerby's retirement, the board struck a "special reorganization committee" on which Garden sat whose report in July 1942 focused on the role of the board, the authority of the principal, and finances. New board committees were established for relations with staff, finances, physical plant, residences, publicity, scholarships, and affiliation with the university. Two "associate" board members from Lethbridge were added to "act principally as good will ambassadors"; the president of the Educational Club, Mrs. J. E. Hallonquist, was named "a corresponding member" to bring the club "into closer association" with the board. The accounting system would "show more accurately the true profit or loss of each department."[8]

While George Walters remained business manager and Galperin remained director of the Conservatory, Garden clarified their reporting line to him. He established three new academic departments, each headed by a Director. The School of Commerce was led by

Glen B. Hinchey, a former high-school principal in New Brunswick, head of the bookkeeping program of "one of the largest business colleges in Montreal."[9] The University Department was led by Ralph McCready, principal of Ponoka high school, holder of a B.Sc. (Alberta) and M.Sc. (Illinois) in chemistry.[10] And the High-School Department was led by Owen Kelly, principal of the high school in Three Hills, a former Mount Royal student, holder of a BA and MA (Alberta) in English.[11] McCready and Kelly were to remain linchpins in the senior administration for the next thirty years. In 1948, two other key members joined the senior administration. When George Walters retired, he was replaced as registrar and business manager by W. G. Maxwell Rae, then an accountant and business manager working for a lumber milling company in Vancouver.[12] Rae, who remained with the college for the next three decades, was to provide critical continuity in business and financial affairs as the college moved from private to public standing. The Evening College established in that year was led by W. John (Jack) Collett, a former teacher and United Church Minister in Claresholm; he was to become academic dean and Garden's successor.[13]

THE SECOND WORLD WAR

For the college, the Second World War was not the financial disaster the First World War had been; in fact it was just the reverse. Wartime economic activity, together with programs for soldiers, spurred enrolment. By the end of 1942, there were 596 students, above the 499 reached under Kerby.[14] In May 1943 Garden said there were 630 "in all departments," 200 in academic programs, including 43 in university courses; their average age was nineteen.[15] In December 1944, he reported that "this Fall has seen a very large attendance of students . . . , many coming from distant points in British Columbia, Saskatchewan, and the Alaska Highway. . . . The college dormitories are filled beyond capacity, and many students were turned away because of insufficient accommodation. The largest increase has been in the Academic Department, which indicates a growing interest in higher education."[16] Greater enrolments improved revenues from $53,000 in 1940–41 to $142,000 in 1946–47. The

Mount Royal College cadets, ca. 1940s. Mount Royal University Archives *Commemorative Yearbook 1971–72.*

college balanced its budget in 1943 and maintained a balance thereafter.[17]

Garden vigorously supported Canada's war effort. In September 1942 male college students were given the choice of taking the University Air Training Corps (UATC) or the Officers Training Corps (OTC). Most opted for the UATC, and a flight squadron was formed with Garden as commanding officer. "All students in Grade 12 must belong and any student over seventeen may belong on a voluntary basis. Those who do not keep up to standards must go active." "Each member of that Squadron draws pay up to 30 days. He takes drill, aircraft recognition, first aid, sanitation, mathematics, signals, navigation, airmanship, administration, discipline, organization and other subjects." In 1942–43 forty-two students participated. In 1943 several students "went active" – some by choice, others because their grades were too low. It was mandatory for women in the university stream to join the Women's War Services, though voluntary for those in other streams. In December 1942, about fifty female students were "organized in the Women's War Services (Civilian)," where they were trained "in First Aid, A.R.P. and Drill, three afternoons a week."[18] A report in the *Varshicom* on the activities of former students (1939–41) indicated that in 1942 seven were in the army, 23 in the RCAF, nine were teaching, four were farming, two were in the Normal School and two in a Nursing program, forty were clerks and stenographers, and thirty-nine were in university.[19]

Apart from some tutoring in English undertaken by a part-time English teacher, the first program for active forces was a course in clerical skills offered to forty students in the fall of 1941; in September 1944 the college added a twenty-five–week "terminal course" in journalism for military personnel.[20]

As with the First World War, so the Second took a toll among students who enlisted. A scroll recorded the names of over three hundred who served in the war effort, with red crosses signalling death on sixteen names. "We remember their names and sacrifice with deep gratitude," Garden said.[21]

COPING WITH ENROLMENT GROWTH

From 1941–42 to 1957–58, Garden's last academic year as principal, enrolment nearly tripled, rising from 584 to 1,647 students.[22] By the mid-1950s the college had to reject applicants because of "cramped quarters." "This situation has its satisfactory aspects," Garden explained, "but it is also unsatisfactory in not being able to expand while the opportunity for doing so is presented."[23]

In the mid-1950s about two-thirds of the students were enrolled in high-school courses, notably in the bridging program. By 1965–66, when the private college ended, the balance had shifted. In 1965, "the percentage of the total student body which is in junior college has been slowly rising from 19 per cent in 1958 to the present 38 per cent. The percentage in secretarial school has dropped slightly from 11 per cent to 8 per cent. The percentage in the high school has dropped from 69 per cent to 53 per cent this year."[24] The transition in the college's role was reflected in library holdings, most of the 5,874 volumes in the library in 1964 consisting of post-secondary works; there was also evidence of greatly increased book loans over time.[25]

Much of the growth was due to rising demand, still focused heavily on the universities, as seen not only in the growth of universities but in the emergence of junior colleges in Alberta. By the early 1960s, governments were contemplating creating new kinds of institutions – community colleges, technical institutes – to respond to other dimensions of the soaring demand. "In the affluent post-war world, many young people from families with no university tradition were now choosing to attend. In September 1951, universities and colleges in Canada were enrolling forty-two of every one thousand young Canadians of university age. The following year it was fifty, and ten years later it was seventy-five. Today [2005], the figure is four times greater than that."[26] At Mount Royal, a private institution, enrolment growth was also facilitated by aggressive student-recruitment tactics. Among the "field representatives" who received commissions for student registrations was Gerald L. Knowlton, a former student, graduate of the University of Alberta and of the MBA program at the University of Western Ontario, and later a well-known realtor. The notice of his appointment in 1955 indicated that his mission was "again" to visit "high schools, parents and students in Alberta, British Columbia, and Saskatchewan."[27]

The steady growth in the college's enrolment, together with growing variety in its programs in the late 1950s and early 1960s, required additional facilities. So long as it could, the college renovated and added to the old Barn. But it needed constant attention – in 1942, six classroom floors were resurfaced, in 1944 smoke damage forced redecoration, and in 1946 a leaky roof was repaired. In 1946, when there were 763 students, Garden declared that "our accommodation is taxed even beyond capacity." In November 1950, he said that the residence in the Barn had "about outlived its usefulness." "It costs us a good deal each year in renovations to keep it in a usable condition." In 1957 the dormitory section was renovated again, with new linoleum adding "a bright cheery atmosphere to an otherwise drab and depressing cell block." The patching and filling was to continue until the college abandoned the building in 1972.[28]

To increase space, the college periodically acquired more houses, including Kerby's, which was turned into a dormitory for senior girls.[29] In 1946, with provincial funding assistance, it acquired five wartime huts on the Mewata Armoury site from the War Assets Corporation, and relocated them to the campus for use as classrooms, laboratories, and reading rooms.[30]

But none of this met the needs. Deciding to use the well of respect for Kerby, who had died earlier in the year, and his wife Emily, the board announced a $100,000 fundraising campaign in December 1944 to build the Kerby Memorial Building.[31] Viscount R.

B. Bennett donated $25,000.[32] By the end of 1945 it had raised most of the money.[33] But then the question of site arose. During a visit Bennett "strongly recommended" abandoning the downtown location in favour of the site at the Institute of Technology offered by the government in 1929, as it "would provide a more satisfactory campus and with greater room for expansion." Stanley and Garden raised the matter with Premier Manning, who "seemed to be favourable but wished to consult with his cabinet."[34] Once again, the government offered the college a long-term lease for land at the site "at a nominal fee of $1 per year, providing, however, that before any construction work is started, the plans and specifications of any buildings must be submitted . . . for approval."[35] The board's property committee recommended accepting the offer, but then second thoughts led to a reversal of board opinion: "the college would not own its own campus," downtown "buildings would be closer together and would tend to reduce overhead expenses," and the old campus remained "nearer the centre of the city and better located for good attendance at symphony concerts and other musical performances."[36] So the Kerby Memorial Building was built across the street from the existing campus, at 7th Avenue SW and 11th Street.

In the realm of might-have-beens, the college's decision to maintain its own site may have spared the private college from being merged with the Institute of Technology when it became a publicly funded institution.

The decision to build was made in January 1947. The building was dedicated in June 1949, with Premier Manning praising the college for its values-oriented curriculum.[37] In February 1948 the old gymnasium burned down and the construction project was expanded to build a new one.[38] The new gymnasium, which opened on 18 November 1949, was named after George Stanley, the long-standing chair of the board. Garden reported that the Stanley gymnasium "made a big difference" to college life. For intramural programs, "students are divided into three

The memorial stone honouring Dr. George Kerby (donated by E. S. Somerville of Calgary) was installed over the entry to the Kerby Memorial Building in November 1948. Dr. W. H. Swift, Alberta Deputy Minister of Education, commented on Dr. Kerby's "colourful character and inspiring career." Photographer the *Calgary Herald*; Glenbow Archives NA-2864-4068b.

Kerby Memorial Building and Stanley Gymnasium. Mount Royal University Archives G524.

'houses,' the Stanley House, the Kerby House, and the Garden House, and these form their own league" that plays in the gymnasium.[39]

Further expansion of college facilities consisted of acquiring more houses and adding wings to the Kerby Memorial Building – one in 1957 to create five classrooms and "a first unit in a plan to replace the residence in a period of years," another in 1961 that included a library, classrooms, laboratories, a cafeteria for 120 people, a snack bar, and tiny student's lounge.[40] In February 1959 Jack Finlay, president of the Junior College Council, proposed "that a new building be built on the present Kerby house location, financed entirely by student funds," based on a loan from the board that would be repaid over five years.[41] The board referred the issue to the Property Committee with the directive that, while recognizing "the need for a Students' Union building," the board should provide it.[42] The board then assigned a rented house for student use.

One other facility development of note was the small chapel built in the Kerby Memorial Building and dedicated on 26 May 1951. At Garden's initiative, it included four leaded, stained-glass panels honouring James H. Garden, Henry M. Jenkins, A. Melville Scott, and William G. Hunt, all former board members. The windows were later moved to the new campus of the public institution.[43]

Despite the additions, the college remained inadequately housed. A report in the early 1960s described the lamentable situation: a "severe shortage of classroom space"; "office space . . . too crowded in all areas"; the chapel was "very inadequate," seating only sixty students; the gym was undersized, designed for a campus with three hundred students; the dining facilities were "very overcrowded." The "lack of campus grounds, playing fields, and student car parking facilities [is] detrimental to the public image of the college, student morale and athletic accomplishment." "Student Union facilities are housed in make-shift accommodation, and students' offices, boardroom and lounge are in separate buildings." "The lack of funds is the main cause of inactivity."[44] If there was any consolation in the space shortage, it may have been the sense of community generated by shared hardship. However, it was becoming more evident by the year that Mount Royal was finding it hard to provide the facilities and equipment it needed.

MOVING BEYOND AFFILIATION

Another of Garden's major preoccupations during his first decade in office was the relationship with the University of Alberta. Within months of taking office he proposed adding first-year courses in engineering, nursing, and education, but the university responded negatively.[45] President Newton explained, "We doubt the wisdom of your attempting to put on the first year of a strictly professional course. In such courses, it seems to us advantageous to the student to enjoy the professional atmosphere of a large group of students working in the same field. . . . " One purpose of first-year nursing was "weeding out" unsuitable students, a task that could not be delegated. So far as I know," Newton wrote, "it has never been proposed that junior colleges should develop into professional schools."[46]

But Stanley and Garden were not prepared to abandon their ambitions, and in February 1943 the college approached the University of Alberta again about offering first-year engineering, arguing it was a matter of wartime urgency. The college would "serve as a feeder of mature students to the university."[47] Dean R. S. L. Wilson of the Faculty of Applied Science, asked to review the college's capacity and the potential for "collaboration with the Institute of Technology for this purpose,"[48] concluded in March 1943 that renovations and judicious hiring – for example, of a surveying teacher from among "practicing engineers and surveyors in Calgary" – would enable the college to offer first-year engineering courses. The college then asked for permission to offer the courses and committed to "meet the recommendations in Dean Wilson's report." At this point, however, the faculty members in Engineering at the university opposed the idea and the General Faculties Council (GFC), as Newton put it, "contented itself with recommending that your proposal be deferred, pending further study of the whole question of junior college work in professional fields." When the college persisted, Newton asked the GFC to respond.[49] The GFC's report was frank: "We believe that the provincial Institute of Technology and Art together with the Normal School at Calgary, these being tax-supported institutions, should have their functions developed to include junior college work preparatory to senior university Arts courses as well as 'general education.' We doubt the practicability of broadening the existing basis of junior college work in Calgary without tax support." Moreover, while it had "no objection" to Mount Royal "teaching first-year Engineering as a temporary war measure," the university planned "to launch a junior college of its own after the war, at which time it would presumably take over most, if not all, of the university work presently carried on at Mount Royal College."[50]

Chafing at the constraints, the college set the goal of freeing itself from university control. In December 1942 the board formed a committee to review the legal charter and to determine whether the charter of Calgary College would be "available."[51] After meetings with Manning and Newton, Clinton Ford, who chaired the committee, reported that these ideas had been "well received."[52] By January 1944 the revised

charter was ready.[53] At that point, however, conflicting understandings came into play.

For Mount Royal, inspired by the Calgary College and American models, a junior college offered its own programs in university-transfer and career programs, and universities were free to recognize whatever course credits they wished toward their own degrees. For the university, a junior college offered all university-level courses under its direction and could not affiliate with other universities without its approval. Potential misunderstanding appeared in a memorandum that Newton wrote after his meeting with Ford in December 1943. The college wanted to revise the charter "to bring it into line with the work they are actually doing." "They do not propose to ask for authority to exceed their present scope with reference to university work, although they called attention to the charter of Calgary College . . . which they stated gave authority to conduct practically all kinds of university work short of conferring degrees."[54] When the draft Mount Royal bill omitted any reference to the university, Newton reacted with alarm. "If the junior college work of Mount Royal is to be independent of the University of Alberta," he wrote to Solon E. Low, the minister of education, "Mount Royal ceases to be particularly a junior college of this university and can affiliate with any university it selects. . . . " As "the university is bound to do its utmost to protect the unity and integrity of higher education in this province," he wrote, it "must therefore oppose the Mount Royal draft bill in its original form."[55]

A meeting of college and university officials held in minister Low's office on 2 March 1944 led to the insertion of the phrase "subject to the general regulations of the University of Alberta" into section 2 of the charter. The bill was passed a few days later. Section 2 read as follows:

> The Corporation shall have and be deemed to have had power and legal authority to establish, equip, maintain, and conduct . . . an institution of learning for the education and instruction of youths of both sexes, or of either sex, in the elementary and secondary branches of knowledge, and for education and instruction in music, art, speech and drama, journalism,

business, technical and domestic arts and such courses as may be arranged for the rehabilitation of ex-service men and women, and, subject to the general regulations of the University of Alberta, to establish courses of study of the junior years of a university, with the status of a junior college, and to do all such acts, matters and things as are incidental or conducive to the attainment of the said objects.

In presenting the new charter to the board, Garden referred also to an "important amendment in Section 10, Clause 4, where the board of governors is given authority to enter into any arrangements with any educational authority that may seem conducive to further the objects of the school." Together, "these amendments make it possible for the college to widen the scope of its work and render better service to the young people of southern Alberta. . . . Mount Royal College has now the status of a junior college by act of parliament. These amendments make it possible for the college to widen the scope of its work and render better service to the young people of southern Alberta."[56]

In practice, the insertion of the clause desired by the university did not have the intended effect. While it maintained the status quo in Alberta, it had no effect on the college's ability to arrange for the transfer of its course credits to universities in other jurisdictions. Indeed, the university's attempts to confine the college encouraged it to become a vehicle outflanking the university's monopoly in Alberta, a monopoly that generated a clientele for what Mount Royal had to offer.

The ineffectiveness of the clause inserted into section 2 became evident within days. An advertisement in the *Western Examiner* on 24 June 1944 announced that, "in cooperation with the University of Oklahoma," Mount Royal was launching "a Special Two-Year Course . . . open to students who can enter from Junior Matriculation."[57] "The inference seemed rather obvious," Newton wrote to Garden, "that, having been denied approval for the present to carry first-year Engineering work in cooperation with this university, you turned elsewhere for an outlet." "The absence of a written agreement of affiliation with the University of Oklahoma did not alter the fact that

In the 1950s, Mount Royal College promoted its university-like attributes to prospective students. Mount Royal University Archives *Varshicom 1955-56.*

you were actually playing the part of a junior college to that university." Thus, he said, "I can do no other than disapprove completely of the action announced in your advertisement. In my opinion, at the very least you should have made formal application to us for consideration by our Committee on Junior Colleges."[58] Garden replied that this view was "entirely wrong." "We have not turned to any other university seeking the privilege of offering first-year Engineering and are still hoping that Alberta University [sic] may yet be able to grant our request in this regard." Inquiring students had been told by Oklahoma if they took "certain specific subjects," they could be admitted. These requirements could be satisfied by grade 12 courses already offered by the college together with "the first-year BSc courses which we are authorized to offer by the University of Alberta and hence there seemed to be no problem involved."[59] The college had neither sought affiliation nor added courses. The entrance requirement was "Junior Matriculation (Grade 11) and at the end of the first year," which included Latin or French, "a student can gain his Alberta Senior Matriculation as well as qualifying for the first year of the Oklahoma University course."[60]

In 1944, the "Engineers of Calgary" proposed to the University of Alberta that first-year Engineering courses "might be available at Mount Royal College," but, as Garden explained, "unfortunately we were unable to take any action on this suggestion on account of our present lack of accommodation."[61] By 1946, the college found the necessary space and under some pressure from the Department of Veteran Affairs and local demands, the university permitted the college to offer its first-year Engineering courses. Sixty students enrolled for the first year.[62] The college then advertised "courses in applied science leading to degrees of B.Sc. in Civil, Chemical, Electrical and Mining Engineering. Priority will be given to married returned servicemen resident in Calgary."[63] While the arrangement lasted only a short time, because of the university's resistance,[64] the courses became the core of the college's Engineering transfer program to American institutions. By 1953 the college claimed that its courses led to "about eight engineering" streams.[65]

For five years, the college had the best of both worlds – deliverer of the university's courses, and provider of university-transfer pathways to American institutions. This happy situation ended in 1951 when the university opened the University Centre in Calgary. Upon learning of the coming centre, the college offered itself as a partner, pointing to "the new Kerby Memorial Building" and "well-trained instructors who have been approved by the university."[66] At the same time it discreetly explored "further expansion on our part along the lines of affiliation with other universities,"[67] and contacted McGill and other institutions.[68] The University Centre opened in September 1951 to offer first-year arts and science courses and the first two years of Education.[69] Thereafter it grew steadily, extending the range of arts and science courses and later adding courses in Commerce (1953), Physical Education (1956), Engineering and Education (1957).

The opening of the University Centre had both short-term and long-term implications for Mount Royal. In the short run, the college had to cope with the fact that better students in arts and science now registered at the University Centre, leaving it with smaller numbers and weaker students. Enrolment dropped from thirty-one in 1950–51 to eighteen in 1951–52; for 1952–53, the college advised students in arts and science to "go to the Calgary branch of the university."[70] The de facto end of the affiliation agreement was another consequence. In December 1954, the college's board declared that "the original purpose of the affiliation no longer exists" but left formal discontinuation to be "instituted at such time as the Executive [Committee] may decide."[71] The administration ceased seeking approval for new faculty members and reporting students in university-level courses. In response to a query from the university in 1954, the college responded: "We have no students registered in first year Arts and Science with the University of Alberta at Mount Royal College this year. That is … why you are unable to find names for the list for the first-year committee."[72] The affiliation agreement became a fiction, useful for advertising and credit transfer purposes but having no practical effect.

Noting that when the college entered into the affiliation agreement in 1931, "it had been encouraged to do so by the university and the government" and had proceeded only because "assurances were given that this would not be a temporary arrangement,"[73] Garden made a case for compensation. Premier Manning promised that "everything would be done to try to protect the college from too severe [a] loss."[74] In the end, the university hired one faculty member, purchased some laboratory equipment, and provided $3,600 compensation for lost revenue.[75]

The longer-term implication of the opening of the University Centre for the college was foreshadowed by Garden in September 1951: " . . . in time we can find other ways of expanding the college's work that will compensate for any loss in this regard."[76] Finding those other ways was to lead to a redefined college – one serving as a "community" rather than as a "junior" college. In the immediate future, however, the one remaining program rooted in University of Alberta courses – Petroleum Engineering – became a vital financial support for the college.

A Footnote: Petroleum Engineering

In most years the Petroleum Engineering program admitted seventy to ninety students a year. However, there was a sleeping clause lurking below the surface that became visible when the graduates of the Mount Royal/Oklahoma program applied for admission to the engineering profession in Alberta. At that point the statutory role of the University of Alberta in overseeing admission to the professions precipitated a crisis, for the Board of Examiners of the Association of Professional Engineers of Alberta was chaired by the dean of Applied Science, R. M. Hardy, and he and the board decided that any applicants must first meet the admission requirements of the University of Alberta. The University's requirements included a minimum grade average of 60 per cent in high school, no academic deficiencies, a senior course in a foreign language, and no senior matriculation courses accepted for university credit. By contrast, the requirements for the Mount Royal/Oklahoma program did not specify a grade average for high-school work, permitted academic deficiencies that had been overcome, and allowed up to five senior matriculation courses for degree credit.[77] The lack of congruence led the board to require all of the graduates of the Mount Royal/Oklahoma program to take a year of study to fulfill the university's admission requirements.

Faced with graduates' complaints, Mount Royal's board in 1955 established a committee to discuss the situation with university officials, while Garden travelled to Oklahoma to secure continued support.[78] On 7 December 1955 Garden and Hardy, who was wearing his hat as chairman of the Board of Examiners rather than as dean, agreed that college students whose high-school records would not enable them to be admitted to the university Engineering program would have to make up any academic deficiencies and complete two full years of college after high-school graduation *before* transferring for a further two full years of study at an American institution.[79] In correspondence, Hardy observed that the college's second-year courses were "identical" to those of the university and were unacceptable only because they were not offered under an affiliation agreement.[80] "It is most unlikely," Hardy added, "that the Board . . . would require additional examinations in such cases where the candidate subsequently successfully completed the degree requirements at an American university."[81] Garden advised his board that "we arrived at a compromise agreement which Dean Hardy has given us in a letter that may prove satisfactory."[82] In 1956, he said that Hardy had "approved our engineers being admitted to a two-year course . . . with a high-school diploma, without the requirement of the last unit of a foreign language."[83]

However, the Hardy-Garden agreement dealt with the future, not with Oklahoma graduates who had been told to take a further year of study to meet Alberta's requirements.[84] The issue soon became contentious. On what basis had the board rejected degrees from an engineering program accredited by the same body that accredited Alberta's program? Why did a high-school course in a foreign language or one's high-school record trump a completed engineering degree? In response to a query, Hardy responded that, yes, Alberta high-school graduates who had taken all four years at Oklahoma would be admissible to the profession, even though Oklahoma's admission standards differed from Alberta's, but Albertans who had passed through Mount Royal without meeting the university's requirements were not admissible.[85] Embattled, he grew truculent: "The affiliation arrangement . . . has been effectively used to nullify our judgment on the matter. Moreover, the university . . . has been placed in the position of cooperating in the Engineering course offered at Mount Royal, which is of lower standard than any offered in Canada. To the extent that this impression is created, the reputation of the university . . . in the field of engineering is weakened."[86] However, there were over two hundred graduates of the Mount Royal/Oklahoma program, and Hardy and the board had to blink.

The process began when the university Senate addressed the issue in May 1957. Garden described his agreement with Hardy: "it was decided that Mount Royal would not insist on . . . a foreign language, and Dr. Garden said he had prepared in Dean Hardy's office the statement currently appearing in the prospectus of Mount Royal College." Furthermore, Hardy "had subsequently taken the matter up with the Professional Society, in which he reported that they were satisfied with this arrangement." Surprised to learn of the understanding, president Stewart requested

Clinton J. Ford, Chairman of the Board 1955–61. Photographer Lane's Studio; Mount Royal University Archives E317-1.

an explanation from Hardy, who said that he had met with Garden as board chairman, not as dean.[87] The executive committee of the university's board of governorsG met with Hardy on 9 December 1957 to review the matter. After the meeting, Hardy wrote that "if the board [of governors] . . . consider that the decisions of the Board of Examiners have been sound in principle but that further efforts should be made to reduce the inconvenience to individuals concerned by the requirements of examinations, it would be quite possible to reduce the number which have been required by the original rulings. The principles . . . will be protected as long as some additional requirement, even one examination, is maintained for these applicants. All things considered, this perhaps would be the best solution of the problem."[88] In fact, after a few more

tergiversations, the Board of Examiners approved the applicants without any further requirement.

The controversy briefly dimmed enthusiasm for the college's Petroleum Engineering program. Most students continued to transfer into third year in Oklahoma – twenty-five of thirty-five students in 1953.[89] Registration peaked at eighty students in 1954–55 and eighty-six in 1955–56, slumped to sixty-eight in 1956–57, and then soared to ninety-seven once the issue was resolved. In 1957, there were ninety-six former Mount Royal students in Oklahoma's program.[90] However, the long-term prospects were dim. The death knell sounded when the University of Alberta began offering first-year Engineering in the University Centre in 1957. Enrolment in Mount Royal's program fell to sixty-seven in 1958–59 and to forty-four in 1959–60.[91] In early 1959, the college negotiated the end of the program with the university, after which first-year students in good standing were able to enter second year at the university.[92] Among the program's graduates were some later leaders in Calgary's "oil patch," including Ed Lakusta, who became president of Petro-Canada, and Bruno Todesco, a Mount Royal high-school graduate of 1948, who held several senior positions, became a member of Mount Royal's board, and was named a distinguished alumnus in 1984.

BECOMING A COMMUNITY COLLEGE

As we have seen, the idea of Mount Royal as something more than a junior college had been articulated since the 1920s. Moreover, in practice, its blend of high-school, career, and university-level courses made it more than a traditional junior college. Just after the war Garden toured colleges in Idaho, California, Nevada, and Utah. He was impressed by the fact that, in addition to a university-transfer role, "the larger and probably more distinctive work [of junior colleges] is in providing higher education and vocational training for young people who do not propose proceeding to a university. Their departments of terminal courses are large with many courses being offered."[93] He was also intrigued by American approaches to "adult education," which "is really part-time education carried on after the regular work hours or in holiday periods." "It recognizes the fact that education is a lifelong

A HIGH SCHOOL LIBRARY PERIOD

Library period for Mount Royal College high school students, ca. 1950–51. Mount Royal University Archives *Prospectus 1950-51.*

process."[94] In 1946, Mount Royal joined the American Association of Junior Colleges (AAJC). Thereafter the college progressively embraced the idea of itself as a "community" rather than as a "junior" college. Though the groundwork was laid in 1948 or earlier, the opening of the University Centre in Calgary accelerated the broadening of the mission. There were five dimensions to the enhanced mandate.

First, the college converted its programs into *two-year "associate diplomas" to provide a terminal credential which was also transferable to universities in other jurisdictions.* The Associate in Arts course for students taking arts and science courses, introduced in 1948,[95] was followed in 1956 by the restructuring of most of the post-secondary curriculum into two-year tracks such as Associate in Engineering, Associate in Business Administration, and Associate in Fine Arts. The Business Administration track led to the University of Western Ontario and American universities. Plans were afoot to introduce other diploma programs, all of them leading to a diploma "which could be negotiated, if desired, for transfer to a university for further study."[96] This was model for new two-year programs thereafter.

Second, the college continued to *develop "terminal courses" intended to "equip young people for various vocations,"* such as Secretarial Science, Stenography, Business Administration, and Medical and Dental Assistants.[97] In some cases, these became diploma programs too, but some were also delivered as one-year certificate programs. Some of these were aimed at young women. "Step into a well-paid job!" one ad declared, with a picture of a business-dressed woman; another, showing a woman at desk, said: "Plan now to fill a well paying job in the world of commerce.... All the cultural and social advantages of an academic college are yours while taking your course at Mount Royal."[98]

Third, the college *developed a large high-school-to-post-secondary education bridging program.* In 1948 the college had introduced a "bridge course between grade 12 and university" for students with "only three or fewer subjects to complete their matriculation requirements for university entrance." Its aim was not only to fill the deficiencies but to help students raise their academic performance: "Even some students who have completed their matriculation are obviously not well enough prepared for university, and should spend additional time in preparation instead of taking the risk of failing in their university work." This stream was separate from the high-school stream: students "with more than three matriculation deficiencies [should] register entirely in the high school department."[99] While the combined body of students in these programs made up nearly two-thirds of college students in the mid-1950s, the overall total shrank to barely more than half by 1965–66. The high-school dimension focused on grades 11 and 12, especially 12, and within the total the bridging program became the main activity. Agreements with the Calgary Rural School Division and Bowness School District, both lacking high schools, to encourage students to attend the college increased the high-school enrolment.[100] "We have students in both grades ten and eleven," Garden said, "but the large group is in grade twelve, many coming from more isolated areas in Alberta, Saskatchewan and British Columbia where they are not able to get the senior year of high-school training."[101] One noteworthy innovation introduced in 1954–55 was the "enriched" courses in grades 11 and 12 to enhance preparation for university admission.[102]

Fourth, in September 1948 the college launched its Evening College *continuing education program aimed at part-time adult students*. "All over America the junior colleges are doing special work in this field," Garden said; "there are thousands of adults continuing their education in the junior college. In fact it is becoming a distinctive contribution of the junior college movement." Tulsa College, for example, had a continuing education enrolment of over a thousand students in a city smaller than Calgary.[103] The courses were intended for "adults desiring to continue their education beyond the years of formal schooling." "No course will be started with less than six students. Each will consist of a two-hour lecture period a week."[104] Collett, who headed the operation, found the task of building the program hard slogging. It took a later generation, and perhaps a different urban demography, for continuing education to become the large function it later became. Though "more than 170 turned up" on 6 October 1948, opening night, for two-hour courses in such topics as "the rise and fall of human affairs," Russian, English, and Spanish, music appreciation, car driving, the life and times of Jesus, public speaking, geology, bookkeeping, and business administration,[105] enrolment remained small. To stimulate repeat enrolment, Collett introduced a diploma for students who completed eight courses; ninety-one were awarded in June 1951. However, he said, "the citizens of Calgary do not appear to be as 'adult education conscious' as citizens in some other cities. It will take some years before the citizens generally become aware of their needs and of the fact that the courses are available."[106] Indeed, the college was to find that the most popular courses it offered through the Evening College were high-school and bridging courses. In 1959, registrations reached 292, with 166 in high-school courses, and 126 in adult education courses.[107] In the early 1960s, the Evening School included university courses.

And fifth, *the college introduced the semester system* to capture a fresh intake of students twice a year. In May 1952 Garden reported that the province's superintendent of high schools was open to the idea and that there would be three goals: to attract grade 12 students who wanted to complete their senior matriculation (including make-up courses); to provide an opportunity for students "required to assist in the harvest fields"; and to enable a "more efficient mastery of each subject."[108] After the minister of education approved the idea, the college announced its intention to introduce semesters in September 1952.[109] However, the announcement was premature. The college found it had to negotiate the matter on two sides – with the Department of Education, which had its own view on the length of semester and related matters, and with the faculty, concerning workload implications. Though the semester system was introduced in 1953–54, with the unequal semesters the government required, it took until January 1955 for the government to agree to two semesters of twenty weeks each and for the workload and compensation effects for faculty to be thrashed out. One of the advantages of the semester system was the capacity to complete entire grade 12 courses within a five-month semester. Though the semester system increased registration of grade 12 students in the second term, one unexpected consequence was a rise in truancy. In place of "the average type of youngster," Collett said, "we were picking up students who had not been successful in high school and a lot of them had habits of skipping classes." There was a "growth in discipline problems and it wasn't a matter of misbehaving; it was a matter of missing classes and getting behind."[110]

While there was a good deal of internal consensus on the new directions, the college's lack of a working relationship with the University of Alberta and its orientation toward American universities raised questions within the college itself. Why, an internal report asked in 1959, "in spite of high fees and makeshift facilities," did the college have more university-transfer students than it had had when it was affiliated with the university? There were two obvious reasons. The university's rigid admission requirements denied access to many students who found its foreign language admission requirement "ridiculous" or who, "for want of one subject, . . . are required to wait out another year before starting their career." By contrast, the college provided a "more adult environment" and offered a flexible curriculum, permitting students to make up a matriculation deficiency while also taking university-transfer or career program courses; moreover, students who took the "pre-professional" programs could either carry away a career credential or seek transfer credit in a university.[111]

Clearly, both the college's growth and its experience suggested that there was a significant demand for a more open and flexible university education than was on offer in Edmonton and that there was also need, in an age of soaring demand for higher education, for the flexible, multi-faceted institution that Mount Royal had become. By this time, the government itself had begun to pay greater attention to the narrow range of educational opportunities available in the province, notably in the form of the Public Junior College Act, 1958, opening the way to junior colleges around the province. However, the government, the proponents of colleges in towns across the province, and the university itself were still some distance away from recognizing that such institutions could or should be more than deliverers of the university's first-year courses.

AFFILIATION – LAST CHAPTER

In May 1957, anticipating the government's intention to pass the Public Junior College Act in 1958, the university Senate proposed new rules for affiliation that were clearly designed to prevent junior colleges from having the latitude enjoyed by Mount Royal. The rules stipulated that all "courses and programs of studies for university credit must be approved by the University Committee on Junior Colleges," that "junior colleges affiliated with the University of Alberta may not have or enter into affiliations or accreditation arrangements with other colleges or universities without the permission of the General Faculty Council," and that "all documents which an affiliated institution proposes to issue for public information and which purport to contain a statement of the institution's relationship with the university or other universities shall be submitted before printing for the approval of the president of the university."[112]

In response, the Mount Royal board of governors resolved on 13 May 1957 that, while it was "completely satisfied with the affiliation with the University of Alberta and feels that it adds to the prestige of the college," it would not accept such constraints.[113] On 26 May 1957 Garden presented a report to the Senate entitled "The Affiliation of Mount Royal College with the University of Alberta" in which he explained the college's role in offering university-level courses. They were for "students who do not achieve the matriculation standards required by the University of Alberta but who should not be denied the privilege of some higher education" and who "can be graduated with an Associate Diploma which gives them some educational standing in the community." "A large number of American universities . . . take these students and allow them to advance towards degrees, granting varying amounts of credit for the work done in the junior college."[114] Finding that the new rules would limit the college to offering courses leading only to degrees in history and economics, the college's board voted on 25 March 1959 "to end the affiliation and carry on our own junior college program of terminal courses." Though some members wondered whether the college's credibility would be jeopardized, others "felt that our reputation and standards would be sufficient to maintain the relationship with American universities."[115]

At the same time, however, the college managed to persuade the university to consider a more specific form of affiliation – this for students who had only one matriculation deficiency that could be made up while taking university courses.[116] The university agreed. Once again, the college agreed to university control over the content of its courses, the qualifications of the faculty, and the assessment of student work, but these constraints did not relate to any of the college's arrangements with other universities or the transfer of students to American or other Canadian jurisdictions. The new program began in September 1959 with a first class of fifty students.[117]

Meanwhile, the evolution of the university's branch campus into the University of Alberta–Calgary continued. In July 1959, the university announced an expansion of arts and science offerings for the fall term.[118] In 1963, when responsibility for affiliation agreements shifted from Edmonton to the

Calgary campus of the university, the college found a much more welcoming partner in the new institution. Collett warmly greeted the change: "Our instructors now have direct access to the heads of the departments at the university and we have found there an interest and concern that has been very helpful. The college has also been given membership on the Council of the Faculty of Arts and Science which meets monthly and is a very valuable contact."[119] Thereafter the affiliation issue faded as an irritant for the remainder of the life of the private college.

FACULTY

From 1944 to 1959, the faculty complement more than doubled, rising from eleven to twenty-eight; of those, three were women in 1944 and ten were women in 1959. There was high turnover. Beginning with the war, but continuing thereafter, the college found itself in open competition with school systems for faculty members. Doris Anderson, who later became well-known as a feminist and author, was a student in 1943. Her memory was not entirely positive: "The classes themselves were dreary, the instructors uninspiring. To make up for what I was certain was inferior schooling, I worked extremely hard, and not only passed with distinction in all my subjects but also won two bursaries – one in English and one in history. At the end of the final term, I gave the valedictory address."[120]

Not surprisingly, there was a lot of faculty turnover. In 1956, only seven of the eighteen faculty members had been there in 1952; in 1959, only nine of the eighteen on staff in 1956 were still there. As a result, the administration devoted considerable time to recruiting faculty. The longest-serving faculty members were the department heads – Owen A. Kelly (English, 18 years); Ralph W. McCready (Science, 18); Otto H. Deutsch (Science, 9); Albert T. Thompson (Mathematics, 9); A. A. Ariano (Language, 10); and J. Walter Hepburn (Business, 14 since returning in 1946).

Teaching for the private college always entailed a financial sacrifice compared to teaching in public school systems. The instructors were either there, like the unit heads, because they were committed to its mission or because they had no alternative. To compete, the college needed to become more systematic and open in its compensation practices. In 1947, a board committee recommended adoption of a salary scale based on degrees held, ten (later eleven) annual steps, a range from $2,000 to $3,000, and annual increments of $100 to the top of the range.[121] It also recommended "a definite plan of pensions" in the form of "the Government Annuity Plan which provides for a maximum of $100 per month on retirement," with the individual contributing 5 per cent of salary and the board 5 per cent.[122] The hope of being included in the Alberta Teachers Retirement Fund was dashed, as it was limited to public institutions.[123]

Though there was a history of informal discussions, formal collective bargaining with academic staff began in 1953–54. It was triggered by the lack of consultation of faculty members when the board had decided upon compensation in the previous year and by the introduction of the semester system, whose originally unequal semesters triggered a proposal to raise faculty teaching hours from 21 to 25 a week.[124] The board was at first reluctant to engage in negotiations, passing a motion "that the teachers be advised that the board is not in a position to accept their proposals and that the following schedule is the maximum to which the board can go; and that a letter be sent to the teachers accordingly."[125] Seeking bargaining assistance, the faculty group associated with the Alberta Teachers' Association (ATA), formed a bargaining team, and demanded the right to be consulted about workload and compensation.[126] Some of the resentments had to do with Garden's parsimonious outlook. (Collett later said that Garden "was a hard man so far as salaries were concerned; he didn't like to pay out any more money than he had to."[127]) The board finally agreed "to a meeting with the academic teachers of the college, the board to be represented by the chairman, the principal, the dean of the college and four or five other members to be named by the principal."[128] The resulting agreement for 1955–56 included the addition of a step on the salary grid (to 12 steps) and a board commitment to contact the minister of education "regarding the possibility of something being done to get our teachers on the Teachers' Pension Fund."[129]

The Conservatory of Music

The number of students registered in Conservatory lessons rose from 245 in 1941 to 660 in 1960, a growth rate similar to that of the college as a whole.[130] Adjusting to that growth, with the problems of finding studio spaces so student practice did not disrupt other activities and the fit between young children and adult students, was not easy. On the main campus, "every available corner [was] being used to its limit" and the Conservatory was "greatly handicapped with unsatisfactory accommodation where the student and faculty are mixed with the resident students." In 1954, the Conservatory opened a branch on the North Hill of Calgary for up to one hundred students.[131] Board member Grant MacEwan led a campaign to raise funds for space in the 1957 addition to the Kerby Memorial building.[132] However, space and noise problems related to the Conservatory remained a constant concern.

In the meantime there was some staff turnover. Leonard Leacock, the pianist and composer, remained – and stayed for four more decades. Among the noteworthy additions in the early 1940s were Norma Piper, the diva soprano who had made an international career,[133] and Gladys Egbert, a long-time piano teacher in the community (and Leacock's teacher).[134] As the Conservatory lived off fees, the recruitment of students was vital. After "a lengthy and animated discussion on the advantages and disadvantages … of house-to-house canvassers or agents as a means of getting students" in 1942, the members decided to canvass themselves.[135] In the same year Galperin revived affiliation with the Toronto Conservatory and made the college a testing centre.[136] He added new musical instruments to the teaching roster. With Ruttan, for example, he attracted some two hundred students for classes in violin, banjo, and Spanish and Hawaiian guitar.[137] Galperin was a grand promoter of music and music education in Calgary, greatly raising the college's local and national profile.

As part of his reorganization of the college, Garden formalized the relationship to the Conservatory, which was supposedly a financially self-sustaining enterprise, but with the college, liable for any deficits or legal consequences. He initiated the board's Conservatory of Music Committee (Stanley, Ford, and Garden) to establish "closer cooperation between the Conservatory of Music and the board of governors" and to "bring about a closer affiliation of the orchestra [fund-raising] committee with the college." A job description and employment contract were drawn up for Galperin and form appointment letters for faculty.[138] Policies adopted in 1944 "recognized" the Conservatory "as a definite branch of Mount Royal College" which must have a "definite budget" and seek "to balance the budget each year." "The engaging and dismissing of teachers is in the power of the board of governors on recommendation of the director through the principal," and there must be contracts for everyone.[139] The director was put on salary rather than paid a percentage of revenues. The budget for the Conservatory was to include "a proper percentage of the overhead expenses of the college" to be approved by the Finance Committee, all proceeds from recitals and lessons were to be "carried in the books of the college, and all transactions in connection with the Conservatory of Music. . . recorded therein"; and a "ticket system" was to be "inaugurated, whereby the students purchase tickets at the office admitting them to lessons with teachers of their choice." The financial records of the Mount Royal College Symphony Orchestra were to be audited annually, and the "music and instruments which are now available to the present Symphony Orchestra shall be held in trust by the college so that they may be made available for the use of the present and succeeding orchestras."[140]

When Galperin left for Vancouver in late 1944, he was replaced as director of the Conservatory by Cyril Mossop, the Choir Master of Knox United Church and a member of the Conservatory faculty. Under Mossop, the Conservatory broadened its mandate to include a ballet program which lasted until the end of 1950, when he departed for another post.[141] He was followed as director from 1951 to 1957 by Harold Ramsay, a former Conservatory student who had performed for years in New York and London and returned to Calgary in 1950 as organist-choirmaster of Wesley United Church.[142] Ramsay sought to lay the groundwork for a degree program, for which he arranged an affiliation with Trinity College; he also introduced an examination system leading to certificate and diploma awards and an external examiner system.[143] (This practice was continued: in the 1960s the examiners were from the University of Alberta in both Edmonton and Calgary,

McGill University, Regina College, University of Manitoba, and University of British Columbia, as well as select independent teachers and government inspectors).[144] Ramsay broadened the scope of instruction to include accordion, tympani, and xylophone, and "the popular style of piano courses,"[145] and mounted a pioneering "folk Mass" for a graduation exercise.[146]

Clayton Hare replaced Galperin as head of orchestras. Hare was a violinist who was often accompanied on tour by his wife, pianist Dorothy Swetnam. With a view to drawing on a wider pool of talent than the Conservatory could provide, over the resistance of Garden, he changed the name of the MRC Junior Orchestra in 1949 into the Calgary Symphony Orchestra.[147] From the demise of the Calgary Symphony in 1939 to the development of a new community orchestra in 1955, the college's orchestras played a singular role in Calgary's music life.[148] In 1955 the Calgary Symphony Orchestra merged with the Alberta Philharmonic to form the Calgary Philharmonic Orchestra, ending the college's singular role in orchestral music in the city.[149]

Following Hare's departure in 1951,[150] John S. Bach became head of the Junior Symphony. A descendant of the great composer, Bach had studied at the Royal Academy of Music and taught in Sydney, Australia, before joining Mount Royal to work with the Junior Symphony. A Mason and a Methodist, Bach belonged to key social networks in which the college was embedded. His wife, Georgina, also worked in the college, replacing Jean Garden, the principal's wife, in food services.[151] With the evolution of the former Junior Symphony into the Calgary Symphony Orchestra in 1955, he had to restructure and regenerate the orchestra program. In 1965, he developed an ambitious program for "orchestra training in Calgary," including a junior orchestra, an intermediate orchestra, and the Southern Alberta Youth Orchestra. Frank Simpson was then hired to oversee this swarm of activities. In the 1970s, the college was to initiate development of the Canadian Association of Youth Orchestras (CAYO).[152]

Of the fourteen Conservatory instructors in 1943–44, only one had a degree; the others held specialized credentials, such as the Alberta Teaching Certificate in Music (ATCM).[153] Two decades later, the core faculty was three times the size but the range of musical credentials was higher, some holding degrees,

most holding multiple forms of music accreditation. Over the years, moreover, the college had developed fourteen "associated branches" where affiliated faculty members taught. The programs consisted of pianoforte, organ, strings, woodwinds, brass, harp, percussion, classical guitar, singing, and music theory.[154]

Some of the turnover in the music staff was due to the 20 per cent administrative levy, some to female instructors having children, some to personal relocations, still others to disputes. When instructors took students with them, the college lost revenue.[155] Among those who joined the Conservatory in the 1950s were Knight Wilson, a violinist and former department head of the Conservatory in Regina; Queena Hawke, who taught voice and became Garden's wife after the death of his first wife Jean; Peter J. Hodgson, who taught piano; and Mary Munn, a concert pianist who had been blind from birth.[156] Despite the turnover, the Conservatory produced students who scored high in examinations and won prizes at the annual Provincial Music Festival.[157]

While speech arts and drama had been part of the college's curriculum since 1911, the appointment of Leona Francis Paterson in 1944 had brought a new scope and dynamism to them.[158] "I was given a studio in the basement of the old college building," she said later, "and it had the pipes all running above which leaked when the weather was cold." She recruited students and hired two faculty members to assist her. Her drama lessons were "so popular that we had to lock the doors for the rehearsals because they [the students] all wanted to come in and see what was happening and sometimes to participate."[159] Among her initiatives were the introduction of Children's Theatre in 1951 (with Jack Medhurst),[160] the Readers Theatre (a very popular activity), a course for radio and TV presenters (Clarence Mack),[161] a speech-therapy program for children with hearing difficulties (with Reta Wilk and Laura Muir),[162] and a new theatre arts program (with Tom Besse). Explaining why she prepared a special course for Petroleum Engineering students, she said: "I feel so strongly that it is necessary for young people to know how to present themselves in front of an audience, whether the audience is one or two [people] or three hundred. They have to know how to sell themselves."[163] Emulating the external examiner system in music, she introduced also a board of examiners for

Conservatory Symphony Orchestra, 1958. Mount Royal
University Archives C3-5.

speech arts.[164] As a pioneer in speech arts, she published a textbook, *Creative Communications*, and articles on topics such as voice production, readers theatre and choral speech. She was founding member and served as president of the Canadian and Alberta Speech Associations. Among her other associations, she was an active member of the Knox United Church.[165]

When Ramsay resigned as director in April 1957, twelve Conservatory instructors urged the board to hire a replacement with a musical background.[166] However, Collett, who described the staff as "restive, perplexed" and roiling with "poor personal relations," was vexed by being "constantly confronted with dissatisfaction on the part of the teachers."[167] He established a committee consisting of himself and members of the staff to oversee activity. Within four years each of the music and theatre departments had its own director – first Hodgson (1962–64), and then Bach

(1964–74) in music, while theatre and speech arts were led throughout by Leona Paterson. Reflecting the new reality, the Conservatory of Music became the Conservatory of Music and Speech Arts in 1961–62. In the hope of building diploma programs in music and theatre, the college established the Fine Arts Division in late 1965, with Hodgson as overall director (1966–67), followed by L. C. Purnell (1967–69). However, the venture did not succeed, and in 1969–70 the Speech Arts and Conservatory directors were listed separately and equivalently in the calendar under the Conservatory of Music and Speech Arts label.[168] In 1974, when Bach retired, the two sides were reunited in the Conservatory of Music and Speech Arts, with Paterson as director (1974–77).[169] Thereafter there was to be only one director.

Throughout, however, the Conservatory played a major role in promoting community awareness of the college. Thousands of students who had no other contact with the college took music lessons there, and thousands of others attended the college's concerts, plays, lectures, and art shows. Under Paterson, the Speech Arts program became a seedbed for similar programs across the country. After retirement, she observed that there were at least twenty private teachers in Calgary who had passed through the college "and others in Edmonton, Red Deer, Lethbridge, and Medicine Hat"; indeed, "we have them all over the country and that's because we started it at Mount Royal. It is very important and I am just delighted to be able to say that to somebody."[170]

STUDENT ENROLMENT AND CAMPUS LIFE

The social and recreational life of students reflected both continuity and change. Young people would have fun. Patricia Roome, after assessing the content of student yearbooks, observed that "the snake dances, powder puff football games and dribblethons of the late 1950s and early 1960s welcomed Mount Royal students into a lively youth culture, but the seeds of these wonderful traditions were sown in previous eras."[171]

Student publications were recurrently overhauled. In 1942, the student yearbook was renamed *Varshicom* and, with the help of advertising revenues, became a notably improved publication. In the fall of 1949 the *Scratch Pad* was replaced by *Emarcee*.[172] In the 1950s several new publications emerged, all in mimeographed format. In 1953–54 there was the *206 Peeper* and the *Tattler*, in 1954–55, the *Acquaintance* and the *Pennant*, in 1955–57, the *Ink Spot*, and from 1957 to 1959, *Collews* (college plus "news"),[173] "edited and published by Mount Royal College Press Club." Their content was much the same – essays on idealistic or critical matters, stories on social and athletic events and the history of the college, profiles of students and staff, stories and jokes, cartoons, wry commentaries, and letters to the editor. Toward the end of the 1950s there was an effort to include literary content, including stories, poems, book reviews, and spoofs.[174] In February 1960, student publications began to take on a more permanent character. The *Royal Reflector*, later followed by the

Reflector, introduced a weekly organ that reported on in-house activities, such as the establishment of a High School Dormitory Students Council – an informal council, the publication indicated, because the organization had not been "officially designated as such."[175] More critical student reporting had begun.

One sign of creeping Americanism in Canada, and in Alberta, was the introduction of cheerleading in 1951–52.[176] It was a female activity and lasted only until the early 1960s, when the college had a short-lived Canadian football team. The next effort to enliven attendance at games consisted of "Calvin Cougar," a mascot introduced in 1980–81 to enliven college athletic and recreational events.

After a brief hiatus arising from the war, drama productions were resumed in 1942–43 under Grace Trinder, director of the Department of Dramatics and Elocution. The club chose the name "The Mount Royal College Masquers." Its first production was a one-act play, *The Minuet*, followed by *In Spite of Our Families* and a version of the Pygmalion story, *The Carved Woman*.[177] The drama program continued through the 1950s.[178] The Conservatory continued to offer concerts, recitals, and players for dance bands. Indeed, so long as the college remained in its downtown facilities, student life was permeated by the sound of music. Isabel Munro Wishart, a student in 1942–43, remembered fondly listening to orchestra practices and recitals.[179]

During the war the question arose whether young women should attend dances without a male escort. A survey by the *Scratch Pad* found that 55 per cent of the respondents thought they should, 45 per cent that they should not. "Why can't something be done about the shortage of men?" a female columnist lamented. In the same year a "Varsity Ball" was held in Lethbridge for "all those who have or are attending university or college; there was a remarkable turnout and Mount Royal College was well represented, the college being affiliated with the University of Alberta."[180] As a result of the more adult student population, there was also a new rule for student residences in 1944: "The use of intoxicating liquor is absolutely prohibited" and would lead to expulsion.[181]

After the war, student social life became more vigorous. In 1945–46, for example, *Varshicom* referred to an initial reception and dance ("a first 'mingling of the masses'"), a Sadie Hawkins dance, a Basketball dance, the "little red school house" dance, Christmas dinner, a New Year's formal, the Varsity Hop, and the Donnybrook Ball.[182] An Engineers Ball, with selection of a queen, emerged in the 1950s.[183] There were competitions to name Mr. and Miss Mount Royal College.[184] Earl Wilmott, dean of Residence for more than a decade, reported that "residence life is a tough job. I tried to treat the students with democratic discussions. . . . " The panty raids were "organized to the hilt. . . . They organized the raids like a battle—fuses were pulled and tossed out in the snow so it would all happen in darkness. And water fights—they'd fill up solid metal waste paper baskets. . . . The water would slosh down the stairs. . . . "[185]

Cheerleaders added to sporting action, ca. 1955. Mount Royal University Archives G29.

Though the war disrupted activities, some sports continued, and team achievements were recorded in the *Scratch Pad*. The 30 November 1942 edition, for example, carried stories on the girls' basketball team, entry of the boys' hockey team into the city's Junior Basketball League, and the results of hockey games.[186] The basketball, hockey, and bowling teams played in local leagues against high-school teams, the Institute of Technology, the Normal School, Olds Agricultural College, and community teams. Intramural sports included badminton, bowling, and ping-pong. However, as UATC and other wartime obligations became more demanding, athletics suffered. In January 1944 Garden said that "the war situation is playing havoc with our sports and games."[187] At the end of the war, with the influx of more men, sports regained a prominent place in campus life. Basketball became the most publicized sport. The men's team played in the Senior City League, which included teams from the military bases and community teams from Calgary, Lethbridge, and other cities. The Stanley Gymnasium was filled with intramural competition based on the house system introduced in 1951.[188] The leagues included girls' volleyball, bowling, basketball, badminton, gymnastics, and cheerleading, and men's teams for skiing, curling, boxing, badminton, ping-pong, and bowling.[189]

The Student Council operated like a student club. Only after the college became public did the board of governors, conscious of its duty of care when collecting funds to transfer to the Student Council, require the formation of a formal corporate body. The role of the council fluctuated. In 1944–45, in addition to its own officers (president, vice-president, treasurer, secretary, and sports and social editors), it included the presidents of students in the university, commercial, and high-school programs.[190] In 1947–48 there were two presidents – one before Christmas (David E. Mitchell), the other after Christmas (Richard Irvine). In 1949–50 a representative of the Petroleum Engineering program appeared, plus one from each of the five high-school home rooms.[191] In 1957–58, the council was divided into the High-School Council, and the Junior College Council.[192] Each council then set a social schedule, which for the junior college group in 1958–59 included the "Sweetheart of Mount Royal College" ball, a bus excursion to Banff, and a graduate banquet and dance,[193] and in 1959–60 nine dances and the selection of a school sweater.[194]

In addition, there were class clubs. High-school students were often organized in a Hi-Y club, a Christian leadership development group. However, as the college grew larger, students felt a decline in "school spirit." In 1954, Angeline Poppel deplored the situation: "Good Old MRC's school spirit would put to shame even a kindergarten! Where is it?" Some students worked hard to organize events, such as the recent Athletic dance, she added, but few attended. "What is the matter with us? Are we too high-hat to do anything for a little fun? Or is it that we're so used to having everything handed to us that we won't work for it?"[195] In 1959 Allen Garrett, the editor of *Collews*, also lamented the decline, attributing it to a reduced number of student "assemblies," poor notice of events, and the semester system, which "tends to break up the pattern of school life just when it should be at its best."[196] A few months later "orchestra dances" were replaced by "record dances" because "of poor turnouts."[197] At

year's end, "a disgusted student" wrote: "I would like to see this school 'pop' with genuine school spirit next year. Wouldn't you?"[198] But the good feelings students associated with their high-school experience could not be replicated, due to the scale and diversity of the college and its scattered facilities.

The Christian Environment

"The outstanding opportunity of a church-related college," John Garden said, "is the freedom that we have for teaching religion and for relating it to the whole life of the college."[199] Maintaining the semblance of a Christian environment was a preoccupation. Initially, Garden gave daily chapel sessions. In 1944, he reported on "the Daily Assembly and Bible Training": "Each morning from 10:30 to 10:45 the students assemble in the auditorium for a bright brief service conducted by the principal assisted on occasion by outstanding ministers and leaders . . . There is always a good attendance and the students seem keenly interested," though "we would like more student participation."[200] Students were required to take ten one-hour courses in religion and Bible study.[201] The one-hour included topics such as "The Parables of Jesus," "How We Got the Bible," "The Story of the Old Testament," "The Sermon on the Mount," and "Science and Religion."[202] In 1943, the *Scratch Pad*, in a survey of the student body, found that 80 per cent were Protestant and 15 per cent Catholic and that most students attended church three times per month. As another sign of the moral environment, on the question of whether girls should go unescorted to dances, 55 per cent thought that, in wartime circumstances, they should while 45 per cent said no.[203]

The college still attracted students intending to become United Church ministers. Bill Sayers, a student from 1948 to 1951, recalled that "we formed a theology club when I was there because . . . there were three or four or five of us heading into the ministry. . . ." Informally, he said, "you were aware of the church connections of most of the teachers: Owen Kelly active over at Wesley, Don Smiley . . . at Trinity, John Garden . . . [at] Scarborough." Otherwise the connection to the United Church was not visible.[204] Some students belonged to campus organizations such as the Student

Christian Movement, the Intervarsity Christian Fellowship and the Young People's Union.[205] However, as the student body became older, the temper of the times grew less religious, and more students enrolled on a part-time basis, "it became increasingly difficult to herd everybody into the [morning] assembly," Collett said, and "finally we abandoned it as it became unmanageable."[206]

To provide a Christian "emphasis" in the college, Garden proposed several measures, including: hiring Christian instructors "whose teaching is done in an atmosphere of intellectual honesty, reverence and respect for religious truth"; "conducting assemblies, morning devotions in each class, vesper services, white gift pageants, study groups, and definite Bible courses in the regular curriculum of the college"; and making facilities available for religious organizations. Garden created the position of Director of the Religious Education Department, to which he appointed the Reverend Sydney R. Vincent in 1955. A year later Vincent reported on what he had found: "Many and weird are the concepts of the students as to what is actually in the Bible and what the Bible teaches. . . . Add to this that in each class there may be up to six or eight Protestant denominations represented, and you will see that at times it is a little ticklish in answering questions without giving offense."[207] One result of his appointment was the Christian Education program using ministerial volunteers. Vincent also developed a "Christian Leadership Certificate" awarded "for the successful completion of Religious Education courses." Two hundred and ninety were awarded in 1955–56.[208]

The multi-denominational approach included classes for Protestants organized by the Canadian Council of Churches and the availability of priests for Roman Catholics. Religious education courses for Protestants included "Introduction to the Bible" and Science and Religion, while Catholic students took "Natural "Apologetics" and "Christian Apologetics." There was also an open course on the "World's Living Religions." A diploma program in religious education was introduced in 1962–63.[209] Thus, despite the diversity and secularism of the time, the college's leadership strove to maintain a certain a religious tone on campus.

A CHANGE OF GUARD

In the fall of 1958 Garden announced his retirement effective at the end of the calendar year.[210] Like Kerby, he had been a tireless booster of the college and given to some exaggeration. During a fundraising event, Wilmott said, a faculty member leaned across to ask: "Earl, is he talking about the college we're working in?"[211] But Garden was much more than a booster. Under his stewardship, the college had been reshaped. It had secured a broader legal mandate. He had established a coherent academic administrative structure and recruited qualified department heads. The college had introduced new programs, credentials, and delivery methods – the two-year diplomas that were either "terminal" or transferable; one-year certificates; continuing education courses; the semester system; the bridging program from high school to university; the Evening College. It had survived the end of its special relationship with the University of Alberta and reoriented its programs toward American universities. It had nearly trebled in enrolment and facilities. Garden left the college in a sound financial position. Moreover, he had raised the college's profile across the country and in the United States. In sum, Garden had provided noteworthy leadership to the college in a trying time.[212] In 1962 he moved to Victoria, where he died on 24 December 1969. His leadership was later remembered in two forms – initially in the Garden Meditation Centre on the campus of the public college, later in the Dr. John H. Garden Memorial Park.

JANUARY 1959   *William John (Jack) Collett becomes Principal*

1964   *University and College Assistance Act provides funding for university courses offered by private colleges in affiliation with the University of Alberta*

1965   *Board seeks conversion to a public college under the Junior Colleges Act, with a board representing the public and Catholic separate boards and existing board of governors*

1966   *Mount Royal College Act amended to change name to George W. Kerby College, freeing name for use by a public college*

30 AUGUST 1966   *Mount Royal Junior College Act passed and proclaimed*

CHAPTER 5

COMPLETING THE MISSION, 1959–1966

Most will agree that Mount Royal Junior College has fulfilled the original purpose and has been a valuable asset to the citizens of Calgary for the past fifty years. However, as a private college, Mount Royal can no longer provide the programs demanded of the comprehensive junior college at reasonable cost to the students. In order therefore to continue the purpose of the founding fathers of Mount Royal College and the efforts of so many public spirited citizens over the years, the present board of governors of Mount Royal College is prepared to turn over the operation of the present college, together with all assets and liabilities, to a new public junior college under the name of Mount Royal Junior College.

– L. A. Thorssen, Board of Governors, 1966[1]

When Dr. William John (Jack) Collett became principal on 1 January 1959, Mount Royal was entering its final phase as a private institution. This was not immediately apparent. The board of governors and Collett anticipated sustaining the college into the indefinite future. However, changes in the post-secondary sector were placing serious limits on its capacity to continue as a private institution, and the roiling waters of change were eroding the sands under the college's feet. For the next six years, the board and senior administration teased every possibility out of the college's mandate and opportunities. They increased recruiting efforts and enrolled more students, trimmed existing programs and introduced new ones, raised fees, tried fundraising. But it was all to no avail. Facing increasingly sharp financial problems and rising competition from heavily subsidized public institutions, the private college was in a battle it could not win.

The 1960s saw a continent-wide proliferation of public colleges of various kinds. Ontario developed Colleges of Applied Arts and Technology (CAATs) to offer terminal career-oriented programs with no transferability or integration with the universities. Quebec resolved the issue differently, with its Collèges d'Enseignement Général et Professional (CEGEPS) offering, after grade 11, two years of university transfer and three years of career preparation.[2] By contrast, the western provinces were influenced by California's master plan, which provided for a laddered but coordinated post-secondary system extending from community colleges through teaching-oriented state colleges to research-intensive universities. The development of the higher education system in Alberta was influenced by, without emulating, the California model. However, it was to take some time to break the junior college mould, which limited the conception of most Alberta colleges to the idea they should offer only University of Alberta courses to fully matriculated students. The head of a government task force on junior colleges, Andrew Stewart, declared in November 1965 that such colleges "were not doing the proper job of a junior college since they accepted only matriculated students and taught only first-year University of Alberta courses;" "junior colleges should be comprehensive."[3] This was not a problem for Mount Royal but for the emerging college system.

PRINCIPAL COLLETT

Collett, who had enthusiastically embraced the community college model, steered the private institution through its final phase and the initial stages of its conversion into a public institution.[4] Like his predecessors, he had deep roots in the United Church and in the social gospel. Born in England in 1910, he had been raised in Calgary, graduated from the Normal School, and begun a teaching career. Deciding to seek more education, he earned BA and BD degrees at the University of Alberta and an MA at Columbia University. Entering the ministry, he served in St. Paul, Taber, Lethbridge, and Claresholm, where he was when appointed director of the Evening College in 1947.[5] He was a leader of the Alberta Tuxis Parliament, a boys' organization fostering Christian leadership skills,[6] and a dedicated member of the Masonic Lodge.[7] Working with Garden, he said later, "you never knew what your responsibilities were," except they were always expanding. Over time, "the responsibility for administration just fell on my shoulders and ultimately, when I became the dean of the college, for the whole of the academic program."[8] He shared his predecessors' view that education was a form of ministry: "Education and intellectual reclamation of young people is an essential part of spiritual salvation," he said; "to this task is the church college called."[9] His community engagements including serving on the boards of the Calgary Public Library and the Community Chest and for twelve years as an elected trustee on the Calgary Board of Education, becoming chairman in 1961. This background was to become important when the college began looking for public support in the form of association with local school boards.

In 1961, when Clinton Ford stepped down as chair of the board of governors, Howard Phin Wright, a lawyer from Airdrie on the northern flank of Calgary, replaced him. A member of the board since 1955, Wright was thoroughly familiar with the college and was a valuable ally to Collett and to his successors during the major transitions of the next decade.[10]

Not long after becoming principal, Collett told the board that "there has been an extensive decentralization of authority during the past month, and an attempt made to delegate responsibility to individuals

William John Collett, Mount Royal College Principal 1958–67. Mount Royal University Executive Records GO010-05Col.

Howard P. Wright, Chairman of the Board 1961–70. Courtesy of Howard Wright.

of ability and proven loyalty to the college. This is a principle to which I enthusiastically subscribe and believe that it will do much to add to the efficiency of the operation of the college."[11] Sid Vincent, Director of the Religious Education program, replaced Collett as dean of the college. Max Rae continued as business manager and Earl Wilmott remained as registrar. In addition, Ralph McCready remained the Director of the Junior College Division, Owen Kelly, Director of the High School Division, Walter Hepburn as the Director of the Secretarial School, and F. James Hawkes as Director of Counseling Services. (Hawkes later became a professor of psychology at the University of Calgary and the Conservative federal MP from Calgary West from 1979 to 1993.) Collett worked with and through an Administrative Advisory Council. "Composed of the principal, dean, registrar, business manager, the director and heads of departments," he explained, "it exercises advisory, executive and disciplinary functions."[12]

In addition to internal challenges, Collett also had to cope with a rapidly changing post-secondary environment in Alberta and with the general cultural tone of the 1960s, which was not favourable to paternalistic institutions like the college and in which authority of all kinds was called into question.

PROGRAM INNOVATION

It is not clear whether the proliferation of new programs during the last five years of the college's private existence was due simply to the gathering momentum behind the community college vocation or whether it was due to a desire to offer yet more programs to entice fee-paying students. In either case, the result was expansion in the scale and variety of programs.

The Business Administration Department added more courses, evening delivery, a correspondence course, and extension to Red Deer in co-operation with local businesses.[13] Enrolment grew from 81 students in 1960 to 125 in 1962 and 425 in 1963, not counting the 100 students in Red Deer. The courses included marketing, business law, salesmanship, supervision, organization, accounting, human relations, public speaking, public relations, and executive secretarial skills.[14] By 1965, 40 per cent of college tuition revenue came from courses offered by the commercial, career, and secretarial programs and business development projects.[15]

In 1962 a two-year petroleum land-management diploma program was launched in collaboration with the Alberta Association of Petroleum Landmen to prepare negotiators of land leases and purchases for energy companies.[16]

A radio and TV broadcasting program was begun in 1963, supported by a one-year Speech Arts certificate program for announcers. Starting in 1963 with five students and increasing to thirteen in 1964, it provided training in "basic techniques for work in the field of broadcasting." Students in the television stream took courses in business administration, English composition, speech (voice production and training), and secretarial science (typewriting), while those in the radio stream studied the fundamentals of broadcasting, drama, history of the theatre, music appreciation, script writing, and announcing.[17] The radio and TV broadcasting programs required extensive practical experience, initially at CFAC, later at the college's studios on the new campus opened in 1972.

Commercial class, 1961. Mount Royal University Archives HA47.

The wartime Journalism program had faded away but was revived in 1963 as a two-year diploma program. Shaped by local practitioners, including John Howse, formerly of the *Calgary Herald*, and Peter Hepher and John Balcers of the *Albertan*, the program started with fourteen students and grew to twenty by 1966.[18] Students got practical experience through writing for and laying out or "making up" the student newspaper, the *Reflector*, and through on-the-job experience at the *Albertan*; following the relocation of the college in 1972, the students began producing their own organ, *Journal 3009*, named after the room in which it was assembled (and in 1992, it was to become simply the *Journal*). The principal aim of the program was to "develop the skills and attitudes that we thought necessary to get them [the students] into a small weekly newspaper to start off their careers . . . ," but another was to equip them to transfer to four-year journalism programs in universities, such as the University of Washington.[19]

Interior Design emerged to address the need for designers to lay out workspaces and select office furniture and décor for businesses. Interior design was becoming increasingly professionalized, and the college program was to play a part in that regard. Beginning with ten students in 1963, the program grew to fifty-seven in 1966. In addition to a core arts-and-science requirement, the courses included art history, architecture and architectural history, furniture design, colour theory and harmony, and the use of various materials and textures; much of the program was studio-based.[20]

In 1964, the college introduced a program to prepare leisure and recreation coordinators for communities and corporations. Starting with a class of eleven students; the program reached a total of eighty-three in 1966.[21] Many of the practical experiences took place in city of Calgary facilities. The program included the methods and skills for organizing indoor and outdoor activities, working with groups, preparing outdoor-education programs, the administration of recreational organizations and activities, and skills in arts, crafts, music, and dance.[22]

Like most universities at the time, the private college required courses in physical education. However, also like the experience on most other campuses, the requirement was abandoned in 1967.[23] Building on the compulsory courses, college introduced a two-year diploma in physical education in 1965 as both a terminal-credential and university-transfer program. The initial class of twelve grew to thirty-one a year later.[24]

Two other curricular initiatives were begun but failed. In 1964, building on the Speech Arts' program for the hearing impaired, a Speech Clinic, with a focus on stuttering, was opened in 1964 under the direction of Laura Muir. Referrals came from physicians, health personnel, and psychologists. It was the first clinic of its kind in Calgary, and a considerable caseload developed. However, the University of Calgary hired Muir away, and the clinic ceased operation.[25] In 1964 the college also introduced a library-clerk program. Though one of the instructors was W. R. Castell, head of the Calgary Public Library, the program was cancelled for want of students in 1967.[26]

All of the other new programs were to be continued through the transition to a public institution. Yet other curricular ideas were also bubbling up. Don Thonger, who was a graduate of the college and had served as student council president, undertook a feasibility study for the development of a "police science" program, and such a program was to be launched after the conversion of the college to public standing. In 1964 the Evening College introduced a course in English for the benefit of "new Canadians."[27]

Describing Mount Royal's unique features in 1963, Collett flagged:

- the semester system, which among other things enabled students to complete high-school courses in five months;

- the matriculation/university program offered in affiliation with the university;

- the career programs "for students who may not aspire to a university degree but feel the necessity of studies beyond the high school level;"

- the Evening College, which was now offering "both high-school and university courses on the semester plan"; and

- an admission policy which "attracts students who may not be able to find a place in the public system," including "adults who wish to return to school but would not be at home in a public school, students who have been problems to their schools and themselves and must find other ways of obtaining an education, and students whose home situation makes it necessary for them to be sent to a residential school."[28]

To assist weak students and those making choices in the face of proliferating options, the counselling function, which had begun in 1955, was finally separated from the religious guidance service provided by chaplains and established as an independent function in 1964.[29] The Director of the Student Services Division was responsible for counselling, residence supervision, student discipline, student affairs (including non-academic athletics), and remedial programs. Both of the initial directors had come from the YMCA – first Bud Gamble, then Jim Hawkes. They brought a professional approach to the role and assumed responsibility for relations with the student associations and student activities.[30]

Flexibility and innovation were the strengths on which the college built during its last days as a private institution and that were to continue into its public stage. However, there were costs attached – the front-end costs of mounting new programs, the higher costs of recruiting faculty with particular specializations, in some cases the need for customized space and special equipment, and coping with the advising and academic support needs of weak adult students. These added to the weight of mounting financial difficulties experienced by the college.

The Students

From 1958 to 1965–66, college grew from 593 students in academic programs to 1,452, an increase of 145 per cent. In proportional terms, the college grew nearly as much in those seven years as it did in the period from 1941 to 1958. Though high-school enrolment also grew (from 411 to 768 students) in those years, the proportion of students in the high-school division fell from 69.4 to 52.9 per cent of the total enrolment. By contrast, the junior college – or post-secondary – division doubled (from 19.5 to 48.6 per cent) of the total. The pace of post-secondary growth greatly accelerated with the addition of the new career programs in the early 1960s.

Surveys of the student body in 1962 and 1964 showed that about 56 per cent gave a Calgary home address, 33 per cent came from elsewhere in Alberta, 6 per cent from British Columbia (and rising rapidly), 2 per cent from Saskatchewan, and some 2 per cent from elsewhere. More than half (61 per cent) were male, but with a revealing distribution within the divisions: boys outnumbered girls 324–127 in the high-school matriculation program and by 162–45 in the junior-college program, while the girls dominated the non-matriculation high-school program (mainly commercial studies), 88–1. There was as yet little indication of the much higher participation rate of women that lay ahead. Their expectations appeared to remain traditional. In terms of age, 4 per cent of the 747 students in 1962 were 15–16; 47.2 per cent, 17–18; 29.4 per cent, 19–20; and 19.4 per cent, 21 years of age or older. "The student body is gradually getting slightly older—fewer under 18 and more over 20;" "there are about two boys to one girl."[31] The religious profile was still heavily Protestant but Catholics and others now constituted nearly one-quarter of the total. Another

FIGURE 5.1 ENROLMENT TRENDS, 1958–65, BY MAJOR DIVISIONS

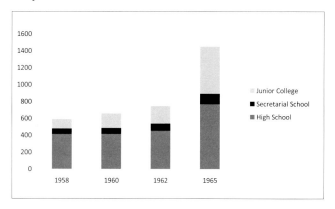

SOURCE: Based on data in the Principal/President Reports to the Board of Governors.

FIGURE 5.2 ENROLMENT BY MAJOR CATEGORY, 1958–66

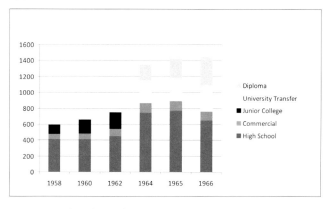

SOURCE: Based on data in the Principal/President Reports to the Board of Governors.

survey of students in 1964 generated similar numbers and noted that "enrolment in Arts and Science and in Career programs has increased year by year; enrolment in Business Administration has varied slightly" within a narrow zone (71–82 students); "enrolment in Engineering [had] decreased" since the end of the Petroleum Engineering program (falling from 44 in 1959 to 9 in 1962 and 10 in 1963).[32] In 1962, 172 students lived in residences (including 48 housed in the YMCA), the vast majority of them male.

Despite the "second-chance" nature of the student body, some students did reasonably well where

FIGURE 5.3 REGIONAL ORIGIN OF STUDENTS, 1962 (%)

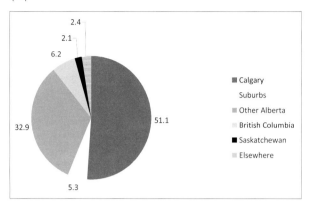

Calgary
Suburbs
Other Alberta
British Columbia
Saskatchewan
Elsewhere

2.4
2.1
6.2
32.9
51.1
5.3

SOURCE: Report of a survey of students, minutes of the Board of Governors Annual Meeting, 29 November 1962.

FIGURE 5.4 MALE AND FEMALE STUDENTS, 1962 (N=747)

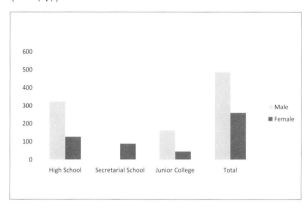

Male
Female

High School   Secretarial School   Junior College   Total

SOURCE: Based on a survey of students, minutes of the Board of Governors Annual Meeting, 29 November 1962.

comparisons were possible. In 1962, for example, "the results obtained by Mount Royal College students [on provincial examinations] are the best we have had in the last five years," Collett reported; students did better than the provincial standard in three subjects (English 30, Physics 30, Biology 32), and the percentage of college students scoring 50 per cent or over was 56 per cent, "which approaches very closely the provincial standards of 60 per cent."[33] Those who passed through the college's university courses or transfer programs appear to have done well. Of the 50 students in the combined matriculation/university program in

1962–63, 33 completed matriculation and 20 received university standing in four subjects. Of the latter, 17 transferred at the end of the year to the University of Alberta-Calgary, of whom 11 secured a pass to a full program and 5 were required to write a supplemental exam; only one failed. A former student at in Oklahoma reported that "of the class that left Mount Royal in 1960, twelve are here at the University of Oklahoma and five students have made the Dean's Honour Roll . . . I was thinking that this is a pretty good representation from Mount Royal College."[34]

However, Collett conceded, "our results are not always better than the provincial average. We have a rather high percentage of students who have failed previously and are trying to make up" and "we do not weed out students who are not doing well."[35] Serving weak students was a huge challenge, Jim Hawkes, Director of Counselling Services, told the board. "This is frequently a very personal, time-consuming job with frequent setbacks. . . . Poor reading skills, inadequate study habits, lack of motivation, mathematics problems etc., these, and many others, are problems shared by large numbers of our student body."[36] To cope with student needs, the counselling function expanded and a learning skills specialist was added.[37] However, the growing strain raised the question whether a private college resting on student fees could successfully implement an "open door' or "second-chance" admission strategy with limited resources. This was to be an issue for the college even after it became a public institution. The college was not funded, then or later, at the level required by an "open door" admissions mandate.

STUDENT ACTIVITIES

In 1962, the high-school and junior-college student councils agreed to merge "in the interests of more efficient student government," but it took two referenda for the change to be approved finally in 1965.[38] The constitution of the merged bodies provided for an Executive Council of seven members plus elected representatives from five program councils (Business, Engineers, Arts and Science, Commercial, and Career); the officers were given extensive powers, including the enactment of bylaws and the administration of funds.[39]

THE ROYAL *Reflector*

The Student's Voice of Mount Royal College

VOL. 1, No. 1   CALGARY, ALBERTA   NOVEMBER 30, 1962

BANFF CONFERENCE
FIRST AT M.R.C.

COMMERCIAL COMMENTS

The commercial society of M.R.C. is now in full swing for the school term of 1962-1963. The new executive elected in October consists of Sharon Hammer as President, Carol Maran as Secretary, and Bonnie Robertson as Treasurer. The Society Representatives are Sally Storey and Charlene Norberg.

The annual Sadie Hawkins Hard Times Dance, sponsored by the Commercial Society, will be held on Friday, November 30th, in the Mount Royal College Gymnasium. Music is being supplied by the Kmonsters from KMON radio in Great Falls. The Platter Party will begin at 8:30 p.m. with doors closing at 10:30 p.m., and the dance will continue until midnight. The admission will be 75 cents per person and one dollar per couple.

Due to the fact that the Gym floor has just been varnished, the Students' Council would appreciate it if the students would wear sneakers or soft-soled shoes.

This open dance has been the biggest success of the school in past years, so let's hope for the same this year. Come and support the school and the Commercial Society at the Hard Times Dance on Friday, November 3rd. Everyone welcome.!

AROUND TOWN

St. Mary's—To celebrate a successful junior football year, St. Mary's is sponsoring a banquet, to be held November 28, at 6:00 p.m. in the Stampeder Hotel. The price is only $2.50, and you are invited to help celebrate a victorious year, while having a real good time.

St. Mary's is sponsoring a debating team which will be sent to Lethbridge to test the mettle of St. Francis' debators on the question of Canada's position in the Cuban Crisis. As this is a matter of concern to all, we wish St. Mary's the best of luck in their search for insight into this problem.

Central—November 22, 4:00-7:00 p.m. was Coney Island Day for the students of Central and surrounding schools. A miniature midway, set up to raise money for the underprivileged in North-Eastern Brazil, was promoted by the Central Y Teen, which also provided a special guest speaker in the person of Mrs. Catto, President of the Y.W.C.A. She spoke on the conditions in present day Brazil and proved very interesting. Hats off to Central for a job well done.

All educational institutions and other worthy groups are invited to submit news to the Reflector. We hope the lack of off-campus news is remedied by the next issue, as we shall be glad to receive your material.

A precedent was set the weekend of November 10 this year when the first annual Mount Royal College Student Government Conference was held at the Banff School of Fine Arts. The purpose of the conference was to make student government at Mount Royal College a more efficient and more effective learning process for all concerned, a purpose which was admirably fulfilled. Delegates have expressed unanimously the feeling that they are much better equipped to handle those jobs for which they were elected, and they have expressed the hope that future delegates will gain as much.

Student Board of Directors. Front Row (left to right): Georgina Gref, Linda Crimp, Charmaine Wagner. Back Row (left to right): John McCardell, Roger Askey, Don Thanger, Dave Smeal, Bob MacIntosh, Jim Hawkes.

Present at the conference were the High School Council, with the exception of two, the Junior College Council Executive, along with the presidents and one council representative from each society, three staff advisors, one principal, one girls' chaperone, one guest speaker, and one slightly weary chaplain.

The conference began Saturday morning at approximately 11:00 a.m. with the official welcome of all delegates by the chairman, Bob McIntosh, who then introduced M.R.C.s (no sarcasm please. Principal, Dr. W. J. Collett. Dr. Collet proceeded to officially open the conference, expressing hope for its success, and pride in the maturity and responsibility of the delegates. He stated some of the problems which have faced student government at M.R.C. through the years, and his hope that

some of them would be solved, as some already had been.

With the conclusion of this highly inspiring talk, which helped immensly to set a successful theme for the delegates, the chairman introduced Mr. E. Tyson, who gave a very educational lecture on parliamentary procedure. Mr. Tyson proved himself an expert in this field, and later made admirable contributions as an advisor when controversies arose over correct procedure.

This conference was then adjourned for lunch, at which the kitchen staff of the school excelled highest expectations, and convened again one hour later. A film supplementing Mr. Tyson's lecture followed.

(Continued on Page 3)

USE ONLY FOR WRAPPING FISH

Mrs. Bach formally requests all those who have Christmas cards being saved to come and pick them up immediately, before she sells them to someone else . . . how to brainwash a texan . . . give him an enema . . . we hope the person who took the sign off the students' lounge and nailed it to Mr. Hansen's door will pick it up at the Students' Council office and replace it . . . best of luck to the basketball team . . . we wish the students would clean up their tables in the canteen . . . Don Thonger had a fascinating partner for one dance a week or so ago . . . have you ever tried to put out a paper without a staff? We hope we will get some help on the next issue . . .

Inaugural issue of The Royal Reflector student newspaper, November 30, 1962. Mount Royal University Archives N2.

In February 1960 the Press Club sponsored a new monthly publication, the *Royal Reflector*. By that time it was a tradition that each new publication must lament the deplorable state of school spirit: "School spirit? Yes, we at Mount Royal have school spirit all right, but whose? The loyalty of the vast majority of MRC students is still firmly rooted to their ex alma maters," the high schools.[40] That publication was superseded in January 1962 by the *Reflector*, a fortnightly. "Why does MRC not have a printed newspaper comparable to UAC's *Gauntlet* or UAE's *Gateway*?," the *Reflector* asked. "There are two basic obstacles, both of which could be overcome" – money, and management – to which it added apathy, "the canteen disease." "Where is the enthusiasm usually found in an institution of this caliber? What can be done to stimulate interest and to arouse latent enthusiasm?"[41]

The answer, it turned out, was student radicalism.[42] In November 1965 the *Reflector* took on a completely new orientation: "The initial problem facing the staff at the beginning of the year was one of policy. We had to decide whether we would publish the type of paper the students would like to read or one that we thought the students should read. . . . We had to eliminate one section of our potential readership as we could not bring ourselves to publish a paper composed wholly of comic strips." The other two editorials then got down to business, addressing "the election game" in Canada and Rhodesia's break with the United Kingdom, "the most foolish mistake of her life." Cultural articles focused on Dave Brubeck and the Modern Jazz Quartet, folk and blues music. Student poems included one by Harvey Moscovitch that began:

Before we go

    Roll with me once more

Across the snow

    For we are dressed and hot

and grew much more steamy before its end.[43] The growing assertiveness of students affected the college in other ways as well. Students became more vocal about their needs for better study space and parking. Some complained about the bourgeois constraints incarnated in the rules, such as the one against gambling in card games in the student lounge. There were also calls for the legalization of marijuana and suggestions that a new student lounge should allow the consumption of alcohol.[44] The "1960s" had arrived at Mount Royal.

In November 1961 a closed-circuit student radio station, CMRC, began. Established by Charles Cook, an instructor in the Radio-Television Broadcasting program, the station initially broadcast to the college's food service areas. Operated by radio-television students,[45] it broadcast news, interviews, and commentaries, and covered student council meetings. In 1964 it claimed to have three thousand listeners.[46] Its choice of music became contentious in the mid-1960s, when tastes were fragmenting.[47]

A Film Club emerged. With a membership of eighty-three, it offered a series of films in the fall of 1968, including *The Virgin Queen*, *Who's Afraid of Virginia Woolf?*, *The Grapes of Wrath*, *Carry on Teacher*, and *The Collector*.[48] In addition, while the Drama Club continued, a Folk Singing Club and a Social Dance Club emerged. A Foreign Students Club appeared, as did political clubs. In 1966, the Young Liberal Association sponsored a slave-girl auction, at which twenty-five girls (and two men) were "sold."[49]

Dances remained a favourite student diversion. Most were organized by program-based student clubs, though there were a few college-wide occasions organized by the councils. Halloween became the occasion for Sadie Hawkins dances, hootenannies, and masquerade dances, while Valentine's Day inspired pajama and Roaring Twenties dances. Some were held in the college's canteen (to the sound of the nickelodeon) and others in the gymnasium, but the more formal ones occurred in dance halls. Sometimes the entertainment stretched the idea of what a religiously affiliated college might endorse. In February 1964 the students held a Monte Carlo night and two years later a Las Vegas Night, including bunny girls and a casino with business students as dealers.[50] On campus, the college's dress code – for example, women's slacks so long as they were tailored – was abandoned in favour of "come as you want" or "casual dress" days. Some young men went unshaven during exam periods.[51] The annual athletic banquet, known as the Blue and White Night dinner after the college's colours, continued, including the crowning of a Miss Cougar, but the "Ice Princess" or "Miss MRC" contest, seen as a beauty contest, succumbed to criticism.[52]

In 1964, the clubs functioning under the auspices of the Junior College Council included the Engineering Society, the Business Administration Club, the Arts and Science Club, and the Career Society. The High School Council was also busy organizing social functions, usually by grade.[53] "A highly successful Cheerleaders Club has accompanied our football team to Edmonton and Saskatoon. Other clubs which are, perhaps, in not such a flourishing state, include a Camera Club, a Ski Club, and an embryo United Nations Club."[54] As new programs came along, new clubs were added, such as the Physical Education and Recreation Club, the Nursing Club, the Social Welfare Society, and the Radio-Television Society.

The most dramatic athletic event of the period was the creation of a football team on 20 May 1960.[55] The Stampeders Football Club supplied the team with uniforms and equipment. Under the leadership of John Borger and John Casanova, players such as Larry Robinson, Gerry Shaw, Barry Pugh, Jack Turand, Bill Owens, Glen Hartley, and others, playing at Mewata Stadium, excited enormous popular support by winning the Alberta championship, defeating the Vancouver Blue Bombers in interprovincial competition, but losing in the Western championship against the Saskatoon Hilltops.[56] Attendance ranged from 1,500 for their first game to 8,000 and 12,000 for later games.[57] The college had never enjoyed such press and popular attention. But it was too much to expect continued dramatic success on the field, and, with the cost coming just as the college was heading into bankruptcy, the great adventure was ended in 1964.[58] Memory of the team and its glories lingered on, and in the 1980s efforts were made to revive it, but again the cost to the college, in a time of fiscal retrenchment, made it impossible.

Basketball was the least costly and the next most popular and effective promotional vehicle for the college. Jack Kenyon, a mathematics instructor who

Mount Royal's first football team, launching the Cougars team name, 1960. Mount Royal University Archives HC13.

1960 Mount Royal College Cougars Football Team
Alberta – British Columbia Junior Football Champions

Left to Right:
Front Row: 50 Wayne Patriquin; 53 Keith Hembroff; 92 Larry Robinson; Ken Morrison, Equipment Manager; Bill Casanova, Coach; Al Valdes, Coach; Coach; John Borger, Head Coach; Dr. W.J. Collett, President; Stan Matlashewski, Manager; 73 Chuck Mckenzie 40 Ken Bray.
Middle Row: 54 Barry Randall; 65 Ron Moore; 71 Craig Makin; 61 Tom Cormack; 47 Bob Chow; 64 Ernie Ross; 56 Jim Watson; 84 Gerry Shaw; Carl Surrendi; 81 Bill Eshom; 66 Eric Fairley; 74 Ron Smith
Back Row: 58 Trevor Ekdahl; 86 Moe Martin; 85 Glen Hartley; 98 Jack Truran; 99 Jim Leach; 97 Ro Riley; 94 Bill Goods; 82 Dennis Stiles; 70 Bob Rohaly; 89 Clarence Tomanik; 88 Terry O'Connell.
Missing: Tom Jones, Dick McKenna, Mike Pannett, George Slater, Don Watson, Joe Seriduk,, Alec Recsky, Vern James.

One of the early Cougars team insignias, which made its debut in the 1960s. Mount Royal University Archives *Cougar Nite Program*, ca. 1977.

Men's basketball action in the Stanley Gymnasium, ca. 1959. Mount Royal University Archives HC8.

remained in the post until he retired at the start of the 1990s), assembled first-rate teams that competed within Alberta against teams from other cities and eventually in college leagues provincially and nationally. Kenyon's teams won national college championships and defeated university teams. He also coached the national junior basketball team. Kenyon's cumulative record as a coach was a remarkable 198 wins and 26 losses, and posthumously he was inducted into the Canadian Basketball Hall of Fame in 2003.[59]

In December 1960 the college celebrated the fiftieth anniversary of its legal charter. Some two hundred alumni gathered in the Dr. George D. Stanley Gymnasium for a buffet supper and reunion on Saturday evening, and a jubilee service was held in Central United Church on Sunday. On Monday evening, the Conservatory presented a jubilee concert to about three hundred people. The good feelings led to re-establishment of the alumni association.[60] However, the association appears not to have received much attention, for in 1964 its secretary wrote to the chair of the board of governors, Howard Wright, and Harold Vaughan, secretary of the United Church's Board of Colleges and Secondary Schools, to remind them that section 15 of the college's charter required the naming of up to five alumni to the board of governors. Max Rae replied that the charter limited the number of board members to forty, and thirty-nine were already in place; he invited the alumni to nominate one member. The United Church replied that it had recently appointed new members and would not appoint more without consulting the principal.[61] However, the college was on the eve of becoming a public institution, with its new board membership stipulated in legislation that did not include an alumni representative. In 1967, the absence of a viable alumni organization to file annual reports with the government in accord with the Societies Act prompted the college to step in to organize at least that activity. Thus, while the college helped ensure its legal continuation, the alumni association existed only on paper until the 1980s.

THE CHURCH CONNECTION

The fiftieth anniversary celebration also inspired discussion of the college's connection to the United Church.[62] While the college continued to receive an annual grant "for Christian education" purposes ($3,100 in 1958–59, $3,600 in 1959–60 and 1960–61, $5,000 from then to 1966), the connection had become a formality. When asked by the Stewart Commission in 1965 to describe its links to church, the college replied that the relationship was "a little vague. There is some general policy relationship, some small financial assistance from General Council, but the real power would appear to be vested in the board of governors of the college." Appointments to the board were "rubber-stamped" by the General Council. Similarly, the local branch of the church, the Presbytery, "has no authority and the college no definite responsibility in this area." It was as if fifty-five years of the relationship between the college and the church had left everything in the same state of suspended animation found by the Massey Commission back in 1921.[63]

Still, as we have seen, college leaders remained committed to religious education and to collaboration with the religious community. When asked by the Calgary Presbytery of the United Church in 1964, the college introduced a two-year diploma Christian Education program to train church workers and prepare students for the seminary.[64] The college still charted the religious orientation of students. In 1964, 40 per cent of all students had a United Church connection, 14.5 per cent an Anglican background, 28 per cent "other Protestant," 13 per cent Roman Catholic, 0.5 per cent Jewish, 2 per cent "other," and 0.5 per cent "none."[65] The Protestant/Catholic balance remained unchanged from what the Scratch Pad had found in 1943 (85 per cent Protestant, 15 per cent Catholic). However, there were never many students in the religious education courses: in 1965–66, when enrolment was mandatory, there were about three hundred registrants; 1966–67, seventy-five registrants; in 1967–68, fifty; and in 1968–69, fifty-six students.[66] Following the departure of Vincent, the new Director of the Religious Education Division, the Reverend Jack Wallens, oversaw the religious education courses, the new Christian Education program, the coordination of chaplains, and contacts with local churches.[67]

Barry Pashak, who joined the college as a teacher in 1962, described the atmosphere at the time as a mix of Christian observances (morning prayers and events in the chapel "that would go out on the kind of daily information sheet that would go out to all of the faculty") and a commitment "to what you might call a Social Gospel" on the part of Collett and other senior administrators. "There was a kind of broad liberalism . . . throughout the institution in terms of hiring and sensitivity to the needs of the community and in trying to present . . . the best sense of the Christian message."[68]

THE FACULTY

In the early 1960s the faculty was divided between instructors in the high-school courses who required certification as teachers and had a higher teaching load, instructors who were certified but taught only post-secondary courses, and post-secondary instructors, the latter two groups with a lighter reaching load. Each had its own association.

The ATA-MRC consisted of the certified teachers who taught in the high-school program; its name reflected its affiliation with the Alberta Teachers' Association (ATA), which provided advice in collective bargaining and pension matters.[69] In 1965, Bill 65 amended the Local Authorities Pension Plan (the Teachers' Retirement Fund Act also needed to be amended) to enable all certified teachers in the college, whether or not they were teaching high-school courses, to participate in the Teachers' Retirement Fund.[70] This divided the faculty into two pension camps – those with a teachers' pension, and those without an employer-based pension. It was only in 1970, with a further revision of the Local Authorities Pension Plan, that the non-teachers became eligible for a pension and both groups were brought into the new plan.[71] The Mount Royal Faculty Association was established to represent the post-secondary, non-teacher faculty. In practice, however, the agreement between the board and the ATA-MRC contained the provisions governing appointments, classification, compensation, teaching load, and responsibilities for both categories.[72] On several occasions Collett advised the two groups of faculty to unite, as in a letter to Douglas J. Turner, the chairman of the College's ATA group: "I have long held the opinion that the Teachers' Association has been ineffective in its negotiations because it is not all inclusive. And suggest that your group take steps to create a stronger body than at present exists."[73]

In 1963, the faculty consisted of 19 full-time equivalent (FTE) faculty teaching 276 full-time equivalent students in junior college courses and 22 full-time equivalent faculty teaching 573 full-time equivalent students in high-school courses. (The actual totals were 31 full-time faculty and 26 sessional instructors.) It is difficult to describe the teaching load because individuals carried blends of junior college and high-school offerings as well as administrative and counselling functions. In general, however, the template was as follows: 21 hours in high-school courses, about 15 hours in junior college courses, 21 hours in counselling services, and 24 hours in Secretarial programs. The FTE student-faculty ratio in junior college programs was 14.5 to 1 and in the high-school program 26 to 1.[74] At that point the calendar contained 130 university-level courses.[75]

By 1962–63, the board had ceded some control over teaching load to the Academic Teachers' Association of Mount Royal College. Article 5(b) of the agreement stated that "teachers will assume a reasonable number of hours of teaching and daytime supervision. Proposed schedules shall be submitted to a committee of the Teachers' Association for approval at least one week before the opening of any semester." In addition to instruction, teachers "agree to supervise and share in the extracurricular activities of the student body" and to "participate in religious activities of the college and will open the first class in the morning with an appropriate devotional period." The salary scale (fifteen steps, in three categories determined by degrees) ranged from $4,900 to $8,500. Full-time librarians were included in the academic staff.[76]

As the affiliation agreement with the University of Alberta required faculty university courses to have at least a Masters degree in the subject they taught, the result was a general rise in faculty credentials in the early 1960s – and, of course, in the costs attached to them. In the four years the college's calendar published the names of faculty approved by the university, a total of twenty-eight Mount Royal faculty were approved – six in 1960–61, ten in 1962–63, eight in 1963–64, and four in 1964–65.[77] The sources of their academic credentials indicated that the vast majority came from Canada, with only a sprinkling from the United States and elsewhere.

At this point, the category of "college instructor" was far from well established in Canada, and people entering into the field experienced some status anxiety as their professional identity evolved. Because of the variety of institutions, including the technical institutes, the role was not fixed in law until the Colleges Act of 1969. Moreover, circumstances at Mount Royal, which was manifestly sinking financially by 1963, did not encourage faculty to linger. Already, in 1960, the board committee for negotiations with the faculty had discussed problems with faculty morale. "The college is not meeting competition for instructors." It was being used "as a stepping stone to better positions," and at the end of each term there has been a larger percentage turnover resulting in a loss of efficiency."[78] Things did not change thereafter. Indeed, the annual turnover rate was about 33 per cent in the first half of the 1960s.

The Mount Royal Faculty Association decided to seek recognition as a bargaining agent in early 1966, and the Board of Industrial Relations, by a letter dated 2 March 1966, advised Collett that "the applicant trade union is a proper bargaining agent" under the article 63 of the Alberta Labour Act.[79] Given that circumstance and the pending end of the private college, the parties failed to approve a collective agreement to serve as a benchmark, though they sketched out many of its terms. In June 1966, two months before the transition to public status, Collett wrote the leaders of "the two Teachers' Associations . . . to express the board's regrets that have made the conclusion of negotiations for salaries in the 1966–67 academic year impossible."[80] The draft "faculty agreement" that had been developed included two categories – Instructor, "a member of the Mount Royal Faculty Association and teaches at the post-secondary level," and Teacher, "a member of the Academic Teachers' Association and teaches on the High School Level."[81] The consolidation into one group remained for the public college.

FINANCIAL UNCERTAINTY

Though the private college's revenue nearly tripled from 1957–58 to 1965–66, the institution sank steadily toward insolvency. Some of this was due to the cost of facilities expansion, some to new programs, and some to the higher salaries needed to compete with the school boards.[82] In addition, as Collett recognized, the college was expensive by its own nature: "We attempt to keep our classes small, give the students close supervision, locate and deal with individual problems and difficulties, and to give individual tutorial help to the student in academic difficulty."[83]

In 1961–62 the college needed a $250,000 bank loan to carry on. A year later, with operating revenues of $640,000, its liabilities had reached $282,000, or 45 per cent of revenues. Though it raised tuition fees and though growing enrolment increased revenues, the debt kept rising. In 1964–65, the last normal year of the private college, operating revenues had reached $1,212,000 and the debts stood at $424,000 ($34,500 overdraft, $209,000 bank loan, $181,000 "deferred bank loan"), or 35 per cent of revenues. The final financial statement for 31 August 1966 indicated that revenues in the previous twelve months had reached $1,344,000, while the deficit and loans had reached $507,000, or 42 per cent of the revenues.[84]

The college tracked the bottom line by area of activity. From 1959 to 1965, only the university transfer, Evening College, and Secretarial programs generated a positive bottom line. Every other sector – High School, Junior College, Business Administration, Engineering, Career Programs, and the Conservatory – lost money.[85] The Conservatory's deficit was to roll forward as a policy question for the public college – how much of the government grant or student fees, whether for credit or non-credit courses, should be used to subsidize the Conservatory?

Faced with growing insolvency, the board launched a series of fundraising efforts. In January 1962, a public-relations firm hired to study "the college situation as pertaining to public relations," recommended approaching the premier for capital funding "based on the principle of Provincial Government Aid to Junior Colleges," approaching the city, and launching a fundraising campaign involving 1,000 donors willing to pay $5 a month for three years (yielding

FIGURE 5.5 MAJOR SOURCES OF REVENUE, 1912-1964: % OF TOTAL INCOME

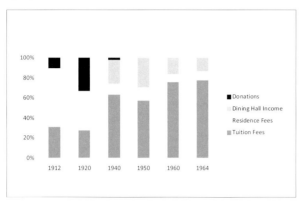

SOURCE: Based on a chart in EC minutes, 30 November 1939; supplemented by reference to the available audited financial statements (1922 forward).

FIGURE 5.6 SALARY COSTS AS % OF EXPENDITURES, 1920-1964

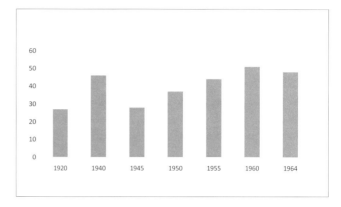

SOURCE: Based on a chart in EC minutes, 30 November 1939, supplemented by reference to the available audited financial statements (1922 forward).

TABLE 5.1 REVENUES AND EXPENDITURES, 1912-1965: MAJOR CATEGORIES

	Total Income	Tuition Fees	% of Total	Residence Fees	% of Total	Dining Hall	% of Total	Total Expenses	Staff Costs	% Spent on Staff
1912	42,210	13,186	*31*	25,024	*59*			39,020		
1913	64,929	18,750	*29*	30,633	*47*			65,722		
1915	39,884	9,951	*25*	26,095	*65*			37,960		
1920	70,152	24,576	*35*	35,539	*51*			71,257	19,528	*27*
1940	53,583	28,434	*53*	5,045	*9*	10,453	*20*	53,583	24,568	*46*
1945	116,931	54,176	*46*	14,975	*13*	30,011	*26*	116,391	32,625	*28*
1950	150,961	78,857	*52*	18,776	*12*	40,293	*27*	150,961	55,191	*37*
1955	242,888	150,272	*62*	24,872	*10*	54,883	*23*	242,888	106,428	*44*
1960	432,490	296,342	*69*	31,548	*7*	65,859	*15*	432,490	219,487	*51*
1964	880,813	600,061	*68*	68,005	*8*	104,137	*12*	880,813	424,365	*48*

SOURCE: Audited annual financial statements.

$180,000). But the requests to the province and the city were denied,[86] and the fundraising campaign generated only $15,000 in cash and pledges against a goal of $300,000.[87] In the fall of 1962, the college formed a Committee of Eleven whose task was to find 1,000 people to help raise $500,000, but neither good will nor hard work sufficed to raise enough money to keep the college afloat.[88] To add to the woes, the Ministry of Municipal Affairs in 1964 removed the college's tax-exempt status (granted by an amendment to the college's charter in 1950), requiring it to pay "for services such as police and fire protection and garbage removal."[89] Despite its best efforts, the college was on a downward fiscal slide that it could not reverse.

What lay behind the fiscal crisis? Was it the front-ending of new programs? Salary increases? The cost of serving weak students requiring extra attention? Lack of proper heed to the bottom line? The lack of private funding in an increasingly secular age? The explanation lay in part in all of these things, but there were other factors too, including the expansion of publicly subsidized programs at the Institute of Technology, recently re-baptized as the Southern Alberta Institute of Technology (SAIT),[90] the continuing growth of the public university across the river, and the high cost of programs requiring specialized equipment. For similar reasons, private institutions across the country were being converted into public ones.

THE ANDERSON REPORT

In 1962 Collett engaged Dr. Robert N. Anderson, an assistant professor of education at the University of Alberta–Calgary, to serve as "academic advisor" and to "conduct a major study of Mount Royal's academic program and . . . report to the board of governors of the college."[91] Struck by the fact that there was no Senate or GFC to engage the community or the faculty, Anderson began by recommending the establishment of a Senate. His vision of that body was of one made up of external experts, people who could help "assess existing activities and organization in their relationship to the accomplishment of objectives; identify both the strengths and weaknesses of the various educational programs; and provide a set of feasible recommendations for overcoming the weaknesses and

strengthening the total program."[92] Following consultation with the University of Alberta, the University of Alberta–Calgary, and the Calgary Board of Education, and having received their agreement to send representatives, Collett persuaded the board of governors to establish the Senate. Its mandate was "supervising the academic program of the college. The Senate is responsible directly to the board, recommends to the board matters of policy, and has no power in financial matters."[93] It held its first meeting on 13 November 1964.[94] However, the Senate disappeared with the establishment of the public college in 1966.

Meanwhile, Anderson had been preparing his report on the college. Completed in 1964, it was comprehensive and concluded with nineteen pages of recommendations. The board worked through the report in a special meeting in October 1964. Much the most important of Anderson's recommendations was that the board should explore the potential under the Schools Act for becoming a junior college under its auspices – in other words, converting itself into a publicly funded institution. It also recommended the establishment of a GFC, separating governance and administration functions, proper terms of reference for the board and a job description for the principal, who should serve as president and CEO, and clearer job descriptions for the dean, directors of divisions, and department heads. All communications to the board should be "through the president."[95] In the end, the impact of the Anderson report was less its recommendations on management or governance (the principal now became the president) than the impetus it gave to the idea of exploring the potential for becoming a junior college in league with the two local school boards. This was the route the board of governors was to choose.

TRANSITION TO PUBLIC COLLEGE

Though the Anderson Report helped start the modernization of the governance and management of the college, it did not and could not resolve the basic challenge, which was that of perpetuating a private college in an era when public institutions were expanding. In the minds of board members, the transition from private to public college may have begun earlier, but it became an explicit goal in the months following a meeting of board members with the Minister of Education, A. O. Aalborg, on 9 May 1963. Board members made the case for public funding. Responding sympathetically, the minister "suggested that some criteria would no doubt be the nature of the educational program and how it is related to other institutions such as the university, the size of the institution, and the extent of its services, and the specific services being given which are not rendered elsewhere." Asked "whether, since no public junior college is being contemplated for Calgary, Mount Royal College could receive funding like Lethbridge Junior College," the minister replied "that it might be reasonable if Mount Royal College were organized along the same lines as Lethbridge" – that is, operated under the auspices of one or both Calgary school boards. The minutes noted: "The disadvantage here of course would be our loss of connection with the United Church of Canada and possible loss of control and freedom of independent action."[96]

The meeting led to three initiatives. First, responding to the minister's encouragement, the board submitted a funding request in July 1963.[97] The following spring, the legislature approved the University and College Assistance Act (1964), which extended funding ($630 per student) to private junior colleges for full-time students enrolled in university courses offered in affiliation with the university; it also provided access to a provincial guarantee of up to two-thirds of loans for capital purposes approved by the minister. "This is the first step in a continuing program to recognize materially the work of the private colleges," Collett said. One of the first Mount Royal projects undertaken with a small government grant was the conversion of an old house into a student centre. Wyckham House, named after Robert Wyckham, an instructor and coordinator of student activities (1962–64), helped the students "redefine their organization and establish firmly the building and planning fund."[98]

Second, in anticipation of securing a loan guarantee for capital purposes, the board began reviewing sites on which "a worthwhile campus may be planned." In April 1964, Collett wrote to the Minister of Public Works, F. C. Colbourne, saying that press reports had indicated that the Lincoln Park airfield site in southwest Calgary might become available. "Should Lincoln Park become available to the Provincial Government I am certain that our board would be eager to discuss with you and the Government the possibility of an exchange of properties whereby we would take over Lincoln Park and the government assume possession of the buildings and land which are now a part of Mount Royal College."[99] He also raised the idea with the city, the minister of economic affairs, and the president of the Crown Assets Disposal Corporation.[100] In September 1964 he advised the board of the availability of the Lincoln Park site and that he had written a letter to the Chief Commissioner on 28 May 1964 "indicating an interest in the area and suggesting that an exchange of some of our property for Lincoln Park might be considered."[101] Without deciding on a site, the board voted unanimously to "view with favor moving from its present location." Developing a new campus was now a formal goal,[102] and the college's interest in moving to Lincoln Park was included as a potential element in the city's planning for the area.[103]

The third initiative was the decision to strike a committee to study the prospects of becoming a public junior college.[104] Chaired by L. A. Thorssen, the committee began discussions with the public and separate school boards in September 1964. The committee drafted a brief entitled "MRC – Proposal for Development" that foreshadowed what was to follow. It recommended creation of a "new" Mount Royal Junior College with the following salient features:

- the governing board would include representatives from the college, the Calgary Board of Education, the Calgary Separate Board of Education, and the boards of surrounding regions;

- the college would develop a new campus, supported by public funds and administered by the college board;

- the public and separate school boards (like those in Lethbridge and Red Deer) would contribute to the tuition fees of Calgary residents attending the college;

- the governing board would request that college course credits be evaluated, and its students considered for transfer to the University of Alberta, in the following cases: (a) students having matriculation standing; (b) adult students admitted to MRJC after successfully passing 2.0 GPA over the period of their attendance at the college ("it was also assumed that MRJC would be responsible for its own standards, since to recommend inadequately prepared students would be disastrous both to the student and to the relationship between the junior college and the university"); and

- the college would establish a provisional committee to study the above proposals and submit a report to the various interested boards.[105]

In a report dated 14 February 1965, Thorssen advised the joint committee that the minister of education had indicated that the government would amend the University and College Assistance Act to permit a junior college operated co-operatively by public school authorities, SAIT, the university, and the college to access operating and capital funding. A committee consisting of one trustee and one administrator from each school board, a member of the college's board and an administrator, and representatives of SAIT and the University of Alberta–Calgary, then undertook a more detailed feasibility study.[106] Its report recommended "the joint operation of Mount Royal College as a public community Junior College, by a board made up of three members representing each of the Calgary Public School Board, the Calgary Catholic Separate School Board, [and] Mount Royal College Board." Subsequent discussion led to the idea that the current college board would be transformed into the board of a Mount Royal Foundation that would "(a) become the trustees of the present property, (b) appoint three members to the joint board, and (c) administer net proceeds of the property and/or raise funds for special projects and programs within the new college which could not be done with public funds."[107]

In January 1966 the Mount Royal board agreed to ask for a revision of the college's charter to free the college's name for a new public junior college, to consent to the conversion of the old governing board

into the board of a new foundation, and to establish the framework for the transfer of assets. On 18 April, royal assent was granted to replace the words "Mount Royal" with the words "George W. Kerby" in the college's charter, thus establishing the foundation.[108] The board agreed to transfer to the foundation the sum of $140,000 "or the net assets of Mount Royal college, whichever is the lesser" and "to provide supplementary pension benefits to some long-time members of the present Mount Royal College staff for whom present pension provisions are not adequate, any surplus thereafter to be used for purposes that the Kerby Board may determine." The board also recommended that "the members of the present board be nominated to the General Council of the United Church of Canada for appointment to the George W. Kerby College Board of Governors."[109] Howard Wright, chair of the Mount Royal board, was to serve on that new public board from 1966 to 1970, providing a valuable linkage between the new college and the new organization.

On 18 April 1966 the legislature granted assent to the Mount Royal Junior College Act, 1966, which allowed the Board of Trustees of Calgary School District No. 19, and other school districts and school district in the vicinity of Calgary that wished to participate, to establish a public junior college with the name Mount Royal Junior College. The new college would fall under the provisions of the Public Junior Colleges Act, "except as otherwise provided in this Act," which focused only on transitional matters. These included: enabling the participating boards to make an agreement with the private college to take over its assets, liabilities, and staff; requiring them to agree on sharing initial and ongoing costs; giving them responsibility for determining the membership of the board of governors; and exempting Mount Royal Junior College for two academic years from the provision of the Public Junior Colleges Act that forbade offering courses taught by schools. The new college would come into being by an order-in-council following the negotiation of all of the details.[110]

The negotiations with the school boards culminated in an agreement approved by the board on 12 May 1966, signed by the parties on 18 July 1966, and sent to the minister of education for approval. On 26 July, the minister reported to the cabinet that the agreement was satisfactory and had his approval. The cabinet in turn gave its approval on 30 August 1966 and proclaimed the Mount Royal Junior College Act, 1966, enabling establishment of the new college by an order-in-council signed by Lieutenant Governor Grant MacEwan, the former board member. The private board held its last meeting on 31 August 1966.[111] The same day, the University of Calgary assumed sole responsibility for the affiliation agreement with the new public college.[112]

The public Mount Royal Junior College came into existence on 1 September 1966 with a governing board consisting of nine members – three each designated by the Calgary Public School board (Martha Cohen, L. A. Thorssen, Harvey Bliss), the Calgary Catholic Separate School Board (Joe Commessotti, William James, Bruce MacDonald), and the outgoing college board (Howard Wright, Lloyd McPhee, E. B. Lyle).[113] Meeting on that day, the new board named Wright as chairman and continued the appointment of Collett as president. Wright declared that "we are particularly pleased that after a year of negotiations, this has finally become an accomplished fact. We look forward to developing the junior college program." Collett said that he was "delighted" and that the college would be able "to serve the education needs of the community much better than in the past, and will give it a firmer financial basis. I look forward to the selection of a new site and the building of a college that will do justice to the needs of Calgary and district."[114] On 2 September, Wright advised employees of the name of their new employer: "Mount Royal Junior College is the legal name of the Public Junior College which was established by Order-in-Council on August 30th 1966."[115] On 9 September, he wrote to Minister of Education R. H. McKinnon, to conclude the process of conveying assets to the new college. In accord with the agreement, the public college would contribute $293,884 and the government $797,136 to acquire the land and property from the private college (appraised at $1,091,021). "The condition is that any balance remaining from sale and pension benefits for long serving staff would be used for scholarships and other assistance to the new college."[116] On 4 October 1966, Lieutenant Governor Grant MacEwan proclaimed the act changing the name from Mount Royal College Board of Governors to George W. Kerby College Board of Governors.

MISSION COMPLETED

Over the five decades of its existence, the private college had been a pioneering institution. On occasion, it had also been controversial. Its commitment to the individual progress of students, to taking them where they were on their learning curve and leading them as far as they could go, sometimes raised concerns about the quality of its standards, as expressed by government inspectors in the early years and by the University of Alberta in later years. At the same time, its commitment to a campus characterized by "Christian democracy" had not always pleased conservative Methodists, who preferred a sterner approach to religious education and discipline.

Through those five decades, the college remained primarily a deliverer of high-school courses rather than of post-secondary courses. For its first twenty years, it had also offered elementary schooling (grades 4 to 9), but, following its affiliation with the University of Alberta in 1931 and conversion to a junior-college role, it abandoned the lower-level classes in favour of university courses. Breaking the original mould also encouraged thinking about adding terminal-career programs for adults who did not intend to go on to university. By the end of the 1930s, the college was foreshadowing its later adoption of a community-college mandate.

Of possible futures, the option of becoming a four-year degree-granting institution would probably have been preferred by the college's founders and leaders, many of whom had championed the cause of a public university in Calgary and were frustrated by lack of success in getting one. However, given the province's one-university policy, that was never a realistic prospect. Indeed, even the college's role as a junior college offering the university's first-year courses was clearly transitional, dependent upon decisions by the province not to fund the expansion of the existing university or to build a new one in Calgary.

The college took on new colorations as circumstances changed. Finding it difficult to expand its junior college role in affiliation with the university, it had secured a change in its charter in 1944 that enabled it to offer courses accepted for advance credit by American universities. When the university established a centre in Calgary to offer arts and science courses in competition with the college, Mount Royal redesigned its curriculum around career programs and two-year diplomas in both career and liberal arts programs. When the university finally accepted that its admission standards denied many Albertans with minor academic deficiencies the opportunity to overcome them, the college negotiated an arrangement to prepare students to meet those standards and to complete the first year of study.

The change in the college's self-conception, from a junior college operating in affiliation with the University of Alberta to a community college offering a wide span of programs and its own credentials could be seen in the way the college's administrators measured success. Kerby was proud of the superior achievements of graduates when they took provincial examinations or performed in University of Alberta programs. Excellence against external standards was the measure of success, though he had also broached the idea of continuing education without such benchmarks. By contrast, Collett was proud of the college's role as a "second chance" institution. Added value to individuals was now seen as being at least as important as success against external standards.

Nearly continuous enrolment growth indicated that college programs were needed or wanted by Calgarians and others. The college's flexibility enabled thousands of Albertans to overcome educational deficits, prepare for careers or employment, or secure a foundation for degree-level studies – people who otherwise would not have had such opportunities in Alberta at the time. The college's decision in the mid-1950s to require general education in two-year career programs incorporated elements that continued the "civilizing" mission of the college in practical studies but also incorporated elements that were recognized for credit by American institutions, making the programs bridges to other options, not career training cul-de-sacs.

Orienting the university-transfer programs to American universities entailed risks. For students who transferred to U.S. universities, the risk was that of returning to Alberta and finding they could not enter the University of Alberta. In fact, however, other than in petroleum engineering, such problems were rare. For the college, the risk was that orienting university-transfer activities to American universities made sense

so long as the University of Alberta had no presence or only a modest presence in Calgary; it was to be unsustainable when the University of Calgary appeared.

Many practices adopted by the college derived from its experience and values but were reinforced by contact with American institutions after 1945. In the 1950s and early 1960s the college became a transmission belt into Alberta for U.S.-style ideas, practices, and values, notably with respect to the ideal of the community college and the implications of lifelong learning for educational institutions. In the end, however, the college could not generate the resources to continue with so ambitious a mandate in the face of a soaring participation rate in higher education that inspired the spread of public post-secondary institutions.

Had the college's founders been present at the end of its private existence in 1966, they might have wondered whether it had succeeded in its primary purposes – providing educational opportunities to people who otherwise might not have had them, and doing so in an educational, character-building environment permeated with Christian values. The answer to the first question was clearly yes. For five and a half decades, the college had served some thirty thousand students in its academic and commercial programs and nearly that many in music lessons. Its curriculum had evolved steadily, providing educational opportunities not otherwise available. Its former students, moreover, showed considerable satisfaction with their education. The founders would have had many reasons to conclude that the college had fulfilled its first purpose.

Had it also provided a Christian environment and a moral education? Here the United Church distinguished in its own deliberations between two types of institution – "an institution calculated to give a liberal education in a religiously conditioned atmosphere, the other an institution calculated to impart religious education in an intellectually conditioned atmosphere." Mount Royal belonged to the first category.[117] The distinction was in effect between a faith-tinged and faith-based institution. The college had exposed generations of students to the fundamentals of the Christian faith. Though chapel services had become optional in 1931 and were attended thereafter by only a small minority of students, they continued. In 1964–65, the services were interdenominational in nature and conducted by different people each day of the week. In the 1960s there were three chaplains who shared an office and were available at different times – a United Church minister, an Anglican minister, and a Catholic priest. In that period Robert Anderson wrote that, though there was no statistical evidence and he could only venture an opinion, the small classes and close faculty-student relations created a "religious atmosphere and a religious learning situation in which most of the students participate." Moreover, the environment encouraged thinking about large-order questions: "Perhaps a much more complete educational process is possible where young people at this vital state of their development are allowed to consider religion as one of the intellectual challenges they must face. There is not only the opportunity of free enquiry in this area but there is stimulation toward this kind of enquiry."[118] Indeed, it was never easy to fulfill the original religious and moral goals because of the college's diverse clientele and its non-denominational nature (which implied keeping the religious dimension at a general level) and the growing secularism of popular culture. Whether the college's religious environment, in turn, affected student values or behaviour is impossible to assess. Thus, all one can say is that the college provided the elements for a moral and religious education and that students had the opportunity to make of them what they would.

As a loosely church-affiliated institution, Mount Royal was subject to many of the trends affecting other religious colleges. In 1966 the Danforth Commission published a report entitled Church-Sponsored Higher Education in the United States. Many formerly religious post-secondary institutions were being converted into public institutions or closing down. The review of 817 colleges (12.5 per cent of them Methodist) found their strengths to be "freedom to experiment and to serve special purposes; responsiveness to able leadership, when provided; close student-faculty relationships; a good record (in some colleges) of preparation for graduate and professional study; concern for the progress of individual students; and espousal of humane values." Their weaknesses were "insufficiently strong in scholarly attainment of faculties, financial support, selection of students and faculty in relation to educational purposes, curricular design, implementation of religious aims, and self-evaluation." Most of these findings would have applied to Mount

Royal. The chief purpose served by religious colleges, wrote the commission, was that "they belong to the great tradition of collegiate education in the arts and sciences illuminated by the Christian faith. . . . At its best it is a broad and general education in that it stresses the arts of thought and communication and the principles which should govern personal and public affairs. It is the most useful kind of education, in the best sense of the word 'useful,' for its worth is not restricted to a particular occupation, a particular time or place, a particular stratum of society.... It should provide good preparation for responsible living in a rapidly changing world such as ours. Soundly conceived, it gives the student an understanding of the values that are most worth conserving in our heritage and of how they may be the guiding principles of the future."[119] Catholic institutions were finding the same challenges. "At the end of the 1960s," the historian of Saint Francis Xavier University has written, the "heritage of forming Catholic young people through a liberal arts residential program" had become "problematic." "Expanding enrolments, the imitation of trends elsewhere, the increasing religious pluralism of the faculty, the elimination of a prescriptive curriculum, and the dismantling of *in loco parentis* fractured the university's vision of education and its image of the ideal person."[120]

Even while it was adding more utilitarian programs, Mount Royal's aspiration to expose students to the broad perspectives of the liberal arts, religious studies, and languages so as to provide them with a heightened awareness of "the values that are most worth conserving in our heritage," while also cultivating their critical and reflective capacities, was an enduring legacy. In the public college, it took the form of a mandatory liberal-arts component in university-transfer and diploma programs. The general-education requirement was the residue of the original religious motive, that of civilizing and Christianizing the masses. It is a healthy residue. The overwhelming characteristic of modern higher education has been its utilitarian focus, as manifested in the weakening, if not disappearance, of liberal-arts requirements in undergraduate curricula and the proliferation of narrow applied programs preparing practitioners for occupational fields. It is testimony to the vision of Mount Royal's founders, administrators, and faculty that, even as the institution became a community college offering career-oriented programs, it continued to maintain its commitment to the liberal arts. It was the gift of the private college to the public college that followed it.

SEPTEMBER 1966	*Mount Royal Junior College commences operations, under guidance of Board of Trustees*
JANUARY 1967	*First two-year, diploma-based nursing program in Canada begins*
MARCH 1967	*President Collett departs; replaced by Ralph W. McCready, Acting President*
1 JULY 1968	*President Walter Pentz takes office*
1968	*Students Association of Mount Royal College incorporated (SAMRC)*
1969	*The Colleges Act passed; Colleges Commission established*
1970	*First Board-MRFA collective agreement under the Colleges Act*
	Faculty and student members join the board of governors
	Lincoln Park site for new campus approved and construction begins

CHAPTER 6

BECOMING A PUBLIC COLLEGE, 1966–1972

Liberation was in the air. . . . Young people everywhere were in revolt. . . . The rebellion kept metamorphosing. . . . Class politics gave way to cultural politics, then sexual politics, and, finally, ecological politics. . . . Historical consciousness and abstract talk of dialectics, materialism, and imperialism began to lose resonance to therapeutic consciousness . . . politics became group therapy. Talk of political revolution gave way to the quest for more personal spiritual transformation. By the early 1970s, process had all but trumped ideology.

– Jeremy Rifkin, *The European Dream*[1]

In the 1960s, Alberta governments crossed an important watershed in post-secondary education. Until then Alberta had pursued a single-university policy, regarded colleges as junior colleges under university control, and offered apprenticeship and other forms of training primarily from one site in Calgary. With large-scale federal government funding for training after 1960, Alberta turned the technology institute into the Southern Alberta Institute of Technology (SAIT) and established the Northern Alberta Institute of Technology (NAIT) in Edmonton.[2] It came to realize that colleges could also deliver job readiness, – vocational and career programs along with university courses. The shift in policy was articulated in Premier Ernest Manning's *A White Paper on Human Resources Development* (1967): "All individuals and organizations should have equal access to its programs and services," it said; "in education, this requires the expansion, decentralization and diversification of post-secondary and continuing education in all forms and development of co-ordinating mechanisms to ensure effective delivery."[3] The University of Lethbridge and Athabasca University were soon established, more public colleges were established (several including technical programs), and the technical institutes were expanded. Other innovations followed, including further education coordination councils, the Alberta Education Communications Corporation (ACCESS), and Alberta Vocational Centres for job readiness programs and basic training.[4]

These changes paralleled similar restructurings and expansions of higher education taking place across Canada and the United States. The proliferation of Canadian colleges of various types led in November 1970 to the establishment of the Association of Canadian Community Colleges (ACCC) to serve as a clearing house for information about colleges.[5] The changes also occurred amidst rapid population and economic growth. The population of Alberta was urbanizing, with Edmonton and Calgary alone absorbing "all [of] Alberta's population increase" between 1961 and 1971, almost all of it from people moving "from surrounding rural areas."[6] The first high-rise buildings appeared in Calgary, the Imperial Oil Building (1964), the Guinness Complex (1965), and the Husky Tower (1967). The city introduced the "Plus 15" internal walkway system to link the downtown core. New public institutions emerged, including the Glenbow Museum, the

Convention Centre, the central library, a performing arts centre, and the Centennial Planetarium. The city sprawled outward, with the suburbs linked to the core by highways. The downtown became a rather barren place, made up of large buildings and windy canyons, showing signs of life only during business hours.

The six years from Mount Royal's change into a public institution in September 1966 to its occupation of its new campus in September 1972 were filled with critical events. The province identified the college model it wanted. The college articulated is own vision to guide its development and to influence the shape of the emerging college system. Despite cramped temporary facilities, it mounted many new programs, designed a new campus, and nearly doubled the student, faculty, and staff complement. These events occurred at a time when generational revolt was rampant, and the college was not exempted. The period was rife with struggles over governance as the faculty, students, and governing board sought to establish their roles in relationship to one another in the new institutional context.

THE BOARD OF TRUSTEES

In accord with the college's new legal foundation, the board of Mount Royal Junior College became the Board of Trustees, and its membership, nominated by the three parties to the agreement (the old college board, the public and separate school boards), was appointed by the government. Howard P. Wright was named board chair.[7] The Board of Trustees inherited the administration, support staff, and thirty-six faculty members.[8]

Determined to protect Mount Royal's distinctive nature, the board's first significant declaration, one month after taking office, was a statement entitled "Mount Royal Junior College: Its Character, Philosophy, Aims, Programs and Instruction, and What Problems May Arise in Maintaining These in the Forthcoming Legislation for the Establishment of Regional Colleges in the Province." The college, it said, was concerned "firstly because of the effort that has been expended in attaining its character, and secondly because of its strong convictions of the rightness of its character."[9] This was followed by a "General

Martha R. Cohen, Chairman of the Board 1970–74. Mount Royal University Executive Records GO010-05Coh.

Russell H. Purdy, Chairman of the Board 1974–75. Mount Royal University Archives E216-1.

Statement of Policy" that Collett submitted to the board in December 1966 that defined Mount Royal as a "community college" whose "policy is to serve the community in areas where needs in education are discovered." It would strive to raise "the level of education in the community" by serving adults, whatever their educational background. There were to be no admission requirements. A student would "be able to discover an area in which he may profitably study" and that "this may mean a frequent change of program or readjustment." "The faculty must be devoted to teaching the student and not the subject. Each student is an individual seeking fulfilment and never loses the potential of success." Indeed, "the college will have failed in its commitment to the community if a student leaves its halls without having found some dimension of personal growth." Provided as information, the statement was not formally approved by the board, though there was probably a good deal of consensus in favour of it. Had the statement been approved, language about the religious dimension of education (not cited above) would have had to be removed.[10]

In 1969, the Colleges Act of 1969 altered the composition of the board to consist of the president, ex officio, a board chair and six public members chosen by the government, one member nominated by the Students' Association, and one member nominated by the Faculty Association. All were appointed by the government. The change in membership came in July 1970.[11] Martha Cohen replaced Wright as chair, the first woman to be formal head of a higher educational institution in Alberta; she served until 1972. The new members in 1970 included Glenn E. Holmes, a chartered accountant, elected vice-chair by fellow board members; Russell H. Purdy, a partner in Deloitte, Plender, Haskins and Sells, who replaced Cohen as chairman in 1972 and served until 1975, Ward A. Steckle, former principal of Canada Western High School, and Patrick J. Burns, manager of the Burns Foundation, heir to a ranching and meat-packing fortune. In 1970, P. Neil Webber, a mathematics instructor, became the first faculty member, and Marvin Symons the first student member.

Choosing a College Model for Alberta

Perhaps the most influential development relating to colleges in the 1960s was the approval of the California Master Plan for Higher Education in 1960. Described by Dr. Neil Smelser, a distinguished sociologist, as "among the two or three most important and influential innovations in higher education in the 20th century,"[12] it provided a coordinated set of institutions in three systems (junior/community colleges, four-year colleges, and research-intensive universities). The plan facilitated role differentiation (permitting each sector to build on its strengths and uniqueness) while providing a framework for credit transfer and credential recognition and in effect making a major step toward a system designed to facilitate lifelong learning.

The Canadian approach varied from one part of the country to the other, with the western provinces showing the influence of the plan and the rest of the country, fully aware of the plan, deciding on other models. In 1966 Ontario introduced colleges of applied arts and technology to offer one-year certificate and three-year diploma programs in career fields, without any connection to the university system; their diplomas were supposedly to enjoy "parity of esteem" with three-year university "General" degrees. Quebec's collèges d'enseignement général et professionnel (CEGEPs) offered two-year programs leading to university (three years of study in Quebec) or three-year career programs. While British Columbia and Alberta were influenced by the California model, they did not emulate it exactly.

Through a lengthy process involving study commissions, workshops, and conferences, the Alberta government slowly developed a conception of the kinds of colleges it wanted. In the process, it demonstrated "leadership of a kind not apparent earlier in matters regarding post-secondary education. After 1965, the government reversed the trend of local initiative, forced communities to revise their aspirations for their college becoming a university, insisted upon a diversification of college curricula and modified, to some extent, university control of colleges."[13] The Banff Regional Conference of School Administrators in November 1966 on the role of the junior college,[14] and a meeting on potential legislation in 1967,[15] set the

broad directions. Dr. Henry Kolesar, later Director of the Colleges Commission and the first Deputy Minister of the Department of Advanced Education, said that "the general functions of the two-year college are: (a) to broaden the base for higher education in Alberta; (b) to ease the problem of access to higher education; (c) to advise students according to their capabilities; (d) to provide a 'salvage function' to those students who have dropped out of school; (e) to assist students to adjust their aspirations in ways that make their potential and the requirements of specific programs compatible; and (f) to serve in some geographical locations as a cultural center for the community in which it exists."[16] The Provincial Board of Post-Secondary Education wanted the colleges to have an "eclectic" mandate to serve both personal development and societal needs.[17]

The Colleges Act of 1969 described the mandate of the "public colleges" in spare language: to provide "(a) courses of general, academic, vocational, cultural or practical nature, subject to the approval of the minister, and (b) short courses or short programs to meet the needs of special interest groups" (section 27). This description left great latitude for variety in the program mix and nature of the colleges. Another departure made the colleges members of "the public college system," a new and undefined entity.

From 1967 to its electoral demise in 1971, the Social Credit government developed two intermediary bodies. The first, the Provincial Board of Post-Secondary Education, established in 1967, was responsible for coordination, planning, and making financial recommendations, including developing draft legislation for the college system and negotiating affiliations with Alberta universities.[18] This was to this point "the most important government initiative in the eventual establishment of a public college system in Alberta."[19] It was replaced in 1969 by the Colleges Commission, whose role was to coordinate the development of the colleges, develop facilities and financial recommendations for the government, and serve as a buffer between them and the government and the universities on credit transfer issues.[20] The college system now bore "a very close resemblance to junior college systems in the western United States."[21]

Given their junior college origins, some colleges harboured the goal of becoming a university. The aspiration reached the point in Red Deer that, following the 1971 election, the minister named an administrator (replacing the board) to reorient the institution to a college mandate.[22] Inspired by the vision of itself as a workplace-oriented institution, Grant MacEwan College in Edmonton, established in 1970, offered only career programs.

The Conservative government that came to power in 1971 took more authority into its own hands. It established the Department of Advanced Education ("and Manpower" was soon added) to provide government coordination, terminated the University and College Commissions, and established the Council on Admissions and Transfers (ACAT), to coordinate the credit transfer fit between the colleges and the universities, ending the need for general affiliation agreements.[23]

In 1971 there were six public colleges – Mount Royal, Lethbridge, Red Deer, Medicine Hat, Grande Prairie, and Grant MacEwan, with three others being planned. Olds Agricultural and Vocational College became Olds College in 1970; in 1975, Alberta Vocational Centres were converted into board-governed Keyano and Lakeland colleges. College enrolments still reflected the junior college role: about 66 per cent of students were in university-transfer courses.[24] Looking ahead, government officials projected that 30 per cent of high-school graduates would seek university admission, 56 per cent college admission (in both career and university-transfer streams), and 14 per cent a job right out of school.[25]

IMPLEMENTING THE COMMUNITY COLLEGE VISION

This was a rare, yeasty time in the life of the college when the bubbles of change were working at all levels. There were lively debates over the nature and size of the required liberal arts component in career programs, whether the general education requirement could be met through university-transfer courses or other non-transferable courses, and over team teaching and mediated forms of delivery.[26] While the notion of open-door admissions was popular, the practical questions arising from it raised the issue of the balance between post-secondary programs and preparatory or remedial activities. Barry Pashak later recalled the

time: "There was a lot of conflict within the college in terms of what kind of institution we should be or become. There were those who wanted to get rid of the high school completely; there were those that wanted it to be a career training centre; there were people like myself that felt that whatever happened it should have an Arts and Science component that could stand alone but could also service . . . career students"[27] Ken Robson also recalled the debates: "The issue of the so-called 60-40 split that was the target for career and arts and science offerings in the new college put a lot of dust in the air. . . . The curriculum of the day was very fluid. Not only was Interdisciplinary Studies a venue for sometimes wild experimentation but the regular curriculum was also something of a moveable feast. There was very little standardization of curriculum. . . . Sections of the same course could vary enormously in content and requirements. . . ."[28] In 1970, the General Education component in all diploma programs was set at twelve of sixty credits, or 20 per cent, distributed across four areas of study, "namely, Communication, Behavioural Sciences, Natural Sciences and Humanities," and consisting of both non-transferable and transferable courses "from the appropriate Arts and Science" courses."[29]

Unlike the debates at the University of Regina, which shared Methodist roots with Mount Royal, the definition of the core liberal arts requirement was driven at Mount Royal by faculty members rather than by students.[30] While students at Mount Royal demanded participation on the board of governors and the *Reflector* carried stories intended to scandalize the orthodox, most showed little interest in what Steven Langdon, president of the Canadian Union of Students, advocated – "a more humane, critical and socially responsible curriculum."[31] No doubt many of the college's students wanted a practical education leading to a job and were not interested in theoretical considerations. Many, moreover, were only loosely coupled to Mount Royal at that point because they were registered in one-year certificate programs, in the first year of new diploma programs, or in evening classes. In such circumstances, it was difficult to be engaged in campus debates even if one wanted to be.

From the fall of 1966 to the fall of 1971, the college's last year downtown, enrolment rose from 1,506 to 2,706 registrants, an increase of 80 per cent. The

FIGURE 6.1 ENROLMENT TRENDS, 1963-67

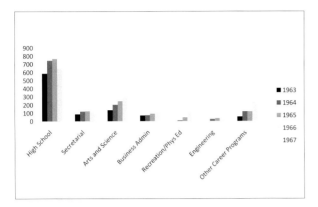

900		
800		■ 1963
700		■ 1964
600		■ 1965
500		1966
400		1967
300		
200		
100		
0		

SOURCE: Based on the Principal/President's Reports to the Executive Committee and, after August 1966, the Board of Trustees.

pace was quickening. Alberta college enrolments in 1969 and 1970 grew "by 12 and 37 per cent respectively."[32] New programs proliferated. In 1966, the college had offered eighteen programs; by 1968, the number had grown to twenty-five; by 1969, to thirty-four; and by 1970 to thirty-seven. Of the thirty-seven, ten were one-year certificate programs and twenty-seven were two-year diploma programs. In 1968, the Provincial Board of Education announced a policy that, "for at least five years, and until non-university programs are more fully developed, only transfer programs of the equivalent of one year to an Alberta university should be approved."[33] As a result, all of the new program additions were in career programs. To accommodate the growth, the college sprawled into nineteen buildings.[34]

In 1970, there were 2,216 freshmen at Mount Royal, and only 490 sophomores.[35] The dropout rate was high: in 1969–70, 670 of the 1,735 full-time students (38.6 per cent) "left school before completing a planned program." The reasons were "personal problems or concerns, followed in frequency by financial reasons and employment opportunities or interference." About one in eight explained that either the college or the courses they were taking "did not contribute to their educational plans as they had expected."[36]

Some of the new programs were pioneering in Canada. Hitherto nursing had been taught either in four-year university programs or three-year

hospital-based programs.[37] After attending a workshop on two-year nursing programs held in 1963 by the Northwest Association of Junior Colleges,[38] Collett persuaded the board to pursue the idea. In the same year, the government undertook a survey of schools of nursing in Alberta.[39] Collett quickly learned how complicated the issue was: responsibility for all nursing education was under the control of the University of Alberta; the government had commissioned Dr. E. P. Scarlett to undertake a study of nursing education and he had recommended leaving nursing education in the hospital setting; meanwhile, the Alberta Association of Registered Nurses was "inclined to be favourable" to moving nursing education to educational institutions. After the 1964 federal Royal Commission on Health Services recommended establishing two-year nursing programs in colleges,[40] the national and Alberta nursing associations promoted shifting the hospital-based programs to the colleges.[41] However, there were questions about how much clinical training college-based nurses would receive, whether the hospitals would provide internships, and whether the university would accept courses for credit if students wished to move to its degree program.

Collett met with the university's Committee on Junior Colleges, its Committee on Nursing Education, the Alberta Association of Registered Nurses (AARN), and Calgary General Hospital to explore the idea. On 8 March 1965 the college held a day-long workshop of all of the interested parties to advance the idea, and in August 1965 Jean Mackie, formerly of Calgary General Hospital's School of Nursing, was appointed director. An advisory committee consisting of key representatives of the various stakeholders provided advice on how to proceed.[42] In October 1966 the board of governors approved the launch of the program.[43] The first cohort, admitted in January 1967, consisted of twenty-five students;[44] by 1968 there were sixty-five students and nine faculty members; and in January 1969, the first class of nineteen graduated.[45] Clinical training was provided in Calgary hospitals and the Ponoka hospital for the mentally ill. Following a brief period of uncertainty,[46] Mount Royal's program was approved for continuation and replicated in five other colleges. Thereafter the transformation in nursing education occurred quickly: in 1969, there had been one university program, one college program, and eleven in hospitals; by 1973, there were two university programs (with 121 students) , six college programs (with 321 students, and six hospital programs (with 516 students).[47] In later years, the curriculum was expanded to include certificates in specialties – for example, operating room and intensive care nursing certificates for registered nurses in 1973, later mental health nursing.

Judith Lathrop, who joined the nursing program in 1973, observed that the main difference between hospital-based teaching and the college program was that in the hospitals "the real focus of our education was not on learning but on providing services whereas at the college the focus was on the student and earning and less so on providing extra staffing to the hospitals;" moreover, the general education component was unique and critical for lifelong learning.[48] Thus, nursing became the first regulated profession to be offered as a college program. Strikingly, nursing was to be later the first college program to be merged into a university program – and Lathrop was to be the key figure in that later transformation as well as the college's move into degree granting more generally.

Another notable curricular departure was the introduction of the Correctional Careers program in 1968 on the initiative of instructors Dick Wallace and Lyle Howarth. It was the first of its kind in Canada, as was the Police Science certificate program introduced in 1970 with forty students and offered in affiliation with the Calgary Police Department.[49] Ken Hollington, coordinator of the Police Science program, said that, with elements drawn from philosophy, psychology, sociology, and anthropology, the program focused on "the 'whys' of police work, leaving the 'hows' to the police departments."[50] Together with his colleagues, Hollington, who became chairman of the Department of Justice Administration and Youth Development in 1976, made the department a national centre of professional development in justice administration.[51] The department negotiated agreements with universities outside the province, as a result of which its diploma programs were accepted for two years' credit at Simon Fraser University, the University of Ottawa, Carleton

Nursing class, 1969. Mount Royal University Archives HA185-2.

University, and the University of California at Long Beach. Its Child and Youth Care diploma program, which prepared graduates to work "with maltreated and behaviourally disoriented youths between the ages of seven and eighteen," was transferable to the University of Victoria.[52] Like nursing, these programs became strong points on which the college later built applied degree programs.

Another notable innovation in 1970 was the Aviation program for training commercial pilots. Its faculty consisted of RCAF veterans. Though students could take the courses for normal tuition costs, they had to bear the cost of operating the planes. The radio and television broadcasting programs were also a new breed of academic programming, preparation for "our society's huge and voracious appetite for knowledge."[53]

One new venture failed, as we have seen – the development of a Division of Fine Arts, with Peter Hodgson, then director of the Department of Music in the Conservatory, as the initial director. However, students for the theatre and music programs did not materialize in the required numbers and the experiment ended by 1969–70.[54]

The college also addressed some legacy issues. In June 1968, it submitted a brief to the Board of Post Secondary Education noting that the draft Colleges

Act did not mention the courses in religious studies that it intended to offer. These were not the five religious education courses the college had stopped in 1969.[55] Margaret (Peggy) Brydon, acting head of the Humanities Department, explained that those courses had been removed because they had "a specific doctrinal content. In the opinion of the administration here, the problem presented by such courses, in a public institution preparing students of all creeds for work in their own dogmatic areas, is almost insuperable." Some of the non-doctrinal content was now included in courses in Moral Philosophy, the Sociology of Religion, and Biblical History.[56] A. W. Vaughan, secretary of the United Church's Board of Colleges and Secondary Schools, said it made sense, given the small number of students, the cost, and the new orientation of the college, to terminate them – the last time the church was consulted by the college.[57]

Sweetheart Queen Connie McColl, 1967. Mount Royal University Archives *Varshicom 1967*.

The faculty was expanding as well and changing in nature as new career programs were added. The thirty-six faculty members on staff on 31 August 1966 became the core faculty for the public college.[58] The new faculty members added over the next five years joined them in the core, as hiring thereafter slowed down considerably.[59] Most of the faculty members hired in the 1960s may have expected, like Ken Robson, that their stay would be short-term but were to find that the retrenchment in higher education in the 1970s cut off opportunities, and they were to spend the remainder of their careers at the college. Like Robson, they came for a job, "with no real understanding of this new institutional type called the community college" and found that circumstances made them permanent members of a new kind of institution.[60]

By 1969, there were 90 full-time instructors; a year later, 106, and in 1972–73, 127, plus 106 part-time faculty members. In 1970, "60 per cent" of the faculty held "at least a Master's degree, [an increase] of

FIGURE 6.2 CITIZENSHIP OF FACULTY MEMBERS AND
COUNSELLORS, 1970-71
N=122

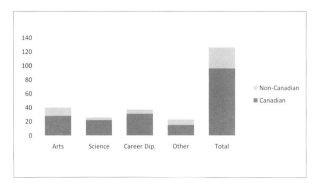

SOURCE: Based on Alberta, Committee of Inquiry into Non-Canadian Influence in Alberta Post-Secondary Education. Report of
the Committee of Inquiry into Non-Canadian Influence in Alberta
Post-Secondary Education. 1973, p. 113, Table B-10.

FIGURE 6.3 COUNTRY ORIGIN OF DEGREES HELD
BY FACULTY MEMBERS, 1970-71
N=114

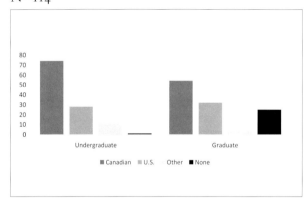

SOURCE: Based on the Principal/President's Reports to the Executive Committee and, after August 1966, the Board of Trustees.

8 percent from last fall; 43 percent have tenure, even
though 60 percent have been with Mount Royal for
two years or less. The average faculty member is 37
years of age and the average income is $11,554 per
year." In 1970–71, the government undertook a review
of the supposed foreign influences, which showed that
77.2 per cent of Mount Royal's faculty were Canadian, that 65 per cent had earned their undergraduate
degree in Canada, and that 47 per cent had earned a
graduate degree in Canada.[61] See Figures 6.2 and 6.3.

The Conservatory's complement grew from 38
instructors on-campus and twenty-five branch studios

in 1970 to 42 instructors in 1972–73 and more branches.[62] In May 1973, the college had a total of 649 employees, including 189 full-time and 113 part-time or
casual support staff and 72 employees in food services.

CLARIFYING ROLES IN CALGARY

While the parts of the new public college were testing
one another and working out their internal relationships, the college also had to determine its relationship to the University of Calgary and the Southern
Alberta Institute of Technology (SAIT). In music,
it also sought to clarify the relationship between the
credentials it offered and those offered by the public
schools and other musical bodies.

The University of Calgary inherited the University of Alberta's affiliation agreement with Mount Royal
on 1 September 1966.[63] Two weeks later the chairman of the university's Committee on Junior Colleges
asked for the college to provide "a rather complete
statement. . . . concerning your understanding of the
present relationships which prevail between our two
institutions." [64] In 1967–68, the calendar described
several pathways for students, including those offered
"under the affiliation agreement . . . for students who
desire to obtain the equivalent of the first year at the
University of Calgary." But the calendar warned that
the students would be "in no way considered as students of the university" and had no guarantees of admission there.[65] In March 1968 the board received an
"intimation from the university" that the agreement
would end on 30 June 1968.[66] It did, for there was no
reference to an agreement in the 1968–69 calendar. By
1969–70, and more fully by 1970–71, a new agreement
was worked out: "All courses taught at Mount Royal
Junior College for which University of Calgary credit
is given must be University of Calgary courses in the
first of Arts and Science or of Physical Education. . . .
In order to transfer . . . the student must complete the
matriculation requirements of the Faculty in which
he intends to enrol." The courses were listed in the
calendar.[67]

As new government coordinating bodies came
along, the affiliation agreement requiring direct negotiations with the university declined in importance.
In 1972, when the Alberta Council on Admissions and

Transfer (ACAT) was created, the affiliation became a formality without much substance; the calendar section did little more than outline the rules and conditions for students, without guaranteeing access.[68] While the vast bulk of the students who transferred to other institutions did so in Alberta, the college claimed in 1970 that it also had "good two-year transfer arrangements with many U.S. universities, particularly in the Pacific NW."[69]

Questions arose about the fit between some college programs and their university counterparts. In 1969 G. H. Tyler, head of the School of Social Welfare at the University of Calgary, raised the issue because the university was planning to introduce a new BA program in social work and found that the colleges and NAIT had already introduced "two-year programs in child care, recreation, social services and related fields." This led to several meetings involving the university, the colleges, government officials, and agency administrators to discuss the requirements for different jobs. The result was detailed learning objectives for the college's Community Service program.[70] That the relationships were sorted out reasonably was suggested by the college's 1977 report on graduate outcomes: that seventeen of that year's twenty-nine graduates in Social Service Careers had found related jobs, two had unrelated jobs, eight were still looking, and two were continuing their education.[71]

A study of the transfer students to several Canadian universities in the early 1960s had indicated notable success.[72] By the end of the decade, however, Mount Royal's students were not faring as well when they got to Alberta universities. A study of 509 students in 1968–69 and 1969–70 transferring into the second year at the University of Alberta, the University of Calgary, and the University of Lethbridge concluded "that in a majority of instances examined, there were significant differences in academic performance between transfer and native students [students who enrolled initially in the university]."[73]

In this period, one other important connection to the university emerged. As the university developed graduate programs, many Mount Royal faculty members enrolled in masters and doctoral programs. By 2002–3, twenty-six faculty members had Ph.D.s from Calgary.[74]

Meanwhile, the fit between the college and SAIT, which was growing and extending its activities, was a matter of concern both to the college and the Department of Education. At the initiative of Collett in the fall of 1966, a joint committee was struck with SAIT "to discuss matters of mutual interest such as parallel programs presently being offered and policies for planning of future course to avoid unnecessary duplication." The committee agreed to establish a standing committee to review new program proposals and recommended these guidelines: "(a) all science-based programs which require extensive or industrial laboratory and shop facilities [shall] be offered at SAIT; (b) all programs which require an arts and science core [shall] be offered at MRJC; (c) certain programs for which there is extensive employment for graduates may be offered at both MRJC and SAIT after thorough investigation of the employment possibilities and training facilities."[75] A review of existing programs indicated there were no unwarranted overlaps. Courses offered by the Alberta College of Art were different from those offered by Mount Royal. While both SAIT and Mount Royal offered business administration, secretarial arts, and marketing programs, "the employment opportunities were sufficient" to allow them to continue. Both also offered programs in television and radio broadcasting, recreation, theatre arts, and journalism, but they were informed by different purposes – SAIT generally producing technicians, Mount Royal generally producing content practitioners. Nor was there duplication between SAIT's two-year computer training program, which produced "graduates eventually becoming junior systems analysts" and Mount Royal's one-year program, which focused on "business applications of data processing only." Mount Royal did not duplicate any of SAIT's technology and trades courses. The committee also agreed that SAIT would refer students to Mount Royal for preparatory education.[76]

As we shall see in the section on planning the new campus, the government briefly contemplated the potential for merging Mount Royal with SAIT, or at any rate locating them on the same campus. In 1967, acting president McCready, responding to the idea of a potential second technical institute in Calgary, proposed combining it with Mount Royal to create "one community college with technical and academic arms."[77]

There were two other options the college was to explore in the years ahead – broadening its role as an open admissions college, and becoming a degree-granting institution. In the meantime, the college was to build higher on its foundations in white-collar and semi-professional career and university-transfer programs.

Fitting into the public context also affected the Conservatory, which asked the government to approve its music courses and examinations recognized for high-school credit. Because the government relied on the Music Committee of the University of Alberta, which recognized the examinations of the Western Board of Music, the issue took years to resolve. The Music Committee held that "there are enough examining boards available," in effect nullifying Mount Royal's statutory and historic role in examinations. This was a practical matter, as some six hundred students were taking the examinations annually. In 1968 the government finally accepted the argument that the college's standards were identical to those of the Western Board, enabling the examinations to be accepted for credit in public schools.[78]

FERMENT ON CAMPUS

In the midst of pell-mell growth, there was an unexpected change in leadership. It was the result of new standards for transparency deriving from the conversion from private to public status. The first casualty was President Collett, who was dismissed over his handling of certain financial matters.[79] Collett explained his departure in a memo to "all members of the Faculty and Staff" dated 22 March 1967: "In view of the rumours and speculations that appear to be circulating throughout the college I should let you know that the board of trustees has indicated that it wishes a change in the presidency of the college."[80] On 28 March the board issued a press release: "While the board acknowledges the personal attributes of Dr. Collett and his sincere and human approach to the problems of the college, we have been forced into the unpleasant situation of arriving at a decision that involves the future of the college. We can only say that it is with the deepest regret that we asked Dr. Collett to resign in order that the position can be offered to someone who we feel will be better able to carry out the diversified and heavy burden that we are demanding."[81] After determining that Ralph McCready, the "executive vice president," was willing to serve as acting president, chairman Wright announced the news on 29 March, adding that "no further changes in teaching or administrative staff are contemplated."[82] Fiscal management was assigned to Max Rae.[83]

The news struck the campus like a thunderbolt. Suspicions surged. Had the board rejected Collett's community-college philosophy? Had board members from other religions forced him out? A group of students marched to Joe Comessotti's office to present him, as acting board chairman (and Catholic representative), "a 150-name petition" demanding an explanation. Bud Gamble, president of the MRC Administrators' Association and assistant to the president, was puzzled: "I personally find it difficult to interpret the statement issued by the board."[84] McCready wrote to the board "to get written confirmation of the conditions under which I am to work," notably whether he would have "to betray" Collett's community-college vision. He also declared that "I am to be in complete charge over the academic affairs of the college within established policy approved by the board. The board of trustees will exercise its control only through finances."[85]

To complicate matters further, the board decided not to advertise the position. As McCready advised the internal community: "The Board of Trustees wishes it to be known that the position of president of Mount Royal Junior College is not being publicly advertised but is now open and any member of the faculty or staff may apply."[86] Even in tranquil times, secrecy surrounding the departure of a president combined with a confidential search process for a replacement would have sparked calls for transparency. Both the Students' Executive Committee and the ATA-MRFA demanded membership on the board to give them a window on machinations, to which the board responded that it could permit observers but that its membership was set by statute.[87] The faculty urged the board to "use every means at its disposal (including advertising publicly) to determine a successor." It also declared that it no longer wanted "the present method of communication [to the board] through the president."[88] Both associations also asked for membership on the presidential search committee but the board explained that its committee was already established.

Collett's departure ended the leadership of one of the major shapers of the institution for nearly two decades. He would be remembered in the college for his community-college philosophy, warm relations with individuals, and public service.[89] Max Rae, who worked closely with both Garden and Collett, later said they had each brought strengths to the college – Garden, notably on the business side, and Collett on the academic side, that enabled the college so survive and to evolve into the public college.[90]

From April 1967 to July 1968, when the next president took office, McCready presided over an institution roiling with change. He was to contend with both the new young faculty and students in a time of continent-wide campus dissent. That he was in for rough ride was suggested by one of the first published student comments on his appointment: "they've got to be kidding."[91] Yet he was a man of the times in some ways, favouring a greater role for faculty members in decision making. He immediately scrapped a reorganization proposed by Collett because of its "pyramidal power structure," winding up with a structure that had at least two dozen people reporting to him in some way.[92] In 1966–67, there had been three vice-presidents (McCready as executive vice-president, Kelly as vice-president, academic, and M. A. Low as vice-president: extension, development, research, public relations). In 1968–69, the senior administrative structure consisted of McCready, serving as both acting president and dean of Instruction, and two administrative assistants to the president (Kelly, J. Yates).[93] The fluidity of working relationships in this period was one of its striking characteristics, according to Jean Mackie, the new head of the Nursing program.[94]

This was not entirely of McCready's doing. Everybody in the institution was mobilizing in a group – students, faculty, support staff. The directors formed a Coordinating Committee and in February 1967 all administrators formed the Mount Royal Junior College Administrators' Association whose purpose was "to act as the official bargaining unit." In March 1968 the Chairmen's Council produced a draft job description which, as McCready noted, lacked any reference "to your relationship to your immediate superior."[95]

Everyone was responsible for everything and no one was responsible for anything in particular. Responding to grass-roots proclamations, Vice-President Owen Kelly advised "all academic personnel" that "only the president and the academic vice president have the authority and right to issue memoranda affecting the whole of the Academic Division."[96]

Initially, McCready worked through the existing administrators but quickly changed their titles, as indicated above. Kelly remained as vice-president, academic for a year, was then made assistant dean of Instruction responsible for library audiovisual services, "curriculum planning, interviewing of students, providing information to students, student complaints, and the office of the Registrar," and then ducked out, returning to full-time teaching in 1968–69.[97] Responsibility for academic personnel was assigned to Frederick Dunn, an American who had the "authority to hire new academic staff, provide them with in-service training and orientation, as well as implementation of programs." Bud Gamble, who had returned to the college in July 1965 as assistant to McCready, then executive vice-president,[98] was "placed in the line structure by giving him additional responsibilities," which included "campus planning, research and acting as representative of the president's office on the Board of Trustees Property Committee," public relations, and residences. In addition to serving as acting president, McCready, who no doubt thought his tenure would be brief, continued as administrative vice-president for Personnel Services. Max Rae was given "dual responsibilities as Scheduling Officer under the supervision of the Academic Vice President and was reassigned as well to assist the Personnel Officer." Richard Cooke supervised the Evening College.[99] Reporting to the acting president, they collectively constituted the President's Advisory Group (PAG).[100]

While the administration was being reorganized, the faculty was also reorganizing. When collective bargaining resumed after September 1966, board members rather than the president led the employer's team, while the Mount Royal Faculty Association (MRFA) became the bargaining unit for the entire faculty, though the next agreement continued to distinguish between Instructors and Teachers.[101] On 18 April 1967, the two faculty groups – the MRFA and the ATA – held a meeting "to decide whether they are in favour of the amalgamation of the groups or not."[102] This was followed by negotiations in which the combined employees group was described as "The Mount Royal Faculty Association (acting on behalf of its members employed by the board) and The Alberta Teachers' Association (acting on behalf of the teachers employed by the board)."[103] In 1968, the faculty groups and the board reached a one-year agreement to enable early response to proposed legislative changes. The agreement applied to "all full-time and part-time academic instructors and all professional personnel excluding those employed in a managerial capacity or employed in a confidential capacity in matters relating to labour relations." The salary grid distinguished between holders of one bachelor's degree, more than one bachelor's degree, one year of study toward a master's degree, and a master's degree. "The normal instructional load shall be twelve hours per week; the maximum instructional load shall be fifteen hours per week"; for instructors in high-school courses, the range was fifteen to eighteen hours per week. "Full-time instructors shall, in addition to instructional hours, participate in student guidance, discipline and other duties relating to their course responsibilities."[104] Thereafter there was in fact just one body representing the faculty in their relations with the board.

The MRFA's formal objects were "to regulate relations between full members and associate members of the Association and their employer," "to bargain collectively, . . . to enter into agreements concerning terms and conditions of work and employment, . . . to seek certification as a bargaining agent . . . under the Alberta Labour Act and to exercise all powers thereto appertaining under the said act . . . [and] to promote and maintain the academic, social, recreational interests and general welfare of its members."[105] In the fall of 1968 it introduced an Ethics Committee to address "academic freedom" issues and govern communications by one faculty member about another.[106] In 1969, the board accepted an MRFA proposal to establish a joint Professional Standards Committee to make recommendations on tenure and professional leaves.

THE INTERIM GENERAL FACULTIES COUNCIL

"By tradition," the Anderson Report had observed, Mount Royal's "faculty has been asked to make decisions on certain administrative details" through Faculty Councils for each of the four academic units (high school, junior college, secretarial, and Conservatory), with the principal as the chair of each. He recommended establishment of a GFC.[107] Though the private board had asked for a legal opinion on developing a GFC,[108] the issue was left unresolved. At the time, there was a nation-wide discussion of faculty and student participation in decision making, as statutes were need for new institutions and religiously affiliated institutions converted into public ones. The challenge was that of converting from a patriarchal to a more collegial model of governance. Much of the discussion of the time was over the composition and powers of collegial bodies. In 1966, the Duff-Berdahl Report recommended bicameral governance for universities, including student representation on senates, and its approach had a formative influence throughout the country.[109] Bicameral governance implied two bodies with statutory authority – a Senate, GFC, or Academic Council with determining authority in academic matters, and a governing board responsible for selecting the president, for property, and for the overall financial and other health of the organization.

At a two-day retreat in Banff including faculty members and administrators, on 21–22 October 1966, to discuss the future of the public college, the lack of a collegial body emerged as a major item on the agenda. "It was the general feeling that faculty members below the rank of director were not kept informed about college policy nor were they consulted while it was being formulated. As a result many faculty members expressed a desire to participate in the governance of the college."[110] Collett advised the board that "a very frank discussion dealt with the difficulties of communication and the ways in which the faculty could become involved in policy decisions" and that "it is likely that a General Faculty Council will be organized so that faculty problems may receive adequate discussion."[111] He probably did not think this was much of a change from past practice. In 1964, he had outlined the program approval process: "if a new program is proposed it will be discussed first in the Division Council and then taken to the Dean, then to the General Faculty Council, and ultimately to the Senate."[112] After the Banff retreat, he launched what became known as the Interim GFC, pending necessary approvals. The "faculty" soon organized a survey on its potential role. There was near unanimity among the thirty-five respondents that the GFC should concern itself with curriculum, admissions, academic standards, student affairs and services, alumni and community relations, long-range planning, and capital improvements. However, the vote was nearly even (19–16) on whether it should approve appointments, promotions, and tenure. On the question of whether the GFC's role should be "advisory" or "legislative," a great majority favoured "advisory."[113] Membership was to be open to both full- and part-time faculty members; "under special circumstances," students "may be asked to serve on committees."[114]

Apparently Collett did not advise the board of developments, for it first learned of the Interim GFC in January 1968. In December 1967 McCready had submitted a draft budget to the Finance Committee and was told to balance it. He took the matter to the President's Advisory Group (PAG), which decided that it would make sense to eliminate "poorly attended courses" in philosophy and drama. The department and program heads learned of this through reading minutes.[115] Program directors Barry Pashak and Edwin Pitt mobilized support, deploring the process for making the budget and the "emasculation of the present liberal educational program" which threatened "Mount Royal's decline from the status of a junior college to that of a technical and training school, since such a decline follows inevitably upon the removal of liberal course offerings."[116]

This letter reached the board in January 1968, along with minutes that referred to the Interim General Faculty Council. Asked by Wright, McCready explained that the Interim GFC consisted of fifteen people – five program chairs, five department heads, three faculty members, a student, and himself – and that the PAG consisted of the administrators reporting to him.[117] The board approved a resolution "to form a legal General Faculty Council as soon as possible, and that a special committee of the board be charged with the formation of such Council." It also asked for "all

responsible organizations within the college [to] be made known to and approved by the board."[118]

McCready then advised department heads that "our long-range plans include the formation of a legally constituted General Faculty Council from which no doubt a Curriculum Committee will emerge."[119] Back-pedalling, he issued a memorandum calling for a vote of all faculty members on the "various course deletions proposed by the administration," stating that "the administration will recommend to the board . . . only those deletions that receive a majority vote."[120]

Inspired by the faculty's protest, a group of students immediately formed the January 11th Movement, whose purpose was "to organize future student participation in Faculty and Trustee meetings and consolidate student involvement in every pertinent area of college affairs."[121] The movement soon faded away, but its existence added heft to the demand for student representation on governing boards.

McCready spent weeks trying to find an elusive middle ground between the Interim GFC and the board. On 8 February the Interim GFC called for "the faculty to be recognized as active participants in all matters of policy formulation and administration"; through the Interim GFC the faculty and board would jointly set policy and hold the administration to account. (This was later described as "co-determination.") It elected an ad hoc committee of six members "to meet with the board regarding (a) legalization of Interim General Faculty Council, (b) selection of a new president."[122] It asked for "two members of the faculty [to] be allowed to sit on the board screening committee to select a new president."[123] On receiving this news, the board told McCready to inform the Interim GFC that it had no standing. McCready then attempted a compromise. He merged the PAG and the Interim GFC into a new body, the "Faculty Forum," thus fusing administrative coordination with an advisory collegial body. "The Faculty Forum," he advised the board, "has agreed to abolish the body known as the General Faculty also Council . . . [and] I have also agreed to abolish the President's Advisory Committee. I have agreed to use the Faculty Forum as an Interim General Faculty Council which I will chair and carry on the usual business as I had previously done with the President's Advisory Committee." This new body was drafting terms of reference for committees that would be paired with board committees. "When these have been approved . . . , I will inform the board of trustees."[124]

McCready's report did not sit well with the board, which directed him to tell the new body that it had no authority and that final decision-making power rested with the board. A month later McCready reported that the Interim GFC – which had not faded away – had "agreed that the power delegated to it concerned *recommending* policy NOT its *implementation* and that the president must retain sole power to recommend the delegation of authority for implementation of policy." This concession was immediately offset by a demand for "representatives from the [IGFC's] Curriculum, Planning, Finance and Personnel Committees . . . to be appointed to the corresponding committees of the board" and for administrators to sit on the committees of the Interim GFC.[125] The board refused the request: administrators "cannot be responsible to two people or committees at the same time" and the "interaction between administrative officers and the Interim GFC committees would be one of communication only." In March 1968, when the board struck a committee to consider terms of reference for a GFC,[126] the Interim GFC struck a six-member faculty committee chaired by Gary Dean to work with the board "on the structure and formation of a legalized" GFC. As the board had not invited such collaboration, it agreed only "to ascertain the purposes and wishes of this committee."[127] The "Office Workers Association" (a new unofficial group) declared that it also wanted to be represented on the Interim GFC.[128] On 15 May 1968, the board deferred further discussion of the new GFC "until a new president is in office."[129]

Meanwhile, relations with the students become acute. A loan to the former president had raised legal questions. Did the Students' Union or its Executive Council have the authority to make a loan? Who was liable if the loan were not repaid? Had the board of trustees exercised due diligence in passing over student funds it required students to pay to an inappropriately structured student body? The board refused to transmit any funds to student bodies until an association was incorporated.[130] Ron Prokosch, president of the Students' Executive Council, then initiated the process of securing incorporation under the Societies Act of Alberta in March 1968 the Students' Association

Students protest the inadequacy of the Library, Spring 1969. Students took part in a campaign to check out all of the Library's books. Mount Royal University Media Services.

of Mount Royal College (SAMRC).[131] The board and SAMRC then negotiated an agreement for the college to collect "student union fees at the time and place of registration, and that these fees be turned over to the student business manager as soon as it is possible," while SAMRC agreed to "supply, annually, an auditors' report showing the manner in which all funds received by the Students' Association have been dealt with. Such report shall be furnished the board not later than the 1st day of September in each year."[132]

Another issue related to the *Reflector*, whose writers, seeing themselves as countercultural critics of the status quo and champions of the student interest, sometimes stretched the limits of propriety and good taste. No one and nothing was exempt from criticism – student organizations, the board, administrators, faculty members, government leaders, the city, parking policies, the Vietnam War.[133] In September 1967, the *Reflector* offended the board by advising freshmen that they were joining a college with "the kind of board of trustees that fires good presidents."[134] In October McCready wrote an article in the publication expressing unhappiness with its "hippy values."[135] However, scandalous articles continued, and in November the board asked McCready "to restore respectability to the college paper." "Why one person, the editor of the *Reflector*, should have the power to tarnish our institution through thoughtless vulgarity which serves no purpose whatsoever, other than to shock his readers, seems beyond all reason," McCready wrote to Prokosch. "The editor, like all others on this campus, must, in some way, be made responsible for his actions."[136] Rallying behind the editor, the Student Council voted unanimous support for him.[137] Yet more offensive material appeared, inspiring widespread complaints on and off campus.[138] Though it had no legal responsibility for the publication, which was technically owned by SAM-RC, it did own the campus and could have blocked circulation. On 3 January the board resolved "that immediate action be taken to restore to responsibility our college paper . . . and that our acting president be instructed to take the necessary steps. Failing this, the publication should cease as from now."[139] "As if the administration and board of governors did not have trouble enough," the *Albertan* weighed in: "the college was precipitated into the public spotlight some weeks ago when a young and immature 'editor,' and one or more equally immature supervisors, produced an issue of the college newspaper which contained vulgar and offensive content."[140] However, it was not an easy matter, as McCready explained; the association was an incorporated body and the administration "cannot ban the newspaper as you have suggested, but I will do all I can to change the 'tone.'" He worked with Ron Prokosch to develop an agreement requiring the editor-in-chief to "consult with a faculty advisor who shall be recommended by the president of the college." The first advisor was John Howse of the journalism program.[141]

The new editorial system led to a more subdued but still lively publication reflecting the times. In October 1968, the *Reflector* published articles on Dick Gregory ("Man in a suitcase"), a story about "Acid Mouse" by Steve Schoemaker ("the mouse digs ACID!!!"), and another by Keith Neufeld, "Cosmic Consciousness," which concluded: "Existence is the body of energy and energy can be neither created nor destroyed." Yet there were some conventional sides as well – every issue contained the picture of a comely young woman, and social notes included a warning: "Boys beware Sadie Hawkins."[142] It was during this period that the gulf between the student newspaper and SAMRC first appeared. The organizations attracted students with different interests and values.

Those interested in student government were more conventional, while those attracted to the newspaper identified themselves as critics of the status quo, even as crusaders for countercultural or alternative views. The divide grew through to the early 1980s, when it became too wide to bridge.

"Fortunately for me and the college," McCready wrote years later, after the passions had cooled, "Dr. Collett left it in such good order that it practically ran itself until a new president could be found."[143] It was not quite that simple. In the 1960s, even experienced college and university presidents found it difficult to ride the tempestuous waters, and McCready did as well as an acting president could in resolving issues or in maintaining sufficient ambiguity to prevent all-out conflict. While he tried to respond creatively to the faculty demand for a bicameral form of governance, he did not have the authority to carry it out and the board was unwilling to relinquish control or to prejudge the legislation that would govern the public colleges. That the institution was no longer willing to accept old ways was suggested when, just before leaving office, he appointed himself dean of Instruction, inspiring a major faculty backlash that forced him to back off.[144] Instead, the new president appointed him Director of Institutional Research and Liaison with the University of Calgary, in which role he oversaw the introduction of some of the new programs and program advisory committees until he retired in 1972.[145]

A NEW SENIOR ADMINISTRATION

Dr. Walter Bruce Pentz (1928–92) became president on 1 July 1968.[146] An American with a Methodist background, Pentz had earned a BA at Maryville College, an MA in political science and American history at Vanderbilt University, and an Ed.D. at UCLA. His academic appointments included terms as assistant professor of political science at Adams State College (Colorado), instructor of political science and assistant football-baseball coach at Pueblo Junior College (Colorado), and dean of Faculty and director of Athletics at Treasure Valley Community College (Oregon). Prior to coming to Mount Royal, he was the executive secretary of the Junior College Advisory Panel of the California State Board of Education. Apart from his

Walter B. Pentz, President 1968–75. Mount Royal University Executive Records GO010-05P.

personal qualities, the board was attracted by his familiarity with the California college system, the jurisdiction then exercising the most influence on Alberta.

Discovering that "approximately thirty people were reporting to the president," Pentz quickly reorganized. The senior administration was reshaped around "the three main functions performed in a junior college – instruction, student services, and business services." Effective 1 August 1968, he named three acting vice-presidents, pending later board confirmation: Gary W. Dean, vice-president, Instruction; G. Frederick Dunn, acting vice-president, Student Services; and Max Rae, vice-president, Business Services, and held his first executive committee meeting on that day.[147] Eight months later he replaced Dunn with Douglas M. Lauchlan, the United Church chaplain and part-time instructor in the Speech Arts program, who was given a broader mandate as vice-president, Student and Community Services.[148] Max Rae later said that Pentz firmly believed in and practised real delegation of authority, his first experience of such thorough delegation since his own appointment in 1947.[149] In addition, Pentz combined the twenty-six

academic disciplines and career programs into twelve Divisions, each headed by a chairman (there were two for the Conservatory, Bach and Paterson).[150] As these moves indicated, he brought a more businesslike management style to the college, including clear job descriptions and policies and procedures. As an indication of the procedural laxity he had found, he noted that Collett's "General Statement" appeared in the calendar though it had not been approved by the board.[151]

Pentz's views on the community college mission conformed to those already current at Mount Royal. "The reason for the existence of any community college," he said, "is to meet, within its corporate capacity and as economically as possible, the educational needs of the area in which it is located. In order to make this philosophical mandate operational, Mount Royal is charged with three main objectives: it must provide a comprehensive, flexible and current curriculum; it must accommodate any adult who expresses a willingness to learn; it must provide an active counselling and guidance program." It should be open to "anyone a high school diploma or who is 18 years of age," provide university-transfer courses and "learning opportunities that lead to gainful employment" and "courses leading to the general education of its clients," "and, if the demand exists, the institution will become the cultural and recreational centre for the community it serves."[152] Furthermore, he quickly adopted the pedagogical model and facilities design for the new campus. Gamble, who remained Assistant to the President – Planning, said that Pentz "continued the process that was under way and he never wavered; he made all the critical decisions that made that new creature evolve."[153]

However, his background as an American was held against him by some in the college, and his choice of senior administrators had him relying on non-academics, on people from counselling, and former military officers. "I don't know if you can be well liked if you come into a college culture" from the outside, John Howse said later. "It was one thing for us to get excited about sending our students to the United States but very few of us got excited about having an American president come up here."[154] Along the same lines, Kenneth J. Robson noted that "the early administration lacked a credible academic leader: Walter [Pentz] was seen as an American bureaucrat (and a Californian to boot) who used American consultants and built an American-style institution; Gary Dean was a counselor; Fred Fowlow and Ernie Tyson [other administrators] were old military people. They too easily resembled the kind of authority figures faculty and students were rebelling against across North America."[155]

Pentz stood at the intersection where the views of activist young faculty members met the traditional views of the governing board and prevailing views and values, in the context of uncertainty about legislation that would regulate faculty participation in decision making and set out the terms for collective bargaining. Moreover, his initial appointees, Dunn and Dean, managed to offend the faculty very quickly. In September 1969, Dean informed faculty members that the board "has tried to have a Faculty Agreement ratified for the beginning . . . of the 1968–69 academic year but has been unable to do so because of the demands in other areas, particularly the administrative reorganization. . . . May I remind you that your salary schedule places you in the top ten percent of Junior College instructors."[156] As negotiations were underway, this might be seen as an effort to bargain by other means. Dunn was openly critical of the faculty. In Pentz's first Executive Committee meeting, on 1 August 1968, he objected to the idea of giving budgets to department chairmen because "these people were just not sophisticated enough in this area to handle it wisely"; in January 1969, he proposed stripping department chairs of any administrative authority, leaving them as full-time teachers with program coordination roles.[157] Pentz ignored these suggestions and removed Dunn in March 1969, but the words and attitudes of his senior administrative colleagues during his first crucial months as president contributed to the idea that he was not just efficient, he was "authoritarian."[158]

In early 1969, when Dean dismissed a faculty member, the MRFA reacted strongly. On 16 April 1969 it held an open meeting to air its concerns, which in part arose from disciplinary action in the absence of agreed performance standards and procedures. A slender majority defeated a vote of non-confidence in Pentz, but the assembly was very critical of Dean.[159] Robert McDougall, president of the MRFA, "requested a meeting between a faculty committee and the board to present a faculty request for (a) dismissal

of Mr. Dean as Vice-President: Instruction, [and] (b) formation of a General Faculty Council."[160] Pentz promptly asked the board for support and recommended a "policy on review procedures": "(1) The function of the board is not to be a court of appeal for every decision within the college, but is only to ensure that proper procedures are followed; (2) The board should delegate authority to the president in a very clearly defined manner; (3) Review procedures should be very clearly defined and communicated to the staff." Those with grievances covered by a collective agreement should use the grievance procedure, while administrators and support staff should refer any issue to "a Senior Administrative officer, notifying their immediate superior of their action." The board endorsed Pentz's approach, and affirmed its confidence in Pentz and Dean.[161]

The board responded more positively to the proposal to form a joint committee to review the crisis and "to examine the role of a General Faculty Council in the field of academic policy development."[162] On the crisis, the joint "exploration committee" found that there was "no single outstanding reason" for faculty discontent "but rather many interrelated reasons," such as the role of the vice-president's office in disciplinary matters, the personality of the incumbent, and "a new administration trying to define and implement new policies and at times evaluating by exception." The committee on the academic council was also intended to draft criteria for performance evaluations for faculty and administrators.[163] The performance evaluation issue was soon left to collective bargaining, while it was to take several more years to resolve issues relating to the academic council. By October 1968 talks were "stalled" on "whether the council should have legislative authority, or should only make recommendations to the college's board of governors."[164]

Where the Universities Act spelled out the functions and authority of GFCs, the Colleges Act said only this on the college equivalent: "A college board, the academic staff association and students' council shall enter into negotiations for the purpose of concluding an agreement for the establishment of an academic council for the college, its composition and functions." Thus, while university faculty members had their decision-making role spelled out in law and handed to them, college faculty would have to negotiate their role. Underlying this different treatment was the assumption that universities consisted of disciplines and professions that were more-or-less permanent while colleges were training institutions in which programs and faculty members would come and go as the market required. Since faculty members were not likely to vote themselves out of a job, even if their program was no longer necessary or a higher priority program came along, the act deliberately kept the academic council weak. When this conception was fused with role uncertainty and status anxiety arising from the newness of colleges and of the college instructor category, the result was to be continuing tension on the Mount Royal campus

The discussions at Mount Royal in the early 1970s echoed those in university circles a decade earlier. To quote from an article on the debate over professorial identity in university circles: "Are they a 'cluster of experts,' an 'expert occupation,' a 'group of sub-professions or emerging professions,' a 'professional bureaucracy,' 'skilled craftsmen,' an 'intellectual social class,' an 'aristocracy of the intellect,' a 'community of scholars,' 'captains of erudition,' or maybe a 'collection of personalities' and 'procession of individuals'?"[165] In university circles, the growing homogenization of missions and bicameral governance helped resolve some of the issues, but bicameral governance alone did not satisfy the demands of many faculty members for more control over their workplace. Beginning in the 1970s many university faculty associations became unions.

The role of the college professoriate was equally vexed, and the discussion was in part informed by the earlier debate within the universities. At Mount Royal, many faculty members wanted to be treated like university professors in internal governance, the assignment of teaching workload, and tenure, and like schoolteachers or civil servants when it came to performance review and automatic grid-based compensation without any merit component. Both because it had achieved the right to act as a bargaining agent prior to 1969 and through the Colleges Act, the MRFA was to continue to play a dual role – that of a formal bargaining unit and that of a "professional" organization demanding for itself a role outside of collective bargaining in the governance of the institution.

Seeing itself as the senior faculty association among the colleges, the MRFA played a critical role in developing a provincial faculty organization, or rather two – first, the Alberta Association of Junior College Faculties (AAJCF), and later, the Alberta Colleges and Institutes Faculties Association (ACIFA) – and in challenging aspects of the Colleges Act, though not, interestingly, the academic council. On behalf of the AAJCF, Hugh Macleod, president, wrote to the minister on two aspects of the Colleges Act. Section 2(b) enabled boards unilaterally to define the membership of bargaining units. (This was not a practical issue at Mount Royal, where the MRFA already included librarians and counsellors as well as full- and part-time instructors.) "It is therefore recommended that such designation be made by the board in negotiation with the full time teaching or instructional staff of the college."[166] This had no effect on government policy, despite a finding of the International Labour Organization (ILO) in 1981 recommending negotiation of membership.[167] The other concern was section 47(b), which made collective bargaining subject to negotiated procedures rather than to the terms of the Alberta Labour Act, which set out dispute resolution procedures. AAJCF proposed that "these negotiations be conducted according to the provisions of the Alberta Labour Act."[168] The government did not agree to this change, and each college was free to choose its own method. While all other colleges opted for compulsory arbitration, the MRFA wanted to retain the right to strike, and that right was continued until removed by legislation in 2004.[169]

THE MRFA AND "CO-DETERMINATION"

In a period of rapid expansion, proliferating programs, and fragmented facilities, the MRFA became an important social network for people who otherwise had little contact. Though the college moved into a large mega-structure in 1972, the challenge of keeping in contact continued but the older forms of sociability faded away and new ones developed. For some faculty members the MRFA became an important sub-community. Some of the early leaders occupied leadership positions for more than three decades. They shared some things in common. Several were of United Church background and some were openly active in the New Democratic Party, formed in 1962, which embodied a political version of the social gospel. Perhaps more important, the core group shared a sense of common cause and sometimes shared particular grievances about particular actions or personalities in the struggles with the administration. "Several key leaders had come through the ranks of the ATA with all that that entailed for negotiations, relations with administration, etc."[170] In general, though, faculty members at Mount Royal, like those in most institutions, paid only occasional attention to the activities of the faculty association, and the greatest moments of solidarity were during collective bargaining rounds and periodic confrontations.

Most of the leaders over the decades came from the liberal arts disciplines (notably English, when one takes into account the full complement of officers). Unlike colleges where "general education" was taught by faculty members in career programs, Mount Royal's liberal arts faculty members were aggregated in academic departments.[171] While faculty members in career programs were oriented to external professions and activities, saw themselves as preparing graduates to be successful in the existing social order, and occasionally wanted to reduce the liberal arts content, those in the liberal arts married high-minded idealism with self-interest in defending the liberal education core and focusing on campus life, which they placed in a larger ideological context: campus struggles were part of broader social struggles. Not surprisingly, the MRFA itself was a strong defender of the core liberal arts curriculum, a commitment that in effect put it at odds with some of its own career faculty members.[172]

One feature of the college's faculty by the 1970s was the comparatively high proportion of women (ca. 40 per cent) by comparison with Canadian universities at the time. This was due in part, but only in part, to the presence of the Nursing and Secretarial Arts programs; it was perhaps more due to the fact that the baseline credential was the master's degree, and many of the women were married and had not had time to pursue doctoral degrees. Women were active in the MRFA and from time to time led it. As a result, the preoccupation with overcoming the "chilly climate" for women in Canadian universities never appeared as

much of an issue at Mount Royal, where women were on a trajectory leading them to become the majority.[173]

Among the most prominent leaders of the MRFA in the early years was Barry Pashak, son of a United Church minister and perennial flag bearer for the NDP in provincial and federal elections.[174] After completing Mount Royal's Petroleum Engineering program and transferring to the University of Oklahoma, he abandoned the field, worked for a while, completed a B.Sc. in mathematics at the University of Alberta–Calgary, and joined the college in 1962 as a teacher of mathematics in the high-school program. In 1966–67 he took a leave to complete an MA in sociology, and returned as a sociology instructor. Earlier he had been deeply involved in the ATA-MRC and its negotiations with Collett. "When I got back," he recalled, "I was quickly embroiled in faculty politics again." The transition from private to public institution was not "very smooth at all," he recalled. "Roles weren't clearly defined; there were a lot of entrepreneurs, people with their own agendas that were trying to bring them to the forefront." Against those who wanted to organize the college around career programs, he, Margaret (Peggy) Brydon, and others from the high-school stream who had secured graduate degrees supported the arts-and-science and university-transfer components of the curriculum and "wanted to teach at the post-secondary level and [in their] subject areas." He was unhappy with the administration and with administration itself. Appointed Director of Arts and Science, he worked with Pentz and Dean for a year but "it just didn't work so at the end of that year I resigned and went back to the faculty as a full-time faculty member. The major difference was [that] I was all caught up in participatory democracy and consensus building and all that sort of stuff – not that I support or go along with those ideas to the same degree as I did in those years, but . . . I was kind of committed to those notions and . . . they were contrary to everything that Pentz and Dean stood for."[175] Finally, he won a seat as a Member of the Legislature of Alberta in 1986 and served until 1993, when he was defeated in a restructured constituency.

Hugh Macleod, also son of a United Church minister (Reverend G. P. Macleod of Knox United, who had also been a member of the private college's board), had earned a B.Ed. and was later to earn an MA in history from the University of Calgary. He had joined the college in 1964. One of the prime movers in the earlier GFC cause and the development of the MRFA (he came from the ATA side), he was also a key leader, as we have seen, of the Alberta Colleges and Institutes Faculty Associations (ACIFA).[176] He served twice as president of the MRFA (1972–74 and 1986–88) and for many years on the Academic Council. A stickler for process, Macleod monitored developments to ensure that the administration abided by the rules in every respect; a wordsmith who valued precision in language, he crafted many of the MRFA's communications. He was to remain at the core of the MRFA through a career that lasted for four decades.

Margaret (Mardy) Roberts, another Calgarian of United Church background whose mother had taught makeup to theatre students at the college, joined Mount Royal in 1969 after graduating with an MA in psychology from the University of Calgary. Shortly after starting, she was invited to serve on the MRFA's Economic Policy Committee, "and so my first encounter with the college administration was as adversaries in the collective bargaining." Apart from that, she said, "I don't remember having much contact with the administration; they were in the other building so one never saw them on a day-to-day basis and as I was embroiled in bargaining and provincial faculty issues and things like that and they were often seen as being on the other side of main issues." The experience was formative, for Roberts remained active thereafter in the MRFA, serving at different points as its secretary, treasurer, and vice-president responsible for liaison with other faculty associations in the province.[177] In four decades of service, she also served as department chair and as a faculty member on the board of governors.

In addition, Martin Serediak, a political scientist, guided negotiations for the MRFA. In that respect, he was both a talented tactician and a pragmatist, aware that the ultimate purpose was to reach an agreement, not endless confrontation. Like the others, he sought to translate ideals into action. He was active in the Arusha group, a CIDA-funded organization located on campus whose mission was to build support for developing countries.[178] After about twenty years, he left Mount Royal for a new profession in health policy,

eventually becoming Assistant Deputy in the Ministry of Health in British Columbia.

Not surprisingly, given the MRFA's desire to establish "co-determination" with the board of governors, flashpoints were usually about the role of the administration. The idea of co-determination implied that the administration would be accountable to the MRFA as the incarnation of the faculty interest. The board did not see things that way. It viewed the president as its chief executive officer and the administration, which reported to the president, as a body of professional managers responsible for carrying out plans and policies. It expected the administration to be thinking ahead, to provide leadership in institutional affairs and external relations, to use appropriate discretion in implementing plans and policies, and to be responsible for the overall well-being of the institution and its constituent parts. The MRFA, by contrast, thought administrators should have minimal discretion and act as mere implementers of policies and plans approved by the board and the MRFA, and then be held to account jointly by board and MRFA. Thus, in 1971, June Akerman, MRFA president, wrote to board chair Cohen to "invite a member of the board of governors . . . to discuss the matter of renewal of administrators' contracts, and further advise the board that the faculty is vitally interested in the process of evaluation for future appointments of administrators."[179] Along the same lines, the academic council in April 1972 voted to "go on record as opposing in principle the notion that any group such as 'chairmen' may make decisions regarding budget cuts prior to the official policy-recommending body, i.e., the academic council, has established guidelines for same. . . . " Administrators were to wait for directions before taking any initiatives.[180]

The negotiation of collective agreements brought the clashing conceptions to the fore. Though the parties in the first round after the Colleges Act referred their differences to a conciliation board struck by the Board of Industrial Relations,[181] the MRFA did not accept the outcome and negotiations continued. In the spring of 1970 the MRFA threatened a 24-hour walkout to secure "a total increase in income and benefits of about 20 per cent."[182] To clarify dispute resolution, board chair Wright learned from the Board of Industrial Relations that it was "of the opinion that we are without jurisdiction and that the provisions of the Alberta Labour Act have no application in the above dispute." The MRFA's lawyer then advised the board that, in the absence of an agreement by 1 March 1970, the MRFA "will have to consider means other than negotiation or conciliation."[183] Frustrated, Wright proposed province-wide bargaining, but was told by the department that things would settle down over a few years and, besides, the idea was contrary to the implications of board governance.[184]

Despite the noisy prelude, there was no strike and the parties signed an agreement for the two-year period from 15 August 1970 to 14 August 1972. It retained the faculty's right to strike, as did subsequent agreements. In 1972 negotiations were also protracted, ending in another threat of work-to-rule and the threat of using the clause in the collective agreement leading to strike or lockout.[185] To punctuate its demands, the MRFA dissolved its bargaining team, the Economic Policy Committee. Though the negotiations eventually resulted in a two-year agreement,[186] the dialogue during this round led the board's lawyer to advise it that the MRFA's notion of co-determination implied ending the day-to-day management of the college by an administration that reported to the board and to the board alone.[187] The pattern of confrontation followed by two-year agreements was confirmed by an agreement for the 1974–76 period.[188] Though the MRFA frequently bargained with a lot of publicity (demonstration pickets, withdrawal of participation in committees, declarations), there was never a faculty strike.

Negotiations over the academic council were also fused with the goal of co-determination. In 1970, the first committee on the academic council agreed that it should make "recommendations and/or decisions which as near as possible reflect the views of informed and responsible students, faculty and administration."[189] In 1972, another committee embraced some of the MRFA's agenda when it recommended "a two-fold structure involving: (1) enlarged committees of the board of governors to include members of the academic community; (2) a revised and somewhat smaller academic council, with a more specific mandate."[190] The council would recommend policy, and board committees would monitor performance. The board's standing committees would be restructured to include two faculty members, two full-time students,

one member of the administration with related responsibilities, and two board members, one of whom would be chairman. Despite concerns about the implications, the board approved the recommendations on 25 August 1972.[191]

In September 1973 the parties finally agreed on a role description for the academic council.[192] "Subject to the authority of the board of governors," it began, "the Academic Council is empowered to deal with all academic affairs of the college and, in particular, but without restricting of the generality of the foregoing, the Academic Council may review and recommend policies" on "the educational aims of the college, courses of study, the academic schedule, academic requirements for diplomas, certificates, and other academic credentials, the advisement and placement of persons entering the college as students, the establishment of academic units and programs of study, affiliation agreements with other institutions, the development and implementation of academic plans, and the form and content of the college calendar." The council was also authorized to make recommendations to the board on budgets, building programs, and "any other functions considered by council to be of interest to the college." It consisted of eighteen members – two statutory members (the president, chief financial officer), four board representatives, eight academic staff representatives, and four student representatives. The council also established a number of committees, on curriculum, academic standards, credit transfer, and "procedures and implementation."[193] With minor modification, this was the basis of the constitution approved by all three parties in 1979.

Though it was not by itself contentious, the inclusion of a faculty member on the board raised interesting questions for the board and MRFA. (Mount Royal's board had recommended the inclusion of student and faculty members during discussion of the Colleges Act.[194]) The act stipulated that the faculty member was to be "nominated by the academic staff association of the college," and the MRFA held an election to determine its nominee.[195] Some behavioural balancing was required. If the faculty member were seen as an MRFA emissary, that would devalue his/her role in the eyes of other board members. Yet, if the faculty member's views were far removed from those of the MRFA, they might be taken to be quixotic or more reflective of faculty sentiment than those of the MRFA. Explaining that "we wanted them to be full members [of the board]," Mardy Roberts said later that the shoals were generally avoided: "I think we were served by people who had the association and the college interests at heart and so there was rarely time when they didn't agree with the majority view."[196]

By and large, other board members were positive about faculty members' participation and respected their views and proposals. P. Neil Webber, a mathematics instructor and later a Member of the Alberta Legislature and cabinet minister, was the first of them from 1970 to 1972. He refrained from voting on "contractual matters" on conflict-of-interest grounds because of legal advice from the MRFA.[197] Over the years, board faculty members adopted slightly different strategies in this respect. Some absented themselves during any discussion of compensation to avoid concerns about self-interest or even historic relationships among employee group compensation. Others were satisfied to listen without speaking or voting. At his first meeting, in September 1970, Webber proposed that the board should meet twice a month "so that ample time may be available for the presentation of material by various college areas," and that board minutes should be circulated to faculty members. These suggestions did not appeal to other board members who agreed to send three copies of the minutes of public meetings to the MRFA and the Students' Association. The board considered requesting a copy of the MRFA's minutes but left it "to "voluntary action" by the association.[198] None was forthcoming.

The second member, George Papas, a philosophy instructor and later president of the MRFA, served from 1972 to 1974. His self-description as "the faculty representative to the board" suggested his approach to the role. He promoted the co-determination agenda. Among other things, he recommended that the board should dissolve its curriculum committee in favour of taking advice directly from the academic council and dissolve its finance committee in favour of a budget review committee consisting of the Director of Finance, the VP, Instruction, two student representatives, four faculty representatives, and one support-staff representative. Its mandate would be "the allocation and/or reallocation of all college operating funds; the establishment of budget guidelines and procedures; review

of the budget."[199] Rather remarkably, given its earlier posture, the board agreed, as did the MRFA. On 16 October 1974 Macleod advised the board that "the MRFA hereby approves the proposals to abolish the curriculum committee and the finance committee of the board. . . and to assign the duties of the aforesaid committees to the academic council and the budget review committee."[200]

The Politics of Site Selection

While those internal struggles were going on, the college continued planning for its new campus. In September 1970 Pentz advised the board that the college was currently operating "out of nineteen different buildings," five of them "formerly private dwellings," one "a converted office building," another "the top floor of an electronics outlet," and the like. By comparison with the norm of 200 square feet per student set by the Alberta Colleges Commission, Mount Royal had only 46 square feet per student.[201] The first planning issue was that of site, a matter that became surprisingly political. Though discussions had taken place with city and Department of Education officials since 1964, the college's formal planning for the new campus began in October 1966 when Collett proposed formation of a board campus development committee. "The college," he said, "should be located for convenient, efficient and pleasant operation as an education institution and community facility." The board then struck its Building and Property Committee,[202] with Neil (Bud) Gamble assigned as a "representative of the President's office" to serve on it and provide administrative support.[203] It took until March 1970 for the site of the new campus to be fixed. The major options were an enlarged location in the downtown to be created by created merging the existing site with Mewata Park, a site in eastern Calgary, and the vacant RCAF airfield in the Lincoln Park district in southwest Calgary (the former Currie Field at No. 3 Service Flying Training School).

The Lincoln Park site first came to the board's attention in September 1964, when Collett reported that the RCAF was planning to shut down its base.[204] Others were also interested in the site, such as ATCO Industries and the Calgary Stampede.[205] Mount Royal

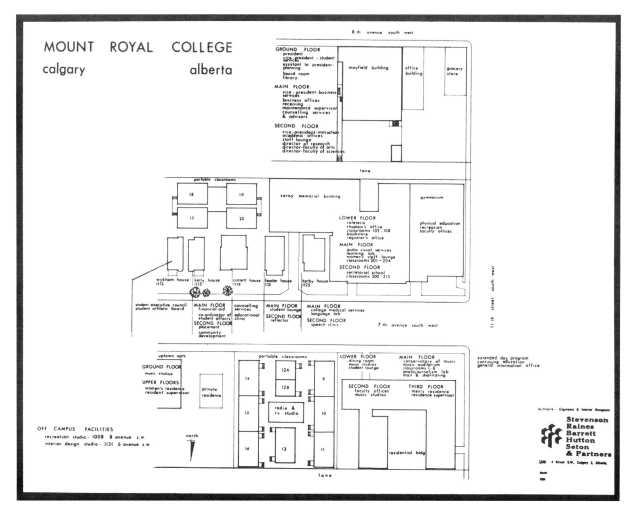

Mount Royal College's downtown "campus" in 1970, following decades of gradual expansion into homes and buildings in the area surrounding the original building. Stevenson Raines Barrett Hutton Seton and Partners; *The Reflector*, 31 August 1970; Mount Royal University Archives N2.

students liked the idea of the Lincoln Park site, and in March 1965 some 140 of them marched to city hall to demand a campus on the Lincoln Park site; the co-chairs of the march, Garry Kohn and John Carstairs, presented a letter to the mayor declaring that "we need a new and a real campus. . . . The students feel that education should have priority over entertainment or industry and that education is the world's largest and finest business investment."[206] In the end, community groups in the region blocked the Stampede though ATCO was assigned land.

The city preferred a downtown site as a campus would be a "people generator" helpful for urban renewal.[207] However, board members exhibited "a definite swing . . . to the Lincoln Park site as opposed to the downtown site,"[208] not so much from an educational as from a political point of view, notably the complications of negotiating land parcel size and location, parking, transportation and access, and whether "other provisions would be kept."[209] Discussion of site also raised the question of size. In March 1965 and again in 1967, city and college officials discussed the possibility of "a downtown site for a community college with a maximum enrolment of 5,000."[210] However, the city's estimates of the land required fell below the college's estimates.[211] Anticipating that the college enrolment might grow beyond 5,000 and that a downtown location would limit capacity, noting as well that the city had done nothing to assemble property for the purpose, the board notified the city in April 1967 that it was requesting 80 acres on the Lincoln Park site. In August 1967 the college hired Stevenson, Raines and Partners to work on the planning and design for the new college.[212]

Meanwhile, the provincial government was thinking more grandly. In 1965 it decided to establish an Alberta Vocational Centre in Calgary, with the issue of its location left uncertain; the AVC was to create a new delivery vehicle for adult upgrading and job readiness programs funded by the federal government. The province was still administering SAIT and enlarging it as well. In September 1967 Minister of Education Robert Reierson raised the possibility of a campus in Lincoln Park to accommodate both Mount Royal and SAIT for a projected joint enrolment of 10,000–15,000 students.[213] Board member Thorssen anticipated that "within two years" the institutions might be merged, "establish[ing] the pattern for the rest of the province." Moreover, he added "the minister . . . has indicated that there is an additional possibility that such an institution could offer the third and fourth year of a degree program."[214]

With that scenario in mind, Mayor Jack Leslie (1965–69), a graduate of the university-transfer program in 1938 who moved on to the University of Alberta,[215] concluded that Mount Royal should be located in Lincoln Park.[216] Thus, "with the full approval of the minister," Mount Royal "made a written request to the city for a joint site of 115 acres in Lincoln Park." But then the temperature cooled. According to a board document, "the city did not respond to this letter and broke off all official contact with the college. The city wanted to defer any decision until the new legislation for Post Secondary Education was presented in the spring of 1968." The college continued to promote Lincoln Park for itself. In February 1968 a citizens' group, Calgary Urban Action, sponsored a forum at the Jubilee Auditorium at which the college presented the case; city officials declined the invitation to participate.[217] However, the Chamber of Commerce also weighed in, favouring a downtown site.[218]

In July 1968 Mount Royal and city officials met with minister Reierson to discuss the site. The minister indicated that the city was not facing an either/or situation and was "definitely placing an adult educational centre [the AVC] in the urban renewal area which will provide upgrading programs for adults and that this would probably provide the type of instruction that the Chamber of Commerce is concerned about." Dr. G. L. Mowat, chairman of the Provincial Board, who was also there, in effect declared in favour of the Lincoln Park site.[219] Following the meeting, the city council "agreed to seek provincial approval for the college" to relocate to Lincoln Park.[220] In a letter dated 21 July 1969, the government allocated the site to the college.[221]

At this point Rod Sykes, the newly elected mayor (1969–77), decided to use the city's site approval power to maximize benefits for urban-renewal goals. The Department of Education was still considering building the AVC campus but had not fixed the site. Concerned that the campus in Lincoln Park might absorb the AVC campus, Sykes linked the city's approval for the college to the development of a downtown campus for the AVC. The minister of education advised Sykes that the college was responsible for selecting its own site.[222] The mayor ignored the letter, and the minister wrote again on 23 December 1969, urging him "to meet with the Mount Royal board at the earliest possible date" to resolve the issue. Sykes then upped the ante, appointing "a committee to study the proposed locations of Mount Royal Junior College, with a view to recommending to City Council that location which the committee considers will best serve the interests of the people of Calgary."[223] In return, the board issued a statement: "In view of the substantially unchanged circumstances governing the availability and suitability of an urban renewal site, the present critical shortage of college facilities, and the expenditure of time, effort and money which has gone into the planning to date, the board of governors must question the rationality of the decision to review the location of the site at this time."[224] The board met with the minister on 13 January 1970, following which Clark advised Pentz that "the government has agreed to make April 8th 1970 the final deadline for submission of proposals by the city of Calgary for a site for Mount Royal College…. We expect continued planning for Lincoln Park. We will only respond to new information."[225]

Students "kidnap" Calgary Mayor Rod Sykes and Chief
Inspector Chris Staff, March 1970, for a student charity
event. Photographer the *Calgary Herald*; Glenbow Archives
NA-2864-5192.

Sykes' ad hoc committee then scrambled matters
further by recommending merger of Mewata Park
with the college's existing properties. Thus, both
the AVC and Mount Royal would be located in the
downtown. Some faculty members, including Pashak,
joined Sykes in his campaign to keep the college in
the downtown because "it would better service lower
income people and that kind of thing and because of
the better transportation into the downtown."[226] But
the college's board stood firm, declaring that it had
"carefully considered the report and having done so
sees no reason to change its original position; . . . we
would like to receive a government decision as soon
as possible."[227]

The cabinet finally intervened,[228] but made con-
cessions to Sykes. The college would be relocated to
Lincoln Park, its enrolment would not exceed 5,000,
and there would be "a significant reduction in the total
size of the Lincoln Park site." The government would
"take ownership of the present downtown lands and
buildings" and "alternative uses of this land and for
these buildings will be explored in consultation with
the City of Calgary."[229] The minister instructed officials "to enter into discussions with the Mount
Royal board and other authorities in the Department
of Education with a view to incorporating the proposed Adult Vocational Centre in Churchill Park into
Mount Royal College at an initial downtown campus"; the AVC campus would cost $3.5 million. Thus,
the reduced size of the Lincoln Park operation would
be compensated for by merging Mount Royal and the
AVC in the downtown.

The Colleges Commission had envisaged a three-
stage expansion process for Mount Royal on the Lincoln Park site: Phase I (to 1972) would culminate in a
campus for 5,000 students with 500 residence spaces,
at a total cost of $25 million; Phase II (1972–77) would
be for 7,500 students, with an additional 200 residence

spaces; and Phase III would take the campus up to 10,000 students.[230] As a result of the cabinet's decision, Phase I capacity was reduced to 3,000 from 5,000 students, the residences were removed, and the budget was cut to $16.6 million. Salvaging what it could, Mount Royal's board persuaded the Colleges Commission to agree that the campus would "be acceptable for physical facilities to be built for 5,000 students as soon as possible after 1972" and that the long-range campus plan would accommodate 10,000 students.[231] Lauchlan explained the downsizing process: "It was agreed . . . to reduce the academic space on the outer section of the building by 2/5ths but leave the entire service core essentially untouched."[232]

Thus, between decisions driven by government priorities and Sykes's manoeuvring, the facilities were reduced and bowdlerized, giving rise to problems when the campus opened – and hastening the time when the next expansion project would be necessary. Indeed, from 1966 to 2010 the government persistently underestimated student demand for Mount Royal, with the result that each construction phase – I, II, and III – was hardly finished when the campus was overflowing. Pentz presciently warned Kolesar, whose hand had been forced by politicians, that there is "a real possibility of a boom in post-secondary enrolments and the limitation on Mount Royal College might need to be reviewed."[233]

Sod turning for the Lincoln Park Campus, June 1970. (L–R) The Honourable Robert Clark (Alberta Minister of Education) and Howard Wright (Chairman, Mount Royal College Board of Governors). Photographer the *Calgary Herald*; Glenbow Archives NA-2864-5771.

Construction underway on the Lincoln Park Campus, 1971. Photographer Hillhurst Studio; Mount Royal University Archives HB83-2.

The Character of the College

While issues of site and size were determined by forces beyond the college's control, other aspects fell within its ambit – the tone, the particular space needs, the spatial relationships, and the design. Mount Royal's planners were bold and innovative, rethinking traditional ways of delivering programs. Its architects looked for a metaphor appropriate to a community college as distinct from a high school or university. In the fall of 1967 the architects and some administrators visited institutions in California, Michigan, North Carolina, Massachusetts, and Ontario to study campus designs.[234] The architects engaged the college community in a dialogue about the goals to be served by the new facility.[235]

In November 1967 the Building and Property Committee approved a statement on "The Character and Guidelines for the Development of Mount Royal College." The new facilities "should reflect an educational institution which is unique, exciting, dynamic and viable – one having an integrity which distinguishes it from other educational institutions." "Every attempt should be made to allow for change . . . This suggests that great zones of adaptable multi-purpose space should be provided rather than highly specialized small zones . . ., designed so that they will retain their usefulness despite organizational changes which may occur." The facilities should include "a variety of teaching spaces . . . to allow for a balance of individual, small group and large learning situations. In most instances partitions and other space arrangement determinants should facilitate maximum flexibility since programs and teaching methods will undoubtedly continue to change."[236] The campus "should contribute towards learning by encouraging involvement and communication as well as aesthetic pleasures. . . . " Thus, "opportunities for the encounter of students with each other and with faculty should be considered of paramount importance. Social, lounging and meeting areas should be provided in a manner that maximizes informal learning opportunities. In addition adequate provision should be made for places of privacy and independent thought."[237]

"Just before we were going to make the final decision," Gamble later related, "we got this one page letter from a fellow by the name of Stan Leggett and it

intrigued both Arnie Fullerton [architect] and myself and so even though we were close to the deadline we invited him up . . . He immediately related to this concept because it fit with his own idea of what should be happening in education. He saw this as a unique opportunity, that half the battle was won, and he could now fit his idea quite nicely into this."[238] Thus, the board retained Engelhardt, Engelhardt and Leggett to elaborate the pedagogical model. Leggett drafted "The Idea of a College" (6 January 1969), in which he proposed a curriculum based on a problem-solving approach in which faculty would either pose problems for students to consider or work with students to define issues and problems, which the students would then address using technology, interdisciplinary methods, faculty advice, and any other resources they found that helped. A "lecture-discussion-independent study model" would constitute "an alternative to the traditional model of small class/small laboratory system of instruction." Students would spend "some" time "in lectures [ca. 30 per cent], some time in group discussion [ca. 15 per cent], and a substantial amount of time in independent work [ca. 55 per cent]." Self-paced learning was a critical feature of the model. Students would be responsible for mastering bodies of information and skills in segments that could be assessed at "testing stations." Moving from one module to another would depend on testing success, on demonstrated competence.

Leggett underlined the implications of his concepts. "Built into the total decision-making apparatus are views as to what truly constitutes an education. This model is based upon the importance of the student as a learner, his reaction to the problems that he must solve, and his acquisition of tools to enable him to attack problems. . . . In a sense, the student, within limits, is expected to get the information he needs and learn by trying to solve the problem. The instructor adopts the position of waiting until he is called upon and, throughout, refraining from telling the student what to do – an admirable restraint." This "enterprise model" involved "an interdisciplinary project-oriented approach to learning in which, as in a continuum, students are able to spin off at any level for career programs or to follow areas of individual interest while a portion of the group of students involved move on into other institutions for more advanced levels of education growing out of the enterprise in which they have been involved." The space implications included the need for "flexible space" to permit "unknown probes into unknown areas" and four "major problem centres involving interdisciplinary approaches."[239] The plan also envisaged a wired facility enabling TV programs to be broadcast from a central media centre into each classroom and student and faculty media-based projects; Leggett anticipated use of computers. "This, very simply," Pentz said when the facilities opened, "is how our Lincoln Park learning model was envisioned and this is the basis on which the new campus was planned and built."[240]

This was a bold plan that implied changes in how faculty members conceived themselves and behaved. To facilitate the transition, the administration organized visits to other institutions, held workshops, and issued *Toward 72*, "guidelines" for instructors "developing their courses for implementation at the Lincoln Park Campus in September 1972."[241]

Meanwhile, the architects had decided that the campus should be modelled on the modern shopping mall. "The central core of the campus is an open mall which allows access to any area. In this, the structure resembles a vast shopping complex." The architects described their efforts to combine functions in large open spaces. "Outside the mall, two sides of the campus open into the learning library – an open L-shaped area which is the primary study area. Scattered throughout the learning library are the resource islands, the learning centres for independent study. Each one caters to a specific discipline with all the resources needed for study readily available . . . The learning library also houses some 200 faculty offices. Being located near the centres of study, instructors are thus in closer liaison with students and are readily available for consultation."[242]

RELATIONS WITH SAMRC AND STUDENT SPACE

There remained the issue of space for student activities. When planning the new campus had begun in the fall of 1967, Ron Prokosch, president of the Students Executive Council of the Students' Union, had advised the board of a desire to build a student centre. . . . "[243]

The size of such facilities soon became an issue. As Lauchlan explained later, "there was a general agreement with the Colleges Commission that there would be government support available for student association facilities but there were no guidelines available to define that participation."[244] Thus, initial planning for students' facilities occurred without government direction on what it would pay for. In October 1969 the association presented its estimated needs – 33,775 gross square feet of space (25,043 for "students' facilities," 9,075 for "shared areas"); in addition, it proposed "9,950 or so" more square feet for "revenue producing areas" (bank, barbershop, collegiate store, and travel bureau) – altogether, some 46,000 square feet.[245] In November 1969, the campus plan was approved by the Colleges Commission,[246] and a few weeks later, on 11 December 1969, the commission finally issued its guideline for what it would pay for in student space. It would permit funding only for Students' Association offices, meeting rooms, and games and lounge areas – about 27,000 square feet. Anything beyond that would have to be paid in full by the association. The association requested a government loan of $1.2 million to pay for extra space but the Colleges Commission refused the request.[247] By the time all of this was clear, in July 1970, the college's tender documents for construction were ready to be issued. They included the 46,000 square feet requested by the association. "For this reason," Lauchlan explained, "the association and the board reached agreement that the college would assume responsibility for the space beyond the provincial support level [i.e., 27,000 square feet] by declaring it academic or administrative space against the requirements of growing enrolment. This would allow the project to go to tender. The students in the meantime would continue their search for financing." This outcome was recorded in the "Pentz-Symons agreement" of 21 July 1970. The architect, J. M. Stevenson, advised the Colleges Commission of the areas affected by this re-description.[248] In October 1970 the Colleges Commission awarded $303,550 to the Students' Association to match a like amount to be raised by the association. In January 1972, the association proposed buying a share of the new campus, but it had no money and the board preferred a non-ownership licensing relationship.[249]

When the campus opened in September 1972, the association occupied the 46,000 square feet. This disturbed the board, which asked in May 1973 for a report on the "exact descriptions of facilities being used by the Students' Association, the amount which they have paid for, an estimate of the square footage cost of utilities and care taking, and a survey of what other colleges and universities are doing in this regard."[250] As the report showed that the association was occupying more space than it was entitled to and was charging rent for commercial space that had been removed from its purview, the board demanded that the association sign agreements for each board-owned space it was occupying. In exchange, it guaranteed that "the Students' Association shall be invited to participate in any planning for expansion of the college so that all alternatives can be fully explored by the association prior to making commitments for the purchase of existing space."[251]

Wyckham House, the first student centre, located at 1113 - 7 Avenue S.W., in a former home across the street from Mount Royal College's original building, 1970. Mount Royal University Archives HA296.

Another space-related irritant arose from the location of student activities at the heart of the open-plan campus. There was a large area centred on the Forum, including the Rathskellar pub, that students used for social occasions. To set policies "to govern the utilization of the Forum, Fireside Lounge, and Games Lounge (Upper Forum), etc.," the board and the association formed the Forum Program Board. Its purpose was to coordinate use, minimize noise, and control liquor. Partygoers with liquor sometimes wandered the hallways. When planning for Phase II began, both sides looked forward to the student activities being located in a separate facility.

The hope that the Students' Association would abide by its commitment to supply financial information was short-lived. In September 1971 Lauchlan reported that the association had not "complied with the terms of our agreement regarding the submission of audited financial statements and budget projections . . . No funds can be released to the students until these decisions are made. Further, in view of the legal status of the present Executive, I believe that the board must consider whether or not they are 'duly elected and constituted' representatives of the Student Body to whom these activity funds can be entrusted."[252] The problems were remedied but uncertain student leadership was a persistent concern. High turnover in the student body meant that few students gained experience in student government; there was little memory of prior commitments.

LOOKING BACK

The period from 1966 to 1972 was both a productive and a contentious time. In terms of transformational experiences, this period had nearly all of them. The college had a new legal footing, a new board, a new collegial body (the academic council), a new administrative structure, legally established faculty and students' associations, a collective agreement with the faculty, a huge change in scale (near doubling of enrolment, trebling in employees), an expanded program roster, a changed student body, and a new public image.

During that period the college was permeated by idealism and inventiveness. It committed itself to a bold new pedagogical approach that would steer the design of its new facilities. Stimulated by the opportunity to design programs and revise old ones, faculty members experimented with team teaching, peer tutoring, and other innovations. During this time, the Colleges Act also formally fixed some attributes of the new college, including the composition and role of the governing board, the context for collective bargaining with academic staff, and the limited nature of collegial decision making. It made Mount Royal a member of a broader system, creating a situation in which its future efforts to be different in response to the rapidly evolving Calgary community would be held hostage to a system responding to the needs of communities with quite different characteristics. To be sure, times of rapid change are also times of stress, and the college's internal relations suffered in the face of growth and many unresolved issues. However, even more stressful times lay ahead, as the move to the new campus was to bring both new opportunities and new conflicts.

TABLE 6.1 PROGRAM PROFILE, 1970s[1]

CAREER DIPLOMA PROGRAMS "To prepare a student for immediate career employment upon graduation."	CERTIFICATE PROGRAMS "To prepare graduates for immediate employment or to assist practitioners in the field in upgrading their skills."
Aviation	Architecture
Broadcasting	
Business Administration Streams: 1. General Business Administration; 2. Accounting & Financial Management; 3. Personnel Management; 4. Marketing Management; 5. Computer Programming; 6. Systems Analysis	Public Administration
Community and Regional :Planning	Community and Regional Planning
Social Justice Careers	Criminal Justice Careers: 1. Correctional Officers; 2. Police; 3. Extension Program
Early Childhood Education	Early Childhood Education and Development
Environmental Quality Control	Environmental Quality Control: (a) Air Sampling and Analysis; (b) Water Sampling and Analysis)
Interior Design	
Journalism	
Recreation and Leisure Studies	
Medical Office Assistant	
Music: (a) Keyboard Instruments; (b) Orchestral Instruments;	
Nursing	
Public Relations	
Secretarial Arts	Stenographers
Social Service Careers	Youth Services
Speech	
Arts and Science Diplomas "To prepare students to transfer to a selected degree-granting university for continuation of studies"	
Applied Social Sciences	Interior Design
Canadian Studies	Journalism
Computing Science	Leisure Education
Criminal Justice	Petroleum Land Management
Drama	Physical Education: 1. General Physical Education; 2. Aquatic Administrator; 3. Community Coach; 4. Physical Fitness Instructor & 5. Evaluator
Engineering	Secretarial Arts
General Studies	Speech

1   Summary of programs, MRC *Calendar*, 1977-79, 51.

TABLE 6.2 ACADEMIC PROGRAMS, BY DEPARTMENT, 1977[1]

DEPARTMENT	PROGRAMS OFFERED "Courses" = open to all students
Administrative Studies	Diploma: 6 Certificate: 1 Courses: 4
Behavioral Science	Diplomas: 3 Certificate: 2 Courses: 5
Communicating and Performing Arts	Diploma: 7 Courses: 3
Criminal Justice	Diploma: 3 Certificate: 4 Courses: 1
Environmental Sciences	Diploma: 3 Certificate: 3 Courses: 7
Humanities and Religion	Diploma: 1 Courses: 10
Interior Design and Architecture	Diploma: 2 Certificate: 1 Courses: 1
Language Arts	Courses: 1
Leisure Education and Physical Education	Diploma: 5 Courses: 5
Math, Physics and Engineering	Diploma: 4 Courses: 5
Nursing	Diploma: 1 Courses: 1
Secretarial Arts	Diploma: 3 Certificate: 1 Courses: 1

1   List based on MRC *Calendar*, 1977-79, 248-49.

TABLE 6.3 CITIZENSHIP OF MOUNT ROYAL COLLEGE ACADEMIC STAFF AND ADMINISTRATION, 1970-71

FACULTY	ARTS	SCIENCE	NURSING	OTHER	TOTAL	%
Canadian	28	22	10	28	88	77.2
Non-Canadian	12	4	3	7	26	22.8
Total	40	26	13	35	114	100.0
Counsellors	Counsellors	Administration				
Canadian	8	11			19	65.5
Non-Canadian	4	6			10	34.5
Total	12	17			29	100.0

Based on Alberta, Committee of Inquiry into Non-Canadian Influence in Alberta Post-Secondary Education. Report of the Committee of Inquiry into Non-Canadian Influence in Alberta Post-Secondary Education, 1973, Table B-10, Citizenship of Staff by Division, 1970-71, 113.

TABLE 6.4 COUNTRY OF UNDERGRADUATE AND GRADUATE DEGREES OF ACADEMIC STAFF, 1970-71

	ARTS	SCIENCE	NURSING	OTHER	TOTAL	%
UNDERGRADUATE						
Canadian	25	16	11	22	74	64.9
USA	11	5	1	11	28	24.5
Britain	0	2	0	0	2	1.8
Other	4	3	1	1	9	7.9
None Stated	0	0	0	1	1	.9
Total	40	26	13	35	114	100.0
GRADUATE						
Canadian					54	47.4
USA					32	28.1
Britain					0	0
Other					3	2.6
None Stated					25	21.9
Total					114	100.0

Based on Alberta, Committee of Inquiry into Non-Canadian Influence in Alberta Post-Secondary Education. Report of the Committee of Inquiry into Non-Canadian Influence in Alberta Post-Secondary Education, 1973, Table B-11, Country of Degree of Academic Staff by Division, 1970-71, 113.

1970–1972	*Negotiations for merger with Alberta Vocational Centre-Calgary*
1971	*Collaboration begins with Old Sun College*
1972	*Lincoln Park campus opens*
	Department of Advanced Education and Alberta Council on Admissions and Transfer established
1975	*President Pentz departs; Douglas M. Lauchlan named Acting President, then President in 1976*
1977	*Board rejects Lincoln Park Development Plan*
1978	*Phase II expansion proposal submitted and ignored*
1980	*Constitution of Academic Council approved*
	President Lauchlan departs

CHAPTER 7

SETTLING INTO LINCOLN PARK, 1972–1980

Every inch of the building suggests new ways of learning things. . . . Physically, the move is a century jump.

– Calgary Herald, 1972.[1]

If a vigorous Mount Royal College community is to develop, it is necessary for each member of the community to recognize that it is a fruitless effort to attempt to impose one's exclusive sense of what the College is and where it is going on others. This has been tried. . . . The most visible outcome to the outsider is a badly stressed organization.

– Ingram et al., "A College in Process," 1975.[2]

The Peter Lougheed Conservative government elected in 1971 moved quickly to launch its "province-building" agenda. This took many forms, beginning with the development of infrastructure (roads, regional colleges, hospitals, schools). It also entailed establishing government authority over the province's oil and gas reserves and advancing Alberta's interests in Canada. Lougheed used force majeure to renegotiate oil and gas leases and to raise the royalty rate to 20–25 per cent of gross profit. This was before OPEC reduced supply in 1973. From 1973 to 1981 the price rose from $10 a barrel to $37. The rising price contributed to inflation, which in 1975 forced the federal government to introduce a three-year wage-and-price controls program. Meanwhile, Alberta experienced rapid economic and demographic growth. In the late 1970s, some 3,000 people a week moved into Calgary in search of employment. In 1976 Alberta established the Heritage Savings Trust Fund, into which it placed 30 per cent of revenues received from non-renewable resource royalties.[3] Inflation roared: the average price of a house sale rose from $103,000 in 1973 to $230,000 in 1981. The downtown burgeoned with developments. High-rise towers dwarfed the Calgary Tower (renamed from the Husky Tower). From 1978 to 1982, Calgary set a record for the volume of office space built in Canada in such a short period. Building permits topped one billion dollars a year. Sprawling into new suburbs, the city added new shopping malls and recreation centres and parks.[4]

Alberta's good fortune raised questions elsewhere in the country. Conflicting opinions about whether oil wealth should be reserved for Alberta or shared nationally led to tensions between Alberta and the federal government, which had to balance regional interests. One of the first venues for the debate was the new Lincoln Park campus of Mount Royal College, which in July 1973 hosted the Western Economic Opportunities Conference organized by Lougheed to present western views to Prime Minister Pierre Trudeau and Finance Minister John Turner.[5]

Though relocation to the new Lincoln Park campus in September 1972 opened the way for fresh initiatives, some of the old tensions continued and indeed became sharper. The move disrupted the college's established relations with the community. Relocated from the bustling downtown to a large tract of empty land in the southwest quadrant of the city, it was surrounded on two sides by military bases and bordered by two freeways, accessible only by automobile and infrequent bus service. Over the next thirty years, the college was to make repeated efforts to work with the city and community groups on a Lincoln Park development plan, with the aim of making the college a focal point and resource for that community. At the same time, the college reached out more vigorously to the wider community, including First Nations peoples. Thus, while undergoing sharp challenges to its internal sense of community, the college focused more intensely on the external community than it had ever done in the past.

"A Century Jump": The New Campus

The Lincoln Park campus into which the college moved in September 1972 was very handsome, solidly built, and modern in form.[6] There were attractive vistas both inside and outside the three-storey building, with lovely external terraces and inner spaces. The external cladding consisted mainly of attractive striated precast concrete wall panels. Expansive terraces near the centre of the structure were well used during good weather. Literally and figuratively, the new Mount Royal was an "open door" institution, a "people place," as the new advertising tagline suggested. The corridors were laid with high-quality glazed terracotta tiles that still gleam. The building was a mega-structure, uniting a wide array of functions under one roof. It consisted of 60,121 square metres of gross space on 86.7 acres of land. Of the gross space, only 33,373 square metres, or 55 per cent, were assignable to functions. The rest consisted of the corridors, stairwells, open spaces, and mechanical and electrical services.[7] The architects had delivered the high-quality academic shopping mall that they had promised.

Flexibility was the dominant motif. The college's open admission requirements were matched by the huge open multi-purpose spaces and wide corridors. There were few enclosed classrooms or offices. Much of the instruction was to take place in open areas where partitions and tablet chairs could be moved around to fit different instructional methods and class sizes. The

Aerial image of the
Mount Royal College
Lincoln Park Campus,
1972. Mount Royal
University Archives
HB82.

The new Lincoln Park
Campus featured the
Kerby Memorial Chimes
carillon. Photographer
Linda Crawford; Mount
Royal University Archives
G1244.

major enclosed instructional spaces were clustered in ten 100-seat spaces divisible by hanging partitions into 25- or 50-seat modules. Faculty offices, located in the huge open Learning Resources Centre, consisted of desks hanging off mobile partitions. Student services, including counselling, were also located there. Spaces for administrators consisted of bullpen offices visible through plate-glass windows. Some large spaces were designed for multiple uses. The Forum, a 1,000-seat open area, divisible by mobile partitions into four large theatre-style classrooms, was also devoted to student use, such as dances, concerts, receptions, and banquets. The major social space for students, the Rathskellar, was located there as well. The 400-seat [Clinton J.] Ford Theatre, a large two-storey room with a balcony on the second level, doubled as a lecture space and black box theatre. The [Walter] Jenkins Theatre, a 200-seat lecture hall with raked benching (no fixed seating), was also useful for theatre purposes. There were also two purpose-built performance spaces – the 297-seat [Leonard] Leacock Theatre, for music, and the 270-seat [Howard P.] Wright Theatre, with a thrust stage, for drama. To encourage discussion and participation, there were two "seminar pits" in the corridors that came to feature everything from wrestling matches to musical presentations and debates. These were located on the ground floor of the open three-storey wells, enabling people on all three levels to see or engage in what was going on in the "carpeted, chair-less, 'people baskets'" on the main floor.[8]

As intended, the corridors and scattered functions facilitated interaction among faculty, staff, students, and administrators. The largest open space, "bigger than three football fields," was the burnt-orange–carpeted Learning Resources Centre. In response to the Leggett model, with its emphasis on self-paced learning, technology, and the role of faculty and librarians as facilitators of learning, most academic personnel were located in the centre. Teaching materials for programs were clustered in "resource islands" where librarians could assist students and faculty. The resource islands were connected by co-axial cable to the audiovisual resource centre that contained videotapes (both made by faculty and purchased from elsewhere) and 16-millimetre film. As claimed by the college, this was probably "one of the most sophisticated electronic library files on the continent" at the time.[9] Faculty "offices"

were clustered around the resource islands. Alan R. Dyment, who became director of the Learning Resource Centre in 1973, later said the resource islands were "very, very popular with the students; they were popular with faculty; they became a gathering place, a social centre . . . for the programs, and each island was a little different," the focal point for a different sub-community of students and faculty.[10]

The spaces designed for particular programs worked well for example, for television and radio broadcasting, for interior design, for science laboratories, and for the performing arts. Downtown, the Conservatory had taught lessons in the old Barn and in "old houses that were empty." As the new facilities did not include music studios, Bach designed soundproof cubicles that were located in the corridors on the third storey and in the landing of a stairwell. "When we moved to the new campus," he said, "it was so big that you only saw some of the people once every two or three weeks. It was cold, whereas the other one was nice and warm." To keep in touch, Conservatory instructors met once a week for "lunch and discussed things." In a melancholy note, he added: "I suppose the others on the academic side did the same thing but we weren't invited to those."[11]

The Leacock Theatre expanded the audience for the Conservatory, which now had five orchestras (three string, two full symphony), five choirs (in place of the one), and a wide range of brass and woodwind ensembles. Similarly, the Theatre Arts program benefited from the Wright Theatre to become a prominent venue for theatre productions. In the 1970s, there were few performance halls or theatres in the city, and Mount Royal now filled a void. Thus, the new campus was a major addition not only to post-secondary education but to the cultural life of the city.

Though the faculty concerns were about the pedagogical implications of the facility, some were critical of the structure. Steve Thompson, a faculty member, described it as "massive in scale, impersonal and functional": "It's like a machine with its lack of colour, its exposed mechanical duct work, the great concrete columns. . . . An efficient machine, humming away, drawing me into its maws."[12] Ken Robson remembered: ". . . faculty offices were arranged in star clusters with no doors. These odd-shaped offices had five-foot hard board partitions, tin file cabinets, fluorescent task lighting and one bulletin board each. The orange upholstery on the office chair matched the thousands of square feet of carpeting throughout the main floor of the building. Initially, these office complexes were situated well back of the windows (which were reserved for student work areas), and under large, pendulous mercury vapour lights. For reasons that were immediately evident, offices began migrating towards the windows and, soon, uniformly rectangular offices, many with a moveable partition-door, began to appear along the entire perimeter of the [Learning Resources Centre]."[13]

There was nowhere to leave books or notes without fear of losing them. For want of privacy and quiet, faculty members found it hard to read, prepare classes, meditate, or talk to one another or with students with any privacy. The same was true of the "classrooms" separated by standing partitions in large open spaces. The babble of lectures, debates, films, and other activities made it difficult to concentrate. The effect was the opposite of that intended: rather than making themselves permanently available to students and colleagues, many faculty attended only for classes, office hours, and meetings.

As employees sought privacy, the partitions multiplied, turning large open areas into confusing mazes of corridors, offices, and meeting rooms. The challenge of coping with open space was not limited to the faculty or academic support staff. To ensure accessibility, the vice-president, Instruction, "complete with typing secretaries," was located "in an open-area group of desks in the library."[14] The president's bullpen lasted only to 1973, when a separate office was hived off to provide a private space for Prime Minister Trudeau at the Western Economic Opportunities Conference.

One of many on-campus eateries, the Stage Door, ca. 1972. Photographer Janet Brown; Mount Royal University Archives B6-3-11.

Unsatisfactory working conditions led faculty members to request a space where they could prepare classes, grade papers, read, and mingle. In November 1974 Thomas L. Wood, the third faculty board member, asked the board "to build an area . . . to accommodate approximately one-third of the faculty to provide facilities for reading, marking, lecture preparation, relaxation, offices, meetings of the Faculty Association and committees thereof and storage of files for same." After plans were drawn up, the board approved funds to develop a Faculty Centre.[15] Thereafter it became an important social centre for faculty members.

The open-floor-plan Library. Photographer Janet Brown; Mount Royal University Archives B6-62-14.

The challenges of the open-plan facilities complicated implementation of the Leggett pedagogical model. The model envisaged a mix of large lectures, lecture-discussion groups, individual instruction, and self-paced student learning. The underlying assumptions were idealistic: students were eager learners capable of assuming responsibility for their own learning, and faculty members would see themselves as learning facilitators rather than as subject authorities, would develop materials for self-paced and competency-based learning and would be available for individual consultations all week long. However, the students were not used to self-paced and competency-based learning and many faculty members found it difficult to make the model work, even with the best of wills. Moreover, there was the question of how the contractual obligation to teach twelve to eighteen hours, depending upon one's field, squared with the full-time job of learning facilitation.

Teaching spaces on the new campus featured movable walls and open spaces. Photographer Janet Brown; Mount Royal University Archives B6-45-32.

Even so, many faculty members made valiant efforts to make the Leggett model work. Recalling "one of the noble pedagogical experiments I participated in," Robson said that "seven of us taught two lectures each in the Ford Theatre to the 200+ students in the survey of British literature. The balcony with its poor sightlines posed a challenge for anyone teaching in the space and prompted all of us to "perform" in order to maintain attention. We each went to the

Media Services area weekly where we recorded audio quizzes on the topics which the students would listen to at the Resource Islands. They would hand in their answers to be collected and corrected by instructors according to a key. . . . I still recollect a colleague finishing his – and our – final lecture in the course with the deliberately out-of-focus slide of Dylan from the cover of his *Blonde on Blonde* album accompanied by the punch-line: 'It's all blowin' in the wind.'" Noting that his memories indicated the inadequacies and absurdities of these early years but also the amount of effort and accommodation individuals brought to the task of implementing the Leggett model, he said that "the model failed and the remainder of the 1970s became a time of searching for pedagogical alternatives. My sense is that, with some notable exceptions, most instructors reverted to more conventional modes of instruction."[16]

Why did the Leggett model fail? There were many reasons: "1) it was far too closely associated with (mostly) non-teaching administrators and it had too few faculty champions; 2) there were unresolved workload implications; 3) it relied upon relatively rudimentary and inflexible technology; 4) it required high levels of infrastructure support; 5) it was very time-intensive; 5) it presupposed an unrealistically high degree of independence among learners; and 6) it incorporated several other controversial pedagogical features (e.g., 'make time the variable and learning the constant')."[17] Mardy Roberts explained that "the self-paced instruction just didn't work" because there was a lack of qualified support staff to test students in a timely way, faculty had received insufficient professional development in self-paced learning, and the students were unfamiliar with "mastery learning" and its implications. Though the campus had a central media production capacity, despite the removal of the wiring for televisions in classrooms, only a few instructors took advantage of the technology and the media centre became a service station for a few individual faculty members rather than a vehicle for the systematic delivery of the curriculum. "We implemented all the instructional changes all at the same time, and people were learning to cope with open area classrooms and self-paced learning and students who had never encountered this kind of learning before. So I think all of those combined to be a real bit of shock to both faculty and the students. . . . I think the technology wasn't sophisticated enough to do TV shows or the people weren't sophisticated enough to know how to best use the technology." Within "five or six years . . . ," Roberts concluded, "we were back to the old ABC classes with one instructor and scheduled exams."[18]

Given such challenges, it was inevitable that the Leggett model would founder. This was due less to the model than to its application in an open admissions college with many "second-chance" students who lacked academic motivation and needed intensive instruction and learning skills support. However, both the internal squabbling and the lack of necessary funding caused the experiment to fail. Only when rising admission standards required students to have completed, or very nearly completed, matriculation in the early 1980s did the gap in student learning skills reach the point where the college could provide an adequate level of support to weak students. The model would be better suited to the first-class undergraduate university Mount Royal aspired to become in the twenty-first century.

The failure of the experiment led to confrontation, conflict, and bitterness. The board had endorsed the Leggett model after seeking faculty support. The board and president Pentz had been lauded for their vision and were committed to the model. They put pressure on the faculty to make it work. Meanwhile, many faculty members only realized the implications of what they had approved when implementation was needed, some were disbelieving from the outset, and others became angry at being blamed for the lack of success in implementing the model. The resulting conflict was to provide a lesson in how not to introduce major change in curricular delivery.

ADDRESSING THE TENSION

In response to the rising tensions, the board sought the advice of consultants in October 1974. A team designated by the Department of Educational Administration at the University of Alberta examined the campus environment and concluded in its report, *A College in Process* (December 1975), that the manner in which the college had adopted the Leggett model had been a mistake. That was not because the model was flawed but because faculty had been denied the alternative of continuing or trying other approaches. "The decision makers" had failed to show sufficient flexibility in planning and in responding to faculty resistance; their "unitary style" had not allowed for variety or nuance: many problems had arisen from "the administration's decision to back an 'instructional systems' strategy as an all-embracing framework. But the responsibility was shared. The administration had turned from "the initial empirical-rational strategy" to "a power-coercive strategy." Faculty members had resolved the contradictory forces working on them "by some combination of the following: by successful application of the 'instructional systems' framework, by 'going through the motions' and reporting compliance, by passive resistance, and in a few instances by aggressive counterattack."[19]

Some senior administrators "held the view that the 'open area' design of much of the instructional space would itself compel innovation in teaching methods. Stripped of access to the familiar self-contained classroom, instructors would search for alternatives that would suit the new environment. Necessity would once again be the mother of invention." However, "what was overlooked was the possibility that creative energies thus unleashed would find ingenious ways to restore the traditional environment." Within two years, the large open spaces had been replaced by complex mazes of partitions. Thus, the consultants wrote, "it appears that the metaphor 'people place' – in the sense of person-to-person interaction – has been operationalized all too well, and that boundaries have been needed to structure this interaction in manageable ways." Conformity "with the model became a goal in itself. The model became the 'end' rather than a 'means'. . . the goal appears to have become 'make the model work' rather than 'achieve the educational goals of the college.'" "It was for reasons such as these, that the attempt to implement a comprehensive systems approach to instruction . . . was subverted, accompanied by deterioration in staff-administration relationships."[20]

"During the period of data gathering," the consultants wrote, "we sensed a posture of implacable confrontation in the relations between these two groups which is entirely inappropriate for a community college." On the one side, Pentz had referred "frequently" to the activities of the MRFA "with evident disdain for what he perceived as its dog-in-the-manger attitude towards bringing his 'idea of a college' to realization. This disdain extended to the mechanism required by the Colleges Act for participation by students and faculty in college governance. His actions in this respect had the effect of a self-fulfilling prophecy." Pentz's disdain, however, was matched by negative faculty attitudes, notably in the leadership of the MRFA: "Whatever the reasons, this attitude

is perfidious and entirely inappropriate to the community college setting." The consultants strongly urged that "every effort . . . be made to eradicate the 'management-union' mental set in addressing the educational issues which face the college. An equal effort is needed to foster commitment to the college as a whole, and to gain widespread recognition within the college of the need to transcend parochial interests when key issues of college-wide significance are discussed."[21]

Among its many recommendations, the report suggested striking a task force consisting of faculty, students, support staff, and administrators "to seek means by which participation in governance and administration of Mount Royal College can be revitalized." The president should "assist the board in seeking means to revitalize and create participatory structures within the college," notably "to enhance the authority and statute of the Academic Council in relation to the board." For its part, the MRFA "should assess its leadership role in fostering a positive college development among its members"; "in particular, it should assess itself against the impressions we have formed regarding its present posture – the 'I'm all right, Jack' attitude with its associated complacency, protectivism, and tendencies toward militant confrontation rather than problem-solving." The college should embrace "a pluralistic concept of teaching and learning," in which faculty members were "responsible in a collegial fashion for the quality of instruction offered at the college as opposed to an individualistic response to a model established by fiat"; "it is incumbent upon instructors to justify to their colleagues the practices they use." Finally, since "the physical plant should be fit to the learning program, not the reverse," the facilities should be retrofitted to provide for "differentiated instructional space" and "quiet and private work areas" for faculty, staff, and students; faculty needed a space where they could relate to one another, and the counselling services needed space to provide for privacy and confidentiality.[22]

In retrospect, this period in the college's life was formative in its organizational culture. Such cultures, once established, are very difficult to change. In faculty memory, Collett was remembered for being collegial, open, and warm in personal relations. However, the institution was then only a third of the size, and the Colleges Act, difficult collective bargaining,

Mount Royal Faculty Association Executive, ca. 1977 (back row, L–R) Steve Thompson, Richard Collier, Syd Goldstein, Charles Killingsworth, Hugh MacLeod (front row, L–R) Lorna Smith, Alexandra Bradley, Rose Marie McLean, unknown. Photographer Janet Brown; Mount Royal University Archives B33-61.

the Leggett model, and the new facilities lay ahead. That notion of Collett's period perhaps intensified the perception that Pentz, with his more businesslike style, was "authoritarian." In reality, tired of the constant hassles, Pentz began to disengage from decision making. Lauchlan said that he "gradually withdrew from things over the last two years. Max [Rae], Gary [Dean] and I started meeting in the little meeting room in the bookstore just to keep from tripping over each other – especially important for Dean and I. At one point I said, we need to regularize this, so I was delegated to go to Pentz and tell him that we wanted to return to the regular Executive Committee meetings, but if he wouldn't do that we would continue to meet and to try to coordinate things on our own. He

said, 'Go ahead.'" In effect, he gave up.[23] Paradoxically, perhaps his lack of visibility made the impression of his "authoritarianism" even stronger. A later dissertation on Mount Royal's "organizational culture" concluded that Pentz's years as president crystallized a faculty "counterculture" of "frustrated, angry and suspicious staff," and that the counterculture lingered on thereafter "in some sectors and in the 'old guard'."[24] Pentz faced a particular challenge: that of leading an institution at a time when the legitimacy of any authority was in question on campus, when there was little congruency between the goals and values of the constituent elements in the college.[25] It was a huge challenge. Not surprisingly, the board did not renew his contract when his term ended on 30 June 1975.[26]

An Uneasy Compromise

The board named Douglas Lauchlan as acting president "for a term ending on the 30th day of June 1976, unless extended for a further period by a resolution of the board." Lauchlan was assigned all of the authority of the president under the Colleges Act.[27] He had the experience and personal style for the job. He was later described as "the insider, well liked, approachable and a permissive leader who relaxed bureaucratic procedures, a healer."[28] Among other things, he had been the chief interlocutor between the board and the faculty and student associations and had handled most external relations. There were no rival internal candidates. Dean had begun a sabbatical leave, and never returned.[67] (Fred Fowlow, the registrar, served as acting VP, Instruction in 1975–76.) Lauchlan quickly reorganized: the Directors of Information and Planning and Development, and the four division heads (Business Services, Instruction, College Services, and Community Services) now reported to him.[29] They would meet as an "interdepartmental committee.... This is the key management group of about a dozen staff with others called in as resource as required. It provides a clearing house for the detail of operations which do not fall within the purview of one single division or department. It also provides an opportunity to discuss operational policies and objectives."[30]

Along with the acting president, two new board members assumed office on 1 July 1975. They were to play important roles in the next six years. Gerald M. Burden, a corporate lawyer from the oil and gas industry, was named chairman. Earlier he had been chairman of Calgary's Board of Education, typically a more interventionist body than the board of a post-secondary institution; moreover, he had served during a teachers' strike and was inclined by experience to see the MRFA as a union rather than as a professional association or co-determining partner with the board. The other new member was Fred Stewart, also a Calgary lawyer, formerly a member of the provincial Colleges Commission, deeply involved in the community, later a cabinet minister, who was more of a conciliator, mediator, diplomat, and problem solver. Concerned about the tense environment in the college, Stewart was to devote countless hours to meetings with faculty representatives and in collective bargaining.

Douglas M. Lauchlan, President 1976–80. Mount Royal University Executive Records ER-GO010-05L.

Gerald M. Burden, Chairman of the Board 1975–81. Mount Royal University Executive Records GO010-05B.

The presidential search began with an "evaluation of the President's Office" that revealed that there was no board-approved job description for the president and that the board had never reviewed Pentz's performance. Burden organized a board retreat in October 1975 "to discuss and agree on board priorities for 1975–76," including "the presidential search, budget policy, a statement of goals and objectives, and the role of the college." In his view, "the board should challenge the administration regularly on its continuing process of implementing the goals and objectives" and "should publish its terms and standards of academic excellence" for the institution.[31]

In September 1975 the board agreed on a presidential job description.[32] It then approved an advertisement and established a "screening committee." The latter consisted of three board members from the Personnel Committee (one student, one public-sector member, and one academic-staff member), the chairman of the Academic Council or a council designate, and one member from the non-faculty staff at large.[33] Through George Papas, the MRFA asked for the right to screen the short-listed candidates. Burden responded that "he was unwilling for the board to give a commitment to seek the advice of the Faculty Association but advised Mr. Papas that the board may well decide that they wish the help of the Faculty Association . . . in various areas. However, no advance commitment or undertaking can be made."[34]

In due course, the presidential search narrowed to two candidates – Lauchlan and Dr. Daniel J. Cornish, a member of the Department of Advanced Education. The board divided, with the chairman on one side and the majority on the other. The result was a compromise reached on 14 April 1976. Lauchlan would serve as president for a three-year term while Cornish would serve as Executive VP, Academic Affairs. The vice-president was to have "responsibility as Dean of Instruction and for coordinating the Division of Instruction, the Division of Community Services, and the Division of College Services." The board simultaneously reclassified "the position of vice president, business services presently held by Max Rae . . . to that of executive vice-president, business affairs effective July 1, 1976."[35] Thus, Lauchlan and Cornish found themselves in an uneasy partnership, with the president operating on a short time frame and a potential

successor acting as vice-president. In September 1976 the board specified the duties of the two roles. Those of the president were "the implementation of the policies of the board and the interpretation of those policies to the faculty, staff and students of the college," and "active participation with the board of governors in the interpretation of the role and program of the college to the community it serves." Those of the executive vice-president included "development, implementation, and planning activities related to programs of study and other supporting services. The vice-president works closely with the vice-president, business services, deans, department chairpersons, and other directors in developing programs, arranging their finance, and maximizing learning opportunities for students. Through familiarity with the philosophy of the institution, its capabilities, alternative learning strategies, and a variety of management techniques, the vice-president provides leadership, coordination, and facilitation in Academic Affairs as well as representing Academic Affairs on a college-wide basis." In short, the president was to focus on external matters, the vice-president on internal matters.

While the divisions and departments reporting to the president remained unchanged, the internal structure of the Division of Academic Affairs was elaborated. There were twelve academic departments (the same as before), with each chairperson reporting to the vice-president. As Lauchlan explained in the annual report, the novelty was a reorganization "to facilitate the development of three major thrusts: the professional development of our faculty, an integrated learning skills program to effectively address the needs of inadequately prepared students, and the extension of our educational services to the community."[36] There were two new "theme" deans: Jeanette Demicell, named in January 1977 to serve as dean of Academic Affairs (Learning Skills), and Robert Gervais, dean of Academic Affairs (Personnel, Budget-Making).[37] The position of Officer for Faculty Professional Development was established. In addition, Norman Burgess replaced the retiring Leona Paterson as director of the Conservatory, and Edward P. Schmidt, director of Finance, replaced Max Rae as secretary-treasurer and executive vice-president, Business Affairs on 1 September 1977.[38] Further restructuring led to the development of a separate continuing education division and the appointment of Thomas Stevens as the first dean of Continuing Education in the spring of 1980.

In the Academic Affairs Division, Cornish worked closely with Demicell, Gervais, and the twelve department chairs. They did so in a context in which the MRFA, perhaps sensing an opportunity to expand its influence, protested the promotions of Schmidt and Burgess on the grounds that there should have been national competitions and the establishment of the two theme deans as managerial rather than as academic staff positions[39] – in effect challenging the legitimacy of the appointments of four senior administrators. Even so, Cornish and his team improved the effectiveness in the learning skills and counselling units, implemented the policy requiring all career programs to have program advisory committees, initiated internal program reviews in career fields, and began to narrow the open door admissions policy to students whose needs the college could actually handle. As Cornish was at the centre of the academic action, while Lauchlan concentrated on external matters, he was to become the lightning rod for some of the continuing faculty unhappiness.

COMMUNITY EDUCATION SERVICES

From the start of his association with the college, Lauchlan had made community development one of his principal concerns. He understood that phrase broadly. It encompassed not only Calgary but also Alberta and Canada. As vice-president, he had initiated establishment of a standing board Committee on Government and Community Relations and served as its secretary. The committee became the vehicle through which he promoted his idea of the college's role in community development. In April 1972 the board approved his proposal for the Killarney Baptist Church to use college facilities for its weekly services.[40] In the same year, he secured board approval to turn the Kerby Memorial Building into a facility for the Senior Citizens Council.[41] In 1973 he arranged participation in the Servicemen's Opportunity College, a vehicle enabling servicemen to accumulate academic credits in colleges across the country (it required waiver of residence requirements).[42] With Leona Paterson, he

was a founder of the Canadian Speech Association and of the Alberta branch of that organization.[43]

In October 1971 Lauchlan spelled out his vision of the college's role in community development. Commenting on a paper on a proposed funding plan by the Colleges Commission, he noted that it "supports very traditional kinds of effort in the Continuing Education Field, and does not provide for any support pattern for creative experiments in Community Service. It must be clearly stated that Community Service cannot be understood exclusively in terms of courses and programs which may conform to the formula. . . . For example, the college must make provision to be a resource for many of the things which the community may decide to do for itself." The "present negotiations with the Federation of Calgary Communities is an example of this kind of option. If the Federation locates in [the] Lincoln Park [campus], they will carry on many programs which are designed and directed by themselves for which we will simply provide space and resource personnel, either students or faculty. The creative use of space is another factor which is not covered in the formula. All the colleges have an opportunity to provide real services to the communities simply by allowing the community to make advantageous use of their facilities." College funding should include an allowance for community-service activities.[44]

Though he never persuaded the government to fund community-education services, including the Conservatory, or to provide some funding for the flight-training dimension of the Aviation program,[45] Lauchlan found alternative ways to translate his vision into practice. He helped organizations establish themselves as legal entities entitled to funding from various sources. "We have experimented with this option in a couple of instances," he said. "The Calgary Youth Orchestra is incorporated under the Societies Act of Alberta in order that it may receive funding support from various cultural agencies, like the Calgary Region Arts Foundation. The Canadian Festival of Youth Orchestras has been incorporated under the Societies Act of Alberta to achieve charitable donation status."[46] (In 1977, with Frank Simpson, the new director of orchestras, he initiated the Canadian Association of Youth Orchestras.) The college could serve as a physical host and provide core administrative services while recovering costs from the organizations involved. Moreover, such partnerships could feed into the development of credit programs.[47] In short, the college could serve as a catalyst for the formation of community groups, assist them in securing funding, provide them with space and services, and recover its costs from their revenues.

This thinking led to two initiatives. In January 1974 the board approved Lauchlan's proposal to form an Institute of Cultural and Linguistic Development under the Companies Act to serve as the focal point for community and cultural organizations.[48] A few months later it approved his proposal to establish an Alberta Business Centre as a non-profit society that would seek funding from the provincial Department of Industry and Commerce. Its purpose was "to provide a centre for the business community to identify and solve its own problems; to provide a meeting place for business, government, labour and public groups to examine specific problems and propose practical solutions; to provide a method of gathering national and international human resources for the assistance of the Alberta Business community; to provide a service and training centre for small business enterprise in Alberta."[49] Neither venture endured for long, but they were signs of Lauchlan's imaginative approach to community development.[50]

Lauchlan was also concerned about marketing the college. At the beginning of each semester, the college printed large newspaper ads describing its credit, non-credit, and Conservatory offerings. On an ongoing basis, smaller ads were published on new courses, programs, and activities. Two themes were found in all promotions: "The People Place," and "Exciting Things Are Happening." Lauchlan explained: "As a significant percentage of our students arrive here with no specific goals – it is to this market that the general institutional advertising is directed, if they become oriented toward the college and make decisions about goals after they arrive in consultation with counselors, faculty or fellow students."[51] As part of the outreach program spurred by Lauchlan, Harry Alston and other faculty members in the radio and television broadcasting program negotiated an agreement with Community Antenna Television (CATV) to carry the college's radio station (along with that of the university) beginning in October 1973.[52]

In 1973, Pentz and Lauchlan persuaded the board to join the new Association of Canadian Community Colleges (ACCC). This later led to a difference of opinion with Burden, who proposed withdrawing from the ACCC in 1977. The result was a compromise – a letter to the ACCC suggesting how it might become more effective.[53] In 1979, Lauchlan negotiated an agreement with "Co-op College of Canada and Regional Board of Co-op College of Canada."[54] As these examples indicate, Lauchlan sought to parlay isolated activities into collective strengths, to foster specialized associations in the broader community, to establish networks.

POTENTIAL MERGER WITH AVC-CALGARY

In some ways the most significant development of the decade was the negotiation relating to the potential integration of Alberta Vocational Centre–Calgary into the college. This was when the potential for the college to become a broader open-door institution was addressed explicitly. For reasons other than college intentions, the negotiations failed. Thereafter the college had no choice but to build higher on its postsecondary base.

The Vocational Centres had come into existence in the 1960s to administer federal training funds and supplementary funding from the provincial government.[55] In 1970, AVC-Calgary offered two streams of courses on a "four-week block system": Vocational Preparatory and Business Education. It was in the process of adding "a basic literacy program for persons presently functioning below the Grade 6 level."[56] As the AVC was funded primarily by federal grants, the provincial government was slow to address its facilities needs.[57] There was also the issue of whether such programs should be located in colleges. In 1970–71, Ontario had assigned them to its CAATs. Thus, as plans to develop a facility for some seventeen hundred AVC students in the Churchill Park area of Calgary were made, it was natural for the Department of Advanced Education to consider a potential merger with Mount Royal, though SAIT might have been a more appropriate partner.[58] Merging Mount Royal and AVC-Calgary arose in part because both required government funding for new facilities.

In May 1970 the minister directed officials to explore a potential merger of AVC-Calgary and Mount Royal. Henry Kolesar, head of the Colleges Commission, asked the college to identify its terms for a merger. The college responded that it would accept responsibility for the AVC only if its governance was "within the purview of our board and the colleges system." Employees would "be required to follow the existing personnel policies in effect at our institution," and the college would want to see whether it would absorb all of the curriculum or whether some would be better located at SAIT and/or the agricultural schools. The facilities implications must be resolved "well before the completion of the building."[59] In September 1970, the board agreed to take over the new AVC but wanted "the right to plan the programs and the authority to offer programs at either campus"; it also wanted the AVC to "be integrated with the college in respect to both administration and faculty" and suggested assembling "sufficient land . . . east of the new Alberta Vocational Centre to permit building of a second community college when needed."[60]

A joint AVC–Mount Royal committee was formed to work on amalgamation. In early 1971 the committee, which included Pentz, Lauchlan, and Dean on the college side, and C. Barry Virtue and R. W. Hahn (acting director) on the AVC side, recommended "an organization plan designed for inter-locking the two campuses" based on as much decentralization "as possible" – "because each institution has a history and because each will be located in a different part of Calgary, the identity of each should be preserved"; and "because people closest to the ground are best at making the initial decisions." Business functions would be integrated while academic functions would not. The board approved the recommendations in February 1971, and the college introduced a page on the "Churchill Park Campus" in its calendar.[61]

But then the forces of resistance began. Employees began to get nervous about salaries, benefits, standing, and security.[62] J. P. (Jack) Mitchell, director of the Division of Vocational Education in the Department of Education, stressed the very different roles played by the two institutions. The AVC campus was intended to be "an identifiable training centre for 'disadvantaged'

adults," a place reserved for them where they would feel comfortable attending. "The institution is characterized by a high level of individualized programming and instruction, and facilitates necessary social adjustment of the individual." AVC relied on Canada Manpower funding,[63] and if that funding were withdrawn, the college "could be in a very embarrassing position through no responsibility of its own." The Colleges Commission moved slowly.[64]

However, the minister was determined, and the joint committee continued its work. By January 1971, a draft plan was ready. It made the AVC into a division of the college headed by an executive vice-president Churchill Park (AVC), who would report to Mount Royal's president and be the chief campus administrator at Churchill Park.[65] The minister secured legislative approval for the college to manage the AVC and sent a letter dated 19 March 1971 proposing that as of 1 July 1971 all AVC employees would be transferred and funding provided.[66] On 26 April 1971 the Mount Royal board accepted the proposal, and on 1 July 1971 all AVC employees were to become college employees – on paper. However, on 26 May 1971, a day-long meeting of ministry, college, and AVC officials reviewed every item in detail,[67] and concluded that, with a provincial election in the offing, it would make sense to defer the deadline for a year.[68] However, Barry Virtue, who was named provost of the proposed AVC division within Mount Royal, began planning the new facility ("the Churchill Park Campus") to be located at 332-6th Avenue SE; it was expected to open in July 1972.[69] Pentz circulated a memo to all staff declaring that "effective August 1, 1971, Mount Royal College will consist of three campuses," two in Calgary and Old Sun Campus of Mount Royal College on the Blackfoot reserve near Gleichen.[70]

Following the election, which brought the Conservatives to power, the new minister of education, James L. Foster, also initially supported the merger. However, the concerns of key department officials and among AVC employees gave him pause.[71] The delay led Mount Royal's board to send Foster a letter dated 24 February 1972 proposing that Mount Royal should take over the AVC "on or before April 1, 1972, under the conditions set forth in the resolution passed by the board . . . on July 5, 1971." "If you agree, please return a signed copy of the proposal by March 15, 1972. If no word is received by this date, the board . . . will assume that the Department of Advanced Education does not wish to proceed with the merger and would therefore consider the matter closed."[72] Foster was angered: "I do not appreciate the tactics of your letter . . . and may I further suggest that your board are not entitled to assume that if no word is received by March 15th that this Department does not wish to proceed with this merger."[73]

To finesse the issues, Mitchell proposed that instead of a merger, the college could operate the AVC under a management contract or order-in-council. In May 1972 Mount Royal's board agreed to accept either method, "provided the centre be operated under the policies of the Mount Royal College board"; moreover, this interim step would last only "until a complete merger has been attained."[74] Nothing happened on 1 July, and continuing AVC employee opposition led the minister in September 1972 to appoint a lawyer to review the situation "and to iron out any legal wrinkles."[75] Publication of the Colleges Commission's draft "Master Plan Number One" heightened tensions by proposing that both the Calgary and Edmonton AVCs should be merged into the colleges, doubling the voices of concern.[76] Mitchell now openly opposed mergers, which "could lead to loss of identity and perhaps even the abandonment of the present unique services they [the AVCs] provide for underprivileged persons. . . . [W]e have been attempting for over two years to amalgamate AVC, Calgary with MRC. To date, we have not identified significant benefits nor improvement of effectiveness nor efficiency which will result from such amalgamation."[77]

Though Mount Royal's board voted in January 1973 to accept the most recent agreement with the government, the prospect of merger drained away. The minister was unwilling to act. Work proceeded on the new AVC campus in downtown Calgary. The Colleges Commission was wound up and its functions transferred to the new Department of Advanced Education. In the end, one small joint project came out of the discussions. The warden of the penitentiary in Drumheller had asked for programs to be offered at that site. Virtue and Lauchlan did an academic-needs survey, and Roger Tierney and David Morphy of the college's counselling staff assessed guidance needs.[78] In February 1972 the board approved a mix of college and AVC offerings.[79] After merger negotiations with the AVC ended, the college continued to offer its own courses for a few years, but the need was steadily diminishing because of AVC's expanding role.

For Mount Royal, the significance of the failed negotiation was that AVC-Calgary would progressively occupy academic upgrading and work readiness training space previously occupied in part by the college, narrowing the need for it to occupy that space. This was to generate some tensions over the years, as the college faced the fact that there was another institution capable of providing a service for "second chance" and adult students. One can see the trend in the 1970s. In 1972–73, the college announced its "Program for Student Success" for full-time students "who are encountering difficulties." It set out what the college would and would *not* do for such students, a recognition that it could not do everything.[80] In 1976–77, the idea of "open door" admissions was clarified – one needed to have a high-school diploma to be considered for admission to eleven of forty-eight programs, while being either eighteen years of age or having a high-school diploma was necessary for the others.[81] In 1977–79, the admissions policy was modified slightly: "The 'Open Door' policy of the college makes it possible for anyone 18 years of age or older to enter and attempt most programs. It does NOT guarantee a diploma after two years of study, as one may need an extra semester or more to gain an adequate background."[82] When they attempted to secure other modifications to the policy, such as admission of students who could be prepared for full post-secondary study after just one semester of upgrading, Cornish and Demicell ran into faculty resistance. However, rising student demand, limited spaces, and the need to select only one of every three applicants in the 1970s ended the open door in practice. Practice was to trump ideology.

Thus, while the University of Calgary limited the college's role in university work, SAIT confined any technology ambitions, so over the next two decades the evolution and growth of AVC-Calgary removed the need for the college to focus on adult upgrading. Circumstances were increasingly confirming Mount Royal's post-secondary and academic character.[83]

OLD SUN COLLEGE

Another link to the community in which Lauchlan was a key player was the relationship with Old Sun College. There are four reserves for Native peoples within commuting distance of Mount Royal's campus, and for many purposes they are linked in a grouping known as the Treaty 7 Management Corporation. Wanting to ensure that those peoples are aware of its programs and are able to access them, the college has pursued three different strategies since it became a public institution: special programs on campus for Native students; Native student centres on campus to enable students to meet with one another and with Native counselors or tutors; and offering or participating in programs on the reserves. Over time there have been successes and failures on all three fronts. In this respect, it is important to note that both the college and the Native communities have been constantly changing – the college abandoning its large academic upgrading program and raising the level of its admission requirements, the Native peoples growing more rapidly than the general population and becoming better educated, more integrated into the general economy, and more urban.

The first approach – bringing Aboriginal students to the campus and providing them special courses and support – began in the fall of 1968. Canada Manpower approached E. G. (Ernie) Tyson, a college instructor, to explore the potential for a program for Aboriginal students that would help them overcome academic deficiencies and prepare them for occupations. "Project Go Ahead" was launched as a pilot project. "Mount Royal will supply the training, Canada Manpower will handle costs, and the Indian Affairs Department will provide residences." The project involved bringing fifteen native students to campus to fill "the gaps between elementary and high school in one year." As Tyson said, "It would give the college a chance to live up to the philosophy of rendering a service to the community and giving educational opportunity to all. It's a chance for the Indians and it's a chance for us."[84] However, the pilot project was not renewed.

One fascinating by-product of the college's association with Native students in that period was a rodeo series from 1969 to 1971. The rodeo club joined with similar groups from the University of Alberta and Olds Agricultural College to establish the Canadian Intercollegiate Rodeo Association. In 1971 the association had eight members, including the original partners and the universities of Calgary, Lethbridge, and Saskatchewan, Lethbridge Community College, SAIT, NAIT, and AVC-Vermilion. Apart from promoting interest in rodeo, it enabled full-time students to compete for prize money in such events as saddle bronc, bull riding, steer wrestling, bareback bronc, calf riding, ladies' barrel race, goat tying (mixed event), and ribbon roping. The Mount Royal students' association made the arrangements – for example, in 1969, with the Sarcee band for use of its rodeo grounds, with a horse provider, and with a rodeo clown.[85] The activity faded away when the initiators graduated.

In 1970, the college undertook the second approach to its relations with Native peoples, offering programs on reserves. In this case, the college established a partnership with the Blackfoot Nation to provide programs in the former residential school on the Blackfoot (Siksika) Reserve in Gleichen, east of Calgary. The school had been part of the federal residential school program since 1929, administered by the Anglican Church until the 1950s and thereafter by federal authorities. This venture was to lead quickly from an association to the development of a separate Native-based institution. As funding Native education was a federal responsibility, the college approached the Indian Affairs branch with a proposal. It included a Native teacher aide position, Native studies (Blackfoot history, culture and crafts), adult upgrading tutoring, secretarial and business courses in areas such as budgeting, homemaking, and child care, carpentry, recreational leadership, university transfer courses, and early childhood education (kindergarten, day care). Mount Royal was to administer the campus on a fee-for-service basis.[86] In 1971 the residential school was transformed into Old Sun College and then incorporated in 1973 as Old Sun Community College.[87] In Mount Royal's 1973–74 calendar, the "Old Sun Campus" was described as "one of the campuses that makes up Mount Royal College. It is committed to meeting the expressed needs of the native people and is administered in partnership with the Blackfoot Band. The curriculum is directly related to meeting those needs."[88]

Old Sun College opened as a Mount Royal College satellite campus in 1971 on the Blackfoot Reserve in Gleichen, Alberta, operating until 1978 when it became an independent institution run by the Blackfoot Nation. Mount Royal University Archives HA255-2.

A "semi-autonomous institution," Old Sun had a governing committee made up of representatives of the federal and provincial governments, the band, and Mount Royal (initially four, including president Pentz and board chair Martha Cohen, but later only two Mount Royal members). The first class in September 1971 included 123 students.[89] In April 1972, "Lieutenant-Governor J. W. Grant MacEwan, with the help of Chief Leo Pretty Young Man, unveiled a plaque marking the official opening of the Old Sun 'Partnership' Campus of Mount Royal College." It was said to be "a first for Canada." President Pentz announced that the college had been given $163,000 to operate the new campus in that year.[90] The campus consisted of the "brick school building of the original Old Sun missionary school, barns and other structures."[91]

At one level, Old Sun Community College provided a successful model for adult education in Native communities. The band would identify local needs, arrange for external institutions to deliver courses, and use its influence to ensure that students attended classes. However, as Lauchlan wrote in July 1975, the completion of courses was insufficient: "The critical issue for a determination of the effectiveness of the college training relates to the aspirations of the people themselves. At present the more successful vocational preparation programs at Old Sun create skills which must be marketed in white society. The social adjustment problems facing the successful graduates of these programs are profound, perhaps in some cases insuperable." He pointed out that there was "evidence of a strong desire on the part of many of the Blackfoot people to remain within their own society and create a better way of life for themselves in a style consistent with their own traditions." He suggested that the college should "take an initiative with the provincial government to request that a major consultation involving the Federal and Provincial governments, the Band council, and Mount Royal College take place as soon as it can be arranged to review options for the future of the Blackfoot people."[92]

In 1972, the board named Cohen, Purdy, Stickle, and Pentz to serve on the Old Sun board for a two-year term; later, Lauchlan, Cohen, and Purdy continued to serve on the oversight board of Old Sun College.[93] Indeed, Purdy remained on the Old Sun board for sixteen years and Cohen for twelve years (part of the time as vice-chair).[94] However, the connection to the college grew more tenuous. Gerald M. Burden, the next chair of the board, resigned from the Old Sun board because the college was already well represented.[95] Moreover, Old Sun was on a trajectory from "semi-autonomous" to "independent status" in 1978. As a result, "the last ties of governance in the required appointment of two members of the Mount Royal College Board to Old Sun's Board were severed." Even so, Lauchlan added that "Mount Royal College continues to provide support services in administration on a fee-for-service basis, maintains close ties with Old Sun, and is the link with the provincial system. We welcome this sign of full maturity of an important centre in which we take some measure of credit."[96] However, the business connections to Old Sun were soon ended as well. In October 1997 Old Sun Community College became a founding member of the First Nations Adult and Higher Education Consortium (FNAHEC).[97]

Where the college offered courses on reserves without the kind of local control found in Old Sun, as on the Stoney reserve in the 1970s and early 1980s, the results were much less successful and the college abandoned them. The most effective way to offer such programs, experience showed, was through local educational councils like Old Sun's that could bring local social pressures and authority to bear on the project. The question of serving Native communities was to continue, and in its third approach to the issue of Native education begun in the late 1980s, the college was to enter into an agreement with the Treaty 7 Management Corporation for special programs and a Native centre on the college's campus.

THE STUDENTS

From 1972 to 1979–80, the number of full-time equivalent (FTE) students grew from 2,888 to 3,441, an increase of 18 per cent. This growth was not as great as one might have expected, given the new campus. However, by the end of the decade, the college had exceeded the design limit for its facilities.

As indicated in Figure 7.1, enrolment in diploma programs grew from 45 to 56 per cent of total FTE enrolment, while that in university-transfer programs, though remaining constant in size, declined from 42 to 35 per cent of the total. Figure 7.2 shows that business administration was the most popular career program, as measured by proportion of enrolment (11.7 per cent), followed by police science (5.0 per cent), social service (4.4 per cent), interior design (3.8 per cent), leisure education (3.5 per cent), early-childhood education (3.4 per cent), nursing (3.3 per cent), and a host of others with smaller enrolments – for example, physical education (2.8 per cent) and journalism (1.6 per cent). Within the university-transfer stream, as indicated by Figure 7.3, 60 per cent of the students were enrolled in "general arts and science," 13 per cent in the BA stream, 6 per cent in the B.Sc. stream, 7 per cent in the business stream, and 5.5 per cent in the engineering stream.[98]

When the college moved to Lincoln Park, the student experience changed from that of a crowded, cramped array of temporary downtown facilities to one informed by the spacious environment on the Lincoln Park campus. The college tried to keep the same sense of school spirit by continuing the tradition of "Frosh Week," issuing T-shirts, organizing "flicks" in the Forum, and offering half-price tickets for cabarets. In 1973, "Frosh Week got on the road . . . with the society membership drives and a few words from Big Brother Gary Dolha. Monday night, midst beer and wine, Rose Marie Walker and Thirsty Boots performed in [the] Rathskellar [one of the social spaces]. Yesterday were the added attractions of flicks with Mae West (free to students wearing Frosh Week T-shirts)."[99]

Following the initial dispute over the Students' Association's occupation of spaces, relations between the association and the board settled down. In January 1975, the board and the association signed an agreement

FIGURE 7.1 ENROLMENT TRENDS: DIPLOMA, UNIVERSITY-TRANSFER, OTHER PROGRAMS, 1972–79

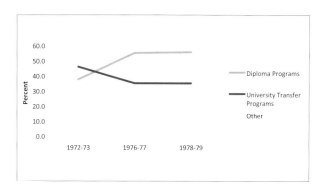

SOURCE: Based on enrolment figures, Board minutes, 24 September 1973, 14 January 1980.

FIGURE 7.2 ENROLMENT IN LARGEST CAREER PROGRAMS (% OF TOTAL CREDIT ENROLMENT), 1979–80

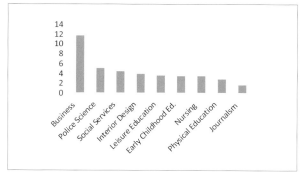

SOURCE: Based on enrolment reported in Board minutes, 14 January 1980.

FIGURE 7.3 PROGRAM ORIENTATION OF UNIVERSITY TRANSFER-STUDENTS, 1979–80 (%)

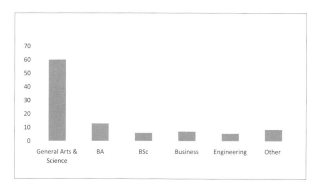

SOURCE: Based on enrolment report, Board of Governors minutes, 14 January 1980.

establishing the Wyckham House Board "to initiate ideas for improved use of association facilities; to initiate ideas for improvements in the rental of association facilities; to initiate ideas for new revenue property; to initiate ideas for investments; to approve expenditures to pursue the above noted responsibilities and to approve policy relative to the same; to consider proposed policies and projects relative to the above presented by Students' Council and shall approve or disapprove in writing; to select the staff of the association upon recommendation of the Personnel Committee of the

[college's board of governors]." Consisting initially of Michael Smith, a lawyer, Douglas Brewster, a chartered accountant, Douglas Kuwahara, a businessman, and Steve Thompson, a faculty member, the board was named in honour of Robert Wyckham, the former faculty member who was remembered for advocating student facilities during the private college years.[100] It was to provide important stability during a period in which turnover in student leadership was high. As we shall see, it was replaced at the end of the century by another arrangement.

ACADEMIC PROFILE

Following the relocation to the Lincoln Park campus in 1972, the college's program base remained largely stable. In 1978–79 two new diploma programs were added (rehabilitation services, petroleum and mineral-resource land management) along with certificate programs in computing-science programming and petroleum mineral-resource land management.[101]

By the end of the 1970s, there were 148 full-time faculty members and 65 FTE part-time faculty members, for a total of 213 FTE faculty members. Instructional support included 58 full-time positions. The 1974–75 calendar recorded that the highest academic credentials held by faculty members (n = 119) was distributed as follows: Ph.D., 4 per cent, MA, 66 per cent, BA, 24 per cent, diploma/other, 6 per cent.[102] By the 1970s, in short, the master's degree had become the effective minimum credential for new hires in most fields. The academic complement constituted about one-third of the total FTE employee complement: in 1980, there were 36 administrators and 180 FTE clerical staff. Altogether, there were 486 full-time positions and 146 part-time ones, yielding a total FTE complement of 644. In addition, the Conservatory employed 75 hourly instructors on the campus and 27 instructors in neighbourhood branches.[103]

The development of the career programs led to periodic reconsiderations of the general education requirement in 60-credit diploma programs. In 1978, the requirement was re-stipulated: "All diploma students must complete a minimum of 12 credit hours of Arts and Science Core Courses. At least one course must be presented from each of any four of the seven Arts and Science Core Areas," defined as follows: (1) Behavioural Sciences, (2) Communications; (3) Fine Arts and Physical Education; (4) Humanities; (5) Mathematics and Physics; (6) Natural Sciences; and (7) Social Sciences.[104] In addition, some of the new career programs did not fit easily within workload templates developed for people teaching in liberal arts programs. The Nursing program, for example, required negotiation with the MRFA over teaching workload and such other matters as compensation for travel and parking, use of sessional appointees, and vacation periods.[105] Similarly, Interior Design and the Radio and Television Broadcasting programs, both of which required

a good deal of hands-on instruction, did not fit easily within the template.

During the 1970s the college experienced tight operating funding.[106] During the negotiations for the new campus, one of the arguments for the Leggett model was that, by shifting more responsibility onto students for their own learning, it would be less costly than a traditional model.[107] That may have led to departmental expectations for economies that did not materialize. In addition, the college was expanding community-education services, notably the Conservatory and continuing education, and those were supposed to be self-sustaining. As a result, Lauchlan's pleas for funding for community-education services went unanswered. In December 1978, Burden, Lauchlan, and Cornish met with Assistant Deputy Minister Bosetti and Alexander S. Dobbins, a financial analyst, to review the college's proposal for a $736,500 increase in its operating budget: $209,000 to bring support staff salaries up to AUPE government salaries, $227,500 to provide "administrative support to the Music Conservatory and [their] extensive community service operations," and about $300,000 "to accommodate growth in specific program areas."[108] No increase was granted, nor did Lauchlan's campaign for Conservatory funding, though it reached the minister, yield any result.[109]

By the end of the 1970s the college's enrolment in credit programs was stabilizing. Lauchlan explained that "this was not a result of lower demand for our services. It was a result of deliberate planning related to budget constraints."[110] Some programs, such as Interior Design and Justice Administration, had reached their desired enrolment limits and the growth of other programs was being held back by the lack of funding for faculty. The government's priority at the time was building up the capacity of the new regional colleges, and, in its view, Mount Royal, with its new facility, could wait a little longer for more resources. In words reminiscent of those of Pentz earlier, Lauchlan wrote that "the college is convinced that additional facilities and additional resources are necessary to meet the needs of the fastest growing city in Canada."[111] Though denied permission for its Phase II expansion project, the college benefited from $9 million from the Heritage Fund to improve college libraries over three years, leading to an increase in the book collection from

82,600 in 1978–79 to 105,827 in 1981–82 and in its microform collection from 46,200 to 112,400.[112]

The Nursing program offered by the Allied Health Department remained somewhat apart from the rest of the institution, both by the extent of external regulation and the amount of time faculty and students spent in hospitals. Enrolling sixty students a year, it was now one of five diploma-level nursing programs offered by Alberta colleges. A report to the board indicated that "two-year nursing education remains the subject of considerable controversy" but that "programs such as ours have nevertheless established themselves in the Canadian nursing education system." The accreditation review in 1977 led to the addition of a faculty position and to other reforms. Its graduates continued to improve in registered-nurse examinations, as indicated by the dropping failure rate: 33 per cent in 1969, 19 per cent in 1973, 12 per cent in 1975, and less thereafter. By 1979, the nursing department was planning to add a number of post–basic-certificate programs in mental-health nursing, occupational-health nursing, extended-care nursing, and/or gerontological nursing.[113]

Meanwhile, continuing education enrolment in non-credit courses was soaring. In 1978–79 there were 5,843 registrations; in 1980–81, 11,805; and in 1984–85, 20,005.[114] Offering courses on speculation required the timely termination of undersubscribed courses, and in 1978 the college introduced a "minimum enrollment policy" to deal with that issue: "One basic premise of the policy is that each course must stand on its own, financially." The pay rate was too low to attract full-time faculty members and few taught in continuing education.[115] Instructors were found from the community and the division grew rapidly, filling the campus at night and on the weekends. Over time, with changes in the city's economy, demand shifted from "lifestyle" to professional-development courses. The college's success was in a context in which all levels of education competed for continuing education students, placing the college in some areas in competition with the university, SAIT, the school boards, and private career colleges.

In 1980 the relationship of continuing education programming to the Academic Council was clarified. The exemption of continuing education courses from council scrutiny first had been raised in 1972 by P.

Neil Webber, who had asked why recommendations on the non-credit fee structure did not come through the Academic Council.[116] However, nothing changed, and in December 1979 Thomas Wood, the faculty member on the board, also "expressed concern that community education services was operating outside the ambit of the Academic Council." The board approved his motion directing the administration "to meet with the appropriate committee of the Academic Council to ascertain if it is feasible to develop a relationship which will place all academic matters in and relating to Continuing Education within the regular purview of the Academic Council."[117] The discussions culminated in an agreement in March 1980 that the broad directions, not each course, would be submitted for review and recommendation.[118] In April 1980, Thomas J. Stevens, a veteran administrator from Seneca College in Ontario, was appointed dean of continuing education and community services.

THE CONSERVATORY

During the 1970s the Conservatory began to grow rapidly. In 1978–79 there were 4,367 registrations in music courses; in 1981–82, 4,991; and in 1983–84, 7,181 – an expansion of 64 per cent in five years.[119] At the end of the 1976–77 year, Leona Paterson retired after working at the college for thirty-one years and Dr. Norman E. Burgess replaced her as director.[120] A graduate of the University of Saskatchewan's music program and holding a doctorate in music from the University of Indiana, Burgess was an accomplished violinist, as was his wife, Joan Barrett, who played with the Calgary Philharmonic Orchestra. He was to bring a musician's concerns to planning. In April 1980, in a document entitle "A Proposal for the 'Coming of Age' in Our Conservatory System," he foresaw three streams of students – the roughly 90 per cent who belonged to the "preparation for life – enrichment" stream; those aiming at "preparation for music careers;" and those engaged in "preparation for receiving of 'finishing' music institutions which are career oriented."[121] The latter stream, which became known as the Academy of Music stream, was to provide "a carefully constructed competency-based curriculum that is definitely career oriented. Emphasis would be

Conservatory students, ca. 1972. Photographer Janet Brown; Mount Royal University Archives B6-109-2A.

music, also added to the Conservatory's profile. The Calgary Fiddlers not only performed at the College and elsewhere in Alberta but toured internationally and played for Queen Elizabeth, who later requested a repeat appearance.

PLANNING LINCOLN PARK DEVELOPMENT

As planning for the Lincoln Park campus had proceeded, Lauchlan became concerned about the absence of an agreed plan for the development of the community to be built around the college. In 1970 he asked architect Ted Raines of the firm designing the college to draft a report on uses of the land around the site. With that in hand, he approached officials in the Department of Education, the Alberta Housing Corporation, Alberta's minister of public works, and senior officials of Central Mortgage and Housing in Ottawa and Calgary to promote the idea of Mount Royal as the core of a Lincoln Park community. "At that stage there was a universal approval of the idea," he said later, but progress on the idea was delayed by skirmishing with Mayor Sykes, the 1972 provincial election, and the need to establish contacts with new players. In the spring of 1973 he contacted Denis Cole, chief commissioner of the city, and they agreed it would be desirable to form a committee "on the model of urban renewal programs" to plan the future of Lincoln Park. In July 1973 he wrote Dr. Walter Worth, deputy minister of the new Department of Advanced Education, to initiate a review of the issues. "The future effectiveness of the college can obviously be enhanced, or seriously restricted," he wrote, "by the kind of development that takes place around it . . . If . . . Lincoln Park became the kind of sterile institutional community involving shopping centres, hotel/motel complexes and specialized institutional housing, such as the Retarded Children's Village, which has already begun, this could create a kind of geographic and sociological isolation for the college. . . . Similarly, if the area were devoted to upper middle class residential development it could place the College in isolation from many of the people it is designed to serve." He noted that the city's Planning Department was proposing a development of "combined high

on performance skills; aural, theoretical, style and historical skill needs would be spread out over a long period and related to practical needs. . . . An audition would be required to enter the program and juries to maintain continuance." A "core faculty" would teach the Academy program: "The concept would be similar to 'principal' players in an orchestra."[122] The Academy program soon became a noteworthy beacon in music training in western Canada. It began to attract gifted students from as far away as Winnipeg and Vancouver. Its musical prodigies began to play as soloists with symphony orchestras, to appear on national radio programs, and to be admitted to Juilliard and other outstanding schools.

One of Burgess's other innovations, the "Calgary Fiddlers," a group of young people devoted to fiddle and low density housing making provision for a wide economic spectrum of the population of about 3,000 people." Mount Royal would be "the sociological key to the mixed community, providing a range of educational, recreational, cultural, and to some degree commercial services which provides the social adhesive to bind divergent groups together."[123]

As Lauchlan wrote, "the proposal could change the nature of the college in that the emphasis on Community Service and Continuing Education could become much more prominent, and indeed could become the major functions associated with Mount Royal." The future size of the college would be constrained and future expansion would reflect "community requirements for recreational facilities, the role of the college as a community centre, and the impact of that role upon service units like food services, and other services operated by both the college and the student's union." The college could serve as a venue for health services, a transportation depot, a meeting and conference centre, and, since "the wired city is now technically feasible," a focal point for "an integrated communications system for the community."[124]

Patiently, Lauchlan built agreement among city, provincial, and federal officials to co-operate in planning the future of the Lincoln Park.[125] In February 1974 Mayor Sykes responded favourably to a request from the college board to participate in the planning. In June 1974 a meeting with two cabinet members (Dave Russell and Jim Foster) and department officials, notably Dr. Milton Fenske, who was responsible for property matters, led to support and a letter from Foster, as minister of advanced education, to the minister of the federal Department of Urban Affairs urging participation. This was followed by meetings with federal officials. Finally, on 22 January 1975, the federal authorities agreed to join and Lauchlan declared a procedural "victory."[126] The board authorized Pentz and Lauchlan to represent the college but "with the explicit understanding that no commitments will be made without prior reference to the board."[127] The parties formed a Steering Committee, with Cole as chair and Lauchlan as secretary.[128] Lauchlan kept the board apprised of developments and of issues needing response, such as the traffic planned for the 50th Avenue right-of-way adjacent to the college. He initiated a series of "Lincoln Park Planning Task Groups" in the college to address particular matters.

The initial report of the Steering Committee was presented to the board of governors in September 1976.[129] The next version, entitled "Draft Position Paper – Lincoln Park Task Force in Community Cooperation, January 17, 1977," addressed the fit between the college and the community around it. "If Mount Royal College cannot be physically and functionally integrated into Lincoln Park, the result will be quite a different community from that currently envisioned. This is particularly important in early phases when the college could be viewed as the keystone of the community; that is, the development relies on Mount Royal to provide some facilities and services and act as a catalyst for the creation of some community institutions." The report continued: "Mount Royal College will be the focus of a mixed use, educational-based village centre. The magnificent college facility will become in fact, the centre of a community where education, living, recreation, and employment all exist in a highly integrated single location." Indeed, the college was part of an area that encompassed the Currie military base and ATCO facilities, all of which would become "the major cultural, educational, recreational, and social centres for Lincoln Park and surrounding communities."[130]

The drift of the report was of concern to Gerry Burden and some other board members concerned about locking the college's future into a small part of the total community of Calgary. In April 1977 Burden wrote to the minister, A. E. Hohol, saying that "we have reached a point where we are unable to proceed without clarification of Department policy regarding several vital issues." The agreement reached between Minister Clark and Mayor Sykes in 1970 ("to which the board of governors was not a party") reduced the site of the college from 123 to 86 acres, leaving the department holding two parcels of approximately 20 acres each "which were originally designated for Mount Royal College use"; an enrolment cap of 5,000 students was set; and the college was directed to assume responsibility for AVC Calgary "and establish a full college operation in the downtown core." "This arrangement was nearly completed but at the last moment, was suspended by your predecessor, the Honourable James Foster, in the face of resistance from the AVC staff." Burden then posed these questions:

- Does the enrollment limit of 5,000 students still apply? If it does not, can we reacquire the 40 acres to return the site to its original size? We cannot protect the future of this institution beyond an enrollment of 5,000 students on this site without more land.

- If the enrollment limit does apply, is the Department prepared to commit to the development of this institution on other sites in the City of Calgary as the demand requires?[131]

In response, William Yurko, Minister of Housing and Public Works, and Hohol refused to transfer more land to the college. Hohol wrote to Yurko: "I agree with your assessment that any specific move at this point will have implications for the whole of the development proposal. It could well be that the college people would have their aspirations met, if as you suggest, alternate land of equal size were to be made available to them some time in the future. I also agree with you that the park development has to include student housing."[132] The ministers in effect sided with Lauchlan and against those concerned about binding the college into a small property and part of the Calgary community, presumably in the expectation that Mount Royal's future would take a multi-campus form.

In the college the task groups were perceived to be partisans of the evolving plan. Criticism surfaced when details became known. When the board held a special meeting on 2 February 1977, faculty critics (John Howse, Gerry Bruce, Hugh Macleod) argued that total integration into one neighbourhood implied that the college might lose or diminish its connections to the broader community. Richard Collier "emphasized the importance of exercising care not to alienate the community by non-involvement; nor on the other hand damage the educational process by over-involvement." Some board members expressed reservations. Alexander G. (Sandy) Cameron, a public member, asked whether Mount Royal could accommodate demand for services when its facilities were taxed to capacity. Burden, concerned about future growth, suggested that the Steering Committee

should recommend more land for the college. Mount Royal, he said, would not "give up even one acre" for the project. "We are not in the housing business. Our priorities are to preserve Mount Royal as an educational institution and our right to expand."[133]

Finally, the board reached a conclusion on the plan at a special meeting on 5 October 1977.[134] With only Lauchlan dissenting, the board voted to advise the Steering Committee "that the college will not participate in the development of the conceptual design of Lincoln Park as submitted by the consultants through the Steering Committee, the primary reason being that the board is of the opinion that to preserve the flexibility of the college for future growth and change to enable it to fulfill its potential as a unique post-secondary educational institution in this province, the college must retain full use of and control over the land it presently owns in any Lincoln Park development plan." The resolution was conveyed to Mayor Sykes in a letter dated 11 October. In response, chief commissioner Cole wrote to the board on 10 November 1977: "Your letter . . . addressed to Mayor Rod Sykes has been forwarded to me for my information and such action as may be deemed appropriate. The decision of your board is very disappointing to the City of Calgary in that the initiative to work together on developing a comprehensive proposal to include college lands was originally taken by the college, and the Steering Committee was under the impression that the board of governors had been kept advised regarding the progress of its work." He noted that the city also had some concerns about loss of control but "it was our view that this was the negotiable item."

Though both the board and city indicated that they were open to other approaches, the Lincoln Park development plan was a dead letter. Twenty years later, in the late 1990s, the plan was dusted off (with the help of Art Froese, formerly of the city's Planning Department) when planning began for Phase III expansion. By that time, however, the Canadian Forces Base adjacent to the college was closed, housing projects were underway on the former base's lands and in other parts of Lincoln Park, commercial developments were planned, and the college had managed to secure more land, including one of the twenty-acre parcels.

Planning Phase II Expansion

By now the college was becoming space-short, and Lauchlan chaired a committee to draft a Phase II plan to accommodate 5,000 full-time day students (i.e., about 7,000 individuals).[135] The documents submitted to the government in January 1979 indicated that the college wished to add 15,290 square metres of space for "growth of the traditional element" that "provides certificate and diploma programs for students of our community who attend generally as day-time students and 7,250 square metres for "growth of the community service element" which "provides services of the college to those students who, for various reasons, cannot attend in the traditional manner." The examples included programs for policemen, government officials, and nurses, a small business training and service centre, "a fitness centre for the development of the individual and of leaders in industry," "a recreation centre," and office space for Conservatory community choral and band programs and community groups. The request also included "a short term residence facility of one hundred units to support the community service element."[136]

Despite the fact that in February 1978 the minister had approved $32,500 "for preparation of a master plan of activities with a target enrollment of 5,000 students," and a further $20,000 for "investigation of possible alternate program delivery sites and methods in urban and rural areas,"[137] the college soon met resistance. Lauchlan and board member Ron Nicholls met with Deputy Minister Kolesar on 16 July 1979 to discuss funding to initiate detailed planning. The response was discouraging. Not only would there be no planning money but the minister's priorities were established by cabinet and "no funds have been allocated for critical pre-design work technically referred to as programming." Mount Royal was not on the list.[138] Whether Kolesar's response reflected political currents, his own sense of what the system needed, or the contentious nature of life at Mount Royal is not clear. What is clear is that he personally did not favour the expansion. When the minister had approved planning money for the college, he had asked Bosetti, the assistant deputy minister: "Is there any likelihood in the foreseeable future we shall build at Mount Royal College?" Bosetti replied that Campus Development Services had "incorporated

Phase II construction in their five-year plan," with a cash flow anticipated of $100,000 in 1979–80, and $6,000,000 in each of 1980–81, 1981–82, and 1982–83. Kolesar's private response on 2 March 1978 was blunt: "I suggest that we begin consideration of using vacant school facilities rather than building an addition."[139] The Phase II project was dead on arrival. In a press interview, Burden declared that he was "very disturbed" about the "lack of action and lack of response" from the government; the project "doesn't have the priority" it should have "despite all the good words. . . . Sometimes matters dealing with the development of humans don't get the same priority as those dealing with the development of things."[140]

The Board and the Department

While the debate over the Lincoln Park plan was occurring, a department request to post-secondary institutions to define their roles precipitated a discussion about the fit between board governance and the role of the Department of Advanced Education. At Mount Royal, with its long tradition of board governance and programs that pre-dated its public status and the department, the idea that department officials in Edmonton would tell the board whether there was a real community need in Calgary for a program or whether its mission was appropriate to its community raised fundamental questions.[141]

In response to the government's request, Lauchlan developed a draft mission statement for discussion by a special board meeting on 14 November 1977. "The general objective of Mount Royal College," it said, is "to continually enhance its unique position within the Alberta system of higher education" in ways that included "reaffirming its commitment to the community college concept as a vital and desirable element in the total spectrum of post-secondary education," "developing innovative and imaginative programs which anticipate or respond to the changing needs of the communities and environments which the college serves through its mandate," "continuing to emphasize the quality of its programs and its ability to apply its resources to the educational needs of adults, particularly those who traditionally have difficulty taking advantage of conventional opportunities for higher education," and "reaffirming its commitment to the development of the instructional process and its personnel; to the development of the learning skills of its students; and to quality in the context of a liberal education." Lauchlan's views were visible in the passage on "program/service objectives." The college would respond to community needs through both "the traditional element" ("formal diploma and certificate programs for students who attend generally as day-time students") and "the community service element" (for students who "cannot attend in the traditional manner. These students are any persons we can assist in reaching their highest growth potential").

Before these "Long-Range Planning Objectives" were approved in December 1977, the board debated committing to the community college role and to the college system. Not everyone wanted to cap the college's potential, and as the department began asserting itself it inspired resistance from boards concerned about their independence in setting direction for institutions. To bring things to a head, Lauchlan moved "that the board . . . affirm its commitment to the community college system of Alberta and its determination to provide the leadership required to encourage the growth and improvement of the system and the unique requirements of each institution within it." The motion passed 8–2. Burden moved, supported by David Walker, a public member, "that Mount Royal College [should] initiate steps to petition the Legislature to afford the college authority to establish three or four-year programs leading to the granting of degrees in certain specialized areas where there is no competition within Alberta from other colleges or universities." The motion was defeated 8–2.[142] This, however, was the first formal consideration of degree granting by the board.

However, the board was unanimous in feeling the constraints of government policy, approving the following statement: "Mount Royal College believes that it must possess the capability to respond flexibly to the needs of the community it services, including the evaluation of present programs and the initiation of new programs and services. This capability can only be realized through greater informed local decision-making. Mount Royal College believes that decisions related to the delivery of services should be made at the local level."[143] Lauchlan's transmittal letter

indicated that Burden had voted against approval of the document on the basis of his disagreement with the proposed "commitment to the community college concept as a vital and desirable element in total spectrum of post-secondary education."[144] "I feel it is only fair to tell you," Burden wrote the minister, "that I cannot personally support, and I did not support the reaffirmation of a commitment to the community college system of Alberta. . . . In my view there are many questions to be answered and issues to be raised with respect to this system and such a 'commitment'… would violate my sense of credibility with respect to initiating action in these matters. I believe it to be in the best interests of Mount Royal College to pursue these issues and questions."[145] In effect, Burden was responding to the centralizing function of the department, whose mandate, approved by cabinet in 1973, was "to provide the leadership, service and coordination necessary to ensure the efficient development and functioning of an effective system of advanced education responsive to the needs of all Albertans.[146]

Two earlier reports had spurred the ministry's interventionist agenda. The Worth Commission recommended that the responsibility for university and college programs and all educational or training programs under the supervision of other ministries, such as nursing and other health programs, apprenticeship programs, private trade schools, and forest technology, should be transferred to Advanced Education. It also recommended the dissolution of the existing commissions and a more direct government role in coordinating developments – "buffer bodies" by their nature are less open than the government to public influence and tend to "open up convenient avenues for avoidance of responsibility by government."[147] Meanwhile, the Colleges Commission published its Master Planning Project report. Where the Worth report had recommended coordination directly by the department, this one also recommended dissolution of the two commissions but recommended establishment of a Planning and Review Board under the minister to function as the planning, coordinating, and policy-making body, for which the department would provide executive functions. Not needing much encouragement, the government dissolved the two commissions and transferred the powers to the department effective May 1973.

Desmond E. Berghofer, the assistant deputy minister responsible for planning and program coordination, responded to Burden: "With respect to local autonomy, we would support the principles of institutional initiative and flexibility; however, these must be implemented within a province-wide framework." He was looking forward to a dialogue about "role clarification" through a review of existing and future program directions.[148]

The significance of the latter remark soon became clear in a spreadsheet circulated by the department entitled "Current and Recommended Service Parameters for Post-Secondary Institutions in Alberta." It mapped out the current and proposed activities of all universities, colleges, institutes, and vocational centres in degree-granting, university-transfer, and certificate- and diploma-level programs. Mount Royal would operate on a comprehensive basis in only four areas: health and allied service programs, business administration, community services, and continuing education. Its roles would be reduced in university transfer (only first-year courses in selected areas, no second-year courses) and its offerings in music, arts, and communications would be limited. Astonished, Lauchlan replied immediately. Noting that Mount Royal was the largest college, he wrote: "Of all the institutions in the college system, the proposals of the Department offer Mount Royal College the narrowest opportunity to expand in the whole system. I cannot understand the reasoning behind this position." He was especially concerned about the omission of any role in adult upgrading: "it is impossible for a community college with an open door admission policy not to be involved in some form of upgrading. Our learning skills staff and the people at AVC Calgary work in the closest consultation. There is no duplication. . . . We simply cannot function without an upgrading component."[149] Lauchlan's protest led to some scurrying around and to a revised version which restored the mandate to include comprehensive first-year and selected second-year university transfer courses and comprehensive programming in arts, music, communications, and academic upgrading.[150]

But the change in language in a document did not change the intention of the coordination function to restrict Mount Royal's programming. In March 1978, it rejected a proposal for a Theatre Crafts and Design diploma program because "a similar program already exists in the province. Since this is a specialized field in which employment opportunities appear quite limited, we are not prepared to approve another program." Refusing to deal with Berghofer, Lauchlan told Kolesar that "there is no similar program in existence. If what [Berghofer] is referring to is a recent approval of a proposal from Grant MacEwan College, that is a different question. We have no desire to hold back [its] the development. . . . However, there are . . . issues regarding programming in Fine Arts in the colleges which are not being dealt with openly and fairly. When Department officials appear surprised to learn that we have two theatres and support facilities in place, our confidence in their decisions in this area is considerably eroded."[151]

Speaking at the April 1979 convocation, Burden apologized to the graduates for any shortcomings they may have experienced. This led to a kerfuffle. Some faculty members assumed he was speaking about their performance, and Reva Stilwell, MRFA president, conveyed their dismay: "The effect of your 'apologies' was to denigrate the achievements of faculty, administration, and students. Some of us were dumbfounded."[152] Burden, who had criticized the government for failing to provide adequate funding and new facilities, responded that "it is obvious that there are many areas in our total system that are deficient, in which shortcomings exist and which need bolstering. Some examples . . . are: (a) limited enrollment in certain courses; (b) omission of certain courses for various reasons; (c) lack of substance in the content of certain courses; (d) deficiencies and inconsistencies in delivery systems; (e) organizational problems, particularly in the time-tabling of courses." Some deficiencies resulted from the lack of funding but others derived from individual and collective performance.[153]

Burden's explanation did not satisfy those looking for offence. MacLeod told the board that the exchange "had raised serious questions about the relationship between the board and the rest of the college, and that 'action, or lack of action, would send a very clear message to the college at large.'" Stewart supported Burden's description of his motives and regretted the implication "that a single incident might destroy the kind of relationship the board had worked at so diligently over the years."[154] The more important audience, however, was in Edmonton, where criticisms of government policy by a board chair and continuing signs of tension were viewed coolly.

Summing Up

By 1980, the college had completed the troubled transformation from private to public institution. It had consolidated its curriculum, expanded continuing education, forged new links to the community, mapped out a new direction for the Conservatory, adapted, if awkwardly, to the new-style campus in Lincoln Park, and accepted a constitution for the Academic Council. Lauchlan had been at the centre of these accomplishments. He had embraced an expansive notion of the role of a community college and translated it into many areas of activity. His major disappointment was the rejection of the Lincoln Park area plan that he had so assiduously developed. Ironically, twenty years later, when the college was to secure its Phase III expansion, the later plan resembled the one he had developed, with the college at the core of a local community, but for the larger area of Lincoln Park once the Canadian Armed Forces base adjacent to the college was closed.

Though Lauchlan was a consensus builder, he found himself in awkward circumstances. He was at odds with the chairman of the board on the neighbourhood planning issue, his relationship with the executive vice-president, academic was unfortunate for reasons beyond his control, and the Phase II expansion project was far from receiving approval in Edmonton. Some faculty members saw the institution as deadlocked.[155] In the circumstances, Lauchlan had little desire to linger, and in September 1979 he notified the board that he would not seek a further term. He reflected with pride on the work he had done, including restoring calm to the college's internal life, facilitating adaptation to the new facility, developing community education, expanding adult education, promoting the Conservatory, and initiating preparations for the next expansion – all considerable contributions. For Mount Royal, he concluded, "the future has never been more interesting."[156] Dan Cornish was an obvious candidate to replace Lauchlan. However, his role had become contentious. There were lingering faculty concerns about the nature of his original appointment and the division of responsibilities with Lauchlan; there were concerns that the board had anointed him as the heir apparent, or that he saw himself that way, or that others saw him that way. The hassles with the MRFA over whether the positions held by Demicell and Gervais should have fallen in the MRFA category tarnished the perception of his senior team. Given the recent internal history of Mount Royal, it was not surprising that some faculty members wished to block his appointment as president.

July 1980	Dr. Donald N. Baker becomes president
1981	Academic reorganization: formation of Faculties
1982	Government approval for Phase II expansion project
	Major donation enables launch of the Academy of Music program
1985	75th Anniversary Fund Campaign launched
1985–87	Ten per cent reduction in operating grants
1986	Calgary Centennial Arenas open; new policies on academic qualifications of faculty members and periodic review of programs and services; first work-study/co-operative program introduced
1987	Wyckham House Student Centre opens
1988	Board approves the "College Goal" (student academic success and student/client satisfaction), and exploration of degree-granting possibilities
1989	Mount Royal Court residences open (legacy benefit of 1988 Winter Olympic Games)
August 1989	President Baker departs

CHAPTER 8

SEEKING A NEW IDENTITY, 1980–1989

For Mount Royal College, the past has been characterized by constant change—by almost imperceptible sea changes in some periods, by rapid and even revolutionary changes at other times. Sometimes the change has been deliberately induced from within, at other times it has been imposed from without. In general, the direction of change seems ineluctably to have been steered by the evolution of the community the college strives to serve.

– Donald N. Baker, 1982.[1]

From the mid-1960s through the 1970s the post-secondary education system in Alberta was transformed. Huge expenditures on new post-secondary facilities and operations had led to new campuses around the province. The expansion was made possible by soaring oil revenues. In the eight years before OPEC raised prices in 1973, 28 per cent of Alberta's government expenditures derived from resource revenues, while in the eight years after, 54 per cent did.[2] By 1980, both the rising price of oil and Alberta's rising fortunes had become a national issue. A debate began over whether charging the Canadian consumers, businesses, and manufacturers the "world" price made sense or whether a two-price policy (internal, external) would be better. In October 1980 the federal government introduced the National Energy Program (NEP) to establish a federal role in managing energy resources.[3] The energy policy debate immediately became entangled in the constitutional negotiations arising from the Parti Quebecois' 1980 referendum on "sovereignty-association." Prime Minister Pierre Trudeau initiated a process to "patriate" the constitution from the parliament of the United Kingdom. This required negotiations over an "amending formula," and these gave Premier Peter Lougheed the opportunity to rally other premiers behind provincial rights. As a result, the provinces gained greater control over natural resources and the right to opt out of federal programs (including the Canadian Charter of Rights and Freedoms).[4]

After peaking in 1981 at $37 a barrel, the price of oil dropped to $25–$29 and in 1985 collapsed to $14–$18, where it remained for fifteen years. Between them, the drop in oil revenues and the NEP caused a sharp economic downturn in the early 1980s. Oil companies ceased exploration and service industries came to a halt. Construction starts in Calgary fell in half from 1981 to 1982, and housing prices plummeted from an average of $230,000 in 1981 to $125,000 in 1985.[5] Some regional banks and credit institutions collapsed.[6] Though the North American economy began to revive in the late 1980s, much of the stimulus in Alberta derived from publicly funded projects such as the 1988 Winter Olympic Games, Calgary's Light Rail Transit (LRT) system, and the Phase II expansion of Mount Royal College. From 1985 to 1994, the province experienced nine consecutive years of deficit, leaving a total debt of $20 billion.[7] The government raised income taxes in 1983 and 1987, increased medical care premiums, froze ministry budgets, and slashed grants to institutions. It diverted earnings from the Alberta Heritage and Savings Trust Fund earnings to general revenues (1982–83), reduced the share of royalty revenues invested in the fund from 30 to 15 per cent (1983), and then reduced contributions to zero (1987–88).[8] Yet the need for larger expenditures continued, as the population continued to grow, raising the demand for infrastructure and services. Calgary grew from 592,000 in 1981 to 754,000 in 1991, an increase of 21.5 per cent. Despite fiscal stringency, government expenditures nearly doubled during the decade.[9]

The economic downturn caused thousands of Albertans to turn to higher education to improve their credentials, leading to high levels of demand. Much of it was met by simply incorporating more students or doing so with enrolment growth grants at half the basic grant level per student. Twice in a decade there were serious cutbacks in grant levels – a 10 per cent cut in operating grants over three years in the mid-1980s, and a 21 per cent cut over three years in the mid-1990s. Partly in search of sector rationalization and partly in search of a mission, the Department of Advanced Education and Manpower began requiring the institutions to submit their institutional development plans for approval.[10] Anxious to reduce the number of civil servants, the government devolved authority to governing boards at SAIT and NAIT in 1982, the Alberta College of Art (ACA) in 1985, and AVC-Calgary in 1992 (as Bow Valley College). Informing government policies and department behaviour was a strongly instrumental view of education, in which the primary aim of post-secondary education was to develop the workforce.[11]

This was the institutional context in which Mount Royal reached the limits of its community-college mandate. However, the community it served was a fast-growing head-office city with one of the best-educated populations in Canada and with the highest proportion of managers and business professionals in the country. As a geophysical research centre, moreover, Calgary also had one of the largest concentrations of computer power in the world. Meeting the needs of that community with one-year certificate and two-year diploma programs was not easy, or entirely adequate, and by the end of the 1980s the college was planning to expand its mandate to include degree programs, stretching the established notion of what a community college was,[12] beginning a two-decade tussle with department officials and other post-secondary institutions.

REGENERATING THE ADMINISTRATION

Chaired by Fred Stewart, vice-chair of the board, the presidential search committee included representatives of all constituencies (board, faculty, support staff, students, and administrators).[13] The list was narrowed from forty to three. The finalists were visited at their

Donald N. Baker, President 1981–89. Photographer
Magelle's Studio; Mount Royal University Archives E8-5.

home location for three days by a sub-committee, and
the finalists met on campus with the constituencies.
In the end, the position was offered to Dr. Donald N.
Baker, a historian at the University of Waterloo, who
became Mount Royal's sixth president on 1 July 1980.
Where Kerby, Garden, and Collett, and Lauchlan had
come from a ministerial background and Pentz had
specialized in educational administration, Baker was
the first scholar to lead the college.[14] Born in Vancouver in December 1936, he had earned a BA in history
and international studies at the University of British
Columbia and an AM and Ph.D. in history at Stanford
University, where he also served as a faculty member
for three years (1962–65). He then taught at Michigan State University (1965–70) and the University

of Waterloo (1970–80). Among other roles, he had
served two terms as an elected trustee on the Waterloo
County Board of Education.

In his inaugural remarks, Baker said that "the
ingredients are there in our traditions to make this a
model institution for the public college system in Alberta and across the country. Mount Royal's blend of
the useful and humane disciplines suits it admirably to
meet the lifelong educational needs of Albertans. . . .
If we act together, if we stimulate each other to realize
our collective ideals, I don't see how we can fail."[15] His
views on the role of the college were coloured by the
California Master Plan (1960) adopted while he was at
Stanford. It provided for a coordinated set of institutions, each set with its own mission but linked to provide ladders of educational opportunity.[16] His career
had led him through three innovative universities,
from each of which he had learned – from Stanford,
about the importance of strategic planning, the value
of a research-intensive university for undergraduate
education, and the added value that a rising institutional reputation provides graduates; from Michigan
State, about the community-focused land-grant tradition, extension, and the role of precincts within a large
institution; and from Waterloo, about co-operative
work/study education and distance delivery. These
lessons influenced his behaviour as president.

The board asked Baker to address several matters, including the expansion proposal, which had
been developed in the optic of the defunct Lincoln
Park plan and was weighted to the non-credit community education side, reclassification of the support
staff, a perceived decline in faculty teaching loads, and
development of a professional development program
for "management-exempt" staff and administrators.
Gerry Burden, the chair of the board, advised him to
focus on the academic quality and development of the
college.

Beyond addressing the initial issues raised by the
board, the major themes of Baker's presidency were
planning, reorganization, facilities expansion, coping with lean operating funding, improving quality,
reaching out through continuing education and extension and international activities, introducing the
work-study co-operative model of delivery, fundraising and institutional marketing, and degree granting.

Planning and Reorganization

"On arriving at Mount Royal College, I made it a priority to establish the importance of planning and evaluation in the college's procedures and administration," Baker said in his State of the College remarks in September 1981, but his first challenge was coping with a flood of administrative departures. Dan Cornish, the executive vice-president, academic and disappointed candidate for the presidency, resigned immediately.[17] The two theme deans, Bob Gervais and Jeanette Demicell, also resigned within weeks for positions elsewhere. The outflow continued with the resignation of Ed Schmidt (vice-president, finance and administrative services), the director of Computing Services, and the head of personnel, all lured by options in the red-hot local economy. These departures forced Baker to name a number of acting appointees, including academic vice-presidents: first Ken Hollington, chair of Justice Administration and Youth Development, then Emmett Hogan, chair of Social Services.

Given the absence of a senior management team, his absorption in management details arising from vacancies, and his desire to launch a strategic planning exercise, Baker struck a seven-member Task Force on Future Directions in November 1980 "to study evolving and projected educational needs in Calgary and region during the 1980s, to assess the ability of Mount Royal College to meet those needs with its present human and other resources, and to recommend changes in programs, staffing, physical plans, policy or procedures to meet the anticipated needs."[18] Chaired by Thomas L. Wood, a philosophy instructor and the faculty board member, the task force included two external board members (Fred Stewart, Diane O'Connor), three faculty members (Dennis Leask, environmental science, Kenneth J. Robson, English literature, and Don J. Stouffer, leisure and physical education), and one administrator (Dean Thomas J. Stevens, Community Education Services).[19] Baker participated in the meetings of the task force as often as he could. The team met with government officials, including assistant deputy ministers (Reno Bosetti, Desmond Berghofer) and experts on planning and institutional renewal. The task force received more than forty submissions. Its recommendations were to build higher on the existing curricular base (by extending university transfer work to two full years, by adding programs in business, informatics, health sciences, and social services), and to incorporate computer technology in delivery. It proposed becoming a wholly post-secondary institution. Its work was to feed into planning for the Phase II expansion.[20] In addition, Baker struck a special committee headed by Hugh Macleod to address issues arising from counselling and the registration process.[21]

While the task force was at work, Baker restructured the administration and recruited new senior administrators. "You can have the best plans and policies but if you don't have really good people to carry them out," he said later, "you don't have much."[22] The restructuring occurred in two steps. After discussing the issue with the Task Force on Future Directions and developing "some suggestions for change," Baker struck an Organization Review Committee chaired by Judith Lathrop and including David Thomas and Alan Dyment, all future administrators, to solicit opinion from the college and "to assess responses and to make its own recommendations."[23] Its report was discussed in a series of meetings with various groups with a view to "settle on a structure that will endure in its main lines for several years, although I have no doubt that various adjustments will be necessary as we go along from one year to another."[24] He submitted his own recommendations (and the report) to the Academic Council for approval and to the board, which approved the changes in April 1981.[25] The aim, Baker said, was to provide "more responsible and responsive academic leadership to plan, evaluate and operate."[26] The new administrative structure continued the three existing Divisions – Academic Affairs, Community Education Services, and Administrative Services – but established eighteen academic departments (formerly twelve) organized in four Faculties.[27] The reorganization was inspired by the desire to provide more coherent units for planning and evaluation, to lay the groundwork for the larger college that was anticipated, and to strengthen administrative support for the work of the faculty. The two "theme dean" positions were eliminated. In addition to the four new faculty deans, the dean of Student Services and the director of the Learning Resources Centre reported to the vice-president, academic. Because Baker wanted a periodic refreshment of the administrative cadre, all of the new positions set five-year terms for normal appointments, and a maximum of two terms except in extraordinary circumstances.

The Organization Review Committee report had identified the fit between the credit and non-credit operations as an "issue for further discussion" and recommended that a review "should be undertaken immediately."[28] The second step occurred in September 1981 after the appointment of the new vice-president, academic, approval of the Phase II construction project, and financial difficulties arising from budget management in Continuing Education and Extension that suggested the need for a reorganization.

The Division of Continuing Education and Extension was merged into Academic Affairs, under a dean reporting to the vice-president, academic. This reorganization also brought the director of the Conservatory into Academic Affairs. Thus, effective in the fall of 1981, all academic functions and academic services reported to the vice-president, academic.[29]

Following a national search, Thomas Wood was appointed vice-president, academic in May 1981. Wood had earned a BA in English at the University of Alberta, begun studies at Cornell University on a Woodrow Wilson Fellowship, but, at the request of his church, moved to Brigham Young University to teach for three years. He then relocated to Calgary, where he entered graduate studies in philosophy at the university. Part-time teaching at Mount Royal quickly led to a full-time job. During the tempestuous 1970s he had been a moderating influence and twice served as the faculty representative on the board. Baker and Wood were to work closely together. Sharing intellectual interests in common, they sought ways to make Mount Royal an innovative community college responding to the particularities of Calgary and an exemplar of its institutional type; by the mid-1980s, they also shared the conclusion that the college needed to raise the level of its credentials in response to local needs. Following Wood's appointment, Ken Robson replaced him as chair of the task force.

By the summer of 1981, following internal searches, the four deans of the Faculties, the dean of Student Affairs, and the director of Academic Services had been appointed following internal searches. Given the extent of change, Baker had waived the requirement for external searches for this first round of decanal/director appointments; the appointments were staggered in length to permit more orderly search processes in the future. Three of the deans had begun as chairmen, and two were former presidents of the MRFA; one had been a faculty member on the board; all held degrees from Alberta universities; two held Ph.D.s and two earned the degree later. Following some reshuffling because of the changes in Continuing Education, the decanal/director complement in Academic Affairs by 1982 was as follows:

Dean of Arts: Robert McDougall, BA, B.Ed. (Saskatchewan), M.Ed. (Calgary) (started 1967), former MRFA president (1969–70), chairman of the Humanities department (1973–80); followed in 1982 by Robson, the chairman of the English department, as well as head of the Task Force;

Dean of Science and Technology: Dennis Leask, B.Sc. (Alberta at Calgary), M.Sc. in Geology (Calgary) (1971), member of the Association of Professional Engineers, Geologists and Geophysicists of Alberta, former Environmental Science department chairman;

Dean of Community and Health Studies: Don J. Stouffer, former chair of the Leisure and Physical Education department;

Dean of Business and Applied Arts: David Thomas, BA (Wales), MA in political science (Calgary), Masters in Curriculum Design (Sussex) (1972), former president of the MRFA (1975–76), faculty board member (1976–77), Professional Development Officer (1980–81);

Dean of Continuing Education and Extension: Judith (Eifert) Lathrop, RN (University of Alberta Hospital), B.Sc. in Nursing (Calgary), Masters of Nursing (Calgary), and Masters in Nursing and Allied Fields (Columbia), chairman of the Nursing and Allied Health departments (1976–80), Dean of the Faculty of Community and Health Studies, 1981–82;

Director of the Conservatory of Music and Speech Arts: Norman Burgess, BA (Saskatchewan), Ph.D. in Music (Indiana), director of the Conservatory since 1977;

Dean of Student Affairs: Robert R. Rose, Ph.D., a long-time counsellor and learning skills instructor, co-author of an influential study of college management focusing on Miami-Dade College;[30]

Director of Academic Services: Alan Dyment, director of the Learning Resources Centre (library) since 1973.

This was a credible group that would represent Mount Royal well in relations with the community, other institutions, and the professions. Demonstrating its energy and a sense that the college had been idling, the team soon prepared fourteen letters of intent for submission to government, including nine new programs.[31] Most of these people were to play key roles over the next two decades.

The search for a vice-president, finance and administration ended in early 1982 with the appointment of Alexander S. Dobbins, the financial analyst in the Department of Advanced Education. Dobbins reorganized the Administrative Services Division to parallel the academic side, with directors reporting to the vice-president, and managers reporting to directors.[32] Among other changes, the Personnel Office was recast as Human Resources and Bruce Mahon, Ph.D., a psychology instructor, became director, a role he played for two decades, becoming over time an important interlocutor with the faculty and staff associations. One other long-serving appointment from the period was Steven Foster, the director of Physical Resources.

Several overlapping committees were the chief vehicles for administrative teamwork. The Dean's Advisory Group (DAG) consisted of the department chairs and the continuing education coordinator for the faculty. Each vice-president's advisory group (VPAG) consisted of the deans and/or directors reporting to the vice-president. The Executive Committee consisted of the president, vice-presidents, and others reporting to the president. In addition, the President's Advisory Group (PAG) consisted of the vice-presidents, deans, and directors and met on a quarterly basis, and for a two-day annual retreat in the fall semester devoted to strategic planning and management development and another later in the year "to review achievements and discuss interim adjustments in our operational goals and priorities."[33] The committees facilitated coordination, communications, and the development of a stronger shared vision and comprehension of collective priorities. With a view to the importance of reflective practice, Baker and Wood brought in a stream of external experts to acquaint the faculty and administration with current academic planning and management issues– such as John Roueche and George Baker on the importance

of shared vision and exemplary administrative practices,[34] George Keller on strategic planning,[35] Patricia Cross on the role of the community college,[36] Richard Chait on governance,[37] and, as we shall see, Robert Birnbaum on collective bargaining.[38]

Impressed by the role of the Secretariat at the University of Waterloo, where a professional cadre supported the board, senate, search committees, and the president's committees, Baker hired Philip J. Musclow from there to establish the College Secretariat and as College Secretary. (One effect was to divide the responsibilities of the old Secretary-Treasurer function held by George Walters, Max Rae, and Ed Schmidt into two parts – the Secretary function for the board now being lodged with the College Secretary; and the vice-president, finance and administration focusing on business matters.) To provide management and planning information, Baker established the Office of Institutional Analysis and Planning (OIAP), with Lynda Wallace-Hulecki as director.[39] Concerned to ensure accurate and timely communications, he initiated a regular internal newsletter. Cathy Nickel, who was to continue to play a key role in college communications for decades, published the *Reporter* and its more ambitious successor, *MRC News*, and the *MRC Bulletin* for special announcements.

The other issues of concern to the board – reclassification of the support staff and professional development for the management/exempt staff group – quickly became agenda items for the new vice-president, finance and administration, and the director of human resources. They were to be accomplished quickly.

FACILITIES EXPANSION

By 1982, the college was serving 5,471 students in a facility designed for 3,000. Driving the growing demand was a combination of the growing 18–24 age cohort and the onset of the recession. The college accommodated the growth "through the filling of vacant seats and the negotiated increase in faculty workload." Even so, there were physical limits: in 1983–84, 87 per cent of the seats in the institution were occupied.[40] The March 1982 budget announcement of funding for the Phase II expansion was very welcome. In a letter dated 18 March 1982, Minister

Roy V. Deyell, Chairman of the Board 1981–87. Mount Royal University Archives E58-2.

James Horsman advised Roy V. Deyell (who had been appointed board chair in July 1981) that the college would receive up to $63 million to add or renovate 25,000 square metres of space.[41] "We can barely shoehorn another student or staff member into our present building, so the government's decision is very timely," Baker said.[42] The timing was also propitious, for, had it been delayed, the recession might have postponed the project for another decade. Even so, the grant was reduced in June 1983 to $61 million and in March 1984 to $60 million.[43]

Baker struck a committee to consider how to operate when construction began – whether to rent portables, rent space, or move to a trimester system to relieve pressure on the available facilities, and how to timetable more efficiently.[44] After considering the

scope of the project, the board asked the government for the adjacent 18.17-acre parcel of land then held by Alberta Housing as it presented a logical entry point to the expanded college.[45] However, discussions with Alberta Housing proved fruitless,[46] and, though the college asked the government to acquire the land for it,[47] expansion planning proceeded without the parcel. The aim was to produce facilities capable of accommodating 7,500 FTE credit students plus one-half the expected increase in continuing education.[48] The board appointed Cornerstone Planning Group Ltd. to serve as functional programmers, William (Bill) C. Duff to serve as project manager,[49] the Chandler Kennedy Architectural Group (CKAG) to provide architectural services, and two firms for structural and electrical engineering (Reid Crowther and Partners; Simpson, Lester and Goodrich Engineering Partnership).

As in the 1960s, the project entailed a great deal of discussion within the college, including displays and workshops and many detailed responses.[50] In January 1983 the culminating document, *Education Plan: Facility Expansion Supplement* in January 1983, recommended a comprehensive community college model that amounted to continuing to build on the college's current program base, yet leaving "sufficient flexibility to move in alternative directions, both in program and of delivery, before and after it [the college] reaches its enlarged capacity in the 1990s."[51] The other models under consideration would have conflicted with the roles of AVC-Calgary and SAIT. The architects projected that "80 per cent of the expanded campus will accommodate existing . . . programs (expanded in size in most but not all cases), 20 per cent new programs."[52]

The design included structured "precincts" in both renovated and new facilities to house the Faculties and other major administrative functions. These were intended to form the physical basis of sub-communities within a much larger and more extended set of buildings. Each was linked to the new "main street," an enhanced corridor running from the east to the west side of the mega-structure on two levels. Along that street were "gates" leading to the precincts, both within and outside the mega-structure. In each precinct there was a "commons" doubling as study space, meeting rooms dedicated to the precinct, and a department home for faculty and students.[53]

If the shopping mall metaphor and open-space plan no longer seemed appropriate, what would replace them? Community college campuses reflected very different self-conceptions and missions. Some looked like high schools; others looked like a mix of office and warehouse space; and still others looked like universities. Senior administrators, board members, and the architects visited campuses in the United States to look at how campuses similar to the Lincoln Park model (e.g., Bunker Hill College in Boston) had fared, consider projects involving the fit between new and old facilities, and build a shared "architectural vocabulary." The board decided to adopt a "collegiate" metaphor to associate the college with higher educational tradition, to underline its high purpose, and to enhance the sense of dignity of users. The buildings would be on "a human scale" (3–4 stories high). Among other things, there would be courtyards, high-quality commons spaces, cathedral-style major entrances, and woodwork to soften the otherwise hard surfaces

The first building, the Arts Wing, designed by Paul Merrick, reflected the collegiate style in its purest form. Built around a courtyard, the wing included a reading room evocative of a similar space at Massey College in Toronto; each department was provided a small common room and designated meeting space; and each faculty office contained built-in bookshelves. There were classrooms of various sizes and configurations and well-equipped lecture theatres with raked seating. Work on the wing began in December 1984 and was completed in the summer of 1986.[54]

Then the construction process was slowed by the architects' declaration of bankruptcy on 30 June 1984.[55] Though the board chose another firm within three weeks (Cook, Culham, Montgomery, Pedersen and Valentine Architects and Engineers, with Fred Valentine as the new design architect),[56] picking up a complex project in midstream was bound to take time. A few months later, Deyell wrote to Minister Dick Johnston requesting his "serious consideration of returning the total grant to the original $63 million for the reason that construction costs are now rising markedly. I regret having to ask you this, but the delay caused by the bankruptcy has apparently placed our tendering of construction into a rising rather than a falling market."[57]

There were two other large wings to be built – Roy V. Deyell Hall, including the Douglas M. Lauchlan Reading Room, for community and health studies completed in 1987, and George W. Kerby Hall for student and administrative services, completed in 1988. New precincts were established within the original mega-structure to serve as home bases for the Faculty of Business and Applied Arts and the Faculty of Science and Technology. The Forum was converted into lecture halls, classrooms, and food outlets. The entire project was finished in early 1989. It encompassed 27,000 square metres of new space, nearly as much renovated space, at a revised cost of $73 million. It added 42 per cent to the college's facilities and increased student capacity by 63 per cent. The end was celebrated in an open house held on 24–25 November 1989.[58]

To enhance the completed project, Baker launched a Signature Sculpture Competition funded by Amoco Canada Petroleum Company Ltd., the Alberta Foundation for the Arts, and the Alberta Advanced Education Endowment and Incentive Fund that led to the selection of two large sculptures by Derek Michael Besant, an internationally renowned artist. "Enigma" and "Homage" were located at the East Gate and West Gate entrances, respectively.[59] He also arranged for the acquisition of a winning piece produced by graduates of the Alberta College of Art.

There were three other major facilities additions in this period. After years of discussion focusing on size, money, and the bar, while students built their building fund, the board and Students' Association agreed on the terms and conditions for the Wyckham House Student Centre.[60] In June 1983, the board agreed to provide $1.9 million for 1,720 square metres of space.[61] Two years later, however, new student leaders demanded more space (2,400 square metres) and more money. While the board ignored the associated theatrics, it recognized that construction costs were rising and looked for ways to assist the students. Alex Dobbins undertook to determine whether a donation from the association would be matched under the government's matching-grant stream. It would, and so the association donated $700,000 and Minister Dick Johnston matched it, on two conditions – that "the money will be used to construct a student facility and

Signature sculpture *Enigma*, by artist Derek Besant, was installed in 1989 at the East Gate entrance. Photographer Leigh Dehaney; Mount Royal University Archives G412-2-7.

on the condition that the facility will be owned by the college."[62] The centre's budget rose to $4,152,000.[63]

The second building project was the construction of a two-surface ice arena complex, the Calgary Centennial Arenas, on Crowchild Trail near the college. This project began when an older neighbourhood arena collapsed and a group of volunteers, including the college, CFB-Calgary, and several neighbourhood associations developed a consortium to build a new one. It opened on 15 November 1986. The federal, provincial, and city governments provided 75 per cent of the cost, while the rest was raised. Dean Don Stouffer, whose duties included serving as coach of the Cougars hockey team, was one of the principal organizers. The arena contains two ice surfaces – one of international hockey size, the other smaller. The project cost $3.8 million, of which the college contributed $150,000.[64] The college then negotiated the donation

of an electronic sign that enables Cougar news to be advertised to passers-by on Crowchild Trail.[65]

The third was a student residential complex, a "legacy" benefit from the 1988 Winter Olympic Games. On several occasions the college had volunteered use of its facilities to the organizing committee. In 1984 it had suggested building "media accommodations at or near" the college.[66] During the games the college hosted the Finnish Broadcasting Network, which used the college's TV broadcasting facilities.[67] After the games, the organizing committee awarded the college some of the housing built for the print media on nearby ATCO property. After the provincial government agreed to provide the 18.17-acre site the college had sought earlier and funding to service the site, the housing was relocated to that land. Mount Royal Court opened in September 1989, at a cost of $12 million. It included 39 furnished modular town-house

Mount Royal College's East Residences opened in 1989 as a legacy of the Olympic Winter Games held in Calgary. Photograph courtesy Greg McKernan.

Douglas E. Thomson, Chairman of the Board 1988-90. Photographer Magelle's Studio; Mount Royal University Archives E273-2.

units consisting of 74 four-bedroom units, 64 two-bedroom units, and 10 single-bedroom units.[68]

In addition to on-campus developments, the college established a presence in downtown Calgary through leased facilities. The original site of the Professional Development Centre at 1010-8th Avenue SW had lasted only a year, thanks to the economic downturn. To provide "swing" space for the expansion project, the college in 1984 leased 32,000 square feet on three floors at 1019-7th Avenue SW. The site was convenient because it was located along the new LRT rail system linking the northeast and southeast quadrants of the city.[69] It also became a major venue for continuing education activities. In 1987, the lease was renewed for a further three years.

Some facilities ideas were not realized, notably a satellite campus in northeast Calgary. In 1981, noting that "63 per cent of the college's clientele comes from the western side of the city," Baker advised Minister Horsman that the board might include a proposal for a northeast campus in future requests to serve a community filled with recent immigrants and working people.[70] In 1986, he returned to the idea. Learning from Jon Havelock, chair of the Calgary Board of Education, that it was considering building a secondary school in the northeast, they agreed to propose a joint-use site. Both boards approved the idea.[71] But the timing was not good. The province had just slipped into a deficit, and Minister Dave Russell said that "I

am not optimistic that in the current fiscal climate we would be able to support this project in 1987–88."[72] After meeting Russell, who explained that "Mount Royal has done quite well for the time being, and we're in tough economic times," Havelock told the press: "The province was penny wise and pound foolish in turning down Mount Royal College's pitch to build a satellite campus in partnership with a new northeast high school."[73]

In 1989, the continuing absence of a Lincoln Park development plan came to the fore when BCE Development applied to develop a regional shopping mall beside the college. Board chair Douglas E. Thomson asked the City not to approve any development until a plan was approved.[74] A college delegation led by Baker made a case to the City Council, which denied BCE's application. The lack of a plan continued until closure of the Canadian Forces Base Calgary forced the need for one in the next decade. Meanwhile, the college took "the position that the sooner planning . . . is started, the better."[75]

The Financial Challenge

From 1966 to the early 1990s there were two major periods in government policy for funding institutions. From 1966 to 1976, funding was ad hoc, driven by the needs of new programs, institutions, and local circumstances.[76] Beginning in 1976, institutions were given "base operating grants" that were adjusted annually by a "price factor," with "supplementary funding . . . to support new programs, the operation of new facilities and to recognize special circumstances (strong enrolment growth, institutional development, institutional size and other circumstances)." In 1981–83, the Supplementary Enrolment Fund was added to provide "marginal rather than full-cost funding" to enrolment changes above a base year (initially 1981–82). These funds were reviewed each year and remained outside base operating grants.[77] The college found itself coping increasingly with targeted funding. For example, in 1981–82, it negotiated $200,000 in "growth supplement" funding to increase the Nursing program from 80 to 120 students. By the end of 1982, the sum of conditional funding was $627,300, at the end of 1983, $1.45 million, at the end of 1984, $1.7 million; though the total fell when the conditions were met and the funding was rolled into the base operating grant, it soared again to $1.8 million in 1987–88 – about 7 per cent of the operating grant of $25.5 million.[78]

As a result of reduced financial support, as the college's Long-range Institutional Plan stated in 1988, "most colleges recognized that to avoid dying of a thousand cuts they would need, in some measure, to reinvent themselves."[79] The hardest financial period was from 1985 to 1988, when the operating grant was cut by 10 per cent. To minimize expenses and maximize revenues, the college made several changes. In 1984 it contracted out its food services, turning that function from a net draw to a net contributor while guaranteeing that everyone was offered a job and guaranteed their college-level salary for so long as they continued to work.[80] Vacant positions were eliminated. Fortunately, Continuing Education began to make a profit and that helped; the Conservatory was given a firm bottom line and required to manage to it. The board approved a four-for-five–year leave plan for faculty and extended the program to the staff and redistributed workloads rather than replacing

people on leave. To improve cash handling, the board in January 1987 approved investing funds with Bissett and Associates Investment Management Ltd.[81] To generate additional revenues, the college entered into a partnership in 1984 with Long Drive Company, a group of businessmen who mounted a driving range on the college's vacant land, with a 50/50 split of profits.[82] The agreement generated about $50,000 profit a year and lasted until 1989 (the college then continued the operation on its own until the space was required for student housing). Because of complaints from the University of Calgary that it was not being treated equally with the University of Alberta, on the basis of per capita grants, an Ontario political scientist, J. Stefan Dupré, was hired by the province to undertake a review; it did not lead to much change but Mount Royal benefited to the tune of a $100,000 increase in its grant.[83] Thanks to the three-year time frame for managing the budget challenge and the fact that the college was growing on the basis of discounted grants, the budget challenge was met without terminations of people (except in food services). Indeed, though much of the change came with "lights-on" funding for the expansion at the end of the decade, the college's government grants doubled, rising from $18.7 to $36 million. The per capita student funding, however, fell from about $4,637 to $3,000 (1988 dollars). In 1980–81, government grants had constituted 64 per cent of college revenues; in 1987–88, with the Arts Wing completed, 69 per cent, and in 1989–90, when Phase II was completed, 75 per cent. The board of governors was persuaded that the college was generally underfunded. Though Mount Royal taught over one-quarter of the students in the college system, it received only "15 and 19 per cent of both the operating and capital allocations" to the colleges.[84]

On 1 July 1980, the college had introduced a computerized financial accounting system. Shortly thereafter, the people who had presided over its introduction in both finance and the computing centre left, thanks to the heated local economy, and before long someone made undocumented changes in the software, severing linkages between ledgers. As a result, the system began generating misleading reports. This came to light at the end of the 1981–82 year at which time the board and senior administrators were astonished to learn that there had been a net year-end deficit of $497,000, though the deficit in Continuing Education had been $1.1 million for the year. Though the financial system disguised the reality, the cause of the deficit was not in the financial system but in budget management in Continuing Education, which had not responded quickly enough to the sudden recession.[85] Alex Dobbins, the new vice-president, finance and administration went into overdrive. The board retained Deloitte Haskins and Sells Management Consultants to review the situation, and the board approved its recommendations for new procedures, policies, and job descriptions, including establishment of the position of Controller to oversee all revenues and expenditures.[86] The Department of Advanced Education provided a special $500,000 grant to help offset the deficit, and that grant, plus $150,000 in enrolment growth funding, the downsizing of Continuing Education, and tight management quickly turned the situation around. Indeed, with the department's approval, the college was soon able to put $1.2 million into reserve funds for particular purposes (program development, data base development, and the Canadian Centre for Learning Systems). Continuing financial prudence enabled the college to add two more reserve funds (to develop a fundraising function, and for initiating the international office).[87]

For the first time since its private phase, the college began fundraising in the early 1980s. There were some initial obstacles. Fundraising was new in Canadian higher education, and there were few people with experience or training to be hired. Many colleges were still thought of as training institutions and had not yet established themselves in the public mind as institutions requiring private support. The rather dim prospects brightened in 1981, when the government introduced the 1980s Alberta Advanced Education Endowment Fund to provide matching grants for donations to colleges, technical institutes, and universities. The availability of matching grants inspired all manner of informal and amateurish fundraising activity, but in the longer term it contributed to the development of strategic planning (so requests could be placed in the context of strategic goals and priorities), spurred the growth of professional fundraising functions in Alberta institutions, and over time yielded major financial benefits for Mount Royal and other institutions. The initial donations eligible for

John Kadz, Manager of the Conservatory's Academy of Music Program for gifted students, works with a young musician, ca. 1985. Mount Royal University Conservatory.

matching grants were simply targets of opportunity. In September 1981, James Horsman, the minister, notified Mount Royal of its first matched funds – $2,000 for a scholarship donation of the George W. Kerby College Board, and $35,400 for donations of cash and equipment from the Alberta Heart Foundation for the nursing program.[88] In November 1981, it received $775,000 for a computer donation by BP Exploration Canada Ltd. and Sperry Univac Computer Systems.[89] In early 1982 the position of Development and Alumni Officer was established but it proved impossible to recruit an experienced fund raiser. The early incumbents came from other fields – a former university professor and a businessman.[90]

In the 1980s the Conservatory became the principal beneficiary of fundraising. This was due to the Conservatory's deep roots in the community. In 1981, Burgess and John Kadz, head of the strings unit, learned that the Kahanoff Foundation would consider a grant to support the proposed Academy of Music program.

This led to an agreement with the foundation in January 1982 that provided for $730,000 in endowment funds over three years (1981–84) and $145,147 in operating funds – a total of $875,147.[91] Through contacts made through Roy Deyell's "Chairman's Challenge," President Harry Carlyle and Vice-President Tom Simms of Gulf Canada Resources hosted a luncheon in which musical prodigies brought tears to eyes and on the spot raised $250,000 more for the Conservatory.[92]

The celebration of the 75th Anniversary in 1985 was the point of departure for the first comprehensive fundraising campaign, the $2.5 million 75th Anniversary Fund campaign. One of the first donations was $100,000 from the Heart and Stroke Foundation to support the CPR program.[93] The $2.5 million target was achieved within two years.[94] As of 1988, the college had received matching grants from the 1980s Fund of $484,411 for operating purposes and $2,242,202 for capital and endowment purposes, for a total of $2,726,614.[95] Including the original donations (cash, in-kind), the total was about $5.5 million. That success led to preparations for the Ninth Decade Fund campaign. Hunter Wight was recruited in 1988 to serve as director of public relations and information services development and to oversee the Ninth-Decade fundraising campaign.[96] Wight, in company with later presidents, was to develop the fundraising activity to a much higher level over the next two decades.

The Calgary Fiddlers, led by Conservatory Director Norman Burgess (back row, second from left), were popular community performers, 1984. Photographer Janet Brown; Mount Royal University Archives B1-90-15.

CURRICULUM AND QUALITY

Although adding programs was difficult during construction, the college proposed new programs in order to be ready when space and funding became available. As a result, it received funding approval in 1986–87 for a new diploma program in Computer Sales and Marketing and four certificate programs: Applied Information; Gerontology; Office Systems Operation and Administration; and Systems Analysis and Project Management. Their combined enrolment was projected to be five hundred students.[97] In 1988–89, a Professional Writing certificate was added. Funding was added to expand enrolment in Business Administration, Child-Care Worker, Criminology, Music Performance, Physical Education, the university-transfer BA program, and the General Arts and Science and Compensatory program. Then, responding to a strong surge in demand, the government in 1988–89 and 1989–90 added funds to expand the university-transfer programs significantly.[98]

At the end of the decade, the college's curriculum consisted of thirty-four career diploma programs, twenty-two certificate programs, ten streams in its general arts and science diploma program, and university-transfer programs leading to BA, B.Comm./BBA, B.Ed., B.Eng., B.Phys.Ed., and B.Sc. degrees.[99] In addition, Continuing Education offered certificates in a variety of fields (e.g., Fitness Studies, Recreation Therapy, Wilderness Survival, Travel, Applied Public Relations, Fashion Merchandising, Telecommunications, and Tour Management). Continuing Education also offered programs in association with such professional associations as the Canadian Association of Petroleum Production Accountants (CAPPA), the Canadian Institute of Management (CIM), and the Building Owners and Managers Association (BOMA).[100] Thus, despite constraints, the college continued to develop its curriculum within the parameters at its disposal.

Of significance for the future was the introduction of the co-operative work-study delivery of programs, a form of delivery with which Baker was familiar from his experience at the University of Waterloo, where the approach was pioneered. He encouraged its adoption at Mount Royal and initiated the appointment of a coordinator for the purpose. In 1986 the college received federal funding for the co-op model for a diploma program in General Insurance and Business Administration. This entailed the addition of two work terms to the four-semester diploma programs. This mode of delivery spread to other programs and became a distinctive feature of the college's move into degree granting in the 1990s.

Meanwhile, the administration focused on raising the quality of programs and services. Baker drafted proposals for two critical new policies to launch the discussion, one on educational qualifications for faculty members, another on the periodic external evaluation of all programs and services. His concern was to strengthen the college's academic profile and its reputation for quality. In the course of deliberations by the Academic Council, the draft policy on educational qualifications (1985) underwent several iterations. In its final form, the policy stated that "the appropriate hierarchy or ranking of desirable qualifications to be used by selection committees when hiring would be: doctoral degree preferred, especially in university-transfer areas; master's degree to be considered the normal minimum for all areas of the college; bachelor's degree and/or experience and professional qualifications allowable in exceptional circumstances." The guidelines were to be "applied to all hiring in the academic areas, including counselors, librarians, and academic officers of the college (chairmen, deans, vice-president, academic, president)."[101]

In May 1986 the college adopted a policy that required the periodic external review of all programs and services. In professional fields, such as nursing and interior design, there were accrediting bodies whose assessments against clear standards were of value, but not all of the career programs had such external reference points. Moreover, there were no external bodies for assessing university-transfer programs or for most administrative and student services. Where there were other external review bodies, the college required the establishment of assessment teams made up of a mix of insiders and outsiders. The aim was "formative" – "to bring about systematic improvements in programs, to identify resource needs, and to assist in staff and curriculum development." By requiring units to undertake self-evaluations prior to the visit of external reviewers, the policy was intended to encourage ongoing reflection about quality.[102] A Coordinator of Evaluation Services was added to support the reviews.[103] Though such policies later became common, few Canadian universities then required the evaluation of programs, much less external evaluation of student or administrative services.[104] Though the word benchmarking was not yet common, "visible signs of success" included "evidence of . . . current and high-quality academic programs possessing academic standards at least comparable to those in other institutions offering similar programs.[105] On the services side, the college arranged for a review of its Information Systems department by the Canadian Information Processing Society (CIP). In addition, the college developed partnerships with professional associations to ensure the appropriateness of its standards.[106]

Another way of adding credibility was to secure transfer credit through ACAT for as many courses as possible. By 1988, 326 of 788 courses, or 41 per cent, were so recognized. Thanks to constraints on admissions at the two major universities, the college experienced a sharp rise in demand for its university-transfer programs and expanded all of its transfer programs to a full two years.[107] Additional funding in 1988 and 1989 accelerated the process.[108]

The aim of formal quality assessment was to enhance the credibility of the credentials awarded by the college, a lifelong benefit for graduates. It was supplemented by vigorous marketing which took several forms, beginning with a new logo (based on a stylized M with a symbolic head above it), a new legend, "Calgary's Community College," and guidelines for the use of the college's brand in all publications and advertisements.[109] To raise its profile, the college began advertising all vacant positions nationally, each advertisement containing a brief description of the college. The marketing program also built up the importance of the city – and thus the college's students. Using the 1981 national census, the Office of Institutional Analysis and Planning prepared a brochure demonstrating that Calgary's population was one of the best-educated in the country, a point that drew national attention. Over 49.3 per cent of the population over fifteen years of age had completed some form of post-secondary education, surpassing all other urban centres; moreover, 23 per cent of the workforce was engaged in management, technical, or professional jobs. In addition, as a geophysical centre, Calgary had one of the largest concentrations of computer power in the world. Hence the college's proclamation that Calgary was "the knowledge capital" of Canada.[110] The college positioned itself as a necessary facilitator of the knowledge society looming on the horizon.

Engaging in research in pedagogical technology was another way to advance the institution's reputation, and the college moved into that field. However, its principal venture in computer-related software development yielded only modest results. In 1984,

it entered into partnership with the University of Calgary, SAIT, the Calgary Board of Education, the Calgary Catholic Separate School Board, Control Data Canada, Honeywell Canada, Reid Chartwell Company, and later AVC-Calgary to establish the Canadian Centre for Learning Systems (CCLS). CCLS began at the initiative of President Norman E. Wagner of the University of Calgary, who invited local educational institutions to combine activities. "CCLS will be a place where students, teachers and researchers can work with up-to-the-minute courseware and delivery systems ranging from traditional CAL courseware to sophisticated laser disc technology."[111] Using a reserve fund set up for the purpose, the college committed $100,000 for a five-year period to the collaborative venture. Despite high hopes, CCLS played a larger role in basic computer awareness and training than in research.[112] Mount Royal's major projects were a courseware package for use by foreign students preparing to write the Test of English as a Foreign Language (TOEFL) developed by David Daum, coordinator of ESL activities, and work on computer-based music instruction. The CCLS board wound up the operation at the end of five years.[113]

Among other activities intended to raise Mount Royal's national profile was its co-hosting with SAIT the Association of Canadian Community Colleges 1986 conference in Calgary.[114] Because of presidential turnover at SAIT, the other co-host, the work fell to Mount Royal.[115] The conference was a popular success, enabling the college to showcase its campus and otherwise draw attention to its faculty and programs.

The Student Community

Despite the fiscal and facilities constraints, enrolment nearly doubled during the decade and student campus activity gathered momentum, thanks to the increased dynamic density of students, the expanded facilities, and the new student centre.

The slow enrolment growth of the 1970s (18 per cent from 1972 to 1980) gave way to much faster growth in the 1980s (79 per cent). Continuing education registrations almost doubled (98 per cent).[116] By the middle of the decade the college was swamped by applications and had to reject 2.7 applications for each one it accepted.[117] High-school students could no longer find easy jobs, and the unemployed wanted to strengthen their credentials. In 1988, a college report noted that "students in Alberta have been flocking back to grade 12 to upgrade their education, taking more advanced courses and bringing up their grades. This return has been so significant that the number of grade 12 students now far exceeds the number of grade 11 students. Similarly, the grade 12 population has just recently begun to outnumber the 18-year old population in Alberta. Two-thirds of potential university-level candidates have recently been spending more than one year in grade 12." "The parents of current Calgary high-school students are among the most highly educated in Canada," and "are likely to have high aspirations for their offspring and will be highly influential in the choices these young people make."[118] Faced by more demand than it could accommodate, the college gave priority to full-time over part-time students. As a result, full-time students rose as a proportion of the whole from 47.4 per cent in 1980–81 to 61.1 per cent in 1983–84, before dropping back to the 57 per cent level for the rest of the decade.[119]

Many of the general statistics concerning students in the period are summarized in Appendix 1. However, a few points are worth noting here. The average age of entering students was in the 23–25 range in the 1980s, a clear indication that few came directly from high school. In 1988, a report found that "the university transfer students are, on average, the youngest group, and the certificate students are the oldest. The mean age of a university transfer student is 19.9; the mean age of a certificate student is 32.2." The average age of full-time students was 22–23, while that for part-timers was 27–28. Only 10–14 per cent came directly from high school, most of them going into the university-transfer stream. "In all other programs, most of the students came to the college directly from the workforce. This is particularly true of those in certificate programs – over 85 per cent of these students were working full-time in the year before they enrolled at the college"; "over two-thirds" have "some post-secondary education, and almost one-third have a university degree." Interestingly, given the fact that institutional and personal agendas may diverge, two-thirds of the students in certificate programs intended to complete them while 20 per cent "plan to take only

a few courses." One-third of part-time students held full-time jobs, and a growing number possessed diplomas or degrees and were seeking an applied education or a new career. The percentage of students listing Calgary as their place of origin (85 per cent) was above the level of earlier decades. Indeed, a study of multiple applications showed that, of all colleges and technical institutes, Mount Royal now drew most heavily on its immediate geographic region. In 1980, women constituted 55.5 per cent of full-time students, and 58.1 per cent in 1987–88, on a trajectory leading to higher levels in the future. Strikingly, "almost three-quarters (71.1 per cent) of the certificate students are female, compared with less than half (43.1) per cent of the university-transfer students."[120] Almost 60 per cent of the credit students by the end of the 1980s were receiving financial aid in the amount of $11.9 million in the form of loans or grants.

"The day of the college as a finishing school for adolescents is over," Baker told the Rotary Club in 1989. "Competition for entrance is keen: we turn away two applicants for every one we admit. And good performance is required to stay. Several years ago we raised our continuation standards, knocked out 12 percent of the student body, and made it plain we expect commitment. Our students are serious-minded adults, often with deep roots in the community."[121]

Mount Royal was indeed still a "second chance" institution, not in the sense that its students had failed at other forms of education but rather in the sense that many had taken time to do other things after graduating from high school and were picking and choosing to improve their credentials.

The opening of the Wyckham House Student Centre in September 1987 provided students with a precinct of their own.[122] "Thirsty's Bar and Lounge" became a focal point for student social life. The proceeds from the bar, the food court, and other commercial enterprises in the centre soon transformed the financial situation of the Students' Association. Its revenues rose from $108,000 in 1980–81 to more than a million by the end of the decade. In 1988 the *Reflector* reported that "where the SA previously employed six people, it now employs forty."[123]

Even so, students showed little interest in their association. In December 1980 eighty-one students attended its annual general meeting, and in November

The ribbon cutting formally opening Wyckham House (L-R) Robert Wyckham, Doug Henderson (President, Students' Association of Mount Royal College), Bill McManus (Member, Mount Royal College Board of Governors), The Honourable Dave Russell (Alberta Minister of Advanced Education) and Donald Baker (Mount Royal College President), January 29, 1988. Photographer Roberta Staley; Mount Royal University Archives G984.

Students in Wyckham House, 1992. Mount Royal University Archives E92-7.

1981 only fifty.[124] In 1983, 14 per cent of students voted in the Student Council elections – up from 6 per cent in the previous election. In addition to student apathy, the association was handcuffed by the immaturity of some leaders. Eligibility to hold office was a recurrent issue, exacerbated by the fact that salaries for executive members inspired candidates whose interests in student affairs were marginal. In 1986, the incoming president appointed two ineligible election candidates to vice-presidential positions, precipitating a crisis. On another occasion, a successful candidate was declared ineligible for failing to remove campaign posters.[125] Inability to maintain a 2.0 GPA led to frequent turnover.[126] In the previous year, the *Reflector* reported in 1988, one president, two vice-presidents and one replacement for a vice-president had resigned because of academic deficiency. It called for adoption of a 3.0 cumulative GPA standard,[127] but such "elitism" was not appreciated and the idea fell flat.

The association's constitution underwent some modifications in the 1980s. As presidents and vice-presidents were directly elected, they did not believe themselves accountable to the Student Council, which wanted to hold them to account. Thanks to an exercise that began in a Political Science class in 1983 and was carried forward by Larry Lee, the vice-president external, the association adopted new objectives, established the executive's responsibility to the council, and set terms of reference for committees.[128] Questions also arose about the fit between the association and the Wyckham House Board, which existed on the basis of an agreement between the association and the college.[129]

There was occasional friction between the college and the association. In the fall of 1981, for example, the association terminated its auditors because their report had suggested mismanagement of revenues from bars and cabarets. Asked to explain, the association told the board of governors that "some students claimed the numbers were wrong,"[130] an explanation that was persuasive only to interested parties. Keeping order at student events was another issue. In the early 1980s the college and association agreed that the college's security department would train and compensate security people designated by the association. There was also tension within the association, notably between the student leaders and the editors of the *Reflector*, who were rarely flattering in their reports on student politicians. The publication's provocative content offended some students and exposed the association to liabilities it did not want to have. In 1981, the *Reflector* finally became an independent entity, based on a separate student fee that students could choose not to pay.[131]

Despite high turnover and other challenges, the association achieved several things in the 1980s. It oversaw the planning and construction of Wyckham House and successfully championed the introduction of a Reading Week (1983) and adoption of a Statement of Student Rights and Responsibilities. The latter, initiated by Lise Hamonic, reached the Academic Council in 1985. The MRFA, linking student rights to faculty obligations, initially asked the board to reject the proposal.[132] However, the discussions continued, and in 1986 Jim MacNeil, Director of Student Services, reported that the draft had undergone sixteen revisions. The final version contained this disclaimer: "It is not the intention of Mount Royal College to create a foundation for civil proceedings in the courts of the province of Alberta."[133] It was approved by the board in January 1987.[134]

Apart from blockbuster social events organized by the Students' Association for venues such as the Max Bell Arena, safely away from the campus and reducing risks to the college's liquor licence, most social life revolved around student societies related to programs. It was more difficult to organize arts and science students but, after a hiatus, the Arts and Science Society was reconstituted in the fall of 1980.[135] The societies organized parties, pubs, and recreational events, often in co-operation with Campus Recreation and/or the association. The sports included archery, badminton, basketball, bowling, curling, football, floor hockey, gymnastics, judo, skiing, table tennis, track and field, volleyball, water polo, and wrestling. Program-based societies often organized their own events.[136] Campus Recreation also organized regular events, including sports days and the Winter Carnival.[137]

In addition to their social and recreational activities, the program-based societies organized many other events. They helped mount career fairs,[138] promoted social awareness (e.g., an awareness day on the challenges of wheelchair-bound students on the campus),[139] and philanthropic campaigns such as the Terry Fox Run (cancer research), the Blood Donor Clinic,

and Shinerama (cystic fibrosis research),[140] and the Discovery House, a women's shelter. The Business Society made the Christmas tree in Wyckham House in 1987 the centre of a charity blitz for the Special Olympics; every dollar donated led to one of six hundred lights being turned on.[141]

Externally, Mount Royal continued its high profile in athletic competitions. In 1982, it won the national college volleyball championship. In 1983, the Cougars team reached the national hockey playoffs.[142] Jack Kenyon became coach of Alberta's junior men's basketball team for two years and led that team to a silver medal in the national championships.[143] Some individual athletes also shone. In 1985, for example, Joanne Gillette, a Physical Education student, earned the gold medal and the national title for women's singles in badminton.[144]

On the cultural side, creative writing revived as a public activity. In March 1981, the *Reflector* published the poems of five student writers.[145] In 1982 the English department launched *Skylines*, a publication largely by and for students, though faculty members sometimes published in it; Henri Garand was the principal faculty advisor. The students formed an editorial board, reviewed submissions, engaged in editorial board debates, and managed the production.[146] The students ranged from recent high-school graduates to an "average mid-30s housewife" to a "housewife in her 40s," and included business, social services, and nursing students along with others from the arts and sciences.[147] The contributions included poetry and short stories.[148] As *Skylines* faded, Neil Besner, another member of the English department, launched *Foothills* in 1985 as a vehicle for student work; to ensure its viability, he negotiated a small grant from the administration. It was published three times a year and was circulated with *MRC News*.[149]

Thanks to an initiative of Wade Lorentzon, the United Church chaplain, the college opened a centre for Aboriginal students. It was not to last. Given the small number of students at the time, the lack of an Aboriginal leader, and the challenge of finding dedicated space during the construction project, the centre slowly faded away. In 1988, a more successful approach was launched in the form of an agreement with the Treaty 7 Economic Development Corporation to provide an academic upgrading program. Known as the

Aboriginal Education Project, the program accepted some 150 aboriginal students each academic year. This was much more successful. Among the prominent graduates of the program (1990) was Dale Auger (1958–2008), a playwright and visual artist "whose vividly colored acrylics have captured the attention of collectors worldwide, including leading galleries, corporations and English and Hollywood royalty." The program "opened my potential," he said later. "It was my launching pad. It had an atmosphere of openness and there were mature students like me there."[150]

The celebration of the 70th and 75th anniversaries, held only four years apart because of a difference of opinion over whether the date should be from the December 1910 legal charter or the September 1911 start of operations,[151] contributed to the re-establishment of the alumni association. At the 70th celebration, 12–15 November 1981, a group led by Gordon Coburn, who became the first president, reconstituted the Mount Royal College Alumni Association. The board of governors approved its constitution in April 1982.[152] The association developed slowly but steadily thereafter.[153]

FOCUS ON STUDENT SUCCESS

The College Goal: To render still more effective the college's commitment to student academic success and to student/user satisfaction with college programs and services.

— Board of Governors, 13 June 1988.[154]

Meanwhile, the administration had begun to focus on "student flow" – student experience of the college from first contact through registration and instruction to graduation and beyond. This was to become a pervasive concern leading to the College Goal of "student success and satisfaction" approved by the board in January 1988. The goal arose in part from administrative efforts to improve student experience. Two of the most vexatious issues during the decade were registration and parking, and these both provided schooling in how to focus on student satisfaction.

The main point of the goal of student success was to do as much as possible to support students in achieving academic success and then finding employment or moving on to further study. Community colleges tend to attract people whose personal temperaments or circumstances require them to focus on relatively short time frames in education. They may also tend to attract what might be called academic "tire kickers," people who want to give a program a try at low cost and marginal commitment. As Bill Purves-Smith, an instructor once put it, there may be a conflict between the agenda of the institution which is looking at progression and completion as important indicators and the agendas of individuals who are just curious about themselves or a subject and who leave for reasons of their own. Results from annual graduate surveys showed that at the end of the 1980s the percentage of graduates obtaining full-time employment had increased since a recession low in 1983 to about 70 per cent, that 67 per cent were employed in jobs related to their program of studies, and that the percentage of those going on to further education was in the 10–15 per cent range.[155]

While there were many very successful students, the distinction of being the college's first recipient of a Governor General's Award for Academic Excellence went to Carolyn Bedford, a 1988 graduate of the Recreation Therapy diploma program.[156]

In administrative services, the focus was student satisfaction – providing efficient, effective, and non-obtrusive services that minimized the number of transactions, the time taken by procedures, and other forms of inconvenience. Rapid enrolment growth, combined with cramped space and manual procedures, caused many irritations. The *Reflector* described registration as "a semi-annual combination of circus and Chinese water torture." [157] Unlike institutions where programs were "canned" and one enrolled in the entire program as a bloc, registration at Mount Royal required course selections, and that required advising and resolving timetabling conflicts.[158] Wood, Dyment, and registrar Arunas Alisauskas did time studies and struggled to streamline procedures and shorten lines. [159] The idea of "one-stop shopping" was adopted but could not be realized until a new student information system and better facilities were available beginning in 1986.[160] That was also the point at which the central Academic Advising Centre opened "to provide year-round academic advice to students [and] to facilitate the development of continuous registration activities."[161] The one-stop shopping goal was to be realized when the registrar's office moved into the new Kerby Hall in 1988.

Parking was another source of frustration. There were 1,600 parking stalls for a steadily growing number of students. Construction took 300 of them away for three years. While the expansion project included 500 additional spaces, they were not ready until 1987. In 1983, the board established a parking committee consisting of representative of students, faculty, and staff to set the rules and the fees necessary for the function to be self-sustaining. In addition, the college leased adjacent land for parking and encouraged car pooling and use of the bus system.[162] When the new LRT system reached Chinook Centre, the college introduced a bus shuttle system. During peak hours, student parking overflowed into the surrounding area, and on occasion police issued tickets to parking offenders, enraging students.[163] With the end of the construction project, the parking issue faded, only to return in the next decade as the college continued to grow.

The focus on student satisfaction led to the introduction in 1984–85 of the Student Reaction to College Survey. The surveys revealed a good deal of satisfaction with instruction but uneven responses to the services.[164] To get finer-grained data, the Office of Institutional Analysis and Planning developed other survey instruments that included surveys of faculty and staff opinion as well. In 1986, the college added "graduate follow-up surveys."[165] "Student" and "client" satisfaction now became mantras in the internal life of the college. It was also developing good data on the progress of students through college programs. It became natural to link the idea of success and satisfaction together, though it took Dean Don Stouffer to propose doing so in an administrative retreat.

In his annual state of the college remarks in September 1986, Baker called on the college to set its goal as that of becoming "one of the finest community colleges in the world. . . . We Canadians tend to be modest. We Albertans, despite our outer ebullience, are frequently inclined to think of ourselves as belonging to tributaries rather than to the mainstream. Yet I firmly believe that we . . . should set our main goal as being among the finest institutions in our line

of business to be found anywhere."[166] That implied benchmarking. By 1987, the focus on student success and satisfaction had broadened to include satisfaction of all constituencies with college services. The final formulation was this: "*To render still more effective the college's commitment to student academic success and to student/user satisfaction with college programs and services.*" Known as The College Goal, this statement was approved by the board of governors and made a major commitment in the budget plan for 1988–89.[167]

Adoption of the goal was followed by the mapping out of "visible signs of success" in each area. The president asked each academic and administrative unit "to find ways to serve the educational needs of students still better than has been done heretofore; continue to develop academic policies and administrative practices which will make the college more student-centred, . . . find ways for college services to serve the needs of internal and external clients still better than has been done heretofore; [and] continue to develop policies and operational practices which will make college services more client-centred."[168] This was accompanied by specific benchmarks – for example, "sample studies of individual student work"; comparatively strong performance in standardized tests, licensing or certification examinations, and "comparatively strong academic performance by students who have transferred to other post-secondary institutions"; "repeat business by clients"; and "use of college programs and services as reference points for . . . other institutions and the use of college personnel as evaluators or consultants by other institutions."[169]

The statements of lofty aspiration were not always realized in practice but they encouraged improvements in services, gave precise indications of good practice, sensitized the organizational culture to the importance of being student- and client-focused, and injected an evidence-based dimension into assertions about how well the college or one of its parts was doing or where it needed to improve. The College Goal was to continue to steer administrative behaviour in the 1990s and beyond.

The Faculty and Support Staff

The employee complement continued to grow with enrolment and new programs, rising from nearly 700 in 1972 to 1,000 in the 1980s to 2,000 early in the new century. Appendix 3 charts the changes in faculty and staff employee numbers over those thirty years. Reflecting the changing level of funding and enrolments, the total complement in the 1980s grew by 55 per cent, in the 1990s by 10.5 per cent, and from 2000 to 2008 by 27 per cent. Of the full-time faculty, some 42–45 per cent consisted of women, of the support staff, 72–73 per cent, and of the management, 35–40 per cent. The median age in all categories grew slightly during the decade, from about 42 to 45 for the faculty, from 36 to 39 for the support staff, and from about 42 to 44 for the management cadre. Ensuring good working relations with and among the different constituencies in the college was a constant managerial preoccupation. "Of the need for improving the environment of working relationships between and among students, faculty, support staff and managers," the college's statement of priorities for 1984–85 stated, "there is no end."[170]

The Faculty

In the 1980s, the full-time faculty complement rose from about 150 to 225, or by 41 per cent; the part-time faculty complement (head count) rose by 30 per cent and the student complement by 79 per cent, the latter figure indicating the staffing challenge the institution faced. The growth in part-timers was driven by financial necessity – the conditional funding, enrolment growth funding at less than cost – and not by deliberate strategy, though the college did want to tap into the resources in the community in its career programs where that helped enrich the curriculum and the linkage to the relevant profession.[171] But there was little the college could do to change the financial situation, and, as Appendix 3 shows, the part-time complement was to grow further in the years ahead.

By comparison with the first part of the previous decade and the last part of the next decade, the tensions between the administration and the MRFA were moderate, lower than during the early 1970s or the late 1990s, but they continued. The main flashpoints

were collective bargaining, the academic council, and individual incidents.

In the fall of 1980, the faculty and board bargaining teams invited Baker to meet with them to discuss compensation and workload issues. He explained that he very much liked Walter Reuther's notion of both sides working to identify problems, options for resolving them, etc., between formal bargaining rounds. The main issue on the table at Mount Royal at the time was money, and the arguments were typical of the dialogue in negotiations. The faculty argued their case on the grounds of external indices – the cost of living, salaries elsewhere (notably the school board) – while the board's team focused on the increase in the operating grant as its reference point.[172] To secure a two-year agreement, Baker proposed a cost-of-living adjustment (COLA) for the second year, an idea with which he was familiar from his days bargaining as a trustee in Ontario. In January 1981 the parties signed a two-year agreement, with a cost-of-living clause, and a memorandum of understanding on the teaching workload issue which referred the matter to a committee.[173] A report prepared in May 1980 had shown in great detail how faculty teaching loads had changed since 1972, with teaching loads in several, though not all, programs declining in numbers of students and contact hours.[174] The eventual agreement on workload set the norm for lecture classes as 13.5 hours (four courses one term, five another) and restored the hours in studio and lab courses to 18 hours. This was purchased by a major salary increase. The MRFA, Baker said, was to be congratulated "for doing something very unusual and very constructive . . . that is, accepting a new agreement containing a provision for an increased workload."[175]

Predictably, the next round of bargaining in 1983 was long and hard, as faculty continued to focus on compensation. The EPC organized a demonstration picket and its spokesmen threatened strike action, panicking more than a thousand students into signing a petition calling on the parties to resolve the issues. There was no strike and no compensation breakthrough, but the faculty had exhibited its anger and determination to the board, administration, and provincial government.[176] Perplexed by this behaviour, the administration encouraged trying new ways of bargaining. It purchased copies of *Getting to Yes* and distributed them to the MRFA. At the suggestion of Dean Judith Lathrop, Robert Birnbaum, author of *Creative Academic Bargaining: Managing Conflict in the Unionized College and University*, which argued for single-team bargaining overseen by an external chairman, was invited to give a workshop to both teams.[177] The teams were impressed and agreed to try the process. With Dick Campion of Alberta's Mediation Services serving as the third-party facilitator,[178] they reached an agreement in March, well before the 1 July start of the contract year. This seemed like a great success to the participants, but the process had gone far too smoothly for some faculty members who suspected their delegates had been taken in by the wily administration. So, for the next negotiations, the MRFA rejected the idea of single-team bargaining and kept negotiations going well into the next contract year, with demonstration pickets, faculty withdrawal from committees, press releases, and demands that appeared to be designed for rejection; indeed, they pulled them off the table when their own members began to ask where the agreement was.[179] Thus, the collective bargaining process at the end of the decade was much as it had been at the start.

Despite such moments of *Sturm und Drang*, the bargaining differences between the parties were not very wide. The negotiations were often more about psychic distance than about substance. The major changes in the collective agreement in the 1980s were these: an early retirement clause; introduction of a four-for-five–year leave program; limits on the annual minimum and maximum scheduled instructional hours for full-time faculty members (384 and 576, with a normal load of 432); workloads established "in consultation between the Chairman and the members of each department, after consultation with the Faculty Dean," with workload data audited by the Office of Institutional Analysis and Planning (a change required by the introduction of the Faculty Dean); and permission for faculty members carrying at least "432 approved scheduled instructional course hours, or the department average, whichever is greater," to accept part-time contracts for additional compensation.

In the 1980s there were no tussles over the role of the Academic Council, but some faculty members perceived it to have declined in importance – a decline from what golden age it is hard to say. In fact, Baker attempted to strengthen the Academic Council.

He chaired it personally for three years and regularly attended its meetings and those of some of its committees,[180] assigned the Secretariat to provide administrative support to the council, persuaded the board to delegate a public member to sit as an observer in its meetings, and persuaded it as well to vote up or down on council minutes and recommendations rather than to just receive them for information.[181] Similarly, Wood ensured that documents coming out of his office were properly prepared and had been vetted by his VPAG to ensure that cross-impacts and resource implications had been identified. One faculty member made such advance preparation his cause, on the grounds that it "obviated" the role of the council's program committee.[182] "This process is in no way meant to obviate the work of Program Committee or Academic Council," Wood responded. "It merely provides for multiple forms of scrutiny, which is a healthy process."[183] It sometimes appeared that faculty critics and the senior administrators belonged to parallel universes from which they saw the same events but gave them different meanings.

When the expansion project's *Education Plan* was circulated for comment, the MRFA focused its few remarks on the few lines about the Academic Council. "Under this section, it appears that academic council is the only body which will recommend academic policy to the board of governors. The MRFA recognizes the essential role of the academic council but . . . believes that it should be the vehicle through which faculty-wide college concerns are expressed, that it should participate in decision-making bodies in the college through elected representation, and that it should make representations about such concerns to all college bodies which make recommendations or decisions on such matters."[184] Not surprisingly, the MRFA opposed the establishment of elected faculty councils in each of the new Faculties. The key issue was not faculty engagement in governance, but the MRFA's role in governance. In a wry comment, Melvin Pasternak, chair of Business Administration, once said that "there is almost a delight in resisting the concept that leaders of an organization have legitimate authority."[185]

There were occasionally tense moments outside negotiations. In 1982 Baker learned that the MRFA had called three meetings of department chairmen.

After meeting with Jane Hayes, the president, he wrote: "I see the role of chairman as critical to effective administration and good morale and as very complex because one person is simultaneously an administrative officer of the college and a member of the MRFA. . . . However, if the association tried to turn chairmen into shop stewards or if the administration ignored the faculty standing of chairmen, the chairman's function would be destroyed. . . . I believe that it is inappropriate for the MRFA to convene chairmen for any purpose whatsoever. That practice can only confuse lines of responsibility and authority." The MRFA took the point and did not call any further meetings On another occasion, the board, responding to some strong faculty criticisms of the president in the journalism program's *Journal 3009*, directed the board chair and the chair of the personnel committee, both lawyers, to meet with the people involved to "explain" the board's views on civil dialogue. Discussions then turned to the sources of alleged declining faculty morale and how to strengthen faculty participation in decision making.[186] One other outcome was a policy requiring the board to approve the publisher or editor of the journal (a college-owned publication, unlike student newspapers), "preferably" the chairman or another senior member of the journalism program. The board had received complaints on earlier occasions and was concerned about liability. "We are not trying to censor free speech," Deyell explained. "We are trying to protect the position of the board in its position of liability."[187]

Among other activities of importance to faculty members was the expansion of the position of Professional Development Officer into the Educational Development Centre in January 1982.[188] Its purpose was to facilitate course and program design, the evaluation of student work, and instructional design, under the auspices of a joint committee with the MRFA. One of its early activities was advancing computer literacy among the faculty.[189] The MRFA also participated in the Executive Committee on the Quality of Work Life, consisting of representatives of the administration, support staff, and faculty association, to identify issues relating to the work environment and to strike task groups to address them.[190] In 1986–87, the members of the President's Advisory Group, together with the Presidents of the MRFA and MRSSA, participated

in a two-and-a-half–day leadership management training workshop.[191]

During the 1980s some faculty members pursued graduate study at the University of Calgary, and a number completed graduate degrees there. In addition, the policy on academic qualifications for new instructors accelerated the trend toward higher academic qualifications. There were also few job openings in higher education in Canada in the 1980s and 1990s. Competition for positions rose and the college also benefited from the increasingly strong pools of candidates. Figure 8.1 illustrates the trend line toward more graduate degrees.

Faculty scholarship became more common and steadily gathered steam in the 1980s and 1990s. Among others, Neil Besner, an instructor in English, published a work on Mavis Gallant's fiction in 1988;[192] a year later Darlene Quaife, also in English, published her novel *Bone Bird*, which won the Commonwealth Writers Prize for First Book; and subsequently Beth Everest and Richard Harrison published poetic works.[193] Mahfooz Kanwar began a publishing career in sociology and multiculturalism, including preparing textbooks with colleague Don Swanson.[194] Historian Patricia Roome began producing articles on Alberta political leaders and feminists.[195] The political scientists were prolific: C. Michael Fellows and Greg Flanagan published a book on Canadian economic issues;[196] David Thomas, despite serving in administrative roles, published works on Canadian public policy;[197] and Keith Brownsey was to produce an array of monographs on politics and public policy issues related to the oil and gas industry.[198] John A. Winterdyk published standard works in criminology and national security issues.[199] Izak Paul produced works in biology and physiology. In business, Melvin Pasternak developed a stock market expertise that made him well off and well known.[200] While much of the publishing by faculty members in the 1980s and 1990s consisted of textbooks and reading materials, the trend toward more scholarly production was to continue and to accelerate.

Administrative Staff

In most higher education institutions, the support staff is the largest single employee group, and Mount Royal was no exception. Like an army that relies on a long

FIGURE 8.1 HIGHEST EARNED DEGREE HELD BY
FACULTY MEMBERS, 1967-2009

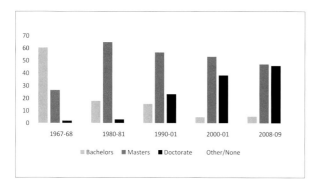

SOURCE: Based on calendar information for 1967-68 and 1980-81;
based on OIAP data for other years.

supply chain, the college requires ample administrative support to deliver good quality instruction in the classroom and service to internal and external clients. In the first two years of the decade, some 170 support staff members left and were replaced. In 1989, 30 per cent of the full-time faculty, 75 per cent of the support staff, and 90 per cent of the management group had been appointed to their position during the decade.

The Mount Royal Support Staff Association represented the support staff, excluding casual employees and the few employees designated as exempt by virtue of the confidential nature of their employment. In 1982–83, there were 266 full-time, 58 part-time, and 300 casual employees, for a total of 624.[201] The range of people involved in the staff association was suggested by the officers in 1985. The new executive committee consisted of Bob Lamarsh (Maintenance), president; Marilyn Siewert (Health Services), vice-president; Dale Scott, (Electronic Equipment Services), treasurer; and Wendy Brown (Economics and Political Science), chairman of the Negotiating Committee.[202] Phyllis Laidlow and Bev Moore, secretaries, were prominent leaders of the association.

As requested by the board, the support staff was reclassified with the aid of a consultant. The new system had fewer categories than the old one. This took place during the last year of generous operating grants, permitting the reclassification to lead to an increase in

compensation for many support staff. In 1981, a two-year agreement provided a major salary adjustment (10 per cent on the grid, 3.5 per cent for progress through the ranks, and 4 per cent for adjustments required for a new classification system). "Of the 217 Association members, 60 people, or 27.6 per cent, received the basic 13.5 per cent increase. The remaining 157 people, or 72.4 per cent of the Association members, will receive in excess of 13.5 per cent. . . . The estimated total cost of the settlement is 16.9 per cent of support staff salaries or $675,000."[203] Reflecting changing grant conditions, later settlements were modest. The agreement in March 1985 provided members with a 1 per cent increase retroactive to 1 July 1984, a 1 per cent increase effective 1 January 1985, and a 1 per cent increase on 1 July 1985, plus $400 lump sum payments. However, the hours of work were reduced from 37.5 to 35 hours, effective 1 July 1985.[204]

First-line managers were often important informal leaders on campus. One of the best-known and most-admired was Stu Gauthier, a military veteran who began at the college in 1974 and became manager of Custodial Services. He was a social animator who organized fundraising events on behalf of good causes, including the Transitional Vocational Program (whose students he often employed); he also organized morale-building Christmas and Easter parties. For his contributions, Gauthier was awarded a 125th Anniversary of Confederation Governor General's medal in 1993 and the college's Distinguished Citizen Award in 1997, a year before his death.[205] "He made a difference at Mount Royal, and he made a difference to all the people who were in contact with him," said Bob Charlton, another military veteran who joined the college in 1982, became manager of Campus Security, and carried on Gauthier's activities.[206] He was joined in his volunteer work by "Big" Jim Chmilar, also of Custodial Services, who became one of the longest-serving employees. Reine Steiner, the grounds manager, also played a key role in setting the tone for the college through landscaping the campus at every stage from its relocation to Lincoln Park through Phase II and Phase III expansion.

The Board of Governors

In the context of rapid and fundamental change, the board was a valuable resource to the college. Because of term limits, there was continual turnover in board membership. Premier Lougheed paid a lot of attention to board appointments. Later premiers played a lesser role, ministers a larger role, and the institutions themselves became more active in identifying the kind of people they would like or need on their boards – for example, for construction expertise or fundraising. One major change in college boards occurred in 1982, when a support staff member was added, raising the total to eleven members. Phyllis Laidlow was the first staff board member.[207]

In the 1980s, the board chairs were prominent community volunteers. Roy V. Deyell, the chairman (1981–87), a lawyer, had served as city alderman, as head of local hospital boards, was a life member of the Heritage Park Society, and served as chairman of the board of directors of Blue Cross Life Insurance Company of Canada while serving on Mount Royal's board. A lifelong Conservative and fundraiser for the federal party, he was a man whose sober and thoughtful style engendered trust. That trust had led to his designation as chairman of the convention when Lougheed was chosen leader and again in 1985 when Lougheed asked him to chair the convention to choose his successor. Among Deyell's initiatives was the establishment the "Chairman's Challenge," a dinner society of locally prominent people on the model of a similar group at the University of Calgary. It met monthly for dinner and to hear speakers and/or entertainment by Conservatory students and was to be a conduit for some fundraising activities.

Deyell was followed as chairman by B. Jean Fraser (1987–88), who had joined the board in 1982 and been vice-chairman since 1985. Like Burden earlier and Anne Tingle later (1990–96), she had also been chairman of the Calgary Board of Education; like Deyell, she had served on a number of health-related bodies.[208] For several years she was the board member who sat on the Academic Council, which gave her a window into the interior life of the college. Doug Thompson (1988–90), a businessman in the aviation field who joined the board in 1984, served for two years before coming to the end of his second term.

The appointments of both Fraser and Thompson as chairman were unusual in that both were already board members.

Max Rae, asked about the style of board chairs, had contrasted Martha Cohen, Russ Purdy, and Gerry Burden. All had done a "good job," but their styles altered – with Martha Cohen, at one end, permitting long board discussions and meetings, Gerry Burden asking each board member to speak on the agenda item followed by a vote, and Russ Purdy, whose style fell between.[209] Asked the same question, Baker noted a difference between board chairs coming from school boards and those from other sectors. "School board members are elected; they are politicians; they have to be seen to be running the enterprise; they have to keep the administrator, chief superintendent, in his place." By contrast, Deyell, coming from the health sector in which doctors are independent professionals, not employees, was more inclined to look to the professional administrators to provide advice and recommendation on their own hook. In practice, the difference was small and never led to problems at Mount Royal, though perhaps Gerry Burden's school board experience, particularly because he was chair of the school board during a teachers' strike, implicitly brought some "political" issues into internal college attitudes.[210]

Four board chairmen in a row were graduates of the University of Saskatchewan (Purdy, Burden, Deyell, and Fraser), three with connections to its law school (Burden and Deyell were graduates; Fraser was the spouse of a graduate). This was not unusual – Saskatchewan exported many professionals. Indeed, Saskatchewanians on the board also included Fred Stewart (1975–81), a lawyer, vice-chairman of the board, and later an Alberta cabinet minister; Alexander G. (Sandy) Cameron (1976–82), who chaired the board's Finance Committee; and Bartlett B. Rombough (1983–86), president of TransCanada Pipeline.

Among the other public members in the 1980s were Edward R. R. (Ted) Carruthers (1982–88), a lawyer, who headed the board's Finance and Property Committee (1982–88), Ron Nicholls (1977–83), manager of an architectural firm, who chaired the board's Strategic Planning and Expansion committees; Joanne McLaws (1984–90), a stockbroker who served as vice-chairman and on the Community Relations

B. Jean Fraser, Chairman of the Board 1987–88. Photographer Magelle's Studio; Mount Royal University Archives E321-2.

Committee; and J. W. (Bill) McManus (1984–90), a retired teacher and businessman who chaired the Personnel Committee and served on the Compensation Committee; Pamela Munroe, Controller of Star Oil and Gas Ltd.; and Terrance Royer, president and CEO of The Relax Group of Companies and former vice-chairman of the board of governors of the University of Lethbridge.[211]

The private college had drawn board members mainly from the United Church network. Board members of the public college came with more varied community roots. Many belonged to the Conservative party, but that connection should not be overstressed – Alberta was a one-party jurisdiction in which many people joined, not out of ideological conviction, but because it was the most influential

network in a province still dominated by face-to-face relationships. Another route was through the Calgary Board of Education: three board chairmen in twenty years had chaired that elected body. A third route was through volunteer work in health and community organizations, perhaps as indication of their commitment to public service. For many public members, the board was only another step in their contributions to the community.

Deyell, Fraser, and Thompson participated in the occasional meetings of board chairmen of colleges and technical institutes while Baker participated in the more active Council of Presidents of the Public Colleges and Technical Institutes of Alberta, serving as its chairman for four years. Tom Wood provided visible leadership in the group of academic vice- presidents. In 1986, Baker became co-chairman, with President Norman E. Wagner of the University of Calgary, of a new joint college-university body whose aim was to discuss issues of common concern. To facilitate good relations with internal constituencies, the board continued to hold an annual dinner with the executive committee of the MRFA. For a brief period it also invited the president of the MRFA to sit in on committee-of-the-whole meetings but within a year decided that the result stultified dialogue and ended the practice. Instead, the board adopted a policy of meeting twice a year with the executives of the faculty, staff, and student associations.[212]

Aware of the work of the Association of Governing Boards on such matters, Baker worked with board members to identify the routine governance information they required on financial, academic, and other performance matters and the best annual cycle for providing it. This led to an annual schedule of fewer meetings with greater substance in each. Baker also proposed, and the board approved in principle, a decision-making matrix showing the fit between the board's and the president's roles, with a view to enabling the president, in turn, to delegate appropriately to the vice-presidents and others in the administrative chain.[213] All of this was intended to enable both the board and the president to perform their functions better.

In 1981, the legacy of the private college – the George W. Kerby College Board – arose when the chairman of that board, Lloyd McPhee, advised Baker, an ex officio member of the board, that its aging members were wondering about its utility. Having addressed the pension issues it had been assigned, having donated funds to the college for the Kerby Memorial Chimes—the carillon—and furnishings for the John Garden Meditation Centre, it now met once a year to approve a donation to the college for scholarships. To wind up the board, the parties agreed that the old board should appoint the members of the college's current board to it, and then resign, leaving the funds and the charter in the hands of the college board. The Kerby board approved this arrangement on 7 October 1981. The Mount Royal board then approved "the proposed trust fund arrangement with respect to the George Kerby College Scholarship Endowment Fund and the merger of the George Kerby College board with the Mount Royal College board, on the understanding that the Mount Royal College board, ex officio, will constitute the entire Board of Governors of the George Kerby College board after the merger has been effected." The George W. Kerby Scholarship Fund was then established with a starting balance of $143,000. Sixteen years after the private college ceased operation, its last official remnant was put to rest.

The Performing Arts

By the 1970s and 1980s, the Conservatory and the Theatre Arts program, with their access to very fine performance facilities, had become important cultural resources to the community. It was only in 1985 that the Calgary Centre for Performing Arts was built. Before then, the huge Jubilee Auditorium and the facilities offered by the university and the college were the main performance spaces. Thus, the college's oldest continuous programs continued to serve both the college and, since the move to Lincoln Park, an even broader sector of the community.

The most notable development in the Conservatory in the 1980s was the progress of the Academy of Music program led by Norman Burgess and John Kadz. It was remarkably successful and attracted students from as far away as Vancouver and Winnipeg. While the Academy was adding lustre to the college's reputation, thanks to the quality of instruction it offered and the skills of its students, long-standing faculty members in the Conservatory were also accumulating honours.

Two Conservatory instructors became Members of the Order of Canada – Dr. Mary Munn, the renowned concert pianist, in 1983;[214] and "Doc" Leacock, who had been on staff for sixty-two years, in 1986.[215]

In 1986, Frank Simpson, conductor and musical director of the Calgary Youth Orchestra (CYO) for sixteen years, retired. An English musician who had relocated to Calgary to join the Calgary Philharmonic Orchestra, Simpson had begun in the Conservatory in 1963 as director of the junior, intermediate, and senior orchestras. These were consolidated in 1967 in two forms, a broader group known as the Southern Alberta Youth Orchestra, and the Calgary Youth Orchestra. Simpson served as the conductor and musical director of the CYO. He estimated that over his twenty-five years some eight hundred young musicians had "passed through" the youth orchestras.[216]

In addition to its continuing performances in the Leacock Theatre, the Wright Theatre, and the "black box" Ford Theatre, the college began mounting off-campus summer theatre productions in the form of "Shakespeare-in-the-Park" productions. They began in Olympic Plaza years before the games were held. Later they were relocated to Prince's Island along the Bow River.

Through Heather Baker, the president's wife, who was president of the board of the Alberta Ballet Company, and Dr. Lloyd Sutherland, who succeeded her, discussions began between the college and the company about the idea of a joint dance school. When the nascent and rival Calgary Ballet Company collapsed in 1984, the Department of Culture arranged for the Alberta Ballet Company to take over the defunct organization's studios in the old Calgary railway station. The college's School of Dance was established in the spring of 1984 by an agreement with the Alberta Ballet Company that made it the company's recognized school of dance in Calgary. Administrative responsibility fell under the Faculty of Continuing Education and Extension. The first classes began in September 1984 with forty-five students taught by Candace Krausert.[217] However, the arrangement with the Alberta Ballet Company proved awkward, since it also wanted to make profitable use of its own studios when they were not used by the professional dancers, and when the three-year lease on the studio ran out, the college decided not to drop its own school.

RELATIONS WITH THE DEPARTMENT

Ever since the establishment of the Department of Advanced Education in 1972 there had been an implicit tension between governing boards and the department over who was fundamentally responsible for the operation of the institutions. Differences flared up periodically, notably when the department attempted to extend its influence over the institutions. In this matter, the 1980s was also a transitional period, one that saw the seeds planted for the department's removal from judgments about programs and mandates in the early 2000s.

In 1974, the department had established a Program Coordination Policy: "Instructional programs in the Alberta system of advanced education will be coordinated to ensure the availability of effective educational experiences and to avoid unwarranted duplication of effort in institutions." Each institution was to develop a "role statement" listing its current offerings and plans for developing new programs. The department would ensure "that role statements collectively reflect the mission and role of the entire system of advanced education" and would identify "gaps or unnecessary duplications in program services in the system."

In 1988, Three Musketeers was one of the Shakespeare in the Park productions to delight audiences at Olympic Plaza. Mount Royal University Conservatory.

In 1980, the department proposed a revision: "To ensure that a comprehensive range of needed, quality post-secondary educational programs and services is developed and maintained and that unnecessary duplication of effort is avoided, the [Department] will facilitate program and service initiatives of institutions and, where appropriate, will approve such initiatives." Thus, the approval of "instructional programs" was broadened into approval of "needed, quality program and service initiatives," all words begging for definition. Institutions were supposed to submit a detailed annual five-year plan for approval.[218] The proposal led to a firestorm of opposition, as the revision would make the Program Services Division of the department the sole arbiter of all funding, reducing the role of the more trusted Administrative Services Division. The crescendo of opposition forced Minister Horsman to rescind the proposal and to return to the 1974 policy.[219]

In 1987, the issue arose again. As Kolesar and Berghofer explained, there was no more new program money so the department wanted to recover funds from institutions that were downsizing or terminating programs so the funds could be reallocated. Once again the institutions reacted strongly, and Minister Russell was forced to rescind the proposal and to re-affirm his support for the "autonomy of institutional boards." As a compromise, he established the Consultative Forum on Post-Secondary Education, consisting of representatives to discuss "system development and coordination and unnecessary duplication." "Given our nearly one billion dollar budget in operating and capital grants," he said, "government must be involved, along with the boards, in decisions about significant program changes and the rationalization of programs between and among institutions."[220] This procedural innovation ended the immediate crisis, but the tensions continued to sharpen in the next decade.

Mount Royal's position was explained by Baker in a letter to the new deputy minister, Lynne Duncan, in 1988. "Community colleges . . . are designed to be flexible, responsive institutions evolving with the communities they serve. In order to fulfill that mandate, they need . . . a good deal of latitude in mounting, upscaling, downscaling and eventually terminating academic programs as the needs of the community change. They also need to be able to move their resources around to meet shifts in student demand." While not opposing system coordination, he suggested that there "are better ways to achieve the government's ends of more effective program coordination and cost savings – namely, a focus on system issues, such as the coordination of institutional mandates, rather than on individual programs within institutions, except where those involve special costs or features, the development of a funding system based on clear and public calculations, and a review of the need for all existing institutions and agencies in the province with a view to appropriate, terminations, mergers and mandate clarifications."[221]

REACHING HIGHER

The idea of becoming degree granting had occasionally surfaced in the college ever since its beginning in 1911. However, from the 1950s through the 1980s the college was deeply committed to its "community college" vocation. Still, given the confined nature of its role, caught between SAIT, the AVC, and the University of Calgary, the college periodically dreamed of reaching higher. The board's brief discussion of degree granting in the late 1970s had been a reaction to the "opportunity" college model implied by the Lincoln Park Development Plan. Had the discussion been more widely known in the college, it would have surprised many. However, it was the board's responsibility to think strategically and, apart from the college's role in university-transfer and career programs, and its diminishing role in high-school programming, one alternative was clearly to become degree granting.

The degree-granting idea did not fade away, despite changing board membership. When the board met with Minister Dick Johnston in 1984, Deyell asked how the government would respond to a proposal to move toward degree granting. Johnston replied "that there is no reason why some public colleges might not move to degree granting status in the years ahead, and . . . Mount Royal has the facilities, staff, programs and resources to contemplate a move in that direction. The question needs to be 'tested' by an actual request." He also said that he would not want to see colleges, "as particularly dynamic and responsive educational institutions, becoming liberal arts colleges." Baker suggested that Ryerson Polytechnic might be "a model" for Mount Royal's professional or career programs, "that the college would not want to abandon its certificate and diploma programs but rather to add the BA and BSc degrees, and that nursing education is an example of a career program in which the college could offer all, or nearly all, of the requirements for the B.Sc. degree in nursing without additional resources." He mentioned the pressure from nursing associations to move in that direction.[222] In November 1988, another Advanced Education minister, David Russell, said that "allowing Alberta's community colleges to grant degrees could be the wave of the future."[223]

The push for degree granting was also coming from some professions. By the early 1980s nurse associations had set the deadline of 2000 for making a degree an entry requirement for the profession. In 1985, Wood met with officials of the Health and Social Service Programs Branch of Alberta Advanced Education "to discuss the feasibility of Mount Royal College's pursuit of degree-granting status for the nursing program." While Wood's subsequent report said that "the most reasonable approach appears to be . . . providing better articulation for our students to degree nursing programs,"[224] the subsequent dialogue in the Academic Council marked the first discussion of degree granting in that body in the 1980s. It was also preliminary to the development of a joint diploma/degree nursing program with the University of Calgary.

By 1985–86 the administration had begun looking beyond the current expansion project. Developing a new long-range strategic plan was one of the goals for 1986–87,[225] a process accelerated by request from the department for an Institutional Development Plan.[226] After review by the academic council and board, the document was submitted in May 1987. However, as the board had not yet taken a position on degree granting, it described the college's future as an elaboration of the present without mentioning degree programs.[227] Meanwhile, the board's goals for 1986–87 directed the administration to "complete feasibility studies on possible new directions for the college and to prepare any consequent action plans for approval."[228] This led to a brief paper by Baker on "degree-granting status" considered by the board in its October 1988 retreat. The options included applied and professional programs on the Ryerson model, a "hybrid" institution offering degrees and diplomas like those proposed in BC, or a liberal arts undergraduate university. The board directed the president to prepare a recommendation "on whether to pursue degree-granting status, and, if so, in what form."[229]

Thus, a combination of external circumstances and internal strategic thinking combined to propel the college toward degree granting. There was clearly a need for university-level courses in the province. The pressure in Edmonton led Grant MacEwan College in Edmonton to reverse its initial strategic decision and to launch a university-transfer program. Former Mount Royal students returned to the college to complain about the large classes and impersonal atmosphere in the universities and urged the administrators to seek

degree-granting capacity. Moreover, responding to the evolution of Calgary into a sophisticated head-office city with worldwide connections, the college's leadership was increasingly convinced that it could not adequately meet the evolving needs of Calgary's information-driven economy with only one-year certificate and two-year diploma programs but needed to add degree programs. Fuelling such thoughts was also awareness that next door in British Columbia the government was planning to convert some of its colleges into degree-program–offering "university colleges." Not to be left behind, but not to lead either, Alberta Advanced Education issued a "discussion paper" in 1989 entitled *Responding to Existing and Emerging Demands for University Education: A Policy Framework*, which set out five potential scenarios for the future: (i) responding by enlarging existing universities; (ii) establishing a new degree-granting institution; (iii) encouraging out-of-province universities to offer programs in Alberta; (iv) establishing criteria to determine which colleges might become eligible for degree-granting status; and (v) developing two-year associate degrees in colleges and technical institutes. The report noted that "several institutions have indicated aspirations toward having degree granting capabilities: Red Deer College, Grande Prairie Regional College, Medicine Hat College, NAIT, SAIT, Mount Royal College, and the Alberta College of Art." The paper led to discussion but to no immediate change in policy. However, the sensed need for some change was evident and certainly not peculiar to Mount Royal, although Mount Royal alone was to pursue the matter in practice.[230]

Thus, developments within Mount Royal itself and developments in the post-secondary sector in Alberta combined to create an internal dynamic that contributed to a growing consensus that degree programs would be appropriate and desirable. Turning the idea into a practical reality, in two different forms, was to be the work of the next two presidents.

Summing Up

As the end of the decade approached, the college had become quite different from what it had been at the start – in size, in structure, in resources, in tone, and in aspirations – but not in its formal mandate. It was more post-secondary and more academic in nature than it had been. It was systematically committed to continuous improvement in its programs and services through periodic external evaluation. Its faculty was becoming better equipped to offer degree programs. Its program base, though not transformed, was becoming more oriented to the demands of the emerging knowledge society and the professions, notably in health care, business, and informatics. Its career programs were increasingly adopting the co-operative work-study delivery mode. It incorporated computers into programs, began distance delivery by technical means, and started international activities. It had begun fundraising and established an alumni association that continued to grow. It had taken institutional marketing to a new level. It had an increasingly professional administration. The goal of facilitating student success and measuring progress in student and client satisfaction was being worked out operationally. Some of those changes were due to circumstance, others to intention, and all in retrospect appear to have been almost inescapable.

Yet, for all the change, the 1980s was more a transitional than a transformational period for college. Fundamental transformation required more than administrative modernization, commitments to quality and student success and satisfaction, and discussion of moving toward degree granting. It required changes in legal mandate, internal governance, and credentials awarded. Those were to come twice in the next two decades. From one angle, however, the college had nearly exhausted its mission as a community college, as defined by Alberta. It was now offering two full years of university-transfer work in the arts and sciences and in many of its career programs, which were oriented primarily to the business, health, human services, technology, and information systems sectors. Because it was limited to one-year certificates and two-year diplomas, it could not keep up with the changing requirements of an emerging knowledge-based society that demanded higher-level skills. It was pretty much confined to finding ways to doing better what it was already doing. From another angle, however, the 1980s marked the "tipping point" when the college began to move toward a new degree-granting mission. What tipped it in the new direction was a combination of factors, including the sense that the college was excessively confined by a college model more appropriate to an earlier industrial society than to the kind of society Calgary was becoming.

Internally, the college settled down from the tussles of the 1970s but began to experience new tensions arising from the presence of a stronger central administration and the beginning of turns in new academic directions. During Baker's tenure, a later analyst of the college's organizational culture (1993) was to write, "the college returned to a more tightly coupled and centralized structure marked by strong policies and procedures, again influencing the essence of the college culture." A "firm" leader heading a strong administration, Baker was seen as having "moved the college toward a university administrative model," entrenched "informal practices . . . into policies and procedures," and made "the pursuit of excellence in operations and outcomes . . . an important value." [231] Not surprisingly, some faculty members, notably in the "old guard," "perceived that their input was not as valued as it could be."[232]

In the spring of 1989, with a year to go in his second five-year mandate, Baker was offered the position of vice-president, academic of Wilfrid Laurier University in Ontario (where, among other things, he initiated a policy similar to that at Mount Royal requiring the periodic review of all programs). Board chairman Doug Thomson offered to renew his appointment for as long as he liked but Baker, at fifty-four, was mindful that, after nine years of his serving as a change agent, the college might benefit from a fresh personality, style, and vision, and that, with a decade or more to go in his professional life, he would either become a very long-toothed college president or could launch another professional chapter. He chose the latter. Looking back, he was proud of his contributions to solidifying academic quality, raising the institution's profile in Canada, and creating a more effective organization led by a cadre of talented administrators. The Alberta college system, he added, was "a model for the rest of Canada and, within it, Mount Royal is the leading exemplar."[233]

Just over a decade after leaving Mount Royal, reflecting his interest in assessing academic quality, Baker became the founding executive director of the Postsecondary Education Quality Assessment Board in Ontario and initiator of its published degree-level standards and quality assessment procedures that were later adopted by the Council of Ontario Universities and that fed into the standards adopted by the Council of Minister of Education, Canada in 2007.[234] That work led him into international activity – as a member of the board of the International Network of Quality Assurance Agencies (INQAAHE), as a consultant in the Middle East for the Canadian Bureau for International Education (CBIE), and later as dean of the Faculty of Humanities and Social Sciences in United Arab Emirates University, an institution which, like Mount Royal but in different ways, was undergoing a major transformation in an effort to become a world-recognized research-intensive institution.

SEPTEMBER 1989	*Thomas L. Wood becomes Acting President; appointed President, 1990*
1991	*Minister advised Mount Royal will seek to become a four-year, degree-granting institution*
1993	*Launch of "Investing in Futures" fundraising campaign*
1995	*"Applied degrees" created for colleges and technical institutes only*
1994–97	*Twenty-one per cent reduction in operating grant; introduction of government Key Performance Indicators (KPIs), targeted funding*
2000	*Phase III expansion project approved by government*
2001	*Board seeks standing as a four-year degree granting college; Launch of "Bright Minds, Bright Futures" fund-raising campaign*
2003	*Board decides to seek university status*
31 AUGUST 2003	*President Wood departs*

CHAPTER 9

BECOMING DEGREE GRANTING, 1990–2003

*Mount Royal College is seeking approval
to be chartered as a degree-granting college
authorized to grant degrees as well as diplomas
and certificates. The College also requests
approval to offer degrees in specific program
areas and the requisite operating and capital
budget support to implement these programs
over the next decade.*

– A Proposal for the Development of Mount Royal College,
July 1993[1]

The period from 1990 to 2003 marked a watershed in the history of Mount Royal College. During that period it secured approval for its first degrees – a new category called "applied degrees" – and set the goal of becoming a full-fledged undergraduate university. The process of institutional transformation accelerated. Its fundraising activities and international activities were greatly expanded. All of this took place in the context of a draconian reduction in its operating grant, a severe space shortage, and the planning and building of more campus facilities.

The signs of economic recovery in the late 1980s did not herald the return of the boom but rather a period of slow growth beginning with a steep recession in the early 1990s. Public finances remained problematic, with government debts soaring. NAFTA inspired some economic restructuring. Exports rose from 25 to 40 per cent of Canadian industrial output while the importation of Mexican produce disrupted agriculture in British Columbia and elsewhere. Despite setbacks, Calgary's economy continued to grow and diversify, and its population reached more than 900,000 by the turn of the century – nearly one million, with the outlying regions. With that diversity, its population fell from the top category in educational attributes to a notch lower. In 2006 "the proportion of adults aged 25 to 64 with a university degree" in Calgary was 31 per cent, above the national average of 23 per cent but below the 34–35 per cent in Ottawa-Gatineau and Toronto.[2] The proportion of Albertans aged 18 to 24 enrolled in post-secondary education was 28.8 per cent in 2000, below the 34.4 per cent national average.[3] Calgary's suburbs continued their outward sprawl. Shopping malls were expanded and new ones built. The average price of a house rose from $190,000 in 1990 to $200,000 in 2000.[4]

Changes in the structure of post-secondary education continued. As we have seen, AVC-Calgary became Bow Valley College in 1992, with a mission to offer Academic Foundations, English as a Second Language, and career-entry programs of one year or less in the health, business, and service industries; its enrolment grew from 3,000 in 1997–98 to 4,000 in 2002–3.[5] In 1997, the three other AVCs were brought under the Colleges Act as well. With these conversions, the post-secondary sector included fourteen public colleges, two technical institutes, and four universities (Calgary, Alberta, Lethbridge, and Athabasca). In addition, an act in 1984 permitting private degree-granting educational institutions led in 1995 to the DeVry Institute of Technology becoming the first secular, for-profit institution to offer a degree program in Alberta.[6] Together with the emergence of college degrees in the 1990s, the growth of the private sector was to raise credential recognition issues of importance to Mount Royal's pursuit of university status.

Challenged by restrained funding and rising student demand, the universities raised their admissions standards, displacing students toward the colleges and the University of Lethbridge. The demand caused Grant MacEwan College in Edmonton to change direction. Hitherto it had deliberately avoided a university-transfer role out of concern that it would dilute its commitment to career programs. In the late 1980s it added a university-transfer function and, with a new campus in downtown Edmonton, grew rapidly from 6,800 Full Load Equivalents (FLE) in 1990 to 10,585 FLE in 2002–3, a rise of 44.7 per cent. By contrast, Mount Royal, hindered by lack of facilities, grew from 6,307 to 7,679 FLE, or 21.8 per cent, in the same period.[7] Though the change in Grant MacEwan's curricular base opened up the potential "to coordinate issues,"[8] its mounting size diluted Mount Royal's role in the college system and made it, along with Red Deer College, the other major university-transfer institution, and thus a player in the dialogue about degree-granting possibilities.

WOOD'S ADMINISTRATIVE TEAM

After a national search, Thomas L. Wood, the vice-president, academic since 1981 and acting president since September 1990, was appointed the seventh president of the college in 1990.[9] His initial term was for six years. He was to be reappointed for another six-year term and further two years, yielding a total tenure of fourteen years as president, a period exceeded only by George Kerby and John Garden. "Tom came to education with a belief that it genuinely makes a difference," his friend and administrative colleague, Ken Robson, said later, "and I think that's kept him motivated in all of the years and in all of the roles that he's played, in the classroom or outside the classroom."[10] On becoming president, he had a clear set of transformational priorities that guided his period in office: the search for degree granting, raising the college's profile and expanding friendships and fundraising activities, preparing for further facilities expansion, and developing the college's international contacts and activities. He threw his heart and soul into the enterprise. His intensity may have made him less collegial than his predecessor or successor, more of a micro-manager, but many of his colleagues saw it as an expression of passionate commitment.

Most of Wood's team consisted of people who were appointed to administrative positions in the 1980s and remained in one role or another during most of his time as president. Judy Lathrop (later Eifert) replaced Wood as vice-president, academic in January

Thomas L. Wood, President 1989–2003. Photographer Magelle's Studio; Mount Royal University Archives E303-18.

1991, and served in that role for the next thirteen years. A very capable administrator, Lathrop managed the introduction of the new degree programs, coordinated strategic planning for the expansion of international activities, and oversaw the restructuring of two faculties and the Conservatory. Given her busy agenda and Wood's goal of facilitating student success through the improvement of services, Alan Dyment, named assistant vice-president, academic and dean of Academic Services in November 1990, became vice-president, Student and Academic Services. When he retired in 2000, his replacement, Ken Robson, dean of arts since the early 1980s, was made responsible as well for residences and the "living/learning" environment – hence his title, vice-president, Student Affairs and Campus Life. This promotion was somewhat controversial, not because of Robson himself, as he was

widely admired in the institution, but because he and Lathrop were married, contributing to the impression that the inner administrative group was too narrow.

Hunter Wight continued to serve as director of External Relations, bringing his wealth of contacts in the business, political, and media worlds to bear on the college's degree-granting agenda. As much as the presidents he worked for, Wight was critical to the success of the college in securing both degree-granting status and the designation as university. In recognition of his large role, he became vice-president, External Relations in 2003. The one vice- presidency in which there was regular turnover was that of vice-president, Administrative Services. In late 1990 Alex Dobbins departed and was replaced by W. Fraser Wilson, who had been hired by Wood to serve as vice-president for a short-lived Division of Arts, Sciences and Academic Services. In 1996, Larry Dawson, formerly of Brandon University, took the position.[11] He was replaced in 2000 by Grahame Newton, a vice-president of CIBC Insurance, who left after two years to head the new stock exchange in Calgary.[12] In May 2003, Richard E. Roberts, formerly vice-president, Finance at the University of Calgary, was appointed to the position.[13]

On the academic side, the structure of the original four Faculties (Arts, Science and Technology, Business and Applied Arts, Community and Health Studies) was modified in the mid-1990s. The separate Faculties of Arts and Science remained but the rest were reorganized into the Faculty of Health Studies, the School of Business, and the Faculty of Community Studies.[14] In 1999, associate deans were added to the Faculties to bolster their administrative capacity as the college continued to grow.[15] Following the resignation of Norman Burgess in 1992,[16] Paul Dornian, a clarinetist who had joined the Conservatory in 1982, became director of the Conservatory of Music and Speech Arts.

A new generation of deans followed the reorganizations of the mid-1990s. Dr. Bryan C. Lane, a specialist in zoology, became dean of Science in 1999. Hillary Elliott, who had earned a Ph.D. in drama at the University of Toronto and came from Red Deer College, became dean of the Centre for Communication Studies in 1998. In 2000, Wendelin A. Fraser, MBA, formerly dean of Business and Administration Studies and Health at BC Open University, became the dean of the School of Business. And in 2002,

Manuel Mertin, who began as a part-time instructor in the college in 1974 and earned a Ph.D. along the way, had been chair of the Department of Economics and Political Science and of its successor, the Department of Policy Studies, and served as associate dean of Arts, became dean of Arts.[17]

There were several other long-service senior administrators. Bruce Mahon, the director of Human Resources since 1981, was a valuable resource and often negotiator in relations with the faculty and staff, notably including the cutbacks of the 1990s. Donna Spaulding, formerly chair of the Department of Nursing and Allied Health, followed Lathrop as dean of Continuing Education and Extension and remained in that position for nearly twenty years. Lynda Wallace-Hulecki, director of Institutional Analysis and Planning for more than fifteen years, assumed responsibility for admission and registrarial services in the mid-1990s.

Wood continued to hold administrative retreats and to invite consultants to update management views and stimulate strategic thinking. Through Robson, who had developed expertise in training academic administrators, the college participated in the Alberta Academy for Leadership Development, systematically building a better-trained cadre of administrators. Thanks to this experienced team, Wood was able to devote a good deal of his time to external relations. Just one month's report (February 1996) indicated the range of his activities. He had been appointed to the federal government's Business, Professional and Educational Services Sectoral Advisory Groups on International Trade and to the Mayor's Advisory Board regarding the selection of sister/twin cities for Calgary, including a proposal for a relationship with Phoenix, Arizona, that he had given in the keynote address to the Community Colleges for International Development, Inc. conference held in Phoenix, and had participated in the Team Canada Trade Mission in January 1996 to India, Pakistan, Indonesia, and Malaysia.

The major challenges faced by Wood during the fourteen years of his presidency revolved around the search for degree-granting and university status, finances, fundraising, and facilities expansion. Perhaps even more than his predecessors, who had been accused of wanting Mount Royal to be treated as an exception in the college system, Wood underlined Mount Royal's singularity.

IN PURSUIT OF DEGREE GRANTING

In December 1989, as acting president, Wood struck a Steering Committee for the Degree-Granting Feasibility Study wanted by the board. Its purpose was "to explore the issues surrounding Mount Royal College's potential for pursuing degree-granting status in select program areas and to examine the implications of adding degree-granting programs to the existing curricular base."[18] In February 1990, he engaged Henry Kreisel and Walter E. Harris, former officials of the University of Alberta, to undertake a capacity review and make recommendations on the feasibility of seeking degree-granting status. Their report, in March 1991, concluded that the college was capable of offering degrees but that it needed to recruit appropriately qualified personnel, add space, and improve its equipment and library.[19] Adding a sense of urgency was the "Discussion Paper on Responding to Existing and Emerging Demands for University Education: A Policy Framework" circulated by the Department of Advanced Education and Manpower in October 1989. Among its options was one to "establish criteria to determine which colleges would be eligible for degree status," while another was to "support the development and introduction of a two-year associate degree at the public colleges and technical institutes."[20] The University of Calgary declared in favour of the associate degree option.[21]

On 19 July 1990, Anne Tingle, chair of the board, advised Minister Gogo that the college had launched a feasibility study of degree granting whose purpose was "to explore the issues surrounding Mount Royal College's potential for pursuing degree-granting status in select program areas and to examine the implications of adding degree-granting programs to the existing curricular base. The study, it must be stressed, addresses long-range planning issues: it is intended to assist the college in determining strategic directions for the next decade."[22]

The college's "Institutional Development Plan, 1991–2000" continued the theme: "The needs of the Calgary region can best be served by gradually transforming Mount Royal College over the next decade from a two-year to a four-year institution. Mount Royal College would be a college, not a university. The college would continue to emphasize teaching

Anne S. Tingle, Chairman of the Board 1990–96. Photographer Arbour Photography; Mount Royal University Archives E276-2.

and learning over research, and would maintain its focus on student success and satisfaction." The idea of becoming degree-granting raised some internal questions. During the Academic Council discussion of the plan, Tom E. Brown, a history instructor, distributed a memo from the MRFA and "spoke to faculty concerns about the mention of future degree granting status" and potential multi-campus operations (including the downtown campus), the future size of the institution, and the anticipated growth in credit-free activities ("would it be a threat to the credit programs?"). "If the proposed changes occur, would not the college become an elitist institution?" another member asked. Randy Genereux, a later MRFA President, "asked whether the college should grow at all. It is important because people who have been here a number of years have seen a lot of changes, including impacts caused

by growth. The pros and cons of this aspect need to be examined."[23] In general, however, the proposal was only mildly threatening to faculty members, as what was envisaged was not the end of certificate and diploma programs but the addition of degree programs.

By the summer of 1991 the idea of becoming a "hybrid" institution was informally supported within the college but not yet formally approved. In July 1991, Tingle advised Minister Gogo that the board would be requesting approval for Mount Royal to become a four-year institution offering certificate, diploma, and degree programs "to provide practical education in response to the needs of the nineties" as a cost-effective response to the rising demand for university programs and to prepare graduates for the new economy. She noted that the board and Academic Council had not yet reviewed the report but would do so upon the resumption of business.[24] As procedural propriety is often more important than, or a substitute for, substance in academic deliberations, the rush to advise the minister led to faculty concerns. In September, when Wood asked the Academic Council to take a position, Marc Chikinda and other faculty members asked for a delay so they could consider the issues at greater length. As the board was not scheduled to meet again until December, Wood and Lathrop urged a vote, and the council split, thirteen in favour of recommending Tingle's request to the board, seven against, and eight abstaining.[25] The council's Planning Committee then took up the issue, and in January 1992 recommended developing Mount Royal "into a four-year institution offering certificate, diploma and degree programs."[26] All proposed degree programs would be in applied areas of study and incorporate the co-operative work-study delivery mode. The recommendation was approved by the council and board.[27] However, the affair left a lingering resentment about taking the council for granted.

In promoting the aspiration to become degree-granting, Wood's message was straightforward. Mount Royal "prepares graduates to thrive in the knowledge economy. Student-centred and progressive, it has forged a tradition of responding effectively to learner need and market demand, working with corporate and educational partners worldwide to provide students with relevant educational opportunities."[28] "It is becoming increasingly difficult to respond in short-cycle programs of one or two years to the growing demand for both general education and specialized skill requirements," Wood said. "Business, to be competitive on an international scale, needs a work force with increasingly higher skills levels. We must build better educational and career ladders for people. That is why the college should evolve into an institution that augments an already wide array of diploma and certificate programs with four-year degree programs in practical, applied areas based on practicums and co-operative study."[29] "Built on the employability skills defined by leading employers and the Conference Board of Canada," the programs would "prepare graduates for employment in fields that require better-educated employees, people with career-specific skills who also had more general knowledge"; offered by colleges, they "would be cost-effective, enabling Alberta students to stay in the province to receive the education they need to compete successfully in the knowledge economy."[30] The knowledge economy and globalization required responses from post-secondary education, including new levels of credential and greater institutional differentiation. Government leaders should apply their conservative principles to higher education – let the market decide what programs the institutions should offer. One-size-fits-all solutions could only stifle innovation and responsiveness.

Wood was a leading spokesman in this regard, but his perception of the changing role of the colleges was far from unique. "By the 1990s, it was apparent that the 1960s concept of the relationship between education and work was becoming outmoded," Michael Skolnik, a specialist in community education has written. "One reason for this was that the middle-level jobs which were the community colleges' bread and butter were increasingly requiring more complex knowledge and skills equivalent or similar to those of university graduates."[31]

To promote its vision, the college reached out to influential constituencies. It found most of them supportive. The Calgary MLA Conservative caucus, Mayor Al Duerr of Calgary, and Margaret Lounds, Chairman of the Calgary Board of Education, all tendered written support for the idea.[32] A survey of 1990–91 college graduates indicated that 90 per cent of them supported degree-granting status (954 of 1,023 respondents).[33] However, there was resistance

in the post-secondary sector. The leaders of colleges and technical institutes, and the politicians representing their constituencies, were concerned that degree granting by Mount Royal might devalue their programs and credentials; it followed that if Mount Royal were able to offer degrees, then all colleges and institutes should have the opportunity as well. The university presidents were skeptical. They suspected that Mount Royal's degrees would be of inferior quality and that college degrees would lead to mission creep in the college system; they were certain that it would increase competition for scarce funding. The University of Lethbridge was particularly concerned because college degree granting could deprive it of a province-wide student clientele to supplement its regional pool. Harold Tennant, the president, proposed offering the third year of some Lethbridge degree programs on college campuses,[34] but this idea did not appeal to Mount Royal.

To strengthen the college's case, Wood pursued five interrelated strategies, each with its own purpose in addition to that of building support for degree-granting status. One was to associate the college with degree granting. This led to an agreement with Athabasca University in 1992 to offer its Bachelor of Nursing program.[35] It also led, in the same year, to a merger of the college's Nursing program with those of Foothills Hospital and the University of Calgary into a "Conjoint Program for a Baccalaureate Nursing Degree,"[36] which began for a "six-year trial period" with a first-year quota of three hundred full-time equivalent students.[37] While the agreement with the University of Calgary entailed teaching on both campuses, that with Athabasca University entailed a whole degree program taught by Mount Royal faculty members. The second strategy was to enlist the participation of a large number of prominent business people and community volunteers in the board of the Mount Royal College Foundation founded in 1991. With Peter Lougheed as a patron and Hal Wyatt, recently retired from the Royal Bank and a very prominent community volunteer, as chair, the foundation helped cast the college's shadow more broadly in the community.

The third strategy was to replace community volunteers on the board of governors with business leaders, the kind who had easy access to the premier

The City Centre Campus at 833 - 4 Avenue S.W. was the last of several downtown satellite campuses. Mount Royal University Archives E343-228.

and members of the cabinet. Wood approached leading businessmen, secured their approval to serve, and then presented the names to the minister, establishing a situation in which the minister would have to explain the rejection of a prominent business leader. The fourth strategy was building support in the press, notably the *Calgary Herald* and the *Calgary Sun*. Wood met with the editors and Wight supplied talking points in a steady flow.

The fifth, and most important, strategy was ensuring a political dimension to the campaign. Department officials could only imagine problems arising from a change of mandate for Mount Royal, but even if they were supportive political approval would also be needed. Wood, board members, and especially Wight, the key contact in political circles, lobbied politicians and cabinet ministers, ensuring they were regularly informed, responding to their reactions, linking the college's goals to their own, and ensuring they knew of the sources of resistance and providing rebuttals to their arguments.[38] The political route took Wood and Tingle to Minister Jack Ady in May 1993 to advise him of Mount Royal's degree-granting plans.[39] In July, they submitted a written submission entitled "A Proposal for the Development of Mount Royal College." "We propose the transformation of the college from a two-year to a four-year institution offering certificate, diploma and degree programs in order to provide practical education in response to the needs of the nineties," the covering letter said.[40]

In short, what Mount Royal was proposing was a mix of career diploma and university-level degree foundation programs, a "hybrid" institution, with the degree programs focusing on applied areas of study and offered in partnership with business and industry through co-operative delivery. Except for the mandatory co-operative delivery, the proposal was similar to what was already happening in British Columbia, where three university colleges were offering a mix of certificates, diplomas, and degrees.[41]

An Awkward Compromise: The "Applied Degree"

Ady liked the vision in the college's proposal and became supportive of adding degrees to colleges. In October 1994, the government published a White Paper, *New Directions for Adult Learning in Alberta*, which proposed the launch of "applied degrees" by colleges and technical institutes.[42] This outcome was not what Mount Royal had proposed. It had wanted to offer university-level degrees focused on applied fields of study and using the co-operative education delivery method. It had not wanted its proposal drowned in a system-wide response and another kind of degree – a degree not even described as a bachelor's degree but simply as an "applied degree," a category found nowhere else in Canada or North America.[43]

A combination of government officials, university leaders, and representatives of other colleges and the technical institutes had united to thwart Mount Royal's aim of becoming degree-granting in response to its own strengths and Calgary's needs. The applied degree was seen as a compromise that would give something, though not everything, to Mount Royal; it would satisfy the other colleges by keeping Mount Royal in the college category while opening the door for them too to participate in offering applied degrees; and it would satisfy the universities by stamping the new credential as different from their own. Premier Ralph Klein, who had succeeded Don Getty in 1992 and had supported Mount Royal's goal, and Minister Ady, both under pressure from the universities and regional colleges, had found what seemed to them like an ideal solution.

On 20 March 1995, Ady announced a six-year demonstration project. Designed to prepare practitioners for fields of work, the applied degrees were to consist of six semesters of study rather than the normal eight semesters for university degrees and would include two semesters of guided and remunerated co-operative work experience. The project would include eight applied degree programs, two of them to be offered by Mount Royal: a Bachelor of Applied Communications (journalism, public relations, and technical writing),[44] and a Bachelor of Applied Small Business and Entrepreneurship.[45] The rest were awarded to other institutions. Mount Royal was immediately "inundated with applications," Registrar Arunas Alisauskas said. Moreover, word that the college was going to offer degrees inspired a surge in applications for university-transfer programs, despite the University of Calgary's dropping of its admission requirement to 65 per cent.[46] The *Calgary Herald* saluted the new programs as "a development worth applauding" because it "underscores the need for post-secondary institutions to develop and offer programs that are more in tune with the real-life needs of employees and employers." The editorial quoted Wood: "We don't intend to be just another university. We will continue our focus on preparing people directly for the workplace."[47]

Hardly had the first applied degrees begun than a new minister was appointed on 29 May 1997. Clint Dunford, whose constituency included the University of Lethbridge, declared that the first round of programs must be assessed before any new ones would be approved: "I am digging my heels in there. There's taxpayers' money going toward them, there's increased time and increased tuition for students, and we want to make sure they're the right thing." Heather Wiley, one of Mount Royal's student leaders, was angered: "This is really frustrating. He's telling institutions to be responsive to the needs of students and then turns around to make such a roadblock for them to be responsive."[48] However, Dunford soon backed down under pressure from regional colleges, and a flood of other programs developed. By 2000, Mount Royal offered fourteen applied degree programs, by 2003, seventeen, and by 2006, nineteen,[49] in such fields as Criminology, Communications, Environmental

Billboards promoted career success and "a Mount Royal education" in 1998. Photographer External Relations; Mount Royal University Archives E98-2.

Science, Computer Information Systems, Interior Design, Nonprofit Studies, and Policy Studies. The applied degrees were strongly featured on the college's new website in 1996.[50]

The Interior Design applied degree program was timely because of pressure from the field's accrediting body, the Foundation of Interior Design Education and Research (FIDER), and the Interior Designers of Canada to raise the program to the degree level. Jacqueline MacFarland, chair of the Interior Design department, explained that the program would provide practitioners with high-level conceptual skills that would enable them to "shape the design profession more than ever before."[51] The new Business and Entrepreneurship program was innovative. "Unique in Canada," it required "a blend of education and training to help graduates succeed in small-business ventures" and "most importantly" required students to "gain first-hand, real-world experience by starting their own small businesses – a graduation requirement of the program."[52] In September 1995, the program was "over-subscribed with twice as many applicants as spaces available."[53] Another novel program, in Public Studies, did not fall initially into what department officials considered an applied area of study, and they prolonged the approval process. Manuel Mertin, then the chair of Political Science, recalled that "the lengths we had to go to get that one through the ministry was something else, since it really was an academic applied degree. It would have been the first undergraduate degree in Policy Studies in Canada, were it not for ministry reluctance. As it was, it followed Carleton [University] by one year."[54] Its aim was to teach "how to develop and implement policies within government, private organizations and non-profit agencies."[55] Another striking applied degree program focused on the management of nonprofit bodies.[56]

In December 1996, a confidential report to the board reviewed the situation. The college had proposed applied baccalaureate degree programs to meet the labour demands it had identified and in fields in which Alberta universities did not offer degrees, and had done so "on its own behalf and did not attempt to represent the interest of other institutions." It had asked for an outcome for itself, not for a change in the system, but the government had decided to change the system. Meanwhile, "Alberta's universities strongly oppose creation of the applied-degree credential and continue to lobby government to eliminate this option. In addition, the college believes that . . . [the] deputy minister does not support applied degrees." By contrast, "Premier Ralph Klein has said he regards applied degrees as one of the highlights of his term in office and . . . Minister Jack Ady has said the creation of the applied-degree credential is one of his most significant decisions as Minister."[57] The latter remark hinted at the reality: Klein and Ady had forced the introduction of college applied degrees over the opposition of government officials, the universities, and some colleges and had accepted the compromise solution because they thought it would give all stakeholders something.[58] They did not anticipate that their compromise contained future credential recognition problems for graduates who wished to go to graduate school, calling the experiment into question. Here the insistence on treating Mount Royal as just another college was to lead to problems that might well have been avoided had the government accepted the notion of differentiation among colleges.

The introduction of the applied degrees accelerated the transformation of the college, as illustrated in Figures 9.1 and 9.2. The applied degree was a new level of credential. The spread of the co-op form of delivery both brought uniqueness to the college's curriculum in Alberta and produced still closer relations with business and industry. The programs attracted Ph.D. holders to the faculty, with all that entailed in expectations

FIGURE 9.1 NUMBER OF REGISTRANTS (HEADCOUNT), 1972–2009

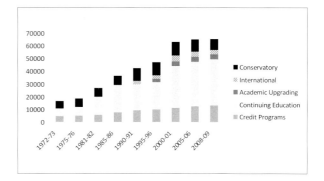

SOURCE: Enrolment reports to Board of Governors, 1972–1980; thereafter statistics developed by the office of Institutional Analysis and Planning.

FIGURE 9.2 ENROLMENT TRENDS BY PROGRAM, 1988–2008

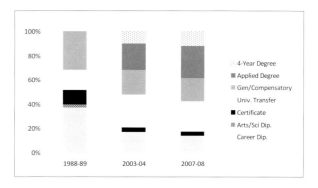

SOURCE: Based on data produced by the Office of Institutional Analysis and Planning.

and values. The programs also attracted students with stronger academic preparation and who stayed longer. Applications from existing degree holders caused the college to adopt a new admissions policy: "Entering students who possess an acceptable degree . . . will be exempt from the four or six arts and science requirements, depending upon the program (students will not be exempted from professional area core courses where they must have current information)."[59]

CREDENTIAL RECOGNITION REQUIRES UNIVERSITY STANDING

With the applied degrees in hand, Mount Royal's board of governors approved a new strategic plan in April 1997. *Vision 2005* anticipated Mount Royal becoming "Canada's leading undergraduate college educating and training individuals for success in the new economy." It would be "a four-year, comprehensive *post-secondary institution* providing personal, intellectual and social education relevant to changing student and community need, and applied education and training relevant to labour market needs." Its "core purpose" would be "to foster the success and satisfaction of our students in the pursuit of their educational goals."[60] The plan's "strategic priorities" included enhancing quality and emphasizing results, including institutional performance measures and benchmarks, resource allocation tied to quality enhancement, and external assessment of student outcomes.[61] Wight developed a *Strategic Marketing Plan to Realize Vision 2005* aimed at "repositioning the image of Mount Royal College within the internal college community and the external marketplace."[62]

The college began to strengthen its capacity for degree granting as resources permitted. It secured a $1.6 million grant to strengthen its library collection and facilities. In 2000, the board approved an "institutional research" strategy which "recognized that integrating teaching and learning is becoming increasingly important as the college continues to expand and diversify its range of programs," including "research in the teaching and learning process." The administration explored "ways of working with faculty so that they can reconfigure their workloads. . . . "[63] To coordinate research activity, the position of Director of Research and Special Projects was established in 2001. Ken Hoeppner, formerly chair of the Department of English and briefly acting dean of Arts, was named to the post. In 2006 the position became that of associate vice-president, Research. The college publicly lamented the "inequity" in Access Fund grants, "whereby grants for associated research costs are built into the program delivery grants for universities but not for colleges and technical institutes."[64]

The first problems with university recognition of the college's applied degrees for admission to graduate and professional programs began in Alberta. Lathrop's efforts to engage Alberta's universities in discussions of potential transfer arrangements fell on deaf ears. Though Mount Royal's programs consisted of many transferable courses, the universities were leery of a general recognition of applied degrees for further study, especially as some graduates began pressing the limits. In general, the universities preferred to deal with each student on an individual basis, mapping his or her academic record to the requirements of the proposed program. However, if the numbers rose dramatically, one could imagine more simplistic approaches being taken. In addition, there were outright opponents of college degrees, including, for example, the president of the Faculty Association of the University of Calgary.[65] As in the past, Mount Royal was more successful in establishing the credibility of its programs in other jurisdictions. Doug King, chair of Justice Studies, reported that two graduates had been "admitted directly into the nationally renowned justice studies masters program at Simon Fraser University."[66]

However, there was a growing problem across the country for the new degree programs emanating from colleges and university colleges. In the absence of a national accrediting system, the public universities, faced with applications for further study from graduates of new degree programs and new degree-granting institutions, made membership in the Association of Universities and Colleges of Canada (AUCC) a condition for their recognition of credentials. The membership criteria reflected the salient characteristics of public universities (as those had been hammered out in the 1960s). As a result, the criteria excluded or marginalized most of the degree programs or degree-program providers authorized by the innovating provincial governments. Reacting to applications from the graduates of colleges in Alberta, including Mount Royal, and BC, Queen's University was to set the pattern in 2003 by taking the position that it would not recognize degrees from Canadian organizations that did not belong to AUCC. Other universities followed, including Dalhousie University, which refused to read the application of a graduate of Mount Royal College. In Alberta, similar behaviour led the University of Alberta to refuse to read the application of a graduate of Kwantlen College in BC.[67]

Responding to university reluctance to accept applied degrees for further study, Mount Royal's board grew concerned about what its programs were doing to the futures of students. Instead of becoming another ladder in the hierarchy of post-secondary credentials, the applied degrees were becoming dead ends. There was also a paradox involved: by 1999, the Alberta government had embraced the idea of lifelong learning and the portability of academic credits, as symbolized by its merger of the two education ministries into Alberta Learning and its adoption of a bold vision of Campus Alberta, a coordinated structure devoted to facilitating lifelong learning. However, in the applied degrees Alberta had established an academic cul-de-sac. By 2001 – only five years into applied degrees – Mount Royal's board of governors decided that the interests of its students required university status.

When Alberta Learning circulated a discussion document entitled *Developing a Blueprint for Alberta's Post Secondary Education System*, the college seized the opportunity to make its case. Hal Kvisle, chair of the board, explained that "it is now time to respond to the burgeoning demand for university education and to take the next step in our journey—to become a student- and teaching-centred *undergraduate university.* In 2002-03, we will hold extensive discussions with internal and external stakeholders and will outline the characteristics, values and ideals of the Mount Royal of tomorrow."[68] The college's formal request was made in a letter dated 12 March 2003 to Minister Lyle Oberg requesting "conversion of Mount Royal from a two-year college to a four-year undergraduate university." "Quality, transferability and credibility—these are the hallmarks of Canadian university degrees. The governors, faculty and students of Mount Royal College are convinced that degrees offered by Mount Royal must be on a par with Canadian university degrees. We do not believe we can deliver on the expectations of our students and communities from a college platform." "We are confident," the letter concluded, "that Mount Royal can . . . grant degrees that will be recognized and valued across Canada."

Don Braid, columnist for the *Calgary Herald*, chimed in with an article entitled "Why MRC should be MRU." Declaring that "the school has made a solid, sensible proposal to the government, to become a four-year, degree-granting university," he noted that

"Calgary and Edmonton are the only cities of comparable size in Canada to have only one university," in recent months more than 5,000 applicants had been turned away from Mount Royal and the University of Calgary combined, and the clincher in Alberta's parochial political environment: "Edmonton has 7,415 more college and university places than Calgary."[69]

So the final formal step had been taken – Mount Royal was committed to becoming a university. And once again it was to find that its argument for an exception would be submerged in a system-wide response.

DOING MORE WITH LESS

Because of sluggish economic growth, government finances at both federal and provincial levels remained dire. In 1994, interest on the national debt consumed one-third of revenues, while Alberta's debt stood at $22.7 billion, "$8,400 for every man, woman and child in the province."[70] Low oil prices drove the share of provincial government revenues from oil royalties from 50 to 25 per cent. Premier Klein decided to balance the budget and eliminate the "net provincial debt" by slashing expenditures and reducing grants to public institutions. Acts were passed making deficit elimination and then debt elimination formal government goals constraining budgeting.[71] In 1993–94, all operating funds to colleges and universities were rolled into a new base grant for each institution, then the combined grant was decreased over a three-year period (1994–95 to 1996–97) by 21 per cent. All capital grants were stopped. An enrolment corridor policy was implemented – holding back the new base operating grant if enrolments decreased below a set amount, refusing to pay more if the top of the enrolment corridor was exceeded.

It is one of the paradoxes of funding for higher education that, as the proportion of institutional revenue from government grants declines, governments ratchet up their demands for "accountability," introduce "key performance indicators" (KPIs), and tie much funding to limited purposes. They apply business models to public institutions. Quite apart from questions of whether KPIs are of value either to governments or the institutions with respect to policy or planning, they have one useful outcome – everyone is perceived to be doing their job. The government appears to be holding the public services to account, while the institutions are seen to be meeting the KPIs.[72] The government then doled out targeted funds: the Access Fund (1994–95, 1999–2000),[73] the Performance Envelope (1997–98), the Learning Enhancement Envelope to support integration of technology, the Research Excellence Envelope to support "quality research outcomes," and the Infrastructure Renewal Envelope for equipment and facility renewal (1996–97).[74] To shift more of the cost onto students, the government revised tuition fee policy to raise the revenue from fees from 20 to 30 per cent of revenues by 2000.[75]

The overall effect on institutional revenues was devastating. Within a few years Alberta fell from being the province with the highest per capita funding for post-secondary education in 1984 to ninth, or second to last, in 2000.[76] The government's share of Mount Royal's revenues fell from 57 per cent in 1993–94 to 41.6 per cent in 1999–2000.[77] From the government's point of view, the strategy worked: its debt fell to $12.5 billion in 2000 and, thanks to rising oil prices and natural gas revenues, was to be eliminated in 2005.[78] However, from the vantage point of public services, the cutbacks created service deficits that had to be addressed when the financial situation turned up. Not for the first or last time, public funding in Alberta swooped and soared rather than following a steady trend line.

Within the narrow limits of the targeted funding, Mount Royal was reasonably successful in accessing small amounts. The projects included equipment purchases (1996–97), some deferred maintenance, (1997–98), a program intended "to develop a college preparation program for immigrants," and $170,000 for faculty recruitment and retention (2000–2001). More significant were grants for enrolment growth in 2002–3 for adding 240 full-time students in university-transfer studies, 60 in business administration and 25 in the Child and Youth Care program for Aboriginal students.[79] The new funding envelope for Key Performance Indicators (KPIs) stirred concern in its initial form, as it assumed that all programs led to employment and ignored continuing education and university-transfer outcomes. However, the final version had indicators for both university-transfer streams and "enterprise funding" activities. The final KPIs

were for the employment rate of graduates, graduate satisfaction level, growth in enrolment since 1993, administrative costs as a share of net expenses, and enterprise revenues as a percent of government grants. The KPIs steered the distribution of 1.5 per cent of total operating grants to the institutions. Official reporting of KPIs began in 1996–97.[80] Mount Royal, the University of Calgary, the Alberta College of Arts and Design, and SAIT "received the maximum awards possible"; Mount Royal scored 98 out of 100 points, and received $676,545 in performance funding.[81] Though the college community was relieved, not everyone saw the KPIs as a good thing. Alberta's faculty associations saw them as a means for displacing "the responsibility for declining educational quality from the provincial government on to institutions."[82]

In 2002–3, the college's base operating grant was $37.4 million while its "conditional," "envelope" and "performance" funding totalled $11.6 million, or nearly 24 per cent of total grants. Fortunately, as the province's financial position began to improve, the performance envelopes were ended (2003–4), with the funds rolled into the base grants.

The college's other efforts to maximize revenues included raising tuition fees and adding or increasing fees for pre-registration, late registration, and co-operative work study.[83] Higher profit targets were set for ancillary services and continuing education. Thanks to fundraising, investment income began to appear in revenues. Partnerships with suppliers led to donations and preferential prices. Xerox Canada, which set up Mount Royal as a "showcase site," donated $300,000.[84] In exchange for becoming an exclusive Dell computer site, the college received preferential pricing.[85] A partnership with IBM made Mount Royal a National Education Services node for IBM, offering training on advanced IBM equipment.[86]

As government grants declined as a proportion of revenue, the college vaunted the result. "No other institution in southern Alberta is under 50 per cent," said Don Ingram, chair of the Finance Committee, observing that even so the $1,475 tuition fee for 1996–97 was lower than that in the universities. This was possible, Lathrop explained, "because teachers are paid less and work 432 actual teaching hours a year, much higher than most university professors. The college also relies

FIGURE 9.3 SOURCES OF COLLEGE REVENUE, BY
PERCENT, 1980-2008

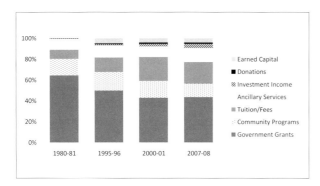

SOURCE: Audited financial statements.

on large numbers of part-time teachers."[87] Figure 9.3 shows the trend lines in revenues.

Minimizing expenditures entailed both downsizing and restructuring. Within the college, the downsizing process began in 1991–92, in a process that included the elimination of twelve vacant faculty positions, five vacant term-certain faculty positions, and the elimination of programs in Community Design and Planning, General Business Administration, and Petroleum and Mineral Resources Land Management.[88] The decisions involved arose from "non-academic" considerations, and the administration apparently thought it did not require the approval of the Academic Council, while the old Budget Advisory Committee had languished. The MRFA protested that the "Academic Council should have been, but was not, active in the process which led to those deletions."[89] There followed several meetings of the administrative, faculty, and student executive committees with a view to improving the process of ensuring that decisions required by financial or other non-academic imperatives were appropriately dealt with, a legal opinion that found that "the college has not violated the Colleges Act, the Constitution and By-Laws of the Academic Council, nor Policy 550-1 by proceeding as it has,"[90] and a recommendation from the Academic Council, by a vote of 16 to 11, with one abstention, that a new Budget Advisory Committee be constituted.[91] (It was, with a membership of two representatives from each of the faculty, staff, and support staff associations, two managers, the college's

vice-presidents, and the director of Institutional Analysis and Planning.) This affair increased faculty suspicions about the administration's view of the Academic Council and contributed to the further polarization of relations between administrative and faculty members on the council.

However, the downsizing process had only begun. It was accelerated in 1992 when Deputy Minister Lynn Duncan advised that the province intended "to restore fiscal balance through expenditure management," that "each institution should expect a 1993–94 grant level that is at or below the 1992–93 level," and that the minister was looking for "creative structural change" in the institutions.[92] There followed department documents entitled "Major Issues Affecting Post-Secondary Education over the Next Decade" and "Accountability: Expectations of the Public Post-Secondary System." In 1993, the department introduced the requirement for the annual submission of a rolling three-year budget plan, and the minister sponsored a roundtable for the institutions on restructuring.[93]

To prepare the college, Wood organized a workshop for administrators, association leaders, and college employees. It was facilitated by Richard Chait, an expert in governance issues, and Ken Chabotar, an expert in financial management, both associated with Harvard's professional development programs for academic administrators. The outcome was a document entitled "First Principles for Retrenchment 1993–94" that was approved by the Academic Council and board.[94] In early 1994, Wood called a meeting of faculty, staff, and student association representatives to address the 11 per cent reduction in grant for the coming year. In the end, the faculty and staff associations agreed to a 5 per cent decrease in salary over two years (1995–97),[95] while the board agreed to restore the 5 per cent in 1997 or as soon as possible thereafter. Faculty members voted 143 to 97 in favour of the plan, support staff, 230 to 55, and the management/exempt group, 72 to 6.[96] In addition, the board froze hiring, collapsed vacant positions, offered a special early retirement plan,[97] and contracted out custodial services.[98]

Rationalization of the curriculum followed, both to secure savings and to eliminate hollow academic shells that could come back to haunt the college when the new accountability systems came into force.

Lathrop warned that downsizing would not be easy: "We cannot expect that all those affected will endorse the proposed changes."[99] As the procedures for "program suspension or deletion for non-academic reasons" stipulated that the vice-president, Academic "shall request a recommendation from academic council regarding the status of a program, prior to processing the recommendation to the president,"[100] Lathrop asked the council to classify programs in categories – to be continued at the current level, increased, downsized, suspended, or terminated. This led in January 1994 to a plan for "program and service rationalization."[101] Programs that did not culminate in a parchment, such as the Canadian Studies program, were terminated as a "housekeeping" matter (because they had no graduates, such programs would count negatively in the KPI system). Three "inactive" diploma programs were also cancelled: Speech, Applied Social Sciences, and Engineering. Low enrolment led to the cancellation of four more diploma programs: Computer Marketing, Business Administration, Leisure Facilities Operations, and two certificate programs: Correctional Officer and Secretarial Arts.[102] In addition, following a recommendation from the renewed Budget Advisory Committee, high-school courses were converted into cost-recovery continuing education offerings.[103] The program rationalization was to continue. In March 2000, three more diploma programs were suspended: Community Rehabilitation, Environmental Technology, and Therapeutic Recreation.[104] Despite an Academic Council resolution opposing the action, the staff-intensive "resource islands" in the library were closed.[105]

Though downsizing reduced the number of employee positions, the targets were achieved mainly through attrition and the early retirement plan. The budget plan for 1994–97 forecast a reduction in the President's Division from 23.0 to 19.8 positions, in Administrative Services from 153.1 to 124.1, and in Academic Affairs from 432.8 to 406.7. Lost faculty positions were to be replaced by part-time and term-certain appointments.[106]

An Organization Review Task Force established by the board in October 1994 set principles for reorganization (forward-looking, flat, flexible, administratively effective, efficient, and accountable). After discussing the issues with the MRFA, deans,

FIGURE 9.4 EMPLOYEE SALARY AND BENEFITS: % OF BUDGET, 1995-2008

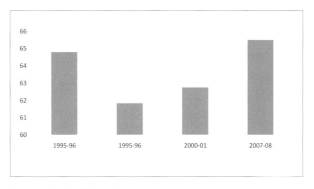

SOURCE: Audited financial statements.

department chairs, and others, Vice-President Lathrop presented the outcome to the board – 79 individuals "providing leadership" would drop to 65.[107] The effects of downsizing and reorganization on salary and benefit expenditures are shown in Figure 9.4.

In addition, the college experienced financial problems in maintaining its facilities. The original mega-structure was nearing three decades of existence and its roof, among other things, needed replacement. To cope with rising problems, the college supplemented its maintenance budget from other funds. As a result, the college's 2001 budget plan observed that "Mount Royal continues to use up its capital assets faster than it has the ability to replace them, posing a significant challenge for the institution." Indeed, the board declared, Mount Royal was "structurally underfunded in comparison to other provincial postsecondary institutions – an issue that remains unresolved."[108]

THE FOUNDATION

Fundraising became a major activity in the 1990s. Hunter Wight, director of Public Affairs and Development, had presented a proposal for a $25 million Ninth Decade fundraising campaign to the board in October 1989.[109] After attending a workshop on fundraising, Wood and Wight decided to establish a foundation to enlist the support of influential members of the community. To avoid problems with a potential rogue body that might not only wish to raise money but to spend it as well, the board agreed to set up the foundation as a stock-based company, with itself as the sole share owner.[110] By September 1991 the Mount Royal College Foundation was legally established and Hal Wyatt was designated chair of the board.[111]

The foundation reviewed the original fundraising proposal and decided upon a more modest $15 million, five-year (1993–98) "Investing in Futures" campaign for a medley of purposes – the small business training centre, scholarships, educational technology, instructional leadership, the Conservatory, and co-operative education . (For a record of major donors over the years, see Appendix 5.) The campaign moved more slowly than anticipated and in 1998 it was capped at $12,333,812.[112] The hard slogging led to an evaluation which concluded that the campaign had relied too heavily on leadership gifts, "without the traditional base of well established donor support enjoyed by most organizations embarking on a major capital drive. Today, the goal of the Foundation is to establish a base of support with a balanced and integrated relationship-driven development process. This involves the building of a large donor base through annual giving, special interest donations, major gifts, alumni solicitation and estate planning as well as special events."[113] This led to a Patrons fundraising program that focused on monthly contributions, the origins of the college's ongoing annual campaigns.

The next major campaign, "Bright Minds, Bright Futures," in 2001–4, reached its $25 million target. It raised $7 million for "investing in student success" (scholarship and bursary funds, library, Centre for Integrated Wellness, Centre for Global Experience), $3 million for investing in teaching excellence (technology, training executives in residence), and $15 million for investing in innovative programs (Institute for Sustainable Development, Institute for Nonprofit Studies, School for Business and Entrepreneurial Studies, Centre for Studies, and baccalaureate development in science and technology). Ron Brenneman, CEO of Petro-Canada, and Rick George, the CEO of Suncor, co-chaired the campaign.[114] This time, there was more support from within the college's own constituency of former students.

Thus, beginning with a small campaign in the 1980s and continuing with the large campaigns of the 1990s and early 2000s, the college demonstrated both the depth and breadth of its support within the community and its unique capacity, as a college, to generate such significant financial support. This was no doubt due in part to the college's location in the head-office city of the oil and gas industry in Canada, but it was due also to aggressive fundraising activity on the part of the college.

Phase III Facilities Expansion

By the mid-1990s the campus was once again overcrowded. Given the financial priorities of the government and the freeze on capital spending, the college's options were to intensify use of the existing facility and leasing off-campus space. "The design capacity of the Lincoln Park campus has been exceeded," the college's March 1999 Long-range Institutional Plan declared.[115] Once again, as in 1981, the college explored the potential for year-round use by introducing a trimester system, and once again decided that, with low and controlled tuition fees, the option was only possible if the government provided a higher operating grant.[116] Some space was "re-purposed." The Ford Theatre, a black box theatre, was converted into a performing arts stage for music, dance, and theatre with the aid of a donation from the Nickle Foundation, with a matching grant from the province. Completed in March 1992, the overhauled theatre was inaugurated by a performance of *Hamlet*.[117] In 1999 and again in 2000, the board approved internal renovations at a cost of $1.9 million to yield about 300 more classroom seats and a number of offices.[118] In 2000, a $2.9 million renovation project added three 55-seat classrooms, spaces for computer and engineering labs, labs for electronic publishing, renovated library space, and space for the Bachelor of Arts "collaborative program" with Athabasca University.[119]

In 1990, when its lease on the downtown campus came to an end, it leased more space for its City Centre Campus. It maintained that site until the expansion project opened space on the main campus. It was used notably by Continuing Education and the Languages Institute, which offered English as a Second Language training for foreign students. In addition, the college leased other spaces. From the city, it leased three of the group homes on Lincoln Lane (across from the

Mount Royal College committed to maintaining small class sizes as it transitioned to degree granting. Photographer Brian Harder; Mount Royal University Archives E345-19.

A. Douglas Rogan, Chairman of the Board 1996–97. Photographer Magelle's Studio; Mount Royal University Archives E230-1.

college), adjacent vacant land for student parking use,[120] and parts of the Holy Cross Centre for health-related continuing education programs.[121]

Following the city's rejection in 1989 of the shopping mall proposal for land on the other side of the 50th Avenue right-of-way from the college, Lincoln Park fell off the city's planning agenda. It reappeared briefly in 1991 during a review of the city's transportation plan which required a review of the 50th Avenue right-of-way along Mount Royal's boundary.[122] But the principal outcome was not a plan but a process – formation of the Lincoln Park Development Committee to advise the city on development applications in the area. Altogether, Lincoln Park consisted of 800 acres with four primary landholders: CFB Calgary, the city, the college, and a private developer.

The announcement in 1995 that the federal government intended to close CFB Calgary was to bedevil planning for years. The prospect of securing land and facilities from the base seized the college's imagination. In response to word that the federal Department of Public Works was planning to hold hearings with community groups,[123] the college retained an architect to develop a plan. It resembled the Lincoln Park Development Plan of the 1970s, except for the larger area. As before, the college would be "the focus for a sustainable community in Lincoln Park that offers a quality of life unique to Calgary." The college would "not be an island, but a heart. Its pulse will set a tempo that resonates through its new environs and echoes through the city itself."[124] Vice-President Wilson foresaw neighbours walking into the college for a "café latte," to shop, or to attend "a performance by the Conservatory or by Shakespeare in the Park."[125] Wood and Wight made the rounds of municipal, provincial, and federal offices in search of CFB Calgary land and buildings, albeit at someone else's expense since the college had no money.[126] The college proposed acquiring ninety-three acres, and did a study on which spaces would fit college functions. However, it was unable to persuade any government to provide land, and the idea fell off the table in 2000 when the college had to focus on its expansion project.[127]

Ground breaking for the East A building (L–R) Barry Erskine (Calgary Alderman), The Honourable Lyle Oberg (Alberta Minister of Advanced Education and Learning), Thomas Wood (Mount Royal College President), The Honourable Ralph Klein (Alberta Premier), David Tuer (Mount Royal College Chairman), Bev Longstaff (Calgary Alderman). Mount Royal University Archives E01-4.

David A. Tuer, Chairman of the Board 1997–2001. Mount Royal University Archives E280-1.

Jack W. Ady, Chairman of the Board 2001–02. Photographer Randy Neufeld; Mount Royal University Archives E2-1.

Detailed planning for Phase III expansion began in December 1997 when the board called for services to develop a campus master plan "to guide the physical growth and development of the college to the year 2005 and provide long-term projections to the year 2020 and beyond. Planning development tasks will include analyzing projections for future growth, establishing planning policies that outline standards for development consistent with the college's *2005 Vision for the Future*, and determining facility requirements, building locations, traffic patterns, open spaces and landscape development that support its educational plan and act as a guide for future change."[128] Art Froese, a former planning director for the city, was retained as the consultant.[129] He recommended that the college should acquire the fifteen acres of land on the 50th Avenue right-of-way owned by the city. Jack Donohue, chair of the board's Implementation Steering Committee, then negotiated purchase of the site at a cost of $2.9 million.[130] On 23 October 1999, the board approved "the direction/concept outlined in the Campus Development Plan." David Tuer, chair of the board, was pivotal in securing approval. He identified the opportunity, galvanized the team, and in the end made the case to government that left the Minister little opportunity to do anything but say yes.

Government approval came on 8 September 2000, with the announcement of a $94 million grant to the college to expand the enrolment capacity in Lincoln Park from 6,500 FLE to 9,000 FLE, or about 38 per cent. Behind the scenes, there was an intriguing squabble over the actual amount of the grant. The college knew that the cabinet had approved $94 million, but when Maria David-Edmonds, the deputy minister, called Wood to advise him of the approval, he was told it would be only for $69 million. Instantly Wood, Wight, and the board of governors took the political route and managed to get the total amount back.[131]

Three major new wings were to be built. The West Wing housing the original athletic facilities was to be expanded into the Physical Education and Recreation Complex, which would include a triple gym, a fitness centre, running track, squash courts, and climbing wall as well as the Department of Physical Education and Recreation Studies, Campus Recreation, and satellite food services. Thanks to a donation, the West Wing also included the Encana Wellness Centre. East

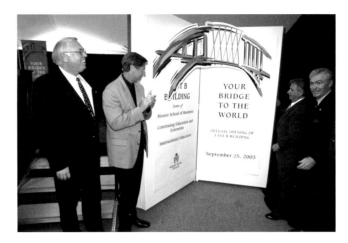

The East B building official opening (L–R) Steve Savidant (Mount Royal College Board member), The Honourable Lyle Oberg (Alberta Minister of Advanced Education), The Honourable Ralph Klein (Alberta Premier) and Dave Marshall (Mount Royal College President). Photographer Mike Ridewood; Mount Royal University Marketing and Communications.

Wing I (12,000 square metres) contained faculty and department offices, classrooms, computer labs, study and leisure spaces, a combined 90-seat lecture theatre and moot court, and satellite food services. It was intended to become the home for the Faculty of Arts. East Wing II (8,300 square metres) was for the Bissett School for Business and Entrepreneurial Studies, the offices of International Education, the Faculty of Continuing Education and Extension, general purpose classrooms, computer labs, and student space.

The campus was redeveloped, with a ring road, additional parking sites, and new playing fields. The outdoors work included an outdoor theatre funded by a million-dollar donation from TransCanada Pipelines. In addition, the board allocated $4.1 million for renovation of the existing facilities, of which $1.7 million was spent on upgrading the Learning Resources Centre and the area for the Communications program. A planned performance hall for the Conservatory for which Wood and Wight sought private donations and contributions from the federal, provincial, and municipal governments was not realized then,[132] but the work they began then led to an agreement in 2009 for all three levels of government to provide their share of the funding.

Scenarios for the project discounted "vertical expansion" and "infill expansion," opting in favour of new buildings.[133] The general strategy was to move the Faculty of Arts, the School of Business, and the Faculty of Continuing Education and International Education into the new buildings, giving them clear new physical precincts in which to develop their sense of identity. The architectural firm of Graham Edmunds was retained for the project.

Government funding for the project reached $100,728,515, including the purchase of the 50th Avenue right-of-way.[134] Another important addition, a residential complex consisting of four apartment-style concrete structures and five townhouse-style wood structures, was built at a cost of $33 million. It accommodated 594 students, raising the total of residential spaces on campus to 1,032. Funding came from the Alberta Municipal Financing Corporation, the loan provider to colleges and universities for such projects.[135]

The East B building, subsequently named the Bissett Building in honour of David and Leslie Bissett. Photographer Pablo Galvez; Mount Royal University Marketing and Communications.

In September 2002, exactly thirty years after the opening of the Lincoln Park campus and just over a decade since the completion of the Phase II expansion project, the first stage of Phase III was opened – the spacious and state-of-the-art athletic and recreation facilities. Premier Klein and Minister Lyle Oberg spoke at the ceremony.[136] In 2006, the final piece of the project was completed – the Centre for Continuous Learning, a two-floor, 4,700-square-metre stand-alone building (with wi-fi access in all rooms, and twelve 40-seat classrooms), funded by large donations honouring Roderick Mah (1929-2007), a college alumnus and prominent businessman (after whom the Centre is named), and to establish Ross Glen Hall. The building was designed to meet

West Residences, apartment-style and townhomes, created on-campus living facilities for almost 1,000 students. Photographer Pablo Galvez; Mount Royal University Marketing and Communications.

Leadership in Energy and Environmental Design (LEED) standards, one of the first "green" buildings in Calgary to secure the "gold" award.[137]

During the space crunch of the 1990s, one historical issue surfaced. In 1996 the college was given a large, expensive, handmade organ by the Calgary Universal Foundation for the Organ. The Carthy Organ at Mount Royal had 1,624 pipes and was 6.1 metres high and 5.8 metres wide.[138] The donation arose from a confluence of roles played by people with a college association. Former president Doug Lauchlan was then the director of the Calgary Centre for Performing Arts and had organized the quadrennial Calgary International Organ Festival. Hal Wyatt, chair of the foundation, was also chairman of the Organ Festival. The donation was intended to make the Conservatory into "Canada's pre-eminent organ academy." However, there were few places for such an instrument and the administration decided that the Dr. John H. Garden Meditation Centre was "the most suitable solution." It proposed locating the organ in the centre, renaming it as the Wyatt Recital Hall in recognition of Hal and Marnie Wyatt, and honouring Garden by naming the new courtyard park adjacent to the Kerby Wing in his name.[139] While the Meditation Centre was a lovely space, it was not much used.

Wade Lorentzon, the chaplain assigned by the Christian Community Church, and other members of its Board of Elders, met with board chairman A. D. (Doug) Rogan, Wood, and Wight to convey concerns about the "loss of a designated meditation centre, possible indifference to the college's history and historical artifacts, possible affront to the memory and family of Dr. John H. Garden, and the need for a dedicated space for religious services and meditation on campus."[140] In the end, a space on the first level near the West Gate was designated, minor renovations

Construction underway on the Carthy Organ at Mount Royal College, 1996. Photographer Mike Ridewood; Mount Royal University Archives E96-22.

were made, and the new meditation centre opened on 4 March 1998.[141] The Dr. John H. Garden Memorial Park—which is used to recognize those individuals in whose name memorial scholarships have been established at the college—was officially dedicated on 21 August 1998. The opening was saluted by an article in *Reflections*, the alumni magazine, entitled "A fitting tribute," which outlined Garden's original intention to study botany and the fact that his uncle, Sir Alexander Garden, had developed "a flower that still enjoys universal popularity" – the "gardenia."[142]

RELATIONS WITH THE STUDENTS' ASSOCIATION

Despite the growing number of students spending a longer time on campus, few showed much interest in the Students' Association. Typically, 6 to 10 per cent voted in elections for the Student Council and other offices.[143] The quorum of 1 per cent turnout for annual meetings was rarely met, and the meetings proceeded only because no one raised the quorum issue. Though the association paid salaries to its officers, the highest in Canada for such positions in 2000 ($26,702),[144] turnover was high, there was often only one candidate for an office, and continuation from one year to another was limited. In 1997, only one person continued in office from the previous year.[145] The most successful route to office in the association was through participation in the Students' Council. [146] In 2000, only one member of the existing executive stood for re-election and several new candidates surfaced;[147] in 2003–4, by contrast, the entire executive was re-elected.[148]

Although uninterested in student politics, many students were interested in tuition fees and parking. In 1997, some 3,000 signed a petition protesting a rise in tuition fees.[149] The periodic increase in parking fees also elicited vocal protests, though no action, notably when the fee was increased to $85 in 2000. (Employees were then paying $350.)[150] Debates about smoking, which had begun in the 1930s over the right to smoke, had by the 1980s moved in the opposite direction, over limits to be imposed on smokers. In 2004, there was a big town hall meeting of students on whether smoking should be continued in the Liberty Lounge.[151] There were also lots of student volunteers

for good causes – for example, the surfeit of volunteers in 1997 for a new Peer Support Centre.[152] In 2003, CRMC The Edge, the students' broadcasting station (FM 107.5), began transmissions into social and dining spaces around the college, including "political debates" among candidats for office.[153]

In the 1990s the association initiated benefits for its members. In 1992, 84 per cent of students voting in a referendum agreed to institute a health insurance plan. In 1996, 92 per cent voted to implement a "managed care" dental insurance plan for students. ("Managed" meant that particular dentists must be used.) Mandatory plans were then implemented for students taking nine or more credits, though those who had a plan already could opt out. By 2001, these plans cost in the order of $175 per person and costs were slated to rise to $190 in 2002–3.[154] To encourage the use of public transit, the association administered a referendum in 2005 to accept a "mandatory" U-Pass for the public system, and 65 per cent approved.[155]

Once again the student newspaper became an issue. On 12 December 1991 the *Reflector* carried a cartoon that led to protests about alleged racism and anti-Semitism. Wood met with various people to address the issue, including the instructor serving as the overseer and a representative of the *Jewish Free Press*. The dean of Arts issued reprimands to the editor, cartoonist, and entertainment editor. The upshot was that the acting chairman of the *Reflector* Publication Society declared that it would hire a full-time editor, appoint an advisory board of journalist professionals to deal with policy matters, and perhaps seek membership in the Alberta Press Council.[156] To provide students with what it deemed more reliable information than was otherwise available about its affairs, the association launched its own publication, *Association Matters*, in 1992.[157] As in the 1980s, and despite student representation on the board of governors, the board's finance committee, and the budget advisory committee, all of which had voted on the matter, the Students' Association also punctuated its opposition to a tuition fee increase by withdrawing its representatives from the Academic Council, bringing the deliberations of that body to a halt.[158]

With growing enrolment, the size and operations of the Wyckham House Student Centre needed to be revisited. Anticipating the need for building more space, the association secured approval in a 1992 referendum to charge a $3 fee per semester to expand the centre and renovate part for a Native student centre.[159] A plebiscite to raise it to $8 failed in 1999 but succeeded in 2000, including an escalating scale of fees to a peak of $33 per semester in 2006–7.[160] Finally, in the fall of 2007, construction began on a $14 million renovation and expansion to enlarge the centre by 45 per cent.[161]

In the meantime, the growing building funds raised questions about the fit between the Wyckham House Board (the body of external advisors) and SAMRC's executive group, and in 1999 the Wyckham House Board was terminated. Through negotiations guided by Ken Robson, an alternative was developed – the Student Centre Liaison Committee, made up of equal numbers of board and association representatives, and empowered to oversee the operations of the licence agreement and other matters.[162]

One issue that inspired some student discussion was the Code of Student Conduct developed over two years in a process coordinated by Ken Robson, vice-president, Student Affairs and Campus Life. The code replaced older policies on academic integrity and disqualification. The issue of concern was its application to off-campus events. After several iterations, it was approved in the fall of 2003.[163] Related to that issue was the question of risk. After 11 September 2001, the association's insurance rates soared, causing it to withdraw from hosting off-campus events. Students wishing to hold off-campus events should refer to themselves as a "group of students" rather than as members of a campus club, society, or the association.[164]

Under the terms of the Colleges Act, the association was obliged to submit its audited financial statements, the name of the auditors, and the auditors' management letter to the board of governors for approval. For some reason, the board only received the association's documents for 1994–95 and 1995–96, without approving them, opening the door to the claim that approval was unnecessary. As "the provisions of the legislation have not been followed for several years," the association told the Student Centre Liaison Committee, it proposed "changing the regulations to reflect actual practice." The committee recommended approval. While it "is not required," Mick Mulloy, the business manager, added, board "support would be useful in

the association's application" to the government to be exempted from the act. President Bryan Boechler sent a letter to the Lieutenant Governor declaring that "this provision is now no longer required. The association is both a corporation registered under The Societies Act as well as a registered charity; as such, the association is required to make detailed returns to both the provincial and federal governments which are open to public perusal; with gross revenues of $2 million, the association is a significant corporation in its own right, with qualified staff and professional advisors to ensure that its fiduciary responsibility to its members and to the public is maintained; finally, the board of the college has no real interest in the detailed financial operations of the association, receiving the audited accounts only as information."[165] After considering the legal and other implications, the board agreed to "indicate to the minister" that it "does not object to an application" from the association, "provided that a satisfactory amendment to the Agreement on Operating Relationships . . . [January 1997] can be concluded." However, the initiative came to naught. Perhaps to avoid a precedent for the college system, the Lieutenant Governor denied the request.[166]

Another sign of a positive relationship was the board's approval for an expansion of Thirsty's Bar and Lounge in 1998. Selling liquor was profitable for the association but involved risks for the college, which held the liquor licence and contended with the effects of rowdy behaviour.[167] In 1998, recognizing the growing size of the student body, the board approved a request to expand Thirsty's by 100 seats. The proposal was cunningly linked to the development of a Native Student Centre in Wyckham House, at a cost of $400,000.[168] To avoid the implications of the old name, the bar was re-baptized *Liberty Lounge*.

But then the relationship soured. Incidents in the bar and at parties, plus concern over leases and other facilities arrangements made without consultation, led the board of governors to undertake a risk assessment. This exercise led to fourteen meetings between association and board representatives and the formulation of policies to govern use of the centre. Citing key documents, Robson said that students should know that "the college owns Wyckham House. . . . The board … is the landlord, hence the licence of occupation. The students are tenants in that space; the board owns it, the Students' Association does not."[169] In the ensuing dialogue about the issues, Sean Fraser, president of the association and a member of the board of governors, declared that, as "the board does not have the authority or jurisdiction to effect the proposed policies, the association does not consider itself bound by the policies, and it will not abide by them since the association believes the policies are beyond the scope and jurisdiction of the board."[170] By a vote of 8 to 3, the board issued an ultimatum: "if the board . . . has not received a letter from the [association] by the end of the week indicating that the board has the full authority to enact the policies just approved, that the association will comply with those policies, and that it will resume the consultation process with the college administration in order to work toward implementation of those policies and build a framework for the expansion of Wyckham House, the board of governors will serve notice to the Students' Association that the board will move to terminate the Licence of Occupation Agreement between the board of governors and the Students' Association of MRC."[171] The association would be ousted from the centre. If the association thought it had a case, it would have to go to court. It did not.

There matters rested for a few years. Finally in May 2007, with board approval, the association commenced a 45 per cent expansion of Wyckham House that included an expanded link to the college's circulation system, a larger food court, a peer support centre upstairs, additional study space, recreational and lounge space, a larger *Liberty Lounge*, and more space for clubs. The project was completed in two phases, the first in fall 2008, and the second in fall 2009.[172]

As Appendix 1 indicates, the composition of the student body continued to change. As the new applied degree programs attracted more students straight from high school, the average age of full-time credit students declined, as did the proportion of those with academic deficiencies. With the longer programs, students stayed longer in the college. The proportion of those completing programs continued to rise. The trend toward greater female participation also continued.

One notable change was the more visible presence of Native students. From 1994 to 1997, the college and the Treaty 7 Economic Development Corporation mounted the three-year Aboriginal Education Project.[173] Its purpose was "to help meet the educational needs of aboriginal people by offering learning opportunities and community activities" and "to enhance cross-cultural understanding within an institutional setting." Levels one and two of the project were designed to meet the needs of students for advanced upgrading, especially in Math and English, study skills, college preparation, and Aboriginal culture courses. Level three offered college and university courses for students aiming at diploma or degree programs. Level four was designed to assist students with the transition "into the mainstream post-secondary education community." Beginning with a cap of seventy-five students in 1993, the program had about ninety when it was cancelled in 1997. Treaty 7 nations provided about 65 per cent of the funding while the province provided 35 per cent. The reason for the cancellation, according to Cate Hanington, the Program Liaison Coordinator, was that "Treaty 7 Economic Development Corporation and the Métis Nation didn't feel that the program led directly to jobs."[174] What the project showed, however, was a new level of Native interest in post-secondary education on the campus. It was in this context that the new Native Students Centre was opened in Wyckham House in 1998. Leona Badger, a Native student, was responsible for running the centre. "The Native Student Centre thrives on being a bridge between Native students and the other students in the college," she said. Physically, the centre was designed as "a representation of the circle of life and the four directions, based on the medicine wheel concept."[175]

Student social life continued along well-grooved pathways − parties, dances, volunteer activities. In 2001, "Carnipaloozafest" was inaugurated to celebrate the association itself − its departments, volunteers, and student leaders. It was intended to be an annual event. The theme in 2003−4 was a "cruise ship and included cruising-style activities such as 'Fun Money Casino,' Karaoke, a shuffle board tournament, and a mock treasure hunt." Entertainers included "members from the T & T Organettes who dazzled the audience with their amazing steel drum cover songs, 34 and Karamoko and his band added a jazzy sway to the ambience with their Afro-Francophone style." Students were encouraged "to learn about all of our services

Mount Royal College Athletics was awarded the Canadian Colleges Athletic Association Supremacy Award in June 1999, recognizing Mount Royal College as the top overall athletic college in Canada, based on national medals accumulated in all sports over 25 years. (L-R) Thomas Wood (Mount Royal College President), Alan Ferchuk (Alberta Colleges Athletic Conference President), Don Stouffer (Mount Royal College Dean of Community and Health Studies), Mark Kozak (Mount Royal College Athletics Director). Mount Royal University Archives E392-52.

and the locations of everything from the Native Student Centre to the Wycked Kitchen to the CopyWrite."[176]

The college's athletic teams continued to flourish. One of sixteen participants in the Alberta College Athletic Conference (ACAC), Mount Royal routinely won much more than its share of prizes. In 1997, a reporter for the *Reflector* observed that the length of the 33rd annual Cougar awards ceremony was due, not to the number of speakers, but to "the sheer volume of awards and accolades." In Alberta, the college's Cougar teams had won nine gold medal championships, two silver medals, and two bronze medals. For the eighth year in a row, the college won the ACAC Supremacy Award for leading the conference. Furthermore, the average GPA for the College's teams was 2.96, "the best in the province." At the national level, where Mount Royal participated in Canadian Colleges Athletic Association (CCAA) competitions, Mount Royal teams also did reasonably well. In 1995–96, for example, they won two silver medals and two bronzes, and six Cougars were selected for CCAA All-Canadian awards, "more than any other school in Alberta."[177] In June 1999, Mount Royal received the CCAA Sports Supremacy Award for achievements over 25 years – a total of 44 CCAA medals (18 gold, 16 silver, and 10 bronze). Of the eighteen national championships, six were in men's volleyball and three in men's hockey. In 2000, the women's basketball team added its first national championship. "There are 175 community colleges and technical institutes in Canada, and we're number one, so we take a lot of pride in that," said Mark Kozak, the college's athletics manager.[178]

As the college looked toward achieving university status and entering into competition with universities, Denny Neider, academic support co-ordinator, anticipated that "the prestige of the [university] league . . . might make sponsorship a little bit easier. There might be some sponsors that are more willing to get behind it." Joining the university leagues, moreover, would require more travel and higher-level competition.

Ron Wuotila, the athletics manager, remarked on the benefits of stronger competition: "We are a dominant athletics program. One of the things that we are suffering from is the quality of our competition. Just like a student, if you are not challenged as an athlete, you don't get any better." Moreover, the development of four-year programs might staunch the flow of excellent athletics from the college to universities in shorter programs.[179]

RELATIONS WITH THE FACULTY

It would have been remarkable for the college to have undergone the changes in self-conception and faculty credentials associated with degree granting without a return to the polarized environment of the 1970s. The adoption of a new mission required firm leadership, courage, occasional peremptory action to make things happen, and changes in policy and priority that threatened the recently established concept of the college instructor and stretched the idea of what the recently established public college should be.

A dissertation on the effects of leadership on Mount Royal's organizational culture completed in 1993, based on interviews with faculty, staff, and administrators, distilled the collective memory of past administrations. "The current organizational culture has historical roots but has been reconstructed and shaped by successive leaders and individual staff and group members' values and beliefs." The transition from the private religiously affiliated college to the public community college and the building of the Lincoln Park campus had moved "the college culture . . . from a small, collegial family to the post-1972 large complex 'cul de sac' and visually structured institution." "The post-1972 transitions resulted in tumultuous upheavals in the college culture, structure and leadership." Leadership styles had differed, affecting the culture, with the stronger central administrations generating the strongest faculty responses. In the 1990s, the centralization grew further, as did the nervousness. This was partly because of the senior administration's intense management style, partly because of anxiety induced by the degree-granting agenda, partly because of the retrenchment activities of the time, and partly because the sheer longevity of senior administrators made

them all too familiar while depriving other faculty members of the opportunity to rise in the administration. "In order to have power here, you need to be visible in meetings, committees, and the association," one faculty member explained.[180] The author of the dissertation remarked perceptively that "the presence of strong subcultures harbouring localized behaviours and a counter-culture perspective creates the potential for counter-productive behaviours."[181] "Overall," he noted, "the faculty subculture was characterized by strong tendencies toward anarchy, a need to excel in their individual activities, and an anti-administration stance exemplified in the political activities of the faculty association."[182]

In this context, the Academic Council was a "significant symbol through which the faculty exerted an influence and power over college academic affairs and college governance."[183] Indeed, its importance grew in the 1990s because of the gravity of the matters it had to consider, such as program terminations, and because of concerns about administrative behaviour, both with respect to its advancement of the degree-granting agenda that would change the institution profoundly and in its approach to the role of the Academic Council. As one senior administrator said in confidence, the new regime was "less collegial" than that of the previous decade. The signs of growing polarization quickly emerged. In 1991, faculty members proposed and secured a subtle but important change in the council's constitution: members were now described as "representatives" of a "constituency," no longer as members drawn from a constituency.[184] Faculty members of council began to caucus before council meetings to discuss agenda items. In 1991–92, two MRFA leaders, Hugh Macleod and Marc Chikinda, became chairs respectively of the Program and the Planning committees; in 1992–93, Chikinda became chair of the council.

The major issues of the 1990s – degree granting, financial cutbacks, program terminations, contracting out, and employee layoffs – prompted faculty nervousness while requiring the senior administration to initiate bold action. Thus, circumstances contributed to wariness on both sides. The faculty wanted to scrutinize all administrative proposals and procedures in detail while the senior administrators, concerned to produce effective and timely responses to external challenges and opportunities, chafed at faculty resistance to change. There were perhaps two other general factors at work. First, Wood had set aside the policy limiting administrative appointments to two five-year terms, with the result that until well into the 1990s the administration had a familiar rather than a fresh face; unable to rise in the administration, some faculty members became active in the MRFA and Academic Council, ways of dealing with strategic questions by other means. There is an old saying that in administration one's friends come and go but one's enemies accumulate, and years of saying no to people, inadvertently giving offence, or paying insufficient heed to every sensibility exacts a price. Second, many of the college's activities during the period fell outside the immediate purview of the credit faculty – fundraising, facilities planning and development, international activities and connections, and continuing education and extension work. The increasingly wide span of the college's activities may have reinforced the already strong sense of marginalization felt by the most activist faculty members – a sense accentuated for some by the focus on degree granting that threatened to devalue their credentials or activities.

Whatever the causes, there was no doubt that there was an increasing polarization between the administration and some faculty members that was expressed in several forms. The periodic survey of faculty opinion in all colleges and technical institutes undertaken by ACIFA provided some straws in the wind, though the survey never drew responses from more than 20 per cent of faculty members. In 1995, the responses suggested the effects of the cutbacks and notable concerns about the effectiveness of the Academic Council, which was "perceived to continue to remain below average in terms of its effectiveness."[185] In 1996, T. J. MacAlister, president of the MRFA, explaining the survey responses to the board, pointed to the question on whether "administration clearly understands day-to-day problems faced by instructors": 33 per cent disagreed, and 33 per cent more strongly disagreed.[186] The 2000 results on the question of whether "senior administration communicates openly with faculty" were sobering: 3.4 per cent strongly agreed, 9 per cent agreed moderately, 25.5 per cent neither agreed nor disagreed, 26 per cent disagreed, and 35.9 per cent strongly disagreed.[187] In other words, about 86 per

cent of the respondents were either non-committal or negative. "The survey results reflect a faculty anticipating transition," Jerry Paquette, president of the MRFA explained; "faculty [members] view preparing for new roles as a major issue."[188]

Another contributor to tension was collective bargaining. As a result of the first 11 per cent operating grant cut, the board and MRFA had taken eight months beyond the start of the contract date to agree on terms in February 1996.[189] "Disappointed and discouraged," the board and MRFA established a joint committee consisting of Bruce Mahon and Ken Robson for the board, and Judy Collins and Greg Flanagan for the MRFA, to review options for "a more mutually beneficial and expedited process." The result was a three-year pilot project for a continuous bargaining process that involved a joint standing committee to address non-salary issues and establish memoranda of agreement that would have force until the end of the contract, at which point the parties could either ratify or reject them. Salary and cost items would be dealt with separately.[190] The first fruits were memoranda on service credit for faculty members who had held prior term-certain appointments and "the status of chairs within the newly created School for Business and Entrepreneurial Studies, the Centre for Health studies, and the Centre for Communication Studies."[191] However, it turned out that there was a lot of work for little yield. "The living agreement was somewhat inconvenient," Mahon recalled, "as negotiations never ended – there were always meetings and ongoing discussions, and often not a lot of significant outcomes (e.g., it was not easy trying to have a board member at all the meetings, and you may recall how important that was to the MRFA. . . . It sounded fine in theory but in practice it was more limited."[192] At the end of its three-year trial, the experiment lapsed.

In 1998, following negotiations that led the MRFA to "work-to-rule" and to launch a "demonstration picket,"[193] the parties agreed "to strike a committee to explore the feasibility of creating a formula or alternative way to arrive at a figure for compensation settlements."[194] It led nowhere, and negotiations in 2001 and 2003 also led to deadlock, mediation, and faculty withdrawal from committees.[195] In both rounds the faculty sought salary increases well above the increase in operating grant. By 2003, faculty members were looking forward to a change in status and eye-ing the compensation of university professors. Randy Genereux, citing the top salary of "over $130,000" for faculty members at the University of Calgary, noted that the top rate for a Ph.D. holder at Mount Royal was $74,000, while "high-school teachers make 16 per cent, on average, more than college instructors."[196]

One might wonder what was achieved by the psychodrama of negotiations at Mount Royal. In fact, after decades of negotiations in which the MRFA had routinely provided its bargaining team with the right to strike without returning to the faculty for a vote, buttressed by demonstration pickets and withdrawal of various services, the MRFA had achieved little not granted in other institutions where the right-to-strike did not exist. Given the fact that both operating grants and tuition fees were set by government, it was hardly surprising that faculty compensation and workload were similar to those in other Alberta colleges. Mount Royal's board could not give away what it did not have. In the mid-1990s, the salaries of Mount Royal faculty members holding doctorates ranked fifth out of ten colleges ($57,532 vs. $62,532 at Keyano College) and second for faculty members holding master's degrees ($55,056 vs. $56,677 at Grand Prairie).[197]

Twice in fifteen years the board and the MRFA had agreed on a novel bargaining approach – the first involving the external chair of a single bargaining team, the second a form of continuous bargaining – and both had lapsed after a single experiment. Indeed, the confrontations had grown worse in recent years. It was time for another approach to collegial governance and working relations. The old ones had exhausted their value and were causing unnecessary and wasteful tensions. While that may not have been apparent to members of Mount Royal's association, it was abundantly clear in Edmonton. It was hardly surprising that when the government introduced the Post-secondary Learning Act in 2004, sections 88 through 92, followed by Regulation 53/2004 (Model Provisions Regulation), ended the faculty's right to strike at Mount Royal in favour of the compulsory arbitration required in other post-secondary institutions; the act also continued to exempt post-secondary institutions from the provisions of the Employment Standards Code and the Labour Relations Code.

INTERNATIONAL EDUCATION

In 1990, the Office for International Relations became the Office of International Education. Under the guidance of the director, Lorna M. Smith, the office steadily expanded Mount Royal's international contacts. Funded initially by a small reserve fund, the office was given the mandate to operate on a self-sustaining financial basis, if not a profitable one. Its guiding principles included creating opportunities for faculty and staff for professional development and renewal, creating opportunities for international activities for students, contributing to the social and economic development of Calgary, and providing opportunities for international students to visit/attend the college. For the next decade the office established the framework for what became a large theatre of activity. In 1995, the office received the Internationalization Excellence Award of the Association of Canadian Community Colleges (ACCC).[198]

In 1989, the office developed the Languages Institute at the City Centre Campus to deliver credit-free ESL and language training to local and international students, customized language training to Calgary companies working overseas, study tours, and international contract programs. The institute began with 60 international students and grew to over 1,500 a decade later. From 1994 to 1998, international students constituted 2.5 per cent of semester enrolment (208 students in the fall of 1998). They paid tuition fees double those of domestic students. In 1997–98, the Languages Institute generated revenues of $2.3 million. In addition, the office coordinated development projects in Gaza, the West Bank, Guyana, and Jordan, all funded by the Canadian International Development Agency (CIDA) and the World Bank. It negotiated a $1.3 million contract for language training for Mexico and other contracts and grants totalling $1 million. In that year, the total revenue was $4.6 million, with a net profit of $250,000 – a benefit when the college was still reeling from the 21 per cent cut in its basic operating grant.[199] In 2008–9, working with a $300,000 budget draw, the office generated some $4 million in activity.

Wood took a personal interest in the college's international activity. In 1992, he was appointed by the Canadian government as one of five Canadians working with equal numbers of American and Mexican educational leaders to the Trilateral Task Force on North American Higher Education Collaboration. Its purpose was to increase "educational mobility," including bringing Mexicans to Canada for study. Those contacts led to a partnership in 1992 with the Instituto Tecnológico y de Estudios Superiores de Monterrey (ITESM) in Monterrey, Mexico. A private institution with one of the most computer-intensive environments in the world, ITESM was also internationally active. As a result of Wood's involvements, the Third Trilateral Conference was held in Banff in 1994. That meeting contributed to the formation of the Consortium on North American Higher Education Collaboration (CONAHEC) as a U.S.-Mexico Educational Interchange Project. It was expanded to include Canadian institutions in 1997. In 1998, Wood participated in a Team Canada mission to Mexico that led to another agreement with ITESM for the language and culture preparation of Mexican teachers at Mount Royal.[200] Wood served a term as president of CONAHEC and brought its 2002 annual conference to the college.

Wood also participated in other Team Canada and Team Alberta missions intended to sell Canadian goods and services in other countries. A Team Alberta mission to Japan and China in the fall of 2002 led to agreements with Gifu Shotoku Gakuen University in Japan (an informal partner for the previous ten years). The same trip included discussions regarding the expansion of programming with the Shanghai University of Finance and Economics (SUFE). "The Chinese economy is expanding at an astonishing rate," Wood

International students from Instituto Tecnológico y de Estudios Superiores de Monterrey (ITESM) in Mexico attend a Stampeders football game in 2001 while taking part in International Education programs. *Mount Royal University International Update*, Issue 1, September 2001.

said. "There is considerable interest in the Canadian post-secondary education system and in Mount Royal College." Subsequently fourteen Japanese students enrolled in the Languages Institute, all billeted in local homes to enhance exposure to English and local culture.[201]

Thanks to the off-campus nature of most of the international activity and the location of the Languages Institute at the downtown campus, most faculty members knew little about the college's international activity.[202] A 2001 review concluded that "internationalization had not yet truly become part of the institution's core activity: teaching and learning." As a result, the priority in the next "Strategy for Internationalization" aimed to integrate international programs and activities "into mainstream campus life, including teaching and learning, research activities, and the delivery of student services."[203] In articulating its plans for the next decade, the college used Jane Knight's definition of internationalization as "the process of integrating an international/intercultural perspective into the teaching/learning, research and service functions of higher education."[204] To that end, the new plan included six strategies: building institutional partnerships, providing students with international experiences, bringing foreign students to campus, informing the curriculum with international perspectives, international development and training assistance, and international contract training. The number of faculty involved in foreign missions grew. By 2009 the college had seventy partnerships with other institutions, agencies, and companies. It had received three major donations (Royal Bank, Scotiabank, and PetroCanada), secured funding from the Canada-European Union Mobility Program, which provides up to $4,000 support for students in partnerships involving three European and three Canadian partner institutions, and, as of 2009, $750 provincial grants to 67 individual students to help with the costs of such activities.[205] The sites ranged from many parts of Europe (e.g., Austria, Spain, and the United Kingdom), China, and Latin and South America (e.g., Peru). In 2009, the Global Television Network and Canwest Global Foundation awarded $150,000 to assist students in Communication Studies to undertake directed field studies on a global scale.[206] In the summer of 2009, fifteen faculty members were delivering credit courses on student tours.

The college also focused on immigrants to Canada. In 2003, the federal ministry of Human Resources Development (HRDC) announced $1,526,900 in funding over three years for a major study involving Mount Royal, Ryerson University, and New Brunswick Community College to make it easier for Licensed Practical Nurses and foreign-credentialed nurses to advance toward a nursing degree to help alleviate the shortage in the field. The foreign-trained were then receiving no credit for prior learning, and the task was to develop appropriate prior learning assessment and recognition (PLAR) tools.[207]

Internationalizing the curriculum included Carolyn Anderson's project for a "web-based International Community Development course" funded by the Canadian Bureau for International Education (CBIE). "We needed to provide students with more information about community development issues worldwide," she explained, "to look at international issues within the context of their particular discipline and community development."[208] The course began in September 2002.

Thus, as the college entered the twenty-first century, it had substantially raised its level of international activity and its international profile. To be sure, there was the continuing challenge of sustaining an increasingly large bubble of activity resting on short-term fees and project funding. There was also the challenge of relating that bubble to the core activities, teaching and research. And there was the further challenge, not necessarily related to any of the projects, of internationalizing the curriculum itself, making students aware of "the tension between the social and cultural diversity of knowledge and its universality,"[209] and preparing them for an increasingly globalized economy and culture.

By the end of the first decade of the twenty-first century, and facing the third decade of its existence, the office was developing a new strategy for the next decade. Reflecting the conversion from college to university, that new strategy will place greater emphasis on research activities and aim at being more firmly dovetailed with classroom course delivery.

Conservatory instructor Kum Sing Lee works with Tamara Niekludow, a piano student from Poland, in the annual Morningside Music Bridge program for gifted young musicians from around the world, 2003. Photographer Ted Jacob; Mount Royal University Conservatory.

The Performing Arts

The Conservatory's musical and theatre arts training and artistic performances were to continue to bring considerable attention to the college. Its purpose was lofty: "Our long-term mandate is to transform The Conservatory into a world-class centre for arts education and training, focusing on youth."[210] The core strategy on the music side had been to build on the broad base of music lessons for a large clientele, to stream students into Kodaly and Suzuki programs where appropriate, to select the best students for admission to the high-powered Academy Program with its master classes with world-class musicians, and to forge links with the leading music schools around the world. In North America, the focus was on links to the Curtis Institute of Music in Philadelphia, the Colburn School in Los Angeles, the New England Conservatory, and the Juilliard School in New York.

In 1996, the effort to form links became international, thanks to the support of Andy Chan, a member of the Morningside Group, a Chinese international investment company, who wanted to expose both Chinese and Canadian music students to outstanding North American music teachers and to broaden their cultural as well as their artistic horizons. The program consisted of annual summer workshops which brought together outstanding students from leading music schools around the world for a month of private lessons in violin, viola, cello and piano, master classes, and chamber music and recitals. The students came from China, Poland, Japan, Taiwan, the Netherlands, Russia, and the United States. Sessions were also held in China and Poland.[211] The teachers were prominent musicians such as János Starker.[212] Former students continued to the leading music schools and/or professional careers. Andrea Case, a young Canadian cellist who experienced the program, explained that she had learned about differences in Chinese and Canadian music education: "They put great emphasis on technical perfection … whereas in Canada the emphasis is more on diversity and musicality."[213] Beginning in 1997, performances were recorded, and became a standard college gift to visitors.

The activities stemming from the quadrennial international organ festival became an important part of the Conservatory's calendar. Lessons were taught in Wyatt Recital Hall and performances were held in Jack Singer Concert Hall in downtown Calgary. For example, Neil Cockburn, head of Organ Studies, and Marcel and Elizabeth Bergmann, Conservatory piano instructors, were performers at the fourth Royal Bank Calgary International Organ Festival and Competition in August 2002.[214] As one might expect, the Conservatory's students flourished in music competitions.[215] Many went on to distinguished professional careers.[216]

The Suzuki program was very popular. In 2001 the Conservatory added a Certificate of Achievement in Suzuki Piano Pedagogy for students who completed the courses;[217] in 2002, the Suzuki Piano Summer Institute included the first videoconference interaction between instructors and that year's "composer in residence," Rémi Bouchard, in Manitoba; in 2004, videoconference lessons were offered to students across Canada; and in 2005 upgraded technology enabled three-way teleconferencing, to allow music students in two locations to connect with one instructor.

The incorporation of the Theatre Arts program into the Conservatory was accompanied by an expansion in the range of its activities. The theatre program had two streams, one for training actors, the other for training technical staff for theatre and TV. Under Doug Rathbun, chair of the Department of Theatre and Speech, students not only mounted productions on campus but participated in professional productions in downtown Calgary and elsewhere. In the spring of 1997, the Year of the Refugee, the Theatre Arts program mounted Euripides' *The Trojan Woman*, "a metaphor for our time."[218] In 1997–98, the first production of the year was Shakespeare's *As You Like It*

directed by Lorne Kennedy, who had spent twelve seasons as an actor and director in Ontario's Stratford Festival.[219] That was followed by *The Children's Hour* and *Nicholas Nickleby*.[220] In addition to the on-campus diploma program and theatre productions, the summer Shakespeare in the Park series continued to be a marked success. In 1997, the series attracted more than 35,000 people and an "award was granted to it by Calgary's Downtown Business Association for the contribution the production made to the city's cultural community." In 2002, for the first time, it also offered productions on the campus. Shakespeare Survivor, "a touring show produced by student actors from Shakespeare in the Park," offered productions in the Kerby Centre (a senior citizens' organization located in the Kerby Memorial Building, which was part of the original Mount Royal campus) and the Alberta Children's Hospital, among other locations. It blended "pop culture with some of the Bard's best work to tell the tale of eight well-known characters who will do anything to outwit, outplay and outlast each other."[221] The Theatre Arts program also mounted travelling productions for schools, known as Have Theatre, Will Travel.

END OF A LONG RUN

Thomas Wood's period as president was marked by profound change in the nature of Mount Royal, though the final transformation into a university still lay ahead. His personal passion and commitment had driven much of the change. He had managed both the internal and external processes for securing applied degree-granting status for Mount Royal (and triggered the change for other colleges and technical institutes). His promotion of the applied focus of the degrees had determined the template for applied degrees across the province, increasing the fit between college programs and the business and industry sectors they were designed to serve. He had initiated changes required for the college to become a university, including its progressive adoption of the idea that it needed to become a university for the sake of its students. With the addition of more faculty members holding Ph.D.s, the college's sense of itself changed and it added research to its mission. Wood had also overseen the completion of major new academic buildings, recreation facilities, and student residences. He had raised the college's profile considerably both nationally and internationally and enhanced global awareness on campus. With Hunter Wight and others, he had developed a fundraising function that was the most successful among colleges in the country. In short, Wood was a transformational leader – he wrought changes in the institution at fundamental levels – in mandate, aspiration, organization, operation, clientele, and faculty qualifications. Not surprisingly, such energetic leadership also exacted a certain price in internal comity, as indicated by signs of rising faculty alienation.

During the period, Mount Royal did not get all it wanted. The applied degree was a compromise, not the kind of degree the college had wanted. Though the board of governors made the best of the situation, it soon returned to what it believed the community really needed and what the college should offer – four-year undergraduate degrees, and university standing to ensure their credibility.

Though Wood regretted leaving the presidency in August 2003 without achieving the university standing he believed was imminent, his accomplishments

were considerable. Being a change agent, he admitted in a retirement interview, had not been easy. "Inertia, a reluctance to change, has been a challenge, as has been persuading government to support education in general and Mount Royal College in particular. . . . That's not to say that there has been no support." Funding for the expansion project was "a remarkable indicator of government support, and another high-water mark in government support was approval of applied degrees." He anticipated that the goal of transforming the college into a university would continue: " . . . higher levels of education are required and we must educate a broader spectrum of the population. Calgary badly needs an undergraduate university, combining degree programs with a broad array of post-secondary opportunities."[222] In recognition of his contributions, the University of Calgary awarded Wood an honorary doctorate and ENMAX donated $1 million to establish a lecture series in his name.[223]

After leaving Mount Royal, Wood became the founding president of the Asia Pacific Institute for the Tec de Monterrey (ITESM) and helped found Quest University, a private liberal arts and sciences university in British Columbia.

2003	David G. Marshall becomes president
	Bill 43 enables colleges to offer "foundation degrees" from a college platform
2006	Learning Act amended to permit "alternative academic councils"
2007	Nursing baccalaureate program commences
2008	Post-Secondary Learning Amendment Act sets out new institutional categories
2009	Post-Secondary Learning Amendment Act allows Mount Royal and Grant MacEwan Colleges to request the use of the word "university" in their name by an order-in-council.
	Premier Ed Stelmach presides over ceremony to launch Mount Royal University

CHAPTER 10

BECOMING A UNIVERSITY, 2003–2009

One who has not studied the practice of degree granting might assume that the main determinant of whether a postsecondary education institution obtains from the government the authority to grant degrees is the content of its instructional programs. . . . This, however, has not generally been the case. . . . Essentially, a degree is what those who have the legal authority to award one say that it is.

– Michael Skolnik, "Should the CAATs Grant Degrees?" 1995[1]

As we have seen, Mount Royal's board of governors had concluded that graduating ever more students with credentials that would face recognition problems was neither in the interest of Mount Royal's graduates nor of its institutional reputation, and so had set the goal of making Mount Royal into a university. This required both a change in Alberta government policy and transformation of the institution itself. Both events took place in a national context in which there was a certain tension between the innovative provinces that had authorized college degrees and new degree providers, both internal and external, and the public universities that hitherto had enjoyed a monopoly on degree granting. Mount Royal's final conversion into a university was entwined with events at the national level.

Meanwhile, Alberta underwent another tumultuous period of boom and bust. For seven years provincial revenues burgeoned because of the rising price of oil and growing gas exports. The annual average price of oil rose steadily from $27 a barrel in 2000 to $50 in 2005, $64 in 2007, and then $96 in 2008 (with a peak of $147 in October). Meanwhile, royalties from natural gas exports rose steadily, becoming the single largest source of revenue. By 2005 the government had liquidated its debt, and Premier Klein announced a "prosperity bonus" of $400 (tax-free) for every person in Alberta, at a cost of $1.4 billion of the province's $6.8 billion surplus.[2] Calgary's population continued to grow, reaching 961,000 in 2008,[3] and the city sprawled out further in all directions. Thanks to high-rise developments and lengthening transportation times, the downtown revived as a residential node of its own. Mirroring the price of oil, the average price of a single-family home soared to $474,000 in 2008, double the 2000 level.[4] The economic boom was facilitated by easy credit arising from the deregulation of financial institutions in the United States and elsewhere, credit that fuelled a boom in home construction and real estate prices as people sought to use such easy credit to acquire a property or a better one.

In the fall of 2008 the boom collapsed, with the effects spreading immediately from the United States to the rest of the world thanks to the "securitization" of loans involving many financial institutions. Within weeks the price of oil fell from $135 a barrel to $34 in early 2009 and only slowly rose in 2009 to the $65–$75 range and in 2010 to the $70–$90 range. This entailed a huge loss of royalty revenue. Equally serious, the price of natural gas exports fell to about one-third of what it had been because a new technology enabled Americans to recover gas from plentiful shale deposits. Yet Calgary's economy was only moderately affected by the financial crisis. In March 2009, the unemployment rate was a comparatively low 4.5 per cent,[5] and the average cost of a home had fallen to $420,000, down 11 per cent from a year earlier.[6] However, in-migration nearly ceased,[7] and government revenues collapsed. In his 2009–10 budget, the minister of finance declared that "Alberta is facing our first recession since 1986."[8] The post-secondary institutions were advised that they would receive zero change in their operating grants for 2010–11 and 2011–12. Indeed, it soon became clear that the deficit projection was underestimated and another period of fiscal retrenchment in government services began. As before, the demand for admissions in colleges and universities rose as people who had deferred education during the boom years sought to strengthen their credentials.

THE NEW PRESIDENT

On 1 September 2003 Dr. Dave Marshall, formerly president of Nipissing University, became president of Mount Royal College – the first former university president to hold the post. Born in Fergus, Ontario, Marshall had earned a B.Sc. in chemistry at the University of Western Ontario, an M.Ed. and a Ph.D. in Educational Administration at the University of Alberta. Along the way he held a series of interesting jobs in far-flung locations, serving as an instructional designer for Athabasca University, an instructional technologist in the Gordon Robertson Educational Centre in Frobisher Bay, as director of a CIDA-sponsored project in St. Lucia in the Caribbean, and as Director of Regional Services Branch in the Department of Education. His academic career began as a high-school teacher in Collingwood and Sault Ste. Marie, where he taught math, physical education, biology, chemistry, physics, and instrumental music. His university career began in the Department of Education Administration at the University of Manitoba, after which he moved to Nipissing University College in 1985 as the dean of Education. In 1990 he became president of Nipissing and served in that capacity for thirteen years.[9]

At Nipissing, one of his major responsibilities was completing Nipissing's transformation from a university college affiliated with Laurentian University into an independent undergraduate university, Nipissing University. In addition, as chair of a joint college-university committee, he had played a key role in relations between Ontario's colleges and universities, a complex relationship because of the lack of university-transfer programs within the colleges and a weak credit transfer

David G. Marshall, President 2003-2011. Photographer: Brian Hawkes Photographic Inc.; Mount Royal University, Office of the President.

body. He was familiar with the debate in Ontario over Queen's University's invocation of AUCC membership criteria to screen out students with degrees from non-conventional providers. He had been involved in discussions relating to issues raised by Ontario's college degrees. Moreover, as a scholar, he made credit transfer, credential recognition, institutional recognition, and related matters the focal point of many publications – and continued to publish on such topics as president of Mount Royal. On taking the job, he remarked: "The chance to see a college undergo the change to a unique kind of university is an opportunity I couldn't resist. I am excited to have the chance to do it all over again."[10] As if Mount Royal's proposed transformation into a university were not enough of a challenge, the college's announcement of his appointment promised even more: "Dr. Marshall will be instrumental in affirming Mount Royal's place among Canada's premier institutes of higher learning.

He will be a powerful advocate for the institution's transformation into a learning- and teaching-centred undergraduate university and will guide the creation of one of North America's finest teaching and learning environments."[11] Because of his range of experience and familiarity with system issues, he was also to become a member of the Higher Education Quality Council of Ontario (HEQO), a body responsible for assessing and reporting on the quality of higher education in Ontario.

In an all-college meeting held on 12 September 2003, Marshall said that his three main priorities would be mandate change, the budget process, and better communication.[12] Among other things, he tried to quiet fears that the transformation would entail the dismissal of faculty and lead to the end of applied degrees. On the latter point, he said: "We'd probably want to change some part of the applied degrees, or at least have a stream in the applied degrees, that would be more of a liberal arts stream, a little more of an academic component. Make them a little more university level."[13]

Marshall worked well with the senior administrators in place when he arrived – Judy Eifert (formerly Lathrop) as vice-president, Academic, Hunter Wight, as vice-president, External Relations, Ken Robson, vice-president, Student Affairs and Campus Life (2000), and Richard E. M. Roberts, vice-president, Administrative Services, who had just begun. In September 2004 he advised the board that he wished to renew Eifert for a further term and to name her as Provost.[14] However, things then came apart. Earlier in the year budget cuts had been required to reach a balance for 2004–5. During the budget deliberations that spring the initial scenarios showed a major deficit, leading to a plan of retrenchment that entailed, among other things, "the restructuring of faculty positions or adjustments to course delivery. Full-time faculty positions will be left vacant or filled with part-time instructors, some courses will be reduced, program quotas will be adjusted and other courses will set increased capacity," including English courses.[15] Calling a town-hall meeting to explain the situation, Marshall said that "you can't cut $5 million from our budget and not affect somebody's experience. Let's not be naïve. The whole goal of what we're trying to do of course is damage control, not damage zero. We have to find a lot of money out of our budget and everyone will have that effect their quality of life and their quality of experience in some way, shape or form and to say otherwise would be naïve and misleading."[16]

It was against this backdrop that in October 2004 the board received the 2003–4 financial statements, which revealed that in the previous year the three veteran vice-presidents had received "retention payments" to stay and make "all reasonable effort to ensure that they contributed to the [new] president's success and transition." The story in the *Reflector* erroneously linked the payments to the budget cuts for 2004–5[17] but the facts were irrelevant. For their own reasons, the MRFA and Students' Association organized protest meetings and passed resolutions of non-confidence in the board, which had approved the payments.[18] Responding to the agitation, Marshall called an all-staff meeting to defend the board and the vice-presidents publicly and to answer questions, but this did little to quiet the tempest. The chairman of the board, Harold Kvisle, then invited representatives of the faculty, staff, and student associations to a special board meeting to discuss their concerns and "agendas," including whether their goals were to change "the decision-making process, to dismiss the board, to change the governance practices of the institution." Though the representatives claimed that the only issue was the money involved in a time of financial constraint, there were signs of other issues, such as an emotional complaint that faculty members were not respected by the administration. The discussion also revealed that since the mid-1990s the board had assigned the determination of administrative compensation to a committee of "public" members and that the committee had neither informed the rest of the board nor asked for its confirmation of its decisions.[19] The board agreed to refer the matter to the provincial auditor (who eventually found against the practice), providing one outcome to the meeting that everyone could agree on.[20] However, it was clear that the board and Marshall were coping with historical baggage, with grievances real and imagined focusing on continuing members of the senior administration.

The only way out, without jeopardizing the transformation agenda and continuing if not worsening the polarization, everyone recognized – including Eifert and Robson, who discussed alternative ways

Harold (Hal) N. Kvisle, Chairman of the Board 2002–7. Mount Royal University Executive Records ER-GO010-05K.

to proceed with Marshall – was to effect changes in personnel. This led to the departure of both people – Robson, in a reorganization in November 2004, and Eifert, following a brief leave, by resignation in February 2005. The Library and Enrolment Services were assigned to the vice-president, Academic, while Health Services, Athletics, Residences, the Learning Skills Centre, and the Career Centre were united a new unit, Student Affairs and Campus Life, "under the temporary watch of current campus life director Brian Fleming."[21] Eifert's resignation opened the way for a search for a new vice-president, Academic and Provost.[22] "Judy's long and distinguished career at Mount Royal spans more than 30 years," Marshall said. "Her leadership in vital administrative roles has been instrumental in achieving significant advances at Mount Royal and in post-secondary education across Alberta and beyond."[23] The departures of Robson and Eifert marked the end of an era, for both were exceptional administrators who had played formative roles in making the college what it was in 2004.

The search for a new vice-president, Academic and Provost culminated in the appointment of Dr. Robin Fisher, who began his duties in September 2004. A New Zealander by origin, Fisher had earned his Ph.D. at the University of British Columbia in First Nations and BC history.[24] His career then took him through three universities in their formative stages: Simon Fraser University in 1972, the University of Northern British Columbia in 1993 as dean of the College of Arts, Social and Health Sciences, and, in 2002, the University of Regina, as dean of Arts. His experience in new institutions, the latter one of the original western Methodist colleges, made him a natural choice for his new position at Mount Royal. By the start of the 2004–5 academic year, the senior administration consisted of Marshall, Fisher, and Richard Roberts, the new vice-president, Administrative Services, Hunter Wight, vice-president, External Relations, and Brian Fleming, Executive Director, Student Affairs and Campus Life, responsible for student experience.

The style of the new administration was markedly different from that of the outgoing one. Wood, Eifert, and Robson had spent more than thirty years at Mount Royal, came from within the faculty family, were familiar with the details and history of every issue that came to the fore, and carried the scars of old tussles.

By contrast, Marshall and Fisher were outsiders, free of the taint of the past, and committed to a transformational agenda that required considerable delegation of authority, higher faculty salaries, and lower teaching loads – all popular outcomes. Their main focus for the next six years was to secure approval for the transformation of the college into a university and to set the internal foundations for that transformation.

In the summer of 2003 the leaders of the college – including Wood, Wight, and Jack Donahue, a board member and friend of Premier Klein – had believed that the decision to make Mount Royal into a university was at hand. That turned out to be an illusion. Resistance to the idea was gathering behind the scene and caused the government to back away. Thus, instead of a sprint to new institutional status, Marshall and his team were to find themselves involved in a six-year marathon. In the process, Marshall was to exploit the question of national credibility to great effect.

THE CHANGING POST-SECONDARY SCENE

Ever since the conversion of most religiously affiliated universities into publicly supported secular institutions in eastern and central Canada, the credibility of Canadian degree programs had been a simple matter. Degrees were offered by public universities. Their public standing, their growing similarity of mission and governance structures, and their shared use of faculty members in evaluating research projects, and in some cases programs, were taken to be a sufficient gauge of quality.[25] This picture began to change in 1983 when Ontario's Degree Granting Act, regulating degree granting for the first time and requiring degree-granting institutions to rest on an Ontario statute, opened a loophole for the granting of a "ministerial consent" for individual degree programs offered by other institutions, whether from within or without the province, whether public or private. The act did not establish any vehicle for considering applications, so the process remained a "black box." In 1984, Alberta's Private Colleges Accreditation Act opened up the local post-secondary market to external and private universities but required all applications to pass through the scrutiny of the Private Colleges Accreditation Board (PCAB), an arms-length advisory body that made recommendations to the minister.[26] Thus, in both provinces, control of degree granting was no longer solely a legislative prerogative but was also now a matter of ministerial discretion. NAFTA made Ontario's "black box" operation unacceptable, and in 2000 the Post-secondary Education Choice and Excellence Act remedied that deficiency by establishing the Postsecondary Education Quality Assessment Board (PEQAB), an arms-length agency, to make recommendations on all applications for a ministerial consent in the light of public criteria and procedures.[27] The New Brunswick Degree Granting Act of 2001 also opened the way for private and external institutions to operate, with the assessment role, after a period of confusion, delegated to the Maritime Provinces Higher Education Commission.[28] In 2003, BC also opened its market to private and external public institutions and established the Degree Quality Assessment Board to review all new degree programs from all sources, public and private.[29]

Across the country, public universities which had previously enjoyed a near monopoly on degree granting looked askance at these new forms of degree-granting authority and the programs and institutions authorized by them.[30] Since the 1950s, public universities had been largely homogenized in their missions, internal structures, and self-conceptions (though funding them as if some were not much more research-intensive than others became an issue).[31] Their formally shared characteristics were enshrined in the membership criteria of the Association of Colleges and Universities of Canada (AUCC), a national clearing house and promotional body for universities, not an accrediting body. (It reviews institutions applying for membership but not its existing members.) When many public universities made membership in AUCC a "proxy" measure for institutional acceptance, the effect was to exclude most institutions and programs approved by the innovating provinces. Its position was that, given the lack of institutional accreditation in Canada, "historically, the appropriate provincial charter plus membership in the Association of Universities and Colleges of Canada have stood in lieu of institutional accreditation in higher education. . . . Canadian universities have a shared understanding of the value of each other's credentials."[32] Faced by a medley of potential applicants, AUCC soon tightened its membership requirements.

The behaviour of some public universities claiming that membership in AUCC was a proxy for accreditation, or general recognition, raised hackles in the provincial governments that had introduced college degrees, opened the doors to new private and external providers, and established quality assurance agencies to review the organizations and proposed programs of all new degree program providers. Government officials knew that the public universities did not undergo organization or in most cases program reviews comparable to those established by their new quality assurance agencies. Moreover, the universities' refusal to recognize the credentials of new institutions and programs appeared to challenge the authority of the provinces. This was particularly true in Alberta, whose strategic vision for lifelong learning was at odds with the behaviour of universities for whom lifelong learning meant only access to part-time study in their own courses, not a laddered or coordinated higher education system involving many players, public and private.

In 1999, as we have seen, Alberta had become the first province in Canada to make lifelong learning a formal government goal. "Our vision, a vision and set of proposed practices for providing integrated ladders of educational advancement," Premier Klein said in announcing Campus Alberta, "is for Alberta to become like one big campus where students enrolled in one post-secondary institution can take courses from any college or university in the province, either on-site or on-line from their homes, or on the job. We want to make lifelong learning a reality in this province." Campus Alberta would provide Albertans "access to a seamless system of adult learning, where institutions collaborate to deliver quality lifelong learning—where and when Albertans need it—to address their social, cultural, and economic needs."[33] Such sentiments went hand-in-hand with the notion that education could take many forms and be delivered in many settings and that credits for learning should be cumulative and portable. In 2004, the Post-secondary Learning Act established the Campus Alberta Quality Council (CAQC), an arms-length body whose responsibility was to undertake the review of all new degree programs offered by any institution and to review the organizations of institutions new to Alberta or new to degree granting. Credential recognition would be assured through the Alberta Council on Admissions and Transfers. Subsequent legislative changes empowered the CAQC to review proposed changes in institutional mandate. CAQC was to become the vehicle through which Mount Royal, among others, was to pass on its way to university standing.[34]

Alberta's comprehensive and flexible approach to lifelong learning found echoes in the deliberations of the Council of Ministers of Education, Canada (CMEC). Beginning with a meeting convoked by Ontario's Postsecondary Education Quality Assessment Board in February 2004, the government-based quality assurance agencies in British Columbia, Alberta, and the Maritimes tried to refocus the discussion of academic credibility by developing generic learning outcome standards for degrees and the principles and procedures for acceptable quality assurance activities required to generate trust that the standards were met in practice.[35] These were modelled on PEQAB's standards and procedures, which, in turn, reflected those used in Europe, the United States, and a growing number of other countries.[36] The working group was expanded to include representatives from all provinces and evolved into the Pan-Canadian Committee on the Quality Assurance of Degree Programs, a standing committee of CMEC. The first major upshot of its work was the *Ministerial Statement on Quality Assurance of Degree Education in Canada* approved by CMEC in 2007 as a guideline for *government* decisions relating to new programs or degree-granting institutions.[37] Alberta was deeply involved in this enterprise. Its PCAB provided administrative support for the Pan-Canadian Committee while Minister Dave Hancock strongly supported the *Ministerial Statement* as a step toward a national accreditation system.

Alas, the effort to deflect the discussion of academic credibility away from the input measures in AUCC's membership criteria (resources, policies, structures) to the demonstrable learning outcomes of programs had little immediate effect. CMEC is a talk shop, the ministers have little influence on university policies, and no change in credential recognition policies or practices resulted from its declaration. However, Canada at least now possessed published degree-level standards that could be compared with those in other jurisdictions, even if they had only a hortatory standing.

For the story in this book, the important point to note was Alberta's involvement in this national effort to deepen the discussion of academic credibility from the salient features of public universities to learning outcome standards and the quality assurance procedures necessary to demonstrate that they are met in practice. This background was to have some repercussions on the dialogue about Mount Royal's ambitions.

A Transformational Process

Comparing the challenge at Mount Royal to the situation at Nipissing University, which had begun as a teachers' college and evolved into a university, Marshall said in 2008 that they were "very different." Unlike Mount Royal, Nipissing had never offered non-degree–level courses. Its development had started with "university transfer in 1967 and [it]

then started doing first year and then it gradually did second year and then in the 1970s started doing full four-year degrees, but they weren't theirs. Laurentian University put their stamp on top of the degree," just as Mount Royal had delivered Athabasca programs but "Athabasca put the stamp on it." Nipissing "was always considered a university-level institution, . . . and as such it always had in place the university-level environment" in "its governance process" and "in faculty expectations, roles and responsibilities." "So it was a developmental process but not a transformation process. Mount Royal's, on the other hand, is indeed a transformation process, a process in which we are actually transforming a college-level environment into a university-level environment. To my knowledge, what we are doing here has not been done anywhere in Canada."[38] Thus, the process entailed more than a change of name or a change in the credentials being awarded. It was not an accretive but a transformative process that was required.

There were changes to be made by the college to adapt to AUCC admissions criteria where the decisions lay within its power and changes to be made that required government action. At bottom, the college needed: a legislative foundation for offering degrees and engaging in research, a bicameral governance system, a preponderance of students in degree programs, a qualified faculty, and an adequate library, faculty workload, and other policies enabling active faculty research. The first two (mandate, bicameralism) required government legislative changes while the others (faculty workload, library) required additional government funding.

Thus, Marshall, Fisher, the board, and others at Mount Royal found themselves campaigning on three fronts – carrying out the changes that could be made internally, both before and after government approval; persuading the government and ministry officials that legislative and funding changes were necessary, desirable and not as costly as they feared; and coping with the concerns of other colleges and universities.

Just as Wood had found it hard to secure the support of colleagues in other colleges, so did Marshall. Indeed, when he argued that legislation should be amended to permit colleges offering degree programs to opt for an "alternative Academic Council" (a GFC by another name) to satisfy AUCC admission requirements, not a single college or technical institute president supported him. In the end, Marshall argued that "each institution and each community should decide for their own reasons which types of degrees they wish to offer. And the aspiration or constraints of one institution should not hinder the development of another." As for Mount Royal, it would continue to seek designation as a university, including adjustments needed to create a GFC, and prepare an application for AUCC membership to ensure its programs would receive Canada-wide recognition.[39]

That the college was facing an uphill battle at the political level was suggested in December 2003 when Minister Lyle Oberg told the *Edmonton Journal* that he was opposed to creating more universities. "Realistically, we don't need any more universities in this province," he said, adding that giving college degree-granting status was enough. "He's wrong about that, and sadly misinformed," the *Calgary Herald* editorialized in response. "For students who are entering the job market directly after graduation, a college degree may be all they need. However, a college degree is a different animal than one granted by a university. College grads who want to continue their education at a university often find that college document doesn't carry equal weight."[40]

Marshall joined the issues in a campaign to modify Bill 43 (the Post-secondary Learning Act), which was under consideration when he arrived. Bill 43 combined and updated in one piece of legislation the four separate acts that governed Alberta's post-secondary institutions – the Universities Act, Colleges Act, Technical Institutes Act, and Banff Centre Act. Among other things, it established the Campus Alberta Quality Council to review all new degree program proposals and all new degree-granting organizations. It also enabled colleges and technical institutes to offer four-year foundation baccalaureate degrees. Marshall immediately flagged the dangers involved. "While Bill 43 will allow Mount Royal to seek approval to offer foundational baccalaureate degrees as a college," he wrote the minister in April 2004, "the institution now believes that the degrees that will best serve the needs of students cannot be offered from a college platform." Mount Royal would not offer degrees, he wrote, that were "not of the highest quality (*determined by recognition of the credential by other post-secondary institutions and by employers*)"; such recognition would only come "if the institution operated from a university platform"; hence Mount Royal needed to "be designated an undergraduate university." Things had changed since 1991, when the college had asked to become a degree-granting college. "Today . . . more than a decade of marketplace change, knowledge economy expansion, population growth and post-secondary diversification has led to further thought, research, consultation and discussion. The conclusion is that the two issues—the granting of undergraduate degrees and university status—are in fact, inextricably (and appropriately) linked."[41]

As the italicized phrase above indicated, Marshall stressed the importance of unquestioned acceptance of Mount Royal degrees across the country. This required working with the Alberta government on the "four pillars of government support that are required to develop a baccalaureate degree granting institution" capable of belonging to AUCC: "(1) approval of our proposed Alternative Academic Council model; (2) approval of new baccalaureate degree programs; (3) capital funding for enhanced infrastructure such as library and labs; and (4) approval of an appropriate level of operating funding for our new baccalaureate programs."[42] Marshall also noted "three conditions that college-level funding has not allowed Mount Royal to meet" AUCC requirements: "(a) undergraduate programs taught by senior academic staff; (b) a proven record of scholarship, academic inquiry and research; and (c) a library and other learning resources appropriate to the institution's mission, goals and programs."[43] The changes required of government, in sum, came down to three things: statutory authorization of bicameral governance, broader degree-granting authority, and additional capital and operating funding.[44]

As a matter of strategy, the college positioned its campaign for university standing in terms of accessibility, on meeting demand not otherwise met by the existing universities.[45] Its submissions to government flagged the statistics: the number of degree holders in Alberta was 17 per cent below the national average; it ranked eighth in the country in the proportion of 20–29-year-olds earning a degree; Calgary had thousands fewer post-secondary places than Edmonton; far too many students were being turned away by the University of Calgary (6,337) and Mount Royal (5,130 in 2002–3). The world was changing; society needed, and the college therefore needed, to offer higher level credentials.[46]

Marshall's emphasis on AUCC membership was not what Alberta government officials wanted to hear. Given that Ontario universities (including Nipissing) had refused to recognize Alberta's applied degrees, Marshall's mention of Ontario universities and AUCC criteria stirred criticism. However, he persisted. Why would a government be willing to permit Mount Royal to offer undergraduate degrees but not be willing to give it the conditions necessary for those degrees to be recognized by Canadian universities? For Marshall, "'Mount Royal University' is the only appropriate designation." Moreover, he wrote, continuing the line argued by Tom Wood, "Mount Royal proposes to be a very different kind of university, one focused on undergraduate teaching and learning. Its undergraduate programs will meet societal needs and workplace demands. Its model of faculty work and reward and its governance structure will ensure that it will continue to be a student-learning centred institution."[47]

Adding to the difficulty of making the case was the fact that there were four different ministers from 2003 to 2009, all from small towns and wary of appearing to give something to Calgary. When Klein was replaced as leader of the Conservative party in 2006, the "Calgary candidate," Jim Dinning, endorsed the idea of Mount Royal becoming a university while the "rural candidate," Ed Stelmach, who won, opposed the idea. The goal receded – but the college's campaign was to continue, raising the political heat on politicians who faced the public exposure of depressing accessibility statistics and broadsides from the Calgary press.

PREPARING INTERNALLY

Meanwhile, Marshall began the internal transformation of the college. He framed the process in terms of meeting the membership criteria of AUCC and benchmarking against other universities. In June 2004 he established the Transition Steering Committee to oversee the work of what became nine task forces and sub-committees. Its "strategies" included developing or acquiring "the tools necessary to gain AUCC membership," developing an Academic Plan and new

Mandate Statement, submitting new degree program proposals to government, communicating "Mount Royal's image in transition and prepar[ing] to brand a new Mount Royal," and both continuing the work of various task forces and implementing their recommendations.[48] Over the next three years the reports of the task forces fell like confetti.

Vision and Mandate

Throughout the transition, the college's "vision" remained that of becoming "Canada's leading undergraduate university educating and training individuals for success in the knowledge economy." Its core purpose "is to foster the success and satisfaction of our students in the pursuit of their current and future educational goals." Its "institutional values" are to be "relevant" in curriculum and credentials, "student/client-centred," "results-oriented and quality-focused," "creative, innovative and supportive," and "accessible," an "institution of first choice in a growing and diversifying post-secondary market."[49]

The Academic Planning Committee developed a new "mandate" statement that was approved by the board of governors on 16 September 2006 and by the Ministry of Advanced Education on 31 October 2006. It began: "Mount Royal is a learning community that focuses on instruction informed by scholarship. Its mission is to develop excellence in baccalaureate and applied degrees along with certificate and diploma programs. Mount Royal's programs combine liberal and applied studies in order to develop informed and thoughtful citizens and to provide individual fulfillment, opportunities for further study and employment to its graduates." To make the point clear, the document added that among the credentials Mount Royal would award were "university-level baccalaureate degrees and transfer programs."[50] Related statements declared that Mount Royal would be an undergraduate university "that focuses on instruction and is informed by scholarship" and committed to individual learning, general education, the value of experiential learning, and the achievement of program outcomes.[51] "Its main focus is on instruction and to foster the success and satisfaction of students in the pursuit of their educational goals."[52]

In January 2007 the Academic Planning Committee published a five-year academic plan (approved by the board a month earlier) which declared that Mount Royal would be "an institution different from what we are, but also different from many other universities in Canada." With recommendations in each category, the plan addressed the student experience, the faculty ("part of Mount Royal's difference from other universities will be that the balance between teaching and research will be different"),[53] programs ("a strong emphasis on general education, . . . experiential learning that integrates theory and practice, reference to outcomes in the development and evaluation of programs, the integration of teaching and scholarship"), scholarship and research ("scholarship that will … contribute to student learning and the student experience"), student services and support, technology, communities (alumni affairs, advisory committees), structure and organization ("no changes" except introduction of Faculty Councils in all Faculties, Schools, and Centres), resources, and implementation (an ongoing implementation committee).

On student experience, the linchpin of the new university, the plan elaborated familiar themes in the college's history.[54] On how programs are delivered, the Academic Plan stressed the value of "experiential education" of the kind found in the applied degrees; "we wish to maintain this approach in all our baccalaureate degrees" while recognizing that there are also other forms of "learning by doing," including participation in scholarship and research. In addition, the college was committed to lifelong learning and would enable students to transfer to other institutions, would strive to become "more creative" in integrating credit and credit-free programming and credits, and to be "judicious" in distance education, where its "face-to-face learning experience" would be diluted.[55]

As part of this reconsideration of its identity, the college redefined its general education requirements – the core syllabus of learning required of all degree-level students. The Committee on Program Definition and General Education recommended that all degree programs must include general education courses in four clusters: Numeracy and Scientific Literacy; Community and Society; Values, Beliefs, and Identity; and Communication. Students must take a one-semester foundation course in each cluster, followed by other general-education–denominated courses in years two and three. No student could satisfy the requirements without taking at least two courses in Mathematics or Science.[56] One unusual feature of the requirements was that they required "vertical" completion of the general education requirement, the first-year year courses becoming the gateways to those at the second year, and the second-year courses gateways to later courses. The clusters implied that general education courses would be taught by several Faculties, distributing not only the teaching load but also the shared sense of engagement in the core curriculum.

Governance

The Task Force on Institutional Governance recommended a new governance model ("the appropriate bicameral governance structure required for Mount Royal College, both present and future") and a transitional arrangement pending the eventual full establishment of bicameral governance.[57] Its report, filed in September 2005, recommended "key principles" for change: "The ultimate responsibility for the operation of the institution is vested in the board of governors"; "there must be a clear distinction between the powers and duties of the governing body and academic decision-making body"; "faculty, support staff and students, as well as public members should be represented on the board," and in greater numbers (three faculty, two staff, two students) to permit more diversity of opinion; "accommodation should be made for alumni participation on the board of governors"; "the academic decision making body should be representative of all academic constituents," with academic staff comprising "at least two thirds of the total number of members of the academic governing body"; and "the president should be the chair of the academic governing body."[58] In addition, the report recommended a change in the size and composition of the governing board.[59] The board concluded that the new board should consist of 19–22 members, with two-thirds external members (the inverse of the Academic Council, which would be two-thirds internal members).[60]

One of the particularly sensitive issues involved in this restructuring was the role of the MRFA in designating faculty members for collegial bodies. As we have seen, the MRFA had always opposed any form of election or selection other than through its auspices. This practice, however, did not square with what most people in universities consider to be collegial governance, wherein faculty members directly elect their own representatives to an academic council in their unit or to the GFC at the collective level. This was not an easy transformation for the MRFA and required a level of trust that initially did not exist. Indeed, it took a good deal of good-faith dialogue to persuade the leadership of the MRFA to accept the idea. Robin Fisher worked closely with David Hyttenrauch, president of the MRFA, to build the necessary level of trust. As part of the effort, the administration and the MRFA co-hosted a lecture series on "Building a Different University."[61] That the full implications of bicameral governance were subtle and not immediately grasped by the MRFA became evident when it asked for certain standards assigned to the new GFC to be enshrined in the collective agreement with the board of governors – an act that would have made a matter fully within the control of the GFC, which had two-thirds faculty membership, subject to the approval of the board, which otherwise had no role in that regard. Marshall persuaded the MRFA to drop the idea. Advised that the faculty members were caucusing in advance of meetings, he asked whether he could join them for the discussion.

Other Changes

By contrast with the shift in governance, the other transformations were equally necessary but less dramatic. The Climate for Change Task Force examined "potentially contentious and divisive issues surrounding change." The Credit Accounting Task Force examined the nature of course credits and the length of the semester and reading week, and recommended standardizing course credits on a three-credit basis (per semester) rather than by contact hours. The Task Force on Research recommended establishment of a Research Advisory Council for "policies, programs and other activities related to encouraging, recognizing and supporting RSA" (Research, Scholarly Activity, Artistic Activity). It identified "three indicators … of progress in developing a culture of research": proportion of faculty engaged in research, external research grants, and student involvement in research. The purpose of research would be "similar to that at most Canadian primarily undergraduate universities." Some 15–20 per cent of the faculty was currently engaged in research and the task force projected

that 80 per cent would be by 2012, plus about 10 per cent of senior students.[62] The Task Force on Faculty Roles and Responsibilities recommended that faculty members should choose every three years between two "patterns": "the teaching/scholarship pattern or the teaching-intensive pattern." Faculty members selecting "the teaching/scholarship pattern would teach six (three-credit) [semester] courses or equivalent and those selecting the teaching-intensive pattern would teach eight (three-credit) [semester] courses or equivalent."[63]

The Institutional Accreditation and Review Task Force examined AUCC's criteria for accreditation and Campus Alberta Quality Council's requirements with a view to ensuring that the college would meet the necessary requirements. The Institutional Positioning Task Force developed a seven-year plan to position Mount Royal's undergraduate-university vision in the marketplace. The Program Task Force sought to align programs with degree-granting criteria across Canada. (Marshall asked it to address the degree-level standards of Ontario's PEQAB.) The Student Recruitment and Retention Task Force developed proposals to ensure that the college retained its current market share.[64] And the Strategic Technology Planning Committee recommended ways to enhance college operations through the use of technology in teaching, learning and scholarship, administrative services, and communications and community relations.[65]

The Task Force on Library Transition benchmarked the library against those in comparator institutions, assessed the learning resource needs of anticipated new programs, addressed the growing use of digitized databases and initiatives for sharing library resources in Alberta, and proposed major additional expenditures and new facilities. Despite annual increases and special supplements (e.g., $1.36 million from 2000 to 2003, $550,000 in 2003–4, $450,000 in 2004–5), the expansion in student numbers and the weeding out of outdated materials had left the college at the same standard throughout the period – 25 volumes per student, "far short of all Canadian undergraduate universities and B.C. university colleges."[66] Thereafter the college steadily increased its allocation for acquisitions (it was just over $1.2 million in 2008–9). From 2000 to 2009, the physical holdings in the library rose from 117,709 to 216,490, while electronic journal holdings nearly doubled as well. In February 2006, Marshall advised Minister Hancock that the "enhancement of our library is Mount Royal's highest facility priority."[67] While this was happening, Alberta institutions were collaborating on the development of the Lois Hole Campus Alberta Digital Library linking thirty-five post-secondary libraries, including Mount Royal. In December 2008, the government agreed to provide $2.8 million to plan a new library facility. As one would expect of an institution offering new degree programs, the library's holdings, when compared with those in fourteen peer institutions, were smaller than those of the peer group libraries as a whole but consisted "of quality materials that have been carefully chosen to match the programs offered at the institution." The comparison also indicated that Mount Royal "ranked second highest in the number of student contacts at reference desks. In terms of instruction sessions offered to students by library staff, Mount Royal ranked significantly higher – in fact, more than double – compared to its peer institutions."[68]

Meanwhile, the college had been undergoing some other forms of transformation. One notable addition was the establishment of a Faculty of Teaching and Learning, "where students become educators and educators become students, exploring new ways to enhance their already exceptional teaching talents. Through the Faculty of Teaching and Learning, Mount Royal students can begin their journey to becoming teachers, while faculty can draw on resources and support to explore and enhance their instructional practice. Unique in Canada, the Faculty of Teaching and Learning provides institutional leadership in teaching and learning, and is a significant milestone in Mount Royal's aspiration to becoming a university." The faculty consists of four units, all focusing on student learning and teaching excellence:

- The Department of Education and Schooling, which offers the first two years of a Bachelor of Education degree leading to another institution;

- The Department of General Education, which coordinates and ensures the effectiveness of the general education component that normally consists of

twelve semester courses or 30 per cent of course credits in a program;

- The Academic Development Centre, which supports "the professional development of Mount Royal faculty through programs and services intended to foster teaching excellence and innovation," including expertise and support "in the areas of classroom teaching, learning technologies, curriculum design, online and blended delivery, media production, audio/video conferencing and scholarship related to teaching and learning"; and

- The Institute for Scholarship of Teaching and Learning, a body that "encourages the teaching-learning process by facilitating teaching-learning research, creating a culture of inquiry, and advancing our understanding of teaching and learning. Scholarship and practice are brought together in creative ways by locating the Institute in the Faculty of Teaching and Learning."

The point of establishing this cluster as a faculty was to underline the college's commitment to effective learning and innovative and excellent instruction and to mark its distinctive character as an undergraduate university.

Another notable innovation was the development of a new centre for Aboriginal students, who, by 2000, numbered 400–500 on campus. In 2007, an agreement between the college and Treaty 7 nations led to establishment of the Iniskim Centre as a "community within the community, a place fostering the academic success of aboriginal students and also welcoming the entire MRC community." Jolain Foster, a Mount Royal graduate, was named director. While a student at the college, she said, "I was really trying to figure out who I was in this new community and what my community expected of me, what my family expected of me and how my culture played a role in it." Robin Fisher, the vice-president, Academic, himself a specialist in Native history, said that "in our time and

Aboriginal students raise a tipi at the East Gate Entrance.
Photographer Anika Van Wyk; Mount Royal University
Marketing and Communications.

place, Mount Royal has a particular responsibility to provide educational opportunities for Aboriginal students. This responsibility arises from our past and will determine our future. It is time that Aboriginal people had equal opportunities in Western Canada and post-secondary education is perhaps the most important doorway to those opportunities."[69]

Thus, the college developed not only a better idea of what the transformation into a university implied but also a stronger consensus about what new directions should be taken. Faculty participation in the planning was so comprehensive that opposition was muted. By this time, moreover, many of the generation of faculty hired in the 1960s and early 1970s had retired and the new faculty members who replaced them were looking ahead rather than backward.

Collective Bargaining

The transformation to university standing also had implications for collective bargaining. Indeed, without the flexibility of the leadership of the MRFA in this regard, notably the good offices of David Hyttenrauch, the president, it would have been nearly impossible to make the changes needed to transform the college into a university. Even so, there were limits on what the leadership could accept. Imbued with the egalitarian values of the college, in which faculty members were paid according to seniority and qualifications rather than performance, in which everyone held the same Instructor rank, in which the concept of merit pay was heretical, MRFA's bargainers would go only so far in accepting the more meritocratic views attached to work in most universities. The final collective agreement with the MRFA under the college, covering the period from 1 July 2008 to 30 June 2010, embodied the resulting compromises. In this respect, it was fortunate for Mount Royal that collective bargaining took place within an institutional framework rather than at the provincial level, as in Ontario or Quebec. As members in the evolving college culture, permeated increasingly with the desirability of degree granting and becoming a university, the Faculty Association was able to respond in ways unimaginable if, say, a provincial body encompassing all colleges and technical institutes had been in place.

As in the past, the work year in the new agreement was described as "eight (8) months of teaching responsibility, two (2) months of intersessional period developmental responsibility, [and] two (2) months of vacation" (article 11.2). The proposed "work patterns" were built into the agreement: "Teaching-Service Pattern – a full-time workload" (defined as "normally . . . 384 scheduled instructional course hours annually" (article 11.4.1); and the "Teaching-Scholarship Pattern – a full-time workload" ("normally 288 scheduled instructional hours annually," article 11.5.1). Marshall described the weighting for faculty responsibilities as 60 per cent for teaching, 30 per cent for scholarship, and 10 per cent for service – a break from the standard university model of 40–40–20.[70] Article 4.2 specified faculty ranks: Lecturer, Assistant Professor, Associate Professor, and Professor. The salary scale ran from $52,322 (lowest of five categories based on academic qualifications) to $112,505 in the highest category (twenty-five years of service) (article 10.1). Though, for "reasons deemed valid and approved by the board" (article 10.3.1.3), it could appoint someone above the normal step for his/her credentials and experience, the compensation system rested essentially on the mix of seniority and qualifications (article 10.3). There was no mention of merit pay. The major categories of leaves were continued: four-for-five, professional, and sabbatical. Professional development funds were distributed, on a per capita basis, to elected faculty committees in each academic unit for their distribution. As we have seen, the right to strike had disappeared with the Post-Secondary Learning Act of 2004, so the dispute-resolution procedures in the agreement largely replicated the process in the Labour Act – mediation, followed if necessary by compulsory binding arbitration (article 18).

An important addition, one resisted by the MRFA earlier, spelled out the process for the review of tenured faculty members by "the appropriate Dean/Director . . . in consultation with the Chair, based on the [faculty member's] Annual Report and current curriculum vitae." Where performance was found unsatisfactory, the report was submitted to the Faculty Review Committee, a standing committee of Faculty Council. Allowing for dialogue, this process could lead either to a revised performance plan or to a report that performance was unsatisfactory, after which the matter fell into administration hands for action (article 19).

The AUCC managed to make it into the collective agreement in the clauses on initial appointments: "if a candidate for a tenurable [or associate professor] appointment has previously attained the rank . . . at an AUCC accredited [sic], or equivalent institution, the selection committee may recommend appointment" with tenure or at that rank. Each academic unit was to elect Tenure and Promotion Committee (article 5.3); there was also an Institutional Tenure and Promotion Committee (article 5.4) chaired by the vice-president, Academic and elected by the Academic Council. The criteria for tenure included: "evidence of effective teaching, evidence of scholarship, where applicable, evidence of service, and evidence that the duties have been carried out in a responsible and professional manner" (article 6.2). An addendum on teaching, scholarship, and service defined the activities involved and by implication the evidence required.

The fact that the agreement was seen as unfinished business was suggested by several appendices. Appendix B, "Principles of a Tenure, Promotion and Rank System at Mount Royal," set out guidelines that essentially ensured that people in the Teaching-Service track would not be discriminated against in promotion and other matters – a gesture to the residual college component. By contrast, the Memorandum of Understanding dated June 2008, "regarding faculty work patterns and other transition issues," declared that "the college's goal is to maximize the number of faculty on the Teaching-Scholarship-Service (TSS) work pattern in any given year and that the college would "fund no less than 55 per cent of all tenured and tenurable faculty to enter the TSS work pattern" – an indication of where the predominant allocation of resources would be in the future. Another Memorandum of

Understanding dated 30 May 2008 set up a committee to flesh out the content and structure of the faculty member's annual report. Another memorandum dated 30 June 2009 dealt resolved the rank issue as follows: as of 1 July 2009, all tenured faculty members would become Associate Professors, while all tenurable faculty members would become Assistant Professors. Yet another memorandum (30 June 2009) agreed that the parties would ask the Appointments, Promotion and Tenure Committee of the General Faculties Council "to undertake the development of detailed criteria and standards for promotion to the rank of Professor." That work was completed in early 2010, with the GFC's recommendation being approved by the board of governors.

A combination of replacement hires and new positions implied that by 2010 up to fifty new faculty members would be hired, with more to come, raising interesting questions about the extent to which newcomers change the nature of faculty culture at Mount Royal and the extent to which they are absorbed into it.

GRUDGING GOVERNMENT POLICY CHANGES

While readying itself internally, Mount Royal pursued critical transformation issues with the government and officialdom. There were three key changes required – the legal capacity to establish a bicameral governance system, approval to change the institution's name to "university," and appropriate capital and operating funding.

The process took much longer than anyone in the college had imagined. Thinking that the decision was near in the fall of 2004, Marshall, Wight, and board members asked Minister Dave Hancock for an early decision to permit timely planning for the conversion in 2006–7. He received documents on themes such as "The Tools of Accreditation as a University-level Institution," "Implications for Mount Royal of Not Becoming a University-level Institution," "System Implications of Not Establishing Mount Royal University," "System Concerns Regarding the Establishing of Mount Royal University," and "Options for Increasing Access to University-level Degrees in Calgary."[71] However, in April 2005, Hancock advised the college that the decision would be deferred pending a "comprehensive review" of the post-secondary educational system. Premier Klein, who had earlier indicated support in discussions with college officials, now backed away. The college, he said, had claimed that "the university and the academic community support them in this endeavour. I'm finding out otherwise."[72] Apparently the presidents of the University of Calgary and the University of Lethbridge had criticized the proposal for reasons "ranging from program duplication to sparse provincial funds being stretched to accommodate a new university."[73] In response, Marshall said that the college was only requesting $5 million more for operating costs and another $17 million in capital costs to grow by 2,500 students, hardly numbers that justified alarm. "Whatever time the minister needs to decide on the approval is fine with me, as long as it's the right answer," Marshall said. 'We can wait until the mandate comes and then develop our degree proposal or we can develop our degree proposal and wait for the mandate. We'll wait for the advice of the minister before we decide anything. They're well aware of our timelines."[74]

The *Calgary Herald* did not need to be diplomatic. Columnist Don Braid reacted strongly: "Absurdities abound in the government's latest denial of university status for Mount Royal College. Here's just one: Every year when Mount Royal College has its graduation, a group of students are handed full university degrees in nursing, history, psychology or English. Those grads have taken all their classes at Mount Royal from college faculty members. But the sheepskins don't mention Mount Royal. Instead they say 'Athabasca University,' and they're handed out by the Athabasca provost." He quoted a Liberal MLA, Dave Taylor, to the effect that the rural part of the Conservative caucus opposed any decisions in favour of Calgary. "Throw in Dave Hancock's widely rumored candidacy for the party leadership," Braid added, "and you have a recipe for more delay. No pretender to Ralph Klein's throne wants to annoy the rural kingmakers."[75]

Wounded, Hancock explained that the decision required "full involvement of stakeholders and Albertans," without explaining why he did not already have such information in hand or what issues he expected the consultation to address. One could imagine alternatives for Mount Royal, he said, though he mentioned only one: "college degree-granting status … without it becoming a university."[76] Braid called him to discuss the issues, and following that interview, in a piece entitled "Hancock's politics not Calgary's concern," reiterated his conclusion that Hancock's motive was his leadership ambition and his fear of offending rural party members by making a concession to a Calgary institution. As a result, Braid wrote, "by August this year, as many as 3,000 rejection slips will go out to qualified Calgary students for whom there's no space. Edmonton has no such problem because the capital has far more post-secondary spaces than Calgary. To be precise, it has 8,387 more places. That isn't just a large discrepancy between two cities of roughly equal size – it's monstrous. . . . With such a severe crunch at U of C, Mount Royal has geared up to provide more degree transfer programs. Fully 80 per cent of MRC students are now in these courses. The most seamless solution is to make Mount Royal a university so students can earn their entire degrees there."[77]

Discussions with Hancock continued, and in December 2005 the minister wrote Hal Kvisle to respond to issues raised by the college. On the question of establishing the legitimacy of degrees, he wrote: "Granting Mount Royal university status on the basis that such status is the only way to give its degrees credibility goes directly against the fundamental rationale of the [Postsecondary Learning] Act, undermines the concept of degree granting as provided in the Act, and undermines the process we have engaged in nationally" to "establish through the Council of Ministers of Education, Canada, a national accreditation process." "I . . . could not and would not recommend university status on that basis." Yet, he acknowledged, "in the absence of national accreditation standards in Canada, some institutions use AUCC membership as a proxy measure." Accordingly he would help Mount Royal meet the requirements, "provided that it is always fundamentally clear that the rationale sees this as an enhancement and not as the sole mechanism for degree recognition." He added that the government planned "to define the roles and responsibilities of each institution within a comprehensive advanced learning system." "Prudence would suggest" the naming issue should "be kept in abeyance until completion of the roles and mandates discussion contemplated by the Alberta Learning process." As for AUCC membership,

he recognized the importance of the bicameral issue. To that end, "I have introduced an amendment … that would allow us to create a structure under which a board can create an academic council to which appropriate responsibilities for academic decisions can be delegated and which has a membership that reflects its responsibility."[78]

Indeed, the issue of collegial governance had in fact been sharpened by the Post-secondary Learning Act of 2004. Section 46, which spelled out the membership and authority of the Academic Council, scrapped the requirement that the faculty and student associations and the board would negotiate its role in favour of a body which "shall make recommendations or reports to the board with respect to any matter that the board refers to the academic council." This was a step backward in terms of the idea that collegial governance was in some degree a negotiated matter among institutional partners.

In 2006, an amendment provided for "Alternative Academic Councils," and Regulation 219/2006 enabled colleges and technical institutes with more than 40 per cent of their students in degree programs to apply to the minister "to dissolve" their existing academic council and to establish "an alternative academic council." The new "model" must include the president, the academic vice-president, "not more than ten senior officials appointed by the board of the college or technical institute," and "sufficient academic staff members of the public college or technical institute, elected in accordance with a process determined by the board of the public college or technical institute," "additional members appointed by the board of the public college or technical institute," and "the academic staff members elected . . . must comprise the majority of the members of the alternative academic council." The powers of the Academic Council would be like those of the GFC. "Subject to the authority of the board," it would be responsible for "determining programs of study . . . , determining standards and policies respecting admission," "providing for the granting of degrees, other than honorary degrees, where the public college or technical institute has been designated as an institution that may grant degrees," "making rules respecting academic awards," "making recommendations and providing advice to the board of the public college . . . on academic programs and other matters considered by the academic council to be of interest to the public college or technical institute." "The president of the public college or technical institute, or the person designated by the president from among all of the members of the alternative academic council, must act as chair of the meetings of the alternative academic council."[79] On the basis of this change, Mount Royal moved quickly to establish its own General Faculties Council and to commence its bicameral governance system in the fall of 2008.[80]

Historians of the early years of Mount Royal University will want to assess the extent to which the new forms of governance led to a change in organizational culture, hopefully in a less polarized direction than existed in the public college. Certainly, the new forms of governance hold out some promise in that regard. They imply a reduced role for the MRFA, its functions narrowed to negotiating and administering the collective agreement on the faculty side. They imply a narrowed role for the board, formerly responsible for the entire operation but now focusing primarily on financial and property matters, collective agreements, and hiring and firing presidents. They empower faculty members both by assigning significant responsibility to collegial bodies they dominate and by requiring the direct election of faculty representatives to collegial decision-making bodies. The increased responsibility, moreover, implies the level of respect that some faculty members had felt was lacking under the old system. The new forms of governance also imply a less "managerial" role for senior administrators, less sheer "position power," and a larger need to exert a "collegial leadership" style.

While passing "the Mount Royal clause" permitting Alternative Academic Councils to be formed, the government moved in other ways to confine the institutions aspiring to be universities. In November 2007, it introduced a new classification scheme for post-secondary institutions which became the basis of the Post-Secondary Learning Amendment Act, 2008. The act distinguished between two categories of institution of relevance to Mount Royal:

Comprehensive Academic and Research Institutions (CARI). This category includes the University of Alberta, University of Calgary, University of Lethbridge, and Athabasca University.

Such institutions offer a comprehensive range of baccalaureate and graduate programs and have a mandate for comprehensive research activity.

Baccalaureate and Applied Studies Institutions (BASI). This category includes Mount Royal College and Grant MacEwan College. Such institutions offer foundation baccalaureate degrees in specific areas as well as certificate, diploma, and applied degree programs. Their research is limited to applied research and scholarly activity.[81]

The obvious purpose of this distinction was to keep Mount Royal and Grant MacEwan in the college category even as they offered four-year degree programs. They would be undergraduate universities but without the name university—or to reverse Mount Royal's earlier description of itself as "a college with a university atmosphere," they would be "universities with a college atmosphere." From Mount Royal's point of view, the distinction was another half-step that only meant that its struggle for fuller recognition would continue. It began a new campaign – to redefine the research constraint from one focusing on "applied" research (who can control what individual faculty members do?) to one focusing on the question of how "research-intensive" an institution is.

In 2007, with the change in bicameral governance in hand and with the expectation that it would meet AUCC requirements before students graduated, the college began its first four-year degree programs. The very first initiative, as in the past expansions of credentials, was Nursing. As a result of the college's own Bachelor of Nursing program, the collaborative nursing program with Athabasca University was to be phased out by 2010–11, and all students enrolling as of 2007 (graduates in 2011) would be in the Mount Royal program.[82] The announcement was made by Minister Horner at a large meeting on the college's campus; "Mount Royal College is now a degree-granting institution," he declared, upon which, the *Calgary Herald* reported, "the crowd went wild" and Marshall, who "became a little misty-eyed," declared that "I was absolutely over-whelmed by the moment

(L) Dave Marshall (Mount Royal College President) and The Honourable Doug Horner (Alberta Minister of Advanced Education and Technology), celebrate the formal announcement of Mount Royal College's first degree program, Bachelor of Nursing, March 15, 2007. Photographer Anika Van Wyk; Mount Royal University Marketing and Communications.

an actual cost-based approach rather than trying to compare costs with other institutions.

In recognition of the significance of the occasion, the college published in March 2007 a large "Certificate of Birth" in the *Calgary Herald* announcing "the birth of the first Mount Royal university degree."[85] A month later, "already recognized as a national leader in addressing the nursing credential issue" because of the grant received in 2003 to establish a means for incorporating foreign-trained nurses, "Mount Royal College received a grant from a forum of western provincial and territorial governments to show other western jurisdictions how to set up similar programs."[86] The Nursing program was also well on its way.

However, behind the scenes, things were not progressing so well. The long-standing tension with the department surfaced again. In December 2007 Marshall received a letter from Minister Horner that he was "unable to make further funding commitments for new programs or expansions" and that "system requests for program funding will substantially exceed whatever funds may be provided in Budget 2008."[87] This was stunning news to Marshall and Fisher, who had prepared five more applied degree programs for conversion into four-year programs for September 2008. The government's log rolling inspired the *Calgary Herald* to publish an acidic editorial: "With all of its oil wealth, [Alberta] has the lowest university participation rate in Canada. . . . Mount Royal's degree will be further diluted once British Columbia converts five colleges to universities. . . . Why should Alberta students pay the price of a devalued parchment?"[88]

When the department asked the college to add fifty more students to the nursing program, Marshall, with the aid of such comments, took advantage of the request to meet with Assistant Deputy Minister Philip Gougeon to go over the costs – about a million

and by the crowd and by the emotion. I realized this isn't just a press conference, it's a moment in history." Horner said that the government would provide a one-time $10 million investment for recruiting and program delivery.[83] The process of negotiating the funding had been challenging, Marshall said, as the college had resisted "85-cent nurses," a reference to the department's effort to get the college to accept a lower level of funding than the universities for the same program. "We've made it clear that unless we get comparable funding to other university programs, we just can't do it. Funding affects quality," he said. The funding was expected to provide for 980 students in all four years, but a later funding addition raised that number by about 200.[84] In the end, as part of the funding deal Marshall and the government agreed on dollars for the first year – and managed to persuade Gougeon that it made no sense to freeze the college in place when one could launch five programs for that amount of money.[89] Gougeon agreed, and persuaded the minister – or perhaps the officials had been the source of reluctance anyway. In any event, on 11 April 2008 Minister Doug Horner, along with the college's Minister of Justice and Attorney General Alison Redford (Mount Royal university-transfer BA-stream graduate, 1984), the MLA from the Calgary-Elbow riding in which the college was located, returned to campus for another large meeting to announce that Mount Royal would receive funding for five university programs:

- Bachelor of Arts, with majors in Anthropology, English, History, Policy Studies, Psychology, Sociology, and Spanish;

- Bachelor of Arts in Criminal Justice;

- Bachelor of Communication, with majors in Information Design, Journalism, and Public Relations;

- Bachelor of Science, with majors in Cellular and Molecular Biology, General Science, Geology, and Health Science; and

- Bachelor of Business Administration, with concentrations in Accounting, General Business, Human Resources, and Marketing.[90]

Thereafter the college could offer a reasonable span of foundation baccalaureate programs.

In addition to new programs and the other activities already mentioned, the college developed new activities to assist its conversion and satisfy not merely AUCC but best practice considerations. In 2007–8, for example, it introduced the Office of the Ombudsperson "to promote a respectful workplace by providing support and ensuring that all members of the campus community are treated fairly and equitably." It enhanced programs for "employee wellness" based on the Encana Wellness Centre which also served

Cathy L. Williams, Chair of the Board of Governors 2007-present. Photographer: Brodylo Morrow Photography; courtesy of Enbridge Inc.

members of the community for a fee. The Learning and Development program for employees offered courses in change management, time and meeting management, and other matters, including coaching sessions for individuals.[91]

In addition, the college enhanced its commitment to student success and high-quality services for students. The Division of Student Affairs and Campus Life (SACL) brought in an external team of three professionals to review its operations and committed to periodic review of both student and career services.[92] As there was a policy requiring such reviews for all academic programs and all services established in the 1980s, this renewed commitment indicates the short shelf life of such commitments.

The final steps in the college-to-university conversion took place in 2009. Minister Horner secured passage of the Post-Secondary Learning Amendment

The creation of Mount Royal University was announced on September 3, 2009. (L–R) Dave Marshall (Mount Royal University President), The Honourable Ed Stelmach (Premier of Alberta), The Honourable Doug Horner (Alberta Minister of Advanced Education and Technology), Cathy Williams (Chair, Mount Royal University Board of Governors). Photographer Mike Ridewood; Mount Royal University Marketing and Communications.

Board of Governors Chair Cathy Williams presents Mount Royal University's first honorary degree to Alberta Lieutenant Governor Norman L. Kwong (a 1949 graduate of Mount Royal College's Commercial program) on September 3, 2009. Photographer Mike Ridewood; Mount Royal University Marketing and Communications.

A special "transitional logo" was used as Mount Royal College became Mount Royal University. Design by Mount Royal University Marketing and Communications.

Act, 2009, which allowed members of the BASI institutional category to request the use of the word "university" in their name by an order-in-council.[93] Assessing the situation, Don Braid, in the *Calgary Herald*, described the bill as "one shrewd piece of political engineering by Doug Horner's Advanced Education Department. The wording allows Mount Royal to become a university very quickly because it already has seven degree programs that will, I'm told, fit nicely into the 'specified areas' . . . Mount Royal will become Alberta's fifth public university." Moreover, Minister Horner had "guided the whole process with considerable wisdom, by making sure Mount Royal was ready to be born as a first-class university, not some inferior wannabe."[94] The road had been long, with many obstacles and diversions. "The biggest barrier," Braid said, "was always the rivalry from other colleges and universities that didn't want one school – especially a Calgary one – to get a leg up. . . . Once it was even voted off the island at a meeting of post-secondary officials. A straw poll showed that nobody wanted Mount Royal to rise."[95]

Seizing the opportunity provided by the new situation, Cathy Williams, chair of Mount Royal's governing board, promptly requested permission to use the word 'university'. In a letter dated 15 July 2009, Horner responded that he was prepared to accede to Mount Royal's "request for a change to its name to include the term 'university,'" on the condition that it recognized that "it would continue to be a member of the BASI [college] category" and that "a name change should not be interpreted as an opportunity to broaden the breadth of programs or credentials currently offered in the BASI sector or to expand degree programs at the expense of certificate and diploma programs." "The BASI sector," Horner's letter went on, "focuses on teaching intensity while conducting scholarly research activity and where appropriate applied research, a strong focus on instruction will continue to be the mainstay of these types of institutions."[96] Once Williams signed on 22 July that the college accepted the conditions, the road was clear for the minister to seek the order-in-council to declare Mount Royal University.[97]

On 3 September 2009, in a special assembly and celebration at Mount Royal ("Mount Royal University Day"), Premier Ed Stelmach said that it "was very important for me to be here today for this special celebration because it's a great example of what Campus Alberta stands for and it's a big step in our government's plan to build the next generation economy in Alberta." "By the power of An Order in Council of the Government of Alberta," he declared, "from this day forward, this fine institution will be known as Mount Royal University." "As Calgary's oldest post-secondary institution Mount Royal has a strong history of serving the community . . . with top-quality, meaningful programs. Alberta is full of enterprising Mount Royal graduates who have made their mark on the social and economic face of our province." He came bearing a gift – the province would "provide funding for the development of Mount Royal University's new seal."[98] Lieutenant Governor Norman Kwong, a one-time student, was awarded the first honorary degree awarded by the new university – an honorary Bachelor of Arts degree. In an emotional address, he declared that "this school has achieved such great things, and I'm confident Mont Royal University will continue to make contributions in its new role."[99]

THE CHANGING STUDENT AND FACULTY PROFILE

The transformation of the college was reflected in its students and faculty, as reflected in the charts in Appendix 1 and Appendix 2. Some of the more salient trends are highlighted below. From 1966 to 2009, the credit student population had grown from 1,500 to 12,600 students, or 8,000 FLE (the new definition of a full-time student adopted in 1991). The introduction of the applied degrees beginning in 1996 changed the composition of the credit student body, and the introduction of four-year foundation programs in 2005 accelerated the change. These were among the more salient changes:

- A rising proportion of applicants entering directly from high school: 10–14 per cent in the 1990s, 37–38 per cent after the introduction of the applied degree programs, 45 per cent after the introduction of the foundation degree programs (2008);

TABLE 10.1 DISTRIBUTION OF STUDENTS BY TYPE OF PROGRAM, 1988–2008

Type	1988-89	1995-96	2003-04	2007-08
Career diploma	37.3 %	30.5 %	17.1%	13.9%
Arts & Science diploma	2.2	4.9		
Certificate	11.8	7.9	3.8	3.5
University Transfer	16.8	23.7	26.9	25.0
General & compensatory	31.8	26.8	20.4	19.1
Applied degree			21.8	26.7
4-year degree			10.0	12.0

- Changing enrolment patterns as students opted for higher over lower academic credentials (see Table 10.1);

- Longer programs implied spaces for fewer new students, and the total number of individual students stabilized at the 12,600 level in the early 2000s. Longer programs also implied fewer graduates, and the total of parchments awarded dropped from 1,461 in 2000–2001, to 995 in 2006–7 and 712 in 2007–8.[100]

- A rising proportion of courses accepted for transfers to other universities: from 45 per cent in 1989–90, 54 per cent in 1995–96, 74 per cent in 1998–99, and 85 per cent in 2005–6;[101]

- A growing integration of the college into degree-granting activity in the province, as shown by in-transfers from universities and out-transfers to universities: some 1,000–1,200 in-transfers a year in the early 2000s, about 50–58 per cent from Alberta universities and 27–29 per cent from another Alberta public college. And some 950–1,100 transfers a year to other institutions, 73–80 per cent to Alberta universities and 10–15 per cent to other colleges;[102]

- A rising appeal to students from further away: the proportion fell from the 83–84 per cent range from the 1960s through the 1990s to 77 per cent in the early 2000s.

Reflecting the general trend in post-secondary education, the proportion of female students continued to rise, reaching 63.5 per cent in 2007. In general, college students are older than university undergraduates, and the introduction of the degree programs and the higher proportion of students entering directly from high school led to a downward age trajectory. The average age of full-time students was 22 in 1980, rose to 25 during the recession in the mid-1980s, fell back to 22 in 2002–3, and then declined to 21.5 in 2007–8. It appears likely that the average age will further decline, as the proportion of students entering directly from high school rises. Whether it will affect the cultural tone of the campus will be seen, but one might anticipate problems associated with a younger student body.

The college always had a strong part-time student component. In the 1980s, about 28–30 per cent of the total consisted of part-time registrants in credit programs. Reflecting the appeal of the longer degree programs, the proportion declined slightly, to the 25–27 per cent range, beginning in the 1990s. Student satisfaction with their education has always been remarkably high – in the 94–98 per cent range. And, of those students looking for jobs, following the recession of the 1980s, over 90 per cent have found one within

Mount Royal College's first Instructor Emeritus Awards were presented in 2006 to (L-R) Mahfooz Kanwar (Sociology), Ken Hoeppner (English), Wayne Haglund (Geology) and Mike Fellows (Economics and Political Science). Photographer External Relations; Mount Royal University Marketing and Communications.

The Library has become increasingly popular with students who seek access to digital and online resources. Photographer Pablo Galvez; Mount Royal University Marketing and Communications.

six months of graduation, over 70 per cent in their field of study.[103]

Of the students giving Calgary as their home, about two-thirds come from the western quadrants: 41 per cent came from the southwest, 25 per cent from the northwest, 22 per cent from the southeast, and 11 per cent from the northeast. It was for that reason that in 1999–2000, the board had again discussed the issue of a campus on the eastern side of the city. Perhaps, as the college completes its next building projects and saturates its current campus, the thought of a satellite campus on the eastern side of the city will reappear. A survey of student characteristics in 2007 indicated that 89 per cent spoke English as their mother tongue, and 90 per cent were single. Aboriginals made up 1.8 per cent and "visa students" about 2.2 per cent.[104]

Government financial aid for students was especially needed during economic hard times. The total amount rose from $11.9 million in 1988–89 to $21.6 million in 2003–4, and stabilized in the $19 to $21 million range thereafter. In 1988–89, 48.7 per cent of the full-time students received loans; the proportion peaked in 1993–94 at 56.7 per cent and then fell to 42.1 per cent in 2003–4 and 35.2 per cent in 2007–9. The curve mirrored the economy – recession in the 1980s, slow recovery in the 1990s, and a boom in the first decade of the twenty-first century. The average loan (1992 dollars) was in the $4,600–$4,800 range. The number of scholarships grew from 400–450 in the 1980s to 1,770 in 2003–4, and 2,683 in 2007–8. The total pool of scholarship funding rose dramatically – from $331,000 in 1988–89 to $1,900,000 in 2003–4 and $2,700,000 in 2007–8, testimony to vigorous fundraising activity. In 2003–4, scholarship funds constituted 0.41 per cent of the college's operating budget, in 2007–8, 1.03 per cent.[105]

The credit-free areas of activity also expanded. Continuing Education course registrations rose from 22,000 in 1988–89 to a peak of 35,000 in 1999–2000, dropped to 31,000 in 2003–4, and then, after the relocation to the main campus, rose to 38,600 in 2007–8. In 1993–94, the college began tracking students in the Languages Institute – 2,200 in that year, 3,300 in 1998–98. After that the category was changed to students in "international programs," beginning with 3,234 in 1988–89, rising to a peak of 4,320 in 2002–3, and then stabilizing in the 3,800–4,000 range.[106]

Encompassing all extension and credit-free activities, there were 54,591 registrations.[107]

Just as the student profile of the college underwent steady changes, some driven by the changing level of the credentials it offered, so the faculty profile changed. In 1974–75, as we have seen, the highest academic qualifications of faculty members were as follows: 7 non-degree credential, 30 BA, 78 MA, and 5 Ph.D. By 2002–3, the numbers were: 11 non-degree credential, 10 BA, 130 MA, and 99 Ph.D. By 2005–6, 193 of 293 full-time faculty members, or 66 per cent, held Ph.D.s. However, the Ph.D.s were unevenly distributed – well over three-quarters of the faculty in the humanities, social sciences, and natural sciences, only handfuls in the professional fields where Ph.D. credentials were less available – but also where the applied degree programs were being offered.[108] Hiring more faculty members for 2009–10 and 2010–11 changed the proportions further.

Meanwhile, to accommodate the growth, the college committed itself to developing new facilities, notably a new library and learning centre (estimated cost of $187 million) for which it received government planning money, an expansion of space for the science and technology programs to enable greater enrolment and the addition of research activity (projected cost of $25 million), and a parkade to cope with growth and to replace parking space lost through construction on old parking lots.[109]

THE CONSERVATORY

The number of students in the Conservatory rose during this period to about 4,000 individuals taking some 10,000 lesson courses. The number of music teachers rose from 100 on campus in 1990 to 240 in 2005, while affiliated instructors at other locations rose from 40 to 50.[110] Its musical reputation continued to grow through the Academy and the Bridge Program, the one producing graduates who aim at professional careers in music, the other establishing international linkages, notably in Poland and China. As Paul Dornian explained, its activities included "eight orchestras, two ensembles, six choirs, a vibrant jazz program, and each year we attract some of the best international teachers and students to programs like the Morningside Music

Bridge and the International Organ Workshop.... Our Academy program has produced most of the Rose Bowl winners at the Kiwanis Music Festival for the past 25 years, and its alumni are employed by the finest music organizations in the world." He also noted that the Conservatory was sustained by "the visionary long-term support from Mount Royal College," which had received "no provincial support for its extensive community programming." Noting the underfunding of music and arts organizations, he lamented that Alberta has "an environment that encourages gifted young artists to see Calgary as a nice place to be from, rather than a professional destination to aspire to."[111]

The Conservatory's success was marked by the growing stream of graduates attending elite American institutions – Yale, Harvard, Boston's New England Conservatory, New York's Mannes College, and Juilliard. As John Kadz, the cello instructor, put it: "Yes, it means we are losing our best and brightest, but it is the only way they can achieve recognition on a worldwide basis." "The cream flows where the opportunities are," said Michael Hope, an assistant bassoonist with the Calgary Philharmonic Orchestra. "We live in a global community where people circulate. It's like the Calgary Flames; hardly any of the players are from Calgary."[112] Among the graduates were Michael Kim, who became dean of Brandon University's School of Music, and Daniel Okulitch (1995), who earned degrees from Oberlin's Conservatory of Music and began an operatic career in 2002.[113]

Finally, in the summer of 2009, all of the funding pieces fell into place for the new Conservatory performance and practice centre for which Wood and Wight had begun seeking funding a decade earlier. It would be for music and theatre performance, plus practice space and offices. The project budget was for $60 million, $20 million from each of the provincial and federal governments, $10 million from the city, and $10 million from the private sector.[114] The architects' initial sketch was of a stunning addition to the most striking architecture in Calgary.

The Theatre Arts program also continued to draw large audiences. The Shakespeare in the Park productions which had begun in Olympic Plaza were moved to Prince's Island. On the twentieth anniversary of the series in 2004, *Julius Caesar*, sponsored by the Alberta Foundation for the Arts, 66 CFR, Lite 96, the Calgary

Flames, and the *Calgary Herald*, ran from 2 to 11 July, drawing a total audience of some 40,000.[115] In October 2004 the program offered *Somewhere over the Rainbow*," featuring Conservatory students, as part of its "Feast of Sound and Song" series.[116] In 1990, the program presented Peter Shaffer's *Equus*. The director explained that "each audience had a different reaction" and that in the final nude scene the "finesse and timing were impeccable."[117] Many of the graduates became professional actors.[118]

Admission to AUCC

In March 2008 the college had submitted its application for membership to the Association of Universities and Colleges of Canada (AUCC). A Visiting Committee chaired by President Jack Lightstone of Brock University and including President Roseann O'Reilly Runte of Carleton University, Rector Yvon Fontaine of the Université de Moncton, and Ms. Christine Tausig Ford, Corporate Secretary of the AUCC, prepared the report. It met with a broad cross-section of the college community, held an open meeting attended by "more than 110 faculty members," and reviewed Mount Royal's history and legal authority, governance and administration, administration, mission and objectives, academic programs, academic quality assurance, faculty, academic freedom, students, enrolment, student services, scholarship, research and creative activities, funding and tuition fees, and library/learning resources. The committee's report was unqualified: "The Visiting Committee to Mount Royal College strongly recommends that Mount Royal be admitted to institutional membership in AUCC. The Committee believes that the institution meets the criteria for membership in the Association as set out in the [AUCC] By-laws." It noted particularly that "the shared governance model . . . is appropriate and effective, with the Board, General Faculties Council and the administration fully understanding where the authority for various decisions is vested." It found the library resources limited but concluded "that this is mitigated by the sharing of resources within the Alberta postsecondary system, and by the increasing access to electronic resources." The "programs and services offered by the institution provide

the necessary breadth and depth of studies leading to university degrees, with highly qualified academic staff, a strong quality assurance policy, academic integrity policies, and a framework of high quality services that meet students' needs." The new "streams of work patterns—teaching/service and teaching/scholarship/service—provide support for faculty research." The committee noted that "the research culture had been building at the institution for the past two decades, with many staff hired as early as 1989 with the assumption that the institution would transform into a full undergraduate university, and that research and scholarship would be an important component of their work." "In fact, the Committee stressed that in its visit to Mount Royal, it found a mature and flourishing university culture."[119]

The Visiting Committee's report concluded that the three-year applied degree programs, with two semesters of guided work experience, were "university level three-year degrees with appropriately rigorous academic content and standards." In some of the applied degrees converted to four-year degrees, the mandatory work-experience component had been replaced by "an optional co-op program and a commitment to service learning." On 28 October 2009, Mount Royal was welcomed into the AUCC as a full-fledged member.[120]

David Bissett (second from right) and his wife Leslie donated $12 million to Mount Royal, the largest ever donation to a Canadian college. Celebrating the naming of the Bissett School of Business is (L-R) Wendelin Fraser (Dean of the Mount Royal College Bissett School of Business), Denis Herard (Alberta Minister of Advanced Education and Technology), David Bissett and Dave Marshall (Mount Royal College President). Photographer Pablo Galvez; Mount Royal University Marketing and Communications.

DEFINING A GREAT UNDERGRADUATE UNIVERSITY

Having achieved undergraduate university standing in fact and in name, how was the college going to develop its distinctive excellence as an undergraduate university? Building on the college's long-term commitment to the theme of student success and satisfaction, planning for the future made the theme of its "transformative change" into becoming "one of Canada's best undergraduate universities on every measure related to student satisfaction." What that would mean in practice was spelled out in the case statement for

TABLE 10.2 HALLMARKS OF EXCELLENCE

Graduates who are prepared for the next stage in their lives	… and see value in the breadth and depth of their post-secondary education, seeing their time devoted to higher education as superior preparation for life and work success.
Responsiveness and Endurance	… that proves an institution's ability to stand the test of time as an integral part of a community's economic and social development; being flexible in order to offer programs students and the community need, and credentials that take graduates where they want to go.
Emphasis on teaching and learning	… that heightens the transfer of knowledge from passionate, scholarly-informed teachers to eager and able students; creating dynamic, interactive environments that take learning to higher levels and that enrich knowledge by thorough 'real-world' learning that pouts theory in practice.
Availability of student scholarships and bursaries	… that help remove the financial barriers to education and that reward academic achievement, encouraging students to pursue higher education and to continue through graduation
Interaction with knowledgeable and scholarly faculty	… engaged in scholarly activities, highly knowledgeable and skilled in offering individualized attention that takes student learning to new heights
Leading-edge centres of excellence	… that create knowledge and advance student learning by delving into issues and practical applications for today's pressing issues, sharing what's learned across Canada and around the world
High-quality learning facilities	… that help students learn by meeting their individual and group study needs and integrate educational technology

the $105 million fundraising campaign intended to facilitate the transformation: "Changing the Face of Education: A Centennial Fundraising Campaign for Mount Royal University." The university's "vision" was of "creating exceptional learning experiences for a world of possibilities," while its "promise" was to provide students with "a high quality education enhanced by smaller class sizes, personalized learning and a single-minded dedication to premier undergraduate learning."[121]

The fundraising campaign, launched quietly on 1 July 2007 and announced publicly in December 2010,

had three principal priorities: Learning Opportunities (scholarships), the Learning Environment (faculty and academic support), and Learning Spaces (facilities and equipment). The campaign began with the recognition of previous donors. In April 2008, the foundation held an event to name the School of Business building in honor of David and Leslie Bissett, who had donated $12 million to the school. A month later it held another event to recognize the combined $5 million donations of Dr. Norman Wong, Donald McCaffrey, and Wayne Chu by naming the Roderick Mah Centre for Continuous Learning in honour of their friend, a college alumnus who had served on the foundation's board and been named a "distinguished citizen" by the college.[122]

The institution's goal, the fundraising literature declared, is "to become an undergraduate university that excels from a student, community and school perspective—an institution that exhibits the hallmarks of a great undergraduate university." To make the goal more specific, Marshall identified some "hallmarks" of greatness. Such hallmarks, he recognized, are not inscribed anywhere, but his review of "institutions widely held to be at the top of their game—based on student feedback from the Canadian University Report, the independent third-party reviews, and polls such as those conducted by *Maclean's*, the *Globe and Mail*" indicated the characteristics outlined in Table 10.2. To build on the college's existing strengths and underline its special character as a new university, Marshall also stressed the importance of demonstrating pedagogical success through results on the National Student Survey of Engagement in the learning process, the best "proxy of learning outcomes" in a field hard to assess: "Our goal is to be the number one ranked university in Canada on all measures related to student success and satisfaction; the best 'next step' university in the country. We will have to crawl over about 60 great undergraduate universities in Canada to get there, but the fun is in the trying!"[123]

The Centennial Campaign had three major targets. The largest amount, $40 million, was intended to supplement the scholarship endowment fund and to generate some $2 million a year for bursaries and scholarships. The next largest, $35 million, was targeted to supplement government funding for "state-of-the-art learning spaces," including $20 million toward the $113 million cost of a new Learning Centre and Library, and $15 million toward the $152 million cost of enhanced Science and Health labs. The most novel feature of the campaign was the $30 million target to establish "six thematic Centres of Excellence in areas of academic priority." The aim was to develop vehicles for bringing advanced students and faculty members together in "multi-disciplinary, issues-based institutes: hubs of scholarly activity that spur exciting new discoveries and ignite a passion for learning in students and faculty alike." The centres would also encourage scholarly activity related to strengths and themes in

the college's curriculum. "Each Centre will mark the intersection of community need, student learning and the advancement of knowledge—a collaboration among faculty and students in an open and exploratory environment" creating "an unparalleled learning environment for students," strengthening "the pivotal connection between Mount Royal and the community by: engaging in real-world problem-solving relevant to business and the community, involving senior undergraduate students in research projects, a powerful learning tool typically available only to postgraduate students in a traditional university environment;…. creating a trans-disciplinary critical mass of faculty and students who will delve deeply into questions important in today's world." Endowed chairs in the centres would serve as "sparkplugs … building excitement within Mount Royal and the broader community and attracting an ever-widening circle of expertise." The chair holders would be "high-profile faculty with proven scholarly accomplishments—people from across North America whose vision and insight will set Mount Royal apart and offer an outstanding educational opportunity for students."

The $125 million campaign was much the largest fundraising venture ever undertaken by the institution. As the government will match up to $3 million annually, the college managed to secure that match in 2007 and 2008. Among other activities its annual Pearls of Wisdom lobster fest (with Rodney Clark of Rodney's Oysters in Toronto providing the fare) has become a major social event and steady contributor to annual revenues. In addition, the government provided funding to plan a major new library. In 2007–8, the foundation received donations of $10.1 million, earned $299,000 from fundraising events, and $470,000 from a "levy on gifts." Its total expenses were $1.8 million. In 2006–7 it transferred just over $4 million to the college and in 2007–8, $7.4 million. (The foundation's administrative costs were respectively $940,000 and $1.1 million.)[124] With the announcement of the change of name in September 2009, the campaign went into high gear.

Looking Back

It took most of a decade for the board of governors' goal of achieving university status to be realized. In September 2009, when Mount Royal University was officially baptized, much had been done to turn the college into a university in its inner core. Had it become a university in 2003, as seemed likely at the time, the result would have been a change of name, but with critical changes still to be made. As things worked out, those changes, the internal transformation from college university, occurred before the fact was officially recognized in the name. While it is difficult to weigh all of the responsibilities for the achievement, given the long history and the many people involved in the issue, there is little doubt that President Marshall's experience in university leadership, his firm convictions on the importance of meeting AAUC criteria, his national connections, and his sustained determination not to accept second-rate funding or second-rate standing for Mount Royal's degree programs were indispensable to the outcome. This is not to devalue the critical role of others who made necessary decisions in the last phases of the campaign the ministers of higher education and the premier of the province, key civil servants, the board of governors, and the faculty association, among others. However, the generative force in all of this, as in the past, derived from within the leadership of the college, which successfully managed to condition the environment in a way conducive to its goals.

CHAPTER 11

THE FINAL TRANSFORMATION

For the past two decades, Mount Royal has been on an evolutionary path towards becoming a university-level institution. . . . In fact, the Committee stressed that in its visit to Mount Royal, it found a mature and flourishing university culture.

– Report of AUCC Visiting Committee, June 2009

When the University of Regina was formed in 1974, after a long evolution similar to that of Mount Royal College, one of the commissioners who had recommended it was asked "Why should there be a university in Regina?," to which he answered: "Because it's there now."[1] The same could have been said when Mount Royal College became Mount Royal University by an order in council in September 2009. It had been there for some time awaiting recognition. The wait had been worthwhile: it enabled the institution to undertake a nearly complete transformation in governance, mandate, credentials awarded, programs offered, patterns of student enrolment, faculty qualifications, public profile – and, not least, immediate recognition by other universities in the form of membership in the Association of Universities and Colleges of Canada (AUCC).

Evolving with the Community

Colleges and universities are social constructs – the creation of people with particular visions and values responding to the conditions in which they find themselves. As they evolve, they both reflect their community and help to shape it. Thus, Mount Royal's development reflected the development of Calgary from a small regional entrepôt in an agricultural region into one of the world's major energy centres linked to a globalized economy. Developing in symbiotic relationship with that dynamic community, the college experienced nearly constant change, often slow, sometimes more dramatic. There were moments along the way, indeed, where the college changed its very essence, its mission, when one might speak of transformation rather than of transition or even of evolutionary change.

After twenty years of existence as a small college primarily serving students from rural regions and small towns, the college underwent its *first transformation* when it affiliated with the University of Alberta in 1931 and became a junior college offering the university's courses. This transformation probably saved the college's life. It had probably completed its mission in serving a rural population, both because of the spread of public schooling and because the Depression decimated the farm population from which it drew half of its student body. To survive, it needed the new clientele that post-secondary courses attracted. In short, the transformation was not just desired subjectively but required objectively.

The transformation entailed a number of the characteristics of fundamental change. The affiliation agreement altered the mandate of the college and its governance. The board of governors yielded up most of its control to the university over faculty qualifications, the hiring of faculty members, the content of the university courses, the preparation of examinations, and the assessment of student work. Thanks to the elimination of grades 4-9 and the addition of university-level courses, the student body changed, as did the tone and texture of campus life. Earlier, the residence had served as the core for campus life but older students did not want to live there or accept the restraints it implied. Originally the "junior college" role played by the college rested entirely on

the affiliation agreement with the university, but in 1944 it secured an important change in its legal charter that made it a "junior college" in name and function. Though the University of Alberta sought to hedge in its role as a junior college by making its offerings subject to its authority, the fact was that Mount Royal was content to let that constraint apply to its offering of the university's courses while focusing increasingly on transfer to American institutions where the constraint did not apply. Now called Mount Royal Junior College, it advertised itself as "the college with the university atmosphere," though the majority of its students remained in high-school courses.

For two full decades, the college served as the private proxy for the public junior college that Calgarians had demanded and that the government, primarily for financial reasons, had repeatedly rejected.

The *second transformation* was less thorough but still involved major changes in curriculum, self-conception, and public identity. It was also triggered by a change in external circumstances. In 1951 the University of Alberta opened its own University Centre in Calgary, in effect (though not legally) depriving Mount Royal of its unique role in offering its introductory courses in Calgary. Following the opening of the University Centre, the college reoriented its university-transfer programs (including its University of Alberta courses) to universities in other provinces and the United States, added diploma programs in business, expanded its high-school matriculation program and enabled students to mix high-school and college-level courses, created continuing education and extension operations, and embraced the notion of itself as an American-style community college. Along with that new self-conception went the idea of "open door" admissions and serving "second-chance" students – those who had not succeeded as students earlier. What mattered was not the admission standard but the ability to move students successfully through a program to meet the graduation standards. If there was a problem with this mission, it was the heavy commitment to student support services it implied, and the private college never had the resources to fulfil that mission adequately. Faculty members dedicated to teaching individual students made up the difference, to the extent that it was made up. Toward the end of this transition period the college began offering new career programs, leading to the hiring of faculty with qualifications other than the standard teacher credentials used in the past.

The *third transformation*, begun in 1966, was a response to another threat to the college's survival. Indeed, this time the board of governors accepted that the college could not continue as a private institution and decided to seek public support. It declared that the college had fulfilled its original mission, which was that of filling educational needs not met by other organizations. By the early 1960s public institutions had grown or emerged to provide programs in areas previously served by the college, with the development of the University of Calgary, enhanced funding support for SAIT, and new vocational centres to provide job readiness programs, all of them taking space in the local educational market, narrowing the college's options. The ensuing transformation was from a private, religiously affiliated institution bearing many marks of its emanation from the Methodist/United Church community to a secular, publicly funded community college with all that eventually entailed in governance, transparency, curriculum, faculty, students, and campus life.

This was a bumpier, noisier, and longer transformation than the earlier ones. Early in this period the Mount Royal Faculty Association and the Students' Association of Mount Royal College were formed, giving a more formal character to their roles in the institution. Thanks to government funding, the college expanded its career programs, enrolment, and faculty and built a new campus. Governing boards, senior administrators, and employees drawn from the Methodist/United Church community gave way to people without such connections and appointed by the government. Internal constituencies were added to the board in 1970, initially a member of the faculty and a student, and in 1983, a support staff member. With additional funding, and with a new campus in 1972, the college was better equipped to play the community college role it had claimed earlier. But it was a community college with a difference. Thanks to its evolution as a private institution, it prized its general education requirements for diploma programs, maintained Latin and religious studies in the curriculum, and otherwise carried on some of the older traditions – a gift from the past to the future.

However, the transformation proved unsettling. It began during a time of ferment on campuses when authority and old ways were being challenged and more participative decision-making processes including faculty members and students were spreading. By the time the Colleges Act of 1969 set out the terms and conditions for the college system, the Faculty Association expected that the college would have a bicameral form of governance like an Alberta university – an equivalent to the General Faculties Council (GFC), a body with statutory authority in academic matters, and a board of governors devoted chiefly to financial and property matters, with the president coordinating activities between them. However, the statute and government policies were rooted in a different conception of the colleges as training institutions where programs would come and go as the economy changed, and faculty members with them. To avoid faculty self-interest impeding the termination of programs, the academic councils were made advisory to governing boards. It was to counterbalance that structural weakness that the Faculty Association sought a role in "co-determination" of policy, direction, and supervision with the board of governors.

The idealistic pedagogical and facility models embraced in the 1960s did not work as intended on the new campus opened in 1972. The pedagogical model was too optimistic about the capacity of students, while the open-plan facility, with its lack of walled classrooms and offices, absorbed a lot of energy and time as mobile partitions or walls and furniture were shoved around with changing uses, giving everyone also a sense of impermanence.

Clashes arose between the president, eager to implement the idealistic models for which he and the board had been praised, and faculty members trying to make things work in less than attractive circumstances. The polarization reached the point in 1975 that the president was not renewed and consultants were hired to review the situation and make recommendations for the future. The result was an organizational culture permeated by faculty mistrust that rose and fell but was never entirely absent thereafter. In the 1990s, an outside observer commented on the faculty's "strong tendencies toward anarchy . . . and an anti-administration stance exemplified in the political activities of the faculty association."[2]

Though they did not contribute to the transformation within the college directly, negotiations with both the Southern Alberta Institute of Technology (SAIT) and the Alberta Vocational Centre–Calgary (AVC-Calgary) were important defining elements in the college's evolution. In 1967, the college agreed with SAIT that it would not move into trades and technologies or fields where there would be unwarranted duplication between them. Failed merger discussions with AVC-Calgary led to another boundary on the college's potential role, or, to make the point differently, opened the way for the college to develop as a mainly post-secondary institution. AVC-Calgary continued as a separate agency, growing into Bow Valley College in 1992, offering job readiness and adult upgrading courses, while Mount Royal, despite its "open door" admissions policy, began to reduce the scope of its services in that regard. In effect, Bow Valley College was to pick up pieces left behind by Mount Royal as it continued along its trajectory toward degree-granting and university status. Thus, the arrangements with AVC-Calgary and SAIT helped focus Mount Royal on its role in university-transfer and white-collar career programs. This was the case, even though once the local board of education reduced its programs for adults in the 1990s the college offered high-school courses on a continuing-education, fee-for-service basis.

From 1966 through the mid-1990s the college pursued its community college vocation and teased out many of its implications. It became systematically community-focused and student-centred. It made its primary goal that of student success and student and client satisfaction. It expanded its program base explicitly to meet the needs of professional groups in health care, business, and information technology. It incorporated the work-study co-operative mode of delivery into some of its programs and set plans to expand the method to many more programs. However, by the mid-1980s, responding to the needs of a dynamic, high-tech, globally oriented employer pool, the college concluded that it could not fulfil its mission with one-year certificate and two-year diploma programs. The emerging knowledge society and modern economy required higher levels of knowledge and skills than the college could provide with those credentials. Another sign of the need for more advanced

credentials was the fact that Alberta's major universities were swamped with applicants, raised their admission standards, and diverted hundreds of students toward the university-transfer programs in the colleges, including Mount Royal. By the end of the 1980s the government had twice provided additional grants for the college to take in more university-transfer students. Students who transferred from the college to the large universities frequently came back to ask the college to seek degree-granting status because of the huge class sizes and impersonal environment they found in the universities.

In retrospect, it seems almost ineluctable that the next transformation would involve degree granting. In the 1980s the college fleshed out its university-transfer offerings to a full two years; it sought and secured transfer credit for many courses through the auspices of the Alberta Council on Admissions and Transfers; it adopted a new faculty qualifications policy for university-transfer programs: "Ph.D. preferred, master's required." Unable to deepen its base because of the AVC or to broaden it much because of SAIT, the college built higher on its existing foundations – which implied an increasingly academic vocation – and eventually degree granting. Moreover, the idea of degree programs being offered by colleges was spreading throughout North America.[3]

The formal roots of *the fourth transformation* began in 1988, when the board of governors, after discussing options for the college's future, directed the administration to develop a report on degree-granting options. However, the aspiration became a practical plan in 1992 when the board made a formal request to offer four-year bachelor degrees in applied fields of study that universities were not addressing, including the co-operative work/study method of delivery. That request led to skirmishes with government officials who were nervous about mission creep and precedents, to university opposition to college-based degrees and the funding implications, and to the opposition of most of the other colleges and technical institutes that lacked the capacity to offer degrees or feared a loss of standing by comparison. The college was able to persuade the government, but the result was a compromise – a new category of degree, the "applied" baccalaureate degree to be offered only by colleges and technical institutes. To differentiate them from university degrees, they would involve six semesters of study and two semesters of work experience. Thus, Mount Royal's initiative was diluted and generalized to the whole college and technical institute system.

Having no option, the college introduced its first "applied degree" programs in 1996 and eventually offered nineteen of them. While college- and institute-based "applied degrees" were welcomed by students and employers, they were viewed with suspicion by universities that anticipated dealing with applied degree holders seeking admission for further study; from their point of view, the new degrees were "terminal" rather than pedestals for further study. (While more than half of all of Mount Royal's courses were already accepted for transfer to Alberta universities, and while its applied degrees consisted almost entirely of such courses, that was not the case in most other colleges and technical institutes.) The applied degrees inspired changes in the college. Instead of two years, students now had to spend three years of study and a year of monitored work experience; this required students with longer time horizons than those earlier. More students sought entry directly from high school, and more students sought to transfer into Mount Royal. It was becoming increasingly a first-choice institution for high-school graduates. Degree granting also enabled the college to recruit more faculty members with Ph.D.s, giving rise to changing notions of the faculty's role and the importance of research.

However, Alberta's decision to launch applied degree programs – a category of degree not found anywhere else in Canada – raised issues that eventually reduced their appeal. Within five years, those issues led the board of governors to take the next step – to request a change to university status.

The *fifth transformation* entailed the nearly decade-long campaign to change the college in ways that would satisfy the sometimes conflicting requirements of government leaders, department officials, and the membership criteria of the Association of Universities and Colleges of Canada (AUCC). During this phase, with a view to maintaining its special intellectual quiddity, the college redesigned its general education requirement to provide for both breadth and depth through "vertical" course requirements over three years of study. In this way it prepared for its new role by ensuring that the strong liberal arts strain – the

secularized heir to the Methodist moral education – was provide a central thread in the tapestry being woven.

At this point the story of Mount Royal merged into the broader political tussle in post-secondary education in which Alberta was to play a noteworthy role. In different ways, Alberta, British Columbia, and New Brunswick opened their post-secondary educational markets to new private institutions and external providers in the early twenty-first century. Except for New Brunswick, they did this through statutes that established quality assurance agencies to review the proposed programs and the organizations of applicants for approval. In addition, colleges in Alberta, BC, and Ontario were permitted to apply to offer particular degree programs. These statutes opened the way for individual degree programs to be offered. Opening a new avenue to degree granting, one that bypassed the public universities, was not welcomed by the universities and so, when holders of degrees from colleges and other new degree providers applied them for admission to further study, they were told that their applications could not be accepted because the degrees had not been awarded by a member of AUCC. In the absence of a national accrediting body, they said, membership in AUCC was a "proxy" way of determining credibility. The AUCC promptly tightened its membership criteria. In effect, this was at least a reproach, if not a challenge, to the authority of the provincial governments involved. It was perhaps no accident that within a short time the innovative western provinces required their public universities to submit all new programs to their quality assurance agencies for vetting.

For Mount Royal, some of whose graduates were rejected on the grounds the college did not belong to AUCC, this turn of events gave it crucial leverage to force changes in Alberta legislation enabling the college to meet the membership criteria of the AUCC, a condition the college set for offering four-year degrees. The government made the changes grudgingly. Like other colleges, Mount Royal was permitted by legislation in 2004 to mount four-year degrees if it wished, but the college took the position that it would not offer such degrees until it met the requirements to belong to the AUCC so that its graduates would not run the risk of having their credential unrecognized (or devalued entirely) if and when they wished to continue their studies. In 2006, legislation (the "Mount Royal clause") permitted colleges to develop an "alternate" Academic Council – to implement a bicameral governance system. In 2008, legislation establishing six categories of post-secondary institution, and placed Mount Royal and Grant MacEwan College in the second category, which enabled them to engage in research but not to be research-intensive or to call themselves a university. In the spring of 2009 further legislation enabled the college to apply to use the word 'university' in its name, and following a request and acceptance of conditions intended to tie down the college's aspirations to those in the second category of institution, an order-in-council on 2 September 2009 changed the college's name to Mount Royal University.

Meanwhile, the college had been transforming itself internally. It had developed terms of reference segregating the roles of the board of governors and the General Faculties Council, establishing genuine bicameral governance. It had negotiated a new role and responsibilities and workload policy for faculty establishing a balance among teaching, scholarship, and service. It introduced a rank system for faculty. It overhauled the core general education requirements to fit the new degrees. It began to replace most of the applied degree programs with four-year degrees. It enhanced library holdings and began a $100 million fundraising campaign to assist with the transformation. It set the goal of becoming the leading undergraduate university in the country and identified the hallmarks of that standing.

Except for the college's conversion from private to public standing, every major initiative leading to changes in its mandate came from within the college. Indeed, many of them were resisted by the Edmonton-based department responsible for higher education. The attitude of government officials was reflected in the words of a former deputy minister who advised college presidents that he would rather have one college or university angry at him for refusing a request for what might be deemed special treatment than to have all the rest angry at him for making an exception. While it is the job of officials to enforce policies and to avoid unfortunate precedents, that view, if taken seriously, was a recipe for keeping Mount Royal at the level of institutions working with very different

capacities and in very different environments. The witticism also suggested a hard reality – to get some things done, the college had to go beyond the bureaucracy, to add a political dimension to the other layers of its consultation and cajoling. Of course, governments must coordinate their public systems, and some of Mount Royal's views and ambitions raised problems of precedent and policy. However, it was far from being the only college or university to resort to political lobbying. Indeed, as we have seen, other institutions used political influence to thwart Mount Royal's campaign for degree-granting capacity. In Alberta's political system, the politics of envy, characterized by the rivalry between Edmonton and Calgary and by concerns of the "rural" caucus about benefits flowing to the cities, creates an environment in which negative lobbying is easier than lobbying *for* something.

Not surprisingly, in a context in which all post-secondary institutions importune politicians directly, the relationship between the institutions and the government also underwent changes. From 1968 to 1972 the Colleges Commission and the Universities Commission coordinated the sectors separately, a situation which treated the two sectors as isolated silos even though the colleges offered primarily university-transfer programs in the early years. Beginning in 1972, the Department of Advanced Education (later the Department of Advanced Education and Manpower) coordinated government policy for post-secondary education. In 1974 the department introduced a program coordination policy under which it required progressively more detailed information over the years. The more detailed the requirements became, the greater the concern in institutions became about the adequacy of the criteria, the transparency of the procedures, and the qualifications of government officials to make system-wide decisions by comparison with those of institutional governors and officials. Perhaps it was inevitable that at some point a new arms-length coordinating body would be established to take over some of the department's role. In any event, the Campus Alberta Quality Council established in 2005 replaced the department in matters relating to program and mandate approvals. The council changed the game by including representatives of the institutions, establishing public criteria and procedures, and including third-party evaluations. The department's role, as a result, focused more on financial and property matters than on institutional mandates. Consequently, it has become more difficult to lobby for purposes that must go through the council.

Because in other jurisdictions colleges have been transformed into universities overnight, with transformational changes to follow, the fact that Mount Royal undertook most of the basic transformation before having its name changed is worth stressing. Only the conversion from private to public college standing came close to the same transformational scope. Profound transformations of this sort entail significant changes in most of the following: (i) mandate, whether in the legal charter or through affiliation; (ii) governance, whether in the authority, role, or composition of the governing board or of the collegial academic body responsible for decisions or advice on academic matters; (iii) the level of programs and credentials awarded; (iv) the spectrum of programs offered; (v) the source of primary funding; (vi) the level of admissions and/or learning outcome standards; (vii) student academic achievement levels; (viii) faculty responsibilities and the collective agreement; (ix) faculty qualifications; (x) the composition of the student body; (xi) the quality of the campus experience; (xii) the scale of operation; (xiii) the means for delivering programs; (xiv) the nature of linkages to the community; and (xv) and policies guaranteeing academic freedom. The conversion from college to university standing in Canada, moreover, includes the addition of a research mandate and in practice introduces academic rank, with all that implies in terms of performance evaluation and may imply in changes to compensation procedures. The final transformation of Mount Royal College included all of those elements but the source of primary funding. Transformations on that scale are not easy and no doubt there will be some unintended consequences. But there should be many fewer than in institutions scrambling to become what Mount Royal already was prior to its name change.

The government's recognition of the change of name to Mount Royal University in September 2009 marked the end of the process in Alberta. A month later, in October 2009, AUCC, finishing an application process that had begun in 2006, voted to approve membership for Mount Royal University, marking its formal introduction into the national circle of universities. The

history of Mount Royal College had come to an end, and the history of Mount Royal University began.

Before hastening on, let us note that, from a public policy point of view, Mount Royal's history involved four significant moments: (i) making the small, underfunded, private college a proxy for the public junior college wanted in Calgary; (ii) transforming the private college into the public community college; (iii) converting the public community college into a public university; and (iv) deciding what to do for the people who were left behind by Mount Royal's conversion from a college into a university.

One can understand the reasons for governments making these decisions, but they may or may not have been the wisest decisions. For example, there are both opportunities and problems attached to launching a new institution *de novo*, but there also problems, along with opportunities, in resting new public institutions on foundations designed for other purposes.

- While Mount Royal benefited from becoming the proxy for the public junior college in 1931, a public institution might well have been able to offer better facilities and programs.

- While "Mount Royal" survived in 1966 thanks to a transformation in its legal and financial footing, it inherited problems in its organizational culture that complicated its development.

- While Mount Royal was ready to become a university in 2009, it remains to be seen whether its internal culture and the conditions attached to its conversion by government will prevent it from becoming the first-class undergraduate university it aspires to be.

In addition, there are always resource issues, both in funding the institution's new mandate at the level necessary to ensure success and in ensuring that the students left behind with the last transformation are served by other providers. That there will be people left behind is indicated by the college's enrolment plans for the immediate future: because of limited funding, the total number of seats will remain about the same but as students move into the third and fourth years of degree programs the first-year admission level will be reduced, causing enrolment in credit programs to fall from 10,000 in 2008–9 to about 7,200 over time.

In short, while the story of Mount Royal's series of transformations may be seen as the story of the "little engine that could," it must also be seen as the story of government decisions made and of consequences for other institutions, including but not limited to the mandates of Grant MacEwan College in Edmonton and Bow Valley College in Calgary and perhaps university enrolments in Calgary and Lethbridge.

Looking Back in Comparison

Mount Royal's century-long history in some ways recapitulates the history of other private religiously affiliated institutions that evolved into public universities but was also markedly different in some respects. The differences are visible in the different trajectories of Mount Allison University and the University of Regina, both also of Methodist origin. It is also useful to consider the effect of different institutional histories on Grant MacEwan College, which became a university at the same time as Mount Royal.

Mount Allison University, whose roots trace back to 1839, was originally intended to prepare ministers through theological and arts education and to raise the level of lay education from elementary through higher education.[4] In 1862, it was established as a degree-granting college but it retained two secondary schools, one for boys, and the other for girls. It was the first university in the British Empire to award a B.Sc. to a woman (1875) and a BA to a woman (1876). Following the model of the University of Toronto (1906), it adopted a bicameral governance system. Yet, as a committee of the Carnegie Corporation in New York found in 1922, Mount Allison remained "embedded in secondary organizations that divide the attention and interest."[5] (This was about the time when George J. Trueman, who became president of Mount Allison in 1923, visited Mount Royal as a member of the Massey Commission and found that Mount Royal, perhaps because it lacked the ballast of degree programs, was chasing off in too many directions in search of a

clientele.) Just as the effort to establish a public community college in Calgary failed in the 1920s, leaving the private Mount Royal to play a proxy role for a public institution, so contemporaneous efforts in the Maritime provinces to create a federated, publicly supported university system collapsed, leaving Mount Allison and other small religiously affiliated institutions to provide much of the higher education in the region.[6] Like Mount Royal, and about the same time, Mount Allison was eventually forced to seek public funding and became publicly supported in 1963.

Unlike western Methodist institutions that operated in provinces where degree granting was monopolized by government-based universities inspired by the American land-grant initiative and where diversity, to the extent it was permitted, was sheltered within the degree-granting power of public institutions, the small private, religiously affiliated institutions in the Maritime provinces retained their degree-granting power and defined themselves more or less as they pleased until forced to seek public funding. Following closure of the girls' school and the boys' academy by the mid-1950s and "a period of crisis" from 1957 to 1963, Mount Allison assumed its current character as a small, residential liberal arts university.[7] Today it offers degree programs in Arts, Science, Commerce, Fine Arts, and Music. Its strength lies in its nature as a small liberal arts university, its capacity to attract a national clientele, and its location in a small town – a student body of 2,250 students in a town of just over 5,000 people. "Small classes, a sense of community, and personal dialogue between students and faculty are ingredients that can best be provided by the small university and that make a unique contribution to the intellectual development of students."[8] (Location in a small community is also a weakness, since there is a limited pool of part-time talent to enrich the curriculum and minor campus perturbations become community events, magnifying their significance.) In short, Mount Allison developed in ways that were impossible in the more regulated degree-granting environment and much larger urban centres of western Canada.

Founded at the same time as Mount Royal and with a similar mission, Regina College managed to persuade the University of Saskatchewan to permit it to offer its first-year Bachelor of Arts courses in Regina in 1925, making it a "junior college" by affiliation. This precedent undoubtedly influenced the decision of the University of Alberta to accept Mount Royal as an affiliated junior college in 1931.[9] While the single university policy was to be maintained in both provinces until the 1960s, the trajectories of the two Methodist colleges diverged. Unlike Mount Royal, Regina College went bankrupt during the Depression. After disaffiliating from the United Church in 1934, it was "taken over" by the University of Saskatchewan.[10] Thereafter its development was comparable to that of the University of Calgary – first operating as a centre offering only first-year courses, expanding to meet Baby Boom growth, adding more courses and programs over time, becoming the focal point of local demands for an independent university, and finally, in 1974, becoming the University of Regina. As a public institution, moreover, it could not nurse a narrow curriculum, like Mount Allison; it had to adapt to the needs, many of them instrumental or social, of the southern half of the province and the Native population. Interestingly, its enrolment size has remained similar to Mount Royal's through much of its history; today, in the early 2000s, both had about 9,000 full-time and 3,000 part-time students, and a similar range of activities, including special educational linkages to the Native community. As Regina approached the twenty-first century, it held a symposium on the future, but beyond addressing local Native educational needs, little was said that would mark it off from any other regional university.[11]

Thus, there is much about context that has defined and will continue to define all three institutions. Moreover, all of them have retained some elements from their Methodist origins – a strong liberal arts core and identity, academic disciplines separated from professional programs and not subsumed in them, and concern for individualized student attention and good quality instruction. However, there are some obvious constraints on Mount Royal. Because of its size and commuter campus nature, Mount Royal can never provide the kind of campus environment available at Mount Allison, a small residential institution whose rich on-campus environment routinely enables it to top university in rankings of high-quality small undergraduate universities and whose distinctive character enables it to draw students from across Canada.

Nor will the government fund Mount Royal for the foreseeable future to compete with the much larger research-intensive universities in Calgary and Edmonton. It will need to position itself in other ways – "to do by design what others do by default," as Marshall puts it.[12]

It is also worth noting the somewhat different trajectory of the other college that became a university along with Mount Royal. Grant MacEwan College had deliberately eschewed a university-transfer role until the late 1980s, when, in response to soaring demand and a request from the government, and with advice from Mount Royal, it introduced university-transfer programs. A new campus in downtown Edmonton enabled its university-transfer function to grow rapidly thereafter, surpassing that of Mount Royal in size. Though both began with the same formal mandate and operating under the same legislation, their histories were quite different, as were their internal cultures. At no point did the members of the public college's board, senior administration, or faculty regard Mount Royal as similar to most of the other colleges in its fundamental mission or character. Until the 1990s, only Red Deer College was very close to Mount Royal in profile. Until Grant MacEwan began its university-transfer work, it seemed closer to an Ontario CAAT than to Mount Royal. That sense of being an institution apart informed Mount Royal's early promotion of applied degrees for itself and then university standing, not for the system as a whole but for itself. Though its initiatives can be seen as part of a continent-wide trend toward college baccalaureate degrees, Mount Royal did not see itself as promoting or contributing to that broader cause. It was all too conscious of its own long history of developing and extending its university-transfer programs over decades, its internal battles over the content and size of the liberal arts curriculum, its long campaign to secure recognition for most of its university-transfer courses, and the tensions arising from changing requirements for faculty credentials. Its arguments were rooted in the claim of institutional exceptionalism, not in arguments about college degree granting in general.

By contrast, Grant MacEwan College moved in little more than a decade from being an institution offering only career programs into one offering university-transfer programs, applied degrees, and then foundation degrees. Throughout that period of rapid change its self-conception, leadership, and faculty members remained steeped in a career-oriented version of the community college vocation. Perhaps as a result, Grant MacEwan was more comfortable offering degree programs from a college platform than Mount Royal was. Indeed, while presidents Wood and Marshall of Mount Royal were pursuing university status, Grant MacEwan's president, Paul Byrne, was actively promoting the idea of college baccalaureate degrees provincially, nationally, and internationally, serving among other things as a board member of the Community College Baccalaureate Association, a body that Mount Royal did not join. Reflecting that view, the *Edmonton Journal* suggested that Mount Royal was "hung up on titles."[13] Functionally, though not necessarily deliberately, Grant MacEwan was aligned with Advanced Education, which warned Mount Royal that other institutions felt "threatened" by its desire to be called a university.[14] Michael Skolnik, an OISE professor who strongly advocates the college baccalaureate, said that "GMC was quite ambivalent about university status. It identified strongly with the community college movement, whereas I'm not sure that was exactly the case at MRC – which would be understandable given the difference in their histories." Skolnik elaborated:

> I don't fault MRC for choosing to advance only its own interests rather than support a wider movement for university acceptance of the community college baccalaureate, because I think that Dave [Marshall] believes that the wider movement is both pedagogically wrong and politically futile. My impression is that disagreement over that belief was at the heart of the difference in strategies between the two colleges. If one accepts that either belief is reasonable, then the strategies of each college look honorable and proper in the context of their respective beliefs. The problem is that it was not feasible for either institution or

for the government for these two colleges to have different institutional status. So long as MRC would not rest until it got university status, GMC could not remain a "baccalaureate granting college" even if that would have been its preference, at least for another decade. In that sense GMC was as much a hostage to MRC's aspirations as a freeloader on its coattails. In any event as a supporter of the community college baccalaureate movement, I am sorry to see the loss of a strong and effective advocate for that movement.[15]

Where Mount Royal made meeting AUCC requirements its talisman, GMC did not follow. Indeed, it took no significant public role in the campaign for university standing waged by Mount Royal. It was awarded the title of university because of the political requirement for parity between Calgary and Edmonton institutions and because its standing would be anomalous rather than because it had actively sought it. Thus, the issue of offering full-fledged degree programs from a college platform in Alberta was finessed rather than addressed squarely by the transformation of the largest two colleges into universities (albeit with restricted mandates), a process similar to and a bit later than similar legal transformations in British Columbia. As Skolnik suggests, the outcome was no doubt a setback for the overall cause of upgrading the level and credibility of college-level education in a context in which university standing remains "the coin of the realm," as president John Tibbits of Conestoga College once put it, despite the fact that some college degree programs are clearly more intellectually demanding than some university programs.[16] The college baccalaureate movement, moreover, is and will remain more popular in the United States because "college" does not necessarily have the confined meaning common in Canada, where until recently it implied credentials other than degree qualifications and now may imply a degree that may not be recognized by universities for purposes of further study.

Looking Ahead

Just as Mount Royal has developed through a medley of forces and factors – the visions of its governing boards, senior administration, and faculty; changing societal need, student demand, and economic forces; government policy; the evolution of neighbouring and competitor institutions – so it will continue to be shaped by both endogenous and exogenous forces in the future. It will be partly master of its own fate, and its leadership will need to remain agile to seize new opportunities, to cut losses, and to avoid shoals. At least as interesting as the past five transformations will be the next – the development of a high-quality undergraduate university offering a high-quality education in a university permeated with scholarly activity.

Built on the foundations of a college that did not have a research mandate, the new university will need to develop an organizational culture in which the commitment to generate new knowledge and understanding (i.e., research) permeates the whole – not only in the job description of faculty members but in their self-conception and personal values and aspirations; not only in how students view the institution's purpose but also in their own expectations as learners and potential researchers; not only in the comprehension of administrators and staff members but also in their support for the institution's broader role; not only in the title of the institution but in the public image of the kind of undergraduate university it is. Mount Royal also wants to be distinctive, not another garden-variety secondary provincial university – a "second banana" institution dimly shadowing the research and graduate program profiles of the research-intensive institutions. It aspires to be a student-focused undergraduate university that offers a strong foundation in the liberal arts for all programs, some of which prepare students for further study, others of which prepare students in applied fields of study for admission to practice, using the work-study co-operative mode of delivery and in close partnership with employers. It aims to maximize student engagement in their learning.

There will be challenges, one of them the lingering effects of the college's history on continuing faculty and staff. Many former students who benefited from its open admissions policy and flexible requirements may be proud of the "new" Mount Royal but may not feel as tied to it as they did earlier. This kind of alumni response is not uncommon when institutions shuck off an older skin for a new one. For example, many of the former students of Waterloo Lutheran University, which also had flexible admissions, lost their sense of close kinship with the public Wilfrid Laurier University as its entrance requirements steadily rose after it entered Ontario's public university system. The new Mount Royal cannot take it for granted that the cohort of alumni will always find it easy to identify with the new university, whether for fund raising or other purposes.

There will also be distractions – for example, ranking systems for universities. The dominant models in most such systems are the research-intensive university in the United States and United Kingdom. Jamil Salmi of the World Bank has outlined that model in *The Challenge of Establishing World-Class Universities*. To be truly outstanding, such universities have (a) sufficiently plentiful resources that they can pay whatever it takes to recruit the best students and faculty in the world, (b) a high concentration of globally recruited talent at all levels (faculty, student, staff), (c) a very high proportion of graduate students, especially at the doctoral level, and (d) considerable freedom from external interference.[17] Even oil-rich Alberta will cavil at those requirements. Indeed, few universities anywhere have the resources or latitude required to be world class in Salmi's sense. Yet the model is very attractive, especially for those institutions that can demonstrate their worth to politicians and the public by moving up in the rankings. However, balancing the requirements of a strong undergraduate education and those of becoming research-intensive, in the absence of significant additional funding, has implied a dilution in the quality of undergraduate education, as suggested by books emanating from faculty members of the University of Calgary and the University of Toronto. The titles speak for themselves: David Bercuson, *Petrified Campus: The Crisis in Canada's Universities*, and Bercuson, with Robert Bothwell and Jack L. Granatstein, *The Great Brain Robbery: Canada's Universities on the Road to Ruin*.[18]

There are other models for universities. In the United States, the "Carnegie" classification system differentiates among several types, and in Canada the *Maclean's* ranking aggregates universities in several categories (those with medical schools, those that are comprehensive but lack a medical school, and primarily undergraduate institutions). The *Globe and Mail's* new *Canadian University Report* assesses universities by size (Mount Royal and Grant MacEwan are considered "small," in the 4,000–12,000 student range). President Marshall has written that "there is not only no federal system of education [in Canada] but there is no 'Carnegie' classification of institutions like there is in the United States" and, one might add, no institutional accrediting bodies like those in the United States, with the result that "what is called a four-year liberal arts college in the United States is called a university in Canada, and the label 'college' is almost totally reserved for the community college sector."[19] The result is that the *Maclean's* rankings have a greater impact than similar rankings in the United States. It remains to be seen whether the *Globe and Mail's* rankings will have much steering effect, as they appear designed to make nearly every institution look good: thus, both Mount Royal and Grant MacEwan vaulted to the forefront in their first appearance, in such categories as "most satisfied students," "quality of education," "student-faculty interaction," "quality of teaching," and "class size."[20] In general, it is very clear that ranking systems have a profound steering effect on institutions. In the words of a European Union official in 2009 about the challenge of herding institutional cats across the EU in desired directions, the EU was planning to develop its own ranking system to "mobilize shame" on the items the EU considered important. No institution will want to be at the bottom of any ranking, and no government will want to see its institutions at the bottom.[21] Realization of the importance of rankings led Mount Royal in 2006 to map itself against the *Maclean's* criteria. That governments are also vulnerable to pressures to conform to what others think are important criteria for universities was shown by the fact that Alberta blinked in the face of pressure from public universities to require all new degree-granting institutions to resemble themselves, as described in the membership criteria of the AUCC.

One response to the pressures to conform to other models could be putting pressure on the ranking systems to reflect the characteristics of the kind of institution Mount Royal aspires to be – one that focuses on learning outcomes. This could include advocating the inclusion of the results of "student engagement" surveys, as reported by the National Survey of Student Engagement (NSSE) or its Canadian version, Canadian University Student Consortium (CUSC). Comparing itself to other Canadian institutions on that basis, Mount Royal knows that it will score comparatively high. Marshall believes that the evidence of the link between learning engagement scores and learning outcomes will force the engagement scores onto the public ranking agenda.[22]

There is also another kind of engagement that is crucial – that of the external stakeholders. One of the keys to Mount Royal's success as a public college was the high level of its engagement with the community it served, whether in career programs, music and speech lessons, recreation, concerts, or other activities. This is a feature that Mount Royal University will want to build on, both to take advantage of established linkages and because studies of institutional engagement with communities at many levels clearly demonstrate that there is a "positive relationship between individual stakeholder engagement with the college" and community support rooted in the belief that the institution adds value to the community. "Depending upon the nature of this increased engagement," the studies suggest, "it could lead to better outcomes for students, institutions, and communities."[23] In short, it will behove the university to pay particular attention to the spectrum of its community engagement – to know what it is, to find ways to measure the level of engagement, and to work assiduously at maintaining the former college's marketing edge in that regard.

The new university will also require a large measure of consensus internally concerning its special character and future directions. The authors of a pessimistic work on Canadian universities lament particularly their tendency to "seriously devalue the education of undergraduate students. Undergraduate classes are too large, frequently taught by graduate students rather than professors, and often delivered in ridiculously impersonal and uninspired ways. . . . Although the shape of Canadian universities in the more distant future is unclear, it is not preposterous to hope, as well as to urge, that they become genuine places to learn."[24] The diversion of faculty time and energy away from the teaching function has generated many similar concerns.[25] The massification of higher education combined with the greater emphasis on research has generated a sense that students are not receiving what they deserve. Mount Royal College had limited experience with faculty members who saw themselves mainly as scholars rather than as teachers. That may well change as the new university proceeds along its trajectory.

What will make new Mount Royal's faculty members different from those elsewhere? Why will they behave differently than faculty members in research-intensive universities? Ensuring they behave in ways suitable to the university's mission and special character will require actions such as the following. First, the institution will need to develop a persuasive picture of the institution it aspires to be, to reinforce it internally through rewards and tireless promotion, and to communicate it to potential faculty recruits and to students. Its implications will need to permeate the organizational culture. Second, the university will need to encourage ongoing and systematic reflective pedagogical practice. Beyond the usual workshops on teaching and assessment, this will require paying attention to what students say about their experience. It may give all new faculty members a book such as Richard Light's *Making the Most of College*, which contains student comments on what works in the classroom even with large classes and research-oriented faculty.[26] Third, the university can ensure that its faculty members are both familiar with *and* engage personally in efforts to measure effective teaching and learning, such as drawing conclusions from evidence of student engagement, which focuses on student learning activities, and the Collegiate Learning Assessment (CLA) project, which estimates changes in the skills of students in critical thinking and writing from the start to finish of baccalaureate education – the added value, if any, of the experience.[27] As a public university serving students from diverse backgrounds, Mount Royal will need to remember that "what happens to the students in a college community is what counts, not how smart the students happen to be."[28]

The story of York University's development provides a cautionary tale with respect to idealistic aspirations in the face of pervasive university values and preoccupations that run counter to them. In the words of Skolnik:

York's original vision focused primarily on providing a new type of learning environment and curriculum approach for undergraduate students. But there was no institutional history or set of shared experiences among faculty to support this vision. In the absence of that, the faculty who were recruited mainly from research universities did what came naturally, they re-created a research university . . . If some of MRC's critics were correct that the campaign to become a university was sheer status-seeking, then it wouldn't be a surprise to see the movement to become more like UC begin very soon. If on the other hand, the institution became a university in order to serve undergraduate students, particularly career-focused ones, more effectively, then institutional development efforts will focus on strengthening and consolidating the capability for that. It will be interesting to see how things unfold![29]

For Mount Royal University to succeed in fulfilling its new mission, beyond what it can do itself, it will also require the comprehension and support of the government of Alberta, which must recognize that to offer a face-to-face and small-class environment to students, Mount Royal will require two things: an enduring mandate that specifies its particular character for the foreseeable future; and a defined faculty-student teaching ratio that must be sustained. There will be no supply of cheap graduate student labour to buffer the teaching load (unless it comes from the neighbouring University of Calgary). What Mount Royal embodies for Alberta is a more diverse higher education environment, some real institutional differentiation. It would be a pity if that additional variety and richness in the environment were to be lost for want of government persistence in supporting an institution it insisted must be different from the others.

There are, however, some worrying signs. In 2009 the government agreed to provide operating funding for the third and fourth years of the new four-year programs in 2011 and 2012. However, when the downturn in oil prices occurred, it froze Mount Royal's grant at the 2009–10 level and, instead of providing operating funding, awarded a lump sum of $6 million to enable Mount Royal to manage its enrolment down to the level it could afford with such funding. This implied a reduction of 25 per cent in first-year admissions, and an overall drop from 8,000 to 7,200 students. Some of the special funding for Nursing also evaporated, with enrolment planned to shrink from 320 to 210. The university's plan to grow by a further 2,500 students "is now off the table," Marshall reported, and along with it much of the new faculty hiring that was envisaged. Indeed, the funding situation implied that the vision of the university as one offering different levels of credential was modified: all diploma programs in Business, Arts, and Science were dropped in favour of the degree programs, and the number of spaces for "open studies" was cut in half.[30] Thus, Mount Royal will continue much of its transformation into an undergraduate university through enrolment management, meeting its larger staffing needs for four-year programs by redeploying staff. It will do all of this, moreover, with the suspicion that the minister and perhaps the cabinet are regretting their acceptance of the new mission and their own commitments during the boom times. While there is no going back for the university, proceeding into the future may prove even more challenging than anticipated.

There are two aspects of the history of Mount Royal University's emergence that should provoke wider reflection. The first is the process by which new institutions receive general recognition in Canada. Though it was useful for Mount Royal to claim that AUCC membership was essential for the general credibility of its degrees – and perhaps it was, at least in the eyes of most public universities – that only raises the question of whether the organizational characteristics identified in AUCC's membership criteria are truly related to academic quality. It is at least conceivable that a university organized along different lines can offer programs that achieve higher level learning outcomes than similar programs offered by Canadian universities. Indeed, few European universities would satisfy AUCC's membership criteria. Moreover, as American higher education demonstrates, sharing organizational

characteristics does not necessarily yield high, consistent, or even acceptable academic quality. Ultimately, as the Council of Higher Education Accreditation (CHEA) in the United States has argued, the bottom line in higher education is what graduating students know and can do, and that seems a reasonable starting point for recognition of programs and institutions across jurisdictional or other lines. In this sense, the position taken by the Council of Ministers of Education, Canada, with Alberta in the lead, is worth repeating: "Quality assurance of degree programs has become increasingly important as the landscape of degree providers becomes more diverse in Canada. . . . The lack of national or common standards presents a challenge for student mobility and transferability within Canada and for understanding of Canadian education and institutions internationally."[31]

Are there alternatives to the current reliance on AUCC membership criteria for the recognition of degree-granting institutions or degree programs offered by new or external institutions? If not, there ought to be. There is an obvious conflict of interest involved in AUCC serving as the promotional body and lobby group for the public universities while screening out organizations that do not share the characteristics of the public universities. That is why AUCC applies its membership criteria only to applicants for membership rather than to its existing members, most of whom have never been reviewed by AUCC. CMEC, which has endorsed quality assurance and degree-level standards for universities, is a talk shop unlikely ever to agree on a national agency of some kind. One suspects that it will be effective in post-secondary education when the post-secondary institutions themselves have already largely formed a consensus on matters. Chances of that happening with respect to a national means to insert institutions and programs into a national context of academic credibility are minimal, given the penchant of those institutions for hanging on to the criteria they won in the 1960s – the mandates including research, bicameral governance – and to make them into badges necessary for academic credibility.

In an age when people expect to build on their academic credentials through a lifetime and mobile populations expect to have their prior learning formally recognized, provincial governments have a responsibility to assist people through credit transfer and credential recognition processes. They also have a responsibility to think imaginatively about what sorts of institutions and institutional arrangements are required to maximize the human resource potential of their community through education. In higher education, there should be "no dead ends," as a report in Ontario declared, without much effect on government or university practice. In Canada, only Alberta and British Columbia have set up mechanisms that deal adequately with transfer issues, while Quebec's unusual system rather finesses the issue insofar as internal institutions are concerned. The experiments with college baccalaureate degrees in BC and Alberta – efforts at creating a more differentiated higher educational system – wound up making the principal colleges into universities, in order to safeguard the interests of their students, while the degrees offered by Ontario colleges, thanks in part to university snobbishness, and in part to the comparatively low academic standards of some of the colleges, are becoming seen as second-class credentials. Not surprisingly, there are growing demands for "system redesign" in Ontario and elsewhere, but that may be decades away.[32] It may be triggered only by the realization that will come eventually that our self-regarding post-secondary institutions – now among the few in major industrial democracies that are not subject to serious periodic external program or institutional examination – have not necessarily been the best custodians of the popular interest.

That leaves primarily the federal government. In the United States, the federal government uses its student financial aid programs to require all institutions benefiting from such funding to be accredited by an agency identified by the federal government. Perhaps that practice suggests an alternative for Canada. Perhaps the federal government could decide that all universities receiving funding must be accredited by a federally sponsored agency whose mandate would be to ensure that all "accredited" universities have quality assurance policies, standards, and procedures consistent with those already endorsed by CMEC – and take the results into account in ongoing practice. In short, a new federal agency might focus on the quality of quality assurance activities undertaken by universities, notably including periodic program and institutional reviews by wholly external panels of experts. Thus,

the story of Mount Royal's long development from a tiny Methodist college into a medium-sized public university over a century is one that not only sheds light on the development of Alberta or even on the transformations of a single institution but opens interesting vistas on larger issues.

The second aspect bears on the challenge of transforming a pedagogically-oriented college into an institution whose internal culture is pervaded by a commitment to, and awareness of, the importance of advancing knowledge and understanding through research and creative activities. This will not be easy because of changes within the university sector itself. In an essay on the development of colleges and universities, Michael Skolnik notes that the "binary" system erected in the 1960s, with colleges serving primarily economic roles and the universities focusing on the liberal arts, the professions, research, and graduate study, was bypassed in the 1990s by changes in both sectors.[33] College programs evolved to meet the increasingly complex needs of the workplace while the universities also reoriented themselves to the economy by adding new applied degree and career programs, forming partnerships with business and industry, and becoming more market- and economy-oriented. The university, he suggests, should have "welcomed" rather than fought college degree programs because those programs would obviate the need for the university to serve the economic needs those programs addressed. The university, he says, must seek a balance between an economic role and what it uniquely does best – "the advancement and conservation of knowledge, the search for truth, and . . . 'the ceaseless struggle to see things in relation,' which can easily be jeopardized if it makes service to the economy its primary allegiance."[34] In his work on the University of Saskatchewan, Michael Hayden emphasized much the same point in describing the challenge of "maintaining a balance between creative intelligence and applied intelligence, between study and service," because programs in applied fields of practice may lead to undesirable constrictions on the university's creative capacity. Thus, he concluded, the university will need "the freedom to apply the store of creative intelligence that it has been cultivating for so long in ways that suit its capabilities and in ways that will preserve its nature."[35]

As a largely economically oriented college, Mount Royal had stood out for the strength of its liberal arts requirements. Now, as a university, it will need to find a convincing and continuously refreshed balance among its "economic," "democratic," and "educational" roles. While the liberal arts core curriculum will play a key role in this regard, the capacity to ask big questions, to see the larger implications in details and techniques, exists in all fields. "One of the greatest opportunities of our college," George Kerby wrote in 1912, "is the fact that we have the young people for the most part at the formative period of their lives, and we are able to help them in shaping their ideals and determining their life purposes and work. This, in our judgment, is the greatest mission of our college. The chief function of the college is to discover the man in the student and train him for citizenship and public service. It makes little difference whether the college is state or private endowed, if it only opens up some celestial vision or enables the young mind to catch the gleam."[36] Echoing Kerby's concern about the fundamental purpose of education, Alison Wolf wrote exactly ninety years later: "The contribution of education to economic life is only one aspect of education, not the entirety, and it does not deserve the overwhelming emphasis which it now enjoys. . . . Our recent forebears, living in significantly poorer times, were occupied above all with the cultural, moral and intellectual purposes of education. We impoverish ourselves by our indifference to these."[37]

Indeed, one may hope that, as Mount Royal University enters the next chapter of its existence, it will remain inspired by its founders' view that education is about more than preparing people for the workforce, that it is even more importantly about shaping the best in both the individual and society – that it will continue to see its primary function as that of enabling minds, "to catch the gleam."

This early proposed design for the Mount Royal College badge is believed to have been designed by Alexander Scott Carter, one of Canada's pre-eminent heraldic artists. The motto "quam bene non quantum" means "how well, not how much." Mount Royal University Archives 1912-2.

from Mr. Vincent Massey Toronto

Mount Royal College students presented this silver cup to Principal George Kerby to congratulate him on receiving an honorary Doctor of Divinity from Victoria College, University of Toronto, in 1912. Students held Rev. Kerby in high regard. Photographer Ewan Nicholson; Mount Royal University Archives 1912-1.

Student academic achievement over the decades has been recognized in many ways, including the award of medals. Ida Schrader received a medal in 1915 for shorthand and typewriting and the Henry Birks and Sons Gold Medal was presented to Ron Prokosch in 1968. Photographer Jim Baillies (Schrader medal) and Mike Ridewood (Birks medal); Mount Royal University Archives 1915-1 and Birks medal courtesy Ron Prokosch.

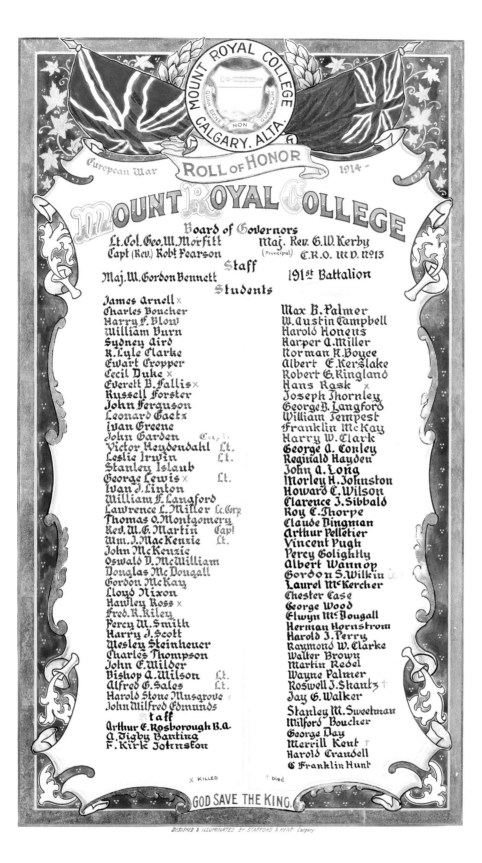

This hand-cal-
ligraphed scroll
commemorates the
service and sacrifice of
Mount Royal College
students, alumni and
employees in the First
World War. Mount
Royal University
Archives 1917-1.

These paintings of Mount Royal College's founding Chairman, The Honourable William Cushing, and founding Principal, Rev. George Kerby, hang in the East Gate entry to Kerby Hall. Both were painted by renowned Canadian and International portrait artist John Wycliffe Lowes Forster, who completed 500 such works during his illustrious career. Upon his death in 1938, his estate formed the nucleus of Canada's National Portrait Gallery in Ottawa. Photographer Jim Baillies; Mount Royal University Archives 1930-1-1 and 1930-1-2.

Designed and stitched by Miss Margaret Carrick, Dean of Girls and House Directress, in 1935, this tapestry now hangs in the Mount Royal University Executive Boardroom. The work captures Mount Royal College's first 24 years of history, including its 1910 date of incorporation, the name of founder and first Principal George Kerby, becoming a junior college of the University of Alberta in 1931, the College's Christian roots, the lamps of learning and the College badge. Miss Carrick worked at Mount Royal College from 1911-1942. She became a close friend of the Kerbys and was well liked by students, remaining in touch with many until her death in 1958. The Margaret Carrick Scholarship was presented by the Mount Royal Educational Club from 1942-1966. Photographer Jim Baillies; Mount Royal University Archives 1935-1.

These two hand-calligraphed scrolls were designed by A.J. Casson, a member of Canada's famed Group of Seven artists. They honour the service of Mount Royal Junior College students, alumni and employees who served in the Second World War, and are on display in the Mount Royal University Alumni Relations office. Photographer Jim Baillies; Mount Royal University Archives 1946-1-1 and 1946-1-2.

Four stained glass windows were installed in the chapel of the Kerby Memorial Building in 1951. Commissioned by Principal George Kerby and created by Robert McCausland Ltd. of Toronto, Canada's pre-eminent stained glass firm and North America's oldest, they pay tribute to four of the institution's founding Board members: James Garden, William Hunt, Henry Jenkins and Melville Scott. The windows currently hang in the East Arts building. Photographer Jim Baillies; Mount Royal University Archives 1949-1, 1949-2, 1949-3, 1949-4.

The original Mount Royal College building in downtown Calgary, ca. 1969. The building was demolished shortly after opening of the Lincoln Park Campus in 1972. Mount Royal University Archives G1102.

The open-concept Library in Mount Royal College's Lincoln Park Campus, ca. 1972. Photographer Janet Brown; Mount Royal University Archives G1103.

Lincoln Park Campus expansion in the late 1980s resulted in
the creation of two new main entrances, the East and West
Gates, that enhanced the building's presence. Photographer
Pablo Galvez; Mount Royal University Marketing and
Communications.

Signature sculpture Homage, one of two by artist Derek
Besant, was installed at the West Gate in 1989 following a
public competition. A second sculpture, Enigma, was installed at the East Gate. Photographer Pablo Galvez; Mount
Royal University Marketing and Communications.

Marnie and Hall Wyatt (Founding Chairman, The Mount Royal College Foundation) at the console of The Carthy Organ at Mount Royal College in Wyatt Recital Hall, 1996. Photographer Paul Coates; Mount Royal University Archives E96-25-1.

Simon Preston (Organist, Westminster Abbey) performed at the inaugural concert of The Carthy Organ at Mount Royal College, 1996. Photographer Paul Coates; Mount Royal University Archives E96-25-2.

The Dr. John H. Garden Memorial Park opened in 1998 in the Kerby Hall courtyard to pay tribute to individuals in whose names memorial scholarships have been established at Mount Royal. To date, more than 150 people have been so honoured. The Park's namesake, John Garden, was one of the first students to enroll at Mount Royal College and later served as Principal. Photographer Pablo Galvez; Mount Royal University Marketing and Communications.

Aerial view of the Mount Royal Campus, 2006. Photographer James Dyck; Mount Royal University Marketing and Communications.

IT'S OUR FIRST.

Certificate of Birth

MOUNT ROYAL

Bachelor of Nursing (BN)

ARRIVED AT 10 A.M.
THURSDAY THE 15TH DAY
OF MARCH, 2007 A.D.

Calgary's oldest post-secondary
institution proudly announces
the birth of the first Mount
Royal university degree:
The Bachelor of Nursing.

Dave Marshall
President, Mount Royal College

Hal Kvisle
Chair, Board of Governors

MOUNT ROYAL
COLLEGE
Calgary, Alberta

mtroyal.ca/nursing

The "birth announcement" ad celebrating the launch of Mount Royal College's first degree program, Bachelor of Nursing, on March 15, 2007. Artwork by Mount Royal University External Relations; Mount Royal University Marketing and Communications.

Students and employees celebrate Mount Royal's official transition to Mount Royal University, September 2009. Photographer Tomas Kraus; Mount Royal University Marketing and Communications.

Mount Royal
College Campus,
2006. Mount
Royal University
Marketing and
Communications.
Photo credit
Pablo Galvez.

Concept rendering for The Bella Concert Hall, the new Mount Royal University Conservatory teaching facility and performance hall made possible by contributions from the Taylor family, Government of Canada, Province of Alberta, City of Calgary and Mount Royal University. Construction of the building, to be located on the east side of the campus near the Roderick Mah Centre for Continuous Learning, is scheduled for Spring 2011 and opening is slated for 2013. Design by Sahuri & Partners Architecture Ltd. (Calgary) and Pfeiffer Partners Architects Inc. (Los Angeles); Mount Royal University Office of the Vice-President, University Advancement.

APPENDICES

APPENDIX 1. CHAIRMEN OF THE BOARD OF GOVERNORS, 1910-2010

NAME	PERIOD ON BOARD	Term as Chairman
William H. Cushing	1910–34	1910–1926
George D. Stanley	1910–54	1926–1954
Clinton J. Ford	1931–64	1954–1960
Howard P. Wright	1955–72	1960–1970
Martha R. Cohen	1966–74	1970–1974
Russell H. Purdy	1970–75	1974–1975
Gerald M. Burden	1975–81	1975–1981
Roy V. Deyell	1981–87	1981–1987
B. Jean Fraser	1982–88	1987–1988
Douglas E. Thomson	1983–90	1988–1990
Anne S. Tingle	1990–96	1990–1996
A. Douglas Rogan	1990–97	1996–1997
David Tuer	1995–01	1997–2001
Jack Ady	2000–03	2001–2002
Hal Kvisle	2001–07	2002–2007
Cathy Williams	2003–10	2007–2010

APPENDIX 2. MOUNT ROYAL STUDENTS, 1981-2009

(Based on data from Office of Institutional Analysis and Planning, Trends-at-a-Glance)

	1981-82	1985-86	1990-91	1995-96	2000-01	2005-06	2008-09
COURSE REGISTRATIONS							
Total Registrations	56,797	72,411	85,220	93,244	109,892	122,043	129,311
Credit Total	35,471	43,470	52,195	56,295	57,998	69,420	77,299
Extension Total	21,326	28,941	33,025	36,949	51,894	52,623	
Continuing Education	14,263	21,748	20,385	21,451	32,824	34,899	36,304
Academic Upgrading				2,597	3,704	4,027	3,821
International Programs			2,759	2,728	4,548	3,901	3,239
Conservatory	7,063	7,193	9,881	10,173	10,818	9,796	8,648
CREDIT REGISTRANTS							
FTE /FLE (see note 1)	3,989	5,077	4,862	5,682	6,611	7,808	7,847
Headcount (Annual Unique)			9,370	10,047	11,265	12,468	13,278
Fall applications	4,931	9,011	12,131	12,027	13.041	14,382	15,519
Targeted admission level		3,846	4,090	4,289	4,430	5,092	4,574
Ratio		2.3	3.0	2.8	2.9	2.8	3.4
Parchments awarded	481	796	995	1,239	1,461	1,679	1,011
Enrolment by program type							
% 4-year degree				4.4%	6.1%	10.5%	30.7%
% 4-year applied degree				1.8%	14%	26.4%	15.9%
% 2-year diploma		43.2%	38.5%	30.5%	25.0%	15.9%	13.2%
% 1-year certificate		12.7%	10.0%	7.9%	4%	3.3%	5.3%
% university transfer		14.7%	19.3%	23.7%	29.3%	27.5%	10.6%
% open/compensatory studies		29.5%	32.2%	26.8%	21.8%	16.4%	24.2%

APPENDIX 2. MOUNT ROYAL STUDENTS, 1981-2009 cont.

	1981-82	1985-86	1990-91	1995-96	2000-01	2005-06	2008-09
STUDENT PROFILE							
% full-time (see note 2)	47.4%	57.7%	49.2%	59.2%	61.1%	69.4	73.8%
% female	55.5%	56.0%	57.5%	60.1%	63.3%	63.0%	62.8%
% new to college	39.1%	30.5%	41.6%	38.9%	38.2%	32.1%	33.4%
% direct from high school			31.2%	33.5%	37.9%	42.7%	44.4%
% Calgary origin	84.2%	85.2%	83.2%	81.8%	82.0%	79.8%	80.1%
Full-time average age (Fall)	22.1	22.7	23.1	23.1	22.1	21.8	21.7
Part-time average age (Fall)	27.6	28.0	26.8	27.5	25.6	25.5	25.5
Entering average age (Fall)		23.4	23.2	22.8	22.2	21.1	21.2
Total average age (Fall)	24.4	24.7	24.8	24.5	23.5	23.1	22.7
% Visa students					2.3%	1.9%	2.6%
LOANS / SCHOLARSHIPS							
No. student recipients of loans		2,591	3,433	3,079	2,268	3,350	3,416
% receiving financial assistance		59.5%	45.9%	49.4%	32.9%	38.7%	34.9%
Est. average financial award		$3,219	$3,611	$4,192	$6,446	$4,671	4.885
Scholarship/bursary funds		$309,934	$332,834	$456,432	$1,208,597	$2,874,049	$5,305,793
Full-time student recipients		462	475	644	1,250	2,303	2,872
PROGRAMS							
Number of program offerings		64	67	53	68	68	68
Number of parchment programs			53	45	59	58	61
Number of course offerings		740	894	959	880	1,007	1,012
% courses ACAT transferable		35.0%	44.7%	54.4%	70.9%	65.9%	76.7%

PLEASE NOTE: Definitions and calculation methodologies changed over time. Data for some categories may not be comparable across the years. Any instance where data field is blank means that verifiable data is not available.

NOTES
1) FTE (Full-Time Equivalent) was based on standardized credit values which are the same for each program. From 1990/91 onwards FTE was replaced by the FLE (Full-Load Equivalent) which is based on program specific credit load.
2) A student is considered Full Time if registered in at least 30% of the program full-course load in any given semester.

APPENDIX 3. MOUNT ROYAL FACULTY AND STAFF, 1981-2009

(Based on data from Office of Institutional Analysis and Planning, Trends-at-a-Glance)

	1981-82	1985-86	1990-91	1995-96	2000-01	2005-06	2008-09
EMPLOYEE COMPLEMENT							
Total complement		1,246	1,816	1,575	1,843	2,017	2,345
Faculty (unique headcount)	463	951	1,350	1,141	1,295	1,388	1,584
Full-time credit (includes librarians, counselors)	149	174	226	202	227	276	334
Part-time credit	314	297	391	326	322	451	520
Continuing Education	--	368	573	423	474	492	490
International programs/Languages Institute	--			30	64	57	60
Conservatory (excluding branch instructors)	--	112	160	160	208	220	294
Support staff (excluding casuals)	347	251	404	380	493	602	722
Management	44	44	62	54	55	77	83
EMPLOYEE PROFILE							
Full-time faculty, credit							
Median age			45.0	47.0	47.5	49.6	49.5
% female			42.7%	50.0%	51.0%	51.8%	56.6%
Median length of service (years)			9.0	9.9	6.71	8.6	8.2
Support staff							
Median age			39.0	42.0	43.0	43.7	42.3
% female			72.4%	71.8%	72.0%	71.4	71.2%
Median length of service (years)			3.1	6.7	4.53	5.8	4.6
Management							
Median age			44.0	47.0	49.8	49.3	51.4
% female			38.6%	38.2%	40.0%	41.6%	48.2%
Median length of service (years)			6.5	9.9	11.91	8.1	9.9
FACULTY QUALIFICATIONS (see note 1)							
BA highest academic credential					8.4%	4.9%	5.4%
MA highest academic credential					53.2%	50.9%	47.2%
PhD highest academic credential					38.4%	43.6%	46.0%

PLEASE NOTE: Definitions and calculation methodologies may have changed over time. Data for some categories may not be comparable across the years. Any instance where data field is blank means that verifiable data is not available. Faculty qualifications are provided for full-time credit faculty only.

APPENDIX 4: STUDENT COUNCIL PRESIDENTS, 1911–2010

Student organizations changed in nature over time. The Students' Association of Mount Royal College (SAMRC) was established under the Societies Act in 1968, after which the president was been elected in annual elections open to all students. Missing data are due to lack of sources.

YEAR	PRESIDENT	ORGANIZATION
1911–12	Percy Morecombe	Students' Council
1912–13	Percy Morecombe	Students' Council
1914–15	Percy W. Smith	Students' Council
1915–16	Harold P. Young	Students' Council
1916–17	Lester McKinnon	Students' Council
1917–18	Mansfield G. Newton	Students' Council
1919–20	Aileen Sibbald	Junior Executive
1920–21	Walter Hymas	Student Council (Boys)
	Helen Schoonmaker	Student Council (Girls)
1921–22	George Chennells	Student Council (Boys)
1930–31	Ken Underwood	High School Class
1931–32	Findlay Barnes	Students' Union
	Kay Short	High School Class
1937–38	Bill Dickie	Student Council
	Bob Anderson	High School Class
1938–39	Don Swanson	Students' Council
	Jeanette Farman	University Class
	Don Francis	Commercial Council
	Bob Anderson	High School Class
1939–40	Maxwell MacCrimmon	Students' Council
	R. W. Brookes Avey	University Class
	Marguerite Carr	Commercial Class
	Harvey Barker (killed in War)	High School Class
1941–42	Don Jones	Students' Council
1942–43	Norman Hovan	Students' Council
1943–44	Robert Treacy	Students' Council
1944–45	Robert McCulloch	Students' Council
1945–46	George Villett	Students' Council
1946–47	Cal Franke	Students' Council
1947–48	Dave Mitchell; Dick Irvine	Students' Council

YEAR	PRESIDENT	ORGANIZATION
1948–49	Bob Gilmour	Students' Council
1949–50	Mike Farrell	Students' Council
1950–51	Roger Lundgren	Students' Council
1951–52	Gordon Kenny	Students' Council
1952–53	Jim Wallace	Students' Council
1953–54	Phil Parr	Students' Council
1954–55	Grant Hinchey; Bill Halliday	Students' Council
1955–56	Early Berry (fall); Pete Rasmusen (spring)	Students' Council
1956–57	Dave Porter	Students' Council
1957–58	Claude Haplin	Junior College Council
	Lew Menegozzo	High School Union
1958–59	Scott Kirk	Junior College Students' Council
	None listed	High School Union
1959–60	Jack Finlay	Junior College Council
	Wayne Harvey	High School Council
1960–61	Kent Lyle	Junior College Council
	Lynn Hickey	High School Council
1961–62	Peter Slaa	Junior College Council
	Mel Gale	High School Council
1962–63	Don Thonger	Junior College Council
	Roger Askey	High School Council
1963–64	John Sleutel	Junior College Council
	Bill Naismith	High School Council

YEAR	PRESIDENT	ORGANIZATION	YEAR	PRESIDENT	ORGANIZATION
1964–65	R. John Carstairs	Junior College Council	1986–87	Kevin Scott	
	Robert Stockhall	High School Council	1987–88	Doug Henderson	
1966–67	Harry L. Moss	Junior College Union	1988–89	Pat Walsh	
1967–68	Ron Prokosch	Senior Executive Council	1989–90	Mark Corbett	
1968–69	Bob Glass	Students' Council	1990–91	Dave Wylie	
1969–70	Brent Winnitoy	Students' Council	1991–92	Sandeep Dhir	
1970–71	Marvin Symons	Students' Association	1993–93	Noreen Branagh; Michele Decottignies	
1971–72	Dennis Docherty		1993–94	Brian McCabe	
1972–73	Kit Rainsforth		1994–95	Brendan Correia	
1973–74	Gary J. Dolha		1995–96	Jackie Fisher	
1974–75	Gary J. Dolha		1996–97	Bryan Boechler	
1975–76	Max Nelson		1997–98	Heather Wilkey	
1976–77	John Hind		1998–99	Heather Wilkey	
1977–78	Greg Ho Lem		1999–00	Bradley J. Bauer	
1978–79	Kris Farkas		2001–01	Sean Fraser	
1979–80	Colleen Albiston		2001–02	James Wood	
1980–81	Scotty McGowan		2002–03	James Wood	
1981–82	Scotty McGowan		2003–04	Jennifer Wietzel	
1982–83	Tom Boettger		2004–05	Jackie Chukrey	
1983–84	Larry Lee		2005–06	Jackie Chukrey	
1984–85	Larry Lee		2006–07	Jonathon Macpherson	
1985–86	Paul Pressel; Adam Dutkowski		2007–08	Jonathon Macpherson	
			2008–09	Travis McIntosh	
			2009–10	Travis McIntosh	

APPENDIX 5: PRESIDENTS OF THE FACULTY AND STAFF ASSOCIATIONS, 1966-67 TO 2009-2010

YEAR	MRFA	PROGRAM	MRSSA	DEPARTMENT
1966-67	Arne Wawruch	Interior Design		
1967-68	Glenn Burgess/Arne Wawruch	Biology		
1968-69	Robert McDougall	Humanities		
1969-70	David MacNab	Mathematics		
1970-71	Wes Akerman	Physical Education and Recreation		
1971-72	David MacNab	Mathematics		
1972-73	Hugh MacLeod	History		
1973-74	Hugh MacLeod	History		
1974-75	David Thomas	Political Science		
1975-76	George Papas/Richard Collier	Philosophy/ English		
1976-77	Richard Collier	English		
1977-78	Alexandra Bradley	Library	Steve Evans	Media Service
1978-79	Alexandra Bradley	Library	Debbie Goudie	Library
1979-80	Reva Stilwell	Mathematics	Debbie Goudie	Library
1980-81	Barry Pashak	Sociology	Ev Pilkington	Physical Education and Recreation
1981-82	Barry Pashak	Sociology	Stan Quick	Physical Education and Recreation
1982-83	Jane Hayes	Secretarial Arts	Diane Munson	Registrar
1983-84	Roger Tierney	Counseling	Diane Munson	Registrar
1984-85	Roger Tierney	Counseling	Bev Moore	Science and Technology
1985-86	Chuck Killingsworth	Physical Education	Bob LaMarsh	Maintenance
1986-87	Hugh MacLeod	History	Kim McKellar	Engineering Services
1987-88	Hugh MacLeod	History	Kim McKellar	Engineering Services
1988-89	Mark Chikinda	Broadcasting	Kim McKellar	Engineering Services
1989-90	Marc Chikinda	Broadcasting	Patti Haines	Nursing
1990-91	Maxine Mott	Nursing	Patti Haines	Nursing
1991-92	Maxine Mott/Wayne Haglund	Nursing/ Earth Sciences	Jan Kruger	Library Services
1992-93	Greg Flanagan	Economics	Jan Kruger	Library Services
1993-94	Greg Flanagan	Economics	Stephen Davies	Library Services
1994-95	John D. Balcers	Journalism	Stephen Davies	Library Services

1995-96	John D. Balcers	Journalism	Maureen Bedard	Library Services
1996-97	Tom MacAlister	Biology	Maureen Bedard	Library Services
1997-98	Tom MacAlister	Biology	Maureen Bedard	Library Services
1998-99	Tom MacAlister	Biology	Maureen Bedard	Library Services
1999-00	Tom MacAlister	Biology	Maureen Bedard	Library Services
2000-01	Jerre Paquette	English	Wayne Hudson	Conservatory
2001-02	Jerre Paquette	English	Wayne Hudson	Conservatory
2002-03	Randy Genereux	Psychology	Maureen Bedard	Library Services
2003-04	Randy Genereux	Psychology	Maureen Bedard	Library Services
2004-05	Randy Genereux	Psychology	Maureen Bedard	Library Services
2005-06	David Hyttenrauch	English	Chris McNelly/ Joy Bilozir	Human Resources/Conservatory
2006-07	David Hyttenrauch	English	Joy Bilozir	Conservatory
2007-08	David Hyttenrauch	English	Joy Bilozir	Conservatory
2008-09	David Hyttenrauch	English	Maureen Bedard	Library Services
2009-10	David Hyttenrauch	English	Maureen Bedard	Library Services

APPENDIX 6: MAJOR DONORS TO MOUNT ROYAL COLLEGE

DONOR NAME	DESIGNATIONS (most significant gifts)	Notes

David and Leslie Bissett
  Bissett Scholarship for Excellence in Business
  David and Leslie Bissett Scholarship
  Future Campus Expansion Bissett School of Business
  Chair Business Administration
  Chair Financial Management
  Executive-in-Residence
  Institute for Nonprofit Studies
  Aviation program – Springbank Hangar
  Conservatory's Connection
	Bissett School of Business	Recognized through the naming of the Bissett School of Business and the East B Building

Donald McCaffrey	Future Campus Expansion Health and Science Facility	Recognized through the naming of the Roderick Mah Centre for Continuous Learning
Dr. Norman Wong	Future Campus Expansion Health and Science Facility	Recognized through the naming of the Roderick Mah Centre for Continuous Learning
Wayne and Eleanor Chiu	Future Campus Expansion Health and Science Facility	Recognized through the naming of the Roderick Mah Centre for Continuous Learning
F. Richard Matthews, Q.C.	Future Campus Expansion	
Joyce Austin	Judy Wish Hamilton Memorial Scholarship for Excellence in Communication	Gift made posthumously
John Simpson	Cougar Statue	
Hal Kvisle Kvisle Scholarship in Biological Sciences	Investing in Futures Campaign: Excellence in Teaching	
James Stanford Investing in Futures Campaign: Excellence in Teaching Investing in Futures Campaign: Innovative Programs Investing in Futures Campaign: Student Success	James M. Stanford Bursary	
Richard and Lois Haskayne Small Business Training Centre	Haskayne Entrance Scholarship	
Anonymous Chief Jack Beaton Bursary in Criminal Justice Studies	Investing in Futures Campaign: Excellence in Teaching	
H. Norman Stewart Small Business Training Centre	Hal Wyatt 90th Anniversary Scholarship in Applied Nonprofit Studies	
Joan Snyder	Joan C. Snyder Academy Scholarship	

DONOR NAME	DESIGNATIONS (most significant gifts)	Notes
Anonymous	Mount Royal Bright Futures Scholarships Centre for Continuous Learning Institute for Nonprofit Studies Institute for Nonprofit Studies Research MRU Kids Future Leaders Program	
Morningside Foundation Limited	Morningside Music Bridge	
Carthy Foundation	Wyatt Artist in Residence Conservatory's Connection Institute for Nonprofit Studies Chamber of Commerce Directed Field Studies R. Michael Mears Scholarship	
Anonymous	Small Business Training Centre	
The Kahanoff Foundation	Dufort Project Learning Technology Fund Music Program General Donations	
Encana Corporation	Encana Wellness Centre Integrative Health Institute Chief Jack Beaton Bursary in Criminal Justice Studies Judy Wish Hamilton Memorial Scholarship Excellence for Communication	Please note new format of corporate name

APPENDIX 6: MAJOR DONORS TO MOUNT ROYAL COLLEGE cont.

DONOR NAME	DESIGNATIONS (most significant gifts)	Notes
Students' Association Mount Royal University	Mount Royal University Students' Association Wyckham Centre Students' Association Bursaries	While SAMRU has a high level of cumulative giving, the most significant gifts were provided just prior to 1990
ENMAX	ENMAX Bright Minds Scholarship ENMAX/Thomas Wood Distinguished Speaker Series	
Mount Royal Cougar Booster Club	Cougar Booster Endowment Athletics Team Travel Intercollegiate Athletics Multiple, significant scholarship donations for student athletes in basketball, volleyball, hockey, badminton, etc.	
The Calgary Foundation	Multiple designations	Funds are receipted by the Calgary Foundation, and redirected to Mount Royal.
TransCanada Corporation	Bright Minds, Bright Futures Campaign Small Business Training Centre Kvisle Scholarship in Biological Sciences	Recognized through the naming of the TransCanada Amphitheatre
RGO Office Products Partnership	Centre for Continuous Learning	Recognized through the naming of Ross Glen Hall in the Centre for Continuous Learning
Nickle Family Foundation	Nickle Foundation Theatre Project Nickle Theatre Lighting Lab	Recognized through the naming of the Nickle Theatre

NOTES

CHAPTER 1: FOUNDING THE COLLEGE

1   W. H. Cushing, Chairman, Charles F. Adams, Secretary, and George W. Kerby, Principal, "Fourth Report to the Alberta Conference, 1914," *Journal of the General Conference of the Methodist Church*, 1914, 221.

2   On Alberta, see Desmond Berghofer and Alan Vladicka, *Access to Opportunity, 1905–80: The Development of Post-Secondary Education in Alberta* (Edmonton: Alberta Advanced Education and Manpower, 1980), 6–7; Lewis G. Thomas, *The Church of England and Higher Education in the Prairie West before 1914* (Canadian Church Historical Society, 1956); A. D. Winspear, "Bishop Pinkham College, Calgary's First," *Golden West* (March–April 1956). See also D. C. Masters, *Protestant Church Colleges in Canada: A History* (Toronto: University of Toronto Press, 1966). On the broader history of higher education in Canada, see Robin Sutton Harris and Arthur Tremblay, *Bibliography of Higher Education in Canada / Bibliographie de l'enseignement Supérieur Au Canada* (Toronto: University of Toronto Press, 1960); Harris, *Bibliography of Higher Education in Canada: Supplement 1981* (Toronto: University of Toronto Press, 1981); *A History of Higher Education in Canada, 1663–1960* (Toronto: University of Toronto Press, 1976); and Harris, ed., *Changing Patterns of Higher Education in Canada* (Toronto: University of Toronto Press, 1966).

3   The reserves were those of the Blackfoot near Gleichen, Blood near Cardston, Peigan near Pincher Creek, Sarcee near Calgary, and Stoney near Morley.

4   For key documents, see Douglas R. Owram, ed., *The Formation of Alberta: A Documentary History* (Calgary: Alberta Records Publication Board, 1979); for general accounts, see Gerald Friesen, *The Canadian Prairies: A History* (Toronto: University of Toronto Press), and Howard Palmer and Tamara Palmer, *Alberta: A New History* (Edmonton: Hurtig Publishers, 1990).

5   "Calgary is named after a small town in Scotland: the word 'Calgary' is of a Gaelic origin and means clear water": *Henderson's Alberta Gazetteer and Directory, 1924*, 7. But scholars disagree: "The true meaning . . . is 'Bay Farm.' It may not sound as apt or attractive as 'clear running water' but at least it is accurate and Calgarians should cease to perpetuate an etymological fraud." George F. G. Stanley, "The Naming of Calgary," *Alberta History* 23, no. 3 (1975): 7–10.

6   Omar Lavalee, "Canadian Pacific," in Stephen Wilk, with Valerie Jobson and Redvers Perry, eds., *100 Years of Nose Creek Valley History* (Calgary: Nose Creek Historical Society, 1997), 114.

7   http://thegauntlet.ca/story/8857 (retrieved 27 Jan. 2010).

8   Cited in Wilfrid Eggleston, Homestead on the Range (Ottawa: Borealis Press, 1982), 7.

9   Simon Evans, "Spatial Aspects of the Cattle Kingdom: The First Decade, 1882–1892," in Anthony W. Rasporich and Henry C. Klassen, eds., *Frontier Calgary: Town, City, Region, 1875–1914* (Calgary: University of Calgary Press, 1975), 41–56.

10 Max Foran, *Calgary: An Illustrated History* (Toronto: James Lorimer & Co., 1982), 180, Table 11: Building Permits Issued in Calgary, 1907–68, and Table 12: The Labour Force of Calgary by Industry, 1911–61; and 174, Table 2: Number of males per 1,000 Females in Calgary, 1891–1971. Also Foran, "Land Speculation and Urban Development in Calgary, 1884–1912," in Rasporich and Klassen, eds., *Frontier Calgary*, 203–20; J. P. Dickin McGinnis, "Birth to Boom to Bust: Building in Calgary, 1875–1914," ibid., 6–19. Foran wrote several other works on Calgary's history, including *Calgary: Canada's Frontier Metropolis* (Burlington, ON: Windsor Publications Inc., 1978);, and, with Heather MacEwan Foran, *Calgary, Canada's Frontier Metropolis: An Illustrated History* (Calgary: Windsor Publications, Inc, 1982).

11 E.g., Judy Bedford, "Prostitution in Calgary, 1905–1914," *Alberta History* 29, no. 2 (1981): 1–11; Terry L. Chapman, "Women, Sex and Marriage in Western Canada, 1890–1920," *Alberta History* 33, no. 4 (1985): 1–12. "Calgary, like Winnipeg, is a city of homeless young men," Bob Edwards wrote in the *Eye Opener*, and "they "must occasionally feel a bit lonesome and long for the … society of cheerful young ladies to enliven the situation." *Eye Opener*, 20 May 1911. Edwards regularly dwelt on evidence of personal hypocrisy and the absurdities of some of the arguments put forward by "moral reformers" and "purity leaguers."

12 For popular accounts of prairie social tensions in this period, see James Gray, *Red Lights on the Prairies* (Toronto: Macmillan, 1971), and *Booze: The Impact of Whiskey on the Prairie West* (Toronto: Macmillan, 1972).

13 On early Methodist development in Canada, see: George A. Rawlyk, *The Canada Fire: Radical Evangelicalism in British North America, 1775–1812* (Kingston: McGill-Queen's University Press, 1974); J. H. Riddell, *Methodism in the Middle West* (Toronto: Ryerson Press, 1946); Neil Semple, *The Lord's Dominion: The History of Canadian Methodism* (Montreal/Kingston: McGill-Queen's University Press, 1996); Goldwin French, *Parsons and Politics: The Role of Wesleyan Methodists in Upper Canada and the Maritimes from 1780 to 1855* (Toronto: University of Toronto Press, 1962); "Methodism and Education in the Atlantic Provinces 1800–1874," in Charles H. Scobie and John W. Grant, eds., *The Contribution of Methodism to Atlantic Canada* (Montreal/Kingston: McGill-Queen's University Press, 1992), 152–53; and "Egerton Ryerson and the Methodist Model for Upper Canada," in Neil McDonald and Alf Chaiton, eds.,. *Egerton Ryerson and His Times* (Toronto: University of Toronto Press, 1978), 45–58.

14   George Whitefield, letter to Dr. Durrell, in George Whitefield, *Works* (1771), cited in *The Compact Edition of the Oxford English Dictionary* 1: 395. On Whitefield's role in the transatlantic spread, see Frank Lambert, *Pedlar in Divinity: George Whitefield and the Transatlantic Revivals, 1737–1770* (Princeton: Princeton University Press, 1993) .

15   Clara Thomas, *Ryerson of Upper Canada* (Toronto: University of Toronto Press, 1969), 16.

16   Richard Allen, "The Social Gospel and the Reform Tradition in Canada, 1890–1928," *Canadian Historical Review* 49 (1968): 382; see also Allen, *The Social Passion: Religion and Social Reform in Canada 1914–1928* (Toronto: University of Toronto Press, 1971).

17   John H. Wigger, *Taking Heaven by Storm: Methodism and the Rise of Popular Christianity in America* (New York: Oxford University Press, 1998), 8, 11–12; also David Hempton, *Methodism: Empire of the Spirit* (New Haven: Yale University Press, 2005). On the frontier's role in shaping social values, see Jackson Lears, "Luck and Pluck in American Culture," *Chronicle of Higher Education: The Chronicle Review*, 24 Jan. 2003, 20: B15.

18   VU/UC 83.051C, Box 68–6, "The Educational Policy of the Church: A Statement Approved by the Board of Regents of United College, Winnipeg, for Submission to the Special Committee on Theological Colleges Appointed by the Board of Christian Education," 1942.

19   Foran, *Calgary: An Illustrated History*, 178.

20   Central United Church, Calgary, Centennial Book Committee, *They Gathered at the River* (Calgary: Central United Church, 1975); Emily Spencer Kerby, "Calgary's Churches Have Developed with Inspiring Rapidity," n.d., reprinted in Anne White, ed., *A New Day for Women: Life & Writings of Emily Spencer Kerby* (Calgary, 2004), 8–14.

21   J. F. Perry, "Central Methodist Church before World War One," in Rasporich and Klassen, eds., *Frontier Calgary*, 181–89; Paul Voisey, "In Search of Wealth and Status," ibid., 221–41; and Foran, *Calgary: An Illustrated History*, 32, 106, 158. For a broad sketch of the church's development, see W. J. Collett, *United Church in Calgary: Activities and Events, 1875–1970* (Calgary: Century Calgary Publishing, 1975).

22   Chapman, "Women, Sex and Marriage in Western Canada, 1890–1920," 1–12; Bedford, "Prostitution in Calgary, 1905–1914," 1–11; Nancy Sheehan, "Temperance, Education and the WCTU in Alberta, 1905–1930," *Journal of Educational Thought* 14 (1980): 108–24"; and "The WCTU on the Prairies, 1886–1930," *Prairie Forum* 6 (1981): 17–34; and Robert Irwin McLean, "A 'Most Effectual Remedy': Temperance and Prohibition in Alberta, 1875–1915" (MA thesis: University of Calgary, 1969); Gray, *Booze*, and *Red Lights on the Prairies*.

23   Central United Church, *They Gathered at the River*, 474: of the 256 voters for prohibition, 178 were members of the Methodist Church.

24   Bedford, "Prostitution in Calgary," 9; Paul Voisey, "The Votes for Women Movement," *Histoire Sociale – Social History* 23, no. 3 (1975): 18.

25   Chapman, "Women, Sex and Marriage in Western Canada," 1–12.

26   Perry, "Central Methodist Church," in Rasporich and Klassen, eds., *Frontier Calgary*, 185.

27   For other perspectives, see: W. Brooks, "The Uniqueness of Western Canadian Methodism, 1840–1925" *Journal of the Canadian Church Historical Society* 19 (1977), 57–74; G. N. Emery, "Ontario Denied: The Methodist Church on the Prairies, 1896–1914," in F. H. Armstrong, A. Stevenson, and J. D. Wilson,

eds., *Aspects of Nineteenth Century Ontario* (Toronto: University of Toronto Press, 1974), 312–26; and A. H. Child, "The Ryerson Tradition in Western Canada," in McDonald and Chaiton, eds., *Egerton Ryerson and His Times*, 279–301.

28   Perry, "Central Methodist Church," in Rasporich and Klassen, eds., *Frontier Calgary*, 187.

29   Thomas, *Ryerson of Upper Canada*, 1; C. B. Sissons, *Egerton Ryerson: His Life and Letters* (London, New York: Oxford University Press, 1947), *A History of Victoria University* (Toronto: University of Toronto Press, 1952), and *Church and State in Canadian Education: An Historical Study* (Toronto: Ryerson Press, 1959).

30   As principal, Ryerson organized the curriculum "to fit the principle in which he believed most firmly, that disciplined education was the path to self-improvement, to usefulness in society, and to service of God." Thomas, *Ryerson of Upper Canada*, 89; also: Sissons, *A History of Victoria University*, 43–66; and Nathanael Burwash, *The History of Victoria College* (Toronto, 1927), 104–27.

31   From J. G. Hodgins, ed., *The Documentary History of Education in Upper Canada* (Toronto, 1884–1910), 5: 240; quoted in Thomas, *Ryerson of Upper Canada*, 100.

32   Quoted in French, "Egerton Ryerson and the Methodist Model for Upper Canada," in McDonald and Chaiton, eds., *Egerton Ryerson and His Times*, 66.

33   French, *Parsons and Politics*, 124; and "Egerton Ryerson," 56.

34   Ryerson lost the battle against a separate Catholic system. His view: "Where there are diversities of religious opinion the method is to have combined secular instruction, and separate religious instruction – the State providing the former, and leaving the latter to the respective parents and religious persuasions of the pupils." Chief Superintendent of Education, *Annual Report of the Normal, Model, Grammar and Common Schools in Upper Canada for the Year 1855* (Toronto, 1855), 10, 23.

35   Robert M. Stamp, "Response to Urban Growth: The Bureaucratization of Public Education in Calgary, 1884–1914," in Rasporich and Klassen, eds., *Frontier Calgary*, 153–68; see also P. E. Weston, "The History of Education in Calgary" (MA thesis, University of Alberta, 1951).

36   Joan MacDonald, *The Stanstead College Story* (Stanstead, Quebec, 1977); the college is now a boarding school.

37   John G. Reid, *Mount Allison University: A History to 1963*, 2 vols. (Toronto: University of Toronto Press, 1984); French, "Methodism and Education in the Atlantic Provinces 1800–1874," in Scobie and Grant, eds., *The Contribution of Methodism to Atlantic Canada*, 152.

38   In 1938 Wesley College merged with the Manitoba College (Presbyterian) to form United College, which in 1967 became the University of Winnipeg. A. G. Bedford, *The University of Winnipeg: A History of the Founding Colleges* (Toronto: University of Toronto Press, 1976).

39   VU/UC 78.103C, Box 11, Resolution of Special Committee on Education, Saskatchewan Conference, Feb. 1910; ibid., letter from J. H. Riddell, principal, Alberta College, to Rev. J. W. Graham, General Secretary, Board of Education of the Methodist Church, 21 Feb. 1910, supported the Regina initiative, calling for "as many centres as possible," while Board member W. W. Andrews of Sackville, New Brunswick protested that "at first sight it seems unwise that local interests should determine a policy, which in the long run, will be sure to be regretted." Letter to Graham, 28 Feb. 1910. On the "hearty endorsement" of the board and the General Conference, see ibid., Box 2:

Minutes, Outgoing Correspondence, Board of Education Minute Book, 1906–1910, 15 Feb. 1910. See also: James M. Pitsula, *An Act of Faith: The Early Years of Regina College* (Regina: Canadian Plains Research Center, University of Regina, 1988), 8–9; W. A. Riddell, *The First Decade: A History of the University of Saskatchewan, Regina Campus, 1960–1970* (Regina: University of Regina Press, 1974); William P. Argan, with Pam Cowan and Gordon W. Staseson, *Regina, the First Hundred Years: Regina's Cornerstones, the History of Regina Told Through Its Buildings and Monuments* (Regina: Leader-Post Carrier Foundation, 2002); Michael Hayden, *Seeking the Balance: The University of Saskatchewan, 1907–1982* (Vancouver: University of British Columbia Press, 1983); J. W. T. Spinks, *Decade of Change: The University of Saskatchewan, 1959–70* (Saskatoon: University of Saskatchewan Press, 1972).

40   Cited in John Howse, "The History of Mount Royal College" (MRUA, unpublished draft, ca.1975), 8–9 (hereafter cited as Howse, "History").

41   VU/UC 78.103C, Box 2: Minutes, Outgoing Correspondence, "Quadrennial Report of College Property," Joint Meeting of Executive Committee and Commission of Seven, Board of Education Minute Book, 1910–21, 1 May 1919.

42   Ibid., Box 13: Incoming Correspondence, 1913–26, Graham to Rev. Stonewall Anderson, Nashville, Tennessee, 14 Jan. 1913.

43   The Provincial Archives of Alberta hold the records of the Alberta Conference of the Methodist and United Churches, including five boxes of materials by and about Kerby: PAA 75.387, United Church of Canada, Boxes 176–181. On Kerby's ideas, see Michael Owen, "'By Contact and by Contagion': George W. Kerby, 1860–1944," *Vitae Scholasticae: The Bulletin of Educational Biography* 10: 1–2 (1991), 131–57, and "Rev. Dr. George W. Kerby: Evangelist for the Home and School"; *Alberta Journal of Educational Research* 39, no. 4 (1993): 477–93. One of his successors who knew him, W. J. Collett, wrote a brief sketch, "Dr. George W. Kerby," in Max Foran and Sheilah Jameson, eds., *Citymakers: Calgarians After the Frontier* (Calgary: Historical Society of Alberta, Chinook County Chapter, 1987), 281–89; there are also remarks in Calgary Central United Church, *They Gathered at the River*, 375–92 and passim; see Kerby, autobiographical sketch, in *Alberta Past and Present* II (1924), 12–17; and the affectionate memoir of Lenore Walters, "In Memoriam" (MRUA, brief unpublished manuscript).

44   PAA 75.387, Box 178, *Acta Victoriana* (Cobourg, Ontario). Kerby published one article under his own name, "The Hope of the Future the Inspiration of the Present," ibid., Jan. 1887, 7–9. Sissons, *A History of Victoria University*, 199.

45   University of Toronto, Torontonensia 12 (1911–12): 310.

46   PAA 75.387.5706: "Dr. Kerby's reminiscences at the complimentary dinner in his honor given by the citizens of Calgary and presided over by his worship Mayor Andrew Davison."

47   PAA 75.387, Box 178 (Kerby's speech notes); file 5717 contains his Masonic speeches, e.g., "Masonic Sermon," 29 June 1913, "Grand Master's Address" [1931].

48   Calgary Central United Church, *They Gathered at the River*, 378.

49   Howse, "History," 6.

50   Quoted in ibid.; on the development of the telephone network, see "Tribute to the Telephone Era," in Wilk et al., eds., *100 Years of Nose Creek Valley History*, 89.

51   Methodist Church, General Conference, *Report of Committee on Sociological Questions, Department of Temperance and Moral Reform*, 1906. On the social gospel, see Allen, "The Social Gospel and

the Reform Tradition in Canada, 1890–1928," 381–99; and G. N. Emery, "The Origins of Canadian Methodist Involvement in the Social Gospel Movement, 1890–1914," *Journal of Canadian Church Historical Society* 19 (1977): 104–18; and, for a broader view, Charles Howard Hopkins, *The Rise of the Social Gospel in American Protestantism, 1865–1917* (New Haven; Yale University Press, 1940); and Phyllis D. Airhart, *Serving the Present Age: Revivalism, Progressivism, and the Methodist Tradition in Canada* (Montreal/Kingston: McGill-Queen's University Press, 1992).

52   Kerby, "The Parting of the Ways; or, Life Stories of Young Men," *Canadian Epworth Era*, July 1901, 202–3; see also: "The Parting of the Ways, or Life Stories of Young Men," ibid., Oct. 1901, 293–94; "In His Steps—Or What Would Jesus Do?," ibid., Feb. 1899, 36; "The Cavan Blazers," ibid., May 1903, 134–37; "The Pastor and the Boys, or How One Pastor Solved the Boy Problem," ibid., July 1903, 197; and "The Boy and the Birds," *Christian Guardian*, 3 June 1903, 10. The issues are in PAA 75.387, file 5814.

53   *Who's Who in Canada, 1938*, 369–70.

54   Owen, "By Contact and by Contagion," 136.

55   Calgary Central United Church, *They Gathered at the River*, 270.

56   White, ed., *A New Day for Women*, ix; biographical sketch, ix–xxi; and White, "Emily Spencer Kerby: Pioneer Club Woman, Educator, and Activist," *Alberta History* 46, no. 3 (1998): 2–9. Alberta's archives hold many materials, including copies of her articles. PAA 75.387, Boxes 181–182. See also Marjorie Norris, *A Leaven of Ladies: A History of the Calgary Local Council of Women* (Calgary: Detselig, 1995), and Holt Reineberg, "Women's Suffrage in Alberta." *Alberta History* 39 (1991): 25–31.

57   E.g., Constance Lynd [pseud.], "Tired of Being a Woman," *New Outlook*, 29 Dec. 1926; cited in White, ed., *A New Day for Women*, 4.

58   PAA 75.387, United Church of Canada, Box 181, Constance Lynd [pseud.], "Ladies—the Bachelors and Birth Control," undated ms.

59   White, *A New Day for Women*, x , and "Emily Spencer Kerby: Pioneer Club Woman, Educator, and Activist" *Alberta History* 46, no. 3 (1998): 2–9; Michael Owen, "'Do Women Really Count?' Emily Spencer Kerby—Early Twentieth-Century Alberta Feminist," *Papers*, Canadian Methodist Historical Society 10 (1995): 170–87; Patricia Roome, Emily Spencer Kerby: Discovering a Legacy," *Journal/United Church* 14, no. 1 (2001): 1–3. On the struggle of women for recognition in the church, see Elizabeth Gillan Muir and Marilyn Färdig Whiteley, eds. *Changing Roles of Women Within the Christian Church in Canada* (Toronto: University of Toronto Press, 1995).

60   David J. Hall, "Arthur Sifton, 1910–1917," in Rennie (ed.), *Alberta Premiers of the Twentieth Century*, 34–36.

61   On her activities on behalf of women's rights, see White, *A New Day*.

62   Valerie J. Korinek, "No Women Need Apply: The Ordination of Women in the United Church, 1918–65," *Canadian Historical Review* 74 (1993): 473–509.

63   Kerby admitted he had "taken the liberty of adding some coloring and shading to give them a better literary value." George W. Kerby, *The Broken Trail: Pages from a Pastor's Experience in Western Canada* (Toronto: William Briggs, 1919), Preface, 7.

64   Ibid., 146–47, 55–56, 186–88; on the immigrant student issue, see Manfred Prokop, "Canadianization of Immigrant Children: Role of the Rural Elementary School in Alberta, 1900–1930," *Alberta History* 37 (1989): 1–10. On denominationalism: Quoted in Calgary Central United Church, *They Gathered at the River*, 378.

65 In 1908 he was involved in discussions to mount "a mission and school" for Japanese settlers near Strathmore. L. G. Thomas, *The Liberal Party in Alberta: A History of Politics in the Province of Alberta 1905–1921* (Toronto: University of Toronto Press, 1959), 65.

66 Ibid., 381. In 1910 the General Conference debated whether to abolish the itinerancy rule but decided not to do so. *Journal of Proceedings of the Eighth General Conference of the Methodist Church held in Metropolitan Church, Victoria, B.C., 14th August to 31st August, 1910*, 381.

67 As new forms of association took shape in secular urban societies, ministers experienced "a crisis of status as their position as moral and intellectual leaders was undermined." Owen, "By Contact and by Contagion,"131. See also Marshall, *Secularizing the Faith: Canadian Protestant Clergy and the Crisis of Belief, 1850–1940* (Toronto: University of Toronto Press, 1992).

68 Calgary Central United Church, *They Gathered at the River*, 382.

69 *Calgary Daily Herald*, 6 June 1910; Cushing, chairman, and Adams, secretary, Board of Governors, "First Annual Report of Mount Royal College," *Minutes of the Proceedings of the Eighth Session of the Alberta Conference of the Methodist Church, held in the Central Methodist Church, Calgary, Alberta, from Thursday, May 25th to Wednesday, May 31st 1911*, 72–73; Howse, "History," 1–7; Robert MacDonald, "A History of Mount Royal College" (unpublished manuscript, 2000), chap. 1.

70 *Methodist Yearbook, 1915*, 97.

71 Coats, "Calgary: The Private Schools, 1899–1916," in Rasporich and Klassen, eds., *Frontier Calgary*, 141–52; and Thomas, *The Church of England and Higher Education in the Prairie West Before 1914*.

72 *Albertan*, 27 July 1910; "College for Methodists," *Calgary Daily Herald*, 3 Aug. 1910.

73 *Journal of Proceedings of the Eighth General Conference of the Methodist Church, 1910*, 68.

74 Minutes, "Meeting, Aug. 2, 1910, of the Provisional Board of Governors of the Proposed Methodist Preparatory College at Calgary"; *Calgary Daily Herald*, 20 Aug. 1910.

75 Calgary Central United Church, *They Gathered at the River*, 157. While recognizing Cushing's personal provity, Edwards was every critical of his political behavior in turning against Rutherford and bringing down his government. *Eye Opener*, 5 March and 18 June 1910.

76 Foran, *Calgary: An Illustrated History*, 70, citing "The 100,000 Manufacturing Building and Wholesale Book Edition," published by the *Albertan*, 1914.

77 Calgary Central United Church, *They Gathered at the River*, 156.

78 George F. G. Stanley, "From New Brunswick to Calgary: R. B. Bennett in Retrospect," in Rasporich and Klassen, eds., *Frontier Calgary*, 242–66. Books on Bennett include: James H. Gray, *R. B. Bennett: The Calgary Years (*Toronto: University of Toronto Press, 1991); Peter Waite, *The Loner: Three Sketches of the Personal Life and Ideas of R. B. Bennett, 1870–1947* (Toronto: University of Toronto Press, 1992); and Robert Saunders, *R. B. Bennett* (Toronto: Fitzhenry and Whiteside, 2004).

79 Patricia Roome, "Alexander C. Rutherford, 1905–1910," in Bradley J. Rennie, ed., *Alberta's Premiers of the Twentieth Century* (Regina: Canadian Plains Center, University of Regina, 2005), 12–14; Cushing's business life is described briefly in Henry C. Klassen, *A Business History of Alberta* (Calgary: University of Calgary Press, 1999), 74, and Klassen, *Eye on the Future: Business People in Calgary and the Bow Valley, 1870–1900* (Calgary: University of Calgary Press, 2002); on Cushing's political

career, see Thomas, *The Liberal Party in Alberta*, 21–22 (election and appointment as Minister of Public Works), and 130–33 (aspiration to be premier, resignation), passim.

80 Calgary Central United Church, *They Gathered at the River*, 159.

81 University of Calgary, *Preliminary Announcement of the University of Calgary, July 1912*.

82 Foran, *Calgary, An Illustrated History*, 155.

83 Ibid., 88.

84 PR, 24 Mar. 1911.

85 In the church, "the brothers seem to have been almost interchangeable, and in fact on at least one occasion A.B. succeeded W.H. as recording steward." Calgary Central United Church, *They Gathered at the River*, 159.

86 The lay members included T. H. Blow, E. H. Crandell, Wesley Hoople, James H. Garden, William L. Hunt, Senator James A. Lougheed, F. G. Marwood, Alfred Price, and H. A. Sinnot, all from Calgary, and W. F. McEwen (Carlstad), W. M. Craig (Olds), E. Michener (the MPP for Red Deer), W. J. Brotherton (Medicine Hat), T. W. Quayle (Claresholm), and George D. Stanley (High River). The Methodist ministers were originally Thomas C. Buchanan (Calgary), Aubrey S. Tuttle (Calgary, later principal of St Stephen's College), Charles H. Huestis (Red Deer), R. J. Johnston (Swift Current), George C. Webber (Okotoks), J. H. Riddell (Edmonton, principal of Alberta College), and T. P. Perry (Lethbridge).

87 Board minutes, 7 Sept. 1910.

88 Board minutes, 4 Nov. 1910. Church records tell a different story: on 8 September "a deputation consisting of Hon. W.H. Cushing and O.S. Chapin from the Calgary College waited on the Board with reference to their call of Rev. Geo. W. Kerby to accept the position of Principal thereof and asking the Board to accept his resignation as pastor at the end of Conference Year. After a short address from Rev. Geo. Kerby, and on the motion of the recording steward and duly seconded . . . the resignation of the pastor was accepted." Calgary Central United Church, *They Gathered at the River*, 382.

89 Quarterly Official Board of the Church, cited in Calgary Central, *They Gathered at the River*, 383.

90 Perry, "Central Methodist Church," in Rasporich and Klassen, eds., *Frontier Calgary*, 187.

91 W. H. Johns, *A History of the University of Alberta, 1908–1969* (Edmonton: University of Alberta Press, 1981), 34–35; A. W. Rasporich, "The University of Calgary's Pre-History, 1912–1966," *Alberta History* 54, no. 3 (2006): 2–11; Rasporich, *Make No Small Plans: The University of Calgary at Forty*. (Calgary: University of Calgary Press, 2007), 1–7; also Norman Leslie MacLeod, "Calgary College, 1912–15: A Study of an Attempt to Establish a Provincially Funded University in Alberta" (Ph.D. diss., University of Calgary, 1970).

92 "The College Bills Passed," *Calgary Daily Herald*, 10 Dec. 1910.

93 EC minutes, "Minutes of Emergent Meeting of the Executive Committee of the Board of Governors of Calgary College," 10 Dec. 1910. Later, Kerby gave more dramatic versions of the story. *Albertan*, 21 Dec. 1933, and this version in ibid., 27 April 1936: "The Premier [Clifford Sifton] … telephoned and asked him to supply another name at once, and he replied 'Call it Mount Royal.' Mr. Sifton replied 'That is a better name anyway.'" Ibid., 27 Apr. 1936.

94 An Act to Incorporate Mount Royal College, 1910 (assented to 16 Dec. 1910).

95 Board minutes, "Minutes of the Provisional Board of Governors of the Proposed Methodist Preparatory College at Calgary," 2 Aug. 1910.

96 Cushing, chairman, and Adams, secretary, Board of Governors, "First Annual Report of Mount Royal College," *Minutes of the Eighth Session of the Alberta Conference of the Methodist Church, 1911,* 73–74.

97 *Calgary Daily Herald*, 3 Aug. 1910.

98 "Mount Allison's standard professorial salary remained at $1,250, and one alumnus from Calgary, paying off his student account at Mount Allison, wrote in 1912 of the much higher sums available in Alberta: 'things do not seem just right with the principal here getting $3600 and a free house while some of you men at Mount Allison with so much more to look after toil for love and loyalty to Mount Allison." Reid, *Mount Allison University* 1: 255–56.

99 "Teaching Staff for New College," *Albertan*, 2 May 1911.

100 Ibid.

101 Cushing and Adams, "First Annual Report," 1911, 74. Aileen Sibbald remembered Mrs. Kerby as a "very good" teacher. MRUA, Sibbald interview (Macdonald-Wilk), 27 Sept. 1998.

102 E.g., article on the hiring of J. E. Lovering, *Chinook*, 1912–13, 9.

103 Howse, "History of Mount Royal College," 14.

104 EC minutes, 7 Sept. 1910.

105 Ibid., 8 Nov. 1910. The legal description was lots 39 and 40, 31 and 38, block 7, plan A. Board Finance Committee minutes, 11 Mar. 1911; cf. Cushing and Adams, Alberta Conference, *Annual Report 1911*, 74. The city's December 1910 records show that the college had been granted permits 1501 and 1502 for lots 910, block 230, section 9 (residence, estimated cost $20,000) and 3340, block 37, section 16 (college, $45,000). City of Calgary Building Permit Register, City of Calgary Archives, City of Calgary, month ending December 1910. I owe this reference to Dr. Donald B. Smith.

106 Charles F. Adams to Sir John Langham, 24 Nov. 1911.

107 Cushing and Adams, "First Annual Report," 1911, 73.

108 EC minutes, 16 Jan. 1912, Kerby, "To the Executive and Members of the Board of Governors, Mount Royal College."

109 Cushing and Adams, "First Annual Report," 1911, 74.

110 PR, 24 Mar. 1911; also "The Schools and the Nation," *Morning Albertan*, 10 Mar. 1911; "The Lofty Ideals of Mount Royal College. Its Work Will Be of National Importance. Million Dollars Needed Eventually for the Equipment of the Institution," ibid., 25 Mar. 1911.

111 Vincent Massey, Diary, 19 August 1911, Vincent Massey Papers, University of Toronto Archives. I owe this reference to Dr. Patricia Roome. On Massey's early life, see Claude T. Bissell, *The Young Vincent Massey* (Toronto: University of Toronto Press, 1981).

112 In all likelihood Massey asked his Oxford friend, Alexander Scott Carter, who became a professional heraldic specialist and the creator of Canada's coat of arms (1921), to design the crest. For illustrations of crests Carter designed for Canadian universities, see R. G. M. Macpherson, article originally published in *Heraldry in Canada*, September, 1990. http://www. heraldry.ca/art/painter/carter/carter.htm; other articles on him include: ": "The Halcyon," 30 (November 2002); and "Paint, Gesso, Silver, Gold and Stone: Alexander Scott Carter, Artist and Architect," published by the Friends of the Thomas Fisher Rare Book Library. For reproductions of the several versions of

the badge over the years, see MRUA: Brigitte Wenn, comp., "Mount Royal University Badge History," July 2010.

113 PR, 24 Mar. 1911; *Albertan*, 25 Mar. 1911.

114 *Calgary Daily Herald*, 15 July 1911.

115 MRC, *Calendar,* 1911–12, 33.

116 Ibid., 1942–43, 30–31.

117 *Morning Albertan*, 6 Sept. 1911.

118 "Mount Royal College Formally Opened," *Calgary Daily Herald*, 6 Sept. 1911; "Mount Royal College's Open'g, Enjoyable Function."

119 MRC, *Calendar*, 1911–12, 10.

120 *Calgary Daily Herald*, 6 Sept. 1911.

121 *Calgary News Telegram*, 7 Sept. 1911.

122 *Chinook*, Christmas, 1911, 25–26.

123 "Thousands attend at Mount Royal," *Albertan*, 6 Sept. 1911; names of the 179 students were recorded in MRC, *Calendar,* 1912–13, 46–50; Kerby, PR, 28 Feb. 1922, later claimed 189 students (perhaps a typographical error). The "Second Annual Report to the Alberta Conference,"1912, signed by Cushing and Adams, said that "total registration of students for the [first] year, 187." It then provided a breakdown of "enrolment," showing a total of 255 students: Academic, 112; Music, 65; Commercial, 53; Expression and Physical Culture, 25." Minutes of the Ninth Session of the Alberta Conference of the Methodist Church, held in the McDougall Methodist Church, Edmonton, From May 31st to June 5th, 1912, 102–3.

124 PR, 16 Jan. 1912.

125 Alberta Department of Education, *Annual Report, 1913*, 117.

126 Board minutes, 12 Jan. 1911. White, ed., *A New Day*, xiv, refers to her as "co-principal" and cites Jean Grant, "In Memoriam" (PAA): the Kerbys "were prevailed upon to accept the responsibility of becoming the Principals of Mount Royal College."

127 Board minutes, 24 Mar. 1911.

128 Ibid., 25 Mar. 1911.

129 *Calgary Daily Herald*, 30 Nov. 1911.

130 MRUA, Admin., Correspondence 1911, Wm. Egbert to Kerby, 2 Nov. 1911; the donation was from him and his brother.

131 EC minutes, 12 Dec. 1911.

132 VU/UC 78.103C, Box 12: Incoming Correspondence, 1911–12, Charles F. Adams, Board of Governors, to Rev. J. W. Graham, 18 Apr. 1912, enclosure: "Information for the General Conference, Board of Education." See also MRC Board, "Second Annual Report to the Alberta Conference," Minutes of the Ninth Session of the Alberta Conference of the Methodist Church, 1912, 103. VU/UC Finding Aid 184, "Administrative History, 4: "Mount Royal College was established with a property of $238,000 and up and reliable subscriptions for $250,000 more."

133 Board minutes, 5 July 1912. "Then we have indefinite promises of land or money from P. Burns and J. Steinbrecker, the promise of one of the new College buildings from W. H. Cushing, $23,000 subscriptions each from O. S. Chapin, Wesley Hoople, Mr. Hextall, $10,000 from W. G. Hunt, with the express expectation of making it $25,000; $5,000 from G. W. Morfitt and H. Riley."

134 *Beating the Odds: A History of the Mannix Family in Business, 1898–1997* (Calgary, 1998), 48.

135 *Albertan*, 6 Sept. 1911.

136 EC minutes, 12 Dec. 1912, including correspondence on the loan guarantee.

137 Ibid., Box 2: Board of Education Minute Book, 1906–1910, 2 Mar. 1910.

138 Ibid., Incoming Correspondence, 1913–26, Principal, Alberta College to Executors of the Lillian Massey-Treble Estate, 20 Apr. 1917. An interesting detail: "The University of Alberta is the only State University in Canada granting a B.D. degree."

139 Methodist Church, General Conference, *Journal of Proceedings of the Eighth General Conference of the Methodist Church, 1910*, 368.

140 Emphasis in original. VU/UC 18.103C, Box 12: Incoming Correspondence, Kerby to Graham September 1911.

141 Ibid., Box 2, Board of Education Minute Book 1910–21, 4 Oct. 1911.

142 Board minutes, "Meeting, Aug. 2, 1910, of the Provisional Board of Governors of the Proposed Methodist Preparatory College at Calgary." (Board minutes are held in Mount Royal's Executive Record Centre.)

143 VU/UC 18.103C, Box 12: Incoming Correspondence, Rev. Arthur Barner, president, Alberta Conference of the Methodist Church, to Graham, 25 Aug. 1911.

144 Ibid., Riddell to Graham, Sept. 1911. Riddell and Kerby were like oil and water. A decade later, Riddell angered Kerby by reporting erroneously on financial matters to the Methodist Board of Education without consulting Kerby. VC/UCC Archives, Box 13, Incoming Correspondence, 1913–26, Graham to Kerby, 3 Dec. 1921, Kerby to Graham, 7 Dec. 1921.

145 VU/UC 78.103C, Box 12: Incoming Correspondence, 1911–12, Kerby to Graham, 1 Nov. 1911.

146 Ibid., Kerby to Graham, 1 Nov. 1911.

147 Ibid., Graham to Kerby, 9 Mar. 1912.

148 Ibid., Kerby to Graham, 18 Mar. 1912.

149 Ibid., "Information for the General Conference, Board of Education," enclosure with letter from Adams to Graham, 18 Apr. 1912.

150 Ibid., Box 12: Incoming Correspondence, 1911–12, Nov. 1911 file.

151 Ibid., Box 13: Incoming Correspondence, 1913–26, Resolutions of the General Conference Special Committee, report by Rev. T A. Moore, secretary of the General Conference, to Graham, 20 Jan. 1913.

152 He joined the board in 1914. Ibid., Box 2, Board of Education Minute Book, 1919–21, Winnipeg meeting.

153 Ibid., Box 13: Incoming Correspondence, Graham to Kerby, 3 Dec. 1921, quoting Riddell's letter; Kerby to Graham, 7 Dec. 1921.

154 In 1910–11 and 1911–12 the connexional grants ran from $1,000 for three colleges (Alberta, Albert, Columbian) to $2,794 for three others (Mount Allison, Wesley, Wesleyan) and $6,147 for Victoria College. Ibid., Box 2, Minutes, Outgoing Correspondence, Board of Education Minute Book, 1910–1921, Annual Statement, Educational Fund, 30 June 1911 and 30 June 1912, minutes of meetings on 4 Oct. 1911 and 31 Dec. 1912.

155 Ibid., Box 11: Nov. 1910, Rev. J. Warner to Graham, 30 Nov. 1910. Earlier, Calgary members had expressed concerns about their donations being sent as connexional funds to Alberta College. Calgary Central United Church. *They Gathered at the River*, 472–73.

156 VU/UC Box 12: Incoming Correspondence, General Board of Education Minute Book, 4 Oct. 1911.

157 A.G. Bedford, *The University of Winnipeg: A History of the Founding Colleges* (Toronto: University of Toronto Press, 1976), 2–3.

158 Report of the Commission appointed to consider the granting of degree-conferring powers to Calgary College (May 22, 1914), 3. See also the accounts in the histories: W.H. Johns, *A History of the University of Alberta, 1908–1969* (Edmonton: University of Alberta Press, 1981), 2; John MacDonald, *The History of the University of Alberta, 1908–1958* (Edmonton: University of Alberta, 1958), 1–5. On the wider context, see Robert Steven Patterson, "F.W.G. Haultain and Education in the Early West" (M.Ed. thesis, University of Alberta, 1961); A. S. Morton, Saskatchewan, *The Making of a University* (Toronto: University of Toronto Press, 1959); and Michael Hayden, *Seeking the Balance: University of Saskatchewan, 1907–1982* (Vancouver: University of British Columbia Press, 1983). On the religious squabbles within the fledgling University of Toronto that influenced Haultain and others, see Friedland, Martin L. *The University of Toronto: A History* (Toronto: University of Toronto Press, 2002).

159 VU/UC Archives, Box 2: Minutes, Outgoing Correspondence, Board of Education Minute Book, 1906–10, 24 Sept. 1906. W. H. Alexander, "In the Beginning (University of Alberta)" *Alberta Historical Review* 8 (1960): 15–20; Rod C. Macleod, *All True Things: A History of the University of Alberta, 1908–2008* (Edmonton: University of Alberta Press, 2008), 1–18. On Tory, see: E.A. Corbett, *Henry Marshall Tory, Beloved Canadian* (Toronto: Ryerson Press, 1954), and *Henry Marshall Tory: A Biography* (Edmonton: University of Alberta Press, 1992).

160 Howse, "History," 7.

161 VU/UC Archives, Box 14, Resolution, "Sept. 24, Montreal" [1905]. Johns, *A History of the University of Alberta*, 5–6. On the split, see VU/UC 78.103C, Box 12, Board of Education Minute Book 1910–1921, meeting of September 1912, "Recommendations to the Board of Education from the Board of Alberta College, Edmonton, regarding the Future of the Educational Work of the Methodist Church in that City."

162 An Act Respecting the University of Alberta, 1910, article 42.

163 Quoted in Howse, "History," 8.

164 Ralph Joseph Clark, "A History of the Department of Extension of the University of Alberta, 1912–1956" (Ph.D. diss., University of Alberta, 1986); Berghofer and Vladicka, *Access to Opportunity*, 3–7; Macdonald, *History of the University of Alberta*, 13ff.

165 *Eye Opener*, 18 Dec. 1909.

166 *Albertan*, 9 Dec. 1910: "Calgary College Bill Endorsed. It is Shorn of Degree Conferring Powers and Name is Changed;" Anthony W. Rasporich, "A Community in Search of a University: The University of Calgary's Pre-History, 1912–66," *Alberta History* 54 (2006): 2–11; R. K. Gordon, "University Beginnings in Alberta," *Queen's Quarterly* 58 (1951–52): 487–96.

167 Max Foran, "William J. Tregillus," *Dictionary of Canadian Biography* 14: 1006–8.

168 University of Calgary, "Our donors," *Preliminary Announcement of the University of Calgary, July 1912*, 13–16; the members of the Board of Governors consisted of Dr. Blow, chairman, W. J. Tregillus, Secretary, J. S. Dennis, James Short, William Georgeson, H. W. Riley (MPP), and R. B. Bennett (MP). In 1913–14 the "Advisory Members" included many boosters of Mount Royal College – e.g., J. A. Lougheed, A. J. Sayre, A. B.

Cushing, and W. G. Hunt. *The University of Calgary, First Annual Calendar, Session 1913*.

169 "University of Calgary," *Chinook*, Christmas, 1912–13, 5.

170 Phyllis E. Weston, "A University of Calgary," *Alberta Historical Review* 11, no. 3 (1963): 2.

171 *Report of the Commission Appointed to Consider the Granting of Degree-Conferring Powers to Calgary College*, 12, recommendation 1; MacLeod, "Calgary College;" Donald B. Smith, "Calgary University's Fight 75 Years Old," *Calgary Herald*, 3 Oct. 1987; Weston, "A University of Calgary," 4.

172 *Report of the Commission*, 12–13: recommendations 2–3; John W. Chalmers, *Schools of the Foothill Province: The Story of Public Education in Alberta* (Toronto: University of Toronto Press, 1967), 205–6.

173 Frank Simon, "History of the Alberta Provincial Institute of Technology and Arts," (M.Ed. thesis: University of Alberta, 1962), 33–40; and on the later period, P. B. Lowe, "Technical and Vocational Training in Alberta: A Descriptive Study of its Development" (MA thesis, University of Alberta, 1962).

174 *Report of the Commission*, 13, and recommendations, 4–5; "History of SAIT," www.sait.ab.ca; and Simon, "History of the Alberta Provincial Institute of Technology and Art."

175 G. Mann, "Alberta Normal Schools: A Descriptive Study of their Development 1905 to 1945" (M.Ed. thesis, University of Alberta, 1961).

176 Chalmers, *Schools of the Foothill Province*, 206–9.

177 *Chinook*, 1913–14, 12. The *Chinook* was the original student publication of Mount Royal College.

178 "Mount Royal College Commencement has large audience," *Albertan*, 17 June 1913.

CHAPTER 2: TAKING ROOT, 1911–1931

1 College aims, *Methodist Yearbook*, 1915, 97.

2 Foran, *Calgary: Canada's Frontier Metropolis*, 153.

3 Censuses, 1921 and 1931, cited in James Gray, *The Roar of the Twenties* (Toronto: Macmillan, 1975), 69.

4 Eric J. Hanson, *Eric J. Hanson's Financial History of Alberta, 1905–1950* (Calgary: University of Calgary Press, 2003), 121.

5 "The value of field crops in Alberta was $142.26 million in 1920, $157.22 million in 1925, $77.31 million in 1935, and, by 1942, $142.13 [million]" The price of wheat, $2.90 a bushel in 1917, dropped to $1.03 in 1929, 47 cents in January 1930, and .35–.39 cents thereafter. The price of beef fell from $4.00 per hundredweight in 1932 to $2.50 a year later. Foran, *Calgary*, 117; Grant MacEwan, *Illustrated History of Western Canadian Agriculture*, 101.

6 College aims, *Methodist Yearbook*, 1915, 97.

7 PR, 27 Jan. 1925.

8 On the Alberta home and school movement, see Owen, "Rev. Dr. George W. Kerby: Evangelist for the Home and School," and "'By Contact and by Contagion,'" and Chalmers, *Schools of the Foothill Province*, 403; e.g., on home as "the experiment of the school," PAA 75.387, Box 179, file 5, 5709, "Fourth Biennial Report of the Canadian Federation of the Home and School, by the President Dr. George W. Kerby." On the broader movement, see Robert Steven Patterson, "The Establishment of Progressive Education in Alberta, 1925–1940" (Ph.D. diss., Michigan State University,

1968), and "Progressive Education: Impetus to Educational Change in Alberta and Saskatchewan," in Howard Palmer and Donald B. Smith, eds., *The New Provinces: Alberta and Saskatchewan, 1905–1980: 12th Western Canada Studies Conference* (Vancouver: Tantalus Research, 1980), 173–98.

9 Kerby, *Keep a Grip on Harry* (Toronto: F.C. Stephenson, 1904), 5–6, 9, 15–16; also Kerby, articles in *The Canadian Epworth Era*, 1901–3.

10 "Welcome," *Chinook*, Christmas, 1913.

11 "Mount Royal College, Report to the Alberta Conference," 21 May 1926; *Record of Proceedings of the Second Meeting of the Alberta Conference of the United Church of Canada, May 17th–24th, 1926, McDougall United Church, Edmonton, Alberta*, 16–18.

12 MRC, *Calendar*, 1911–12, 29.

13 *Methodist Year Book*, 1915, 98–99.

14 MRC, *Calendar*, 1911–12, 19–22; cf. ibid., 1921–22, 19.

15 Ibid., 1922–23, 18, 23–26.

16 Ibid., 1921–22, 18–19.

17 Ibid., 22.

18 UAA 68-9-428: Board minutes, corespondence, 8 Nov. 1916–25 Feb. 1925, George Y. Chown, registrar, Queen's University, to Tory, 8 Nov. 1911.

19 Ibid., Tory to Chown, 15 Nov. 1911.

20 Ibid., e.g., letters on 1914 examinations: Kerby to Tory, 18 May 1914; Kerby to Cecil Race, registrar, University of Alberta, 18 May 1914, and Tory to Kerby, 19 May 1914. MRC, *Calendar*, 1921–22, 18.

21 Ibid., 1922–23, 11.

22 UAA 68-9-428, Tory to Chown, 15 Nov. 1911.

23 Ibid., Tory to Kerby, 7 Dec. 1911.

24 Ibid., Tory to Kerby, 6 June 1912.

25 MRC, *Calendar*, 1912–13, 27.

26 Ibid., 1921–22, 18.

27 *Chinook*, Easter 1927, rear cover.

28 Ibid., Christmas 1911, 20.

29 There were eventually two "yells," ibid., Apr. 1927, inside cover.

30 Ibid., Christmas 1911, 26.

31 Ibid., Christmas 1913, 23.

32 The first was held on 31 Oct. 1911. Ibid., 31.

33 Ibid., 1912, 10.

34 Ibid., Christmas 1912–13, 9.

35 Ibid. Among the Society's early presidents were Wilson Gouge, Florence Jarrett, Anna Reed, Gertrude VanDelinder, Helen Beny, and Gordon Kelly. MRC, *Calendar*, 1913–14 to 1921–22. There are more detailed descriptions of aspects of student in life in Macdonald, "History," chap. 2, and passim.

36 *Chinook*, Christmas 1911, 27.

37 Ibid., Christmas 1912–13, 10.

38 Ibid., Easter 1912–13, 10. In 1927, Kerby declared that the recent debate between grades 9 and 10 had been the best ever held in terms of the quality of public speaking. PR, 15 Feb. 1927.

39 *Chinook*, Christmas 1912–13, 10, 4.

40 Ibid., 1919–20, 17–18.

41 MRC, *Calendar, 1921–22*, 45.

42 Collett interview (Macdonald-Wilk), 16 Oct. 1997.

43 On the role of the YWCA in encouraging girls to commit to a life of service, see Diane Pedersen, "'The Call to Service': The YWCA and the Canadian College Woman, 1886–1920," in Paul Axelrod and John G. Reid, eds., *Youth, University and Society: Essays in the Social History of Highesr Education* (Montreal/Kingston: McGill-Queen's University Press, 1989), 187–89.

44 "The Girl's Bible Class," *Chinook*, 1926, 22.

45 MRC, *Calendar*, 1915–16, 48; *Chinook*, Christmas 1913, 22.

46 MRC, *Calendar, 1921–22*, 46.

47 PR, 28 Feb. 1922.

48 The General Proficiency Medal for 1934–35 attracted numismatic attention: Earl J. Salterio, "A Glimpse of Higehr Learning: Alberta 1994," *Canadian Numismatic Journal*, 1995, 23–27.

49 MRC, *Calendar*, 1912–13, 43–5; ibid., 1922–23, 41–5.

50 *Journal of the General Conference of the Methodist Church*, 1914, 164.

51 MRC, *Calendar*, 1914–15, 14.

52 PR, 15 Feb. 1927.

53 Neil Semple, "'The Nurture and Admonition of the Lord': Nineteenth Century Methodism's Response to Childhood," *Social History* 13 (1981), 157–75.

54 Owen, "By Contact and by Contagion," 150.

55 PR, 28 Feb. 1922.

56 MRC, *Calendar*, 1921–22, 45.

57 Ibid., 1922–23, 47; ibid., 1932–33, 51.

58 The statement that disappeared: "It is expected that all students attend the daily non-sectarian chapel service. On Sunday mornings they attend some one of the city churches. On Sunday evenings a chapel service is held in the College." Ibid., 1931–32, 11–12.

59 Ibid., 4; ibid., 1918, 15; the language was later modified: "Students in Ladies' Residence make their own beds, and all students are required to maintain an orderly room." Ibid., 1922–23, 9.

60 MRC, *Calendar*, 1919–20, 10–11

61 Ibid., 1912–13, 12; ibid., 1918, 16.

62 Howse, "History," 19; *Calgary Daily Herald*, 4 Aug. 1914.

63 VU/UC Archives 78.103C, Box 13: Minute Book, 1910–21, 12 Nov. 1914. On Methodist patriotism, see Methodist Church, General Conference, Army and Navy Board, 1918, *The Church, the War and Patriotism*. On the background, see W. H. Magney, "The Methodist Church and the National Gospel, 1884–1914," *Committee on Archives United Church of Canada Bulletin*, 1968.

64 *Albertan*, 10 June 1916.

65 Methodist Church, Alberta Conference, *Minutes*, 1914, 220.

66 *Chinook*, Christmas 1914–15, 24.

67 *Albertan*, 15 June 1915; MRC, *Calendar*, 1915–16, opposite 32.

68 *Chinook*, Christmas 1914–15, 24

69 Ibid., Christmas 1913, 26–27.

70 *Albertan*, 10 June 1916.

71 *Chinook*, Christmas 1914, 3–7.

72 Ibid., Easter 1919, 22.

73 *Albertan*, 12 June 1916; *Chinook*, Easter 1918–19, 19–20, contains a list of seventy-nine names, including those killed (James Arnell, Cecil Duke, E. J. Fallis, Halwey Ross, H. S. Musgrove, H. W. Clark, G. S. Wilkin and R. J. Shantz).

74 Kerby, "A Message from the Principal," *Chinook*, Easter 1919, 1. The college's cadet corps continued on a smaller scale. The 1922–23 calendar contained a picture of six student prize-winners of the E. D. Adams Shield for marksmanship, awarded to the "champions of the private colleges and schools of Calgary." MRC, *Calendar*, 1922–23, opposite 40.

75 Report of the Educational Society, *Journal of Proceedings of the General Conference of the Methodist Church*, 1918, 193.

76 "Reconstruction," *Chinook*, Easter 1919, 21–22: "Such men are either terribly ignorant of what the Bolsheviki are, or else they are criminals of the blackest dye, and as such should be in solitary confinement, or better, executed."

77 On later reflections on mingling religion and patriotism, see Michael Gauvreau, "War Culture and the Problem of Religious Certainty: Methodist and Presbyterian Colleges, 1914–30," *Journal of Canadian Church History* 32 (1987): 12–31. On the state of the Alberta church, see Robert Macdonald, "The Methodist Church in Alberta during the First World War," *Papers*, Canadian Methodist Historical Society, Volio, 1995, 145–69.

78 VC/UCC Archives, Box 14, Unclassified, "Scope of Work," page on Mount Royal, showed the following enrolments: 1912: resident students, 89, day students, 100; 1913: resident, 113, day, 165; 1914: resident, 71, day, 168; 1915: 39 resident, 153 day. The number receiving a diploma fell from 118 to 7 in the same period. The report indicated that the number of teachers was between 15 and 17. See also the enrolment recapitulation in PR, 28 Feb. 1922.

79 *Journal of Proceedings of the General Conference of the Methodist Church*, 1918, 190.

80 VU/UC Archives 78.103C, Box 2: General Board of Education Minute Book, 1910–21, 3 Sept. 1915. The mandate was to "make such practical suggestions as might direct the Board to effect improvements in our Educational policy and administration." Ibid., Box 13: Incoming Correspondence, 1913–26, Graham to Wm. Sparling, Hamilton, 14 Feb. 1919.

81 Methodist Church, General Board of Sunday Schools and Young People's Societies, *The Constitution of the Local Sunday School*, 1918. On the church's response to the war, see J. Michael Bliss, "The Methodist Church and World War I," *Canadian Historical Review* 49 (1968): 213–33.

82 *Report of the Massey Foundation Commission*; Minutes, Annual Meeting, Board of Education, 14 Jan. 1919, Minute Book, 1910–21, 232–33. For the church's acceptance: UV/UC Archives 78.103C, Box 13, Incoming Correspondence, 1913–25, Graham to Massey, 18 Jan. 1919.

83 Bissell, *The Young Massey*, 80–83.

84 *Report of the Massey Foundation Commission*, quotations respectively from 6–9, 28, 31, 19–20, 11–12.

85 Ibid., 71–77.

86 Ibid.; VU/UC Archives, Box 12, Board of Education Minute Book, 1910–1921, 30 Mar. 1921.

87 EC minutes, 15 Apr. 1921. In response to Kerby's report on the content of the report, the Executive Committee approved a motion to respond. This led to a telegram, 15 Apr. 1921, to Vincent Massey asking for corrections before publication.

88 VU/UC Archives 78.103C, Box 13, Incoming Correspondence, 1913–26, George J. Trueman to Kerby, 26 Jan. 1921.

89 E.g., ibid., Box 14, Minutes of the Standing Committee on Colleges of the Religious Education Council of Canada, 19 Dec. 1921 and 5 Jan. 1922, and the Agenda of the Annual Meeting of the General Board of Religious Education, 24–25 Apr. 1923.

90 The nine: Rev. S. D. Chown, Rev. J. W. Graham, Rev. C. T. Scott, Rev. Dr. George J. Trueman, Vincent Massey, J. H. Grundy, C. B. Sissons, J. C. Robertson, and W. C. Graham. VU/UC Archives, Finding Aid 184, "Administrative History," 4.

91 VU/UC Archives, 78.103C, Box 13, Incoming Correspondence: copy of G. J. T[rueman] to Kerby.

92 Ibid., Minutes of the Educational Society, Annual Meeting, 18 Apr. 1921, Minute Book, 1921–26.

93 PR, 30 Apr. 1923. However, in 1923, the department's private schools inspector wrote: "I was quite favorably impressed with the effectiveness of the organization, and with the type of work accomplished in the different departments."

94 Albertan, 24 Oct. 1926.

95 Kerby, PR, 18 May 1925.

96 "Mount Royal College Story Told in 17 Churches. Prominent Citizens Conduct Mission on Behalf of Institution Which Fills Fine and Important Purpose in Alberta – Record More Than Justifies Its Perpetuation, They Declare." Albertan, 7 Mar. 1927.

97 MRC, Calendar, 1929–30, 11.

98 Ibid., 1918, 35.

99 Albertan, 7 Jan. 1921.

100 PR, 12 Dec. 1921, statistics for the fall term; ibid., 28 Feb. 1922.

101 D. C. Jones, "School and Social Disintegration in the Alberta Dry Belt of the Twenties," Prairie Forum 3 (Spring 1978).

102 PR, 11 Dec. 1923.

103 Quoted in Howse, "History," 27.

104 EC minutes, 26 June 1924.

105 PR, 22 Nov. 1928.

106 EC minutes, 2 Apr. 1925; minutes of the special board meeting, 2 June 1925.

107 MRUA, Admin: Board Correspondence 1929, Walters to Stanley, 14 Nov. 1929.

108 MRC, Calendar, 1912–13, 46–50; ibid., 1921–22, 41–42; ibid., 1922–23, 41–45.

109 Albertan, 9 June 1931, 3 June 1932, 11 June 1934, 13 June 1936, 12 June 1937, 15 June 1938, 20 May 1939.

110 "Students at Stettler Addressed by Dr. Kerby," Calgary Daily Herald, 5 June 1931.

111 PR, May 1933.

112 Chinook, Easter 1927, 21–22.

113 PR, 20 Feb. 1930.

114 Ibid., 21 Mar. 1929.

115 Chinook, Easter 1927, 23; PR, 24 Jan. 1929.

116 Chinook, Easter 1927, 27; PR, 21 Oct. 1926.

117 MRC, Calendar, 1929–30, 3; on rental of the hockey rink, PR, 1 Apr. 1926.

118 Chinook, Easter 1927, 27; PR, 26 Jan. 1928; Albertan, 16 Jan. 1929.

119 Chinook, Easter 1927, 21.

120 There are copies of student publications in MRUA; see Works Cited for a list.

121 MRC, Calendar, 1914–15, 53; ibid., 1915–16, 48.

122 Ibid., 1918, 37; ibid., 1919–20, 38.

123 Ibid., 1921–22, 46. At that point the representatives for each class were: 1912 (Harold Timmons), 1913 (Charles Boucher), 1914 (Maryam Tisdale), 1915 (Lawrence Miller), 1916 (Arthur Clarke), 1917 (Florence Moorehouse), 1918 (Romaine Fox), 1919 (Finlay Ross), 1920 (Aileen Sibbald), and ibid., 1922–23, 48 (Flora Sorge). See also "Scholarship is Planned for the Mt. Royal College," Albertan, 8 Jan. 1921, concerning the establishment of the "Mount Royal College Alumni," with Captain John Garden as president.

124 PR, 28 Feb. 1922.

125 MRC, Calendar, 1929–30, 54.

126 Chinook, Easter 1927, 9.

127 Ibid.

128 MRC, Calendar, 1912–13, 28–30; ibid., 1915–16, 36.

129 Chinook, Easter 1927, 13. On the earlier history of music in Calgary, see N. J. Kennedy, "The Growth and Development of Music in Calgary, 1875–1920 (MA thesis, University of Alberta, 1972); it gives only a brief mention to the Conservatory.

130 Sibbald interview (Macdonald-Wilk), 27 Sept. 1998.

131 Chinook, 1912–13, 23; ibid., Christmas 1914, 21.

132 Ibid., Christmas 1912–13, 10.

133 E.g., ibid., 9, 12–13, 15.

134 Albertan, 14 June 1913.

135 PR, 30 Apr. 1923; Calgary Daily Herald, 18 May and 5 June 1923.

136 Chinook, Easter 1927, 13.

137 Ibid., 1912–13, 33; 1914–15, 37.

138 MRC, Calendar, 1919–20, 30.

139 Ibid., 1921–22, 33.

140 PR, Dec. 1922.

141 PR, 15 Oct. 1925.

142 Chinook, Easter 1927, 13.

143 Description of the Conservatory, Arpi-Huba, 1938–39, 44–45.

144 Journal of the General Conference of the Methodist Church, 1914, 163.

145 MRC, Calendar, 1911–12, 28.

146 Chinook, Summer 1913–14, 11.

147 MRC, Calendar, 1918, 26.

148 Ibid., 1930–31, 39.

149 Chinook, Christmas, 1912–13, 15; ibid., 1913–14, 12–13; ibid., Easter 1919, 20.

150 Ibid., 27 May 1916.

151 MRC, Calendar, 1914–15, 48

152 "Cover Design," Chinook, Christmas 1913, 16.

153 MRC, Calendar, 1918, 25.

154 Ibid., 1929–30, 38.

155 "Mount Royal College Story Told in 17 Churches," Albertan, 7 Mar. 1927.

Chapter 3: Becoming a Junior College, 1931–1942

1   "Depression Is Character Test," *Calgary Daily Herald*, 2 Jan. 1931.

2   "Calgary Greets New Year with Reckless Vigor," ibid.

3   Bennett's government initiated the Canadian Broadcasting Corporation (1932), Bank of Canada (1935), and Canadian Wheat Board (1935). Larry A. Glassford, *Reaction and Reform: the Politics of the Conservative Party under R. B. Bennett, 1927–1938* (Toronto: University of Toronto Press, 1992); Michael David Swift, *R. B. Bennett and the Depression, 1930–1935* (Fredericton, NB, 1964).

4   On the rise of Social Credit, see C. B. McPherson, *Democracy in Alberta: Social Credit and The Party System*, 2nd ed. (Toronto: University of Toronto Press, 1962); Edward Alan Bell, *Social Classes and Social Credit in Alberta* (Montreal/Kingston: McGill-Queen's University Press, 1992); Albert Finkel, *The Social Credit Phenomenon in Alberta* (Toronto: University of Toronto Press, 1988).

5   "Oil Is Great Alberta Asset," *Calgary Daily Herald*, 3 Jan. 1931; David Finch, *Hell's Half Acre: Early Days in the Alberta Oil Patch* (Surrey Heritage House Publishing Company Ltd., 2005).

6   Foran, *Calgary*, 174, Table 1: The Growth of Manufacturing in Calgary, 1891–1971.

7   Ibid., Table 9: Age Composition of Calgary's Population, 1921–1961.

8   Ibid., 138, 170, 173–75.

9   On the parlous state of public schools in rural districts, see: Jones, "School and Social Disintegration in the Alberta Dry Belt of the Twenties"; D. C. Jones, "A Strange Heartland: The Alberta Dry Belt and Schools in the Depression," in R. D. Francis and H. Ganzevoort, eds., *The Dirty Thirties in Prairie Canada* (Vancouver: University of British Columbia Press, 1980), 89–110; and Jones, "We Can't Live on Air all The Time: Country Life and the Prairie Child," in P. T. Rooke and R. L. Schnell, eds., *Studies in Childhood History: A Canadian Perspective* (Calgary: Detselig, 1982), 185–203.

10   David Leighton and Peggy Leighton, *Artists, Builders and Dreamers. 50 Years at the Banff School* (Toronto: McLelland & Stewart, 1982).

11   "Little Hope Held Out for Two-Year Course in Calgary," *Calgary Daily Herald*, 24 Dec. 1924. On Baker's rural preoccupation, see L. R. Wilson, "Perren Baker and the United Farmers of Alberta: Educational Principles and Policies of an Agrarian Government" (M.Ed. thesis, University of Alberta, 1970), and "The Education of the Farmer: The Educational Objectives and Acctivities of the Unied Farmers of Alberta and the Saskatchewan Grain Growers' Association (Ph.D. diss, University of Alberta, 1975).

12   "Answers Framed to Government Queries as to 2-Year Course," ibid., 14 Jan. 1925; University of Alberta Archives (hereinafter cited UAA) 68-9-253, Minutes of the meeting of the General Committee of Citizens of the City of Calgary in regard to establishing two years of university work at the Institute of Technology and Art, 10 Jan. 1925; "The Junior College Project," *Albertan*, 28 Mar. 1925.

13   UAA 68-9-428, Perren Baker, Minister of Education, to Tory, 3 Feb. 1925, and Tory, "Memorandum," undated. On the history of the university during this period of fragility, see R. C. Wallace, *The University of Alberta, 1908–1933* (Edmonton: University of Alberta, 1933).

14   Ibid., Kerby to Tory, 19 Jan. 1925.

15   Ibid., Tory to Kerby, 26 Jan. 1925.

16   UAA 3/2/9/2-4(2), Text of speech, "Junior College at Institute of Technology, Calgary: Statement made by Minister of Education to the Legislature, Mar. 19, 1925"; ibid., Minister: Correspondence, Nov. 27, 1928–Feb.14, 1935; and *Calgary Daily Herald*, 24 Dec. 1924. The state of public education was reflected in the number of teachers in the province – 924 in 1905, 2,651 in 1910, and 5,320 in 1920, with little change from then to 1945. Statistics Canada, Series W1: "Full-time teachers in public elementary and secondary schools, by sex, Canada and by province, selected years, 1867–1975."

17   *Albertan*, 28 Mar. 1925. On what the Calgary school board would need to do to establish a college, see: Tory, "Memorandum for the Chairman of the Calgary School Board on The Junior College," attached to letter, Tory to Scott, 30 Nov. 1925. Because of the recall of some Trustees, Tory's letter was not shared with the full board. Tory to Frederick Selwood, former chair of the Calgary School Board, 14 May 1926, UAA 68-9-253.

18   *Albertan*, 9 May 1927.

19   EC minutes, 7, 16 Apr. 1928; "Mount Royal May Undertake Junior College," *Albertan*, 16 Apr. 1928.

20   "Mount Royal May Undertake Junior College," *Albertan*, 16 Apr. 1928.

21   United Church, Alberta Conference, *Record of Proceedings*, 1928, 36.

22   PR, 9 Aug. 1928.

23   EC minutes, A. M Scott, superintendent of schools, to Kerby, 28 Mar. 1928; EC minutes, 16 Apr. 1928.

24   PR, 24 Jan. 1929.

25   UAA 3/2/4/12-1, MRC: Correspondence, Kerby to Wallace, 30 Jan. 1929, Kerby to Brownlee, 30 Jan. 1929.

26   Board Finance Committee minutes, 19 Apr. 1930.

27   UAA 3/2/4/12-1, MRC: Correspondence, Kerby to Wallace, 10 Apr. 1930.

28   Ibid., Kerby to President and Members of the Senate of the University of Alberta, 13 May 1930.

29   University of Alberta, *Calendar*, Session 1931–32, 243. The background to the policy: UAA 68-1-177.5.1: Junior Colleges and Affiliated Institutions, especially A. E. Ottewell, Registrar and Secretary of the Senate, 19 Nov. 1930, Attachment: "Report on Policy of Junior College Affiliation," and Wallace to Kerr, 20 Sept. 1930.

30   PR, 22 May 1930; Board Special Meeting minutes, 21 Feb. 1931; UAA 3/2/4/12-1, MRC: Correspondence, Wallace to Kerby, 20 Dec. 1930, Kerby to Wallace, 22 Dec. 1930.

31   UAA 3/3/4/12-1, MRC: Correspondence, Kerby to Wallace, 9 Feb. and 9 May 1932.

32   University of Alberta, *Calendar,* Session 1938–39, 226.

33   "University to co-operate with Junior College. Special Committee Alberta University Senate Named for Purpose." *Albertan*, 16 May 1931; the committee consisted of Dr. R. C. Wallace, president, and Dean W. A. Kerr of the Faculty of Arts. On the details, see: UAA 3/2/4/12-1, MRC: Correspondence, D. E. Cameron, librarian, to Wallace, 24 Mar. 1931 (with a long list of books attached and an estimated cost of $1325); Kerby to Wallace, 25 Mar. 1931; Kerby to Cameron, 13 Apr. 1930; Kerby to Wallace, 1 May 1931 (he has raised funds for library acquisition and visited universities re potential faculty members);

Kerr to Kerby, 1 June 1931 (on adequacy of faculty); Kerr to Kerby, 12 June 1931 (faculty ranks).

34 UAA 68-1-1775.1, "Resolution passed by the Board of Governors of Mount Royal College on Feb. 28, 1931"; also "University to Co-operate with Junior College. Special Committee Alberta University Senate Named for Purpose"; "Special Committee to be headed by Dr. R. C. Wallace, President, and Dean W. A. Kerr of the Faculty of Arts," *Albertan*, 16 May 1931.

35 UAA 3/2/4/12-1 MRC: Correspondence, "University to Co-operate with Junior College"; ibid., Kerby to Wallace, 9 Feb. and 9 May 1932.

36 VU/UC 83.051C, Box 68, File 7, Graham to Kerby, 24 Apr. 1931: "It was moved and unanimously carried that the Board of Education grant permission to the Board of Governors of Mount Royal College to add the second year university work to their academic courses, thus giving the College the statute of a Junior College in affiliation with the University of Alberta according to a plan for Junior Colleges drawn up by the University Senate."

37 UAA 3/2/4/12-1, MRC: Correspondence, Kerby to Walker, 5 Jan. 1931.

38 "Plan to Establish Junior College in Calgary This Year," *Calgary Daily Herald*, undated clipping, City of Calgary Library, Mount Royal College newspaper file.

39 PAA, Kerby files, notes for remarks: "The Junior College: The Prelude; The Function of the Junior College; The Junior College in Action; The Mount Royal Junior College; Some of the Advantages of the Junior College."

40 UAA 3/2//5/12-1, Kerby to Kerr, 22 May 1931; Kerr to Kerby, 1 June 1931. The new faculty included: J. Dillon Cornwall, BA (Alberta), a PhD student at the University of Chicago who would teach English and literature; Mrs. Helen Badgley Moller, MA (Washington), who had studied speech and drama at Columbia; Doris Hunt, BA, MA (Manitoba, Sorbonne), French; Mary White, MA (Queen's, postgraduate work at Oxford), the classics; Merle Marshall, BA, MA (Manitoba), Mathematics; C. S. Burchill, MA (Queen's), history; F. B. Friend, BA (McMaster), MA (Rochester), chemistry and physics. The Commercial Department was now led by C. E. Wright. Margaret Carrick, a graduate of the MacDonald Institute of Montreal, taught household science and social etiquette. E. McDonald, a graduate of the Ontario College of Art, was responsible for fine arts in the intermediate and junior levels.

41 "Inaugural Ceremony of the Junior College, in Affiliation with the University of Alberta, Programme, Thursday Evening, Oct. 22, 1931," MRC, *Calendar*, 1931–32; "Impressive Ceremony Marks Inauguration of Junior College. University of Alberta President Delivers Principal Address," *Calgary Daily Herald*, 23 Oct. 1931.

42 Board Staff Committee minutes, 25 Apr. 1932.

43 PR, 18 May 1925; report of Kerby and Walters, 23 Nov. 1925.

44 EC minutes, 19 Mar., 14 May, and 9 Aug. 1928.

45 When he moved to California in 1923, he offered to donate six lots on 8th Avenue SW if the college paid the back taxes of about $1,000. EC minutes, 13 Feb. 1923 (adjourned to 24 Feb. 1923); ibid., 17 Mar. 1923.

46 EC minutes, 27 Jan. 1926, 22 Feb. and 16 June 1927; Board Finance Committee minutes, 13 June, 22 July, and 17 Dec. 1927.

47 Kerby acknowledged that, despite the very "fine" site, the college could not afford to build on the McKay-Shouldice property. EC minutes, 22 Mar. 1928.

48 It took until 1938 to complete the transaction. Board Finance Committee minutes, 9 Mar. 1932; Board AGM minutes, 25 Sept. 1932; EC minutes, 15 Dec. 1938.

49 PR, 24 Jan. and 21 Mar. 1929; Board Finance Committee minutes, 9 Mar. 1932.

50 "Land Loan in Calgary Considered. Appeal from Mount Royal College Received by Government. Reply Made: Province Will Retain Title, Says Premier; Details Not Ready," *Albertan*, 23 Apr. 1929.

51 EC minutes, Kerby to Brownlee, 30 Jan. 1929; "Mount Royal College New Site Is Likely to Be Decided Today. Premier Brownlee and Dr. George W. Kerby Will Be Discussing Having College Established Near Institute of Technology and Art Buildings," *Albertan*, 14 June 1929.

52 "Land Loan in Calgary Considered. Appeal from Mount Royal College Received by Government. Reply Made: Province Will Retain Title, Says Premier; Details Not Ready," *Albertan*, 23 Apr. 1929. Quotations are from PR, 20 Feb. 1930.

53 "Delay Selection of Site for Mount Royal College. Further Sessions Will Be Held Today between Provincial Government Members and College Heads," *Albertan*, 14 June 1929.

54 Board Finance Committee minutes and EC minutes, 25 June 1931.

55 UAA 3/2/4/12-1, MRC: Correspondence, Kerby to Wallace, 27 Oct. 1932; PR, 10 Mar. and 30 Dec. 1932; handwritten notes by George Walters in the MRC, *Calendar*, 1930–31, intended as a revision for the 1931–32 edition, 24: "There is also a special library to meet the requirements of the Junior College"; and ibid., 1933–34, 29.

56 MRC, *Calendar,* 1947–48, 9.

57 PR, 20 Feb. 1930.

58 PR, 25 June 1931.

59 PR., 27 Dec. 1934; ibid., 15 Dec. 1938.

60 PR, 31 May 1939.

61 PR, 21 Jan. 1931; 25 Apr. and 23 June 1932.

62 "Junior College Saved Citizens Heavy Expenses. Made Available Higher Education for Many, States Dr. G. W. Kerby," *Calgary Daily Herald*, 18 May 1932; "The New Junior College in Calgary," report attached to the Board Staff Committee, 25 Apr. 1932.

63 PR, 23 June 1932; "Junior College Students Make Good Progress," *Calgary Daily Herald*, 18 May 1932.

64 Chemistry 1, History 2, Mathematics 1, Physics 7, Philosophy 2, and Greek 1. UAA 3/2/4/12-1, MRC: Correspondence, Memorandum, Shipley to Wallace, 1 June 1934, and "1934–34 Comparisons: Mount Royal College and University of Alberta."

65 *Albertan*, 22 May 1936; PR, 20 May 1939.

66 MRC, *Calendar,* 1938–39, 22–23. The public school board began a related innovation in 1935 – the first "composite or comprehensive" high school in Alberta. Chalmers, *Schools of the Foothill Province,* 213.

67 VU/UC 83.051, Box 68, George W. Kerby, Report to the Board of Christian Education, United Church of Canada, 1938–39.

68 MRC advertisement, *Albertan*, 23 Aug. 1941; ibid., 30 Aug. 1941, ibid.; 15 Aug. 1942; ads in regional newspapers, e.g., *Lethbridge Herald*, 22 May 1943.

69 Robin S. Harris, A *History of Higher Education in Canada, 1663–1960* (Toronto: Toronto University Press, 1976), 371.

70   "The New Junior College in Calgary," Board Staff Committee, 25 Apr. 1932.

71   "Junior College Saved Citizens Heavy Expenses." The same words are used in "The New Junior College in Calgary," attached to Board Staff Committee minutes, 25 Apr. 1932. On similar colleges in Canada, see W. S. Fox, "Report on the Junior College Situation in Canada in 1934," *N.C.C.U.C. Proceedings*, 65–71

72   The board struck a Committee on New Courses to review possibilities. EC minutes, 21 Dec. 1933, 20 Jan. 1934.

73   Reports of the Committee on New Courses, EC minutes, 20 Jan., 12 Feb. 1934; also Kerby to Wallace, 12 Mar. 1934, UAA 3/2/4/12-1, MRC: Correspondence.

74   "Adult Education to Be Organized during Fall at Mount Royal," *Albertan*, 21 Apr. 1934. On efforts to encourage agricultural careers, see J. L. Wilson, "Agrarian Ideals for Canadian Youth, Alberta, 1916–1936: A Case Study," in Alf Chaiton and Neil McDonald, eds., Canadian Schools and Canadian Identity (Toronto: Gage, 1977), 133–49. For another view, see Paul Axelrod, *Making a Middle Class: Student Life in English Canada during the Thirties* (Montreal: McGill-Queen's University Press, 1990).

75   Committee on New Education Project, minutes, 12 Feb. 1934.

76   Committee on New Education Project Report, 14 Mar. 1934; Finance Committee minutes, 23 Apr. 1934.

77   EC minutes, 2 Oct. 1931; on the role of the Extension Department, see Macdonald, *History of the University of Alberta*, 13–14.

78   The subjects included English, economics, sociology, sciences, agriculture, business (accounting, law, filing, business English), household science, arts and crafts, citizenship, physical education, and music, speech, and drama. Length varied from 120 semester hours (cookery) to 60 (agricultural economics), 40 (chemistry, literature), 20 (physical-education fundamentals), and 10 (religious knowledge).

79   UAA 3/2/4/12-1, MRC: Correspondence, Wallace to Kerby, 13 Mar. 1934; EC report, Board AGM minutes, 30 Nov. 1934; Committee on New Educational Project Report, 10 Apr. 1935; PR, 1 Nov. 1935.

80   MRC, *Calendar,* 1935–36, 29, 40.

81   EC minutes, 16 Oct. 1933.

82   PR, 2 Nov., 15 Dec. 1931; 30 Mar. 1932; *Tatler*, 5 May 1932, "souvenir number," marked the Students' Union greeting of the transformation. (The title was spelled as the *Tattler* when a new version appeared in the 1950s.)

83   PR, 25 Nov. 1937.

84   VC/UCC Archives, Box 14, file 6, "Mount Royal College, Calgary," 1921.

85   PR, 2 Nov. 1931.

86   Invitation for Sophomore Prom, ca. 1935, published in *Mount Royal College Yearbook*, ca. 1972, 22.

87   E.g., remarks on social activities in PR, 20 Jan., 27 Feb. 1934; *Calgary Daily Herald*, 3 Mar. 1934; *Albertan*, 9 May 1935, 24 Oct. and 14 Nov. 1936.

88   EC minutes, 2 Nov. 1931, 6 Jan. 1936.

89   MRC, *Calendar,* 1938–39, 17.

90   "The Literary Society," *Chinook*, 1930.

91   MRC, *Calendar,* 1935–36, 33.

92   List of courses and picture, MRC, *Calendar*, 1935–36, 35.

93   Mount Royal College, *Calendar*, 1935–36, 33

94   PR, 30 Dec. 1932.

95   *Albertan*, 30 Nov. 1931.

96   PR, 30 Dec. 1932; section on the Department of Speech and Drama, Summary of work done during 1932–33 season; *Albertan*, 7 Apr., 7 and 13 June 1933.

97   *Albertan*, 27 Jan., 21 and 25 Apr. 1934. Among the many productions was the A. A. Milne farce *The Dover Road*, Shakespeare's *As You Like It*, the burlesque *Lord Allen's Daughter*, the farce *Aunt Samantha Rules the Roost*, and Hildegarde Flanner's *Mansions*. These were all directed by Beth Lockerbie. Ibid., 13 Nov., 15 Dec. 1936, and 15 Mar. 1937.

98   Ibid., 9 June 1933 and 13 Nov. 1936.

99   PR, 26 Jan. 1933 and 22 Feb. 1933.

100 Ibid., 24 Nov. 1933; also PR, 25 Apr. 1934, on debates with Montreal and Alberta universities in French and in English.

101 *Calgary Daily Herald*, 12 Mar. 1936. On 7 March the Germans had occupied the Rhineland, precipitating an international crisis.

102 PR, 19 Oct. 1933 and 2 Nov. 1935.

103 Ibid., 20 Jan. 1934.

104 E.g., ibid., 22 Nov. 1935 and 2 Mar. 1939; *Albertan*, 10 Mar. 1930, 26 Feb., 11 Mar. 1936, and 17 Jan. 1938.

105 "Physical Culture Classes Offered at Mt. Royal College," *Albertan*, 8 Sept. 1934.

106 Ibid., 7 Jan. 1939.

107 *Arpi Huba, 1938–39*. The 1940 issue of *Chinook* was dedicated to "the late Lord Tweedsmuir," Governor General of Canada, better known as the author John Buchan, "one of the finest, kindest, and wisest men that has ever represented the King in Canada." *Chinook*, 1940, 13.

108 The final issue: "The real purpose of this book will not have been achieved until it is read with pleasure in years to come, to bring back the events and friends of Mount Royal College life." *Chinook*, 1940, 9.

109 *Scratch Pad*, 30 Nov. 1942.

110 See Annora Brown, *Sketches from Life* (Edmonton: Hurtig Publishers, 1981). Also:; Eleanor G. Luxton, interview with Annora Brown, 19 June 1957, in the Glenbow Foundation; *Arpi-Hubra*, 1939, 20, 34. See also Freda Smith Mudiman, "Interpreter of the Foothills," *Calgary Herald*, 17 Oct. 1942 [in 1939 the name changed from *Calgary Daily Herald*]; "Love of Flowers Started Painter on Art Career," ibid., 4 Mar. 1957. She died on 2 March 1987. "Annora Brown, artist, author, leaves a wealth of artistry," *Fort Macleod Gazette*, 4 Mar. 1987; she studied with Arthur Lismer and J. E. H. MacDonald of the Group of Seven.

111 *Albertan*, 10 May 1934.

112 Ibid., 4 May 1935.

113 PR, 15 Dec. 1931.

114 PR, 30 Mar. 1937.

115 Methodist Church, Alberta Conference, *Minutes*, 1931, 24.

116 MRC, *Calendar*, 1944–45, 11.

117 "Mount Royal College Operating accounts, 1911–1939," with handwritten notes for 1940, EC minutes, 30 Nov. 1939.

118 VU/UC 83.061.C, Box 68, United Church, Board of Christian Education, Reports and Agenda, 5th Meeting, 18–20 Apr. 1930.

119 VU/UC 83.83.051C, Mount Royal College, Report to the Board of Christian Education, United Church of Canada, 1938–1939.

120 *Varshicom*, 1942, 72–74.

121 On musical life in Calgary, see the articles on "The Calgary Symphony Orchestra" and "Calgary, Alta" in *Encyclopedia of Music in Canada*, at www.thecanadianencyclopedia.com.

122 MRUA, Conservatory minutes, 19 September 1937.

123 Ibid., 20 Oct. [1933].

124 MRC, *Calendar*, 1936–37, 36.

125 MRUA, Conservatory minutes, 1933–34, contain many references to the "Aeolian concerts."

126 PR, 14 Dec. 1937. Conservatory minutes, general meeting, 19 Sept. [1937].

127 MRUA, Admin, Conservatory, Faculty minutes, 2 Mar. [1934]; executive meeting, 19 Mar. [1934].

128 MRUA, Conservatory minutes, 9 Sept. 1935.

129 E.g., "Registrar now for the Baby Symphony Orchestra," with new classes beginning in violin and guitar, *Albertan*, 17 Aug. 1940.

130 Ibid.; PR, 27 Jan. and 24 Mar. 1938.

131 MRUA, Conservatory minutes, 18 June 1937.

132 Ibid., general meeting, 24 Sept. 1940; ibid., 28 Oct. 1940.

133 Newcombe became "director emeritus." EC Special Meeting minutes, 7 Sept. 1939.

134 E.A.M., "History of the Mount Royal College Symphony Orchestra," undated excerpt from a college calendar; Donald B. Smith, *Calgary's Grand Story* (Calgary: University of Calgary Press, 2005), 239; and "Calgary Junior Symphony Has Gone a Long Way Fast," *Calgary Herald*, 5 June 1943.

135 *Varshicom*, 1941–42, 53; and is quoted in E.A.M., "History of the Mount Royal College Symphony Orchestra," 1944.

136 "Juniors now tuning up," *Albertan*, 23 Sept. 1944.

137 *Varshicom*, 1941–42, 53. Kerby noted that the Junior Symphony Orchestra consisted of "some 60 members with ages running from 7 to 17 and 19." PAA 75.387.5706: Kerby, "Address on the Jr. Symphony Orchestra of Calgary given over CFAC, Monday, Dec. 9th [1941]."

138 MRUA, Conservatory minutes, 21 Oct. 1943.

139 Ibid., 13 Jan. 1941.

140 Ibid., 8 Sept. 1942; on Piper, see Jennifer Hamblin and David Finch, *The Diva and the Rancher: The Story of Norma Piper and George Pocaterra* (Calgary: Rocky Mountain Books, 2006).

141 R. Dale McIntosh, "Egbert, Gladys," *Encyclopedia of Music in Canada,* at www.thecanadianencyclopedia.com.

142 MRUA, Conservatory minutes, 8 Sept. 1942.

143 Ibid., report by Galperin. Also MRUA, Admin., Correspondence 1950s, F. C. Silvester, Registrar, Royal Conservatory of Music, to Garden, 18 May 1956, confirming an agreement made in "1942 or 1943 whereby the Toronto Conservatory of Music (now the Royal Conservatory of Music of Toronto) would return to Mount Royal College 20% of the amount of examination fees received from students at Mount Royal College. It was agreed by Mount Royal College that

they would make no charge for the accommodation of these examinations at the College."

144 MRC, *Calendar,* 1939–40, 36; advertisement in the *Albertan*, 30 Aug. 1941.

145 "Mount Royal College Operating accounts, 1911–1939," with handwritten notes for 1940, EC minutes, 30 Nov. 1939.

146 Tuition revenues, $13,186 in 1912, $18,750 in 1913, $16,133 in 1914, $9,951 in 1915. Methodist Church, Board of Education, Accession 78.103C, Box 14: Unorganized Materials, file 4: Survey Form Reports, June 1915, "Methodist Institutions, Assets and Liabilities"; and file 10: Financial Statements of the Department, 1914–25 (record of grants to the institutions).

147 MRUA, "Superannuation Fund of the Methodist Church," prepared after Kerby's death, 9 Feb. 1944: his salary record shows that he never again made over $2,600 (1921–24) and in the 1930s, between $1,200 and $1,500, with a spike to just under $2,000 in 1939.

148 VU/UC 78.103C, Box 2: Methodist Board of Education Minute Book, 1910–21, minutes, Joint Meeting of the Executive Committee of the Education Society and Commission of Seven, 1 May 1919, and "Quadrennial Report of College Property" (hereafter cited as Methodist Board of Education Minute Book, 1910–21 or 1921–26).

149 One mortgage of $31,200 was held by a Mr. O'Callaghan, another of $31,369 by Mrs. A. E. Langford; a bank loan of $6,010 was held by the Merchants Bank.

150 *Report of the Massey Foundation Commission*, 133–37.

151 Methodist Board of Education Minute Book, 1910–21, 30 Sept. 1918, Joint Meeting of Executive Committee and Commission of Seven, ibid., 1 May 1919; Methodist Board of Education Minute Book, 1921–26, 18 Apr. 1922; also "Forward Movement after the War," United Church, *11th General Council Record of Proceedings* (1944), 114–20. By early 1920 the Forward Movement campaign had exceeded its target. Methodist Board of Education Minute Book, 1910–21, 17 Apr. 1920.

152 By 31 Mar. 1921, the college had accessed $46,260; by 31 Mar. 1922, $64,180; by 30 June 1923, $69,159; and by Feb. 1925, $69,439. Alberta College North received the same allocation as Mount Royal. Methodist Board of Education Minute Book, 1910–21, and ibid., 1921–26, 30 Mar. 1921, 18–19 Apr. 1922, 10 Apr. 1923; 30 June 1923, financial statements.

153 VU/UC 78.103C, Box 13: Incoming Correspondence, 1913–26, Kerby to Graham, 7 Dec. 1921.

154 Methodist Board of Education Minute Book, 1921–26, 18 Apr. 1922.

155 EC minutes, 15 Nov. 1923.

156 E.g., the estate of William H. Cushing, EC minutes, 15 Dec. 1938.

157 PR, 25 Feb., 24 Nov. 1923.

158 Ibid., June 1924; EC minutes, 16 Dec. 1926, 14 Apr. 1927, 4 July 1924, and 16 May 1926.

159 EC minutes, 9 Jan. 1923. In 1925 the college owed $5,000 to Kerby and $2,600 to Margaret Carrick. PR, 20 June 1925.

160 Ibid., 17 Dec. 1925.

161 Ibid., Nov. 1923 and 20 Feb. 1924.

162 Ibid., 21 Oct. 1926 and 22 Nov. 1928.

163 *Report of the Massey Foundation Commission*, 133–37.

164 MRUA, Financial Statements, 1910–1960, 30 June 1925.

165 In 1926 there were eleven Normal School students in the dormitories. PR, 21 Oct. 1926; see also PR, 30 Aug. 1926. The staff paid a special boarding rate: EC minutes, 23 July 1925, 26 May 1926.

166 EC minutes, 30 Aug. 1926, 16 June 1927, 18 June 1928, 30 June 1926, 16 Aug. 1928. In 1937 the net profit was $377. PR, 28 July 1927.

167 Board Finance Committee minutes, 12 Oct. 1933, 30 Oct. 1934.

168 Howse, "History," 43.

169 Board Special Meeting minutes, 7 Sept. 1939.

170 UAA 3/3/4/14-3: Affiliated and Junior Colleges, Mount Royal College, Kerby to Kerr, 13 Sept. 1939. However, Kerby's enrolment reports did not indicate a reduction: 434 students in Nov. 1939, 424 in Nov. 1940; 31 resident students in Nov. 1939, 33 in Nov. 1940. PR, 3 Jan. 1941.

171 UAA 3/3/4/14-3: Affiliated and Junior Colleges, Mount Royal College, Kerr to Kerby, 20 Sept. 1939.

172 PR, 21 Dec. 1939.

173 EC minutes, 7 Sept. 1939, 21 Nov. 1940, 3 Jan. 1941.

174 Ibid., 29 May 1942.

175 MRUA, Admin., Executive Committee file, contains documents on the mortgage held by Mrs. A. E. Langford. "Analysis of Payments to Mrs. A.E. Langford on Account of Mortgage," 30 Apr. 1940, and EC minutes, 2 Mar., 4, 10 May , 21 Nov. 1940, 3 Jan. 1941, 31 Jan. 1941, and 29 May 1941. The final mortgage was "backdated" to 1 October 1940, making the last payment due in October 1950; the last reference to the mortgage was in the financial statement dated 30 June 1951.

176 Alberta Conference, *Appendix*, 1913, 201; Alberta Conference, *Minutes*, 1914, 220. In 1933, the federal government described the total at six full-time and nineteen part-time faculty members. Dominion Bureau of Statistics, *Annual Survey of Education in Canada*, 1933, 108.

177 *Albertan*, 15 June 1915.

178 *Chinook*, Christmas 1915, 15.

179 *Varshicom*, 1941–42, 8–9.

180 MRUA, Admin., "Memorandum of Agreement between the Board of Governors of Mount Royal College and J. W. Hepburn, Oakland, Ont.," 14 June 1928; and Hepburn to Kerby, 21 Jan. 1929.

181 PR, 29 Sept. 1932 and 26 Jan. 1933.

182 In 1938 Doris Hunt and M. Ross were denied leave requests. Staff Committee minutes, 2 Feb. 1938; EC minutes, 24 June 1938.

183 E.g., Staff Committee minutes, 10 June 1929; PR, 22 May 1930.

184 Alberta Conference, *Minutes*, 1926, 17.

185 Finance Committee minutes, 31 Jan. 1931 and 20 June 1932; PR, 26 Jan. 1933, 37 Feb. 1936, and 2 Mar. 1939; Report, Board Scholarship Committee, 25 Aug. 1932 and 31 Jan. 1935.

186 *Albertan*, 22 May 1936; Board Scholarship Committee minutes, 31 Jan. 1935.

187 Ibid., 27 Feb. 1936.

188 *Albertan*, 3 Feb. 1936.

189 Ibid., 5 Jan. 1938; *Calgary Daily Herald*, 12 Jan. 1939: PR, 15 Dec. 1938.

190 *Calgary Daily Herald*, 17 Mar. 1934.

191 PR, 24 Nov. 1933 and 30 Nov. 1934.

192 Ibid., 6 Mar. 1934.

193 The invitees included Mrs. Bradley Jamieson, Mrs. J. A Robertson, Miss Margaret Carrick, Mrs. George Webster, Mrs. H. G. Glass, and Mrs. E. W. Skene.

194 194 MRUA: Myrtle Cuyler, "History of the Mount Royal College Educational Club, 1923–1995," attached to Anderson interview (Macdonald-Wilk), 10 Apr. 1998; see also Patricia Roome, Emily Spencer Kerby," *Journal United Church* 14, no. 1 (May 2001): 1–3.

195 *Albertan*, 16 Feb. 1932, 17 Apr. 1934, 17 Apr. and 1 May 1935, 17 Oct. 1935, 17 Dec. 1936, and 22 Mar. 1938.

196 "Mrs. G. W. Kerby Dies, Pioneer Clubwoman," *Albertan*, 4 Oct. 1938.

197 "Mrs. H.C. Alshaw Heads Mt. Royal Education Club," at the 33rd annual luncheon, *Albertan*, 28 May 1955; "Mrs. T.A.W. Reid Was Elected President of the Mount Royal Education Club at the Club's 35th annual luncheon," ibid., 26 May 1958.

198 Quoted in Howse, "History," 48.

199 EC minutes, Special Committee on the Principalship, 3 Dec. 1941.

200 EC, minutes of the subcommittee to recommend a successor, 11 Dec. 1941.

201 The board refused Garden's request for a "moving allowance," a standard practice for ministers, but relented two years later as "expenses had been very considerable." Minutes, sub-committee, 23 Jan. 1942; EC minutes, 14 Apr. 1944.

202 The tributes to Kerby included an honorary LLD from the University of Alberta in 1937 and the naming of the Calgary chapter of the Imperial Order of Daughters of the Empire, formed on 30 Jan. 1942, as "The George W. Kerby Chapter." UAA 3/3/4/14-3, Affiliated and Junior Colleges: Mount Royal College, Kerr to Kerby, 1 Apr. 1937; Kerby to Kerr, 2 Apr. 1937. Glenbow Museum Archives, Imperial Order Daughters of the Empire, George W. Kerby Chapter Fonds. See also the tribute by Grant MacEwan, "A College and its Founder," in *Calgary Cavalcade: From Fort to Fortune* (Edmonton: The Institute of Applied Art Ltd., 1958), 149–55.

CHAPTER 4: BROADENING THE MANDATE, 1942–1958

1 *Calgary Herald*, 13 Dec. 1941; also 22 Aug. 1942, 28 July 1944: "Save a year in starting your career—complete your high school subjects while preparing for business."

2 Foran, *Calgary*, 179, Table 10: Crude Oil and Natural Gas Production in Alberta, 1947–1972.; see also Laura Atkins, Colleen Nicoll and Jody Stewart. "Turner Valley Oilfields," *Alberta History* 32 (1984): 9–18.

3 Sheilagh Jameson, *Ranches, Cowboys and Characters: Birth of Alberta's Western Heritage* (Calgary: Glenbow-Alberta Institute, 1987). Grant MacEwan's books included *A Short History of Western Canada* (Toronto: McGraw-Hill Ryerson, 1974); *Calgary Cavalcade, From Fort to Fortune* (Saskatoon: Western Producer Book Service, 1975); and *Eye Opener Bob: The Story of Bob Edwards*, 2nd ed. (Saskatoon: Western Producer Book Service, 1974).

4 Chapters on Aberhart, Manning, and Strom in Rennie, *Alberta's Premiers*, 125–200.

5   Johns, *A History of the University of Alberta*, 203; Michael B.
    Andrews, Edward A. Holdaway, and Gordon L. Mowat,
    "Postsecondary Education in Alberta since 1945," in Glen A.
    Jones, ed., *Higher Education in Canada: Different Systems, Different
    Perspectives* (New York: Garland Publishing, 1995), 59–60.

6   Looking back, Garden said of his early years: "We were in the
    midst of a World War. Years of depression had left their mark.
    . . . Some of us had misgivings about the future, but the note
    of hopefulness was present, and we set ... some important
    objectives that we thought should be accomplished." PR, 10
    Dec. 1952.

7   *Scratch Pad*, 30 Nov. 1942; see also "Mount Royal College
    Principal Retires," *Albertan*, 22 Nov. 1958; on the DD degree,
    Board minutes, 26 Oct. 1945.

8   EC minutes, 2 Oct. 1942; Board Special Meeting minutes, 28
    Sept. 1942.

9   "Hinchey New Com. Principal," *Scratch Pad*, undated [ca. 1943].

10 McCready interview (Macdonald-Wilk), 23 Oct. 1997.

11 Owen Kelly obituary, *Calgary Herald*, 3 Feb. 1994. Netta Kelly
    and Jim Kelly interview (Macdonald-Wilk), 4 June 1998: "There
    was a surrogate family element to the college that did overflow
    into our family life."

12 PR, 9 Dec. 1949.

13 EC minutes, 18 Sept. 1947; "Mount Royal College Principal
    Retires," *Albertan*, 22 Nov. 1958.

14 PR, 4 Dec. 1942.

15 UAA 68-1-21, Garden, "Report to President Newton re Mount
    Royal Junior College, Calgary, 5 May 1943.

16 Board minutes, 1 Dec. 1944.

17 Auditor's Statement, 30 June 1943; Financial Report, 31 Mar.
    1944; EC minutes, 28 Feb. 1946; Auditor's Statement, 30 June
    1950.

18 "Mount Royal College Students Now Taking Air Force
    Training," Calgary Herald, 25 PR, Mar. 1943; MRC, *Calendar*,
    1945–46, 12; MRC, *Calendar*, 1945–46, 12; F. May, "Women's
    War Services," *Scratch Pad*, 14 Dec. 1942.

19 "News of Ex Students, 1939–40, 1940–41," *Varshicom*, 1942, 73–
    74. Six were listed as married and twelve as in "miscellaneous"
    activities.

20 William Hitchins was "called up for special work in connection
    with the army." UAA 68-1-21, Garden to Newton, 29 July 1942;
    PR, 1 Dec 1944. On the courses: PR, 4 Dec.1942; Finance
    Committee reports, 4 Sept. 1942 and 25 June 1943; EC minutes,
    28 Jan. 1943; "Learn Journalism," *Albertan*, 16 Sept. 1944.

21 Howse, "History" 61.

22 PR, 29 May 1942.

23 PR, 30 Sept. 1955; ibid., 26 Sept. 1958.

24 Enrolment report, 1 Nov. 1965, in McCready report, Report
    of the Executive Vice-President, Board minutes, 25 Nov. 1965;
    charts in Anderson, "Institutional Analysis," 102–4.

25 Robert Newton Anderson, "Institutional Analysis of Mount
    Royal College, Calgary, Alberta" (Calgary: Mount Royal
    College, 1964), 85–93.

26 Hugh J. M. Johnston, *Radical Campus: Making Simon Fraser
    University* (Vancouver: Douglas & McIntyre, 2005), 16.

27 Notice, with picture, *Albertan*, 27 June 1955.

28 Among the many reports on facilities, see PR, 10 Dec. 1952;
    Finance Committee minutes, 31 July, 4 Dec. 1942; PR, 1
    Dec. 1944, 14 June 1946; PR, 5 Oct. 1946; PR, 24 Nov.
    1950; summary of facilities, EC minutes, 30 Jan. 1959; and the
    Collews, Jan. 1958.

29 The house (704 11th St. W) was acquired for $5,150. Finance
    Committee reports, 15 Apr. 1943, 28 Nov. 1944; EC minutes, 22
    May 1944.

30 EC Report, Board minutes, 29 Nov. 1946. In 1949, the portables
    were sold (*Calgary Herald, Albertan*, 9 Apr. 1949), but reliance on
    portables continued; there were still eight portables in 1965. EC
    minutes, 31 May 1965; PR, 25 Nov. 1965.

31 Board minutes, 1 Dec. 1944.

32 Stanley to Bennett, 8 Dec. 1944, Board minutes, 1 Dec. 1944.

33 MRUA, Admin: Kerby Memorial Building Fund. George
    Walters, notebooks and receipt books, "Kerby Memorial
    Building Fund," and "Kerby Memorial Subscriptions from Dec.
    1st 1951"; also MRUA, Admin., file entitled Correspondence
    1940s, E. S. Somerville to K. J. Morrison, 1 Mar. 1945; Garden
    to Somerville, 9 Mar. 1945.

34 EC minutes, 26 Oct. 1945.

35 Board minutes, 7 Dec. 1945; EC minutes, 6 Nov. 1945.

36 Committee on Relocation to Institute site, Board minutes, 7
    Dec. 1945.

37 EC minutes, 22 Jan. 1947. At that point there was $110,000 in
    cash and "a further $35,200 in bonds that [the board] decided
    to reserve in case the Kerby Building cost was more than
    anticipated." "First Sod to Be Turned Thursday," *Calgary Herald*,
    13 Aug. 1947; "Building Dedicated at Mount Royal College,"
    Albertan, 13 June 1949.

38 Board minutes, 5 Dec.1947 and 9 Dec.1949; *Calgary Herald*,
    19 Nov. 1949; and PR, 25 Feb. 1948. On fundraising, see
    PR, 5 Dec. 1947; joint Finance/EC minutes, 11 Dec. 1947;
    EC minutes, 25 Feb., 30 July, 29 Oct. 1948, and 4 Aug. 1949.
    In 1950, when the shortfall was $37,350, J. W. McConnell of
    Montreal agreed "to donate the last $5,000 on the deficit." PR,
    22 Nov. 1951.

39 Evening College report, PR, 22 Nov. 1951.

40 Board minutes, 8 Nov. 1955; the project was expanded in Oct.
    1956. EC minutes, 27 Jan. 1956; Special Committee minutes, 20
    Oct. 1956; PR, 19 Oct. 1956, 1 and 30 Nov. 1956, and 13 May
    1957.

41 "Student Brief," EC minutes, 26 Feb. 1959.

42 EC minutes, 26 Mar. 1959.

43 MRUA, Admin., Robert McCausland Ltd. to Garden, 8 Sept.
    1947, responding to a 3 Sept. 1947 letter; also EC report, Board
    minutes, 22 Nov. 1951. After seeing "very attractive" leaded
    windows in the Pincher Creek United Church, Garden ordered
    three to honour the college's founders. Garden to Robert
    McCausland Ltd., 3 September 1947; EC report, Board minutes,
    22 November 1951; MRC Archive, file on the stained glass.

44 Anderson, "Institutional Analysis," 70–72.

45 UAA 68-1-21, Ottewell to Newton, 10 Sept. 1942, on meeting
    with Garden.

46 The quotations, in order, are from UAA 68-1-21, Garden
    to Newton, 15 July 1942; Newton to Garden, 20 July 1942;
    Newton to Ottewell, 15 Aug. 1942, Ottewell to Garden, 17 Aug.
    1942, and Newton to Garden, 22 Sept. 1942; also PR, 8 Dec.
    1943.

47   Ibid., "Memo, Re First Year Engineering, Mount Royal College, Left by Mr. Garden and Mr. Trowsdale," 8 Feb. 1943; UAA 68-1-1427: Mount Royal College, Hardy to Stewart, 7 June 1957.

48   Ibid., Newton, "First-Year Engineering at Mount Royal College," 8 Feb. 1943.

49   Ibid., Newton to Garden, 23 Mar. 1943; Newton to Wilson, 27 Apr. 1943.

50   Ibid., Report of the Special Committee of the GFC on "First Year-Engineering at Mount Royal College," 17 May 1943; Newton to Garden, 20 May 1943.

51   EC report, 4 Dec. 1942, and Board minutes, 8 Dec. 1942.

52   Board minutes, 8 Dec. 1943.

53   EC minutes, 21 Jan. 1944.

54   UAA 68-1-21, Newton, "Mount Royal College," 7 Dec. 1943; see Newton to Dr. G. F. McNally, Deputy Minister of Education, 8 Feb. 1944, on making the junior college role "subject to the general regulations of the University of Alberta."

55   UAA 68-1-21, "Memorandum to Honourable Solon E. Low from Dr. R. Newton with reference to 'A Bill to amend the Act to incorporate Mount Royal College,'" 25 Feb. 1944.

56   PR, 1 Dec. 1944. The legislation, amended slightly in 1950: An Act to Incorporate Mount Royal College, 1910 (Second Session), Chapter 30 (Assented to Dec. 16, 1910), and as amended by the Fourth Session of the Ninth Legislature of the Province of Alberta in 1944 and as amended by the legislature on March 31, 1950.

57   UAA 68-1-21, advertisement in the Western Examiner, 24 June 1944.

58   UAA 68-1-21, Newton to Garden, 11 July 1944.

59   Ibid., Garden to Newton, 5 Aug. 1944.

60   "Students taking the appropriate subjects at Mount Royal Junior College and passing with at least 'B' standing will be allowed full credit towards the B.Sc. in Petroleum Engineering courses of Oklahoma University." MRC, Calendar, 1945, 22.

61   PR, 1 Dec. 1944.

62   PR, 14 June, 11 Oct. 1946.

63   Advertisement, Albertan, 12 July 1946; description in "Canadian College Prepares Students to Become O.U. Engineers," Sooners Magazine 29, no. 7 (March 1957): 15; the latter reference was provided by Devon L. Yost, Graduate Research Assistant, University of Oklahoma Libraries.

64   PR, 28 Mar. 1947.

65   PR, 2 Nov. 1953.

66   EC minutes, Garden to John M. Hidden, Secretary of the Board of Governors, University of Alberta, 15 Mar. 1950.

67   EC minutes, 12 Jan. 1950.

68   Board Committee on University Work minutes, 16 Mar. 1950. UAA 68-1-1061, Newton to Hardy, 26 Jan. 1951. The college was refused a request to offer Education summer courses. Newton to Garden, 8 Mar. 1951; Garden to Stewart, 13 Mar. 1945.

69   Macleod, All True Things, 145.

70   PR, 11 Nov. 1951, 19 June 1953, 2 Nov. 1953. One of McCready's classes fell to three students: McCready interview (Macdonald-Wilk), 23 Oct. 1997.

71   Board minutes, 3 Dec. 1954.

72   UAA 68-1-1427, Collett to Anne Chernyk, Registrar's Office, University of Alberta, 29 Mar. 1954; also MRUA, Admin., MRC Archive, Collett to Registrar, University of Alberta, 20 Jan. 1956: "We had no students in the Faculty of Arts and Science … during the sessions 1953–54 and 1954–55." PR, 14 Jan. 1955; EC minutes, 22 Feb. 1955.

73   UAA 68-1-1061, Garden to John M. Hidden, Secretary of the Board of Governors, University of Alberta, 15 Mar. 1950.

74   PR, 7 Sept. 1951.

75   Ibid.; report of the EC, Board AGM minutes, 22 Nov. 1951; PR, 30 May 1952; UAA 86-1-21, Garden to Stewart, 4 June 1952; Manning to Stewart, 2 May 1952.

76   PR, 7 Sept. 1951.

77   Justice Ford advised students: "This is not the same course as is given at the University of Alberta…. Regarding the students who attend this course from homes in Alberta, the condition of admittance is a High School Diploma without a foreign language and these students would be unable to enter the University of Alberta where a foreign language is compulsory for Engineering." Garden, "The Affiliation of Mount Royal College with the University of Alberta," undated [1957], UAA 68-1-1427.

78   PR, 30 Sept. 1955.

79   UAA 68-1-1427, Hardy to Stewart, 7 June 1957. Oklahoma ended the practice of admitting students from grade 11 and Mount Royal required a high-school diploma to admit students. Ibid., Hardy, Chairman, Board of Examiners in Professional Engineering, to C. M. MacLeod, chairman, Board of Governors, University of Alberta, 30 Dec. 1957, Summary of Discussions Dec. 9th, re Appeals Board of Examiners in Professional Engineering.

80   UAA 68-1-1427, Hardy to Colonel L. F. Grant, Chairman, Engineers' Council for Professional Development, Toronto, 8 June 1955.

81   Ibid., Hardy to Garden, 12 Dec. 1955.

82   EC report, Board minutes, 18 Nov. 1955; PR, 16 Dec. 1955. Ibid., Garden, "The Affiliation of Mount Royal College with the University of Alberta" [1957].

83   "Brief Report of the Executive of the Board of Governors of Mount Royal College," 30 Nov. 1956. attached to PR, 30 Nov. 1956.

84   UAA 68-1-1427, Hardy to Colonel L. F. Grant, Chairman, Engineers' Council for Professional Development, Toronto, 8 June 1955.

85   EC minutes, 20 May 1955.

86   Memorandum, 24 July 1954, attached to the minutes of the College on Junior Colleges minutes, 27 Feb. 1957, UAA 68-1-1036.

87   UAA 68-1-1427, Stewart to Hardy, 26 June 1957.

88   Ibid., Hardy to C. M. MacLeod, Chairman, Board of Governors, University of Alberta, 30 Dec. and 4 Jan. 1958.

89   PR, 19 June 1953.

90   "Canadian College Prepares Students," Sooner Magazine 29, no.7 (Mar. 1957): 14–15; and Boyd Gunning, "Sooner Scene," ibid., 30, no. 5 (Jan. 1958): 1–2.

91   PR, 21 Nov. 1958.

92   EC, 1 May 1959.

93   Quoted in Howse, "History," 62.

94   PR, 20 June 1947; editorial, *Albertan*, 19 June 1947.

95   MRC, *Calendar*, 1947–48, 22; "College offers new course," *Albertan*, 27 Aug. 1948.

96   PR, 13 Apr. 1956.

97   PR, 20 June 1947; editorial, *Albertan*, 19 June 1947.

98   *Calgary Herald*, 15 July 1944 and 28 July 1944.

99   MRC, *Calendar*, 1948–49, 22.

100   PR, 9 Dec. 1949; Collett interview (Macdonald-Wilk), 5 Mar. 1998.

101   PR, 20 June 1947; editorial, *Albertan*, 19 June 1947.

102   PR, 15 Apr. 1955, 19 Oct. and 30 Nov. 1956.

103   PR, 20 June 1947; editorial, *Albertan*, 19 June 1947.

104   MRC, *Calendar*, 1948–49, 23.

105   "Mount Royal College announces the opening of the Department of Adult Education and Evening Studies," *Calgary Herald*, 7 Aug. 1948; "Mt. Royal Opening new adult education dept.," ibid., 11 Sept. 1948; PR, 26 Nov. 1948; MRC, *Calendar*, 1947–48, 23.

106   Report on the Evening College, PR, 22 Nov. 1951.

107   J. C. Yates, "Annual Report—Evening College, 1959–60," Board minutes, 26 Nov. 1959.

108   PR, 30 May 1952; *Calgary Herald*, 9 Aug. 1952; on the background, see Collett interview (Macdonald-Wilk), 5 Mar. 1998.

109   PR, 27 June 1952; "Two Semester System Planned for the High-School Department," *Albertan*, 12 June 1952.

110   PR, 16 Jan. 1953.

111   Report on Junior College Division, Board minutes, 26 Nov. 1959.

112   The "Statement of the Board of Governors Respecting Expansion of University Facilities in Calgary," 22 Aug. 1956, recommended, inter alia, that "there should remain within the province only one institution which confers degrees, namely, the University of Alberta." Terms of affiliation, University of Alberta, *Calendar*, 1957–58, 40–41, ; Johns, "A Junior Community College as the University Sees It," *The Alberta School Trustee* (Feb. 1956); and Anderson, "Institutional Analysis," 28–29. For Johns' views in that period, see Duncan D. Campbell, *Those Tumultuous Years: The Goals of the President of the University of Alberta during the Decade of the 1960s* (Edmonton: University of Alberta, 1977).

113   EC minutes, 13 May 1957.

114   UAA 68-1-1036, Text of Garden's remarks.

115   EC minutes, 25 Mar. 1960.

116   Report, Special Committee to Review the Future of the Junior College Division, Board Annual Meeting minutes, 26 Nov. 1959. The report suggested co-operation with "other junior colleges in the West [in] setting up a university of [their] own."

117   The conditions: students must have no deficiency in English 30 or Social Studies 30, have only one matriculation deficiency, and take only one matriculation subject. In 1962, the agreement was expanded to include teachers needing to upgrade "in one Grade 12 subject . . . and one university subject, concurrently, at the first-year level." Thirty teachers enrolled, of whom nine combined high-school and university work. UAA 69-123-1837,

H. T. Coutts, Dean, to Collett, 5 Mar. 1962. Board Annual Meeting minutes, 29 Nov. 1962, attachments: Hawkes, Annual Report of the Student Personnel Services Department, Nov. 1962; Report on the Operation of Mount Royal College, Summer Session 1962.

118   Ibid., 23 Feb. 1961, attachment.

119   PR, 28 Nov. 1963.

120   Doris Anderson, *Rebel Daughter: An Autobiography* (Toronto: Key Porter Books, 2002), 73.

121   Board Committee on Salaries and Pensions for Staff, 1 June 1947; EC minutes, 21 June 1947; retroactive remarks, EC minutes, 25 July 1967.

122   Board Committee on Salary Schedule, 18 July 1947; EC minutes, 25 July 1947.

123   PR, 9 Dec. 1949.

124   PR, 19 Mar. 1954; EC minutes, 14 Jan. 1955.

125   EC minutes, 20 Mar. 1953.

126   Ibid., 19 Mar. 1954. Otto Deutsch, a faculty member at the time, described Garden as "an opportunist in many ways and he would try to get the best he could but he wouldn't refuse to change if it was to the advance of the college." The instructors sought ATA help because of their standing as schoolteachers. Otto H. Deutsch, Interview (Macdonald-Wilk), 11 Dec. 1998. On the development of Alberta schools and the ATA, see Chalmers, *Schools of the Foothill Province*, and his *Teachers of the Foothills Province: The Story of the Alberta Teachers' Association* (Toronto: University of Toronto Press, 1968).

127   On salaries and workload, Collett interview (Macdonald-Wilk), 5 Mar. 1998.

128   Ibid., 24 Feb. 1955.

129   Ibid., 15 Apr. 1955; EC Report, Board minutes, 18 Nov. 1955.

130   PR, 29 May 1942 and 6 Dec. 1957 (chart).

131   PR, 19 Mar. 1954, 16 Dec. 1955, and 13 Apr. 1956.

132   "Money begins to roll in for College building fund," *Calgary Herald*, 15 May 1956. Mention of potential engineering space inspired concerns at the university: UAA 68-1-1427, Stewart to Garden, 15 May 1956.

133   She was recruited by Galperin. MRUA, Conservatory minutes, 8 Sept. 1942; Hamblin and Finch, *The Diva and the Rancher,* 213.

134   R. Dale McIntosh, "Egbert, Gladys," *Encyclopedia of Music in Canada,* at www.thecanadianencyclopedia.com. It took two years to complete discussions. MRUA, Conservatory minutes, 24 Sept. 1940; 8 Sept. 1942.

135   MRUA, Conservatory minutes, 8 Sept. 1942.

136   Ibid., report by Galperin; also MRUA, Admin., Correspondence 1950s, F. C. Silvester, Registrar, Royal Conservatory of Music, to Garden, 18 May 1956.

137   MRC, *Calendar*, 1939–40, 36; advertisement in the *Albertan*, 30 Aug. 1941.

138   Board Finance Committee minutes, 2 Dec. 1942.

139   MRUA, Conservatory, "Conference between Mr. Galperin and the Principal, 23 March 1944"; "Report of Conservatory of Music Committee arrived at after Conferences with the Finance Committee and Mr. Galperin"; "Statement of Policy of Conservatory of Music, 14 April 1944." These statements helped clarify the relationship of Conservatory members to the college and the college's liabilities. Conservatory instructors were

considered independent contractors and were liable for the city's business tax. MRUA, Conservatory, Faculty minutes, 21 Oct. 1943.

140 MRUA, Conservatory, "Report of Conservatory of Music Committee," attachment: "Financial Policy," 14 April 1944.

141 Appointment, *Calgary Herald*, 1 and 4 Nov. 1944; *Albertan*, 8 Nov. 1944. On his life, see Clifford Ford and Barclay McMillan, "Mossop, Cyril," in *Encyclopedia of Music in Canada*, at www. thecanadianencyclopedia.com. PR, 7 Dec. 1945; Mossop interview (Macdonald-Wilk), 26 Apr. 1998; on the ballet program, advertisement, Calgary Herald, 4 Sept. 1948; and on its demise, Board Conservatory Committee minutes, 6 Apr. 1951.

142 Leona F. Paterson, "Ramsay, Harold," *Encyclopedia of Music in Canada*, at www.canadianencyclopedia.com; PR, 6 Oct. 1950; Board Conservatory Committee minutes, 13 Oct., 4 Dec. 1950.

143 PR, 24 Oct. 1952, 6 Apr. 1951, 25 July and 10 Dec. 1952. Bach interview (Macdonald-Wilk), 30 Dec. 1997.

144 Mount Royal College, Conservatory of Music and Speech Arts, *Calendar*, 1964−65, 5.

145 PR, 25 July, 24 Oct. 1952; PR, 21 May 1954. On other changes, see Ramsay, "Conservatory of Music," Varshicom, 1956, 69.

146 A recording of the folk mass is available in the University of Alberta library; see also Muir interview (Macdonald-Wilk), 12 Mar. 1998.

147 MRC, *Calendar*, 1947−48, 25. Advertisements in *Calgary Herald* and the *Albertan*, 17 Dec. 1949. On Garden's resistance, Collett interview (Macdonald-Wilk), 5 Mar. 1998.

148 "Mount Royal College Conservatory, Ensembles," *Encyclopedia of Music in Canada*, at www.thecandianencyclopedia.com.

149 "Calgary Symphony Orchestra," ibid.

150 Hare resigned over refusals to permit him to serve as an adjudicator in the Maritimes because of a conflict with college activities. Hare-Garden correspondence, Conservatory of Music Committee minutes, 28 May 1951; PR, 8 June, 7 Sept., 22 Nov. 1951, 20 Mar. and 30 May 1952.

151 Mrs. John S. Bach interview (Macdonald-Wilk), 30 Dec. 1997; PR, 19 June 1953; Bach interview (Macdonald-Wilk), 30 Dec. 1997; "John Bach (1908−2000): A Calgary Musical Cornerstone," *Music Calgary* 1, no. 2 (Apr. 2000). In 1997, Bach was made a member of Calgary's Hall of Fame.

152 MRUA, Admin., Bach, Director of Fine Arts, "An Overall Programme of Orchestral Training in Alberta," 1965.

153 1MRC, *Calendar*, 1943−44, 5.

154 Ibid., Fine Arts Division, 1965−66, 10−12.

155 PR, 22 Mar., 17 Apr. 1952

156 Nadine Mackenzie, *The Light in the Night: The Life of Mary Munn* (Calgary: McQuahaes, 1981); "Munn, Mary," *Encyclopedia of Music in Canada*, at www.thecanadianencyclopedia.com.

157 PR, 30 Nov. 1956.

158 Announcement, *Albertan*, 23 Sept. 1944. Paterson earned her ATCM ("performer's degree") in Speech and Drama at the Toronto Conservatory of Music Memoir by L. Chrumka, "History of the Speech Arts Program at Mount Royal College," 1980, Glenbow-Alberta Institute.

159 Paterson interview (Macdonald-Wilk), 22 Jan. 1998.

160 PR, 10 Dec. 1952; *Albertan*, 8 June 1953.

161 Paterson interview (Macdonald-Wilk), 22 Jan. 1998.

162 Muir interview (Macdonald-Wilk), 12 Mar. 1998. The speech therapy program for children with hearing problems was later embraced by the Calgary school board. Collett interview (Macdonald-Wilk), 5 Mar. 1998.

163 Paterson interview (Macdonald-Wilk), 22 Jan. 1998.

164 MRC, Conservatory of Music and Speech Arts, *Calendar*, 1964−65, 5.

165 Obituary, "Dr. Leona Francis Paterson," *Globe and Mail*, 9 April 2004.

166 Letter to board, 1 May 1957; PR, 15 Apr., 13 May 1957.

167 PR, 26 Jan. 1961.

168 MRJC, *Calendar*, 1965−66, Fine Arts Division, 5; 1969−70, 119.

169 MRC Prospectus, Conservatory of Music and Speech Arts, 1962−63.

170 PR, 10 Dec. 1952; *Albertan*, 8 June 1953.

171 Patricia Roome, "Snake dances, power puff football and dribblethons: Yearbooks chronicle Mount Royal Culture," *Reflections*, Spring 2008, 9.

172 PR, 29 Nov. 1946; *Varshicom*, 1948, 67−68; *Albertan*, 19 Dec. 1949.

173 Allen Garrett, Editor, *Collews*, Jan. 1959, 3.

174 For an interesting personal story, see Anton Colijn, born in 1942 of Dutch parents in a prisoner-of-war camp in Indonesia, recount the story of his family's departure at Christmas 1949 in the middle of a civil war: "A Strange Christmas," ibid., 4.

175 "Boys' Dorm," *Royal Reflector*, no. 1, Feb. 1960.

176 *Varshicom*, 1952, 70, ibid., 1961 ("Cheerleaders" page, unpaginated).

177 *Varshicom*, 1943, 63.

178 E.g., "Social events outside the college," *Collews*, May 1958, 4.

179 MRUA, Alumni Affairs Collection, Isabel Munro Wishart, 1940s Memory Booklet, 1940s reunion in 1996.

180 *Scratch Pad*, undated [content suggests 1943].

181 MRC, *Calendar*, 1944−45, 13.

182 Mary Wardle, "Social Highlights," *Varshicom*, 1946, 45; see the similar reports on events in 1947, ibid., 53, and 1949, ibid., 47.

183 E.g., *Varshicom*, 1959, 42.

184 Ibid., 1950, 56.

185 Earl Willmott interview, Vancouver, 1972, in Howse, "History," 86−89; Garden said "only five" per cent caused most of the trouble. PR, 30 Nov. 1956.

186 Russell Dickson," "The World of Sport," *Scratch Pad*, 30 Nov. 1942.

187 PR, 21 Jan. 1944.

188 *Collews*, Dec. 1957, 1.

189 Ibid., Nov. 1957, 9−10; "Sports Resume," *Inkspot*, Apr. 1957.

190 The Students' Council focused on "social events, Literary Society, Clubs, etc., athletic activities," the yearbook, and the *Scratch Pad*. MRC, *Calendar*, 1945−46, 12.

191 *Varshicom*, 1945, 10.

192 *Collews*, Dec. 1957, 10−11.

193 Jack Finlay, President, "Annual report of Mount Royal Junior College Students Council," Board minutes, 26 Nov. 1959.

194 "Student Council News in a Nutshell," *Colleus*, Jan. 1959; Wayne Harvey, President, "Report of the High School Council," Board minutes, 26 Nov. 1959.

195 Angeline Poppel, "School Spirit in MRC," *Tattler*, 1953–54.

196 Allen Garrett, "School Spirit—What's That?," *Colleus*, Feb. 1959, 1.

197 "Student Council Report," ibid., Mar. 1959, 7.

198 Letter to the editor, "A Disgusted Student," ibid., May 1959, 5.

199 PR, 30 Nov. 1956.

200 Ibid., 21 Jan. 1944.

201 Ibid., 7 Dec. 1945.

202 Ibid., 5 Dec. 1947, 26 Nov. 1948; United Church Yearbook, 1948.

203 *Scratch Pad*, 1943 [undated number].

204 204   Bill Sayers interview (Macdonald-Wilk), 11 Sept. 1998.

205 MRC, *Calendar*, 1949–50, 8–9.

206 Collett interview (Macdonald-Wilk), 16 Oct. 1997.

207 Vincent, Report on Christian Education and Guidance for the Board of Governors, 30 Nov. 1956, Board minutes, 6 Dec. 1956.

208 PR, 30 Nov. 1956.

209 Andrew Stewart, *Special Study on Junior Colleges* (Edmonton: Queens' Printer, 1965), Sayers interview, 77; Anderson, "Institutional Analysis," 192–93.

210 "Mount Royal College Principal Retires," *Albertan*, 22 Nov. 1958.

211 Notes of interview with Earle Mott and Ralph McCready, by John Howse, cited in Howse, "History," 25, 87; and John H. Garden, "Mount Royal Junior College," in Elsie C. Morrison and Peter N. R. Morrison, *Calgary, 1975–1950: A Souvenir of Calgary's Seventy-Fifth Anniversary* (Calgary, 1950), 68.

212 Garden proposed that he be appointed president, "with duties largely of an advisory nature," while Collett would become principal. Instead, the board named him "honorary principal," with a small stipend for three years. Board minutes, 6 Dec. 1957; Ford, "Report of Committee on Reorganization of Administration," EC minutes, 18 Apr. 1958; PR, 20 June 1958. At the end of the period, Garden resigned and later moved to Victoria. EC minutes, 21 Dec. 1961. W. G. M. Rae, Board secretary, to Garden, 28 Dec. 1961.

CHAPTER 5: COMPLETING THE MISSION, 1959–1966

1   Memorandum to the Steering Committee for Junior Colleges, signed by L. A. Thorssen, representative of MRC's Board, 14 Feb. 1966.

2   Overviews can be found in John D. Dennison and Paul Gallagher, *Canada's Community Colleges: Challenge and Opportunity*; Dennison and Gallagher, *Canada's Community College: A Critical Analysis* (Vancouver: University of British Columbia Press, 1986); and Dennison, ed., *Challenge and Opportunity: Canada's Community Colleges at the Crossroads* (Vancouver: University of British Columbia Press, 1995). For the American variant in the 1980s, see Arthur M. Cohen and

Florence B. Brawer, *The American Community College* (San Francisco, London: Jossey-Bass, 1982).

3   MRUA, Admin.: "Report of a Meeting of the Junior Colleges of Alberta," 30 November 1965.

4   "Mount Royal College Principal Retires," *Albertan*, 22 Nov. 1958.

5   Board AGM, 6 Dec. 1947.

6   He was Speaker of the Tuxis Boys' Parliament of Alberta, 1931–33, Alberta Tux: Handbook (Silver Jubilee 1919–1944), 8. Prior to his appointment, the board debated whether it should entice him from the pulpit: "… the church had lost a great opportunity in not taking a greater interest in the important work of her colleges and the appointment of Mr. Collett would help towards correcting this failure." Board AGM minutes, 5 Dec. 1947.

7   W. J. Collett, *History of the Grand Lodge of Alberta, 1905–1980* (Calgary, 1981).

8   Collett interview (Macdonald-Wilk), 16 Oct. 1997.

9   Brian Brennan, "Dedicated Minister Had Role in Education," *Calgary Herald*, 22 Nov. 1998.

10 Awarded an honorary LLD by the University of Alberta in 1954, he was described as Dr. Wright in the college.

11 PR, Jan. 1959.

12 MRC, *Calendar*, 1961–62, 3.

13 "Mt. Royal Course on Semester Plan," *Albertan*, 29 Aug. 1963; "New Technique Used for Business Course," *Calgary Herald*, 10 Sept. 1964.

14 Reports on the Junior College, 23 Nov. 1960, and on the Department of Business Administration, 11 Feb. 1964; see also PR, 25 Jan. and 28 Sept. 1967.

15 MRUA, Admin., Financial statement, 30 June 1965, Statement III: revenues from Business Administration–Day, Business Development Program, Career Department, and Secretarial School as a proportion of revenues from academic activities other than the Conservatory (part of the Fine Arts cluster at the time).

16 McCready report, Board minutes, 26 Nov. 1964; Calgary Herald, 22 Apr. 1964.

17 MRC, *Calendar*, 1962–63, 20, 44–45. There was initially a two-year diploma program but it was abandoned for lack of registration. Registrar's Report, 1 Nov. 1964, 25 Aug. 1966.

18 Howse interview (Macdonald-Wilk), 12 Feb. 1998; he noted a change in the nature of the students when the college moved to its new campus—more former university students, fewer "classic eccentrics and misfits." The enrolment figure is from the Registrar's Report, 1 Nov. 1964, 25 Aug. 1966.

19 Ibid.

20 MRC, *Calendar*, 1968–69, 92–93, 127–30.

21 Registrar's Report, 1 Nov. 1964 and 25 Aug. 1966.

22 MRC, *Calendar*, 1968–69, 98, 147–49; Report, Director of Physical Education, 25 Nov. 1965.

23 MRC, *Calendar*, 1962–63, 43.

24 Registrar's report, 25 Aug. 1966.

25 Interviews (Macdonald-Wilk), 12 Mar. and 10 June 1998; Report, Department of Speech, 26 Nov. 1964.

26 Director of the Evening School, 26 Nov. 1964: Report, Library, 25 Nov. 1965; EC minutes, 21 Feb. 1968.

27 Director of the High School and Evening College Division, report to the board, 26 Nov. 1964, Board AGM Minutes, 25 Nov. 1964; Library report, ibid., 26 Nov. 1965; also EC minutes, 21 Feb. 1968.

28 Board minutes, 9 May 1963. In 1966 the government's Fact Finding Committee on Post-Secondary and Continuing Education in Alberta remarked on the flexibility and innovation, highlighting the academic deficiency program offered in affiliation with the university, the semester system, and the diploma programs: "Graduates … may be admitted to a senior institution and receive a bachelor degree after two years. All the courses parallel university courses." Jonason et al., *Report of the Fact Finding Committee on Post-Secondary and Continuing Education in Alberta.*

29 Anderson, "Institutional Analysis," 194–95; Gamble interview (Macdonald-Wilk), 16 Nov. 1997.

30 For a general review, see P. A. Gordon, "Student Services in Alberta Colleges" (M.Ed. thesis, University of Calgary, 1970).

31 Anderson, "Institutional Analysis," 102–4.

32 Ibid.

33 PR, 29 Mar. 1962.

34 Ibid. See also Brown, "An Analysis of the Achievements of Junior College Students at the University of Calgary."

35 Ibid.

36 Hawkes, "Annual Report of the Student Personnel Services Department," Nov. 1962.

37 Collett interview (Macdonald-Wilk), 16 Oct. 1997.

38 Hawkes, "Annual Report," Nov. 1962; *The Royal Reflector: The Student's Paper of Mount Royal College*, ibid., 10 Feb. 1964; *Reflector*, 24 Nov. 1965.

39 Don Thonger, president of the Junior College Students Council in 1962, letter, *Reflector*, 24 Nov. 1965 and 22 Feb. 1966.

40 Wayne Harvey, Editorial, *Royal Reflector*, Feb. 1960.

41 "MRC Publication has problems," ibid., Feb. 1962.

42 PR, 24 Jan. 1962; *Royal Reflector*, Jan. 1962.

43 Editorial, *Reflector*, 24 Nov. 1965.

44 Ibid., 25 Oct. 1966, 20 Nov. 1968, and 7 Mar. 1969.

45 *Royal Reflector*, Jan. 1962; *Varshicom*, 1961–62.

46 *Royal Reflector*, 10 Feb. 1964 and 27 Mar. 1964.

47 "CMRC disc jockeys polish up presentations," *Reflector*, 22 Feb. 1966. In 1967 the station began broadcasting into the residences. Ibid., 14 Nov. 1967 and 4 Oct. 1968.

48 Ibid., Jan. 1962.

49 Ibid., 22 Feb. 1966 and 28 Nov. 1967; *Albertan*, 28 Nov. and 12 Mar. 1968.

50 Ibid., 30 Jan. 1964; *Reflector*, 22 Feb. 1966.

51 *Calgary Herald*, 23 Jan. 1964; *Albertan*, 2 June 1964.

52 *Varshicom*, 1960–61, 1961–62, and 1962–63; *Reflector*, 4 Oct. and 11 Dec. 1968.

53 *Royal Reflector*, 10 Feb. 1964, organization chart.

54 John A. Brown, coordinator, "Student Activities," Nov. 1960; EC minutes, 3 Nov. 1960.

55 See the story on the founding in the *Reflector*, Dec. 1060; also "MRC Cougars, Canada's Third Strongest Ball Team," *Albertan*, 15 Dec. 1960.

56 EC minutes, 26 Jan. 1961. A special board committee was formed "to review the football situation, look into the academic study of players, and bring back a recommendation to the next meeting of the Executive." It recommended continuation on a year-to-year basis.

57 Ibid.

58 A decade later, Len Thomas, an instructor, declared with some exaggeration: "It cost a lot of money to keep the team going, but they were good PR. That year [1964] it got so bad that we were having to bail the guys out of jail to get them back to school and to playing. That was not the kind of publicity that we wanted. The money for the team just dried up." "Booze drowns M.R.C. football," *Reflector*, 3 Oct. 1973.

59 See the remarks of a student athlete he recruited, Sindlinger interview (Macdonald-Wilk), 27 Nov. 1998.

60 PR, 16 Dec. 1960. Collett told the board that forming an alumni association was "one of our major concerns in this Jubilee Year."

61 MRUA, Admin.: Alumni Association 1960s, L. V. V. Robinson, secretary, Mount Royal College Alumni Association, to P. Wright, 17 Nov. 1964; response from Rae, Board secretary, 23 Nov. 1964; Robinson, 3 Nov. 1964, to Rev. Harold W. Vaughan, Secretary, Board of Colleges and Secondary Schools, United Church of Canada, 5 Nov. 1964; Vaughan to Robinson, 10 Nov. 1964.

62 EC minutes, 26 Feb. 1960; committee report, Board AGM Minutes, 23 Nov. 1960.

63 Later Collett said that the United Church had lost interest in its non-theological colleges. The "amount of financial support indicated the interest that the church had. The secondary schools began to fall away … and the church gradually severed connections." Collett interview (Macdonald-Wilk), 16 Oct. 1997. Earlier, he was more optimistic. PR, 23 Nov. 1960; Board AGM minutes, 23 Nov. 1960.

64 Anderson, Institutional Analysis," 194–95, wondered whether, given the state of college finances, this was "economically possible."

65 Ibid., 101.

66 MRUA, Admin., Correspondence 1968, Max Rae, on behalf of chairman Wright, to Dr. Gordon L. Mowat, Chairman, Board of Post-Secondary Education, 25 June 1968.

67 Anderson, "Institutional Analysis," organization chart, 223; see also the counsellor's role description, 228–29.

68 Pashak interview (Macdonald-Wilk), 23 Oct. 1998.

69 Ibid., Queen M. Linton, secretary, ATA, to Collett, 2 Nov. 1965; also MRUA, Admin., ATA, 1965–1970, Collett to Pashak, 8 Apr. 1964; the board made some changes in response to requests, Collett to Pashak, 15 May 1964.

70 Board AGM minutes, 28 Nov. 1963; PR, 28 Nov. 1963; Principal, memo to the faculty, 23 Apr. 1964; EC minutes, 27 May 1964.

71 The Conciliation Committee struck to resolve board-MRFA differences in collective bargaining in 1969 recommended bringing faculty under the terms of the Local Authorities Pension Plan. Board CoW minutes, 11 Dec. 1969; see also ibid., 22 Apr. 1970, report by Max Rae: "Out of approximately 90 full time faculty members, 31 are members of the Teachers Retirement Fund…. Apart from faculty, however, we have 124 full time

employees, virtually all of them without a pension plan. The administration recommends that the LAPP be made available to these employees as soon as possible." In addition, see: MRUA, MRFA-Teachers' Retirement Fund, 1970 file, Catherine E. Berry, Asst. Secretary-Treasurer, Teachers' Retirement Fund, to Mount Royal College, 28 May 1970; W. G. M. Rae, Vice President, Business Services, to "All Teachers' Retirement Fund Members," 1 June 1970.

72 Agreement between the board and the ATA-MRC, Sept. 1962, in Anderson, "Institutional Analysis," 151–54.

73 MRUA, Admin: Collett to D. J. Turner, M.R.J.C. Chairman, Alberta Teachers' Association, 27 November 1964.

74 Ibid., 156–57, list of teaching loads.

75 Stewart, *Special Study on Junior Colleges*, 77.

76 Reprinted in Anderson, "Institutional Analysis," 151–64.

77 PR, Nov. 29, 1961; University of Alberta, *Calendar*, 1961–62, 617; 1962–63, 618–19; 1963–64, 651–52; and 1965–65, 679.

78 "A Brief Concerning the Contract of Employment between the Academic Teachers and the Board of Governors of Mount Royal College," EC minutes, 23 Feb. 1961.

79 MRUA, Admin., MRFA, 1966–1967, H. C. French, Secretary, Board of Industrial Relations, Government of the Province of Alberta, 2 March 1966, to Collett.

80 EC minutes, 23 Feb. 1961; Collett to E. L. Pitt (Junior College) and B. Lee (High School), 14 June 1966.

81 MRUA, Admin., MRFA Agreements, 1966–1969, "Mount Royal College Faculty Agreement" [1966].

82 EC minutes, 25 Oct. 1962; MRUA, Committee of Eleven minutes, Conservatory of Music Committee minutes, 19 June 1962.

83 PR, 25 Oct. 1962.

84 Special Report on Junior Colleges, written by Andrew Stewart (Edmonton: Queen's Printer, 1965), 76; financial data, Anderson, "Institutional Analysis," 47–58.

85 Based on the chart entitled "Statement of Revenue and Expenditures (including overhead) 1959–60 to 1963–64, in Anderson, "Institutional Analysis," 54.

86 EC minutes, 24 and 31 Jan. 1962.

87 Wright, "Memorandum to the Executive of the Board of Governors of Mount Royal College from the Chairman of the Board," 20 Mar. 1962.

88 Minutes, special subcommittee to arrange contract details with Cecil Cater, 4 Apr. 1962. Cater served as "campaign director" from 1 Apr. 1962 to 31 Mar. 1963.

89 PR, 29 Nov. 1962. Amendment, 31 Mar. 1950: "4.(b): The land, buildings, equipment and furnishings belonging to Mount Royal College so long as the same are exclusively used and occupied by the College shall be exempt from taxation except for local improvement purposes."

90 Alberta Department of Education, Annual Report, 1963, 87–96, describes the growth of SAIT and NAIT in this period.

91 *Albertan*, 19 Aug. 1962.

92 Anderson, "Institutional Analysis," 4.

93 MRUA, Admin., Senate 1962–66, "Mount Royal College Senate," undated [ca 1962], *Albertan*, 19 Aug. 1962; Minutes, Board of Governors Conference, 22–23 Oct. 1964; "Mount Royal College Names Senate," *Albertan*, 21 Aug. 1963; the

members of the Academic Senate are listed in MRC, *Calendar*, 1964–65, 4.

94 EC minutes, 26 June, 26 Sept. 1963. As the Senate's membership differed from that in the college's charter, a board committee was established to prepare an amendment. See also "Mount Royal College Names Academic Senate," *Albertan*, 21 Aug. 1963. MRC Annual Report, 1964–65, 4.

95 Collett later remembered that little but the principal's title had changed. Collett interview (Macdonald-Wilk), 16 Oct. 1997.

96 Board minutes, 9 May 1963 (special meeting with minister).

97 EC minutes, 26 June 1963; Board minutes; and PR, 28 Nov. 1963.

98 "Robert Wyckham special guest; student centre named in his honor," Dispatch, published for Alumni and Friends of the College (1984), 2, 4; Varshicom, 1964, lists him as a member of the Student Executive Board. Wyckham, BA, MBA (University of Western Ontario), later earned a Ph.D. at Michigan State University and joined Simon Fraser University in 1971, where he remained for the balance of his academic career.

99 MRUA, Admin., Correspondence 1964, Collett to Colbourne, 24 Apr. 1964.

100 Ibid., Collett to J. Steele, Chief Commissioner, City of Calgary, 28 May, 13 July and 18 Nov. 1964; and Collett to L. Richard, President, Crown Assets Disposal Corporation, 27 July 1964; Collett to A. R. Patrick, Minister, Economic Affairs, Alberta, 30 July 1964.

101 PR, 23 Sept. 1964; EC minutes, 23 Sept. 1964.

102 EC minutes, 23 Sept. 1964.

103 MRUA, Admin., Correspondence 1965, City Clerk to Collett, 24 June 1965.

104 MRUA, Admin., Thorssen, memo to Steering Committee for Junior Colleges, 14 February 1966. ERC files, Wright, memo to members of the board, 31 Aug. 1964; and PAA 80.202, item 27, correspondence between O. S. Longman and Howard P. Wright.

105 "Mount Royal Seeks School Board's Help. Public Funds Held Key to Expansion of College," *Albertan*, 13 Feb. 1965.

106 EC minutes, 25 Mar. 1965; Board minutes, 7 April 1965, attachment (minutes of the Joint Meeting of the Executive Committee of the Board of Governors and the Special Committee Negotiating with the Calgary Public and Separate School Boards regarding Junior College Development in Calgary, 7 Apr. 1965).

107 Minutes, Special Meeting of Representatives of the School Boards and Mount Royal College, 25 Oct. 1965. The public and separate school boards hired the firm of Cresap, McCormick and Paget of New York "to study the feasibility of the two School Boards and Mount Royal College joining in a cooperative Junior College project." It found the project feasible. Cresap, McCormick and Paget, *A Plan for a Public Community Junior College for Calgary* (Cresap, McCormick and Paget, 1966).

108 EC minutes, 6 Jan. 1966.

109 Ibid., 13 May 1966.

110 An Act respecting the Establishment and Operation of Mount Royal Junior College, 1966. Also MRUA, Admin., Negotiations relating to the formation of Mount Royal Junior College, 1966.

111 Board minutes, 31 Aug. 1966; "Mount Royal Given U of C Affiliation," *Albertan*, 31 Aug. 1966

112 "Mount Royal Given U of C Affiliation," *Albertan*, 31 Aug. 1966; MRUA, Admin., Agreements: MRJC–UC Affiliation,

1966, which includes "Proposed Affiliation Agreement between Mount Royal Junior College and the University of Calgary, 31 Oct. 1966.

113   Board minutes, 31 Aug. 1966.

114   "Mount Royal Board Holds First Meeting as Public Body," *Albertan*, 1 Sept. 1966.

115   Wright to "All Faculty and Staff," 2 Sept. 1966; with minutes of Board meeting, 5 Oct. 1966.

116   Wright to McKinnon, 9 Sept. 1966; the property was acquired by Mount Royal Junior College. Transfer of assets, Board minutes, 10 May 1967. The land transferred consisted of lots 1 to 13 inclusive in block 43 and lots 29 to 40 in block 37, plus lot 14 in block 43, in downtown Calgary. "There is an appraisal for the first transfer of $775,000 plus an estimate of $25,000 for lot 14, making a total of $800,000."

117   VU/UC 83.051C, Box 68, file 6: United College, "The Educational Policy of the Church," submitted to the Special Committee on the Theological Colleges, Board of Christian Education, 1942.

118   Anderson, "Institutional Analysis," 195.

119   Manning M. Patillo, Jr. and Donald M. Mackenzie, Church-Sponsored Higher Education in the United States: Report of the Danforth Commission (Washington, DC: American Council on Education, 1966), 198–99.

120   James D. Cameron, For the *People: A* History *of St. Francis Xavier University* (Montreal/Kingston: McGill-Queen's University Press, 1996), 384.

CHAPTER 6: BECOMING A PUBLIC COLLEGE, 1966–1972

1   Jeremy Rifkin, *The European Dream* (New York: Tarcher, 2004), 1–2.

2   Simon, "History of the Alberta Provincial Institute of Technology and Arts."

3   A White Paper on Human Resources Development, by Ernest C. Manning, Premier of Alberta (Edmonton, 1969), esp. 26, 72–73, 78–89.

4   Berghofer and Vladicka, *Access to Opportunity*, 33–42; Michael B. Andrews, Edward A. Holdaway, and Gordon L. Mowat, "Post-secondary Education in Alberta since 1945," in Jones, ed, *Higher Education in Canada: Different Systems, Different Perspectives*, 59–93.

5   Alan Thomas, "From 'Flower Power' to the Internet: 25 Years of Canadian Colleges," College Canada 3, no. 2: 1997–98.

6   "Nowhere else were [the government's] efforts more concerted, and arguably more futile, than in those made to strengthen the province's rural fabric." Michael Payne, Donald Wetherell, and Catherine Cavanaugh, eds., *Alberta Formed, Alberta Transformed* (Edmonton: University of Alberta Press) 2: 627–30.

7   An Act respecting the Establishment and Operation of Mount Royal Junior College 1966, s. 3.

8   For context, see John D. Dennison and Robert Harris, "Governing Boards in Postsecondary Education," *Canadian Journal of Higher Education* 14, no. 2 (1984): 13–31; the article focuses on British Columbia colleges and technical institutes.

9   Board minutes, 11 Nov. 1966.

10   Collett, "General Statement of Policy," PR, 6 Dec. 1966. The religious passage: "The College believes that the life of the

spirit is an integral part of the really educated man and seeks to help the student grow in faith. While the College can never be without the formal expression of faith and religion as found in its department of Religion and its allied courses, yet the sympathetic expression of faith in every subject, in every classroom and in every activity is of paramount importance."

11   Commessotti resigned to join the Colleges Commission. Board CoW minutes, 11 Sept. 1969.

12   Kathleen Maclay, Media Relations, University of California, "Clark Kerr's legacy: 1960 Master Plan transformed higher education," 3 Dec. 2003; http://www.berkeley.edu/news/media/releases/2003/12/03_master.shtml.

13   John C. Long, "The Transferability Issue in Alberta: A Case Study in the Politics of Higher Education." (Ph.D. Thesis, University of Alberta, 1979), 43. See also: John C. Long, "An Historical Study of the Establishment of College Systems in Ontario and Alberta in the 1960's" (M.Ed. thesis, University of Calgary, 1972); James M. Small, "College Coordination in Alberta: System Development and Appraisal" (Ph.D. Thesis, Michigan State University, 1972). Gordon Campbell, "History of the Alberta Community College System, 1957–1969" (Ph.D. diss., University of Calgary, 1972).

14   J. E. Seger, J. E., and G. L. Mowat, eds. *The Junior College: The Lecture Series of the Banff Regional Conference of School Administrators* (Edmonton: University of Alberta, 1966).

15   Jonason et al., *Report of the Fact Finding Committee on Post-Secondary and Continuing Education in Alberta*.

16   "Alberta's Public College – Current Operation and Proposed Development, submitted to cabinet by Dr. H. Kolesar, Aug. 26, 1970," 4. In 1970, Robert C. Clark, in Post Secondary Education until 1972: An Alberta Policy Statement, 12, expressed a similar view.

17   From "A Summary Statement of Proposals of the Provincial Board of Post-Secondary Education to the Honourable R. Reierson, Minister of Education, and Cabinet Reactions to the Proposals in Principle" (n.d., unpaginated). MRUA, Admin., Box 2, Provincial Board of Post-Secondary Education minutes, 12 Dec. 1968.

18   An Act to Amend the Public Junior Colleges Act, 1967, c. 64, ss. 3–5.

19   Long, "The Transferability Issue in Alberta," 134.

20   Colleges Act, 1969, c. 14, s. 27.

21   Cicely Watson, New College Systems in Canada (Paris: Organisation for Economic Co-operation and Development, 1973), 22.

22   On government policy, see Clark*, Post-Secondary Education until 1972*, 2–3. On Red Deer College, see : R. E.Barrett, *A University for Red Deer* (Red Deer: City of Red Deer, 1969); R. G. Fast, *Red Deer College: Report of the Administrator of Red Deer College* (Edmonton: University of Alberta Press, 1974).

23   Mount Royal contributed to the discussion leading to the establishment of the Alberta Council on Admissions and Transfers (ACAT): "Comments on 'A Report on the Concept of Affiliation,'" 30 June 1971.

24   Gordon Campbell, *Community Colleges in Canada* (Toronto: McGraw Hill Co., 1971), xvii. On the Alberta system, see: Reno A. Bosetti, "A Comparative Analysis of the Functioning of Six Post-Secondary Non-University Educational Institution." (Ph.D. diss., University of Alberta, 1975); G. Loken, "An Analysis of the Junior College in Alberta: Progress, Program and Prospect" (M.Ed. thesis, University of Alberta, 1966); H.

E. Farquhar, "The Role of the College in the System of Higher Education in Alberta" (Ph.D. diss., University of Alberta, 1967); and John Cecil Clarke, "Alberta Community Colleges: Ten Years in Review" (M.Ed. thesis, University of Alberta, 1983). On individual colleges, see: "Grant MacEwan College," *College Canada* 2 (Sept. 1977), 7; "Mount Royal College," ibid. 3 (Apr. 1978), 1, 11; "Old Sun College," ibid. 3 (Apr. 1978), 1, 8; "Red Deer College: Serving Central Alberta," ibid. 2 (Oct. 1977), 1; and D. Wieler, "Regional Commitment and the Community College at Grande Prairie Regional College," ibid. 4 (March 1979): 10–11; and A. G. Markle, "Genesis of Lethbridge Public Junior College" (M.Ed. thesis, University of Alberta, 1965).

25   Watson, *New Public College Systems*, 32–33.

26   Cf. Berghofer, "General Education in Post-Secondary Non-University Educational Institutions in Alberta."

27   Pashak interview (Macdonald-Wilk), 23 Oct. 1998.

28   MRUA, Baker Files, Kenneth J. Robson, note to author, 5 Aug. 2005.

29   Recommendation of the Academic Council, approved by the Board, 22 March 1971.

30   James M. Pitsula, "Cicero versus Socrates: The Liberal Arts Debate in the 1960s at the University of Saskatchewan, Regina Campus," *Historical Studies in Education/Revue de l'histoire de l'éducation* (Spring 2003): 101–29.

31   Quoted in Patricia, "'In Pursuit of Values,' or 'Laugh When You Say That': The Student Critique of the Arts Curriculum in the 1960s," in Axelrod and Reid, eds., *Youth, University and Canadian Society*, 248.

32   *Calgary Herald*, 20 Jan. 1971.

33   Provincial Board of Post-Secondary Education, minutes, 30 Dec. 1968.

34   Board minutes, 10 May 1967.

35   PR, 18 Sept. 1970.

36   "Report of the Attrition Rate," by Karen Gabber, coordinator, Educational Development Services. Board minutes, 22 March 1971.

37   On the college's earlier proposal, see UAA 68-1-21, Newton to Ottewell, 15 Aug. 1942, Ottewell to Garden, 17 Aug. 1942; Ottewell to Crawford, 3 Sept. 1942.

38   Bernice E. Anderson, Nursing Education in Community Junior Colleges (Philadelphia: J. B. Lippincott Ltd., 1966).

39   University of Alberta, Survey of Schools of Nursing in Alberta.

40   *Report of the Royal Commission on Health Services*, 1964, 64–66.

41   MRUA, Mackie, "Proposal for Diploma Program in Nursing at Mount Royal College, Sept. 1966," 1–18 (origins of nursing education); and "The First Decade: Diploma Nursing Program, Mount Royal College, 1963–1973" (includes remarks by Collett, 21–24, and McCready, 25–26).

42   It first met on 10 November 1965. E. Jean Mackie, "The First Decade: Diploma Nursing Program, Mount Royal College, 1963–1973" (1981, revised 1986), 39 (includes names).

43   EC minutes, 5 Oct. 1966.

44   "Register Now for Mount Royal Junior College Nursing Diploma Program," *Edmonton Journal*, 27 Dec. 1966.

45   "Two-Year Nurses Graduate," *Calgary Herald*, 20 Jan. 1969.

46   MRUA, MRFA, 1966–67, "Minutes, Junior Colleges Advisory Committee Meeting, 30 May 1968," item 3; "Shaky Start for Program," *Calgary Herald*, 22 March 1969; "Minister Re-Opens Nursing Bill Row," ibid., 7 Oct. 1969.

47   M. Steed, "Total Student Enrollment in All Basic Nursing Programs in Alberta," Edmonton, 5 Nov. 1973, cited in Mackie, "The First Decade," 178.

48   Judith Lathrop interview (Macdonald-Wilk), 28 Jan. 1999.

49   "'Forward thinking' brings police to college," *Journal 3009* 1, no. 10.

50   Vernon Fowlie, "New look at policing," *Albertan*, 11 Aug. 1970; Monique Gregoire, "'Secure' future for Justice Administration," *Second Tuesday*, 6 Nov. 1979.

51   "Criminal Justice Department active," *Second Tuesday*, 4 Oct. 1977. Edythe Humphrey, "Criminal Justice Extension program is new thrust for MRC," ibid., 9 March 1976; Gregoire, "'Secure' future for Justice Administration," ibid., 6 Nov. 1979. Pat Roome, "Badges, bars and beyond: The early years of Criminology at Mount Royal College," *Reflections*, Spring 2000, 30; "Corrections conference to discuss unifying, correction, enforcing," *Journal 3009*, 2 March 1973; "CJUS Extension graduates first student," Second Tuesday, 10 Apr. 1979.

52   SK, "Special People drawn to criminal justice," *MRC News*, 1 March 1990.

53   Harvey B. Merkley, Department chairman, "A Report on the Radio and Television Department at Mount Royal Junior College," 1966.

54   On the establishment of the new division, see "Peter J. Hodgson New Director," *Calgary Herald*, 12 Feb. 1965.

55   MRUA, Admin., Correspondence 1969, J.W.S. Wallens to Wright, 21 Apr. 1969.

56   Ibid., M. A. Brydon to Dr. K. Harriet Christie, Principal, Covenant College, 18 Apr. 1969.

57   A. W. Vaughan, secretary, Board of Colleges and Secondary Schools, the United Church of Canada, to Rae, Board Secretary, 15 Sept. 1967; with Board CoW minutes, 11 Oct. 1967.

58   They included John S. Bach, Margaret A. Brydon, Gary W. Dean, Otto H. Deutsch, Stanley Myles Feader, Neil Gamble, Arthur Godwin, Owen Kelly, John C. Kenyon, Leonard Leacock, Ralph McCready, Leona F. Paterson, Douglas J. Turner, and Elaine Woytowich.

59   1966: John D. Balcers, Selwyn R. W. Brindley, Norman Edward Brown, Romeo C. Calosing, Robert J. Gervais, Lynn O. Korella, E. Jean Mackie, Riva C. Stillwell, and Arnold C. Wawruch. 1967: Hugh Macleod, David McNab, George Papas, Audrey Plaxton, and Neil Webber. Letter, Collett to Mr. W. B. Macdonald, Board minutes, 8 March 1967.

60   Robson, note to author, 5 Sept. 2005.

61   Alberta, Committee of Inquiry into Non-Canadian Influence in Alberta Post-Secondary Education. *Report of the Committee of Inquiry into Non-Canadian Influence in Alberta Post-Secondary Education*, 1973.

62   PR, 18 Sept. 1970, with Board minutes, 28 Sept. 1970. On the general teaching situation in Alberta colleges, see: R. Fast, "Teaching in the Alberta Public College," Challenge in Educational Administration 10 (Winter 1970–71).

63   "Mount Royal Given U of C Affiliation," *Albertan*, 31 Aug. 1966; MRUA, Admin., "JGW," Chairman, Committee on Junior Colleges, University of Calgary, to Kelly, 16 September 1966.

64   MRUA, Admin, G.F.C., chairman, University of Calgary Committee on Junior Colleges, to Kelly, 16 Sept. 1966.

65   MRC, *Calenda*r, 1967–68, 23, passim.

66   Board minutes, 20 March 1968; "College Defers University of Calgary Affiliation," *Albertan*, 18 Apr. 1968.

67   MRC, *Calendar,* 1970–71, 10; ibid., 187: "Programs in Affiliation with the University of Calgary."

68   But substance is less important than process in academe. In 1980, the Registrar and VP, Academic removed what they saw as unnecessary "affiliation" material from the calendar. As the Academic Council was empowered to approve calendar material, this led to protest and reinstatement of the language. Academic Council minutes, 31 Jan. 1980; Board minutes, 10 March 1980. New language in 1983, when the calendar was rewritten, referred only to university programs which students "may start" at Mount Royal College. MRC, *Calenda*r, 1983–84, 89.

69   Lauchlan, Board CoW minutes, 28 Sept. 1970. In February 1969, there were only 52 former Mount Royal students registered in the University of Alberta. MRUA, Admin.: R. H. Cooke to "All Staff," 28 February 1969, "Previous Students Now Enrolled in the University of Alberta. . ."

70   MRUA, Admin., Community Services Careers, 1968–1969, contains the correspondence and reports.

71   MRUA, Admin., Community Service Careers, 1967–68, 1977, MRC, Placement and Employment Counselling Department, Career Graduate Follow-Up Survey, December 1977.

72   Anderson, "Institutional Analysis," 204–210, found that most university-transfer students in the early 1960s were successful in all universities.

73   Michael A. Powell, "An Investigation of the Academic Achievement of Mount Royal College Transfer Students at Ontario Universities" (M.Ed. thesis, University of Alberta, 1971), abstract, 87, and passim; John Clifford Long, "The Transferability Issue in Alberta: A Case Study in the Politics of Higher Education" (Ph.D. diss., University of Alberta, 1979).

74   MRC, *Calendar*, 2002–3, 274–77.

75   The Mount Royal Junior College – Southern Alberta Institute of Technology Joint Committee, "Progress and Recommendation Report," 20 Apr. 1967. See also MRUA, Dean to Directors and Division Chairmen, "Memo on Articulation of Programs with the Technical Institutes—Criteria for the Division of Programs between SAIT and Mount Royal Junior College," 6 Jan. 1969.

76   MRUA, Admin., Correspondence 1969, G. W. Dean to Directors and Division Chairman, 6 Jan. 1969; Wright to Minister Clark, 3 Feb. 1969, explaining the situation.

77   "Mount Royal Head Advocates Merger," *Albertan*, 28 Sept. 1967

78   "The Case for Mount Royal Junior College Conservatory of Music and Speech Arts," perhaps by John S. Bach, 1968, summarizing the situation. On the outcome: MRC, *Conservatory of Music and Speech Arts Calendar*, 1971–72, 6.

79   Board minutes, 11 May 1967; MRUA, Admin., Correspondence 1967, Ron Prokosch to Wright, 5 Oct. 1967, on student body involvement.

80   Collett, "All Members of the Faculty and Staff," 22 March 1967; cf. Collett's later interview (Macdonald-Wilk), 16 Oct. 1997.

81   Board Special Meeting minutes, 18 March 1967.

82   MRUA, Admin., Wright to McCready, Ralph, Executive Vice President, Memorandum, Wright to "All Faculty and Staff," 29

March 1967; also attached to MRUE Board Special Meeting minutes, 28 March 1967.

83   Board Special Meeting minutes, 28 March 1967.

84   "Collett axed—McCready Acting Pres.," *Reflector*, 31 March 1967; and the editorial, "Nice day, Joe." Some staff members wanted Collett's "community college philosophy" carved in stone. Board minutes, 3 Apr. 1967. The plaque is now in MRUA. In Sept. 1979 Collett wrote that "the board of governors was no longer appointed by the United Church of Canada but by the government of Alberta. This resulted in a change of presidents. . . ." Collett, "Mount Royal College, 1910 to 1967," in Mackie, "The First Decade," 24.

85   Board minutes, 3 Apr. 1967.

86   McCready to "All Faculty and Staff," 4 Apr. 1967.

87   MRUA, Admin.: "Minutes of the Emergency Meeting of the Students' Council of the Students' Union of Mount Royal College, 22 March 1967. McCready to Board, 18 Apr. 1967, and discussion, Board minutes, 18 Apr. 1967. Ibid., McCready to Prokosch, 14 Apr. 1967.

88   MRUA, Admin., MRFA, 1966–67, Letter from the president and secretary of the MRFA, also signed by the ATA president, 10 Apr. 1967; McCready to A. Wahruch, president, MRFA, 14 April 1967. MRUA, Admin., ATA, McCready to Robert Gervais, president, MRC ATA, 14 Apr. 1967.

89   "W. J. (Jack) Collett, 1910–1998)," AB & NW Conference (United Church of Canada) Historical Society, *Membership Newsletter*, 6 (2) (Oct.1998); on the same theme, Gamble interview (Macdonald-Wilk), 16 Nov. 1997. The Kerby College Board signed a separate agreement with Collett. Kerby College Board minutes, 8 Nov. and 11 Dec. 1967, 5 June and 31 Dec. 1968. After working briefly in the Glenbow Institute, he became Deputy Superintendent of Rockyview School Division on the north side of Calgary. After retiring in 1974, he launched Rundle College "with a bank loan and 20 junior-high students." He died in September 1998. Brian Brennan, "Dedicated Minister Had Role in Education," *Calgary Herald*, 22 Nov. 1998; see also "Mount Royal mourns former president," *Reflections*, Fall 1998, 10.

90   Max Rae interview (Macdonald-Wilk), 22 Feb. 1998.

91   "Collett axed—McCready Acting Pres.," *Reflector*, 31 March 1967.

92   McCready, PR [acting president], attached to Board minutes, 12 and 18 Apr. 1968; also Board minutes, 18 Apr. 1967. McCready was referring to a "special study" prepared by Collett "at the request of the Board of Governors" setting out a detailed description of college activities and an organization chart. MRUA, Admin. Files: Collett, "Special Study."

93   MRJC, *Calendar*, 1966–67, 9; ibid., 1967–68, 10.

94   Mackie, "The First Decade," 37.

95   MRUA, Admin., "Constitution," "draft only," 14 Feb. 1967; proposed final draft, 1 Mar. 1967.

96   MRUA, Admin., McCready, Ralph: McCready to Harvey Merkley, Chairman, Chairman's Council, 7 March 1968, on the proposed job description. MRUA, Admin., Kelly to "all academic personnel," undated.

97   MRUA, Admin., McCready to "all faculty and staff," undated [1967] on the reassignment of duties (Neil Gamble became responsible for residences, counselling, student affairs, health services, and physical education); and MRUA, Admin., McCready, 1967–68, McCready to Bruce MacDonald of the Personnel Committee, 24 April 1968, notifying him of Kelly's

intention and recommending that M. S. Feader replace him as "Assistant Dean of Instruction."

98 *Albertan*, March 4, 1965.

99 PR, Board minutes, 11 Oct. 1967.

100 Ibid.

101 Board minutes, 12 June 1967, McCready to Bliss. The early collective agreements are in MRUA, MRFA: Agreements, 1966–1969.

102 MRUA, MRFA 1966–1967: "Mount Royal Faculty Association, Tuesday, April 18, 1967," agenda for meeting and "secret ballot" vote.

103 MRUA, MRFA 1966–67: draft collective agreement, "A.D. 1967." On the discussions, see Collett to E. L. Pitt, 22 February 1967. In a letter to W. M. Macdonald, acting chairman of the Board's Personnel Committee, he proposed development of a policy on the age of retirement (there had not been one earlier). Ibid., Collett to Macdonald, 16 March 1967.

104 MRUA, MRFA 1966–1967: "Suggested Revisions by the Administration of Mount Royal College to the Faculty Agreement," ca. Oct. 1967.

105 Ibid., "Constitution," undated [ca. 1967].

106 "Academic Freedom—A Right or a Fight," *Reflector*, 20 Nov. 1968.

107 Anderson, "Institutional Analysis," 15 (articles 19–21 on the Senate), 148 (his remarks), 229–30 (Academic Senate), 231–32 (references to General Faculty Council).

108 Board AGM minutes, 26 Nov. 1964.

109 James Duff and Robert O. Berdahl, *University Government in Canada: Report of a Commission Sponsored by the Canadian Association of University Teachers and the Association of Universities and Colleges of Canada* (Toronto: University of Toronto Press, 1966); see also David M. Cameron, *More Than Academic Question: Universities, Government, and Public Policy in Canada* (Halifax: Institute for Research on Public Policy, 1991), 299–308; also earlier articles inspired by the freedom of speech crisis at United College in Winnipeg by W. L. Morton, "University Government: The Alienation of the Administration," *C.A.U.T. Bulletin* 9 (1961) 814; and "The Evolution of University Government in Canada," *Canadian Forum* 41 (1962) 243–47; also S. Freedman, "University Government." *C.A.U.T. Bulletin* 13, no. 1 (1964): 14–26.

110 MRUA, MRFA 1966–67: "The General Faculty Council," 12 January 1967.

111 PR, 24 Oct. 1966.

112 MRUA, Admin., Collett, Memo to All Faculty, "1 June 1964, re "Administrative Reorganization."

113 MRUA, MRFA 1966–1967: "Summary of Questionnaire on the Role of the Faculty Council (Submitted by the Faculty, December 1966)."

114 Ibid., "The General Faculty Council," 12 January 1967.

115 MRUA, Admin., Correspondence 1968, memo, Dunn to the board, "Administrative Staff: Description of Assignments," 3 Jan. 1968.

116 Ibid., Pashak and Pitt to Wright, 9 Jan. 1968; Board minutes, 10 Jan. 1968, Board referral to McCready; Board minutes, 22 Feb. 1968, attachment, Pashak, Gervais, Kenyon, Calosing, Deutsch to McCready, 22 Jan. 1968; ibid., McCready to R. N. Anderson, 12 Jan. 1968.

117 MRUA, Admin., Faculty Council minutes 1968, 10 Jan. 1968.

118 Board CoW minutes, 25 Jan. 1968, moved by W. L. James.

119 Ibid., McCready, memo to department heads, 24 Jan. 1968.

120 MRUA, MRFA 1966–67: McCready to All Faculty Members, 23 January 1968.

121 *Reflector*, 12 Jan. 1968.

122 "Election of an Ad Hoc Committee," undated document in MRC Archive.

123 Gary W. Dean, Chairman, Ad Hoc Committee of Six, Report of the Ad Hoc Committee of Six to the Interim General Faculty Council, MRUA, Admin., Faculty Council minutes 1968, Dean to Wright, 8 Feb. 1968.

124 Acting PR, 21 Feb. 1968.

125 MRUA, Admin., Faculty Council minutes 1968, Acting President Report, 20 March 1968 (emphasis added); motion moved by Dean, Interim GFC minutes, 11 March 1968.

126 Ibid., McCready to Wright, 3 Apr. 1968.

127 Ibid., McCready to Wright, 8 March 1968, Interim GFC minutes, 11 March1968; also McCready to Wright, 3 April 1968, indicating that Dean "will make all future communications in regard to the proposed meeting with the board."

128 Ibid., Interim GFC Minutes, 11 March 1968. While it may be unrelated to the Office Workers group, the secretaries signed a petition to McCready calling for a salary raise as they had not received one while other groups had. MRUA, Admin., Petition to McCready, 15 May 1967.

129 Board minutes, 15 May 1968.

130 PR, 22 Nov. 1966. Bliss, as chairman of the Finance Committee, and the college solicitor, Howard Cook, met with the Students' Executive Council to transmit the board's conclusion. Board CoW minutes, 11 May 1967.

131 Ronald Prokosch, "President's Message," *Reflector*, 21 Sept. 1967; Prokosch, report to the board, 20 March 1968.

132 Board minutes, 23 June 1969. In June 1966 Collett had been advised of the implications of incorporation. MRUA, Admin., E. F. Johnston to Collett, 14 November 1966.

133 *Reflector*, 14 Oct. and 28 Nov. 1967, 4 Oct., 7 March, and 5 and 20 Nov. 1968.

134 Ibid., Editorial, 21 Sept. 1967.

135 McCready, "The Content did not Please Me—President McCready," ibid., 4 Oct. 1967.

136 MRUA, Admin., McCready to Prokosh, 30 November 1969, and Correspondence 1967, Prokosch to McCready, 1 Dec. 1967. Board minutes, 11 Dec. 1967.

137 "Council Backs Editor Unanimously," *Reflector*, 7 Dec. 1967.

138 MRUA, Admin., Petition, 14 December 1967, from 28 Conservatory faculty members protesting that and other pieces demonstrating "very bad taste."

139 Board minutes, 3 Jan. 1968.

140 "MRJC. Let's clear the air," editorial, *Albertan*, 26 Jan. 1968.

141 Ibid., 23 June 1969; MRUA Admin., McCready to Leonard Purnell, 5 Jan. 1967; "Editorial Board Policy Statement and Recommendations," 7 Jan. 1967; on Howse's appointment, Board minutes, 10 Jan. 1968.

142 Ibid., 10 Oct. 1968.

143   McCready, "In Support of the Nursing Program," in Mackie, "The First Decade," 25.

144   MRUA, Admin., "Proposed Diagram Indicating Lines of Authority and Administrative Service in the Instruction Division of the College," 9 May 1968; and transcript of discussion of "establishing the position of Dean of Instruction," 16 May 1968. On his later role, see MRUA, Admin., McCready, Department of Instructional Research, "Statement of what the Mount Royal College Institutional Research Advisory Committee and its Function Is," 8 Oct. 1969.

145   MRUA, Admin., McCready, 1967–68, Pentz to McCready, 30 July 1968, advising the board had approved the appointment. McCready, "In support of the Nursing Program," in Mackie, "The First Decade," 26.

146   Board CoW minutes, 7 June 1968; "Mount Royal Post for Dr. Pentz," *Albertan*, 13 June 13 1968: "Dr. Robert Anderson had been unofficially appointed president but resigned before the announcement was made public." Pentz's appointment received full coverage the student press: Dick Bercin, "New President at Mount Royal Junior College," *Reflector*, 10 Oct. 1968. As a sign the 1960s were still on, the masthead bore the legend, "Things Go Better with Cocaine." The printer refused to include a page devoted to a "pornographic" article on birth control. "Reflector Censored," ibid., 21 Oct. 1968.

147   PR, 1 and 15 Aug. 1968.

148   MRC, *Calendar*, 1969–70, 7, and 1971–72, 7. On Lauchlan's appointment: MRUA, Admin., Pentz to "all staff," 28 March 1969; Board minutes, 23 June 1969.

149   Max Rae interview (Macdonald-Wilk), 22 Feb. 1998.

150   MRC, *Calendar*, 1969–70, 119.

151   PR, 21 and 24 Oct. 1968. The manual was not completed.

152   Pentz, "The Community College Concept at Mount Royal," Speech to the Education Progress Club, 22 Oct. 1969; attached to Board CoW minutes, 11 Dec. 1969. Pentz's views were summarized in "Statement of Objectives," MRC Annual Report, 1968–69, 9.

153   Gamble interview (Macdonald-Wilk), 16 Nov. 1997.

154   Howse interview (Macdonald-Wilk), 12 Feb. 1998.

155   Robson, note to author, 5 Aug. 2005.

156   MRUA, MRFA, 1966–67: Dean to "The Members of the Faculty Association," 10 September 1968.

157   MRUA, Admin., Executive Committee, 1968–69, EC minutes, 1 August 1969; draft memo dated 8 January 1969.

158   MRUA, Admin., Executive Committee Minutes, 1 August, 7 October, and 21 October 1968. One of the items on the November 1968 agenda was the potential composition of a new Academic Council.

159   *Albertan*, Apr. 26, 1969.

160   "College Meets Set on Staff Discontent," *Calgary Herald*, 14 Apr. 1969; "Censure vote set at MRJC," ibid., 19 Apr. 1969; Board CoW Minutes, 24 Apr. 1969.

161   Board CoW minutes, 18 and 24 Apr., 18 and 23 June 1969; PR, 24 Apr. 1969.

      Board CoW minutes, 18 and 24 Apr., 17 and 23 June 1969; PR, 24 Apr. 1969.

162   Wright to R. McDougall, 25 Apr. 1969.

163   MRUA, "Report of the Exploration Committee and the Administration to the MRFA," 16 May 1969; "Mount Royal Plans Special Probe Council, Dean Slammed," *Albertan*, 22 May 1969.

164   "MRC Talks Stalled on Academic Council," *Calgary Herald*, 8 Oct. 1969: "Those attending . . . were undecided on whether the council should have legislative authority, or should only make recommendations to the college's board of governors."

165   Paul Stortz and Lisa Panayotidis, "Introduction: 'Have You Ever Looked into a Professor's Soul?' Historical Constructions of the Professoriate in Canada," in Stortz and Panayotidis, eds., *Historical Identities: The Professioriate in Canada* (Toronto: Toronto University Press, 206), 11.

166   PAA, Alberta Colleges Commission, H. L. Macleod, President, AACF, to Dr. M. Fenske, Director of Admin. Services, Alberta Colleges Commission, 6 Oct. 1970.

167   Alberta Association of College Faculties statement, 28 Sept. 1981, re "Section 26(a) (i) of Bill 50, designation clause"; ACIFA's referral to the International Labour Organization was under consideration by the ILO.

168   Board CoW minutes, 22 Apr. 1970, Hugh L. Macleod, president AACF, to Dr. Henry Kolesar, Alberta Colleges Commission, 10 Feb. 1970.

169   C. V. Well, "Alberta Colleges: A Product of Their Times," *College Canada* 2 (Sept. 1977).

170   MRUA, Baker Documents, Robson, note to author, 5 Aug. 2005.

171   Macleod and Pashak proposed 15 credits but accepted 12. Academic Council minutes, 2 Mar. 1971.

172   Board minutes, 24 June 1974.

173   E.g., Jill Vickers and June Adam, *But Can You Type? Canadian Universities and the Status of Women* (Toronto: Clarke, Irwin, 1977); and Chilly Collective, eds., *Breaking Anonymity: The Chilly Climate for Women Faculty* (Waterloo: Wilfrid Laurier University Press, 1995). See also Peter C. Emberley, *Zero Tolerance: Hot Button Politics in Canada's Universities* (Toronto: Penguin Books, 1996).

174   See the biography in Wikipedia: http://en.wikipedia.org/wiki/Barry_Pashak

175   Pashak interview (Macdonald-Wilk), 23 Oct. 1998.

176   MRUA, Admin., AACF History: Note of steering committee meeting, Mount Royal, 17 March 1967; on 25 March, another meeting at Mount Royal approved a constitution and elected officers. Notice, Ellen Krempien, secretary, to "All Instructors at Mount Royal College," 20 March 1967.

177   Roberts interview (Macdonald-Wilk), 4 Nov. 1998.

178   "A Brief History of Arusha from 1972–2007," at arusha.org/file/arusha/A_Brief_History_of_Arusha_Text.rtf.

179   Board minutes, 22 March 1971, J.W. Akerman, president, MRFA, to Cohen, board chair, 4 March 1971.

180   Board minutes, 24 Apr. 1972; Pentz, memo to Academic Council, 19 Apr. 1972.

181   MRUA, Admin.: Faculty/Board Negotiations, J. R. Hutton, Conciliation Commissioner, to Pentz, 24 Nov. 1969.

182   David May, "Mount Royal staff expect pay raise," *Albertan*, 11 March 1970; . "Mount Royal College Aims to Head off Staff Strike," *Calgary Herald*, 10 March 1970. "Mr. |Bob] Gervais [of the MRFA] said faculty will no longer settle for being treated as 'second class citizens.' 'The faculty wants a say in any policy matters,' Mr. Gervais said, 'and we should be dealt with fairly. . . . Money brought the issue to a head, but we will be negotiating

academic council representation and work load as well.'" It accepted 10.7 per cent. "Pay Boost Given College Teachers," *Calgary Herald*, 11 March 1970.

183 Macleod, first president of the Association of Alberta College Faculty (AACF), to Dr. Henry Kolesar, head of the Colleges Commission, in Feb. 1970; Board CoW minutes, 22 Apr. 1970, Hugh L. Macleod, president AACF, to Dr. Henry Kolesar, Alberta Colleges Commission, 10 Feb. 1970.

184 Board CoW minutes, 31 March 1970; see also MRC Archive, Box 1: Miscellaneous Admin., Correspondence 1970, Wright to Kolesar, chair, Alberta Colleges Commission, 8 May 1970; Henry Kolesar to Minister of Education, 28 May 1970, Alberta Colleges Commission agenda, 11 June 1970.

185 Board CoW minutes, 25 Sept. 1972, *Macleod* to Cohen.

186 Board Special Meeting minutes, 9 Jan. 1973.

187 Board minutes, 26 June 1972, William B. Gill, of Gill, Robison, Anderson and Meurin, 26 June 1972.

188 Board CoW minutes, 6 May 1974.

189 MRUA, Admin., 1968–1970, Burns to Pentz, undated [Sept. 1970], Ad Hoc Committee re Academic Council, minutes 25 Aug. 1970, and draft terms of reference prepared by the joint faculty-student committee.

190 D. M. Lauchlan, H. Macleod, and R. Walker, "Recommendations: Ad Hoc Committee on the Academic Council," 26 July 1972, Board minutes, 9 Jan. 1973.

191 Board minutes, 25 Sept. 1972, 9 Jan. 1973.

192 Board minutes, 22 Oct. 1973.

193 Ibid., 28 Oct. 1974, Fred R. Fowlow, secretary to Academic Council, to Max Rae, secretary to the Board, 25 Sept. 1974.

194 Board minutes, 10 Jan. 1968.

195 Colleges Act, s. 32.

196 Roberts interview, 4 Nov. 1998.

197 Communication, Webber to Martha Cohen, on legal advice concerning his role, 26 Oct. 1990; Board minutes, 26 Oct. and 23 Nov. 1970.

198 Board minutes, 28 Sept. 1970.

199 Ibid., 25 March 1974.

200 Ibid., 28 Oct. 1974.

201 PAA, Alberta Colleges Commission, Agenda for 11 March 1971, copy of Pentz, "Report of the President," vol. 3, no. 1, 28 Sept. 1970.

202 Collett, memo to Board, 14 Oct. 1966.

203 Report of the acting president, Board minutes, 11 Oct. 1967.

204 PR, 23 Sept. 1964; two months later "he brought the board up to date on developments re Lincoln Park." Board AGM minutes, 26 Nov. 1964.

205 PR, 23 Sept. 1964.

206 "Mount Royal Students March for New Campus," *Calgary Herald*, March 1965.

207 Joint Meeting minutes, 16 March 1965.

208 A.W. Fullerton, quoting Gamble, memo, 5 Oct. 1967, cited in E. J. Ingram, R. C. Bryce, R. G. McIntosh, B.W. Pickard, and W. L. Workman, "A College in Process: An Evaluative Study of the Mount Royal College Instructional Model"

(Edmonton: University of Alberta, Department of Educational Administration, December 1975), 181.

209 Gamble interview, cited in Ingram et al., "A College in Process," 182.

210 "Board Statement by Harvey Bliss, Chairman of Building & Property Committee," Board CoW minutes, 16 Jan. 1970.

211 *Albertan*, 11 May 1967.

212 Ingram et al., "A College in Process," 187; Board minutes, 18 Apr. 1967; Gamble interview (Macdonald), 16 Nov. 1997; Board minutes, 26 July 1967; the architects accepted by letter, 3 Aug. 1967.

213 Board minutes, 22 Feb. 1968, "Board Statement by Harvey Bliss."

214 Summary of the Joint Planning Committee Meeting, 24 Nov. 1967.

215 *Reflections: MountRoyal College Alumni Magazine*, Fall 2007, 26.

216 *Albertan*, 28 Sept. 1967.

217 Board minutes, 22 Feb. 1968, "Board Statement by Harvey Bliss."

218 " College Site," *Albertan*, 28 June 1968.

219 Board CoW minutes, 9 July 1968; letter to Reierson, 12 July 1968.

220 Board minutes, 17 June 1969.

221 MRUA, Admin., Clark to Pentz, 21 July 1969.

222 Clark to Mayor Rod Sykes, 28 Oct. 1969, included in Board CoW minutes, 11 Dec. 1969.

223 Clark to Sykes, 23 Dec. 1969, Board CoW minutes, Jan. 16, 1970; Sykes to Pentz, 30 Dec. 1969; Board CoW minutes, 16 Jan. 1970. University of Calgary Library: Ad Hoc Committee of the City of Calgary to Review the Location of Mount Royal College, majority and minority reports, 1970.

224 Board CoW minutes, 11 Dec. 1969, "Board Statement by Harvey Bliss."

225 Clark to Pentz, 22 Jan. 1970, Board Committee of Whole minutes, 23 Feb. 1970.

226 Pashak interview (Macdonald-Wilk), 23 Oct. 1998.

227 MRUA, Admin., Wright to Kolesar, 23 April 1971; Board CoW minutes, 22 Apr. 1970.

228 Charles G. Smith, ad hoc committee chairman, to Howard P. Wright, 16 Jan. 1970.

229 "Résumé of Board Meeting with Hon. R.C. Clark, Minister of Education, May 29, 1970. Cf. Calgary Herald, 16 and 21 May 1970. A copy of the minister's press release was given to the Alberta Colleges Commission, 11 June 1970, item 4b.

230 R. G. Fast, "Population Trends – Student Enrolment Forecasts – Future Accommodation Requirements," and R. G. Fast and M. R. Fenske, "Part II," reports of the Provincial Board for Post-secondary Education, 1968–69, 9: "Projected Capital Expenditures of Public Colleges, 1969 to 1977."

231 Board CoW minutes, 17 June 1969. Provincial bodies had to approve the project; e.g., PAA, Alberta Colleges Commission, R. G. Fast, executive assistant, Board of Post-Secondary Education, to Wright, 20 May 1969; Colleges Commission minutes, 11 June 1970; agenda of 10 Sept. 1970; and minutes of the "special meeting" on the project, 23 Oct. 1970, enclosed in the agenda for 25 Nov. 1970.

232 Lauchlan, "History."<what is this? need full cite; can't find elsewhere>

233 MRUA, "Department of Alberta Correspondence," Pentz to Kolesar, chairman, Alberta Colleges Commission, 3 July 1970.

234 Board minutes, 13 Sept. 1967, re authorization of tour.

235 Gamble interview, cited in Ingram et al., "A College in Process," appendix F, "Mount Royal College: Antecedents to 1975, A Case Study," 181; also Gamble interview (Macdonald-Wilk), 16 Nov. 1997.

236 Gamble, "Statement of Character and Guidelines for the Development of Mount Royal Junior College," revised, 30 Aug. 1968.

237 Ibid.

238 Gamble interview (Macdonald-Wilk), 16 Nov. 1997; Gamble, "Ten-Year Development Plan for Mount Royal College Based on a Commitment to Change."

239 Engelhardt, Engelhardt and Leggett, "The Idea of a College," 6 Jan. 1969, 26, 38, 48.

240 PR, undated [1972].

241 MRUA, Admin., W.R. Bate, M. MacNeill, Research and Development Office, "Toward 72."

242 Stevenson, Raines, Barrett, Hutton, Seton and Partners, "Mount Royal College."

243 MRUA, Admin., Correspondence 1967, Prokosch to Wright, 19 Oct. 1967; Board minutes, 11 Oct. 1967, 31 Jan. 1972; Board CoW minutes, 8 Nov. 1967.

244 Lauchlan, "History."

245 Board Student Services Committee, 16 Oct. 1969, in Board CoW minutes, 11 Dec. 1969.

246 Recommendations for Mount Royal College project, Alberta Colleges Commission agenda, 13 Nov. 1969, item 4(a); also Gamble to Fenske, 3 Nov. 1969, in minutes, 11 Dec. 1969.

247 Kolesar to Pentz, 27 July 1970; in Board CoW minutes, Aug. 18, 1970.

248 Board CoW minutes, 29 Sept. 1970.

249 Board minutes, 31 Jan. 1972; the association proposed buying a share of the campus.

250 Board CoW minutes, 28 May 1973.

251 Board minutes, 25 Nov. 1974, agreement with the Students' Association.

252 Memo, Lauchlan to Pentz, 20 Sept. 1971, Board minutes, 25 Oct. 1971.

Chapter 7: Settling Into Lincoln Park, 1972–1980

1 Elaine Verbicky, "MRC jumps a century, space is key to campus," Calgary Herald, 9 Sept. 1972.

2 Ingram et al, "A College in Process," 3.

3 Paul Boothe, "Time-Consistent Data for Alberta's Public Finances, 1968 to 1989," Canadian Tax Journal/Revue Fiscale Canadienne 39, no. 3/n° 3 (1991): 567–88.

4 Harold Coward, Calgary's Growth: Bane or Boon? (Calgary: University of Calgary Press, 1981).

5 Klassen, A Business History of Alberta, 273.

6 J. A. Barrett, "This is Mount Royal College," Canadian Architect (Mar. 1974), and "Mount Royal College," College and University Business (July 1973). With the move to the new campus, the college was "directed to turn over all buildings and contents [on the old campus] to the Department of Public Works after we have removed those portable classrooms and contents we wish to use at Old Sun and Lincoln Park campuses." Max Rae, Board minutes, 25 Sept. 1972.

7 MRC Annual Report, 1978–79, 19: of the 60,121.4 square metres, 33,372 were considered "usable space," including classrooms, 7.9 per cent, laboratories, 16.3 per cent, the library resource centre, 18.1 per cent, office space 15.6 per cent, auditoriums 7 per cent, athletic space, 14 per cent, food services, 6.9 per cent, guidance and counselling, 3 per cent, student activities 10.3 per cent, other, 4.3 per cent.

8 Ibid.

9 Ibid.

10 Dyment interview (Macdonald-Wilk), 11 Dec. 1998.

11 Bach interview (Macdonald-Wilk), 30 Dec. 1997.

12 Ingram et al., "A College in Process," 73.

13 Robson, note to author, 5 Aug. 2005.

14 Ibid.

15 Board minutes, 26 Nov. 1973, memo from Fred Fowlow, assistant vice-president/ instruction, to Pashak, vice-president, MRFA, re MRFA space requirements; memo from Lauchlan to Fred Fowlow, 18 Oct. 1973, "Study Areas for Faculty"; and Papas' remarks. Wood's remarks are in ibid., 25 Nov. 1974; the expenditure authorization is in Board CoW minutes, 11 Aug. 1975.

16 Robson, note to author, 5 Aug. 2005 [MRUA].

17 Ibid.

18 Roberts interview (Macdonald-Wilk), 4 Nov. 1998.

19 Ingram et al., "A College in Process," 3. The upheavals attracted student scholars; see, e.g., Richard Dale Johnson, "Mount Royal College: A Case Study" (M.Ed. thesis, University of Alberta, 1977).

20 Ingram et al, "A College in Process," 33–34 and, respectively, 72 note, 39, and 35.

21 Ibid., 67–68.

22 Ibid., 70–71, 76, 78, 80–81.

23 MRUA, Baker Documents, Lauchlan, email to author, 8 Feb. 2006.

24 Robert Steven Gawreluck, "Organizational Culture in a Community College and its Interrelationship with Leadership and Structure" (Ph.D. diss., University of Alberta, 1993), 115–16. Pashak, a member of "the old guard," remembered him as "very autocratic" and lacking in "people skills" but also unfortunate in his reliance on Gary Dean to be "his go-between between himself and the faculty;" "under Pentz the whole level of leadership was totally isolated from the rest of the faculty." Pashak interview (Macdonald-Wilk), 23 Oct. 1998.

25 For a review of literature on the topic of presidents and congruency in expectations on campus, see Fleming, "Faculty Expectations for College Presidents," Journal of Higher Education (2010): 251: "The myriad duties and character traits attributed by various groups make the job of president difficult and problematic."

26 Board CoW, 26 May 1975; the discussion included a "Proposed Position Description for the Office of the President" dated 7 May 1975. In his email to the author, 8 Feb. 2006, Russell Purdy, chair of the board, asked Lauchlan and Max Rae to give their opinions on Pentz prior to the decision; Pentz told Lauchlan, "Do what you have to do."

27 Board minutes, 9 June 1975.

28 Gawreluck, "Organizational Culture," 116–17.

29 Ibid.

30 PR, Board minutes, 15 Sept. 1975.

31 Board CoW minutes, Lethbridge, 15 Oct. 1975.

32 Board minutes, 15 Sept. 1975.

33 Ibid., 17 Nov. 1975; procedures for the search were discussed earlier: Board CoW minutes, 20 Oct. 1975.

34 Ibid., 16 Feb. 1976.

35 Board Special Meeting minutes, 14 Apr. 1976.

36 MRC Annual Report, 1976–77, President's Report.

37 Board CoW minutes, 8 Sept. 1976, "Proposal for Reorganization of Academic Affairs."

38 Board minutes, 15 Sept. 1975.

39 In November 1976 the Academic Council approved a motion by instructor Gerry Bruce declaring that the theme deans were academic staff appointments, and thus members of the MRFA. The motion was tabled. Academic Council minutes, 10 Nov. 1976. In January 1977, Richard Collier, MRFA president, protested Demicell's appointment. Board minutes, 10 Jan. 1977. The MRFA then warned that "the extraordinary appointment procedure to administrative positions as adopted by the board, Feb. 21, 1977, should not be applied in the appointment of the president of the college or in the appointment of persons to administrative positions having line authority or responsibilities in the Division of Academic Affairs." Ibid., 18 Apr. 1977.

40 Board minutes, 24 Apr. 1972.

41 Ibid., 27 May 1972.

42 Ibid., 5 June 1973.

43 Leona Paterson interview (Macdonald-Wilk), 22 Jan. 1998.

44 MRUA, Admin., VP Lauchlan Correspondence 1969–1972, Lauchlan to Pentz, 20 Oct. 1971, "Comment on Dr. Fast's Paper on Funding Community Service Programs."

45 D. M. Lauchlan to Alexander S. Dobbins, Director, Financial Planning, Alberta Advanced Education, 14 August 1979, re request "to renew our case for a base adjustment associated with our Community Services program and the Public Conservatory."; also D. M. Lauchlan to Honourable James D. Horsman, Minister, 11 September 1979, requesting funding for the Aviation program: "It is the only credit program in the post-secondary educational system in Alberta in which a student must bear the total cost of a major component of the educational program—flight training…. I ask that you consider removing the inequity faced by our students in this program." Correspondence included in Board minutes, 10 Feb. 1992.

46 MRUA, Admin.: VP Lauchlan Correspondence 1969–1972, Lauchlan to Pentz, 18 Jan. 1974.

47 Ibid.

48 Articles of incorporation, Board Government and Community Relations Committee minutes, 21 June 1974, and Board minutes, 24 June 1974.

49 Board minutes, 25 Nov., memo, Lauchlan to Pentz, 20 Nov. 1974, "Alberta Business Centre Proposal."

50 MRUA, Admin., Community Education Services, report, 25 November 1976, summarizes developments and sets out goals for 1977–77.

51 Board minutes, 24 June 1974, memo, Lauchlan, vice-president/ student services and development, "Explanation of Current Advertising Policy," 15 May 1974.

52 Board minutes, 26 Nov. 1973, Flemming Nielsen, program manager, Community Antenna Television, to Harold Alston, 11 Sept. 1973.

53 Board minutes, 21 Feb. 1977.

54 Board CoW minutes, 7 Aug. 1979.

55 For a broad view, see Hayden Roberts, *Culture and Adult Education: A Study of Alberta and Quebec* (Edmonton: University of Alberta Press, 1982).

56 MRUA, Admin., Alberta Vocational Centre, 1968–1970–71, C. Barry Virtue, Coordinator of Vocational Training Programs, Southern Area, to R. W. Hahn, Acting Centre Supervisor, 14 Oct. 1970.

57 The risks were discussed by Mount Royal's Board: Board CoW minutes, 18 Aug. 1970; letter, Fenske to Pentz, 21 Sept. 1970.

58 Ibid. Also: Virtue, "Proposal concerning Mount Royal College and Alberta Vocational Centre," undated; and S. Minuk [Department of Education], memo to L. S. Villett, C. V. Virtue, R. W. Hahn, H. A. Mahon, B. Cunningham and E. Ubaldi, 31 Mar. 1971, re "My visit to Regina, Winnipeg, Thunder Bay, Peterborough and Ottawa."

59 Kolesar to Pentz, and Pentz to Kolesar, 3 July 1970, with Board CoW minutes, 18 Aug. 1970; and Fenske to Pentz, 12 Sept. 1970, with Board minutes, 28 Sept. 1970.

60 Max Rae, secretary to the board, to Dr. Milton Fenske, Colleges Commission, reporting on resolutions passed on 28 Sept. 1970 in response to a 21 Sept. letter from Fenske. Board CoW minutes, 28 Sept. 1970.

61 MRUA, Admin., Alberta Vocational Centre 1970–71, Committee on Amalgamation of Alberta Vocational Centre and Mount Royal College, 22 Jan. 1971; Board CoW minutes, 22 Feb. 1971; MRC, *Calendar*, 1972–73, 14. The idea of using the Churchill Park campus to house related school board programs also arose. MRUA, Admin., Vertical, C. V. Virtue to Pentz, 17 May 1971.

62 Board CoW minutes, 22 Feb. 1971.

63 Jack Mitchell, director, "Some Major Considerations," with Alberta Colleges Commission minutes, 18 Aug. 1970 ("AVC-Calgary and Mount Royal College").

64 Accounts of the meetings of the Colleges Commission and the document prepared by Jack Mitchell, director of vocational education for the Department of Education, on the potential merger, with MRC Board minutes, 18 Aug. 1970.

65 Board minutes, 25 Jan. 1971; PR, 22 Jan. 1971.

66 Clark to Cohen, 19 Mar. 1971.

67 "Summary of Meeting re Incorporation of Alberta Vocational Center (Calgary) into Mount Royal College," 26 May 1971.

68 Clark to Cohen, 19 Mar. 1971, included with report of Board of Governors Meeting with Department Officials, 25 May 1971; Board minutes, 31 May 1971.

69   MRUA, Admin., Churchill Park Campus Building Plan Changes.

70   Ibid., Pentz to all staff, 28 July 1971.

71   Board minutes, 22 Feb. 1971.

72   MRUA, Admin., Alberta Vocational Centre, Correspondence and Other Info Regarding Merger, Cohen to James L. Foster, minister of advanced education, 24 Feb. 1972, with Board minutes, 24 Apr. 1972.

73   Board minutes, Foster to Cohen, 15 Mar. 1972.

74   Motion by Donald C. McMahon, Board minutes, 27 May 1972.

75   MRUA, Admin., Alberta Vocational Centre, 1972, memo from the Minister of Advanced Education to Dr. Henry Kolesar, Chairman, Alberta Colleges Commission, 22 Sept. 1972.

76   MRUA, Admin., Alberta Vocational Centre, 1973, F. L. Anderson, president, AVC Staff Association, to Foster, 8 Jan. 1973.

77   Ibid., Mitchell to Kolesar, 29 Jan. 1973; ibid., Staff Association of the Alberta Vocational Centre, "Brief to the Alberta Colleges Commission," 9 Feb. 1973.

78   MRUA, Admin., Drumheller Institute, 1971–1973, Morphy and Tierney, "Proposal for the Establishment of Educational Vocational Counseling at the Drumheller Institute," 18 Jan. 1972.

79   Board minutes, 21 Feb. 1972, attachment: Provision of the AVC Program at the Drumheller Institution, 22 Nov. 1971. MRUA, Admin., Drumheller Agreement.

80   MRC, *Calendar*, 1972–73, 26.

81   Ibid., 1976–77, 20.

82   Ibid., 1977–79, 7.

83   When the issue of merger of AVC with another institution arose in 1990–91, the discussion focused on SAIT. Ron Collins, "Partnership study touted," *Calgary Herald*, undated clipping.

84   Ibid.; see also "MRC Has an Indian Satellite School," ibid., 15 Nov. 1972.

85   MRUA, Admin., Mount Royal Students' Association Rodeo Club, 1969, 1971.

86   Board minutes, 18 Dec. 1970, undated attachment, in which Pentz reported that the Band planned to ask the Department of Indian Affairs to permit Mount Royal "to operate the Old Sun Campus on a three-year basis."

87   Board minutes, 25 Oct. 1971. It was founded in 1971 and incorporated in 1973: http://www.oldsuncollege.net/history.htm.

88   MRC, *Calendar*, 1973–74, 13.

89   Board minutes, 28 Sept. 1971. On the initial discussions, see Cohen interview, 5 Feb. 1998; list of Old Sun Board of Trustees, MRC, *Calendar*, 1973–74, 13. Martha Cohen Interview (Macdonald-Wilk), 5 Feb. 1998, touches on the issues relating both to the AVC and Old Sun.

90   Les Silver, "Mount Royal and Old Sun Begin College Partnership," *Albertan*, 8 Jan. 1972.

91   "MRC has Indian satellite school," *Albertan*, Mount Royal College, 15 Nov. 1972.

92   Lauchlan, "Role of Old Sun Community College – A Concept Paper," 29 July 1976.

93   Board minutes, 27 Mar., 29 May (including letter from MRFA to board chair, 6 Apr.), 26 June 1972; ibid., 24 Sept. 1973 and 15 Dec. 1975.

94   Purdy interview (Macdonald-Wilk), 20 Sept. 1998; Cohen interview (Macdonald-Wilk), 5 Feb. 1998.

95   Burden to Ron Scrimshaw, director of Old Sun College, 16 May 1977.

96   MRC Annual Report, 1978–79, 4.

97   See www.fnahec.org..

98   Board CoW minutes, 14 Jan. 1980. MRC Annual Report, 1978–79, Fall 1978 enrolment table, 29–33, also 18. On university-transfer functions in Canadian colleges, see John D. Dennison,"University Transfer Programs in the Community College," *Canadian Journal of Higher Education* 8, no. 2 (1978), 27–38.

99   "Frosh Week," *Reflector*, 3 Oct. 1973.

100   Report of Edith Descent, Business Administrator, SAMRC, Board Finance and Audit Committee minutes, 12 Jan. 1982.

101   MRC, *Calendar*, 1977–79, Supplement (1978), 5–7. On their role, see Board CoW minutes, 14 Jan. 1980. MRC Annual Report, 1978–79, Fall enrolment, 1978, 29–33.

102   MRC, *Calendar*, 1974–75, 242–47.

103   MRC Annual Report, 1978–79, Fall 1978 enrolment table, 29–33. On the branch campuses in this period, see "Mount Royal College Moves Into the Community," *Calgary Herald*, 4 Oct. 1976.

104   MRC, *Calendar*, 1977–79, Supplement (1978), 3.

105   Mackie, "The First Decade," 161–62.

106   106   In 1978–79, 1979–80, and 1980–81, it had small deficits, winding up with an accumulated deficit of $61,889. MRC Annual Report, 1981–82, 38.

107   Gamble interview (Macdonald-Wilk), 16 Nov. 1997.

108   R. A. Bosetti to Henry Kolesar, Deputy Minister, 13 Dec. 1978, "Mount Royal College Budget Proposal," including the presentation from the college, dated 12 Dec. 1978.

109   PAA 83.375, Box 1, College Affairs Advisory Committee, Minutes, 9 Sept. 1977.

110   MRC Annual Report, 1978–79, 4.

111   Ibid.

112   Ibid., 19; 1981–82, 39.

113   Board minutes, 10 Dec. 1979, Allied Health Department, "Presentation," appendix, "Registered Nurse Examination Results."

114   MRC Annual Report, 1984–85, 7.

115   Board minutes, 7 Aug. 1979, David Wood, director of Continuing Education, Report to Board on Continuing Education, Year End Summary 1978–79, 5 June 1979.

116   Ibid., 24 Apr. 1972.

117   Board minutes, 10 Dec. 1979.

118   Ibid., 10 Mar. 1980.

119   MRC Annual Report, 1984–85, 7.

120   The appointment was made earlier; Board CoW minutes, 21 Feb. 1977.

121   Ibid., 14 Apr. 1980.

122 Ibid., 14 Apr. 1980, Dr. Norman Burgess, Director, Conservatory, "A Proposal for the 'Coming of Age' in our Conservatory System."

123 Ibid.

124 Lauchlan to Walter H. Worth, Deputy Minister of Advanced Education, 13 July 1973, re "Lincoln Park Development." Lauchlan discusses the planning issues at length in Lauchlan interview (Macdonald-Wilk), 13 Nov. 1997.

125 Ibid. Milton Fenske, the Director of Campus Development Services, identified costs to government (he saw no unusual ones), Fenske to Bosetti, 3 Nov. 1976.

126 Ibid.

127 Board minutes, 22 Oct. 1973.

128 Denis Cole, chief commissioner, to Sykes and city council, re Lincoln Park, 25 Apr. 1975.

129 Board CoW minutes, 8 Sept. 1976.

130 Lincoln Park Development Plan, 24, 36, 52.

131 PAA 87.375, Box 1, Burden to Minister A. E. Hohol, 14 Apr. 1977.

132 Ibid., Minister Hohol to Minister Yurko, 6 July 1977.

133 "Won't yield 'one acre' of its land," *Calgary Herald*, 3 Aug. 1977.

134 MRUA, Admin., Board of Governors Retreat, 1977, Lauchlan to Board, 21 Sept. 1977.

135 PAA 83.385: 19 June 1978, 7 Aug. 1979, also Lauchlan to Kolesar, 30 July 1979, "Mount Royal College Phase II Development."

136 PAA 83.375, Box 2: planning documents submitted by Mount Royal.

137 PAA 83.375, Box 1, Kolesar to Hohol recommending planning funds, 20 Jan. 1978; minister's approval, 30 Jan. 1978; Milton R. Fenske, Director, Campus Development Services, to Richard H. Cooke, MRC Director of Planning and Development, advising of approval, 7 Feb. 1978.

138 Ibid.

139 PAA 83.385, Kolesar to Bosetti, 13 Feb. 1978, Bosetti to Kolesar, 22 Feb. 1978, Kolesar to Bosetti, 2 Mar. 1978.

140 Elsie Ross, "MRC board raps government inertia," *Calgary Herald*, 14 Feb. 1980.

141 In creating the Department of Advanced Education and Training, Alberta was pioneering in extending the mandate of one ministry over colleges, universities, vocational centres, technical institutes, agricultural colleges, and apprenticeship programs. Berghofer and Vladicka, *Access to Opportunity*, 44. For the Canada-wide context, see David M. Cameron, *More Than an Academic Question: Universities, Government, and Public Policy in Canada* (Halifax: The Institute for Research on Public Policy, 1991), 168–70. On the effects of the Worth Report and emergence of the department, see M. Nussbaumer, "The Worth Report and the Developments in Alberta's Post-Secondary Policies and Structures, 1968 to 1976" (Ph.D. diss., University of Alberta, 1990).

142 Board CoW minutes, 17 Nov. 1977.

143 PAA 83.375, Box 1, Lauchlan to Kolesar, 3 Jan. 1978, attachment, "Long-Range Planning Objectives, Dec. 1, 1977."

144 PAA 83.375, Box 1, "Lincoln Park Development" (includes legal advice); Lauchlan to Kolesar, 3 Jan. 1978, with attachment: "Long-Range Planning Objectives, 1 Dec. 1977."

145 Ibid., G. M. Burden, chairman, Board of Governors, to Dr. A. E. Hohol, Minister, 9 Jan. 1978; Hohol to Burden, 23 Jan. 1978.

146 MRUA, Admin., Department of Advanced Education, "Reorganization of the Department of Advanced Education, 20 January 1973.

147 PAA, Alberta Colleges Commission, Commission on Educational Planning, 132.

148 Ibid., 82, 193; and Bosetti, "System Integration–Coordination – Growth, the Alberta System of Post-Secondary Non-University Education: Master Plan Number One," 24–29.

149 Ibid., Lauchlan to Kolesar, 28 Mar. 1978.

150 Ibid., Pickard to Kolesar, 13 Apr. 1978.

151 Ibid., Berghofer to Lauchlan, 9 Mar. 1978, Lauchlan to Kolesar, 17 Mar. 1978; also Neil W. J. Clarke to D. J. Cornish, 9 Mar. 1978. Lauchlan also urged more transparency. Lauchlan to Kolesar, 24 May 1978, Pickard to Lauchlan, 13 June 1978, Lauchlan to Kolesar, 3 Aug. 1978; Kolesar to Lauchlan, 30 Aug. 1979.

152 Ibid., 23 May 1979, Reva Stilwell, president, MRFA, to Burden, 1 May 1979.

153 Ibid., Burden to Stilwell, 7 May 1979.

154 Board minutes, 23 May 1979.

155 Gawreluck, "Organizational Culture," 117. See Lauchlan's assessment of his contributions, Lauchlan interview (Macdonald-Wilk), 13 Nov. 1997.

156 *Journal 3009*, 1 Oct. 1979.

Chapter 8: Seeking a New Identity, 1980–1989

1 MRUA, Baker Files, State of the College Remarks, 1 Sept. 1982.

2 Ronald D. Kneebone, "From Famine to Feast: The Evolution of Budgeting Rules in Alberta," IAPR Technical Paper Series, TP-00508, Aug. 2005. http://www.ucalgary.ca/iaprfiles/technicalpapers/iapr-tp-05008.pdf.

3 On NEP, see John Erik Fossum, *Oil, the State and Federalism: The Rise and Demise of Petro-Canada as a State Impulse* (Toronto: University of Toronto Press, 1997); and on the details, Brian L. Scarfe, "The Federal Budget and Energy Program, Oct. 28th, 1980: A Review," *Canadian Public Policy* (Winter 1981), at http://economics.ca/cgi/jab?journal=cpp&view=v07n1/CPPv07n1p001.pdf, especially pp. 5–6.

4 Allan Tupper, "Peter Lougheed, 1971–1975," in Rennie, ed., *Alberta Premiers of the Twentieth Century*, 220: "Given his substantial popularity in Alberta, his strong political base, and his proven negotiating skills, Lougheed might have transcended the narrow agenda he had embraced." On Alberta's history in constitutional relations and Lougheed's thinking, see Peter Meekison, "Alberta and the Constitution," in Allan Tupper and Roger Gibbins, eds., *Government and Politics in Alberta* (Edmonton: University of Alberta Press, 1992), 247–68.

5 "Calgary Inflation Adjusted Housing Prices, http://img85.imageshack.us/img85/4922/calgaryinflationadjustede7.png.

6 Other reasons included the emergence of efficient agri-businesses, drought, pest infestations, and foreign competition. *Canadian Annual Review*, 1987, 343.

7 Kneebone, "From Famine to Feast," 5.

8   Boothe, "Time-Consistent Data for Alberta's Public Finances, 1968 to 1989," 570.

9   *Canadian Annual Review*, 1981, 435; 1990, 223.

10   See Gail Vallance Barrington, "Do College Presidents and Government Officials Share the Same Perspective?" *Canadian Journal of Higher Education* 12, no. 1 (1982): 43–55.

11   On rising instrumentalism, see Sheila Slaughter, "From Serving Students to Serving the Economy: Changing Expectations of Faculty Performance," *Higher Education* 14 (1985): 41–56.

12   Dennison and Gallagher, *Canada's Community College*, 69–80, identified ten characteristics of very diverse Canadian colleges: curriculum comprehensiveness; student heterogeneity; open admissions; substantial provision of student services; operational flexibility; decentralization of institutional facilities; responsiveness to government; emphasis on teaching and learning; community orientation; and public character. See also John D. Dennison, "The Community College in Canada," in J. Donald Wilson, ed., *Canadian Education in the 1980s* (Calgary: Detselig, 1981), 223–24.

13   Academic Council minutes, 7 Jan. 1980; Barry Pashak to Fred Stewart, 9 Jan. 1980: "Document on Academic and Administrative Leadership," 28 Jan. 1980.

14   Donald N. Baker and Patrick J. Harrigan, eds., *The Making of Frenchmen: Directions in the History of French Education, 1689–1980* (Waterloo: Historical Reflections Press, 1980); Donald N. Baker and George W. Fasel, eds., *Landmarks in Western Culture: Commentaries and Controversies* (Englewood, NJ: Prentice-Hall, 1968), 2 vols.; and scholarly articles on French history.

15   MRUA, Baker Files, "Inaugural Remarks," October 1980.

16   *A Master Plan for Higher Education in California, 1960–1975*. Prepared for the Liaison Committee of the State Board of Education and the Regents of the University of California (Sacramento: California State Department of Education, 1960).

17   "College Vice President Resigns," *Calgary Herald*, 8 July 1980. "'I am not leaving because I'm browned off about not getting the job,' Cornish, 38, said in an interview Monday. 'And I'm not suggesting that Dr. Baker is not a top-notch man, because I believe he is. But the introspection caused by my not getting the job made me decide to try working in the private sector. It is something I have considered for a long time, and I guess this helped me make that decision.'"

18   Academic Council minutes, 18 Sept. 1980; MRC Annual Report, 1980–81, 16.

19   Board minutes, 10 Nov. 1980, 6 Apr. 1981.

20   Kenneth J. Robson, chairman, MRC Annual Report, 1980–81, 16–17. The others included Brent Pickard (Advanced Education), Richard Miller (Cornell University), Bernard Sheehan (University of Calgary), Neil Webber (Associate Minister of Telephones, a former instructor), and James Small (University of Alberta).

21   Sharon Groner, "Baker plans for future," *Journal 3009*, 24 Oct. 1980; Susan Grabau, "Task forces created for improvements," *Journal 3009,* 13 Feb. 1981.

22   "Elsie Ross, "College president leaving post after overseeing growth, *Calgary Herald*, 27 Apr. 1989.

23   MRUA, Admin.: "Proposed Academic Administrative Structure," March 1981. The report contained job descriptions for Chairmen, Deans, and Vice-Presidents (term limits of five years, renewable once) and an appendix containing the Recommendations of the Organizational Development Committee.

24   MRUA, Reports by MRC, 1980–81, Box 2, Memo, 4 March 1981, to Executive Committee, Organizational Development Committee, Agenda Committee and Task Force on Future Directions, calling for a Saturday meeting to discuss the Organizational Development Committee report and recommendations.

25   Board minutes, 10 Nov. 1980 and 9 Apr. 1981.

26   Pat Gomes, "Baker reorganizing," *Journal 3009*, 10 Apr. 1981.

27   Arts (Behavioural Sciences, Economics, English, Fine and Performing Arts, Humanities, Languages); Business Studies and Applied Arts (Business Studies, Communications, Interior Design, Secretarial Arts); Community and Health Studies (Allied Health, Justice Administration & Youth Development, Leisure & Physical Education, Social Services); Science and Technology (Biology, Chemistry, Environmental Quality Control, Geography & Planning, Geology, Petroleum & Mineral Land Management, and Mathematics, Physics, Engineering, Computer Science, and Aviation).

28   MRUA, Reports by MRC, 1980–81: "Summary of Responses to Organizational Review: Some Suggestions for Change, Major Recommendations," 8.

29   MRUA Baker files, State of the College Remarks, 1 Sept. 1982; PR, Board minutes, 20 Sept. 1982; Wood to Baker, 18 Feb. 1983, re "Faculty of Continuing Education and Extension, Operating Budget," Jan. 1–June 30, 1983; Board regular meeting minutes, 21 Feb. 1983; Board Faculty, Staff and Student Relations Committee minutes, 10 Nov. 1982. Gary Gee, "Divisions shuffled to free Baker," *Journal 3009*, 1 Oct. 1981.

30   John E. Roueche, George Baker, and Robert R. Rose, *Shared Vision*: *Transformational Leadership in American Community Colleges* (Washington Community College Press, American Association of Community and Junior Colleges, National Centre for Higher Education, 1989)..

31   VP, Academic report, Board minutes, 8 Dec. 1981.

32   PR, Board minutes, 18 Oct. 1982.

33   MRUA, Baker Files, "Remarks to Senior College Officers," 5 Oct. 1982.

34   Roueche, Baker, and Rose, *Shared Vision: Transformational Leadership in American Community Colleges*.

35   George Keller, Academic Strategy: The Management Revolution in American Higher Education (Baltimore: Johns Hopkins University Press, 1983).

36   K. Patricia Cross, *Beyond the Open Door* (San Francisco: Jossey-Bass Publishers, 1971); *Accent on Learning* (San Francisco: Jossey-Bass Publishers, 1976); and with Annie-Marie McCartan, Adult Learning: State Policies and Institutional Practices (Washington, DC: Association for the Study of Higher Education, 1984).

37   Richard P. Chait, *Trustee Responsibility for Academic Affairs* (Washington, DC: Association of Governing Board of Universities and Colleges, 1984); and, with Thomas P. Holland, and Barbara E. Taylor, *The Effective Board of Trustees* (Phoenix: Oryx Press, 1993).

38   Robert Birnbaum, *Creative Academic Bargaining: Managing Conflict in the Unionized College and University* (New York: Teachers' College Press, Columbia University, 1980). Birnbaum later published volumes on academic management: *How Colleges Work: The Cybernetics of Academic Organization and Leadership* (San Francisco: Jossey-Bass Publishers, 1988), *How Academic Leadership Works: Understanding Success and Failure in the College Presidency* (San Francisco: Jossey-Bass Publishers, 1992); and *Management Fads in Higher Education: Where They Come From, What They Do, Why They Fail* (San Francisco: Jossey-Bass Publishers, 2001).

39 On college planning, see John Lewis Knapp, "Institutional Planning in Alberta's Public Colleges: A Quantitative and Qualitative Assessment" (Ph.D. diss., University of Alberta, 1991).

40 Mount Royal College, "Institutional Information," 21 Mar. 1983.

41 Invited to serve by Lougheed, Deyell agreed to serve as chair only if Mount Royal were to receive a major project during his term. Oral remark, Deyell to Baker, 1982. It was one of the reasons a building was named after Deyell.

42 Cited in *Journal 3009*, 26 Mar. 1982.

43 Duff, Project Manager's reports, 13 June 1983 and 27 Apr. 1984.

44 Horsman to Deyell, 18 Mar. 1982; Board minutes, 9 Nov. 1981; Strategic Planning Committee minutes, 25 Nov. 1981, 25 Jan. 1982.

45 Board minutes, 20 Apr. and 1 May 1982.

46 Deyell, Board minutes, 16 Aug. 1982.

47 PAA, GR 1989.0408, Box 9: Milton Fenske to Henry Kolesar, 13 Oct. 1983, re "Mount Royal College, Update of Land Adjacent to College," Deyell to Minister Johnson, 11 Apr. 1983; Johnson to Deyell, 6 July 1983.

48 OIAP, "Institutional Information," 21 Mar. 1983.

49 PR, Board minutes, 14 June 1982; Board CoW minutes, 14 June 1982.

50 MRUA, Admin.: D. Bennett and David Thomas (comp.), "Draft Education Plan Response: Summary Collation," 16 Dec. 1982; see also the "College Expansion Programme Information Package for User Groups," 27 Sept. 1982. On other background, see Baker, memo to "The College Community" re "Planning Process for the College Expansion," 30 Sept. 1982; Reports on consultations, Dobbins to Baker, 3 Nov. 1982, and Baker to board, Board minutes, 15 Nov. 1982; Workshop Agenda, 1 Nov. 1982; and Academic Council minutes, 16 Dec. 1982.

51 Document 1: Education Plan: Facility Expansion Supplement, Jan. 1983, 66–67, 82–84. Other college planning documents included: 2A, Background Analysis (space implications), 3, Development Strategy Options: Preliminary Guidelines (matching resources to the options) and Document 4, Facility Program: General Fit (directions to the architect). Board College Expansion Committee minutes, 10 Jan. 1983.

52 Mount Royal College Expansion Proposal 1983, prepared by Chandler Kennedy Group, June 1983, 2.

53 Ibid.

54 President's Report, Sept. 1986, a circulated version, not the standard memo to the Board.

55 Board Special Meeting, Minutes, 16 July 1984: Memo, Baker to W. C. Duff, Project Manager, 20 June 1984, re "Bankruptcy of Chandler Kennedy Architectural Group"; Baker to Kennedy, CKAG, notifying him that "the board takes the position that in view of the above circumstances the present contractual arrangement has been terminated as of June 20, 1984." Also PR, 17 Sept. 1984.

56 Board minutes, 16 July 1984.

57 Deyell to Johnston, 9 Oct. 1985; Board minutes, 18 Nov. 1985.

58 *Mirror*, Northside edition, 21 Nov. 1989; "College throws open its doors," *Calgary Herald*, 23 Nov. 1989.

59 MRC Annual Report, 1989–90, 4.

60 Baker to Board, Board CoW minutes, 19 Oct. 1981.

61 MRC Annual Report, 1983–84, 5. Board minutes, 21 Mar. and 13 June 1983, "Letter of Intent for Relocation of Mount Royal Student Association Facilities between the Board of Governors … and the Mount Royal Students' Association." Correspondence between college officials and Tom Boettger, president, Students' Association, 23 and 28 July and 3, 19, 23, and 25 Aug. 1983. The association's lawyer requested the larger space allotment. Finance and Property Committee minutes, 14 Jan. 1985. An ad hoc board committee (Baker, Carruthers, Laidlow) recommended increased funding. Board Special Meeting minutes, 4 Mar. 1985; Finance and Property Committee minutes, 11 Mar. 1985.

62 Baker to Minister Johnston, 11 Oct. 1985, advising the minister of the "agreement with respect to the development and construction of a new Student Centre, including a provision for a donation of $700,000 to the board by the Students' Association." Board minutes, 18 Nov. 1985; Board CoW minutes, 12 May 1986.

63 In 1992, the Students' Association's financial statements indicated that Wyckham House was valued at $3,952,253. Board minutes, 15 June 1992.

64 The other partners were the South Calgary, North Glenmore, and Lakeview Community Associations, Elbow Park Residents' Association, Mount Royal and Rideau-Roxboro Community Associations, Glenlake Minor Hockey Association, and Trails West Hockey Association. "Proposed S.W. arena a plus for MRC," *MRC News*, 18 Sept. 1985.

65 *Calgary Herald*, 13 Nov. 1986.

66 Letter, Baker to Siler, Apr. 5, 1982; in Board Strategic Planning Committee minutes, 14 Apr. 1982; MRC memorandum, "Olympic Winter Games Media Accommodations: An Alternative Suggestion," 8 Apr. 1982; letter, Baker to Pratt, 10 Apr. 1984; Pratt to Baker, 16 Apr. 1984; Board minutes, 16 Apr. 1984.

67 Markku Vainikka (Team Leader) to Baker, 19 Mar. 1987, confirmed that the Finnish Broadcasting Company would pay the $100,000 for use of the TV studio and related spaces; Baker to Vainikka, 23 Mar. 1987, confirming the college's agreement.

68 Elsie Ross, "College students quick to snap up new residences," *Calgary Herald*, 24 Aug. 1989.

69 "MRC has a downtown campus again," *MRC News*, 27 Nov. 1984.

70 Baker to Horsman, 1 Apr. 1982; statistics in MRC, "Institutional Information," 21 Mar. 1983.

71 Baker to Havelock, 18 June 1986; Mrs. J. M. Dubauskas, Secretary, Calgary Board of Education, 25 June 1986, conveying the CBE's 24 June 1986 resolution.

72 Letter, David J. Russell, Deputy Premier and Minister of Advanced Education, to Deyell, 6 Aug. 1986.

73 Jack Hanna, "Province kills plan for MRC campus," *Calgary Herald*, 20 Aug. 1986; Roman Cooney, "Campus decision assailed," ibid., 21 Aug. 1986; *Mirror*, Southside Edition, 28 Aug. 1986. When the LRT system opened new routes to the downtown, the college opted for a downtown campus instead. PR, 21 Mar. 1989.

74 Douglas E. Thomson to Mayor Klein, 9 Jan. 1989.

75 MRC, "History of Land Use Planning in Lincoln Park," 23 Feb. 1989.

76 P. J. Atherton, "Financing Post-Secondary Education in Alberta," *Alberta Journal of Educational Research* 16 (Sept. 1970).

77 "History and Rationale for Current Investment Mechanisms," Alberta, *Investing in Alberta's Advanced Education System*, 10–11.

78 MRC Annual Report, 1982–83, 32; ibid., 1983–84, FS7; ibid. 1984–85, FS3, 7. As funds were rolled into the base grant,

conditional grants fell to $415,781 in 1985, $577,530 in 1986 (ibid., 1985–86, 11) before soaring to $1.88 million in 1988 (ibid., 1987–88, 21).

79 Section on "The Community College," Long-range Institutional Plan, 1988, 15.

80 On support staff concerns, see Letter, Bev Moore, Acting President, MRSSA, 17 Apr. 1984, to Baker; Board Finance and Property minutes, 7 May 1984; Dobbins to Baker, 11 June 1984, memo on "Food Services Options." The revenues from all "ancillary services" were blended in financial reports; the combined revenues generated a $200,000 contribution as of 1986. MRC Annual Report, 1985–86, 7.

81 Deyell to Bissett and Associates Investment Management Ltd., 17 Dec. 1986; Finance and Property Committee minutes, 12 Jan. 1987; Board minutes, 26 Jan. 1987.

82 "City golfers are teeing off on campus driving range," *MRC News*, 18 Sept. 1984.

83 Howard Solomon and Alan Boras, "U of C's beefs on funding claim dismissed," *Calgary Herald*, 8 Dec. 1987. The university side of the story is in Macleod, *All True Things*, 267–68.

84 OIAP, "Mount Royal College Today," 1988, 7, 13; see also MRC, "Institutional Information," 21 Mar. 1983.

85 Gary Gee and Judy Hamill, "No more layoffs during review," *Journal 3009*, 29 Oct. 1982; the layoffs involved five people in Continuing Education (due largely to shutting down the Professional Development Centre in the downtown) and two others. Ella Kalcounis, "Multiple woes led to losses," *Journal 3009*, 9 Mar. 1983.

86 Finance and Audit Committee minutes, 20 Sept. 1982. Deloitte Haskins and Sells, "Final Report," July 1983; Board minutes, 19 Aug. 1983; MRC Annual Report, 1982–83, 2; *MRC News*, 4 Sept. 1983; Carol Howes, "Troubled MRC fires eight . . . and more may follow," and "MRC Staggers under $500,000 debt load," *Calgary Herald*, 25 and 27 Oct. 1983.

87 In seeking government approval for the use of the surplus (because of its size), the college followed the precedent established when it negotiated use of a $510,000 surplus with the Colleges Commission. PAA, Alberta Colleges Commission minutes, 14 Jan. 1971. In 1984, however, the department left disposition of the surplus to the board of governors. Allocation summarized in MRC Annual Report, 1987–88, financial statement.

88 ERC, Letter, Horsman to Baker, 22 Sept. 1981.

89 ERC, Letter, Phil Gougeon, Coordinator, 1980s Advanced Education Endowment Fund, to Baker, 27 Oct. 1981.

90 Mitch Piper, "Lengthy search ends; new fund-raiser hired," *Journal 3009*, 29 Jan. 1982.

91 Board CoW minutes, 11 Jan. 1982.

92 "Housekeeping, shopping list mark fund-raising year," *MRC News*, 25 Sept. 1984.

93 President's Newsletter, 11 Feb. 1986.

94 President's Report, MRC Annual Report, 1985–86, 4.

95 MRC, OIAP, "Mount Royal College Today: Trends and Issues," 1988, 8–9.

96 Announcement, *Calgary Herald*, 24 Nov. 1988.

97 MRC Annual Report, 1986–87, 5.

98 MRC, OIAP, "Mount Royal College Today," 1988, Appendix A.2.

99 Ibid., Appendix A.4, A.8–A.9.

100 Ibid., Appendix A.5.

101 Academic Standards Committee minutes, 13 May 1986 ("Findings of the Committee with Regard to Academic Qualifications"), policy attached; discussions in Academic Council minutes, 15 May and 10 June 1986. Board Special Meeting minutes, 16 June 1986, contain most of the background documents, including: memo, Thomas to Baker, 17 Feb. 1986; Academic Standards Committee (Academic Council) minutes, 27 Mar.and 13 May 1986; and references to meetings of Baker and MRFA with the Professional Standards Committee, 27 Mar. 1985 and 5 May 1986. Also Killingsworth, MRFA president, to Besner, chair, Academic Council, 17 Feb. 1986, Academic Council minutes, 20 Feb. 1986.

102 "Program Evaluation: Policies and Procedures," together with memo, Ron McDonald, Chairman, Planning Committee, to Academic Council, 17 Apr. and 15 May 1986, 10 June 1986. The Planning Committee of Academic Council also developed "selected" performance "indicators" for programs. Academic Council minutes, 10 June 1985. On similar developments elsewhere, see Walter E. Harris and Edward A. Holdaway, "Systematic Reviews of University Programs and Units," *Canadian Journal of Higher Education* 23, no. 3 (1983): 55–76.

103 "Evaluation Activities," PR, Sept. 1986; Laurie Milton became the first Coordinator of Evaluation Services. Her first assignments included formulation of the academic program evaluation procedure and the evaluation of the Learning Skills Centre. The schedule included the Education Development Centre, the Cooperative Accounting Program, and the Nursing Diploma Program (an accreditation review).

104 See Walter E. Harris and Edward A. Holdaway, "Systematic Reviews of University Programs and Units," *Canadian Journal of Higher Education* 13, no. 3 (1983), 55–76.

105 MRUA, Admin: President's Office "The College Goal," November 1988.

106 These included the Association of Records Managers and Administrators (ARMA), the Canadian Association of Petroleum Production Accounts, the Canadian Institute of Management (CIM), the Canadian Micrographics Society, the Chartered Accountants Society, the Purchasing Management Association of Canada, and the Registered Interior Design Institute of Alberta. MRC, "Institutional Information," 21 Mar. 1983.

107 Alan Boras, "Colleges see entry battle," *Calgary Herald*, 17 Nov. 1987: "The tight squeeze ... at the University of Calgary is expected to cause musical chairs at the city's other post-secondary schools next year as prospective students scramble for admission." The University of Alberta had raised its minimum entrance mark to 70 per cent. Elsie Ross, "College enrolment list soars," ibid., 30 Aug. 1988.

108 Additional faculty complement, MRC Budget Plan, 1989–90, 12; MRC, OIAP, "Mount Royal College Today," 1988, Appendix A.8–A9. In 1989, Baker advised the board that the province should consider moving toward "block transfer of credits rather than the current course-by-course transfer arrangement, so that college students can get a clearer message about what is acceptable for transfer and what is not." PR, 21 Mar. 1989.

109 Baker to Board, 8 Oct. 1981: "To facilitate the development of a clear, consistent and cohesive public image of Mount Royal College, the board ... has approved the adoption of a new graphic symbol for the College and the legend 'Calgary's Community College.'"

110 Mount Royal College, *Education in Calgary: A Spectrum of Excellence*, 1986, prepared by Mount Royal College on behalf of the public educational institutions in Calgary.

111 University of Calgary, "A Proposal submitted to the Honourable Serge Joyal, the Secretary of State of Canada: The Canadian Centre for Learning Systems," Apr. 1984; Baker, memo to Board, "The Canadian Centre for Learning Systems," 14 May 1984; memo, Wood to Baker, re CCLS, 2 May 1984; Board Finance and Property Committee minutes, 7 May 1984; PR, 17 Sept. 1984; "Educational technology centre may shape future of learning," MRC News, 4 Sept. 1984; see also the report of the College's CCLS Project Coordinator, Dennis Leask, Academic Council minutes, 10 June 1985.

112 Canadian Centre for Learning Systems, 1985–96 Annual Report, 7; there was an occasional newsletter entitled CCLS, e.g., the one for Fall 1986 [ISSN 0826-7286].

113 Fred J. Speckeen, Chairman, Board of Directors, CCLS, "Report on the Canadian Centre for Learning Systems," attached to PR, 21 Mar. 1989; on later committees, see Note on Committee of CEOs of Calgary Educational Institutions, PR, 21 Mar. 1989.

114 Board minutes, 19 Apr. 1982.

115 Ibid.

116 The statistics included music and speech arts. MRC Annual Reports, 1984–85, and 1989–90.

117 MRC, OIAP, "Mount Royal College Today," 1988, Appendix A.1; also MRUA, Baker Speeches, Remarks to the Downtown Rotary Club, 25 Apr. 1989.

118 MRC, OIAP, "Mount Royal College Today," 1988, 14, 17–18; OIAP, "Entering Students Survey Report," December 1988.

119 MRC, OIAP, Mount Royal College Annual Enrollment Trends-at-a-Glance, 1988-08-15.

120 OIAP, "Entering Students Survey Report, 1988" (Ref. 88-12-93).

121 MRUA, Baker, Remarks to the Downtown Rotary Club, 25 April 1989.

122 Board minutes, 14 July 1986.

123 Lloyd Cliplef, "SA revamps roles for personnel," Reflector, 21 Sept. 1988; Student Association annual financial statements.

124 Reflector, 10 Dec. 1980 and 18 Nov. 1981.

125 Ibid., 17 Sept. and 1 Oct. 1986, 21 Sept. 1988, Journal 3009, 20 Jan. 1985.

126 E.g., "Failing grades force Neilson out," Journal 3009, 29 Jan. 1982.

127 Editorial, "GPA an issue with the SA," Reflector, 21 Sept. 1988.

128 On other changes, ibid., 9 Nov. 1983, and Journal 3009, 30 Jan. 1985.

129 Reflector, 17 Sept. 1986; Journal 3009, 8, 22 Oct. 1986.

130 Board Finance and Audit Committee minutes, 12 Jan. 1982; Gary Gee, "Auditor Controversy Continues," Journal 3009, 26 Feb. 1982.

131 "Reflector wins independence," Calgary Herald, 13 Feb. 1981; the fee became optional, Reflector, 17 Sept. 1986; "Journal unaffected by Reflector vote," Journal 3009, 20 Feb. 1981.

132 Academic Council minutes, 28 Nov. 1985, and 20 Nov. 1986.

133 Ibid., 20 Mar. 1986; T. Wahl, Chairman, Student Affairs Committee, to Besner, Chair, Academic Council, 11 Apr. 1986, together with the Director of Student Services, to Baker, 1 May 1986; memo, Baker to Board, 16 June 1986, MRFA report, 12 June 1986. In 1992, the policy was revised. Academic Council minutes, 14 May 1992.

134 Academic Council minutes, 18 Dec. 1986; B. J. Fraser, Chairman, Ad Hoc Committee on the Statement of Students Rights and Responsibilities, to Board, 26 Jan. 1987, re "Final Draft, Statement of Student Rights and Responsibilities"; MRC, Calendar, 1990–91, 33–34.

135 Reflector, 7 Oct. 1980.

136 Ibid., 11 Nov. 1981; Journal 3009, 14 Oct. 1982.

137 Reflector, 28 Sept. and 10 Oct. 1983; on the Winter Carnival, ibid., 10 Dec. 1980; Journal 3009, 2 and 16 Feb. 1983.

138 Reflector, 23 Feb. 1983 and 7 Nov. 1984.

139 Ibid., 16 Feb. 1984

140 Ibid., 15 Oct. 1982, 21 Sept. 1988, and 13 Sept. 1989.

141 Ibid., 18 Nov. 1987 and 27 Jan. 1988.

142 "Cougars fortunes are looking up!" and "Hockey team won't stand for another losing season," MRC News, 18 Sept. 1984. There is a brief sketch of Mount Royal's athletic activities in Young People of All Ages: Sports, Schools and Youth Groups in Calgary (Calgary: Century Calgary Publications, 1975), "Mount Royal College." 226–29.

143 "Kenyon courts a silver in nationals," Reflector, 25 Sept. 1984.

144 "Badminton ace returns home as Canada's number-one player," ibid., 26 Mar. 1985,

145 "Snow" by Ross Johnson, "The Dawn" by Gloria Doiron, poems by Laura Sikora, "Change" by Evelyn Ferchuk, and "View from the Hilltop" by Pat Gomes. Reflector, Mar. 1981.

146 Skylines, Fall 1982.

147 Ibid., 1983.

148 The poems: Karen Braun, "Odes I, II, III,"; Jan Derbyshire, "Grounded"; Richard Nebb, "Untitled I"; and Cam McKay, "The Plastic Coloured Sky"; and the short stories: Barbara Burton, "Beginner's Nordic Blues"; Jennifer Wilson, "2:30 Train Home" and "The Game"; and Michelle Gould, "J&K Inc." Reflector, 27 Feb. 1984.

149 "New publication to debut," MRC News, 19 Mar. 1985.

150 Cathy Nickel, "In Their Footsteps," Reflections, Fall 2007, 19–20. Auger's daughter, Neepin, also graduated from the program (2006).

151 The organizers of the 75th anniversary celebration decided to hold the festivities in 1985. "Party plans beginning for anniversary bash," MRC News, 12 Feb. 1985.

152 Board minutes, 19 Apr. 1982.

153 Among the presidents were Unni Soelberg-Claridge, 1984–85, and M. M. Jackson, 1985–86. Board minutes, 20 Jan. 1986; also PR, 21 Mar. 1989.

154 The College Goal was included in the Budget Plan for 1988–89 discussed by the board initially in January 1988 and approved, 13 June 1988.

155 Ibid.

156 MRC Annual Report, 1989–90, 4.

157 Reflector, Mar. 1981, 9 Dec. 1981, and 7 Dec. 1983; see also Journal 3009, 26 Jan. 1983, 7 Nov. and 11 Dec. 1984.

158 On course "canning," see Academic Council minutes, 7 June 1984.

159 Reflector, 7 Dec. 1983.

160 Credit Enrollment Planning Sub-Committee, "Packaging Report to Academic Council," Academic Council agenda, 15 Jan. 1987.

161 PR, Sept. 1986; "The Student Flow Model: Issues and Recommendations," 1987.

162 Baker to Board, 29 Aug. 1983, on leasing land from the Alberta Housing Corporation.

163 Student complaints about parking, *Reflector*, 18 Nov. 1987; *Journal 3009*, 1 Oct. 1982, 9 Oct. 1984, and 18 Oct. 1986.

164 MRC, OIAP, "Mount Royal College Today," 1988, 19.

165 PR, 11 Feb. 1986.

166 MRUA, Admin, Ron MacDonald, memorandum and draft article for the *Mirror*, 14 Jan. 1987.

167 Board minutes, 10 June 1968.

168 MRC, OIAP, "Mount Royal College Today," 1988, 4.

169 President's Office, "The College Goal," Nov. 1988.

170 MRC, "Institutional Priorities for Action, 1984–85."

171 Baker, Special Board Meeting minutes, 5 Mar. 1987.

172 Ashok Mathur, "Agreement Still Pending," *Journal 3009*, 31 Oct. 1980; John Balcers, representing the MRFA, said money was the issue. Ibid., Mathur, "Faculty near settlement," 7 Nov. 1980; Mitch Potter, "COLA boosts faculty wages," ibid., 30 Jan. 1981.

173 Mitch Potter, "COLA boosts faculty wages," ibid., 30 Jan. 1981.

174 MRUA, Admin: MRFA 1975–1981 (Miscellaneous), "Final Report Recommendations of the Workload Review Committee," 12 May 1980, submitted to both the Board of Governors of Mount Royal College and the MRFA.

175 MRUA, Baker Speeches: Statement on the Board-Faculty Agreement, August 17, 1982; Baker, "The State of the College," 1 Sept. 1982.

176 On the discussions, see *Reflector*, 9 (petition) and 23 Nov. and 7 Dec. 1983; Bevelyn Park, "Faculty launches protest," *Journal 3009*, 28 Oct. 1983; Bevelyn Park and Donna McConaghy, "Faculty protest gains momentum," ibid., 9 Nov. 1983; "No strike—work as usual," 23 Nov. 1983; Donna McConaghy, "FA, Board shake on it," ibid., 12 Dec. 1983.

177 Birnbaum, *Creative Academic Bargaining: Managing Conflict in the Unionized College and University* (New York: Teachers' College Press, Columbia University, 1980).

178 MRUA, Baker Documents: Mahon to Baker, email, 3 June 2009.

179 The demands included the right for departments to appoint new faculty members without any administrative approval, removing academic advising from the job descriptions and requiring payment for advising services, the addition of "five working days of personal unspecified leave" for all members and its accumulation from one year to the next, and "sabbatical leaves" to be awarded on the basis of seniority alone. PR, 1985.

180 Linnet Benechuk, "Baker resigns as chairman," *Journal 3009*, 8 Feb. 1984. "I thought it was time for someone else to assume the burden so that I could spend more time attending council's committees."

181 Board CoW minutes, 19 Oct. 1981; Board minutes, 7 Dec. 1981.

182 Gary Gee, "Wood rejects beefs of ex-committee head," *Journal 3009*, 1 Oct. 1982.

183 Academic Council minutes, Nov. 24, 1985.

184 The MRFA's document is attached to Baker to Board, 1 Feb. 1, 1983, "Dinner Meeting with the MRFA Executive Committee."

185 Kathy Bell, "Chairman Knocks Faculty," *Journal 3009*, 26 Nov. 1982. He added: "the relationship between faculty and administration is far more strained than that which exists between management and employees."

186 Bevelyn Park, "Faculty, Baker 'At War'," *Journal 3009*, 12 Dec. 1983; Board CoW, 16 Jan. 1984; Bozena Kolar, "Faculty beefs spawn board investigation," ibid.,1 Feb. 1984; Board minutes, 16 April 1984; Carol Harrington, "Faculty appeal slap on wrist," *Journal 3009*, 4 April 1984.

187 Policy on Journal 3009, Board minutes, 16 April 1984; Carol Harrington, "Sides square off in press wars," *Journal 3009*, 28 Feb. 1984.

188 Professional Development Committee and Bruce Mahon, Acting Dean of Educational Development, "A Review and Evaluation of the Position of Professional Development Officer at Mount Royal College," 1981; appointments were made by both the administration and the MRFA. Lynn Korella was followed by Emmett Hogan, and later by Margaret (Mardy) Roberts. *MRC News*, 28 Aug. 1984.

189 MRUA, Admin: Ad-Hoc Working Group, "A Proposal for the Development of an Educational Development Centre," December 1981. Report of the Educational Development Centre, Jan. 1982, Board minutes, 15 Feb. 1982.

190 College and Community Relations Committee minutes, 5 May 1986. It was "conducting interviews with College employees to identify difficulties and/or opportunities regarding the quality of work life at the College."

191 PR, Sept. 1986.

192 Neil Besner, *The Light of Imagination: Mavis Gallant* (Vancouver: University of british Columbia Press, 1988).

193 Beth Everest, *There Will Be Blood & I Will Tell You, Put Your Hand Down Here* (Black Moss Press, 1997); Richard Harrison, *Fathers Never Leave You* (1987); *Recovering the Naked Man* (1991); *Hero of the Play* (1994); *Big Breath of a Wish* (1995); *Worthy of His Fall* (2005).

194 E.g., Mahfooz A. Kanwar, *The Sociology of the Family: An Interdisciplinary Approach* (Hamden, CT.: Linnet Books, 1971); *Murder and Homicide in Pakistan* (Vanguard Books, 1989); and Don Swenson, eds., *Issues in Canadian Sociology* (Kendall/Hunt Publishing Co., 1997); and *Journey to Success* (Blitzprint, 2002).

195 E.g., Patricia A. Roome, "Amelia Turner," in Foran and Jameson, eds., *Citymakers;* "Amelia Turner and Calgary Labour Women," in Linda Kealey and Joan Sangster, eds., *Beyond the Vote: Canadian Women and Politics* (Toronto: University of Toronto Press, 1989); "Remembering Together: Reclaiming Alberta Women's Past," in Catherine A. Cavanaugh and Randi R. Warne, eds., *Standing on New Ground: Women in Alberta* (Edmonton: University of Alberta Press, 1993), 171–202; "The Woman's Suffrage Movement in Canada," in Bob Hesketh and Chris Hackett, eds., *Canada: Confederation to Present: an Interactive History* (Calgary: Chinook Multimedia, 2001); "From One Whose Home is Among the Indians': Henrietta Muir Edwards and Aboriginal People," in Sarah Carter, Leslie Erickson, Patricia Roome, and Char Smith, eds., *Unsettled Pasts: Reconceiving the West Through Women's History (Calgary:* University of Calgary Press , 2005), 47–78; and "Alexander Cameron Rutherford," in Rennie, ed., *Alberta Premiers of the Twentieth Century*, 3–18.

196 C. Michael Fellows and Greg Flanagan, *Economic Issues:* A *Canadian Perspective* (Toronto: Irwin, 1997).

197 David M. Thomas, ed., *Canada and the United States: Differences that Count*, three editions (Peterborough: Broadview Press, 1993), subsequently published in three editions; *Whistling Past the Graveyard: Constitutional Abeyances, Quebec, and the Future of Canada* (Toronto: Oxford University Press, 1997).

198 Keith Brownsey, *Ralph Klein and the Hollowing of Alberta* (Montreal: Black Rose Books, 2005); and Keith Brownsey, L. Bernier, and M. Howlett, eds., *Administrative Styles in Canada's Provinces*

(Toronto: University of Toronto Press and the Institute of Public Administration of Canada, 2005).

199 John A. Winterdyk, *Corrections in Canada: Social Reactions to Crime* (Pearson Education, 2000); *Issues and Perspectives on Young Offenders in Canada*, 3rd ed. (Nelson Thomson Learning, 2004); *Canadian Criminology*, 2nd ed. (Pearson Education Canada, 2005).

200 Melvin Pasternak, *21 Candlesticks Every Trader Should Know* (Columbia, Maryland: Marketplace Books, 2006).

201 MRC, OIAP, "Institutional Information," 21 Mar. 1983.

202 "Support staff elect executive," *MRC News*, 12 Feb. 1985.

203 Dobbins, Board minutes, 23 July 1981.

204 "MRSA, Board reach new agreement," *MRC News*, 19 Mar. 1985.

205 Brian Brennan, Gauthier biography, *Calgary Herald*, undated clipping, 1998; "Bob Charlton takes helm of Security," ibid., 12 Sept. 1985; Alison Delker, "Mount Royal loses a pillar of its community," *Reflector*, 30 Sept. 1999.

206 Brennan, Gauthier biography, undated clipping, 1998.

207 Chris Frazer, president of the Students' Association, proposed a second student member but this would have required a change in the Colleges Act. *Reflector*, Feb. 1981.

208 "Appointment Chairman—Board of Governors," *Calgary Herald*, 28 Oct. 1987.

209 Max Rae interview (Macdonald-Wilk), 22 Feb. 1998.

210 Baker interview (Macdonald-Wilk), 12 May 1999; Burden held that the president should not be a member of the board. Lauchlan, interview (Macdonald-Wilk), 13 Nov.1997.

211 Munroe and Royer announcements, ibid., 30 Nov. 1987.

212 Special Board meeting minutes, 26 Oct. 1981.

213 "Roles of the Board of Governors and the President: An Illustration," Decision Charter; "Annual Cycle of Board Decision Making: A Model for Possible Implementation." Board CoW agenda, 12 Dec. 1983.

214 R. Dale McIntosh, "Mary Munn," *Canadian Encyclopedia of Music*, www.thecanadianencyclopedia.com.

215 *MRC Bulletin* 6, no. 9 (8 Jan. 1986). In 1973 he had received the Alberta Achievement Award for Service to Music.

216 "Simpson: Man of Music Stepping Down," ibid., Sept. 1984.

217 Memo to Baker from Wood, Aug. 19, 1983, on meeting with Sutherland; press release, 20 Sept. 1983: "Conservatory of Dance proposed"; Wood, report attached to Academic Council minutes,7 June 1984; "Candace Krausert will lead Mount Royal School of Dance," *MRC News*, 25 Sept. 1984; "The MRC School of Dance has a place to call home," ibid., 22 Jan. 1985.

218 Board minutes, 16. Mar. 1988.

219 Ibid.

220 Ibid., Russell to the chair of the Board of Governors of the University of Alberta.

221 Baker to Duncan, Board minutes, 19 Feb. 1988. Department requirements sparked more systematic planning; see Knapp, "Institutional Planning in Alberta's Public Colleges: A Quantitative and Qualitative Assessment."

222 Board minutes, meeting with Minister, 18 Sept. 1984.

223 Heather Lynn Montgomerie, "A Prospective Policy Analysis of Degree Granting in Alberta Community Colleges" (Ph.D. diss., University of Alberta, 1990), 140.

224 Memo, Wood to Baker, 13 Dec. 1985; Academic Council agenda, 19 Dec. 1985; see also Academic Council minutes, 28 Nov. 1985.

225 Executive Committee, 12 Nov. 1985, reported in President's Newsletter, 11 Feb. 1986.

226 PR, Sept. 1986.

227 Mount Royal College, Institutional Development Plan, 1987–90.

228 Finance and Property Committee minutes, 1 Apr. 1986; "General College Objectives for 1986–87," PR, Sept. 1986.

229 The agenda was contained in the minutes of the 17 Oct. 1988 meeting; MRC, Budget Plan, 1989–90, 10.

230 The report referred to enrolments in university transfer programs in 1988–89: Mount Royal: 630, Red Deer: 870, Grant MacEwan: 420, Grande Prairie: 435, Medicine Hat: 515, Keyano: 107, and Lakeland: 52.

231 Gawreluck, "Organizational Culture," 117–18.

232 Ibid.

233 Elsie Ross, "College president leaving post after overseeing growth," *Calgary Herald*, 27 Apr. 1989.

234 The standards, based on European and other models, are available at www.peqab.ca; and the national version at http://www. cmec.ca/Publications/Lists/Publications/Attachments/95/QA-Statement-2007.en.pdf. See also Donald N. Baker and Terry Miosi, "The Quality Assurance of Degree Education in Canada," *Research in Comparative and International Education* 5, no. 1 (Nov. 2010): 32–57.

CHAPTER 9: BECOMING DEGREE GRANTING, 1989–2003

1 Mount Royal College, "A Proposal for the Development of Mount Royal College: Presented to the Honourable Jack Ady, Minister, Alberta Advanced Education and Career Development, July 21, 1993," 4.

2 Statistics Canada, Educational Portrait of Canada, 2006 Census: Provincial and Territorial Highlights, http://www12.statcan.ca/english/census 06/analysis/education/alberta.cfm. Calgary was at 51 per cent, while the Canadian average of 48 per cent led the OECD.

3 Statistics Canada, 2000 for 1998/1999, cited in MRC, "Access 2010: Calgary's Post-Secondaries Collaborate on Growth, Quality," 1.

4 "Calgary Inflation Adjusted Housing Prices," http://img85. imageshack.us/img85/4922/ calgaryinflationadjustede7.png.

5 Chris Dawson, "Colleges granted self-governance," *Calgary Herald*, 22 Aug. 1996.

6 Anthony Johnson, "DeVry to grant U.S. degrees," ibid., 8 Mar. 1995.

7 AAE, *A Learning Alberta: Profile of Alberta's Advanced Education System* (2002), 17, Table 1: Full Load Equivalent Enrolment by Institution, 1997–98 to 2002–2003. The government standardized reporting in 1990–91, introducing the concept of the FLE to replace the Full-Time Equivalent student.

8 From an internal Mount Royal document summarizing the Institutional Development Plans of post-secondary institutions, "Institutional Development Plan Summary: Grant MacEwan Community College," Dec. 1990, 3.

9   Board Special Meeting minutes, 28 Feb. 1989. The search committee included board members Donald W. McDonald, John W. McManus, and Patricia R. Munroe.

10 Ken Robson, in *Thomas L. Wood: A Tribute*.

11 Board regular meeting minutes, 12 Feb. 1996.

12 "Newton steps down as Vice-President," *Mount Royal Leader*, 8 Aug. 2002.

13 Blair Riddle, "Mount Royal appoints new Vice-President: Administrative Services," ibid., 27 May 2003, 2.

14 Accompanying these changes were the retirement in 1995 of Don Stouffer, the dean of the former Faculty of Community and Health Studies, and the departure of David Thomas for an academic vice-presidency at Kwantlen College. Before leaving, Thomas served briefly as the first dean of the Faculty of Community Studies.

15 Organizational Restructuring, Board minutes, 6 Mar. 2000.

16 He was to die prematurely of cancer. "Dr. Norman Burgess (1947–2004)," *Reflections*, Fall 2004, 25.

17 Other appointments included Ross Thrasher, MLS, formerly of the University of Calgary, who became Director of the Library in 1999. In response to the requirements of the Freedom of Information and Protection of Privacy Act 1999 relating to the collection and use of data, the position of Information Management and Privacy Advisor was added.

18 "Terms of Reference for Degree Granting Study," Board minutes, 23 Oct. 1989.

19 Kreisel-Harris Report, 1991. Kreisel had been VP, Academic, and Harris, chair of Chemistry and chair of the President's Advisory Committee on Campus Reviews, 1980–1990.

20 AAE, "Responding to Existing and Emerging Demands for University Education: A Policy Framework," Oct. 1989; attached to Board minutes, 24 Oct. 1989.

21 Murray Fraser, "Major Issues…, A Response," Feb. 1993, strategies 2.10 and 2.11. On the university's own aspirations, see Robert Bott, *The University of Calgary: A Place of Vision* (Calgary: University of Calgary Press, 1990).

22 Tingle to Gogo, 19 July 1990.

23 Academic Council minutes, 15 Nov. 1990.

24 Tingle to Gogo, 12 July 1991; Wood to Board, 18 July 1991, Board minutes, 18 July 1991.

25 Academic Council minutes, 26 Sept. 1991; Board minutes, 26 Sept. 1991.

26 Chikinda to Will, Recommendation regarding College Priorities, 1992–1995, Academic Council agenda, 16 Jan. 1992.

27 Lathrop to Board, Board minutes, 18 Jan. 1993.

28 "New president leads Mount Royal College," *Calgary Herald*, 12 Sept. 2003.

29 MRC Annual Report, 1990–91, 2.

30 Ibid., 1994–95, 1.

31 Michael L. Skolnik, "Reflections on the Difficulty of Balancing the University's Economic and Non-Economic Objectives in Period when its Economic Role is Valued," in Glen A. Jones, Patricia L. McCarney, and Michael L. Skolnik, eds., *Creating Knowledge, Strengthening Nations: The Changing Role of Higher Education* (Toronto: University of Toronto Press, 2005), 118.

32 Dianne Mirosh, MLA, Chairman, Calgary Caucus to Wood, 22 Nov. 1991; Margaret Lounds, Chairman of the Calgary Board of Education, to Gogo, Minister of Advanced Education, 13 Nov. 1991; Al Duerr, Mayor of Calgary, to Gogo, 15 Jan. 1992.

33 OIAP, "1990–91 Graduates' and University-Transfer Leavers' Perspectives on Degree Granting Status at Mount Royal College."

34 Board minutes, 16 Nov. 1992.

35 Athabasca University, "College Collaboration Initiative: A Collaboration Initiative to Improve University Degree Access for Albertans, Concept Paper," Academic Council agenda, 1 June 1992; discussion, Academic Council minutes, 24 Sept. 1992.

36 Board of Governors minutes, 30 Mar. 1992. For the sequel, see Geertje Boschma, Faculty of Nursing on the Move: Nursing at the University of Calgary, 1969–2004 (Calgary: University of Calgary Press, 2005).

37 Ady to Tingle, 7 Jan. 1993; Academic Council agenda, 21 Jan. 1993. Some students protested the fee increase. Academic Council minutes, 10 June 1993, copies of agreement and correspondence.

38 Barry Pashak, a former faculty member, pressed the case in the legislature. Barry Pashak, Government of Alberta, Hansard, 23 April 1992.

39 Report, in Academic Council minutes, 3 June 1993.

40 Board of Governors, Mount Royal College: A Proposal for the Development of Mount Royal College, presented to the Honourable Jack Ady, Minister, Alberta Advanced Education and Career Development, 1993.

41 Paul Goyan and Glen A. Jones, "Degrees in Canadian Higher Education," *International Higher Education* 16 (Summer 1999).

42 Initial Board discussion, Board minutes, 24 Oct. 1994.

43 The board had asked for foundation degrees. Board minutes, 24 Oct. 1994.

44 The initial version was amended. Christen Stoesser and Robert Burnett, "Alternate MRC Proposal Submitted for Applied Communications Degree," IABC Network, Feb. 1995; Elaine Dixson, coordinator of the Public Relations program, letter from Beverly Reynolds, APR, Canadian Energy Pipeline Association, writing as a board member, "MRC Board of Governors Clarifies PR Applied Degree Potential," IABC Network, Feb. 1995.

45 Rick Bell and Alex Frazer-Harrison, "Degrees granted for SAIT and MRC," *Calgary Sun*, 21 Mar. 1995. SAIT was approved for a Bachelor of Applied Petroleum Engineering Technology.

46 Andy Marshall, "Post-diploma program attracts only 16 students [to SAIT's new applied degree program in Petroleum Engineering Technology]," *Calgary Herald*, 29 June 1995.

47 Andy Marshall and Tony Johnson, "MRC, SAIT granted applied degrees," ibid., 21 Mar. 1995; also "A matter of degree," ibid., 22 Mar. 1995.

48 Both quotations are from Andy Marshall, "Applied Degree Approval Delayed," ibid., 7 Apr. 1997.

49 Message from the President and Chair, MRC Annual Report, 1999–2000, 2; Mount Royal College, "Self-Study Report: Transition to Degree Granting Status, Submission to Campus Alberta Quality Council, Organizational Evaluation," April 2006, 3.

50 PR, Board minutes, 12 Feb. 1996.

51 Andrea J. Kirby, "New breed of designers," *Reflector*, 8 Dec. 1998.

52 MRC Annual Report, 1994–95, 4.

53 Ibid., 1995–96; see also Louise Kinross, "Where entrepreneurship is king," *Financial Post*, 25 Apr. 1996, about the program.

54 MRUA, Baker files, Mertin to Baker, email, 20 Aug. 2009.

55 www.mtroyal.ca/ProgramsCourses/FacultiesSchoolsCentres/Arts/Programs/BachelorofArts/pstudies.htm.

56 Naheed K. Nenshi, *The State of Nonprofit Management Education in Canada* [electronic resource] (Calgary: Institute for Nonprofit Studies, Mount Royal College, 2008).

57 "Degree Granting: Communications/.Advocacy Strategy," 27 Nov. 1996, Board agenda, 2 Dec. 1996, 128–32.

58 The 1995 decision to permit private universities to offer B.Ed. degrees was also opposed by the public institutions. Dale P. Bischoff, "Extension of Authority to Confer Bachelor of Education degrees in Alberta," *Alberta Journal of Educational Research* 47, no. 1 (Spring 2001): 40–56.

59 Board regular meeting minutes, 7 Apr. 1997.

60 Statement dated 18 Mar. 1997, Board regular meeting minutes, 7 Apr. 1997.

61 Italics added. "Vision 2005," Board regular meeting minutes, 7 Apr. 1997. Brief summary, Board regular meeting minutes, 3 Feb. 1997; Board minutes, confidential session, 7 Apr. 1997.

62 Board minutes, confidential session, 7 Apr. 1997.

63 "Institutional Research Strategy," Board minutes, 5 June 2000.

64 MRC, Budget and Business Plan, 2001/2002–2004/2005, 6, 8.

65 John Baker, president of the University of Calgary's faculty association, saw college degrees and new private degree providers as weakening the public universities. David Loria, "DeVry Degrees Anger Calgary Institutions," *Reflector*, 8 Feb. 2001.

66 Kim Morison, "Education Debate: Two degrees of separation," ibid., 27 Oct. 2001.

67 On cases of individual students finding that their college-based credentials would not even be read by universities, see Kimberley Noble, "College or university?," *Maclean's*, 13 Nov. 2006.

68 Italics added. MRC Annual Report, 2001–2, 3.

69 Don Braid, "Why MRC Should Be MRU," 8 June 2003.

70 Alberta Finance, http://alberta.ca/home/43.cfm.

71 Treasurer Jim Dinning explained that the "net deficit" was the difference between the $31.7 billion owed minus $18.3 billion in provincial assets and another $5.1 billion in pension liabilities; the remaining debt would be paid over a 25-year period. Anthony Johnson, "Dinning reveals plan," *Calgary Herald*, 22 Feb. 1995. See Christopher J. Bruce, Ronald D. Kneebone, and Kenneth J. McKenzie, *A Government Reinvented: A Study of Alberta's Deficit Elimination Program* (Toronto: Oxford University Press, 1997); and, inter alia, Ronald D. Kneebone, "From Famine to Feast: The Evolution of Budget Rules in Alberta" (Calgary: Institute for Advanced Policy Research, University of Calgary, 1 August 2005).

72 For an early review of performance indicadtors for university systems, see Peter T. Ewell and D. Jones, "Pointing the Way: Indicators as Policy Tools in Higher Education," in S. Ruppert, ed., *Charting Higher Education Accountability: A Source Book on State Level Performance Indicators* (Denver: Education Commission of the States, 1994). On the effects of applying business models to academic institutions, and ties between academe and business, see: Janice Newsom and Howard Buchbinder, *The University Means Business: Universities, Corporations and Academic Work* (Toronto: Garamond Press, 1988); Janice Newson, "The

Corporate-Linked University: From Social Project to Market Force," *Canadian Journal of Communication* 23, no 1 (1998); James L. Turk, *The Corporate Campus: Commercialization and the Dangers to Canada's Colleges and Universities* (Toronto: J. Lorimer, 2000); William Bruneau and Donald Savage, *Counting out the Scholars: The Case Against Performance Indicators in Higher Education* (Canadian Association of University Teachers, 2002); Paul Axelrod, *Scholars and Dollars: Politics, Economics and the Universities of Ontario, 1945–1980* (Toronto: University of Toronto Press, 1982); and Axelrod, *Values in Conflict: The University, the Marketplace, and the Trials of Liberal Education* (Montreal/Kingston: McGill-Queen's University Press, 2002).

73 Access Fund Update, Board minutes, 6 Mar. 2000.

74 Ibid. The Learning Enhancement Fund was dropped at the end of 2000–2001. Mount Royal officials prepared an analysis, "Funding Mechanism," for the board of governors summarizing the implications for the college: Board minutes, 12 Feb. 1996. The Performance bonus/penalty was equivalent to plus or minus 2 per cent of the operating grant, or some $540,000 for Mount Royal. For angry responses to a 1997 "summit" on the future, once the deficit was mastered, see: Jerrold Kachur, "Orchestrating Delusions: Ideology and Consent in Alberta," in Trevor W. Harrison and Jerrold L. Kachur, eds., *Contested Classrooms: Education, Globalization and Democracy in Alberta* (Edmonton: University of Alberta Press, 1999), 59–74; Dean Neu, "Re-Investment Fables: Educational Finances in Alberta," ibid., 75–84; and Frank Peters, "Deep and Brutal: Funding Cuts to Education in Alberta," ibid., 85–98.

75 Letter, Jacqueline Fisher, President, Students' Association, to Minister Ady, 9 Jan. 1996, and response, Ady to Fisher, 30 Jan. 1996; Board minutes, 12 Feb. 1996.

76 Alberta Learning, "Alberta's Post-secondary System: Developing the Blueprint for Change, 2002".

77 Dawson report, Board minutes, 7 June 1999. In constant dollars, the student per capita funding fell sharply. MRC, Budget and Business Plan, 2001/2002–2004/2005, 6, 8; OIAP, Mount Royal College: Trends at a Glance, Sept. 2007, retroactive statistics.

78 Rising natural gas shipments to the U.S. (from 3 billion cubic feet in 1985 to 9 billion in 2000) generated significant new revenues. Canadian Association of Petroleum Producers, *CAPP Statistical Handbook*, cited in Greg Stringham, "Canadian Natural Gas – An important part of North American supply, now and in the future," National Energy Modeling System, Annual Energy Outlook 2003 Conference, 23 Mar. 2004. www.eia.doe.gov/oiaf/archive/aeo04/conf/pdf/stringham.pdf.

79 Infrastructure Renewal Envelope, Board regular meeting minutes, 29 Sept. 1997; "Funding from Alberta Advanced Education and Career Development," ibid., 29 Sept. 1997; Andy Marshall, "Technology grants benefit Calgary schools," *Calgary Herald*, 21 July 1998; Board confidential minutes, 26 Mar. 2001; MRC, Budget and Business Plan, 2001/2002–2004/2005, 13.

80 Marshall, "MRC seeks delay in rating system," *Calgary Herald*, 4 Mar. 1997. In April 1997, the board received a department paper on non-credit KPIs. Board minutes, 7 Apr. 1997. On the earlier pilot project, see Board minutes, 12 Feb. 1996.

81 Marshall, "MRC seeks delay in rating system," *Calgary Herald*, 4 Mar. 1997. In April 1997, the board received a government discussion paper on non-credit KPIs. Board minutes, 7 Apr. 1997. On the earlier pilot project, see Board minutes, 12 Feb. 1996; Marshall, "College Loses in Bonuses Sweepstakes, *Calgary Herald*, 30 June 1998; the "loser" was Bow Valley College. The detailed results were reported in MRC, OIAP, Long-range Institutional Plan, Mar. 1999, chap. 3, 10.

82 Robert J. Barnetson, "Changing Definitions and Off-Loading Responsibility in Alberta's Post-secondary System," *Education Policy Analysis Archives* 5, no. 22 (9 Dec. 1997). The college calculated that it received $5,253 in 1994–95, $4,917 in 1995–06, and $4,548 in 1996–97. MRC Annual Report, 1996–97, 15.

83 Report and Recommendations from Tuition Fee Consultation Committee," Board minutes, 12 Feb. 1996.

84 Board minutes, 29 Sept. 1997.

85 MRC, OIAP, Long-Range Institutional Plan, Mar. 1999, chap. 3, 31; "1999–99 Third Quarter Financial Report to Mar. 31, 1999," Board minutes, 7 June 1999.

86 Wood to Board, 12 Aug. 1992, re "Partnership with IBM Canada."

87 Lynda Wallace-Hulecki warned that "the current criteria under-describe what we do." Andy Marshall, "Mount Royal hikes tuition fees," *Calgary Herald*, 30 May 1995; see the October 1993 government discussion paper entitled "Accountability: Expectations of the Public Post-Secondary System," outlining nineteen areas of expected results. In 1994–95, the first phase of the Key Performance Indicator (KPI) reporting system was piloted.

88 Academic Council minutes, 4 Mar. 1991.

89 Maxine Mott, president of the MRFA, to Tingle, 8 April 1991; also Mott to Marilyn Will, Chairman, Academic Council, 3 April 1991, with Board minutes, 9 April 1991.

90 Legal opinion, cited in Board minutes, 17 June 1991.

91 Academic Council minutes, 9 May 1991.

92 ERC: Lynn Duncan, Deputy Minister, to Wood, 5 June and 23 July 1992; John Gogo, Minister, to Anne S. Tingle, Chairman, Board of Governors, 4 June 1992; Duncan to Wood, 25 Sept. 1992.

93 Wood and Tingle, Board minutes, 1 and 17 Nov. 1993, 13 Dec. 1993.

94 The focus was on allocating resources to the college's mission, the Principal Goal and College Priorities, to prioritize "viable academic programs … ahead of other activities and services except where those … are deemed essential for the effective operation of the college," and to cut selectively. Discussion of "First Principles for Retrenchment 1993–94," Academic Council minutes, 17 Dec. 1992; Lathrop to MacAlister, "Academic Program and Service Review and Rationalization," 13 Dec. 1996, section on "Consistency with the Principles for Retrenchment," Academic Council minutes, 16 Dec. 1996.

95 Ron Collins, "College employees voting on salary rollback," *Calgary Herald*, 2 Feb. 1994.

96 Board minutes, 24 Jan. and 14 Feb. 1994. Wood reported that the salary savings amounted to $1.3 million and increment freezes $0.6 million, for a total of $1.9 million.

97 "Early Retirement Incentive Plan for Support Staff Employees," Board minutes, 8 Mar. 1993; Board minutes, 6 Mar. 1998 and 14 Dec. 1998.

98 The Budget Advisory Committee recommended contracting out, then opposed it when it happened. Wood to Eric Fechter, chair, Budget Advisory Committee, 7 Apr. 1994.

99 Lathrop to Macleod, Chairman, Program Committee, Academic Council, re "Procedures for Program Suspension or Deletion for Non-Academic Reasons," 21 May 1992, Academic Council Agenda, 21 Jan. 1993. The board subsequently approved the procedures. Lathrop subsequently invited the Academic Council to classify programs. Lathrop to T. MacAlister, Chair, Academic Council, 8 Nov. 1993, Academic Council agenda, 16 Dec. 1993.

100 Quoted in Academic Council minutes, 13 Jan. 1994.

101 Lathrop to MacAlister, Chair, Academic Council, "Academic Program and Service Review and Rationalization," 13 Dec. 1993; Academic Council minutes, 16 Dec. 1993; Academic Council minutes, 13 Jan. 1994.

102 Academic Council minutes 16 Dec. 1993 and 13 Jan. 1994; "First Principles for Retrenchment," Jan. 1994, Board minutes, 8 Mar. 1994.

103 Eric Fechter, Chairman, Budget Advisory Committee, to Wood, re "Recommendations for Input to 1993–94 Budget Development," in Board minutes, 18 Jan. 1993. The committee had recommended investigating "alternative methods of providing non-college level courses that are currently offered in Academic upgrading and some certificate level programs as a way of maximizing the use of qualified faculty and maximizing revenues."

104 *MRC Leader*, 13 Mar. 2000; Board minutes, 6 Mar. 2000.

105 Rejected by the Council: Council minutes, 27 Jan. 1994.

106 Budget Plan, 1994–1997 (a pamphlet); Board minutes, 20 June 1994.

107 Lathrop, "Organizational Restructuring: A Proposed Strategy," 31 Mar. 1995; and "Responses Received," Board minutes, 10 Apr. 1995.

108 MRC, Budget and Business Plan, 1998–2001, 7; Budget and Business Plan, 2001/2002–2004/2005, 6, 8.

109 Wight, "Synopsis of the Ninth Decade Fund-Raising Plan," Board minutes, 23 Oct. 1989.

110 Wight interview (Baker), 23 July 2008. When in the mid-1990s the college tried to give the Foundation more independence, the government objected, wanting it to "bring all the responsibility back in house and roll the operation of the Foundation in with the college when it comes to balancing the books."

111 Wight, Board minutes, 17 Sept. 1990; PR, 30 Sept. 1991.

112 In 1994–95, the foundation raised $982,894 and in 1995–96, $1,194,554. Mount Royal College Foundation, financial statements, Board minutes, 7 Apr. 1997. Capital Campaign Report, Board minutes, 29 Sept. 1997; MRC Foundation's Strategic Plan, 2001–2004, Board confidential meeting minutes, 26 Feb. 2001.

113 MRC Foundation, "The Mount Royal College Foundation Revitalization Plan," 1 June 1999, Board minutes, 7 June 1999.

114 Ben Curties, "Students Benefit from Bright Minds," *Reflector*, 24 Oct. 2002.

115 MRC, Long-range Institutional Plan, Mar. 1999, chap. 3, 14.

116 "Study of the Implications of Trimesterization at Mount Royal College," Dec. 1991. Trimesterization would apply to "slightly less than one-half of the programs" and was too expensive. Marc Chikinda, Chairman, Planning Committee to M. D. Will, Chairman, Academic Council, 7 Jan. 1992; Academic Council minutes, 16 Jan. 1992.

117 Finance and Property Committee Minutes, 21 Jan. 1991: Wilson to Wood, Memorandum, 31 May 1991; Final Report, 15 May 1992: Interview.

118 Dawson presentation, Board minutes, 7 June1999; ibid., 5 June 2000.

119 Board minutes, 6 Mar., 17 Apr., and 5 June 2000; *MRC Leader*, 13 Sept. 1999, 15 May 2000.

120 "Leases with the city of Calgary," and report of Bruce Mahon, Acting VP, Administrative Services, Board minutes, 12 Feb. 1996.

121 "Lincoln Park Special Planning Study," Board minutes, 14 Dec. 1998.

122 Board minutes, 14 June and 16 Sept. 1991.

123 "Planning for Future Development: Mount Royal College Interest in CFB Facilities"; also Board confidential minutes, 4 June 1996.

124 Mount Royal College, "Proposal for Participation in the Redevelopment of Canadian Forces Base Calgary," 27 Nov. 1996; Board confidential minutes, 2 Dec. 1996.

125 Anthony Johnson, "Mount Royal College eyes growth options," *Calgary Herald*, 27 June 1995.

126 PR, 18 Sept. 1995; also Board minutes 29 May 1995, and Mount Royal College Lincoln Park Study, 1992.

127 Mahon to Wood, 23 Jan. 1996: Finance Committee minutes 5 Feb. 1996; 23 May 1996: Board minutes 12 Feb. 1996. Andy Marshall, "MRC wants building lands," *Calgary Herald*, 7 Apr. 1997. Minister Ady told the college that the province would not pay for any land: ibid.; see also David Jala, "Ady backing expansion cheers MRC," *Calgary Sun*, 27 June 1995; Steven Chase, "Base land for college backed," ibid., 26 June 1995. Responding to an effort by the college to secure CFB land on the basis of precedents (Collège Saint-Jean in Quebec, Royal Roads in BC), Prime Minister Jean Chrétien told Premier Klein that unlike the other institutions, Mount Royal had never been a fully funded federal institution, and the government did not want to set the precedent. Letter, Jean Chrétien to Ralph Klein, 7 Feb. 1997, included in Board minutes, confidential session, 7 Apr. 1997.

128 "Call for Proposal for Supply of Professional services, Dec. 1997," Board agenda, 2 Feb. 1998.

129 "Campus Development Plan Update," Board minutes, 13 Dec. 1999.

130 College Expansion Project report, Board minutes, 9 Apr. 2001; Rachelle Elburg and Allyson Martin, "City allows college to pave over dirt lot," *Reflector*, 29 Mar. 2001.

131 Wood interview (Baker), July 2009.

132 MRC, Budget and Business Plan, 2001/2002–2004/2005, approved by the board on 4 June 2001, 15–16.

133 Board minutes, confidential session, 14 July 1998.

134 The government provided $94 million, an additional $2 million from the Infrastructure Renewal Envelope for refitting the old facilities, and interest on government funds.

135 Report from Robson and Roberts, "Student Residences Revised Business Strategy," Board minutes, 7 June 2004.

136 Glenn Cook, "New rec facilities officially open," *Reflector*, 26 Sept. 2002.

137 Steve Venegas, "New centre under construction," ibid., 29 Sept. 2005.

138 Jill Bryant, "Mount Royal College gets organized," ibid., 19 Sept. 1996.

139 A.D. Rogan, Chair, Board of Governors, MRC, letter to Rae Morgan, Chair, Christian Church, 24 Oct. 1996, attached to

140 Wood, "Chaplaincy and John H. Garden Meditation Centre, 2 Dec. 1996," Board minutes, 2 Dec. 1996. They asked the the board "to find suitable and equitable meditation space to replace the J. H. Garden Meditation Centre." MRFA, ibid., 2 Dec. 1996 and 3 Feb. 1997.

141 Report of Vice-President Lathrop, Board minutes, 7 Apr. 1997; on an amendment to the rules, see Board minutes, 6 Apr. 1998.

142 "A fitting tribute … Dr. John H. Garden, Nurturer of people – and plants," *Reflections*, Fall 1998, 17.

143 In 2002, there was only one contested position; all others were filled by acclamation. Glenn Cook, "Stone squeaks in," *Reflector*, 7 Mar. 2002. Only 6 per cent of the student body voted.

144 Brad Needham, "SAMRC highest paid executives in the nation," ibid., 26 Oct. 2000.

145 Kelly Harris, "The Saga Continues," ibid., 20 Mar. 1997.

146 *Reflector* Staff, "Landslide! Executive races hardly close," ibid., 4 Mar. 2004. The turnout was 8.8 per cent (975 of 11,021 eligible voters), higher than those in 2003 (7.3) and 2002 (6.15).

147 B. Bauer, "Students' Association of Mount Royal College (SAMRC)," Board minutes, 6 Mar. 2000.

148 "Students Use Their Voice to Make Their Choice," *Association Matters*, March 2003.

149 Trevor Prosser, "Student leaders oppose tuition hike," *Reflector*, 16 Jan. 1997; Kelly Harris, "Petition sparks mixed reaction," ibid., 30 Jan. 1997.

150 Stephanie Stewart, "Students debate banning the butt," ibid., 12 Feb. 2004.

151 Aric Johnson, "Oh the parking horrors," ibid., 30 Mar. 2000.

152 Althea Wiesner, "SA wages battle against students' schedules," ibid., 9 Oct. 1997.

153 Aaron Paton, "College radio finds liteners," *Journal*, 17 April 2003.

154 Notice, "Draft, Subject to CRO Approval," ibid., 13 Sept. 2001.

155 Greg Hudson, "Student elections," ibid., 17 Mar. 2005.

156 Wood, memo to Board, re "*The Reflector*," 3 February 1992; Ian Gent, Acting Chair, Reflector Publication Society, to Wood, 24 January 1992; all with Board minutes, 3 February 1992.

157 Association Matters: News for Students' Association of Mount Royal College Members.

158 ERC: Michele Decottignies, president, SAMRC, to Tingle, 12 February and 3 March 1993; Tingle to Decottignies, 11 Feb. 1993; Wood to Chikinda, Chairman, Academic Council, 12 Feb. 1993; Wood to Decottignies, 3 March 1993.

159 Jill Bryant, "Students say yes," *Reflector*, 28 Nov. 1996.

160 Brad Needham, "SA implements hike," ibid., 7 Dec. 2000.

161 "Hamish MacLean, "Wyckham gets $14M expansion," ibid., 27 Sept. 2007.

162 ERC, Student Centre Liaison Committee, Terms of Reference, 1 June 2004.

163 Elske Stuwe, "Code passed by College," *Reflector*, 24 Oct. 2002.

164 Mandy Angeltvedt, "New policy limits off-campus activities," ibid., 17 Jan. 2002.

165   Board minutes, 12 Feb. 1996; in 1994 and 1995 the revenues exceeded expenditures (1995: $1.88 million in revenue, $1.73 million in expenditures); draft letter, 25 Feb. 1997, from Bryan Boechler to The Right Honourable Bert Olson, Lieutenant Governor, "SAMRC's Request for Exemption from Section 26(4) of the Colleges Act.," Board agenda and minutes, 7 Apr. 1997.

166   Board minutes, 7 Apr. 1997; letter, 28 Sept. 2000, attached to Board minutes, 29 Sept. 1997. Correspondence, Board Finance Committee, Board confidential minutes, 20 Nov. 2000.

167   In 1990, the association requested approval to expand Thirsty's Lounge. Campus development Committee minutes, 15 June 1990; Board minutes, 15 Jan. 1990.

168   Board minutes, 6 Apr. 1998.

169   David Loria, "House of the Rising Conflict," *Reflector*, 19 Apr. 2001.

170   ERC: Letter, Fraser to Board of Governors, 9 Apr. 2001.

171   Board minutes, 9 Apr. 2001.

172   Devin Holterman, "Mass expansion coming soon," *Reflector*, 1 Feb. 2007; Jeremy Nolais, "Wyckham ready to roll," ibid., 4 Sept. 2008.

173   The program was described to the board by Hayden Melting Tallow, chairman of the steering committee, Board minutes, 13 Feb. 1995.

174   Brad Bill, "Native education project in limbo," *Reflector*, 11 Sept. 1997.

175   Alison Delker, "Native centre – finally a reality," ibid., 12 Nov. 1998.

176   Students Association of Mount Royal College, Annual Report, 2003–4.

177   Patrick Caron, "Cougars' finest receive accolades," *Reflector*, 15 Apr. 1997.

178   Sean Rooney, "Cougars win national supremacy award," ibid., 16 Sept. 1999. This was the list of national championships at that point: 1979, Men's volleyball; 1979, Men's basketball; 1982, Men's volleyball; 1985, Women's badminton; 1987, Women's badminton; 1988, Hockey; 1991, Men's volleyball; 1994, Men's volleyball; 1996, Men's basketball; 1997, Men's soccer; 1998, Men's volleyball; 1998, Badminton; 1999, Badminton; 1999, Hockey; 2000, Women's basketball. Sean Rooney, "National champions for the first time," ibid., 30 Nov. 2000.

179   Tania Mayhew, "Mandate change may mean more cash, but Cougars can see downside to university status," ibid., 4 Mar. 2004; see also Farrah Fennig, "Cougar Players Make the Grade," ibid., 8 Mar. 2007.

180   Ibid., 180, citing a faculty member.

181   Ibid., 332.

182   Ibid., 318.

183   Ibid., 176–80. The issues were not unique to Mount Royal. See John D. Dennison, "The Case for Democratic Governance in Canadian Community Colleges," *Interchange* 25 (1994): 25–37. There is an international perspective in Alberto Amaral, Glen A. Jones, and Berit Karseth, eds., *Governing Higher Education: National Perspectives on Institutional Governance* (Dordrecht: Luwer Academic Publishers, 2002).

184   MRUA, Admin., "Proposed Revisions to the Academic Council Constitution," Mar. 1992.

185   Report on ACIFA survey, Board minutes (confidential), 1 April 1996.

186   Report on ACIFA survey, Board minutes (confidential), 3 Feb. 1997.

187   Report on ACIFA survey, Board minutes (confidential), 9 Apr. 2001.

188   Board minutes (confidential), 9 April 2001.

189   Board minutes, 12 Feb. 1996.

190   In Feb. 1996 the two parties agreed to explore an alternative process: Board minutes, 12 Feb. 1996. The proposed model was approved by the board. Board agenda, 4 June 1996, 39–40; Special Committee on Negotiations, "Proposed Negotiating Model for Mount Royal College," 23 May 1996, 141–44; Board regular and confidential meeting minutes, 4 June 1996, 84–85, 86–87.

191   MRC Board regular and confidential meeting minutes, 26 May 1997.

192   Email, Mahon to Baker, 3 June 2009.

193   Mark C. Sollis, "Faculty work to rule," *Reflector*, 15 Jan. 1998.

194   Board meeting minutes, confidential session, 2 Feb. 1998. Robson, spokesperson for the board's negotiating committee, reported that a two-year agreement had been reached, including, in addition to the committee, a 3 per cent increase on the salary grid retroactive to July 1, 1997, 3 per cent on the salary grid effective July 1, 1998, and restoration of the annual increment retroactive to July 1, 1997.

195   Asked to explain the polarization, Jerre Paquette referred to the history of confrontation, tensions arising from the transformation, and occasional incidents, such as the occasion when he, as a new MRFA president, had naively signed a document on student access to faculty evaluations that he asked the administration to return, without success. Paquette interview, 11 July 2010.

196   Tamara Oleksow, "Faculty call strike vote," *Reflector*, 13 Feb. 2003; Andrew Parry, "Tentative agreement reached," ibid., 20 Mar. 2003.

197   Dated 25 Jan. 1996: Board agenda, 12 Feb. 1996.

198   Board minutes, 29 May 1995.

199   Report of Lorna Smith, Board regular meeting minutes, 5 Oct. 1998.

200   "Team Canada Trade Mission," *Calgary Herald*, 14 Jan. 1998.

201   MRC, International Update, 5 (Jan. 2003).

202   Wood stressed making international activities a "mainstream" rather than a peripheral activity. Discussion of international education, Board minutes, 5 Oct. 1998.

203   MRC, Internationalization Strategy, Phase II, 2001–2010.

204   Jane Knight, "Internationalization: Elements and Checkpoints," Canadian Bureau for International Education Research Paper 7, 1994, www.cbie.ca/english/media_research2_e.htm and Knight, "Taking the Pulse: Monitoring the Quality and Progress of Internationalization," Canadian Bureau for International Education Research Millennium Series, No. 2, 2000. http://www.cbie.ca/english/media_research1_e.htm

205   Interview, Lorna Smith, 15 July 2009.

206   Tamara Oleksow, "College cashes in," *Reflector*, 29 Mar. 2001.

207 "HRDC announces $1.5 million for national nursing study at MRC," http://www.mtroyal.ab.ca/news/view.php?item=000124. Posted 11 Mar. 2003.

208 MRC, International Update, 5 (Jan. 2003).

209 MRC, Internationalization Strategy: Phase II, 2001–2010.

210 Mount Royal College website, "The Conservatory."

211 MRC, International Update, 5 (Jan. 2003).

212 http://www.mtroyal.ca/conservatory/musicbridge/mmb_sponsors.shtml

213 "Musicians bridge cultural differences," *Reflections*, Fall 1998, 9.

214 Ibid., 24 July 2002, 4.

215 In 2002, for example, the SAY Trio, consisting of Yujia Wang, Arnold Choi, and Shanshan Yao, was awarded the $1,000 Provincial Music Festival Grand Scholarship. Former Conservatory students also won prizes and, like the members of the trio, advanced to the national competition. *MRC Leader*, 10 July 2002, 4.

216 Among the Conservatory's more prominent music graduates were Michael Kim, Dean of Music, Bando University, Daniel Okulitch, international opera star, Dave Pierce, Emmy Award-winning Music Director for the 2010 Winter Olympic Games and the Calgary Exhibition and Stampede; Yuri Hooker, principal cellist in the Winnipeg Symphony Orchestra; Tanya Kalmanovitch, violinist; Rhian Kenny, flutist with the Pittsburgh Symphony Orchestra; Martha Baldwin, cellist with the Cleveland Orchestra; Katherine Chi, CHI pianist, winner of the 2000 Honens Competition; Heather Schmidt, internationally acclaimed composer and pianist; and, from the Theatre Arts stream, Alan Van Sprang, the TV/film actor.

217 Board minutes, 4 June 2001.

218 Rahel Folden, "Theatre Arts stages an emotional twist of epic tale," *Reflector*, 15 Apr. 1997.

219 Brad Needham, "Theatre Arts up to the job," *Reflector*, 9 Oct. 1997.

220 Christopher Lamb, "A toast to MRC theatre," ibid., 15 Jan. 1998.

221 Teresa Wong, "Shakespearean classics collide with Survivor antics," *MRC Leader*, 20 Aug. 2002, 2.

222 Cathy Nickel, "Stepping down," *Reflections*, Spring 2003, 19–20.

223 After leaving Mount Royal, Wood became the founding president of the Asia Pacific Institute for the Tec de Monterrey (ITESM) and helped found Quest University, a private liberal arts and sciences university in British Columbia.

Chapter 10: Becoming a University, 2003–2009

1 Michael L. Skolnik, "Should the CAATs Grant Degrees?" *College Quarterly* 3, no. 2 (Winter 1995).

2 On whether this was a wise use of the surplus and whether royalty rates should have been returned to 1990 levels, see Amy Taylor, "Short-changing Albertans: The Public Share of Resource Revenues Is at an All-Time Low," *Green Economics*, 15 June 2006, http://www.greeneconomics.ca/op-ed/1370.

3 Statistics Canada, CANSIM, table (for fee) 282-0090 and Catalogue no. 71-001-XIE. Last modified: 2009-04-09.

4 Calgary Real Estate Board, monthly reports of mls sales. http://www.creb.com.

5 Statistics Canada, "Labour force characteristics, seasonally adjusted, by census metropolitan area (3 month moving average), Calgary, Edmonton," http://www40.statcan.ca/101/cst01/lfss03-eng.htm.

6 Archives, Calgary Real Estate Board: http://www.creb.com/public/seller-resources/housing-statistics-archives.php.

7 Ibid.

8 Alberta, Fiscal Overview, March 2009. www.finance.alberta.ca/publications/budget/budget2009/fiscal.pdf.

9 "New president sets sights on future," in MRC, *Redefining Undergraduate Education, Community Report*, 2003.

10 Ibid.

11 "New president leads Mount Royal College," *Calgary Herald*, 12 Sept. 2003.

12 Matthew Peterson, "Prez Marshall's support," *Reflector*, 18 Sept. 2003.

13 Ben Curties, "*The Reflector* chats with Mount Royal prez David Marshall about MRC becoming MRU," ibid., 11 Dec. 2003.

14 Board minutes, 17 Sept. 2004.

15 Ibid., 7 June 2004.

16 Stephanie Stewart, "Five-million-dollar meltdown: Teacher cuts, increased class sizes eyed as deficit looms," *Reflector*, 18 Mar. 2004.

17 *Reflector*, 18 Oct. 2004.

18 David Agren, "VP bonus backlash mounts," and Ben Curties, "Students deserve answers to bonus boondoggle," ibid., 11 Nov. 2004; Aaron Paton, "Winter of discontent, MRC students rally against tuition, VP bonuses," ibid., 25 Nov. 2004. Hal Kvisle, "Board of Governors finally responds to bonus concerns," ibid., 25 Nov. 2004.

19 Board minutes, 15 Nov. 2004.

20 Ibid., 13 Dec. 2004; report on discussions with the Auditor General's office, ibid., 7 Feb. 2005.

21 Ibid., 7 Feb. 2005.

22 Ben Curties, "VP let go in admin shuffle," *Reflector*, 25 Nov. 2004.

23 Ben Curties, "AG to review Board finances, VP bonuses payments will be assessed," *Reflector*, 13 Jan. 2005; Janna Kalmakoff, "Auditor general calls for college transparency," *Reflector*, 8 Dec. 2005; the issue contains a copy of the letter: "We recommend that the MRC Board of Governors examine its governance process to ensure that committee decisions, which are not ratifications of management decisions, be confirmed at the board level."

24 His publications included *Contact and Conflict: Indian-European Relations in British Columbia, 1774–1890* (Vancouver: University of British Columbia Press, 1992); and *Duff Pattullo of British Columbia* (Toronto: University of Toronto Press, 1991).

25 For a general review of higher education in the several provinces, see Jones, ed., *Higher Education in Canada: Different Systems, Different Perspectives*.

26 Through its life PCAB approved nine private institutions, all but one religiously oriented. On the varieties of practice across Canada, see Baker and Miosi, "The Quality Assurance of Degree Education in Canada."

27 Post-secondary Education Choice and Excellence Act, S.O. 2000, c. 36 (Sched.), available at http://www.e-laws.gov.on.ca/. On the basis of legal advice, PEQAB developed three different handbooks, one for each category of institution that Ontario recognized (public, private, and government-based). The degree-level standards are posted at the site, as is the Handbook for Ontario Colleges, www.peqab.edu.gov.on.ca. Transparency required also the publication of the minister's criteria for assessing PEQAB recommendations. See: http://www.edu.gov. on.ca/eng/general/postsec/degree/guideline.pdf.

28 Degree Granting Act, S.N.B. 2000, c. D-5.3 (in force 1 Mar. 2001). The background is discussed in the website for the Maritime Provinces Higher Education Commission (MPHEC): http://www.mphec.ca/en/quality/overview.aspx.

29 Degree Authorization Act, 2003, S.B.C. 2002, c. 24. For the Degree Quality Assessment Board's requirements, see http://www.aved.gov.bc.ca/degree-authorization/applicants.htm. The British Columbia Council on Admissions and Transfer has remained a separate organization: www.bccat.bc.ca/transfer/membership.cfm.

30 John Baker, president of the University of Calgary's faculty association, saw college degrees and new private degree providers as weakening the public universities. David Loria, "DeVry degrees anger Calgary institutions," *Reflector*, 8 Feb. 2001.

31 See Cathy Gulli, "Smartening up: Presidents of seven smaller universities take aim at the big five," *Maclean's*, 12 Aug. 2009. David Marshall, a member of the Higher Education Quality Council of Ontario, has observed that "over half the undergraduate population and almost all of the graduate population reside in about 15 percent of the universities," and that "recent research out of one provincial quality council suggests a disconnect between current university instructional practices and learning outcomes." Marshall, "Improving, Assessing and Demonstrating Student Learning," paper presented to the 12th Transatlantic Dialogue: 27 June 2010, New York University.

32 AUCC, "Overview of Provincial and Regional Quality Assurance Mechanisms in Canadian Higher Education," 2007, www.aucc.ca/qa/_pdf/reg_prov_overview_e.pdf. On the medley of jurisdictional approaches in Canada, see the essays in Jones, ed., *Higher Education in Canada*, notably the conclusion by Skolnik, "Putting It All Together: Viewing Canadian Higher Education from a Collection of Jurisdiction-Based Perspectives," 325–42.

33 Advanced Education, "Campus Alberta: The Evolution of Alberta's Learning System," attached to Board minutes, 7 June 1999.

34 In 1992, Barry Pashak, a former faculty member, had suggested in the legislature that the Private Colleges Accreditation Board could be used to assess public institution programs and potential mandate changes: "Maybe the question of whether Mount Royal College, for example, should be given degree-granting status in some programs could be referred to that board as well. I think there would have to be some mechanism like that put in place." Government of Alberta, *Hansard*, 23 April 1992.

35 Key documents can be found at the website of the European Association for Quality Assurance (formerly the European Network for Quality Assurance), at http://www.enqua.eu.

36 "INQAAHE is a world-wide association of some 200 organisations active in the theory and practice of quality assurance in higher education. The great majority of its members are quality assurance agencies that operate in many different ways....": http://www.INQAAHE.org. Then director of PEQAB's Secretariat, Donald Baker, served on its board of directors from 2003 to 2006.

37 "Ministerial Statement on Quality Assurance of Degree Education in Canada," at: http://www.cmec.ca/Publications/Lists/Publications/Attachments/95/QA-Statement-2007.en.pdf. In 2001, CMEC had introduced a policy on credit transfer and established a committee whose second report records developments since then: Report of the CMEC Working Group on Credit Transfer, 2008. http://www.cmec.ca/Publications/Lists/Publications/Attachments/120/CreditTransfer2008.en.pdf. CMEC, "European Higher Education Area (EHEA) – The Bologna Process" (2008) http://www.cmec.ca/Publications/Lists/Publications/Attachments/119/BolognaReport2008.en. Donald N. Baker, then Director of the Secretariat, Postsecondary Education Quality Assessment Board, wrote a background paper for the Pan-Canadian committee and Ontario government officials entitled "Building a Pan-Canadian Consensus on Quality Assurance for Degree Programs," 2005.

38 Ibid.

39 "Twenty Questions: Everything you wanted to know about the mandate change for Mount Royal... and have probably asked!", 14 Jan. 2004, 11.

40 "Province should assist Mount Royal in its quest for university status," *Calgary Herald*, 10 Dec. 2003.

41 "The New 'U': Mount Royal's proposal to serve the post-secondary education needs of an evolving community by creating a distinctive student- and teaching-focused undergraduate university," 10 Apr. 2004; there are two versions, one much longer, from which this quotation comes (15–16).

42 Mount Royal College, Annual Report, 2006–7, 8.

43 Marshall, "The New 'U'," and "The Role of Professional Associations," 18–20, 26. Marshall continued to publish a steady stream of scholarly articles on issues related to degree and credential recognition: David G. Marshall, "Degree Accreditation in Canada: The Degree-Recognition Issue," *Canadian Journal of Higher Education* 34, no. 2 (2004): 69–96; "Access to Degrees in the Knowledge Economy." *Options Politiques* (August 2004): 76–82; "Differentiation by Degrees: System Design and the Changing Undergraduate Environment in Canada," *Canadian Journal of Higher Education* 38, no. 3 (2008): 1–20; and "What's It Worth? The Tiering of Canadian Degrees," *Education Canada* 46, no. 1 (2005): 55–57.

44 Marshall, "The New 'U'," and "The Role of Professional Associations," 25. The "current base contact hours per week" were 13.5 hours, with 90 per cent of the workload in teaching and 10 per cent in service; the future workload profile would be 9–13.5 contact hours, with teaching constituting 60 per cent of the workload, research 20 per cent, and service 20 per cent.

45 Board retreat minutes, 17–18 Sept. 2004.

46 "The New 'U'," "Twenty Questions: Everything you wanted to know about the mandate change for Mount Royal... and have probably asked!", 14 Jan. 2004; and Marshall, "Leading and Learning in Post-Secondary Education," 7 Jan. 2005, a paper he sent to Minister Hancock.

47 Marshall, "The New 'U'," and "The Role of Professional Associations,", 27, 31.

48 MRC, Institutional Priorities and Strategies, 2006–2007.

49 Ibid.

50 MRC Annual Report, 2007–08, 6.

51 Reprinted in MRC, Academic Plan, Appendix 2, Mandate Statement.

52 MRC, Self-Study Report: Transition to Degree-Granting Status, Submission to Campus Alberta Quality Council, Organization Evaluation, Apr. 2006, 3.

53 MRC, Academic Plan, 9, 10, note 2a: "Faculty responsibilities should become 60/30/10 (teaching, scholarship and service respectively) where 60 equals 6 (three-credit courses), or the equivalent, for those teaching in the teaching/scholarship stream, and 90/10 (teaching and service) where 90 equals 8 (three-credit courses), or the equivalent, for those in the teaching stream."

54 Ibid., 6: "The quality of the student experience has been, and will continue to be, the defining feature of Mount Royal. It will, therefore, remain our first priority."

55 Ibid., 12–13.

56 Program Definition and General Education for Degree Programs at Mount Royal College, Final report to Academic Council 18 May 2006, 5; cited in MRC, Academic Plan, 12. General Education courses cannot be "double counted within the up to 60 per cent major core, but they may be used as part of a minor." Mertin to Baker, email, 20 Aug. 2009.

57 Board minutes, 5 Apr. 2004, 4.5.1.1.b/c, 3.

58 Mount Royal College, Report of the Task Force on Faculty Roles and Responsibilities, Dec. 2006, 5–11.

59 Report of the Task Force on Institutional Governance, 30 Sept. 2005.

60 Board retreat minutes, 30 Sept. 2005.

61 The speakers included Dr. Charles Jago, former president of the University of Northern British Columbia, Dr. Bernard Shapiro, Principal Emeritus of McGill University, Professor Bonnie Patterson, President of Trent University, Dr. James Downey, former President of the University of Waterloo and President of the Higher Education Quality Council of Ontario, and Professor Glen Jones of the Ontario Institute for studies in Education.

62 MRC, Report of the Task Force on Research, Nov. 2006.

63 Ibid., 5.

64 MRC, Self-Study Report, 6.

65 Strategic Technology Planning Committee, Strategic Technology Plan, 14 May 2008.

66 MRC, Report of the Library Transition Task Force, Aug. 2005.

67 Marshall to Hancock, 7 Feb. 2006.

68 AUCC, Report of the Visiting Committee, 19.

69 "New Beginnings for Aboriginal Students," Reflections, Fall 2007, 6.

70 Marshall, "Improving, Assessing and Demonstrating Student Learning," 6.

71 These are collected in a binder entitled "Mount Royal in Motion," Mount Royal College archives.

72 Sean Myers, "Mount Royal decision delayed," Calgary Herald, 5 Apr. 2005.

73 "Decision: Other universities around the province have criticized proposal," ibid.

74 Ibid.

75 Braid, "Province fails to do right by college," ibid., 5 Apr. 2005.

76 Dave Hancock, "Minister defends MRC review," ibid., 6 Apr. 2005.

77 Braid's article continued: "The University of Alberta has 29,427 students while the U of C has 23,913. That's a difference of 5,514. Grant MacEwan has nearly 3,000 students more than Mount Royal. NAIT's enrolment is 600 higher than SAIT's. Only Bow Valley College breaks the pattern, just barely. It has more students than Edmonton's Norquest College by a whopping count of 21." Braid, "Hancock's politics not Calgary's concern," ibid., 7 Apr. 2007. Dr. Terrence J. Downey, president of the St. Mary's University College, wrote to remind people about his and two other small private "university colleges" within the University of Calgary: "What about us?," ibid., 8 Apr. 2005.

78 ERC: Hancock to Marshall, Dec. 2005.

79 CanLII, Alternative Academic Council Regulation, Alta. Reg. 219./2006; accessed at http//www,cabkuu,irg/en/ab/laws/regu/alta-reg-219-2006/latest/alta-reg-2319-2006.html (retrieved 29 March 2009). Among other differences, a GFC had the authority to "exercise any power of a faculty council that the General Faculties Council considers desirable to exercise."

80 Mount Royal Briefing Note 6, "The Regulation Concerning a New Academic Council Model for MRC," 2006; Mount Royal College, Annual Report, 2007–8, 21.

81 Alberta Advanced Education and Technology, Roles and Mandates Policy Framework for Alberta's Publicly Funded Advanced Education System, Nov. 2007, 9; Post-Secondary Learning Amending Act, 2008. The other categories: Polytechnic Institution (e.g., SAIT, NAIT) – offers apprenticeship, certificate, and diploma programs for technical vocations, some applied and baccalaureate degrees in specified fields; Comprehensive Community Institution – offers certificate and diploma programs, high-school completion for adults, apprenticeship, and may participate in collaborative baccalaureate programs; Independent Academic Institutions (private); and Specialized Arts and Culture Institutions (Alberta College of Arts & Design, Banff Centre).

82 Deborah Tetley, "Nursing program called a 'landmark' change," Calgary Herald, 15 Mar. 2007; Trevor Greenway, "MRC to offer university degree," Reflector, 22 Mar. 2007.

83 Tetley, "Nursing program called a 'landmark' change," Calgary Herald, 15 Mar. 2007.

84 Braid, "University nursing degrees kick off new era at Mount Royal," Calgary Herald, 15 Mar. 2007.

85 Calgary Herald, 16 Mar. 2007.

86 Sarah McGinnis, "MRC to spread nursing success," Calgary Herald, 10 Mar. 2008.

87 ERC: Minister Doug Horner to Cathy Williams, 30 Nov. 2007.

88 Editorial, "Lack of universities in Alberta cripples the promise of young adults and the province," Calgary Herald, 16 June 2008.

89 Email, Richard Roberts to author, 3 Sept. 2009: "The significant new money for the degrees will arrive as the student population increases in 2010 and 2011 with the full implementation of the new degrees. The grant funding for the five new degrees started at $1.1 million in year one (2008/09) and grows to $13.2 million by 2012/13. Nursing is in addition to this. The tuition fee revenue will also grow both because of the additional students and the additional fees we now charge for the degree programs."

90 On the funding situation, see: Alan Mattson, "University degrees on hold," Reflector, 17 Jan. 2008, "Masters in procrastinating," ibid., 14 Feb. 2008, and "What's happening with MRU," ibid., 3 April 2008. The board had approved the new degree programs

on 8 Feb. 2008. Alberta Media Advisory, 11 Apr. 2008; MRC Annual Report, 2007–8, 11.

91 MRC Annual Report, 2007–8, 15–16.

92 Ibid., 13–14.

93 Quoted in Braid, "Mount Royal College to finally get its wish," *Calgary Herald*, 5 Feb. 2009.

94 Braid, "Mount Royal College to finally get its wish," *Calgary Herald*, 5 Feb. 2009.

95 Ibid.

96 ERC: Letter, 15 July, Horner to Williams, signed back by Williams, 22 July 2009.

97 Order-in-Council 435-2009, modifying the Post-Secondary Learning Act (ss. 36.1, 85, 92, and 122). The college was then offering 43 degree, applied degree, university-transfer, diploma, and certificate programs, including 30 majors or specializations. There were 7 four-year baccalaureate degree programs: (i) Bachelor of Arts in anthropology, English, history, policy studies, psychology, sociology, and Spanish (as well as 17 minors in a wide range of fields); (ii) Bachelor of Arts in criminal justice; (iii) Bachelor of Business Administration in accounting, general management, human resources, and marketing; (iv) Bachelor of Communication in information design, journalism, and public relations; (v) Bachelor of Computer Information Systems; (vi) Bachelor of Nursing; (vii) Bachelor of Science in cellular and molecular biology, general science, geology and health science.

98 MRUA, Premier Ed Stelmach, "Mount Royal University Day," speech, 3 Sept. 2009.

99 "Old College Try Succeeds for MRC," Calgary Sun, 4 Sept. 2009.

100 Ibid.

101 MRC, OIAP, Trends-at-a-Glance, annual publication; Mount Royal College Self Study Report, 34.

102 OIAP, Mount Royal College Student Transfer Pattern Summary, Fall 2000 to Fall 2004 (June 2005).

103 Mount Royal Self-Study Report, 49.

104 Alan Mattson, "Women not a college minority, single ladies populate most of MRC campus," *Reflector*, 1 Feb. 2007.

105 MRC, OIAP, Mount Royal College, Trends-at-a-Glance, Sept. 2007.

106 MRC, OIAP, "Mount Royal College Today: Trends and Issues," Aug. 1988, 3; the annual reports gave most of the figures; ibid., Trends-at-a-Glance, Sept. 2007; also MRC Annual Report, 2007–08, 13, which breaks down the sources of the funding.

107 MRC Annual Report, 2007–08, 9, graph.

108 Mount Royal College Self-Study Report, 29.

109 Alan Mattson, "Build it, and they will come," *Reflector*, 29 Jan. 2009.

110 Florence Musselwhite and Emily-Jane Orford, *Encyclopedia of Music in Canada*, at www.thecanadianencyclopedia.com.

111 Paul Dornian, "Mount Royal boasts big, old music," *Calgary Herald*, 12 May 2005.

112 Deborah Tetley, "Music students U.S. bound," ibid., 10 May 2005. In that year, the two recipients of the very large scholarships were cellist Sonjoy Athparia (Columbia State University, Georgia), and cellist Estelle Choi (Yale University). "Former Calgarian shares prize," ibid., 10 May 2005: the Janeiki Trio, which included former Mount Royal student Arnold Choi,

won first prize in the 59th Alice Colman Chamber Ensemble Competition in Pasadena, California.

113 *Reflections*, Spring 2009, 32.

114 The city's contribution came last. Letter, Mayor Dave Bronconnier to Marshall, 31 July 2009, committing $8 million and indicating a willingness to go to $10.3 million if Mount Royal could not raise its full share of the funding.

115 *Calgary Herald*, 2 July 2004; for the crowd estimate, see Dornian, ibid., 12 May 2005.

116 Ibid., 12 Oct. 2004.

117 *Journal 3009*, 6 Mar. 1990.

118 *Reflections*, Spring 2008, Spring 2009. Among the graduates were Heather Bailey, who later graduated from the University of Alberta and played a role in the Canadian film *Passchendaele*, and a recurring role in the CBC series *Heartland*; Francis Damberger (university-transfer 1977), co-producer of *Passchendaele* along with many other professional accomplishments; Haysim Kadri (1996), who played the Sheriff of Nottingham in Robin Hood for Alberta Theatre Projects; and Alan Van Sprang (1992), who acted in a wide variety of TV and film productions.

119 ERC: AUCC, Visiting Committee, Report, Oct. 2008.

120 ERC: Letter , Christine Tausig Ford, Corporate Secretary, AUCC, to Marshall, 28 October 2009.

121 MRC, *Changing the Face of Education: The Centennial Campaign for Mount Royal*, 2009.

122 MRC Annual Report, 2007–8, 17.

123 ERC: Marshall, "Improving, Assessing and Demonstrating Student Learning," 6.

124 Mount Royal College Foundation, Financial Statements, 30 June 2008.

CHAPTER 11: THE FINAL TRANSFORMATION

1 James M. Pitsula, *As One Who Serves: The Making of the University of Regina* (Montreal/Kingston: McGill-Queen's University Press, 2006), 391.

2 Gawreluck, "Organizational Culture," 318.

3 See Deborah Floyd, Michael L. Skolnik, and Kenneth P. Walker, eds., *The Community College Baccalaureate: Emerging Trends and Policy Issues* (Sterling, VA: Stylus Publishing, 2005). For a general overview of higher education, see Charles M. Beach, Robin W. Boadway, and Marvin McInnis. *Higher Education in Canada* (Montreal/Kingston: McGill Queen's University Press, 2005).

4 Reid, *Mount Allison University: A History to 1963* 1: 286.

5 Quoted in Reid, "Beyond the Democratic Intellect: The Scottish Example and University Reform in Canada's Maritime Provinces, 1870–1933," in Axelrod and Reid, eds., *Youth, University and Canadian Society,* 286.

6 Ibid.

7 On the debate and events leading to this outcome, see Reid, *Mount Allison University* 2: 282–351. For the story of nearby Dalhousie University, see Peter B. Waite, *The Lives of Dalhousie University*, 1: *Lord Dalhousie's College* (Montreal: McGill-Queen's University Press, 1994), 2: *The Old College Transformed* (Montreal: McGill-Queen's University Press, 1998).

8 Christine Storm, ed., *Liberal Education and the Small University in Canada* (Montreal/Kingston: McGill-Queen's University Press, 1996), publisher's note.

9   Pitsula, *An Act of Faith*, 60–61. In Manitoba, Brandon College was also preparing for major changes. See C. G. Stone and F. J. Garnett. *Brandon College: A History 1899–1967* (Brandon: Brandon University, 1969)

10 Ibid., 126–50.

11 K. Murray Knuttala, *Heritage and Hope: The University of Regina into the 21st Century* (Regina: Canadian Plains Research Center, University of Regina, 2004).

12 Interview (Baker), 9 July 2010; also Marshall, "Revitalizing University Education," paper delivered to the Association of Universities and Colleges of Canada workshop entitled "Thinking Forward/Moving Ahead," 14 April 2010.

13 Quoted in Jeremy Klaszus, "MRU still en route," *Reflector*, 15 September 2005.

14 See the article by the president of SAMRC, Jackie Chuckrey, "MRC remains on track after name battle," *Reflector*, 19 January 2006.

15 Michael Skolnik, email to author, 14 June 2010.

16 Consider, for example, the admission requirements for Conestoga's Bachelor of Technology in Manufacturing Systems Engineering: "A minimum of six (6) Grade 12 courses including five (5) required university preparation (U) courses and one additional university (U) or university/college (M) course. The following Grade 12 U courses, or equivalent, are required: Grade 12 compulsory English (ENG4U), Chemistry (SCH4U), Physics (SPH4U), and Grade 12 Math – Calculus and Vectors (MCV4U) or Advanced Functions and Introductory Calculus (MCB4U), plus one of the following: Advanced Functions (MHF4U) or Geometry and Discrete Mathematics (MGA4U) or Mathematics of Data Management (MDM4U)." /www.conestogac.on.ca/fulltime/programoverview.jsp?SchoolID=2&ProgramCode=1066C&v=1001 (retrieved 18 June 2010).

17 Jamil Salmi, *The Challenge of Establishing World-Class Universities* (Washington, DC: World Bank, 2009); see also his earlier *Constructing Knowledge Societies: New Challenges for Tertiary Education* (Washington, DC: World Bank, 2002).

18 David Jay Bercuson, *Petrified Campus: The Crisis in Canada's Universities* (Toronto: Random Canada, 1997); and Bercuson, Robert Bothwell, and J. L. Granatstein, *The Great Brain Robbery: Canada's Universities on the Road to Ruin* (Toronto: McClelland and Stewart, 1984). Perhaps the earliest indictment was that of Hilda Neatby, *So Little for the Mind: An Indictment of Canadian Education* (Toronto: Clark-Irwin, 1953). See also: Jeff Rybak, *What's Wrong with University, and How to Make it Work for You Anyway* (Toronto: ECW Press, 2007); J. Côté and A. Allahar. *Ivory Tower Blues: A University System in Crisis* (Toronto: University of Toronto Press, 2007); and Hughes J. Christensen, and J. Mighty, eds., *Taking Stock: Research on Teaching and Learning in Higher Education* (Montreal, Kingston: Queen's Policy Studies Services, McGill-Queen's University Press, 2010).

19 Dave Marshall, "Improving, Assessing and Demonstrating Student Learning," remarks to the 12th Transatlantic Dialogue, 27 June 2010.

20 http://v1.theglobeandmail.com/partners/free/cur_2010/cur_ezine2011.html.

21 Quoted in Baker and Miosi, "The Quality Assurance of Degree Education in Canada."

22 Marshall, "Improving, Assessing and Demonstrating Student Learning," 4.

23 Lee A. Swanson, "Value Perceptions as Influences upon Engagement," *Innovative Higher Education* 34 (2009): 278.

24 Thomas C. Pocklington and Alan Tupper, *No Place to Learn: Why Universities Aren't Working* (Vancouver: University of British Columbia Press, 2002), 6, 198.

25 For a thoughtful review of the situation, see Derek Bok, *Our Underachieving Colleges: A Candid Look at How Much Students Learn and Why They Should Be Learning More* (Princeton: Princeton University Press, 2006).

26 After I wrote this, I discovered that Mount Royal had already invited Light to campus for workshops. See Richard J. Light, *Making the Most of College: Students Speak Their Minds* (Cambridge: Harvard University Press, 2001).

27 See www.nsse.iub.edu; and www.collegiatelearnngassessment. org. Both sites include studies of uses made of their instruments by institutions, e.g., Jeffrey Steedle, *Achieving Institutional Value-Added Score Estimation* (draft 1 June 2009).

28 Loren Pope, *Colleges That Change Lives: 40 Schools That Will Change the Way You Think About College* (New York: Penguin Books, 2nd Rev. ed., 2006), 7. There is a burgeoning literature on "student engagement," including George D. Kuh, *High-Impact Practices: What They Are, Who Has Access to Them, and Why They Matter* (Washington, DC: Association of American Colleges and Universities, 2008). Beyond improving the learning of all students, the idea has become central to efforts to raise the educational performance of very diverse student bodies: see Shaun R. Harper and Stephen. J. Quaye, eds., *Student Engagement in Higher Education* (New York and London: Routledge, 2009).

29 Michael Skolnik, email to author, 14 June 2010. For internal views, see Murray Ross, *Those Ten Years, 1960–1970: The President's Report on the First Decade of York University* (Toronto: York University, 1970); and, for his broader reflections based on his experience, *The University: The Anatomy of Academe* (New York: McGraw-Hill, 1976); also inside York, from other perspectives, see Michiel Horn, *York University: The Way Must Be Tried* (Montreal: Published for York University by McGill-Queen's University Press, 2009); and John Saywell, *Someone to Teach Them: York and the Great University Explosion, 1960–1973* (Toronto: University of Toronto Press, 2008). The then president of the University of Toronto described the "vigorous and uncompromising idealism" that was present at its start: Claude T. Bissell, *Halfway Up Parnassus: A Personal Account of the University of Toronto, 1932–1971* (Toronto: University of Toronto Press, 1974), 67–70. See also Bissell, ed., *Canada's Crisis in Higher Education* (Toronto: University of Toronto Press, 1957). For the story of two other "new" universities in this period, see A. O. C. Cole, *Trent: The Making of a University, 1957–1987* (Trent: Trent University, 1992), and Kenneth McLauchlan, *Waterloo: The Unconventional Founding of an Unconventional University* (Waterloo: University of Waterloo, 1997).

30 Marshall interview (Baker), 8 July 2012.

31 "Quality assurance" section of CMEC website, http://www.cmec.ca.

32 Ian Clark, Greg Moran, Michael L. Skolnik, and David Trick, *Academic Transformation: the Forces Reshaping Higher Education in Ontario* (Kingston: Queen's School of Policy Studies, 2009), chap. 7: "Conclusions and Implications for the Future," 175–203; also Howard C. Clark, *Growth and Governance of Canadian Universities: An Insider's View* (Vancouver: University of British Columbia Press, 2003), a plea for government action.

33 See Paul Axelrod, *Scholars and Dollars: Politics, Economics, and the Universities of Ontario, 1945–1980; Values in Conflict: The University, the Marketplace, and the Trials of Liberal Education;* and "Challenges to Liberal Education in An Age of Uncertainty," *Historical Studies in Education/Revue de l'histoire de l'éducation* 10, nos. 1–2 (1998): 1–19. See also Janice Newson and Ian Currie,

The University and Globalization: Critical Perspectives (Thousand Oaks, CA: Sage Publications, 1998); Sheryl Bond, *A New World of Knowledge: Canadian Universities and Globalization* (Ottawa: International Development Research Centre, 1999); Howard R. Woodhouse, *Selling Out: Academic Freedom and the Corporate Market* (Montreal, Ithaca: McGill-Queen's University Press, 2009); and Roopa Desai Trilokekar, Glen A. Jones, and Adrian Shubert. *Canada's Universities Go Global* (Toronto: J. Lorimer & Co., 2009).

34   Michael L. Skolnik, "Reflections on the Difficulty of Balancing the University's Economic and Non-Economic Objectives in a Period When its Economic Role Is Valued," in Jones, McCarney, and Skolnik, eds., *Creating Knowledge, Strengthening Nations*, 121–22.

35   Hayden, *Seeking the Balance*, 292.

36   Kerby, PR, 5 July 1912.

37   Alison Wolf, *Does Education Matter? Myths about Education and Economic Growth* (Penguin, 2002), 254.

WORKS CITED

I. ARCHIVES

Mount Royal provides a case study in how not to handle institutional records. The transformation from private to public institution, followed by the relocation from the downtown campus to the Lincoln Park campus, led to old files and artefacts being stored in a room for which no one was responsible. Materials were taken from the room for particular projects and were either never returned, returned but not filed, or misfiled. There are gaps, including the absence of the records of the board of governors during most of the first decade. In 1987 the president consolidated the files of the board of governors, Academic Council, and senior administration in a central repository (now called the Executive Records Centre), had all files photographed (microfiche), and introduced a policy on records management that included the annual reproduction of all new materials. That policy was abandoned in 2007, pending adoption of an electronic documents management system that has not materialized. That central repository, the Executive Records Centre, unless otherwise indicated, holds almost all of the files and correspondence of the board of governors, Academic Council and senior administration referred to in this book.

In 2005 Dr. Patricia Roome, a member of the history department, became the first Director of the Archives (now the Mount Royal University Archives, MRUA); she has been chasing missing records, handling donations of materials, and encouraging reluctant administrators and secretaries to forward materials of historical interest. Though there are plans to integrate the older holdings of the Executive Records Centre and the Mount Royal University Archives,

the unification remains only a hope as this book goes to publication. Items cited in this book and held in the Archives are preceded by "MRUA" in the notes. The "administrative" files bear on a wide variety of matters, mainly in the 1960s and 1970s, including planning for the Lincoln Park campus, the proposed merger with the Alberta Vocational Centre-Calgary in the 1970s, occasional files on relations with the Mount Royal Faculty Association, the alumni association, and program development and review committees. There is also a large collection of photographs from the 1970s and early 1980s. The Archives also contain student publications. These are the student publications cited in or consulted for this book: *Arpi-Huba*, 1938–39 (yearbook); *Bug House Bugle*, 1921 (?); *Collews*, 1957–59; *Inkspot*, 1955–57; *Journal 3009* (journalism program); *Nova*, 1981–82 (yearbook); *Pennant*, 1954–55; *206 Peeper*, 1953; *Reflector/The Reflector*, 1965–present; *Royal Reflector*, 1960–1964; *Skylines*; *Tatler*, 1932; *Tattler*, 1953–54; *The Acquaintance*, 1954–55; *The Pennant*, 1954–55; *The Royal Reflector*, 1960–64; *The Chinook*, 1911–20, 1926, 1928, 1939–40; *The Scratch Pad*, 1942–44; *Varshicom*, 1940–65, 1967 (yearbook). College publications include *Carillon; Imprint*, 1993–95; *International Update*, 2002; *MRC News; Reflections: A Newsletter for Alumni of Mount Royal College; Dispatch, published for Alumni and Friends of the College*, 1984; *Reporter; Second Tuesday; Toward '72; Weekly Staff Bulletin*. There also Conservatory publications, including *Cadenza*, 1983–1991, and *Conservatory Notes* occasionally thereafter, plus some records of musical performances.

United Church of Canada/Victoria University Archives

Since 1940 the archives of the United Church of Canada and its Methodist, Presbyterian, and Congregationalist antecedents have been located at Victoria University on the University of Toronto campus. In 1985, the archives of Victoria University and its antecedents (Upper Canada Academy, 1829–40, Victoria College, 1840–90), were moved to the same location and are jointly managed and funded by the University and the United Church. The archives contain records bearing on the affiliated educational institutions, including Mount Royal College, notably the files of the church's Board of Education. The chief correspondence files for the college during its Methodist phase are found in: Board of Education Accession No.78.103C, Box 2 (of 15): Minutes, Outgoing Correspondence: Minute Book, 1910–1921, and Minute Book, 1921–1926 (the minutes for meetings of the Methodist Education Society's Executive Committee and annual meeting); Box 12: Incoming correspondence, 1911–1912; Box 13, Incoming correspondence, 1913–1926; and Box 14, unorganized material, notably Folders 6 (1921 document on Mount Royal) and 4 (Methodist Institutions and Assets, June 1915). The files of the Alberta Conference of the United and Methodist churches are in the Provincial Archives of Alberta (PAA), with some holdings at St. Stephen's College.

The United Church of Canada/Victoria University Archives also contain the publications of the United and Methodist churches, including the reports and minutes of their annual meetings (*Journal of Proceedings of the Methodist General Conference, Journal of the Methodist General Conference*, later *Record of Proceedings*), annual reports (*Methodist Yearbook*), and special reports, including the following:

1906   Methodist Church of Canada. Department of Temperance and Moral Reform, *Report of Committee on Sociological Questions.*

1911   Minutes of the Proceedings of the Eighth Session of the Alberta Conference of the Methodist Church, held in the Central Methodist Church, Calgary, Alberta, from Thursday, May 25th to Wednesday, May 31st, 1911.

1912   Minutes of the Ninth Session of the Alberta Conference of the Methodist Church, held in the McDougall Methodist Church, Edmonton, From May 31st to June 5th, 1912.

1918   Methodist Church of Canada. Army and Navy Board, *The Church, the War and Patriotism: Report* .

1918   Methodist Church of Canada. General Board of Sunday Schools and Young People's Societies, *The Constitution of the Local Sunday Sch*ool.

1921   Massey Foundation. *Report of the Massey Foundation Commission on the Secondary Schools and Colleges of the Methodist Church of Canada.* Published by the Massey Foundation with the Authority of the Board of Education of the Methodist Church.

1922   Methodist Church of Canada. *Why the Church Maintains Schools and Colleges.* Toronto, 1922.

1926   The United Church of Canada, Record of Proceedings of the Second Meeting of the Alberta Conference of the United Church of Canada, May 17th–24th, 1926, McDougall United Church, Edmonton, Alberta,

1939   The United Church of Canada*, Reports and Agenda, Fifth Meeting of the Board of Christian Education, Toronto, Ontario, April 18th to 20th, 1939.*

1942   The United Church of Canada, Board of Christian Education, "The Educational Policy of the Church: A Statement Approved by the Board of Regents of United College, Winnipeg, for Submission to the Special Committee on the Theological Colleges." 85.051C, Box 68, file 6.

Provincial Archives of Alberta (PAA)

The Provincial Archives of Alberta (PAA) hold the papers of the Methodist and later United Churches for the Alberta Conference of those bodies, including the Minutes of the annual sessions of the Alberta Conference of the Methodist Church, the files of government departments that have been transferred for accessibility to the public, and, among other things, the remaining papers of George Kerby and his wife, Emily Spencer Kerby. The Archives also contain government reports and commissions, though not all have been transferred from government repositories. Among those of particular interest to Mount Royal College were the files of the Colleges Commission. The Provincial Archives also contain the Records of Private and Vocational schools, 1889–1967. The Department of Education produced an *Annual Report* which contains a few remarks on Mount Royal College.

University of Alberta Archives (UAA)

The University of Alberta archives contain correspondence and documents relating to the history of Mount Royal College, notably including the affiliation agreement between Mount Royal College and the University from the 1920s through the 1950s.

Glenbow-Alberta Institute Archives

The Glenbow-Alberta Institute holdings include many items of both direct and indirect interest to the history of Mount Royal. These include newspaper clippings, personal papers, interviews and business records. The Institute holds "fonds" consisting of documents donated by or related to Jascha Galperin, Leonard Leacock, Cyril Mossop, Mary Munn, and George, Norma Piper Pocaterra, and Leona Paterson, all of the Conservatory. The documents include L. Chrumka's "History of the Speech Arts Program at Mount Royal College." 1980. The Institute also holds the central records of some groups related to the Mount Royal story – e.g., the Alberta Federation of Home and School Association, Minutes 1922–1979; Central United Church Minutes, Correspondence and Board Reports, 1883–1975; and the files of the Cushing brother businesses.

Calgary Public Library

The public library contains many works on the history of Calgary and Alberta and a collection of newspaper clippings related to Mount Royal College.

2. ARTICLES AND BOOK CHAPTERS

Allen, Richard. "The Social Gospel and the Reform Tradition in Canada, 1890–1928." *Canadian Historical Review* 49 (1968): 381–99.

Alexander, W. H. "In the Beginning (University of Alberta)." *Alberta Historical Review* 8, no. 2 (1960): 15–20.

Andrews, Michael B., Edward A. Holdaway, and Gordon L. Mowat. "Post-secondary Education in Alberta since 1945." In Jones, ed., *Higher Education in Canada: Different Systems, Different Perspectives*, 59-93.

Atkins, Laura, Colleen Nicoll and Jody Stewart. "Turner Valley Oilfields." *Alberta History* 32 (1984): 9–18.

Axelrod, Paul. "Challenges to Liberal Education in an Age of Uncertainty." *Historical Studies in Education/Revue de l'histoire de l'éducation* 10, nos. 1–2 (1998): 1–19.

Baker, Donald N., and Terry Miosi. "The Quality Assurance of Degree Education in Canada." Research in Comparative and International Education, "Evaluation in Higher Education" 5, no. 1 (2010): 32–57.

Barrett, J. A. "This is Mount Royal College." *Canadian Architect* (March 1974).

Barrett, J. A. "Mount Royal College." *College and University Business* (July 1973).

Barrington, Gail Vallance. "Do Community College Presidents and Government Officials Share the Same Perspective*?*" *Canadian Journal of Higher Education* 12, no. 1 (1982): 43–55.

Bedford, Judy. "Prostitution in Calgary, 1905–1914." *Alberta History* 29, no. 2 (1981): 1–11.

Bischoff, Dale P. "Extension of Authority to Confer Bachelor of Education degrees in Alberta." *Alberta Journal of Educational Research* 47, no. 1 (2001): 40–56.

Bliss, J. M. "The Methodist Church and World War I." *Canadian Historical Review* 49 (1968): 213–33.

Brooks, W. "The Uniqueness of Western Canadian Methodism, 1840–1925." *Journal of the Canadian Church Historical Society* 19 (1977): 57–74.

Bruneau, William A. "'Quiet Flow the Dons': Towards an International History of the Professoriate." In Stortz and Panayotidis, eds. *Historical Identities: The Professoriate in Canada,* 31–60.

Chapman, Terry L. "Women, Sex and Marriage in Western Canada, 1890–1920." *Alberta History* 33, no. 4 (1985): 1–12.

Child, A. H. "The Ryerson Tradition in Western Canada." In McDonald and Chaiton, *Egerton Ryerson and His Times,* 279–301.

Coats, Douglas. "Calgary: the Private Schools, 1899–1916." In Rasporich and Klassen, *Frontier Calgary*, 141–52.

Collett, W. J. "Dr. George W. Kerby." In Foran and James, *Citymakers: Calgarians after the Frontier*, 281–89.

Dennison, John D. "The Community College in Canada: An Educational Innovation." In Wilson, *Canadian Education in the 1980s*, 213–32.

Dennison, John D. "University Transfer Programs in the Community College." *Canadian Journal of Higher Education* 8, no. 2 (1978): 27–38.

Dennison, John D., and Robert Harris. "Governing Boards in Postsecondary Education." *Canadian Journal of Higher Education* 14, no. 2 (1984): 13–31.

Dennison, John D. "The Case for Democratic Governance in Canada's Community Colleges." *Interchange* 25, no. 1 (1994): 25–37.

Emery, G.N. "Ontario Denied: The Methodist Church on the Prairies, 1896–1914." In Armstrong, Stevenson and Wilson, *Aspects of Nineteenth Century Ontario*, 312–26.

Evans, Simon. "Spatial Aspects of the Cattle Kingdom: The First Decade, 1882–1892." In Rasporich and Klassen, *Frontier Calgary*, 41–56.

Emery, G. N. "The Origins of Canadian Methodist Involvement in the Social Gospel Movement, 1890–1914." *Journal of Canadian Church Historical Society* 19 (1977): 104–118.

———. "Ontario Denied: The Methodist Church on the Prairies, 1896–1914." In F. H. Armstrong, A. Stevenson, and J. D. Wilson, *Aspects of Nineteenth Century Ontario*, 312–26.

Ewell, Peter T., and D. Jones(1994). "Pointing the Way: Indicators as Policy Tools in Higher Education." In S. Ruppert (ed.), *Charting Higher Education Accountability: A Source Book on State Level Performance Indicators*. Denver: Education Commission of the States, n.d.

Fast, R. G. "Teaching in the Alberta Public College." *Challenge in Educational Administration* 10 (1970–71).

Fleming, J. Christopher. "Faculty Expectations for College Presidents." *Journal of Higher Education*, 81, no. 3 (2010): 251–83.

Foran, Max. "Land Speculation and Urban Development in Calgary, 1994–1912." In Rasporich and Klassen, *Frontier Calgary*, 203–20.

———. "William J. Tregillus." *Dictionary of Canadian Biography*. Toronto: University of Toronto 14: 1006–8.

Freedman, S. "University Government." *C.A.U.T. Bulletin* 13, no. 1 (1964): 14–26.

French, Goldwin. "Egerton Ryerson and the Methodist Model for Upper Canada." In McDonald and Chaiton, *Egerton Ryerson and His Times*, 45–58.

———. "Methodism and Education in the Atlantic Provinces, 1800–1974." In Scobie and Grant, *The Contribution of Methodism to Atlantic Canada,* 152–53.

Garden, John H. "Mount Royal Junior College." In Morrison and Morrison, *Calgary, 1875–1950: A Souvenir of Calgary's Seventy-Fifth Anniversary*, 68.

Gauvreau, Michael. "War Culture and the Problem of Religious Certainty: Methodist and Presbyterian Colleges 1914–30." *Journal of Canadian Church History* 32 (1987): 12–31.

Goyan, Paul, and Glen A. Jones. "Degrees in Canadian Higher Education." *International Higher Education* 16 (Summer 1999). Gunderson, H. "Decision to Set up Community College Delayed at Least One Year in Alberta." *Canadian University* 2 (1965).

Gunning, Boyd. "Sooner Scene." *Sooners Magazine* 30, no. (January 1958): 1–2.

Harris, Walter E., and Edward A. Holdaway. "Systematic Reviews of University Programs and Units." *Canadian Journal of Higher Education* 13, no. 3 (1983): 55–76.

James, Cathy. "Practical Diversions and Educational Amusements: Evangelia House and the Advent of Canada's Settlement Movement, 1902–1909." *Historical Studies in Education/Revue de l'histoire de l'éducation*, 10, nos. 1–2 (2008): 48–66.

Jasen, Patricia. "'In Pursuit of Human Values (or Laugh When You Say That)': The Student Critique of the Arts Curriculum in the 1960s." In Axelrod and Reid, *Youth, University and Canadian Society*, 254–62.

Johns, W. H. "A Junior Community College as the University Sees It." *The Alberta School Trustee,* February 1956.

Jones, D. C. "School and Social Disintegration in the Alberta Dry Belt of the Twenties." *Prairie Forum* 3 (1978): 1–19.

Jones, D. C. "A Strange Heartland: The Alberta Dry Belt and Schools in the Depression." In D. Francis and H. Ganzevoort, eds., *The Dirty Thirties in Prairie Canada* (Vancouver, 1980), 89–110.

Jones, D.C. "We Can't Live On Air All The Time: Country Life and the Prairie Child." In P. T. Rooke and R. L. Schnell, eds., *Studies in Childhood History: A Canadian Perspective* (Calgary: Detselig, 1982), 185–203.

Kachur, Jerrold. "Orchestrating Delusions: Ideology and Consent in Alberta." In Harrison and Kachur, *Contested Classrooms*, 59–74.

Kerby, George W. "Biography." *Alberta Past and Present* 2 (1934): 12–17.

———. "The Hope of the Future the Inspiration of the Present." *Acta Victoriana* [Cobourg, Ontario], January 1887, 7–9.

———. "The Parting of the Ways—Or What Would Jesus Do?" *The Canadian Epworth Era*, February 1899, 36.

———. "The Parting of the Ways, or Life Stories of Young Men." *The Canadian Epworth Era*, July 1901, 202–03, and October 1901, 293–94.

———. "The Cavan Blazers." *The Canadian Epworth Era*, May 1903, 134–37.

———. "The Pastor and the Boys, or How One Pastor Solved the Boy Problem." *The Canadian Epworth Era*, July 1903,197.

———. "The Boy and the Birds." *The Christian Guardian*, 3 June 1903,

Kneebone, Ronald D. "From Feast to Famine: The Evolution of Budget Rules in Alberta." Calgary: Institute for Advanced Policy Research, University of Calgary, 1 August 2005.

Knight, Jane. "Internationalization: Elements and Checkpoints." Canadian Bureau for International Education Research Paper 7, 1994, www.cbie.ca/english/media_research2_e.htm

———. "Taking the Pulse: Monitoring the Quality and Progress of Internationalization." Canadian Bureau for Education Research Millennium Series, No. 2, 2000, http://www.cbie.ca/english/media_research1_e.htm

Korinek, Valerie J. "No Women Need Apply: The Ordination of Women in the United Church, 1918–65." *Canadian Historical Review* 74 (1993): 473–509.

Lavalee, Omar. "Canadian Pacific." In Stephen Wilk, ed., with the assistance of Valerie Jobson and Redvers Perry, *100 Years of Nose Creek Valley History (* Calgary: Nose Creek Historical Society, 1997), 114.

Lazerson, M. "Canadian Educational Historiography: Some Observations." In McDonald and Chaiton,, *Egerton Ryerson and His Times*, 3–6.

Lears, Jackson. "Luck and Pluck in American Culture." *Chronicle of Higher Education: The Chronicle Review*, 24 Jan. 2003, 49, 20: B15.

MacDonald, Robert. "The Methodist Church in Alberta during the First World War." *Papers*, Canadian Methodist Historical Society, Volio, 1995, 145–69.

MacEwan, Grant. "A College and Its Founder." In *Calgary Cavalcade: From Fort to Fortune*. Edmonton: The Institute of Applied Art Ltd., 1958, 149–55.

MacIntosh, D. F., and J. C. Nelson. "The New Universities Act in the Province of Alberta." *C.A.U.T. Bulletin* 16 (1967).

Macpherson, R. G. M., "Alexander Scott Carter." *Heraldry in Canada*, Sept. 1990, http://www.heraldry.ca/art/painter/carter/carter.htm.

Magney, W. H. "The Methodist Church and the National Gospel, 1884–1914." *Committee on Archives United Church of Canada Bulletin*, 1968.

Marshall, David G. "Access to Degrees in the Knowledge Economy." Options Politiques (August 2004): 76–82.

———. "Degree Accreditation in Canada: The Degree-Recognition Issue." Canadian Journal of Higher Education 34, no. 2 (2004): 69–96.

———. "Differentiation by Degrees: System Design and the Changing Undergraduate Environment in Canada." Canadian Journal of Higher Education 38, no. 3 (2008): 1–20.

———. "What's It Worth? The Tiering of Canadian Degrees." Education Canada 46, no. 1 (2005): 55–57.

McGinnis, J. P. Dickin. "Birth to Boom to Bust: Building in Calgary, 1875–1914." In Rasporich and Klassen, Frontier Calgary, 6–19.

Meekison, Peter. "Alberta and the Constitution." In Tupper and Gibbins, *Government and Politics in Alberta*, 247–68.

Millar, E. "What Is a University Anyways?" *Macleans*. 29 November 2007.

Morton, W. L. "University Government: The Alienation of the Administration." *C.A.U.T. Bulletin* 9 (1961): 8–14.

———. "The Evolution of University Government in Canada." *Canadian Forum* 41 (1962): 243–47.

Neu, Dean. "Re-Investment Fables: Educational Finances in Alberta." In Harrison and Kachur, *Contested Schools*, 75–84.

Newson, Janice. "The Corporate-Linked University: From Social Project to Market Force." Canadian Journal of Communication 23, no 1 (1998), http://www.cjc-online.ca/index.php/journal/issue/view/83].

Owen, Michael. "'By Contact and by Contagion': George W. Kerby, 1860–1944, *Vitae Scholasticae: The Bulletin of Educational Biography* 10, nos. 1–2 (1991): 131–57.

———. "Do Women Really Count? Emily Spencer Kerby—Early Twentieth-Century Alberta Feminist." *Papers*, Canadian Methodist Historical Society 10 (1995): 170–87.

———. "Rev. Dr. George W. Kerby: Evangelist for the Home and School." *Alberta Journal of Educational Research* 39, no. 4 (1933): 477–93.

Patterson, R. S. "Progressive Education: Impetus to Educational Change in Alberta and Saskatchewan." In H. Palmer and D. Smith, eds., *The New Provinces: Alberta and Saskatchewan 1905–1980: 12th Western Canada Studies Conference*. Vancouver: Tantalus Research, 1980, 173–98.

Pedersen, Diana. "'The Call to Service': The YWCA and the Canadian College Woman, 1886–1920." In Axelrod and Reid, *Youth, University and Society: Essays in the Social History of Higher Education*, 187–89.

Perry, J. F. "Central Methodist Church Before World War One." In Klassen and Rasporich, *Frontier Calgary*, 181–89.

Peters, Frank. "Deep and Brutal: Funding Cuts to Education in Alberta." In Harrison and Kachur, *Contested Classrooms*, 85–98.

Pitsula, James M. "Cicero Versus Socrates: The Liberal Arts Debate in the 1960s at the University of Saskatchewan, Regina Campus." *Historical Studies in Education/Revue de l'Histoire de l'Education* (Spring 2003): 101–29.

———. "University of Regina." *Encyclopedia of Saskatchewan*. http://esask.uregina.ca/entry/university_of_regina. html.

Prokop, Manfred. "Canadianization of Immigrant Children: Role of the Rural Elementary School in Alberta, 1900–1930." *Alberta History* 37 (1989): 1–10.

Rasporich, A. W. "A Community in Search of a University: The University of Calgary's Pre-History, 1912–1966." *Alberta History* 54 (2006): 2–11.

Reineberg, Holt. "Women's Suffrage in Alberta." *Alberta History* 39 (1991): 25–31.

Roome, Patricia. "Emily Spencer Kerby: Discovering a Legacy." *Journal/United Church* 14, no. 1 (2001): 1–3.

———. "Alexander C. Rutherford, 1905–1910." In Rennie, *Alberta's Premiers*, 12–14.

Salterio, Earl J. "A Glimpse of Higher Learning: Alberta, 1994." *Canadian Numismatic Journal* (1995): 23–27 (on Mount Royal's 1934–35 General Proficiency Medal).

Scarfe, Brian L. "The Federal Budget and Energy Program, Oct. 28th, 1980: A Review." Winter 1981, http://economics.ca/cgi/jab?journal=cpp&view=v07n1/CPPv07n1p001.pdf, 5–6.

Semple, Neil. "The Nurture and Admonition of the Lord: Nineteenth Century Methodism's Response to Childhood." *Social History* 13 (1981): 157–75.

Sheehan, Nancy. "Temperance, Education and the WCTU in Alberta, 1905–1930." *Journal of Educational Thought* 14 (1980): 108–24.

———. "The WCTU on the Prairies, 1886–1930: An Alberta-Saskatchewan Comparison." *Prairie Forum* 6 (1981): 17–34.

Skolnik, Michael L. "Putting it All Together: Viewing Canadian Higher Education from a Collection of Jurisdiction-Based Perspectives." In Jones, *Higher Education in Canada*, 325–42.

———. "Should the CAATs Grant Degrees? *College Quarterly* 3 (1994): 2. http://www.senecac.on.ca/quarterly/1995-vol03-num02-winter/index.html.

———. "Reflections on the Difficulty of Balancing the University's Economic and Non-Economic Objectives in Period when its Economic Role is Valued." In Jones, McCartney, and Skolnik, *Creating Knowledge, Strengthening Nations*, 106–26.

——— and Glen A. Jones, "Arrangements for Coordination between University and College Sectors in Canadian Province." *Canadian Journal of Higher Education* 23, no. 1 (1993): 56–73.

Slaughter, Sheila. "From Serving Students to Serving the Economy: Changing Expectations of Faculty Performance." *Higher Education* 14 (1985): 41–56.

Stamp, Robert M. "Response to Urban Growth: The Bureaucratization of Public Education in Calgary, 1884–1914." In Klassen and Raspovich, *Frontier Calgary*, 153–68.

Stanley, George F. G. "From New Brunswick to Calgary: R. B. Bennett in Retrospect." In Rasporich and Klassen, *Frontier Calgary*, 242–66.

———. "The Naming of Calgary." *Alberta History* 23, no. 3 (1975).

Stortz, Paul and E. Lisa Panayotidis. "Introduction: 'Have You Ever Looked into a Professor's Soul?'": Historical Constructions of the Professoriate in Canada." In Stortz and Panayotidis, eds., *Historical Identities*, 3–28.

Swanson, Lee A. "Value Perceptions as Influences upon Engagement." *Innovative Higher Education* 34 (2009): 269–281.

Thomas, L. G. "The Church of England and Higher Education in the Prairie West before 1914." *Journal of the Canadian Church History Society* 3 (1956): 1–11.

Voisey, Paul. "In Search of Wealth and Status: An Economic and Social Study of Entrepreneurs in Early Calgary." In Rasporich and Klassen, *Frontier Calgary*, 221–41.

———. "The Urbanization of the Canadian Prairies, 1871–1916." *Histoire Sociale – Social History* 8 (1975): 75–101.

———. "The 'Votes for Women' Movement." 18 *Histoire Sociale – Social History* 23, no. 3 (1975): 75–101.

Well, C. V. "Alberta Colleges: A Product of Their Times." *College Canada* 2 (1977).

Weston, Phyllis E. "A University for Calgary." *Alberta Historical Review* 11, no. 3 (1963): 1–11.

Wieler, D. "Regional commitment and the community college at Grande Prairie Regional College." *College Canada* 4 (March 1979): 10–11.

White, Anne. "Emily Spencer Kerby: Pioneer Club Woman, Educator, and Activist." *Alberta History* 46, no. 3 (1998): 2–9.

Whitefield, George. *Works* (1771). Cited in *The Compact Edition of the Oxford English Dictionary*. Oxford: Oxford University Press, 1971.

Wilson, J. "Some Observations on Recent Trends in Canadian Educational History." In J. Wilson, ed., *An Imperfect Past: Education and Society in Canadian History*. Vancouver: University of British Columbia Press, 1985. 7–29.

Wilson, J. L. "Agrarian Ideals for Canadian Youth, Alberta, 1916–1936: A Case Study." In Chaiton and McDonald, *Canadian Schools and Canadian Identity*. Toronto: Gage, 1977. 133–49.

Winspear, A. D. "Bishop Pinkham College, Calgary's First." *Golden West* (March–April, 1966).

CATCH THE GLEAM

Young People of All Ages: Sports, Schools and Youth Groups in Calgary. Calgary: Century Calgary Publications, 1975, "Mount Royal College." 226–29.

n.a. "Grant MacEwan College." *College Canada* 2 (September 1977): 7.

n.a. "Mount Royal College." *College Canada* 3 (April 1978): 1, 11.

n.a. "Old Sun College." *College Canada* 3 (April 1978): 1, 8.

n.a. "Red Deer College: Serving Central Alberta." *College Canada* 2 (October 1977): 1.

n.a. "Canadian College Prepares Students to Become O.U. Engineers." *Sooners Magazine* 29:7 (March 1957), 14–15.

3. BOOKS

Airhart, Phyllis D. *Serving the Present Age: Revivalism, Progressivism, and the Methodist Tradition in Canada.* Montreal/Kingston: McGill-Queen's University Press, 1992.

Alberta College of Art. *Founders of the Alberta College of Art.* Calgary: Alberta College of Art, 1986.

Allen, Richard. *The Social Passion: Religion and Social Reform in Canada 1914–1928.* Toronto: University of Toronto Press, 1971.

———. ed. *Religion and Society in the Prairie West.* Regina: Canadian Plains Research Center, University of Regina. 1974.

Amaral, Alberto, Glen A. Jones, and Berit Karseth, eds. *Governing Higher Education: National Perspectives on Institutional Governance.* Dordrecht: Kluwer Academic Publishers, 2002.

Anderson, B. *Nursing Education in Community Junior Colleges.* Philadelphia: J. B. Lippincott Ltd., 1966.

Anderson, Doris. *Rebel Daughter: An Autobiography.* Toronto: Key Porter Books, 2002.

Annual Report of the Normal, Model, Grammar and Common Schools in Upper Canada for the Year 1855, with an Appendix by the Chief Superintendent of Schools [Egerton Ryerson]. Toronto: John Levell, Printer, 1856.

Argan, William P., with Pam Cowan and Gordon W. Staseson. *Regina: The First 100 Years: Regina's Cornerstones, the History of Regina Told Through Its Buildings and Monuments.* Regina: Leader-Post Carrier Foundation, 2002.

Armstrong, F. H., H. A. Stevenson, and J.D. Wilson, eds., *Aspects of Nineteenth Century Ontario.* Toronto: University of Toronto Press, 1974.

Association of Universities and Colleges of Canada. *Overview of Provincial and Regional Quality Assurance Mechanisms in Canadian Higher Education.* 2007.

Atherton, P. J. *Alberta Junior College Cost Studies: Financing Junior Colleges in Alberta.* Edmonton: Provincial Post-Secondary Education Board, 1970.

Axelrod, Paul. *Scholars and Dollars: Politics, Economics, and the Universities of Ontario, 1945–1980.* Toronto: University of Toronto Press, 1982.

———. *Values in Conflict: The University, the Marketplace, and the Trials of Liberal Education.* Montreal/Kingston: McGill-Queen's University Press, 2002.

———. *Making a Middle Class: Student Life in English Canada during the Thirties.* Montreal: McGill-Queen's University Press, 1990.

——— and John G. Reid, eds. *Youth, University and Canadian Society: Essays in the Social History of Higher Education.* Montreal/Kingston: McGill-Queen's University Press, 1989.

Baker, Donald N., and Patrick J. Harrigan, eds. *The Making of Frenchmen: Directions in the Study of French Education, 1689–1989.* Waterloo: Historical Reflections Press, 1989.

Baine, Richard P. *Calgary: An Urban Study.* Toronto: Clark Irwin and Company, 1973.

Barr, John J. *The Dynasty: The Rise and Fall of Social Credit in Alberta.* Toronto: McClelland and Stewart Limited, 1974.

Barrett, R. E. *A University for Red Deer.* Red Deer: City of Red Deer, 1969.

Beach, Charles M., Robin W. Boadway, and Marvin McInnis. *Higher Education in Canada.* Montreal/Kingston: McGill Queen's University Press, 2005.

Bedford, A. G. *The University of Winnipeg: A History of the Founding Colleges.* Toronto: University of Toronto Press, 1976.

Bell, Edward Alan. *Social Classes and Social Credit in Alberta.* Montreal/Kingston: McGill-Queen's Press, 1993.

Bercuson, David Jay. *Petrified Campus: The Crisis in Canada's Universities.* Toronto: Random Canada, 1997.

———, Robert Bothwell, and J. L. Granatstein. *The Great Brain Robbery: Canada's Universities on the Road to Ruin.* Toronto: McClelland and Stewart, 1984.

Berghofer, Desmond, and Alan Vladicka. *Access to Opportunity, 1905–80: The Development of Post-Secondary Education in Alberta.* Edmonton: Alberta Advanced Education and Manpower, 1980.

Birnbaum, Robert. *Creative Academic Bargaining: Managing Conflict in the Unionized College and University.* New

York: Teachers College Press, Teachers College, Columbia University, 1980.

———. *How Academic Leadership Works: Understanding Success and Failure in the College Presidency.* San Francisco: Jossey-Bass Publishers, 1992.

———. *How Colleges Work: The Cybernetics of Academic Organization and Leadership.* San Francisco, London: Jossey-Bass Publishers, 1988.

———. *Management Fads in Higher Education: Where They Come From, What They Do, Why They Fail.* San Francisco: Jossey-Bass Publishers, 2001.

Bissell, Claude T., ed. *Canada's Crisis in Higher Education.* Toronto: University of Toronto Press, 1957.

———. *The Young Vincent Massey.* Toronto: University of Toronto Press, 1981.

———. *Halfway Up Parnassus: A Personal Account of the University of Toronto, 1932–1971.* Toronto: University of Toronto Press, 1974.

Bok, Derek. *Our Underachieving Colleges: A Candid Look at How Much Students Learn and Why They Should Be Learning More.* Princeton: Princeton University Press, 2006.

Bond, Sheryl. *A New World of Knowledge: Canadian Universities and Globalization.* Ottawa: International Development Research Centre, 1999.

Boschma, Geertje. *Faculty of Nursing on the Move: Nursing at the University of Calgary, 1969–2004.* Calgary: University of Calgary Press, 2005.

Bott, Robert. *The University of Calgary: A Place of Vision.* Calgary: University of Calgary Press, 1990.

Brown, Annora. *Sketches from Life.* Edmonton: Hurtig Publishers, 1981.

Bruce, Christopher J., Ronald D. Kneebone, and Kenneth J. McKenzie. *A Government Reinvented: A Study of Alberta's Deficit Elimination Program.* Toronto: Oxford University Press, 1997.

Bruneau, William, and Donald Savage. *Counting out the Scholars: The Case against Performance Indicators in Higher Education.* Canadian Association of University Teachers, 2002.

——— and James L. Turk, eds., *Disciplining Consent: The Curbing of Free Expression in Academia and the Media.* Canadian Association of University Teachers, 2004.

Burwash, Nathanael. *History of Victoria College.* Toronto, 1927.

Calgary Centennial Book. Calgary: Provost Promotions and Publications, 1974.

Cameron, David M. *More than an Academic Question: Universities, Government, and Public Policy in Canada.*

Halifax: The Institute for Research on Public Policy, 1991.

Cameron, James D. *For the People: A History of St. Francis Xavier University.* Montreal: McGill-Queen's University Press, 1996.

Campbell, Duncan D. *Those Tumultuous Years: The Goals of the President of the University of Alberta during the Decade of the 1960s.* Edmonton: University of Alberta, 1977.

Campbell, Gordon. *Community Colleges in Canada.* Toronto: McGraw Hill Co., 1971.

Central United Church, Calgary, Centennial Book Committee. *They Gathered at the River, 1875–1975.* Calgary: Central United Church, 1975.

Chait, Richard. P. *Trustee Responsibility for Academic Affairs.* Washington, DC: Association of Governing Board of Universities and Colleges, 1984.

———, Thomas P. Holland, and Barbara E. Taylor. *The Effective Board of Trustees.* Phoenix: Oryx Press, 1993.

Chaiton, Alf, and Neil McDonald, eds. *Canadian Schools and Canadian Identity.* Toronto: Gage, 1977.

Chalmers, John W. S*chools of the Foothill Province: The Story of Public Education in Alberta.* Toronto: University of Toronto Press, 1967.

———. *Teachers of the Foothills Province: The Story of the Alberta Teachers' Association.* Toronto: University of Toronto Press, 1968.

Chilly Collective. *Breaking Anonymity: The Chilly Climate for Women Faculty.* Waterloo: Wilfrid Laurier University Press, 1995

Christensen, Hughes J., and J. Mighty, eds. *Taking Stock: Research on Teaching and Learning in Higher Education.* Montreal, Kingston: Queen's Policy Studies Services, McGill-Queen's University Press, 2010.

Clark, Howard C. *Growth and Governance of Canadian Universities: An Insider's View.* Vancouver: UBC Press, 2003.

Clark, Ian, Greg Moran, Michael L. Skolnik, and David Trick. *Academic Transformation: The Forces Reshaping Higher Education in Ontario.* Kingston: Queens's School of Policy studies, 2009.

Cohen, Arthur M., and Florence B. Brawer. *The American Community College.* San Francisco, London: Jossey-Bass, 1982.

Cole, A. O. C. *Trent: The Making of a University, 1957–1987.* Trent: Trent University, 1992.

Collett, W. J. *United Church in Calgary: Activities and Events 1875–1970.* Calgary: Century Calgary Publishing, 1975.

———. *History of the Grand Lodge of Alberta, 1905–1980.* Calgary: s.n., 1981.

Corbett, E. A. *Henry Marshall Tory, Beloved Canadian*. Toronto: Ryerson Press, 1954

———. *Henry Marshall Tory: A Biography*. Edmonton: University of Alberta Press, 1992.

Côté, J., and A. Allahar. *Ivory Tower Blues: A University System in Crisis*. Toronto: University of Toronto Press, 2007.

Council of Ministers of Education, Canada [CMEC]. *Ministerial Statement on Quality Assurance of Degree Education in Canada*, 2007.

Coward, Harold. *Calgary's Growth: Bane or Boon?* Calgary: University of Calgary Press, 1981.

Cross, K. Patricia. *Beyond the Open Door*. San Francisco: Jossey-Bass Publishers, 1971.

———. *Accent on Learning*. San Francisco: Jossey-Bass Publishers, 1976.

——— and Annie-Marie McCartan. *Adult Learning: State Policies and Institutional Practices*. Washington, DC: Association for the Study of Higher Education, 1984.

Davie, George. *The Democratic Intellect: Scotland and Her Universities in the Nineteenth Century*. 2nd ed. Edinburgh: Edinburgh University Press, 1997.

Dennison, John D. *Challenge and Opportunity: Canada's Community College at the Crossroads*. Vancouver: University of British Columbia Press, 1986.

———, ed. *Challenge and Opportunity: Canada's Community Colleges at the Crossroads*. Vancouver: University of British Columbia Press, 1995.

——— and Paul Gallagher. *Canada's Community College: A Critical Analysis*. Vancouver: University of British Columbia Press, 1986.

Distad, Merrill. *The University of Alberta Library: The First Hundred Years, 1908–2008*. Edmonton: University of Alberta Libraries, 2009.

Drucker, Peter F. *Managing the Nonprofit Organization: Practices and Principles*. Oxford: Butterworth-Heinemann, 1990.

Duff, James, and Robert O. Berdahl. *University Government in Canada : Report of a Commission Sponsored by the Canadian Association of University Teachers and the Association of Universities and Colleges of Canada*. Toronto: University of Toronto Press, 1966.

Eells, Walter Crosby. *Present Status of Junior College Terminal Education*. MacDonnell Press for the Commission on Junior College Terminal Education, 2007.

Eggleston, Wilfrid. *Homestead on the Range*. Ottawa: Borealis Press, 1982.

Emberley, Peter C. *Zero Tolerance: Hot Button Politics in Canada's Universities*. Toronto: Penguin Books, 1996.

Encyclopedia of Music in Canada. www.thecanadianencyclopedia.com.

Fast, R. G. *Report of the Administrator of Red Deer College*. Edmonton: University of Alberta Press, 1974.

Finch, David. *Hell's Half Acre: Early Days in the Great Alberta Oil Patch*. Surrey Heritage House Publishing Company. 2005.

Finkel, Alberta. *The Social Credit Phenomenon in Alberta*. Toronto: University of Toronto Press, 1988.

Fisher, Robin. *Contact and Conflict: Indian-European Relations in British Columbia, 1774–1890*. Vancouver: University of British Columbia Press, 1992.

———. *Duff Pattullo of British Columbia*. Toronto: University of Toronto Press, 1991.

Fisher, Roger, and William Ury. *Getting to Yes: Negotiating without Giving In*. Houghton Mifflin, 1981; 2nd ed. 1999.

Floyd, Deborah L., Michael L. Skolnik, and Kenneth P. Walker, eds. *The Community College Baccalaureate: Emerging Trends and Policy Issues*. Sterling, VA: Stylus Publishing, 2005.

Foran, Max. *Calgary: An Illustrated History*. Toronto: James Lorimer & Company and National Museum of Man, 1978.

———. *Calgary: Canada's Frontier Metropolis*. Burlington, ON: Windsor Publications, Inc., 1982.

——— and Heather MacEwan. *Calgary, Canada's Frontier Metropolis: An Illustrated History*. Calgary: Windsor Publications, 1982.

——— and Jameson, Sheilagh, eds. *Citymakers: Calgarians after the Frontier*. Calgary: Historical Society of Alberta, Chinook County Chapter, Historical Society of Alberta, 1987.

Fossum, John Erik. *Oil, the State and Federalism: The Rise and Demise of Petro-Canada as a State Impulse*. Toronto: University of Toronto Press, 1997.

Fowke, Vernon C. *The National Policy and the Wheat Economy*. Toronto: University of Toronto Press, 1957.

French, Goldwin. Parsons and Politics: The Role of Wesleyan Methodists in Upper Canada and the Maritimes from 1780 to 1855. Toronto: University of Toronto Press, 1962.

Frenette, Marc. *Too far to go on? Distance to school and university participation*. Statistics Canada. Cat. No. 11F0019MIE-No. 191.

Friedland, Martin L. *The University of Toronto: A History*. Toronto: University of Toronto Press, 2002.

Friesen, Gerald. *The Canadian Prairies: A History*. Toronto: University of Toronto Press, 1987.

Frost, S. B. *McGill University: For the Advancement of Learning.* Montreal/ Kingston: McGill-Queen's University Press, 2 vols., 1980, 1984.

Gallagher, Paul. *Community Colleges in Canada: A Profile.* Vancouver: Vancouver Community College Press, 1987.

Ghosh, Retna, and Ray Douglas. *Education and Social Change in Canada.* Toronto: Harcourt Brace, Canada, 1995.

Gibson, Frederick W. *Queen's University, 2: 1917–1961.* Montreal: McGill-Queen's University Press, 1983.

Gidney, Catherine A. *A Long Eclipse: The Liberal Protestant Establishment and the Canadian University, 1920–1970.* Montreal: McGill-Queen's University Press, 2004.

Glassford, Larry A. *Reaction and Reform: the Politics of the Conservative Party under R. B. Bennett, 1927–1938.* Toronto: University of Toronto Press, 1992.

Gray, James H. *R.B. Bennett: The Calgary Years.* Toronto: University of Toronto Press, 1991.

———. *Booze: The Impact of Whiskey on the Prairie West.* Toronto: Macmillan of Canada, 1972.

———. *Red Lights on the Prairies* Toronto: Macmillan, 1971.

———. *The Roar of the Twenties.* Toronto: Macmillan, 1975.

———. *The Winter Years: The Depression on the Prairies.* Toronto: Macmillan, 1966.

Gray, H. L. *Universities and the Creation of Wealth.* Buckingham, UK& Philadelphia: Society for Research into Higher Education & Open University Press, 1999.

Gwynne-Timothy, John R. W. *Western's First Century.* London: University of Western Ontario, 1978.

Hamblin, Jennifer, and Finch, David. *The Diva and the Rancher: the Story of Norma Piper and George Pocaterra.* Calgary: Rocky Mountain Books, 2006.

Hanson, Eric J. *Eric J. Hanson's Financial History of Alberta, 1905-1950.* Calgary: University of Calgary Press, 2003.

———. *Population Analysis and Projections: College Areas in Alberta.* Edmonton: Provincial Board of Post Secondary Education, 1968.

Hardy, Cynthia. *The Politics of Collegiality: Retrenchment Strategies in Canadian Universities.* Montreal/Kingston: McGill Queen's University Press, 1996.

Harper, Shaun R., and Stephen J. Quaye, eds. *Student Engagement in Higher Education.* New York and London: Routledge, 2009.

Harris, Robin Sutton. *Bibliography of Higher Education in Canada: Supplement 1981.*Toronto: University of Toronto Press, 1981.

———, ed. *Changing Patterns of Higher Education in Canada.* Toronto: University of Toronto Press, 1966.

———. *A History of Higher Education in Canada, 1663–1960.* Toronto: University of Toronto Press, 1976.

——— and Tremblay, Arthur. *Bibliography of Higher Education in Canada/ Bibliographie de l'enseignement Supérieur Au Canada.* Toronto: University of Toronto Press, 1960.

Harrison, Trevor W., and Jerrold L. Kachur, eds., *Contested Classrooms: Education, Globalization and Democracy in Alberta.* Edmonton: University of Alberta Press and Parkland Institute, 1999.

Hayden, Michael. *Seeking the Balance: The University of Saskatchewan, 1907–1982.* Vancouver: University of British Columbia Press, 1983.

Henderson's Alberta Gazetteer and Directory. Calgary: Henderson Directories Ltd., 1911–1929.

Hogdetts, J. E., ed. *Higher Education in a Changing Canada.* Toronto: University of Toronto Press, 1966.

Hodgins, J.G., ed. *The Documentary History of Education in Upper Canada.* Toronto, 1884–1910.

Holmes, Mark, and I. Oliver Hugh Winchester. *The House that Ryerson Built.* Toronto: OISE, 1984.

Hopkins, Charles Howard. *The Rise of the Social Gospel in American Protestantism, 1865–1917.* New Haven: Yale University Press, 1940.

Horne, Michiel. *Academic Freedom in Canada: A History.* Toronto: University of Toronto Press, 1999.

———. *York University: The Way Must Be Tried.* Montreal: Published for York University by McGill-Queen's University Press, 2009.

Jameson, Sheilagh. *Ranches, Cowboys and Characters: Birth of Alberta's Western Heritage.* Calgary: Glenbow-Alberta Institute, 1987.

Johns, W. H. *A History of the University of Alberta, 1908–1969.* Edmonton: University of Alberta Press, 1981.

Johnston, Hugh J. M. *Radical Campus: Making Simon Fraser University.* Vancouver: Douglas & McIntyre, 2005.

Jonason et al., *Report of the Fact Finding Committee on Post-Secondary and Continuing Education in Alberta.*

Jones, Glen A., ed. *Higher Education in Canada: Different Systems, Different Perspectives.* New York: Garland Publishing, 1995.

——— and Michael Skolnik. *Degrees of Opportunity: Broadening Student Access by Increasing Institutional Differentiation in Ontario Higher Education.* Toronto: Higher Education Quality Council of Ontario, 2009.

——— and Ian Macpherson, eds. *Building Beyond the Homestead: Rural History on the Prairies.* Calgary: University of Calgary Press, 1985.

CATCH THE GLEAM

————and Patricia L. McCarney, and Michel L. Skolnik, eds. *Creating Knowledge, Strengthening Nations: The Changing Role of Higher Education.* Toronto: University of Toronto Press, 2005.

Keller,George. *Academic Strategy: The Management Revolution in American Higher Education.* Baltimore: Johns Hopkins University Press, 1983.

Kerby, George W. *Keep a Grip on Harry.* Toronto: F. C. Stephenson, 1904.

————. *Milestones of Methodism in Calgary and Canada.* Calgary, 1925.

————. *The Broken Trail: Pages from a Pastor's Experience in Western Canada.* Toronto: William Briggs, 2nd printing, 1910.

Kidd, J. R., ed.. *Adult Education in Canada.* Toronto: Canadian Association for Adult Education, 1950.

————. *Coming of Age: Adult Education in the 1960's.* Toronto: Canadian Association for Adult Education, 1978.

————. *Adult Education, 1915–1982: The Autobiography of a Canadian Pioneer.* Toronto: OISE, 1995.

————. *A Study of the Banff School of Fine Arts.* Toronto: OISE, 1969.

Klassen, Henry C. *A Business History of Alberta.* Calgary: University of Calgary Press, 1999.

————. *The Canadian West: Social Change and Economic Development.* Calgary: University of Calgary, 1977.

————. *Eye on the Future: Business People in Calgary and the Bow Valley, 1870–1900.* Calgary: University of Calgary Press, 2002.

Knuttala, K. Murray, ed. *Heritage and Hope: The University of Regina into the 21st Century.* Regina: Canadian Plains Research Center, 2004.

Kuh, G. *High-Impact Educational Practices: What They Are, Who Has Access to Them, and Why they Matter.* Washington, DC: Association of American Colleges and Universities, 2008.

Lambert, Frank. *Pedlar in Divinity: George Whitefield and the Transatlantic Revivals, 1737–1770.* Princeton: Princeton University Press, 1993.

Lethbridge, Junior College. *Past, Present and Future of Lethbridge Junior College.* Lethbridge, 1965.

Lethbridge Junior College. *Historical Survey of the Lethbridge Junior College.* Lethbridge, 1966.

Light, Richard J. *Making the Most of College: Students Speak their Minds.* Cambridge, MA: Harvard University Press, 2001.

MacDonald, John. *The History of the University of Alberta, 1908–1958.* Edmonton: University of Alberta, 1958.

Macdonald, John B. *Higher Education in British Columbia and a Plan for the Future.* Vancouver: University of British Columbia, 1962.

————. *Choices and Choices: A Memoir.* Vancouver: University of British Columbia and UBC Alumni Association, 2000.

MacDonald, Joan. *The Stanstead College Story.* Stanstead, QC: Board of Trustees, Stanstead College, 1977.

MacEwan, Grant. *Grant MacEwan's Journals.* Edmonton: Lone Pine, 1986.

————. *A Short History of Western Canada.* Toronto: McGraw-Hill Ryerson, 1974.

————. *Calgary Cavalcade, From Fort to Fortune.* Saskatoon: Western Producer Book Service, 1975.

————. *Eye Opener Bob: The Story of Bob Edwards,* 2nd ed. Saskatoon: Western Producer Book Service, 1974.

————. *Grant MacEwan's Illustrated History of Western Canadian Agriculture.* Saskatoon: Western Producer Prairie Books, 1980.

Mackenzie, Nadine. *The Night in the Light: The Life of Mary Munn.* Calgary: McQuhaes, 1981.

Macleod, Rod C. *All True Things: A History of the University of Alberta, 1908–2008.* Edmonton: University of Alberta Press, 2008.

Marshall, David. *Secularizing the Faith: Canadian Protestant Clergy and the Crisis of Belief, 1850–1940.* Toronto: University of Toronto Press, 1992.

Masters, D. C. *Protestant Church Colleges in Canada: A History.* Toronto, 1966.

McDonald, Neil, and Chaiton, Alf, eds. *Egerton Ryerson and His Times.* Toronto: University of Toronto Press, 1978.

McLauchlan, Kenneth. *Waterloo: The Unconventional Founding of an Unconventional University.* Waterloo: University of Waterloo, 1997.

McPherson, C. B. *Democracy in Alberta: Social Credit and the Party System,* 2nd ed. Toronto: University of Toronto Press, 1962.

Morrison, Elsie C., and Morrison, Peter N. R. *Calgary, 1975–1950: A Souvenir of Calgary's Seventy-Fifth Anniversary.* Calgary, 1950.

Morton, A. S. *Saskatchewan: The Making of a University.* Toronto: University of Toronto Press, 1959.

Muir, Elizabeth Gillan, and Marilyn Färdig Whiteley, eds. *Changing Roles of Women Within the Christian Church in Canada.* Toronto: University of Toronto Press, 1995.

Neatby, Hilda. *So Little for the Mind: An Indictment of Canadian Education.* Toronto: Clark-Irwin, 1953.

————. *Queen's University.* Montreal: McGill-Queen's Univeristy Press, 1978.

Nenshi, Naheed K. *The State of Nonprofit Management Education in Canada [electronic resource]*. Calgary: Institute for Nonprofit Studies, Mount Royal College, 2008. Newson, Janice, and Howard Buchbinder, *The University Means Business: Universities, Corporations and Academic Work*. Toronto: Garamond Press, 1988.

Norris, Marjorie. *A Leaven of Ladies: A History of the Calgary Local Council of Women*. Calgary: Detselig, 1995.

Government of Ontario, Ministry of Education and Training. *No Dead Ends: Report of the Task Force on Advanced Training*. Toronto: Ministry of Education and Training, 1993.

Owram, Douglas R. *Born at the Right Time: A History of the Baby-Boom Generation*. Toronto: University of Toronto Press, 1996.

———, ed. *The Formation of Alberta: A Documentary History*. Calgary: Alberta Records Publication Board, 1979.

Palmer, Howard. *Patterns of Prejudices: A History of Nativism in Alberta*. Toronto: McClelland & Stewart, 1982.

———, and Tamara Palmer. *Alberta: A New History*. Edmonton: Hurtig Publishers, 1990.

———, and Donald B. Smith, eds. *The New Provinces: Alberta and Saskatchewan, 1905–1980: 12th Western Canada Studies Conference*. Vancouver: Tantalus Research, 1980.

Patillo, Manning M., Jr., and Donald M. Mackenzie, *Church-Sponsored Higher Education in the United States: Report of the Danforth Commission*. Washington: American Council on Education, 1966.

Payne, Michael, Donald Wetherell, and Catherine Cavanaugh, eds. *Alberta Formed, Alberta Transformed*. 2 vols. Edmonton: University of Alberta Press, 2006.

Pitsula, James M. *An Act of Faith: The Early Years of Regina College*. Regina: Canadian Plains Research Center, 1988.

———. *New World Dawning: The Sixties at Regina Campus*. Regina: Canadian Plains Reseach Center, University of Regina, 2008.

Pocklington, Thomas C., and Allan Tupper. *No Place To Learn: Why Universities Aren't Working*. Vancouver, Toronto: University of British Columbia Press, 2002.

Pope, Loren. *Colleges that Change Lives: 40 Schools That Will Change the Way You Think About College*. 2nd ed. rev. New York: Penguin Books, 2006.

Rasporich, Anthony W. *Make No Small Plans: The University of Calgary at Forty*. Calgary: University of Calgary, 2007.

———. *The Making of the Modern West: Western Canada since 1945*. Calgary: University of Calgary Press, 1984.

———, and Henry C. Klassen, eds. *Frontier Calgary: Town, City, Region, 1875–1914*. Calgary: University of Calgary Press, 1975.

Rawlyk, George A. *The Canada Fire: Radical Evangelicalism in British North America, 1775–1812*. Kingston: McGill-Queen's University Press, 1994.

Reid, John G. *Mount Allison University: A History to 1963*. 2 vols. Toronto: University of Toronto Press, 1984.

Rennie, Bradley J., ed. *Alberta's Premiers of the Twentieth Century*. Regina: Canadian Plains Research Center, University of Regina, 2005.

Riddell, J.H. *Methodism in the Middle West*. Toronto: Ryerson Press, 1946

Riddell, W.A. *The First Decade: A History of the University of Saskatchewan, Regina Campus, 1960–1970*. Regina: University of Regina Press, 1974.

Rifkin, Jeremy. *The European Dream: How Europe's Vision Is Quietly Eclipsing the American Dream*. New York: Tarcher, 2004.

Roberts, Hayden. *Culture and Adult Education: A Study of Alberta and Quebec*. Edmonton: University of Alberta Press, 1982.

Ross, Murray G. *Those Ten Years, 1960–1970: The President's Report on the First Decade of York University*. Toronto: York University, 1970.

———. *The University: The Anatomy of Academe*. New York: McGraw-Hill, 1976.

Rothblatt, Sheldon. *The Modern University and Its Discontents: The Fate of Newman's Legacies in Britain and America*. Cambridge: Cambridge University Press, 1997.

Roueche, John E., George Baker III, and Robert R. Rose, *Shared Vision: Transformational Leadership in American Community Colleges*. Washington Community College Press, American Association of Community and Junior Colleges, National Centre for Higher Education, 1989.

Rybak, Jeff. *What's Wrong with University, and How to Make it Work for You Anyway*. Toronto: ECW Press, 2007.

Salmi, Jamil. *Constructing Knowledge Societies: New Challenges for Tertiary Education*. Washington, DC: World Bank, 2002.

———. *The Challenge of Establishing World-Class Universities*. Washington, DC: World Bank, 2009.

Saunders, Robert. *R. B. Bennett*. Toronto: Fitzhenry and Whiteside, 2004.

Saywell, John. *Someone to Teach Them: York and the Great University Explosion, 1960–1973*. Toronto: University of Toronto Press, 2008.

Scobie, Charles H. H., and Grant, John Webster, eds. *The Contribution of Methodism to Atlantic Canada*. Montreal/Kingston: McGill-Queen's University Press, 1992.

Seger, J. E., and G. L. Mowat, eds. *The Junior College: The Lecture Series of the Banff Regional Conference of School Administrators*. Edmonton: University of Alberta, 1966.

Semple, Neil. *The Lord's Dominion: The History of Canadian Methodism*. Montreal/Kingston: McGill-Queen's University Press, 1996.

Sissons, C. B. *A History of Victoria University*. Toronto: University of Toronto Press, 1952.

———. *Egerton Ryerson: His Life and Letters*. London, New York: Oxford University Press, 1937, 1947.

———. *Church and State in Canadian Education: An Historical Study*. Toronto: Ryerson Press, 1959.

Smith, Donald B., ed. *Centennial City: Calgary 1894–1994*. Calgary: University of Calgary Press, 1994.

Spinks, J. W. T. *Decade of Change: The University of Saskatchewan, 1959–70*. Saskatoon: University of Saskatchewan Press, 1972.

Stewart, Andrew. *Special Study on Junior Colleges*. Edmonton, December 1965.

Stone, C. G., and F. J. Garnett. *Brandon College: A History 1899–1967*. Brandon: Brandon University, 1969.

Storm, Christine, ed. *Liberal Education and the Small University in Canada*. Montreal: McGill-Queen's University Press, 1996.

Stortz, Paul, and E. Lisa Panayotidis, eds. *Historical Identities: The Professoriate in Canada*. Toronto: University of Toronto Press, 2006.

Swift, Michael David. *R. B. Bennett and the Depression, 1930–1935*. Fredericton, N.B., 1964.

Thomas, A. M., ed. *Community Colleges 1966: A National Seminar on the Community College in Canada*. Toronto, 1966.

Thomas, Clara. *Ryerson of Upper Canada*. Toronto: University of Toronto Press, 1969.

Thomas, Lewis G. *The Liberal Party in Alberta: A History of Politics in the Province of Alberta, 1905–1912*. Toronto: University of Toronto Press, 1959.

———. *The Church of England and Higher Education in the Prairie West before 1914*. Canadian Church Historical Society, 1956.

———. *The University of Alberta in the War of 1939-40*. Edmonton: University of Alberta Press, 1948.

Trilokekar, Roopa Desai, Glen A. Jones, and Adrian Shubert. *Canada's Universities Go Global*. Toronto: J. Lorimer & Co., 2009.

Tupper, Allan, and Roger Gibbins, eds. *Government and Politics in Alberta*. Edmonton: University of Alberta Press, 1992.

Turk, James L. *The Corporate Campus: Commercialization and the Dangers to Canada's Colleges and Universities*. Toronto: J. Lorimer, 2000.

University of Alberta, *Calendar*, 1909–2009.

University of Alberta, Strategic Planning Task Force. *Degrees of Freedom: A Strategic plan for the University of Alberta to the Year 2005*. Edmonton: University of Alberta, 1993.

University of Calgary. *Preliminary Announcement of the University of Calgary, July 1912*.

University of Calgary. *First Annual Calendar, Session 1913*.

———. *Calendar*, 1966–2009.

Vickers, Jill, and June Adam. *But Can you Type? Canadian Universities and the Status of Women*. Toronto Clarke, Irwin, 1977.

Voisey, Paul. *Vulcan: The Making of a Prairie Community*. Toronto: University of Toronto Press, 1988.

Waite, Peter B. *The Loner: Three Sketches of the Personal Life and Ideas of R. B. Bennett, 1870–1947*. Toronto: University of Toronto Press, 1992.

———. *The Lives of Dalhousie University*, 1: *Lord Dalhousie's College*. Montreal: McGill-Queen's University Press, 1994; 2: *The Old College Transformed*. Montreal: McGill-Queen's University Press, 1998.

Wallace, R.C. *The University of Alberta 1908–1933*. Edmonton: University of Alberta, 1933.

Watson, Cicely. *New College Systems in Canada*. Paris: Organisation for Economic Co-operation and Development, 1973.

White, Anne, ed. *A New Day for Women: Life & Writings of Emily Spencer Kerby*. Calgary: Alberta Records Publication Board, Historical Society of Alberta, 2004.

Wigger, John H. *Taking Heaven by Storm: Methodism and the Rise of Popular Christianity in America*. New York: Oxford University Press, 1998.

Wilk, Stephen, and Jobson, V., eds. *100 Years of Nose Creek Valley History*. Calgary: Nose Creek Historical Society, 1997.

Witt, Alan A., et al. *America's Community Colleges: The First Century*. American Association of Community Colleges, 1997.

Who's Who in Canada, 1938.

Wolf, Alison. *Does Education Matter? Myths about Education and Economic Growth*. Penguin, 2002.

Woodhouse, Howard R. *Selling Out: Academic Freedom and the Corporate Market*. Montreal, Ithaca: McGill-Queen's University Press, 2009.

Worth, Walter H. *A Choice of Futures*. Edmonton: Hurtig Publishers, 1972.

n.a. *Beating the Odds: A History of the Mannix Family in Business, 1898-1997.* Calgary, 1998.

n.a. *Calgary Cavalcade: From Fort to Fortune.* Edmonton: The Institute of Applied Art Ltd., 1958.

n.a. Southern Alberta Institute of Technology. *Sixty Years '16–'76.* Calgary, 1976.

4. UNPUBLISHED THESES AND DISSERTATIONS

Barrington, Gail Vallance. "The Impact of Environmental Forces on Alberta Community Colleges, 1980-1990." Ph.D. diss., University of Alberta, 1981.

Berghofer, D. F. "General Education in Post-Secondary Non-University Educational Institutions in Alberta". M.Ed. thesis, University of Alberta, 1970.

Bosetti, R. A. "A Comparative Analysis of the Functioning of Six Post-Secondary Non-University Educational Institutions." Ph.D. diss., University of Alberta, 1975.

Boyle, G. A. "Higher Criticism and the Struggle for Academic Freedom in Canadian Methodism." Th.E. thesis, Victoria University 1965.

Brown, D. W. R. "An Analysis of the Achievements of Junior College Students at the University of Calgary." MA thesis, University of Calgary, 1966.

Campbell, Gordon. "History of the Alberta Community College System, 1957 to 1969." Ph.D.diss., University of Calgary, 1972.

Clark, Ralph Joseph. "A History of the Department of Extension of the University of Alberta, 1912–1956." Ph.D. diss., University of Alberta, 1986.

Clarke, John Cecil. "Alberta Community Colleges: Ten Years in Review." M.Ed. thesis, University of Alberta, 1983.

Farquhar, H. E. "The Role of the College in the System of Higher Education in Alberta." Ph.D. diss., University of Alberta, 1967.

Gawreluck, Robert Steven. "Organizational Culture in a Community College and Its Interrelationship with Leadership and Structure." Ph.D. diss., University of Alberta, 1993.

Gordon, P. A. "Student Services in Alberta Colleges." M.Ed. thesis, University of Calgary, 1970.

Johnson, Richard Dale. "Mount Royal College: A Case Study." M.Ed. thesis, University of Alberta, 1977.

Kennedy, N. J. "The Growth and Development of Music in Calgary, 1975–1920." MA thesis, University of Alberta, 1972.

Knapp, John Lewis. "Institutional Planning in Alberta's Public Colleges: A Quantitative and Qualitative Assessment." Ph.D. diss., University of Alberta, 1991

Letts, A. B. "The Characteristics of Students in Alberta Public Junior Colleges." MA thesis, University of Alberta, 1968.

Loken, G. "An Analysis of the Junior College in Alberta: Progress, Program and Prospect." M.Ed. Thesis, University of Alberta, 1966

Long, John Clifford Anthony. "An Historical Study of the Establishment of College Systems in Ontario and Alberta in the 1960s." M.Ed. Thesis, University of Calgary, 1972.

———. "The Transferability Issue in Alberta: A Case Study in the Politics of Higher Education." Ph.D. diss., University of Alberta, 1979.

Lowe, P. B. "Technical and Vocational Training in Alberta: A Descriptive Study of its Development." MA Thesis, University of Alberta,1962.

MacLeod, Norman Leslie. "Calgary College, 1912–1915: A Study of an Attempt to Establish a Provincially Funded University in Alberta." Ph.D. diss., University of Calgary, 1970.

Mann, G. "Alberta Normal Schools: A Descriptive Study of their Development l905 to l945." M.Ed. thesis, University of Alberta, 1961.

Markle, A. G. "Genesis of Lethbridge Public Junior College". M.Ed. thesis, University of Alberta, 1965.

Marzolf, A. D. "Alexander Cameron Rutherford and His Influence on Alberta's Educational Programs." M.A. thesis, University of Alberta, 1965.

McLean, Robert Irwin. "A 'Most Effectual Remedy': Temperance and Prohibition in Alberta, 1875–1915." MA thesis, University of Calgary, 1969.

Montgomerie, Heather Lynn. "A Prospective Policy Analysis of Degree Granting in Alberta Community Colleges." Ph.D. diss., University of Alberta, 1990.

Nussbaumer, M. "The Worth Report and the Developments in Alberta's Post-Secondary Policies and Structures, 1968 to 1976." Ph.D. diss., University of Alberta, 1977.

Patterson, Robert Steven. "F.W.G. Haultain and Education in the Early West." M.Ed. thesis, University of Alberta, 1961.

———. "The Establishment of Progressive Education in Alberta, 1925–1940." Ph.D. diss., Michigan State University, 1968.

Powell, Michael Anthony. "An Investigation of the Academic Achievement of Mount Royal College Transfer Students at Ontario Universities." M.Ed. thesis, University of Alberta, 1971

Simon, Frank. "History of the Alberta Provincial Institute of Technology and Art." M.Ed. thesis, University of Alberta, 1962.

Weston, P. E. "The History of Education in Calgary." MA thesis, University of Alberta, 1951.

Wilson, L. R. "Perren Baker and the United Farmers of Alberta: Educational Principles and Policies of an Agrarian Government." M.Ed. thesis, University of Alberta, 1970.

Wilson, L. R. "The Education of the Farmer: The Educational Objectives and Activities of the United Farmers of Alberta and the Saskatchewan Grain Growers' Association." Ph.D. diss., University of Alberta, 1975.

5. UNPUBLISHED WORKS, REPORTS, PAPERS

Anderson, Robert Newton. "Institutional Analysis of Mount Royal College, Calgary, Alberta." Calgary: Mount Royal College, 1964. [MRUA, University of Calgary Library].

Calgary Economic Development Authority. "Opening Doors – Exploring Options: An Assessment of the Mount Royal College Proposal for University Accreditation." Calgary: Calgary Economic Development, 2004.

Confederation of Alberta Faculty Associations. *Post-secondary funding framework review. Submission of the Confederation of Alberta Faculty Associations, June 2000.* Edmonton: University of Alberta Press, 2000.

Cresap, McCormick and Paget, *A Plan for a Public Community Junior College for Calgary.* McCormick and Paget, 1966 [MRUA, University of Calgary Library].

Howse, John. "The History of Mount Royal College." ca. 1975 (incomplete text) [MRUA].

Ingram, E. J., and Brent Pickard et al. "A College in Process: An Evaluative Study of the Mount Royal College

Instructional Model". Department of Education Administration, University of Alberta, 1975. [MRUA]

Luterbach, Edward J. "Proposal for Degree Programs." Red Deer College, 1990.

MacDonald, Robert. "A History of Mount Royal College." 2000 [MRUA].

Mackie, E. Jean. "A Biographical History of the Nursing Program at Mount Royal College, Calgary, Part One: The First Three Years (1965–1968)." ca 1968 [MRUA].

Mackie, E. Jean. "The First Decade: Diploma Nursing Program, Mount Royal College, 1963–1973." 1981, revised 1986 [MRUA, University of Calgary Library].

Marshall, David. "Improving, Assessing and Demonstrating Student Learning." Paper for the 12th Transatlantic Dialogue." 27 June 2010 [MRUA].

Martorana, S. V. "A Community College Plan—for Lethbridge Alberta." Lethbridge, 1951.

Snowdon, Ken and Elizabeth Hooey. "Report on Governance prepared for Brock University Special Committee on Board Governance." Snowdon and Associates, June 2006. http://www.brocku.ca/university-secretariat/board-trustees/board/snowdonfinalreport.pdf.

Stevens, Raines, Barrett, Hutton, Seton and Partners. "Supplement to The Idea of a College: A Summary of Some Educational Alternatives." 1969 [MRUA].

Tyson, E.G. "An Initial Look at Some of the Needs and Problems of the Culturally and/or Educationally Disadvantaged in the Calgary Area and the Possible Role of Mount Royal Junior College in Meeting These Needs." 1968 [MRUA].

Walters, S. Leonore. "In Memoriam: A Brief History of George William Kerby, B.A., D.D., LL.D. and Emily Spencer Kerby." In "The Book of Remembrance." Calgary: William T. Knights, 1945, 3–4.

6. NEWSPAPERS AND PERIODICALS

Calgary Daily Herald; Calgary Herald; Canadian Methodist Magazine; Christian Guardian; New Outlook; The Alberta Report; The Albertan; The Edmonton Journal; The Mirror; The Telegram; United Church Observer; Western Methodist Recorder

7. MOUNT ROYAL COLLEGE PUBLICATIONS

Annual Reports, 1970–2009
Institutional Development Plans, 1991–2009

Office of Institutional Analysis and Planning

1985   Highlights of Recent Mount Royal Enrollment Trends and Operating Characteristics, February 1985.

1981–2009   Trends and Issues.

1993   Life after Graduation: What Are Mount Royal College Graduates Doing Now? 1991–92 Graduates: Summary. 1993.

1998   Strategic Decision-Making Information: Based on Association of Governing Boards of Universities and Colleges: Key Questions and Indicators for Trustees.

Other College Reports

1963   A Submission to the Cabinet of the Government of the Province of Alberta from the Board of Governors of Mount Royal Junior College. July 1963.

1969   Stanley Leggett, The Idea of a College. Chicago: Engelhardt, Engelhardt and Leggett, Inc.

1969   Stevens, Raines, Barrett, Hutton, Seton and Partners. Supplement to The Idea of a College: A Summary of Some Educational Alternatives.

1983   Education Plan: Facility Expansion Supplement, January 1983.

1983   Operating Resources Requirements: Facility Expansion Supplement, January 1983.

1983   Mount Royal College Expansion Proposal, June 1983.

1984   Planning Handbook, Edition One, January 1984.

1984   Foundation and Strategic Plan, 1984–85.

1986   Funding for Post-Secondary Institutions: Submission to the Education Committee of the Calgary Chamber of Commerce, July 31, 1986.

1987   Institutional Development Plan, 1987–1990.

1987   Task Force on Student Flow Model, The Student Flow Model: Issues and Recommendations, 24 February 1987.

1989   Mount Royal College Image and Issues Study: Final Report (Heffring Research Group)

1989   Response to "Existing and Emerging Demands for University Education: A Policy Framework." October 1989.

1990   Proposal for a Conjoint Program for a Baccalaureate Nursing Degree in Calgary [Mount Royal College, Foothills Hospital, University of Calgary]

1991   Degree-Granting Proposal, July 1991

1991   Position Paper of the Steering Committee for Degree-Granting Feasibility Study

1991   Study of the Implications of Trimesterization at Mount Royal College, December 1991.

1991   Long-Range Institutional Plan, 1991–2000.

1993   Key Performance Indicator Accountability System of Reporting, October 1993

1993   A Proposal for the Development of Mount Royal College, presented to the Honourable Jack Ady, Minister, Alberta Advanced Education and Career Development, July 1993.

1996   Strategic Research Study – Higher Education Values of Learners for the 21st Century.

1998   Business Plan, 1998–2001.

1998–2001   Faculty/School/Centre Academic Plans, 1998–2001.

1999   Long-Range Institutional Plan, March 1999.

2007   The Heart of Learning: A New Library and Learning Centre for Mount Royal, A Proposal for the Government of Alberta."

8. GOVERNMENT PUBLICATIONS

Alberta legislation

University Act, 1907

Act to Incorporate Mount Royal College 1910 (Second Session, Chapter 30)

Act to Amend the Mount Royal College Act, 1944

Act to Amend the Mount Royal College Act, 1950

Act to Provide for the Establishment of Public Junior Colleges, 1958

The Public Junior Colleges Act, 1958 [1958, c. 64, s. 1]

The University and College Assistance Act, 1964 [1964, c. 102, s. 1]

An Act to Amend the University and College Assistance Act, 1965 (revised annually to 1967)

The Mount Royal Junior College Act, 1966 [S.A. 1966, C-19]

Act to Amend the Public Junior Colleges Act, 1967

Act Respecting a Provincial College System, 1969

The Colleges Act, 1969 [R.S.A. 1970, c56. s. 1]; amended periodically, last effective 1 January 2002 [R.S.A. 2000, C-19].

Post-secondary Learning Act 2003 [S.A. 2003, c. P-19.5]; amended frequently (latest 2009).

Department of Education, Advanced Education/Alberta Learning

1913, 1914–15, 1919–20, 1921–22, 1962–65   Annual Report of the Department of Education of the Province of Alberta

1970   Post Secondary Education until 1972: An Alberta Policy Statement. [By] Robert Clark, Minister of Education.

1972   Committee of Inquiry into Non-Canadian Influence in Alberta Post-Secondary Education.

1977   An Examination of Tuition Fee Structures in Alberta: The Student Perspective.

1977   A Financial Plan for Alberta Colleges and Universities: Recommendations and Research Results. (Bernard S. Sheehan, with Eric A., Hillman, Margaret Reti, Barbara J. Serediak).

1987   Post-Secondary Operating Grants in Alberta: An Equity Study. Edmonton: Alberta Advanced Education. 1987. Written by J. S. Dupre.

1989   Responding to Existing and Emerging Demands for University Education: A Policy Framework.

1989   Trends and Issues in Post-Secondary Education, 1989 to the Year 2000

1989   Goals and Priorities of Post-Secondary Education, 1989 to the Year 2000

1994   New Directions for Adult Learning in Alberta

1995   A Proposal for Performance-Based Funding: Promoting Excellence in Alberta's Public Learning System.

1996   Key Performance Indicators Reporting Manual for Alberta Post-Secondary Institutions.

1996   Fostering Continued Excellence in Adult Learning: The Report of the Alberta Vocational Colleges Governance Review Task Force. (Written by Marshall M. Williams)

1996   Education and Career Development.

2002   Alberta's Post-secondary System: Developing the Blueprint for Change.

2007   Roles and Mandates: Policy Framework for Alberta's Publicly Funded Advanced Education System

Provincial Board of Post-Secondary Education, Alberta Colleges Commission

1969–73   Annual Report: The College System, 1969/70–1972/73.

1968   Mount Royal Junior College: An Analysis.

1971   A Report Recommending the Transfer of all Diploma Nursing and Allied Health programs (R. G. Fast).

1972   System Integration–Coordination– Growth, the Alberta System of Post-Secondary Non-University Education: Master Plan Number One (Reno Bosetti).

1974   Report of the Administrator of Red Deer College (R. G. Fast). Edmonton: University of Alberta Press, 1974.

2007   Roles and Mandates Policy Framework for Alberta's Publicly Funded Advanced Education System. Edmonton: Ministry of Advanced Education and Technology.

Government Commissions/Special Committees

1915   Report of the Royal Commission Appointed to Consider the Granting of Degree-Conferring Powers to Calgary College, including a Report on the Recommendations of the sub-committee on Calgary College and Institute of Technology and Art.

1959   Report of the Royal Commission on Education in Alberta (Cameron Commission).

1963   Survey of Schools of Nursing in Alberta. Prepared by University of Alberta, 1963.

1965   Survey Committee on Higher Education in Alberta. Reports 1, 2 and 3.

1965   Special Study on Junior Colleges. Prepared by Andrew Stewart. Edmonton: Queens' Printer, 1965.

1966   Report of the Fact Finding Committee on Post-Secondary and Continuing Education.

1972   A Choice of Futures. Report of the Commission of Educational Planning. Prepared by Wallace Worth.

1973   Committee of Inquiry into Non-Canadian Influence in Alberta Post-Secondary Education. Report of the Committee of Inquiry into Non-Canadian Influence in Alberta Post-Secondary Education, 1973 (Written by Arnold F. Moir.)

Alberta White/Discussion Papers

1969   A White Paper on Human Resources Development

1984   Proposals for an Industrial and Science Strategy for Albertans, 1985 to 1990

1994   New Directions for Adult Learning in Alberta.

1995   Vision for Change

2002   Developing a Blueprint for Alberta's Post Secondary Education System: A Framework for University Level Education.

INDEX

Burns, John, 61
Burns, Patrick J., 113
Business, Professional and Educational Services Sectoral Advisory Group on International Trade, 214
Business Administration, 76, 91, 94, 164, 190, 223–24, 263
Business Administration Club, 97
business models for public institutions, 221
Business Society, 194
Byrne, Paul, 284

C

Cadet Corps, 30
Calgary, 2–4, 23, 276
    computer power, 178, 191
    downtown, 112, 148, 225, 246
    economy, 3, 16, 44, 178, 206, 212, 246
    educational level, 45, 178, 191, 212
    evolving needs of, 206
    frontier town identification, 3, 65
    geophysical research centre, 178
    head-office city, 44, 65, 178, 206
    "the knowledge capital of Canada," 191
    Light Rail (LRT) system, 178
    population, 66, 212, 246
    religious orientation, 3–5
    students from, 34, 94, 192, 268
Calgary Ballet Company, 203
Calgary Board of Education, 191, 201–2
Calgary Catholic Separate School Board, 105–6, 191
Calgary Centennial Arenas, 185
Calgary Centre for Performing Arts, 203
Calgary Chamber of Commerce, 135
Calgary College, 19–20, 45, 71
Calgary Colonization Company, 11
Calgary Daily Herald, 14
Calgary Fiddlers, 168
Calgary Flames, 269
Calgary General Hospital, 116
Calgary Herald, 8, 30, 61, 92, 217, 265, 269
    on applied degrees, 218
    founders of, 4
    on university status, 221, 252, 259, 261–62
Calgary International Organ Festival, 230, 241
Calgary Local Council of Women, 8
Calgary Petroleum Club, 65
Calgary Police Department, 117
Calgary Public School Board, 7, 45, 104–6
Calgary Region Arts Foundation, 158
Calgary Rural School Division, 76
Calgary Stampede, 3, 133–34
Calgary Sun, 217
Calgary Symphony Orchestra, 38, 57, 81
Calgary Urban Action, 135
Calgary Youth Orchestra (CYO), 158, 203
California college system, 127
California Master Plan for Higher Education, 114, 179
California model of higher education, 90
Camera Club, 97
Cameron, Alexander G. (Sandy), 169–70, 201
Campion, Dick, 198

Campus Alberta Quality Council (CAQC), 221, 250, 252, 255, 265, 280
campus dissent, 121–24, 128–30, 277
Campus Recreation, 194, 228
Camrose Lutheran College, 2
Canada-European Union Mobility Program, 239
Canadian Association of Petroleum Production Accountants (CAPPA), 190
Canadian Association of Youth Orchestras, 158
Canadian Bureau for International Education (CBIE), 208, 239
Canadian Centre for Learning Systems (CCLS), 188, 191
Canadian Charter of Rights and Freedoms, 178
Canadian Colleges Athletic Association (CCAA), 234
Canadian Festival of Youth Orchestras, 158
Canadian Forces Base. See CFB Calgary
Canadian Information Processing Society (CIP), 191
Canadian Institute of Management (CIM), 190
Canadian Intermediate Rodeo Association, 162
Canadian International Development Agency (CIDA), 237
Canadian National Federation of Home and School, 24
Canadian Pacific Railroad (CPR), 3
Canadian Speech Association, 158
Canadian Studies, 224
Canadian University Report, 272, 286
Canadian University Student Consortium (CUSC), 286
Canwest Global Foundation, 239
Career Centre, 248
career fairs, 194
career programs, 93–94, 116, 166, 278. See also terminal courses
Career Society, 97
Carleton University, 117, 219
Carlyle, Harry, 189
Carnipaloozafest, 233
Carnegie classification system, 285–86
Carnegie Educational Foundation, 48, 50–51
Carrick, Margaret, 36, 54, 59
Carruthers, Edward R. R. (Ted), 201
Carry on Teacher, 97
Carstairs, John, 134
Carthy Organ, 230
The Carved Woman, 83
Casanova, John, 97
Case, Andrea, 241
Castell, W. R., 93
Catholic Church, 34–35
Catholic colleges, 2, 108
Catholic students, 35, 85, 94, 99
"The Causes of the War," 30
CBC, 57
Centennial Campaign, 271–72
Centennial Planetarium, 112
Central Methodist Church, 4, 8–9, 11, 17, 28, 37–38
Central Mortgage and Housing, 168
Centre for Communication Studies, 236
Centre for Continuing Learning, 229

Centre for Health studies, 236
Centres of Excellence, 272
certificate programs, 76. See also names of specific certificate programs
CFAC (radio station), 92
CFB Calgary, 169–70, 186, 226
Chabotar, Ken, 223
"Chairman's Challenge," 189, 201
Chait, Richard, 181, 223
The Challenge of Establishing World-Class Universities (Salmi), 285
Chambers, Stanley, 34
Chan, Andy, 240
Chandler Kennedy Architectural Group (CKAG), 183
"Changing the Face of Education: A Centennial Fundraising Campaign for Mount Royal University," 271–72
chapel (in Kerby Memorial Building), 70
chapel services, 29, 54, 85, 107
Chapin, Marion, 36
Chapin, O. S., 11–12, 59
"The Character and Guidelines for the Development of Mount Royal College" (1967), 138
Charlton, Bob, 200
Cheerleaders Club, 97
Chemistry Club, 51
Chess Club, 51
Chikinda, Marc, 215, 235
Child and Youth Care diploma program transferable to University of Victoria, 117
Child-Care Worker program, 120, 190. See also early-childhood education
child-centred education, 25
The Children's Hour, 241
Children's Theatre, 81
China, 239–40, 268
Chinese immigrants, 10–11
Chinook, 14, 20, 27–31, 36, 38, 53
Chmilar, "Big" Jim, 200
Chown, George, 26
"Christian Apologetics," 86
Christian Community Church, 230
Christian Education program, 86, 99
Christian Guardian, 5, 7
Christian Leadership Certificate, 86
Christian Science, 35
Christie, Nat, 61
Chu, Wayne, 271
Church-Sponsored Higher Education in the United States, 108
City Centre Campus, leased space for, 225
Clark, Arthur, 37
Clark, Rodney, 169, 272
Clarke, Arthur, 36
Climate for Change Task Force, 255
CMRC (radio station), 97
Coburn, Gordon, 195
Cockburn, Neil, 241
Code of Student Conduct, 232
co-determination, 124, 131–32, 277
co-education, 10, 14
Cohen, Martha, 106, 113, 131, 163–64, 201